Visual Studio® 2005 All-in-One Desk Reference For...

Visual Studio 2005 Keyboard Shortcuts for General Development Environment

Task You Want to Perform	Feature	Keyboard Shortcut	Task You Want to Perform	Feature	Keyboard Shortcut
Browse data types	Class View	Ctrl+Shift+C		Context-sensitive help	F1
	Object Browser	Ctrl+Alt+J		How Do I	Ctrl+F1
Edit code	Format Document	Ctrl+K, Ctrl+D		Index	Ctrl+Alt+F1
	Comment Selection	Ctrl+K, Ctrl+C		Search	Ctrl+Alt+F3
	Uncomment Selection	Ctrl+K, Ctrl+U	Manage project resources	Properties Window	F4
	Insert Code Snippet	Ctrl+K, Ctrl+X		Data Sources	Shift+Alt+D
	Toggle Outlining Expansion	Ctrl+M		Server Explorer	Ctrl+Alt+S
	Collapse to Definitions	Ctrl+M, Ctrl+O		Solution Explorer	Ctrl+Alt+L
	Toggle Designer and Markup	Shift+F7		Toolbox	Ctrl+Alt+X
	View Code	F7		Add New Item	Ctrl+Shift+A
Debug	Start Debugging	F5		Add Existing Item	Shift+Alt+A
	Start without Debugging	Ctrl+F5		Build Solution	Ctrl+Shift+B
	Step Into	F11	Open files and projects	New File Window	Ctrl+N
	Step Over	F10		New Project Window	Ctrl+Shift+N
	Toggle Breakpoint	F9		Open File Window	Ctrl+O
	Restart	Ctrl+Shift+F5		Open Project Window	Ctrl+Shift+O
Find and replace	Find Symbol	Alt+F12	Navigate windows	Close Document	Ctrl+F4
	Quick Find	Ctrl+F		Close Tool Window	Shift+Esc
	Quick Replace	Ctrl+H		Cycle Documents	Ctrl+F6
Find help	Contents	Ctrl+Alt+F1		IDE Navigator	Ctrl+Tab
				Cycle Tool Panes	Alt+F6

Note: Most of these shortcuts work with all environment settings.

Technology and Terminology

Technology	Description	Technology	Description
Assembly	A file for physically storing data types, including the DLL files where code is compiled	Common Type Specification	A set of rules for how programming languages use data types
Base Class Library	A set of managed code that enables developers to create Windows and Web applications that target the Common Language Runtime	Garbage Collection	A feature of the Common Language Runtime that manages memory
Common Language Runtime	A managed environment for running applications that prevents memory leaks	Global Assembly Cache	A repository that stores public versions of assemblies
		Namespace	A unique identifier for the logical organization of data types

For Dummies: Bestselling Book Series for Beginners

Visual Studio® 2005 All-in-One Desk Reference For Dummies®

Common Visual Studio Item Templates

Item Template	Description
Application Configuration File	Stores application settings for a Windows application
Class	Empty class-definition file
Class Diagram	Model of new or existing classes
Crystal Report	Report using Crystal Reports
DataSet	Stores data using the DataSetDesigner
HTML Page	Web page using HTML
Report	Report using SQL Server Reporting Services
Settings File	XML configuration file
Site Map	Describes flow of Web pages in a Web application
SQL Database	Empty database for storing local data
Style Sheet	Cascading style sheet
User Control	Reusable custom control
Web Configuration File	Stores application settings for a Web application
Web Form	User interface for Web applications
Web Service	Code file for a Web service
Windows Form	User interface for a Windows application
XML File	Empty XML document
XML Schema	Describes contents of an XML document

Common Visual Studio Project Types

Project Type	Description
Class library	Component library with no user interface
Console application	Command-line application
Database project	SQL script storage
Device application	Windows application for a smart device
Empty project	Blank project
SQL Server project	Management of stored procedures and SQL Server objects
Web service	ASP.NET Web application with no user interface; technically, no longer a project type
Web site	ASP.NET Web application; technically, no longer a project type
Windows application	Windows application with a user interface
Windows service	Windows application with no user interface

Visual Designers in Visual Studio

Designer	What You Can Do with It
Class Designer	Model classes using a class diagram
Crystal Reports Designer	Create Crystal Reports reports
DataSet Designer	Create typed DataSets
Project Designer	Manage project settings in a centralized place
Report Designer	Create SQL Server Reporting Services reports
Web Forms	Design user interfaces for ASP.NET Web sites
Windows Forms	Design user interfaces for Windows applications
XML Designer	Create and edit XML schemas

For Dummies: Bestselling Book Series for Beginners

Visual Studio® 2005

ALL-IN-ONE DESK REFERENCE

FOR

DUMMIES®

Visual Studio® 2005
ALL-IN-ONE DESK REFERENCE
FOR
DUMMIES®

by Vanessa L. Williams

Wiley Publishing, Inc.

Visual Studio® 2005 All-in-One Desk Reference For Dummies®

Published by
Wiley Publishing, Inc.
111 River Street
Hoboken, NJ 07030-5774
www.wiley.com

Copyright © 2007 by Wiley Publishing, Inc., Indianapolis, Indiana

Published by Wiley Publishing, Inc., Indianapolis, Indiana

Published simultaneously in Canada

For general information on our other products and services, please contact our Customer Care Department within the U.S. at 800-762-2974, outside the U.S. at 317-572-3993, or fax 317-572-4002.

For technical support, please visit www.wiley.com/techsupport.

Wiley also publishes its books in a variety of electronic formats. Some content that appears in print may not be available in electronic books.

Library of Congress Control Number: 2005927616

ISBN-13: 978-0-7645-9775-6

ISBN-10: 0-7645-9775-2

Manufactured in the United States of America

10 9 8 7 6 5 4 3 2 1

1O/RS/RQ/QW/IN

WILEY

About the Author

Vanessa L. Williams is a consultant and author specializing in Microsoft's SharePoint and .NET technologies. Through her Midwest consulting business, Vanessa Williams Business Solutions, she provides custom development, systems implementation, hosting, and training services for SharePoint, .NET, and Visual Studio Team System. She has ten years of business information systems experience spanning several industries including transportation, petroleum marketing, manufacturing, retail, and motor-sports entertainment. Her nontechnical experience — including jobs as a shipping clerk, accounting clerk, and forklift driver — gives her the unique ability to view systems implementations from an end user's perspective.

Vanessa grew up in Indianapolis, where she graduated from the Kelley School of Business at Indiana University with a Bachelor of Science degree in Business Management and Computer Information Systems.

Vanessa is active in the online tech community. She welcomes comments, feedback, and questions via her Web site, `sharepointgrrl.com`.

Dedication

To Mel and Rosie.

Author's Acknowledgments

Writing a book is a lot like developing software. There's no hotshot who does it all. A small team develops the idea, fleshes it out, and ushers it through the proposal process. Once approved, the author and a small team of editors move the manuscript through the editorial process. During the editorial process, the manuscript is developed and checked for technical accuracy and completeness. After the manuscript is complete, it moves through a production process where yet another team turns it into a physical product. A sales and marketing team works on promoting and selling the book to retail stores and other channels.

Like any good software development project, writing a book isn't a waterfall process. Many activities occur in parallel or provide feedback to other phases. It's common to revisit the proposal multiple times to clarify the book's vision or possibly modify the original idea.

I had an exceptionally good team help me move this book from idea to your hands. Katie Feltman supported my vision for this book and helped build the top-notch team to bring it to fruition. Mark Enochs, the project editor, and Becky Whitney, copy editor, were instrumental in developing the manuscript. Like good teammates, they shared their knowledge with me, and I'm a better writer because of it.

I'd also like to thank the readers of my previous book, *Microsoft SharePoint 2003 For Dummies*. I received hundreds of reader e-mails while writing this book. Answering those e-mails kept me hopping between SharePoint and Visual Studio, but each e-mail helped me write a better book for you.

On a personal note, I need to thank my partner, Melody, who was gracious enough to tolerate another book project. Finally, I never would've finished this book without doggy daycare. Thanks to Brigitte and her staff at the Barkalounge for wearing out my crazy puppy.

Publisher's Acknowledgments

We're proud of this book; please send us your comments through our online registration form located at www.dummies.com/register/.

Some of the people who helped bring this book to market include the following:

Acquisitions, Editorial, and Media Development

Sr. Project Editor: Mark Enochs

Sr. Acquisitions Editor: Katie Feltman

Copy Editor: Becky Whitney

Technical Editor: Chris Bower

Editorial Manager: Leah Cameron

Media Development Manager: Laura VanWinkle

Editorial Assistant: Amanda Foxworth

Sr. Editorial Assistant: Cherie Case

Cartoons: Rich Tennant (www.the5thwave.com)

Composition Services

Project Coordinator: Kristie Rees

Layout and Graphics: Claudia Bell, Jonelle Burns, Denny Hager, Stephanie D. Jumper, Heather Ryan

Proofreaders: John Greenough, Susan Moritz, Christy Pingleton, Evelyn Still

Indexer: Valerie Haynes Perry

Special Help: Heidi Unger, Barry Childs-Helton

Publishing and Editorial for Technology Dummies

    Richard Swadley, Vice President and Executive Group Publisher

    Andy Cummings, Vice President and Publisher

    Mary Bednarek, Executive Acquisitions Director

    Mary C. Corder, Editorial Director

Publishing for Consumer Dummies

    Diane Graves Steele, Vice President and Publisher

    Joyce Pepple, Acquisitions Director

Composition Services

    Gerry Fahey, Vice President of Production Services

    Debbie Stailey, Director of Composition Services

Contents at a Glance

Table of Contents

Introduction

If you're like me, you were probably a little perplexed by the announcement of the new Visual Studio and .NET platforms. My immediate reaction was, "Oh, no — not another set of tools to learn." Don't get me wrong. I embraced Visual Studio .NET and, like most of you, I looked forward to the stability of Visual Studio 2003 and version 1.1 of the .NET Framework. And, probably like you, I was comfortable. A comfortable developer is a productive developer. So I put off reading about the new tools as long as possible because I figured that I would have to do nothing more than find all my usual tasks hidden on new toolbars and menus.

Nothing could be further from the truth.

Visual Studio 2005 is more than just the next version of Visual Studio to use with the next version of the .NET Framework. Visual Studio 2005 is Microsoft's first attempt to position Visual Studio as a tool you can use for the upstream and downstream development activities that sandwich actual code writing. For example, you can use Visual Studio to visually model the entities you want to create in code. Unlike other modeling tools that have only a one-way relationship between the model and the code generation, your code stays synchronized with the model.

To be sure, Visual Studio still excels when it comes to writing code — whether you're writing it yourself or using one of Visual Studio designers to generate code for you. As with the designers in previous versions of Visual Studio, you drag and drop icons from a toolbox onto a design surface. Visual Studio generates the code for you in the background. You can then get up and running in using the new Visual Studio designers and code-generation features by simply reusing what you already know from using previous versions of Visual Studio.

If you're new to Visual Studio, you're getting to the party just in time. Whether you need to write mountains of custom code or create a simple application, Visual Studio 2005 can get the job done. Furthermore, Visual Studio supports the latest approaches to software development, including object-oriented design and programming, componentized applications, and model-driven development.

Visual Studio 2005 provides a dizzying array of editors, controls, designers, and supporting tools for developing software. Getting mired in the details of using these tools is a productivity killer. This book uses plain English to show you how to use Visual Studio 2005 to get busy building software while ignoring unnecessary details. Use this book to focus on the work that pays the bills and to

✦ Improve your individual efficiency and productivity as a developer.

✦ Display proficiency in selecting the right Visual Studio 2005 tools required to develop a solution.

✦ Employ Visual Studio 2005 to guide and improve your individual software development practices or those of a team.

✦ Navigate the many project types, editors, and designers in Visual Studio 2005.

✦ Increase your confidence and professionalism in using the development environment of choice for developers of solutions based on the Microsoft platform.

✦ Determine the role of Visual Studio in your software development process, whether you're working solo or on a team of 20.

Who Should Read This Book?

A little something for everyone is in this book, whether you're brand-new to software development or an old pro. No matter what your skill level is, you need this book if you see yourself in any of these categories:

✦ **New application developers** — Whether you're a student or a graduate who just landed your first programming job or a power user looking to expand your horizons, you'll find everything you need to get productive with Visual Studio 2005 Professional.

✦ **Existing .NET developers** — Not sure when you can make the jump to version 2.0 of the .NET Framework? Never fear. You can start using Visual Studio 2005 right now, with previous versions of the .NET Framework. I show you how, in Book II, Chapter 4. Plus, see how to convert your existing applications and use what you already know to get productive.

✦ **Existing developers using other technologies** — Whether you're coming from Visual Basic 6 or Java, you'll find lots of no-frills examples to help you get started with Visual Studio 2005.

✦ **Advanced developers on the bleeding edge** — Even if you used the .NET Framework since it was in beta, this book shows you how to use Visual Studio 2005 for the latest guidance and best practices in software development.

Visual Studio 2005 Professional is a good development environment for developing software in organizations of all sizes. Use this book if you are any of the following:

✦ **A corporate developer** — Use this book to differentiate yourself or your team members from everyone else in the company. Keep yourself relevant — and your job protected from outsourcing — by demonstrating proficiency in using the latest Microsoft toolset.

✦ **A private consultant** — Use this book to improve your return on investment in the software you use to generate revenue. Visual Studio 2005 has many features to help you stay focused on delivering quality software that fulfills contractual obligations.

✦ **A commercial software developer** — Use this book to see how Visual Studio 2005 can help you improve your ad hoc processes and differentiate yourself from competitors.

Visual Studio 2005 isn't just for developers any more. Increasingly, software is developed as part of a team effort. Visual Studio 2005 has increased its scope to encompass more aspects of the software development life cycle. As a result, all roles on the team are increasingly affected. Regardless of your role, you may find this book helpful if you fill any of these roles:

✦ **Managers, leads, and supervisors** need to understand the productivity gains and best-practices guidance offered by Visual Studio 2005. These gains can be useful for improving team processes as well as for evaluating programmer productivity.

✦ **Architects, designers, and analysts** will find new tools designed to improve collaboration among analysis, design, and implementation steps.

✦ **Developers, testers, and technologists** use Visual Studio 2005 to develop and test software. As such, this integral part of the software development process requires you to know how to harness its many features into a set of steps that support a specific project's development requirements.

About This Book

In this book, I show you how to use Visual Studio 2005 Professional Edition to build these types of applications:

✦ Windows applications

✦ Web sites and Web services

✦ Mobile applications

✦ Native applications using C++

You may be surprised that Visual Studio 2005 has moved way beyond building merely traditional applications. You can use it to build and manage solutions for SQL Server databases, SharePoint sites, Windows Workflow applications, BizTalk packages, and many other enterprise server solutions. I touch on most of these topics throughout the book.

The message of this book is mostly how to use Visual Studio to improve your personal productivity as a developer, whether you're working solo or as part of a team.

The book focuses primarily on Visual Studio 2005 Professional Edition, although many examples work in other editions too. Many developers, regardless of the size of their shops, use Visual Studio 2005 Professional Edition. Even if you're using one of the new role-based editions, it provides many of the same features as Visual Studio 2005 Professional.

You can't talk about Visual Studio 2005 without also covering the .NET Framework. This book covers the .NET Framework at a very high level and in the context of demonstrating the features of Visual Studio 2005.

The book is mostly "language agnostic," although (just like in real life) the language best suited for the job is used to demonstrate the material. In most Microsoft shops, there is a preference for either Visual Basic or C#. For that reason, many chapters use Visual Basic examples when they could have just as easily used C# examples.

Despite my preceding statement, this book isn't a learn-to-program book or a language-syntax book. If you're new to programming, consider checking out a beginning programming book or course. If you're a hobbyist or a new programmer, you may find all the tools in Visual Studio 2005 to be overwhelming or outside the bounds of your budget. In that case, consider using a Visual Studio Express Edition, all of which are free.

Foolish Assumptions

You'll get the most out of this book if you already know how to use basic programming constructs, such as `for` loops and `if/then` statements. Even though I don't teach you how to program in this book, I do share some guidance and tips on the use of best practices. Even if you have never programmed, you can still use the examples in this book to start creating basic Windows and Web applications using Visual Studio 2005.

Here are some other assumptions I made about you while writing this book:

✦ You have little or no experience with object-oriented programming (OOP). Becoming an OOP whiz takes many years of hands-on practice. This book can help lay the groundwork for your OOP training and show you the OOP features in Visual Studio 2005. Book V introduces you to OOP.

✦ You have little or no experience in using Visual Studio or the .NET Framework. If you have plenty of experience with Visual Studio or the .NET Framework, you can reuse that knowledge with this version of Visual Studio. Either way, I walk you through all the examples step-by-step.

✦ You don't have formal training in computer science. In this book, I offer technical explanations of what Visual Studio is doing behind the scenes when I think it's relevant to helping you understand the topic.

Conventions Used in This Book

This book uses a helpful set of conventions to indicate what needs to be done or what you see on-screen.

Stuff you type

When I ask you to type something, like a command or an entry in a text box, the text looks like this:

Type me

Menu commands

When I give you a specific set of menu commands to use, they appear in this format:

File⇨New⇨Web Site

In this example, you should click the File menu, choose the New menu item, and then choose the Web Site menu item.

Display messages

If I mention a specific message that you see on your screen, it looks like this on the page:

```
This is a message displayed by an application.
```

All code in the book also looks like this.

How This Book Is Organized

This book is organized so that you don't have to read it from cover to cover. To get the most out of the book, use the table of contents or index to find specific topics. The seven mini-books cluster common tasks for which you might use Visual Studio 2005 to develop software. This section provides a brief overview of what you can find in each mini-book.

Book I: Visual Studio 2005 Overview

Book I is a good place to start if you're new to Visual Studio or .NET or just want a refresher. In Book I, you get the lowdown on the following Visual Studio 2005 and .NET Framework topics:

✦ What Visual Studio is and its role in application development

✦ What .NET is and its role in application development

✦ How Visual Studio and .NET play together

✦ How programming languages fit into the world of Visual Studio and .NET

✦ How to make sense of all the different editions of Visual Studio 2005

Book II: Getting Started with Visual Studio

Use Book II to get up and running with Visual Studio 2005. If you already installed Visual Studio 2005 and are familiar with making your way around the Visual Studio interface, you can fast-forward through most of Book II. I show you how to

✦ Install Visual Studio 2005.

✦ Get the lay of the land in Visual Studio 2005.

✦ Explore the kinds of applications you can create with Visual Studio 2005.

✦ Use Visual Studio to stay in touch with the Microsoft community.

✦ Plan your upgrade strategy to Visual Studio 2005.

Book III: Building Applications with Visual Studio 2005

Visual Studio 2005 is all about creating applications. In Book III, I dig into the kinds of applications you can create. Here are some topics I cover:

✦ Develop Windows, Web, and mobile applications.

✦ Make your Windows applications look and feel like Office 2003 applications.

✦ Create applications with Visual C++.

✦ Design Web sites using themes, master pages, site maps, and Cascading Style Sheet layout.

✦ Explore the membership, profiles, registration, and Web parts providers in ASP.NET.

✦ Create Windows applications and mobile Web sites for smart devices.

Book IV: Getting Acquainted with Data Access

Nowadays, all applications require access to data. Book IV surveys the vast array of data access features in Visual Studio 2005. Even a seasoned ADO.NET programmer should take a fresh look at the new data access code-generation features in Visual Studio because they can help you to

✦ Explore data controls, including `BindingSource`, `BindingNavigator`, and the ASP.NET data source controls.

✦ Use the Data Sources pane and the Data Source Configuration Wizard.

✦ Create and manage connection strings.

✦ Use the DataSet Designer to create and manipulate strongly typed datasets.

✦ Understand and use TableAdapters and stored procedures.

✦ Access data by using objects in a class library.

✦ Use XML documents, XML schemas (XSD), XML style sheet transformations (XSLT), and XPath with the XML Editor and the XML Designer.

✦ Use the .NET Framework data providers with ADO.NET DataReaders and DataSets.

✦ Explore SQL Server 2005 and SQL Server Projects.

✦ Use Visual Database Tools and create database projects.

Book V: Coding

Book V shows you all the major Visual Studio features for designing, writing, and generating code. Whether you're an experienced or novice programmer, you're likely to come across something you haven't seen yet. Here are some topics I discuss:

✦ Use the code editor to format and navigate source code.

✦ Explore the basic language syntax of C# and Visual Basic.

✦ Understand value types and reference types in the .NET Framework.

+ Create custom data types and work with collections.

+ Get a primer in object-oriented programming, and explore the anatomy of classes in .NET.

+ Use the Class Designer to create new classes and explore existing ones.

+ Use Visual Studio to explore and consume events.

+ Understand the life cycles of Windows controls and Web controls.

+ Use FxCop to analyze your code.

+ Explore the new IntelliSense features, such as code snippets and method stubs.

+ Refactor code with the Class Designer and the C# code editor.

+ Create, test, and consume Web services.

+ Handle exceptions gracefully with structured exception handling.

+ Control code execution, and view data with the debugger.

+ Create unit tests, and use the Object Test Bench.

+ Employ best practices with the Enterprise Library.

Book VI: Going the Extra Mile

Visual Studio 2005 provides many features that take your productivity to new levels. At some point, all developers need to explore the topics covered in Book VI:

+ Configure and manage the build process.

+ Explore your deployment options for Windows applications and Web applications.

+ Use source code control with Visual Studio.

+ Create reports with Crystal Reports and SQL Reporting Services.

Book VII: Extending the Family

Visual Studio 2005 is the development platform for many exciting, new technologies being introduced by Microsoft. In Book VII, I help you explore how to

+ Find add-ons from Microsoft and other third parties to extend the features of Visual Studio 2005.

+ Create a rich, Web-based user experience with Atlas.

+ Look ahead to future versions of Visual Studio and how you can start using them now.

✦ Explore Visual Studio Team System and Team Foundation Server.

✦ Sneak a peek at Windows Vista and Office 2007.

Icons Used in This Book

In a book stuffed to the gills with icons, my editors have decided to use — you guessed it — *more icons*. Luckily, however, the book's icon set acts as visual signposts for specific stuff that you don't want to miss.

Tip icons point out advice that might save you time, trouble, and, quite possibly, cash.

These tidbits are completely optional, but if you're really into the technical side of things, you'll find loads of interesting info here.

Always read the information next to this icon! These icons highlight pitfalls to avoid as you deploy your applications or put the power of Visual Studio 2005 into action.

As its name suggests, this icon highlights stuff that you might want to, well, remember.

Where to Go from Here

Many times throughout the course of writing this book, I would stop and try to put myself in your shoes. As I thought about my own adventures with Visual Studio, I tried to anticipate the topics you might need to look for. I'm sure you'll find many interesting and relevant topics in the Table of Contents and index. I suggest you start with the Table of Contents.

As readers of my previous book, *Microsoft SharePoint 2003 For Dummies*, can tell you, I always respond to reader e-mail. If you have a question, comment, or idea that you think will make us both a lot of money, by all means, jump on my Web site and send me a message.

I can be contacted online via my alter ego at `www.sharepointgrrl.com`. There you'll find content on all my books, including the one you're holding in your hands. Be sure to check out my always interesting tech blog, where I share tidbits and tips on everything from hardware upgrades to Vista. But, please, do me a favor. Don't reveal sharepointgrrl's true identity. I don't want to make the SharePoint gods mad.

Book I

Visual Studio 2005 Overview

The 5th Wave   By Rich Tennant

"We should cast a circle, invoke the elements, and direct the energy. If that doesn't work, I guess we'll have to learn C++ after all."

Contents at a Glance

Chapter 1: What Is Visual Studio?

*W*hat does it take to write software? You need, at minimum, three basic items:

+ A text editor, such as Notepad

+ A programming language, such as Visual Basic

+ A compiler that can convert the programming language into a language your computer can understand

A *programming* language is a language that humans can understand and use to write computer programs. Computers understand only machine language, which is why the compiler has to translate the program from the human-readable programming language into machine language.

If all you need is Notepad to write computer programs, why are so many software-building tools, and books about software-building tools, on the market? Why is the software tools industry a multi-billion-dollar-a-year industry? The reason is that building software with little more than Notepad is slow. And, companies aren't paying their software developers to show off how well they can memorize language syntax. No, companies are paying software developers to build working software in the least amount of time possible and with the fewest resources.

To be truthful, building software that does more than just say "Hello world" requires more than just writing a few lines of code in a text editor. Who knew that business software could be so complex?

That's where tools like Visual Studio enter the picture. Visual Studio is a type of software development tool, an *integrated development environment (IDE)*, that allows you to build software more quickly than typing all your code in "longhand" in a text editor.

The Role of the Integrated Development Environment

Language compilers and all the tools you need in order to start writing computer programs are available for free. Most vendors provide *software development kits (SDKs)* that provide all the tools you need in order to

✦ Write code by using a text editor like Notepad.

✦ Convert the code into the 1s and 0s that your computer can understand.

After you run your text file through the compiler, you can execute the file to run your program.

One of the most popular SDKs for software development supports using the Microsoft family of languages, usually either C# or Visual Basic. Sun's Java is another popular language.

You can download the Microsoft .NET SDK for free from the Microsoft .NET Framework Developer Center, at `http://msdn.microsoft.com/ netframework/downloads/updates/default.aspx`. If you already have Visual Studio 2005 installed, the SDK is already installed.

To download the SDK for Java, go to Sun's Java Web site for developers, at `http://java.sun.com/j2se/`.

Software development kits are an inexpensive way to play around with new tools or to keep your skills updated in new or unfamiliar technologies.

Tools beyond the basic three

Developing software requires all kinds of tools. You need, at minimum, a text editor and a compiler, as I describe at the beginning of this chapter. As you might guess, however, that's not all you need. In addition to those two tools, you need tools for

✦ **Testing and debugging** — You can step through your code one line at a time to resolve errors.

✦ **File linking** — Link all the files you need in order to build an entire application.

✦ **Configuration management** — Manage the configuration settings for everything from file locations to compiler settings.

✦ **Code editing** — Write code without having to memorize the syntax for a programming language. These tools, which have some intelligence about how to use the program language, can provide suggestions or context-sensitive help as you write code.

✦ **Deployment** — Easily deploy your compiled application to other computers, where it can be executed.

When you download a software development kit, you get most of these tools and many more. The problem you quickly discover is that managing all these individual tools is difficult. Plus, many of the tools are command-line tools — you get no point-and-click convenience here.

That's when the idea hits you: "Hey, wouldn't it be great if one single tool integrated all these other tools into one place?" That's exactly what an integrated development environment does: It puts all the individual tools — the intelligent code editor, the debugger, and the configuration manager — into a single tool where they can interact with one another.

Enter Visual Studio

The Microsoft integrated development environment is named Visual Studio. Visual Studio 2005 is the latest version of this product. Some of the numerous editions of Visual Studio are better suited to individual developers, and others are geared toward developing software in a team setting. See Chapter 5 in this mini-book for more details on these editions and how to choose the edition that's right for you.

With Visual Studio 2005, you get these features:

✦ **Programming languages, such as Visual Basic .NET and C#** — See Chapter 4 in this mini-book for more details on the languages you can use with Visual Studio 2005.

✦ **Technologies for building high-quality software, such as Windows applications, Web-based applications, Web services, and applications for mobile devices, such as smartphones** — Book III shows you how to use Visual Studio 2005 to build applications.

✦ **Data access tools that allow you to access data from any of the popular database management systems, such as Microsoft SQL Server or Oracle** — You can also access text files and XML files. Book IV covers the data access capabilities of Visual Studio 2005.

✦ **Tools for debugging, designing, testing, and deploying applications** — Book VI covers many of these tools.

✦ **All the features of the Microsoft .NET Framework, which provides a rich set of features that allows you to work at a higher level of abstraction** — Chapter 2 in this mini-book discusses the evolution of .NET, and Chapter 3 describes the services of .NET.

Several IDEs for Java are available. One of the most popular free editors is Eclipse. Like Visual Studio, the full-scale Eclipse development environment bundles into a slick interface all the tools you need for building software. Because Eclipse, unlike Visual Studio, is an open source project, you can download it for free, at www.eclipse.org/.

You aren't restricted to using Visual Studio just for Microsoft .NET, nor is Eclipse limited to Java. You can use Visual Studio to create Java applications or to create .NET applications using Eclipse.

It's possible to use multiple programming languages, thanks to the nature of IDEs. All the various tools that are integrated into an IDE are created by multiple vendors. Rather than restrict you to just the set of tools that comes with a particular IDE, a *plug-in* lets you use additional tools created by third-party vendors or the open-source community.

To download the Visual Studio plug-in named Grasshopper, which allows you to create Java applications, go to http://dev.mainsoft.com/. You can find plug-ins for Eclipse at www.improve-technologies.com/alpha/esharp/.

Why would you want to mix up your languages with your IDE? The answer is productivity. In the same way that using a single tool, such as an IDE, is better than using 12 different tools, using an IDE that you're already familiar with is more productive than switching to a new IDE. So, if you work in a company that develops Microsoft applications primarily using Visual Studio, you can use it to create Java applications also. You don't need to learn to use a whole new tool, such as Eclipse.

Visual Studio as the Hub

As though the integration of tools weren't enough, Microsoft has something else in mind for Visual Studio: It envisions Visual Studio as the hub for all the server applications with which a developer might interact.

For example, rather than access Microsoft SQL Server by using the tools for that server, you can access SQL Server features right inside Visual Studio. The same statement is true for BizTalk. In the future, Visual Studio will integrate with even more server applications. In this way, Visual Studio is the hub of all your interactions with your company's information technology environment — assuming, of course, that you're strictly a Microsoft shop.

Microsoft has another kind of hub in mind for Visual Studio. The company realized that software development involves more than just coding like a madman. In fact, writing code usually involves only one-quarter to one-third of the effort involved in building software. The rest of the project's time is spent gathering and analyzing requirements, creating models that explain those requirements, and refining those models into tangible designs that are ultimately translated into code. After the code is written, the software has to be thoroughly tested and bugs tracked and maintained.

Many developers use everything from pen and paper to third-party tools to perform the rest of the tasks involved in building software. Microsoft saw an opportunity to bring all this activity under the Visual Studio umbrella. In the past, a developer might have used Visio to create models and used Nunit to automate code testing. Now, all these tools are integrated in Visual Studio, and they work together.

The tools work together so well that a model you create in Visual Studio can even generate code. Visio could do that, for example. The model in Visual Studio, however, updates itself to reflect changes that you make in the code itself!

Microsoft also realized that software development doesn't happen in a vacuum. The days of hotshot developers isolating themselves for weeks at a time to build the next big applications are long gone. Companies have finally realized that this approach to software development isn't sustainable.

Instead, a company usually has a team of developers, often with specialized roles, working on a project at the same time. By acknowledging that *software developer* means more than just *programmer,* Microsoft has expanded Visual Studio to become the hub for a company's team development activities. In fact, Microsoft embraced this model so tightly that it created different versions of Visual Studio for the different roles, such as architect and tester, in a software development project. See Chapter 5 of this mini-book for more information about the different versions of Visual Studio.

A team using Visual Studio can log a software bug, associate the bug with a section of code, assign the task of fixing the bug to a developer on the team, and track the resolution of the bug. All this happens in Visual Studio!

Microsoft's goal (in addition to increased profits) is for Visual Studio to become *the* personal productivity tool for software developers. In the same way that Microsoft Office has increased the productivity of office workers by freeing them from typewriters and calculators, Microsoft intends for Visual Studio to create a new standard of productivity for individual software developers and the teams on which they work.

The Keeper of .NET

The .NET Framework is Microsoft's platform for creating modern Windows, Web, and mobile software applications. While the platform provides the steam that makes your applications go, the Visual Studio 2005 development environment allows you to harness that power. The power of .NET is made accessible by Visual Studio, and its widespread use wouldn't be possible otherwise.

Back in the good old days of software development, before frameworks like .NET existed, developers had to write a lot of code in order to do simple tasks like open a file and display its contents on the screen. In an effort to simplify repetitive tasks, many programming languages started providing helper functions that developers could call. Development environments, such as Visual Studio, were often tailored for use with a specific programming language, such as Visual Basic.

Helper functions were created to do just what their name implies: help developers do something they needed to do. Rather than have to interact with the operating system and tell it to find a file and open it for reading, all a developer had to do was call a helper function and tell the function the name and location of the file to open. The helper function would then "talk to" the operating system and return the file's contents. The developer could use another helper function to display the returned contents on-screen. If the developer then decided to give the user the option to print the file's content, another helper function handled all the details of printing the file.

These helper functions improved a developer's productivity and allowed that person to work at a higher level of abstraction. Over the years, companies like Sun and Microsoft that make software development tools realized that developers needed a little more than just helper functions. Common software development problems had to be solved, such as how to

✦ Manage memory.

✦ Ensure that code is secure.

✦ Allow programs to be moved easily from one hardware platform to another, such as from Windows to Linux.

The solution to this problem was to create a virtual hosting environment in which software applications could run. This host, also known as a *virtual machine* or *runtime engine,* provides services such as memory management to the software that is executed inside the host. The Sun version of the virtual machine is Java, and the Microsoft version is the .NET Framework, also referred to as just .NET or Microsoft .NET.

The .NET Framework is more than just a simple set of helper functions. Applications that are created with the .NET Framework are hosted in a virtual machine called the Common Language Runtime. Therefore, before a computer can run an application that you build by using .NET, the .NET Framework must be installed on the computer. The version of the framework that's installed is the *.NET Framework Redistributable,* which is a free download from the Microsoft Web site. Many new computers have the .NET Framework Redistributable already installed, and most corporations are installing the Redistributable on all their computers.

By running your application in the .NET framework, your application can take advantage of all the many services that .NET provides.

As I mention earlier in this chapter, you can download the Microsoft .NET software development kit to get the tools you need to start building software. To fully capitalize on all the many development features of .NET, however, you need Visual Studio.

New Features in Visual Studio 2005

Visual Studio 2005 has many new features:

+ **Support for version 2.0 of the .NET Framework** — Visual Studio 2005 was built to take advantage of all the new features of the .NET 2.0 Framework. Nevertheless, you can build software by using previous versions of the .NET Framework. I show you how in Book II, Chapter 4.

+ **Improved Web development** — In addition to introducing more tools for building and deploying Web applications, Visual Studio 2005 sports the Visual Web Developer, which uses a local Web server to eliminate the need to have Microsoft Internet Information Services on the development computer. New features in Web development make it dead simple to add login, membership, navigation, and other standard Web site features to your Web site. See Book III for more information.

+ **Increased support for developing applications for mobile smart devices** — Visual Studio provides emulators for smartphones and PDAs that allow you to see what your application looks like.

+ **The use of SQL Server 2005** — Although Visual Studio 2005 can work with older versions of SQL Server and competitors' database management systems, it works best with SQL Server 2005. You can even code stored procedures within Visual Studio. Microsoft SQL Server 2000 Desktop Engine (MSDE) has been replaced with a special developers' edition of SQL Server called SQL Server 2005 Express.

✦ **New controls with smart tags** — Many new controls for Web- and Windows-based development are available. Many new controls automate features that previously had to be coded by hand. All the controls feature smart tags that prompt you on how the control is intended to be used.

✦ **A focus on provider model standardization and reusability** — New provider models for common requirements, such as security and logins, allow you to standardize these features across your portfolio of applications.

✦ **Improved code generation and IntelliSense** — New features, such as code snippets and method stub generation, provide intelligent code templates that allow you to fill in your application specification information. New refactoring tools help you transform your code from procedural to object-oriented.

✦ **The ability to work at a higher level of abstraction** — The new visual modeling features allow you to think about your software at a higher level. The models generate the underlying code, which allows you to concentrate on solving your business problems.

✦ **The use of Team System** — In addition to the Professional edition, which is intended for individual developers, the Team System edition of Microsoft Visual Studio provides all the features necessary to manage the entire software development life cycle.

✦ **More integration with MSDN** — Visual Studio 2005 is even more integrated with MSDN, the Microsoft Developer Network.

Chapter 2: Exploring .NET

In This Chapter

✔ **Discovering how .NET has evolved**

✔ **Sneaking a peek at the components of .NET**

✔ **Looking into the future of .NET**

*I*n an attempt to mitigate the increasing complexity of building software, Microsoft released a brand-new set of tools in 2002 for building software: the Microsoft .NET Framework.

.NET is a reflection of the latest thinking about, and best practices for, how software should be developed. Visual Studio is the premiere toolset that Microsoft has created for developing software by using the .NET Framework. Although the road to Microsoft .NET and Visual Studio 2005 has been topsy-turvy at times, most developers agree that using Visual Studio 2005 to develop Microsoft .NET applications is a huge productivity boon.

Following the Evolution of .NET

Microsoft released the first version of .NET in 2002. Because the company tried to append the .NET moniker to all its initiatives, from software development tools to enterprise servers to operating systems, .NET initially suffered from an identity crisis. Thanks to Microsoft's ubiquitous use of the term, however, .NET is now as much a brand as it is a technology.

Three versions of .NET have been released:

✦ **Version 1.0:** Released in 2002 along with the Visual Studio .NET 2002 integrated development environment

✦ **Version 1.1:** Released in 2003 and includes Visual Studio .NET 2003

✦ **Version 2.0:** Released in October 2005 with Visual Studio 2005

Version 3.0 of the .NET Framework will be released in early 2007 with the latest Windows operating system, Vista. You can get more information on version 3.0 and download the beta at `http://msdn.microsoft.com/winfx/`.

Each of these versions represents a milestone in developing software with .NET:

+ In version 1.0, all development — whether it was Windows-based or Web-based and regardless of the language — was integrated into Visual Studio. Prior to the release of .NET, each Microsoft development tool was a separate product.

+ The new object-oriented language C# was created as part of .NET. Visual Basic .NET was completely revamped to be object-oriented. Many Visual Basic developers felt betrayed, and Microsoft had a hard time convincing them to make the leap.

+ Data access was greatly simplified with ADO.NET, and ASP.NET was introduced for developing Web applications. Even though these technologies share the same names as their predecessors, ADO and ASP, that's where the resemblance stops. Like all .NET technologies, ADO.NET and ASP.NET are object-oriented.

+ With version 1.1 of .NET, many 1.0 features that either weren't ready yet, such as the Compact Framework for devices like the PocketPC, or were available separately from Visual Studio, such as ASP.NET, were completely integrated into Visual Studio .NET 2003.

+ Version 1.1 was more stable and more widely accepted. During this time, the Microsoft .NET brand became diluted from overuse.

+ In the two years between the release of versions 1.1 and 2.0, the dot-net community, as the collective of .NET developers is often called, busily wrote applications that demonstrated how powerful .NET could be. Microsoft listened, and many of the suggestions for ways to extend .NET, which were written about in articles on Web sites like `www.gotdotnet.com` and `www.4guysfromrolla.com`, were implemented as new features in the 2.0 version of .NET.

+ For the release of .NET 2.0, Microsoft dropped the .NET suffix from its non-development software. .NET now refers to just the application platform — the .NET Framework.

+ Visual Studio 2005 matures into more than a mere coding environment and can now manage many aspects of the software development life-cycle. The Team System version of the product uses a server-based component as a data repository.

+ C# establishes itself as a rock-solid object-oriented language.

+ MSDN, the Microsoft Developers Network, becomes more tightly integrated with the Visual Studio product.

With the latest version of Microsoft .NET 2.0, Microsoft developers can finally stand toe-to-toe with Java developers and know that they can use almost all the same language and development features. And, with Visual Studio 2005, many developers' favorite third-party tools are integrated with the IDE, which boosts productivity immensely. At the same time, the Microsoft Team System edition of Visual Studio 2005 draws a line in the sand and positions Visual Studio and Microsoft .NET as the tools of choice for enterprise software development.

Getting Acquainted with the .NET Components

To fully grasp how all the pieces of .NET work together, you first should have a basic understanding of all those pieces. At a very high level, I like to think of .NET in terms of:

+ **The .NET Framework** — All the software that makes Visual Studio possible

+ **The .NET Software Development Kit (SDK)** — All the software that enables you to build software applications by using the .NET Framework

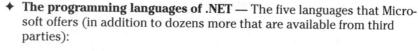

You can download both the .NET Framework and the Software Development Kit for free from the Microsoft Web site at `http://msdn.microsoft.com/netframework/downloads/updates/default.aspx`.

+ **The programming languages of .NET** — The five languages that Microsoft offers (in addition to dozens more that are available from third parties):

  • Visual Basic

  • C#

  • C++

  • J#

  • JScript

See Chapter 4 of this mini-book for more on these languages.

+ A language that can be used to develop .NET applications is said to *target* the .NET Framework.

+ **The technologies of .NET** — All the stuff you can build with .NET, such as Windows and Web applications, Web services, and mobile devices, such as smart phones.

+ **Visual Studio** — The integrated development environment (IDE) that puts access to everything in this list at a developer's fingertips.

The languages of .NET are also free in the sense that you can learn the language syntax and use any text editor to write it. The tool that you need in order to convert the programming language to a language the machine can understand is a *compiler,* which is also free. The compiler is part of the .NET Framework.

To take full advantage of the languages and technologies of .NET, however, you need Visual Studio.

.NET freebies

To start developing .NET applications, all you need is

+ The .NET Framework
+ The .NET Software Development Kit

The .NET Framework provides the bulk of the functionality; however, you need the SDK in order to take advantage of the .NET Framework in your applications.

The Microsoft .NET Framework consists of these three components (all of which are free):

+ **Common Language Runtime (CLR)** — The CLR provides a managed environment for running software applications that prevents memory leaks. Developers access the features of the CLR through the base class library. Some features of the CLR, such as automatic memory management, just happen. (The developer doesn't do anything.)

+ **Common Type System (CTS)** — The CTS sets the rules for how programming languages that use the .NET Framework must behave. New languages can then be developed for use with .NET.

+ **Base Class Library (BCL)** — The base class library is the part of the .NET Framework that developers get to "touch." The BCL enables developers to create Windows- and Web-based user interfaces, access databases, and access services of the operating systems.

Because the .NET Framework is complex, a detailed discussion of every aspect of the Framework is beyond the scope of this book. Knowing all the details of the inner workings of the .NET Framework isn't necessary for most developers, which is part of the reason that Visual Studio is such a valuable tool. It allows developers to access the features of the .NET Framework at a higher level of abstraction and "hides" the implementation details.

If you really want to know more about the inner workings of the .NET Framework, see Chapter 3 in this minibook.

The .NET Framework Software Development Kit provides developers with free tools they can use to access the .NET Framework. The SDK contains, in addition to some general utilities, tools that help you

✦ Manage configuration and deployment and configure the .NET Framework.

✦ Debug software and manage security.

Language compilers are installed with the .NET Framework.

If you're using Visual Studio 2005, the SDK is installed by default. You might still want to use some of the utilities in the SDK to automate build processes or perform other functions that aren't part of the Visual Studio interface.

If you really want to learn how the .NET Framework works, dig into the SDK and use the Framework's command-line compilers. In other words, do some development without using Visual Studio. You can gain a much better appreciation of all the time that Visual Studio saves, and you can better troubleshoot problems that occur in Visual Studio.

No free lunch

Yes, the fundamental components of .NET are free. However, if you expect to be productive, you need to spend some dough. Specifically, get your hands on Visual Studio 2005. With Visual Studio, you're better positioned to take advantage of the languages and technologies of .NET.

Dozens of languages for .NET are available, although only these five are from Microsoft:

✦ **Visual Basic** — Visual Basic has a streamlined syntax that many developers find easy to learn and use.

✦ **C#** — C# is a rapid application development language. Some of the .NET Framework is written in C#.

Although I like to use Visual Basic for user interface programming, C# works best for writing business logic.

✦ **C++** — You can use this more advanced language to build business applications, operating systems, and language compilers.

✦ **Visual J#** — This language is the Microsoft version of Java.

✦ **JScript** — This scripting language is similar to JavaScript.

Here are a couple of third-party languages available for .NET:

✦ Borland Delphi

✦ Cobol

For a complete list of all the languages available for .NET, see `www.gotdotnet.com/team/lang/`. For more specifics on the languages of .NET and how to choose and learn one, see Chapter 4 in this mini-book.

The technologies of .NET are what allow you to build cool applications. With these technologies, you can

✦ Build Windows applications by using **Windows Forms**.

✦ Build Web-based applications by using **ASP.NET**.

✦ Access data from all different kinds of data stores by using **ADO.NET**.

✦ Share data between disparate systems by using **Web services**.

✦ Create software for mobile devices, such as smartphones, using the **NET Compact Framework**.

Peering into the Future of .NET

The world of application development has changed significantly in the past decade. The concept of hosting software inside a runtime engine is now the de facto standard for building most software applications — and Microsoft .NET is a major player.

Visual Studio is all grown up from its days as a meager code editor. You can use it now to manage many aspects of software development. As the keeper of .NET, Visual Studio is poised to take .NET into more aspects of the software development life cycle, such as designing and testing.

As Microsoft looks to the future, it's placing its bets on its new operating system, Windows Vista. Vista, which is completely different from any of the previous Microsoft operating systems, features these completely redesigned subsystems:

✦ A new presentation layer for building Windows applications, graphics, videos, and documents, called **Windows Presentation Foundation**. Applications that target the WPF are called Aero applications, the name of the new Vista user interface. Aero might eventually replace Windows Forms, but that replacement is several years away.

✦ A new communications subsystem called **Windows Communication Foundation** that manages all communications and frees developers from having to handle the details. The subsystem also supports peer-to-peer communications. You'll still be able to use good old-fashioned Web services if you want, but all WCF communications are integrated with Vista.

✦ A new programming model using **version 3.0 of the .NET Framework** to easily access all features of Windows. Previous versions of Windows used a C library interface that was challenging to learn. Previous versions of the .NET Framework provided only limited access to the Windows operating system. Microsoft is positioning version 3.0 of .NET as the programming model of choice for Vista applications which makes it possible to

- Deploy applications to Windows computers and better manage updates to those applications.

- Provide more secure applications by using the security features of Windows.

- Develop more stable applications.

Version 3.0 of the .NET Framework was originally named WinFX. The FX in WinFX is shorthand for the .NET Framework. Microsoft thought the name implied that .NET was "baked" right into Vista. Unfortunately, its customers didn't get it. Microsoft realized that .NET is a stronger brand than WinFX, and decided to change the name.

Vista will be released sometime in early 2007. Many of Vista's components will work with Windows XP.

You can download beta versions for Windows Vista and version 3.0 of the .NET Framework at http://msdn.microsoft.com/windowsvista/getthebeta/default.aspx.

Another exciting area of development is the next version of Microsoft Office. Microsoft has expanded the Office feature set to include new server products, such as SharePoint Portal Server. The new name for SharePoint Portal Server is Microsoft Office SharePoint Server 2007. In the future, Office will include servers for InfoPath forms and Excel reporting. Of course, all these features are extensible with Microsoft .NET.

Microsoft even released a special edition of Visual Studio: Visual Studio Tools for Office (VSTO). VSTO allows developers to create applications by using the .NET Framework and Office.

The next two versions of Visual Studio are expected to more tightly integrate Visual Studio and Microsoft .NET with the new features of the operating system. The next version, code-named Orcas, is expected to be released in late 2006 or early 2007. Orcas will focus primarily on expanding the capability to work with version 3.0 of the .NET Framework and the new Windows Vista presentation subsystem. You'll still be able to do all the traditional business development by using Windows Forms.

Don't expect to see the version after Orcas, code-named Hawaii, before 2010. The expectation is that Hawaii will attempt to deliver on the vision behind Microsoft's software factories (without the unions and the time clocks). The idea behind software factories is that there are similar kinds of software that developers should be able to use a tool to stamp out. For example, an invoicing application is an invoicing application. In how many unique ways can you manage invoices? Microsoft wants to build tools that allow developers to draw pictures or models of their software applications. In this example, you might drop a customer, an order, or an invoice on a modeling screen, and Hawaii could then build a full-blown invoice application.

To read more about **software factories**, go to `http://msdn.microsoft.com/vstudio/teamsystem/workshop/sf/default.aspx`.

With Microsoft making the .NET Framework an important element of its new operating system and Microsoft Office, the future looks bright for both the .NET Framework and Visual Studio. See Book VII for more details on Vista, Office, and the future of .NET and Visual Studio.

Using the New Features in .NET

Here is a list of a few new features in version 2.0 of the .NET Framework that have been long awaited:

+ **Partial classes** — Split code across multiple files. This feature is designed to increase productivity by enabling easier code generation. Partial classes are a behind-the-scenes feature: Visual Studio uses partial classes to separate generated code from the code you write. As a rule, you probably won't create your own new partial classes.

+ **Nullable types** — You can better manage the problem of dealing with null values in a database.

+ **Generics** — Define data types in a generic way and then reuse them. Although the concept of generics is abstract and confusing at first, developers can use it to write reusable code more easily.

Chapter 3: Modern Software Development

In This Chapter

✓ Understanding the professional approach to software development

✓ Building a software development toolbox

✓ Seeing why component-based software is superior

✓ Peeking at how programs are executed in .NET

✓ Learning about automatic memory management

*E*ven if you've never worked in software development, you've no doubt heard about many of the problems associated with software development projects, such as

✦ Frequent schedule and budget overruns

✦ Software that doesn't do what it's supposed to do

✦ Software that's obsolete by the time it gets finished

Over the years, the software development industry has created a number of approaches and tools to help better manage software development. Many of these approaches can be categorized in one of these two approaches:

✦ **Ad hoc, or hotshot** — In this approach, characterized by non-existent development practices, no standard exists for how software is developed. Hotshot programmers often work all night and come in at noon the next day. You usually get no documentation, and only the programmer understands how the code works.

✦ **Rigorous and slow** — As a rejection of the other approach, this one takes an engineering view of software development. The argument is that dotting all your i's and crossing all your t's and then getting proper sign-off at each step along the way gives software development a process that's repeatable and, most importantly, accountable. Unfortunately, the engineering approach adeptly creates mountains of documentation but doesn't adeptly create working software on budget and on time.

After producing many failed projects, software developers have started to get the message that ad hoc approaches are too immature and the rigors of an engineering mentality probably too inflexible. At the same time, most companies have learned that relying on hotshot developers is a recipe for disaster. Instead, many firms now hire developers who write manageable code rather than someone who can write code faster than anyone else.

In this chapter, I offer an abbreviated history of software development by discussing where the process now stands and how it got there. I also discuss some of the inner workings of .NET as it relates to modern development approaches.

Software Engineering in Action

Over the years, a number of methodologies and tools were created in an attempt to solve the problems involved in software development, with each solution promising to deliver software development projects from the evils of scope creep and second system syndrome. *Scope creep* occurs when additional features that weren't originally planned for find their way into the software. If you've ever worked on the second incarnation of an existing system, then you've no doubt experienced *second system syndrome*. In this case, the project quickly gets bloated because developers and users see so many opportunities to improve the existing system. Unfortunately, many methodologies and tools designed to keep projects on track were not only very expensive, but their implementation also required significant overhead. As a result, companies spent a lot of money but didn't always see results.

Now that software developers have had some time to see what doesn't work, they have started to create a living framework of what does work:

+ **Create repeatable processes** — Rather than treat every project like it's shiny and new, developers have started to acknowledge that they should take some common steps. Also, by acknowledging that different kinds of software development projects exist, developers are rejecting the notion of a one-size-fits-all process and instead creating processes that can scale up or down to fit the project.

+ **Follow best practices** — By creating a body of industry best practices, software developers are sharing and reusing their knowledge of how to solve problems.

+ **Use more than one tool** — Developers have learned that no single tool can do the job. Instead, a toolbox of tools from many different vendors and the open source community is a better approach than putting all your eggs in one basket with a single vendor.

Have process, will repeat

When it comes time to starting a new software development project, many developers aren't sure where to begin. Depending on what your role is in the project, the project may not actually start for you until after somebody else completes their responsibilities. Does the project start before or after the kick-off meeting? Should you even have a kick-off meeting, and, if so, who should attend? These questions are answered by the management style and processes your company adopts for developing software.

Managing a software development project tends to fall somewhere in between these two approaches:

✦ **Waterfall** — In the waterfall approach, one phase of the project completely ends before another phase can start. In this way, the project "waterfalls" through the stages.

✦ **Iterative** — Projects that are developed iteratively go through the same phases multiple times. Developers can move backward and forward through the development phases several times to iteratively develop their understanding of both the problem and the solution.

A process for developing software is like any other process. It's a set of steps you go through to achieve an outcome. Your company has a process for paying bills and entering into contracts. Some business processes are more strictly defined and closely adhered to than others. The same is true for developing software. Some companies have strict rules about how projects are initiated and how they progress. Other companies approach each project like it's their first. I describe a few of the popular process approaches in this list:

✦ **Software engineering** — The rigorous engineering approach brings an engineering mindset to software projects. A body of standards outlining the kinds of documentation and processes that should support a project is defined in the Institute of Electrical and Electronics Engineers (IEEE) software engineering standards.

✦ **Agile** — This approach embraces change as part of the software development process. In most approaches, change is usually considered a bad word. Agile developers work in pairs, create many prototypes of their solutions, and incorporate user feedback throughout the entire process.

✦ **Test-driven** — This newer approach to building software involves building test harnesses for all code. These tests, written from the requirements documentation, ensure that code can deliver promised features.

✦ **Rational Unified Process (RUP)** — The RUP commercial process uses the IBM suite of Rational tools to support software development. Its noncommercial equivalent is the Unified Process (UP). RUP and UP are iterative approaches.

What's common to all these approaches is the acknowledgment of a software development life cycle (SDLC). Most processes account for the fact that all software progresses through a life cycle that has similar stages:

✦ **Initiation** — Project planning and justification get the project up and running.

✦ **Requirements gathering** — After the project is approved, developers start talking with users about what they expect the software to do. Frequently, this phase requires reexamining the planning and feasibility efforts from the preceding stage.

✦ **Analysis** — At this stage, developers analyze the requirements they have gathered to make sure that they understand what end users want.

✦ **Design** — Developers start to work out models that describe what the requirements might look like in software.

✦ **Construction and implementation** — Developers write the programs that execute the models created in the design stage.

✦ **Testing** — The programs are tested to ensure that they work properly and meet the requirements that the end user specified.

✦ **Deployment** — Software is installed, and end users are trained.

✦ **Maintenance** — After the software has passed all its tests and been implemented, it must still be supported, to ensure that it can provide many years of service to the end user community.

In a project using a waterfall management approach, the software is likely to progress through the stages of the life cycle in chronological order. A project managed iteratively cycles back through the phases while it makes forward progress. On larger projects, people usually fill specialized roles at different stages of the SDLC. One person often fills multiple roles. Table 3-1 lists some common roles in the SDLC.

Table 3-1	Roles in a Software Project
SDLC Phase	*Role or Job Title*
Initiation	Project manager, project sponsor
Requirements gathering	Analyst, subject matter expert
Analysis	Analyst, subject matter expert
Design	Designer, architect (possibly specialized, such as software architect or technical architect)
Construction and implementation	Programmer
Testing	Tester, quality assurance (QA) personnel
Deployment	Installer, trainer, technician, technical architect
Maintenance	Support personnel, programmer, tester

A software project generally doesn't flow like a waterfall through stages of the SDLC, so that's a big reason that the waterfall approach has fallen out of favor. In most cases, the stages of the SDLC are either

✦ **Iterative** — The stages are repeated multiple times throughout the project. For example, developers commonly loop through the initiation, requirements, and analysis phases several times until they get a handle on what they're expected to build. Each loop delves progressively deeper into the details. You'll frequently question the assumptions of the requirements and analysis stages after you start building models in the design stage.

✦ **Concurrent** — Stages often occur at the same time. For example, a group of developers might analyze requirements while another group starts to build the design models. The design group can start to validate (or invalidate) the analysis assumptions.

 Choosing a process isn't an either/or proposition. Many teams like to combine the features they like best from several different approaches. For example, I like the change-management features of the agile approach. I also frequently refer to the IEEE software engineering standards, though, if I'm looking for some direction on what constitutes complete documentation.

Regardless of whatever approach you decide to take, here's some advice to take into consideration:

✦ **Use a process — any process.** I think that homegrown processes are sometimes better than "store-bought" ones. If everyone gets to participate in creating a process, they're more likely to want to see it succeed.

✦ **Repeat the process.** A process becomes a process only after it has been repeated multiple times. Doing something once and then abandoning it doesn't create a process.

✦ **Improve the process.** You can't improve your process unless it has some means of providing feedback and metrics for measuring. Without metrics, you have no way of knowing when something has improved. If you're unsure of how to do this, take a peek at other methodologies to get some ideas.

Practicing what you preach

A body of knowledge has started to develop around software development. Developers realize that many businesses are trying to solve the same kinds of problems. Rather than treat each project as a one-off experience, developers know that elements of the project are common to other projects that they need to develop. When a problem gets solved the same way over and over again, the solution is often referred to as a *best practice*. In order for a best practice to develop, many people must be trying to solve the same problem. For example, the following list includes several problems that Web site developers try to solve:

+ Providing secure access

+ Logging errors

+ Accessing data

Businesses also need to solve a common set of problems. Every business I have ever worked in needs to

+ Capture and fulfill orders.

+ Manage customer information.

+ Invoice and receive payments.

Rather than try to solve all these problems on your own, an entire community of developers, authors, and companies are sharing their experiences and guidance on how to approach these problems.

This shared knowledge can be called best practices, design patterns, frameworks, or models. Microsoft's own vision for sharing knowledge includes patterns and practices and software factories.

In fact, the underlying premise of runtime environments, such as the Microsoft .NET Framework and the Java Virtual Machine, is that all programs need common features, such as portability and memory management. Frameworks, patterns, practices, and models are all knowledge repositories that enable developers to reuse the work of other developers. Modern software development makes extensive use of all these knowledge-sharing tools.

According to Professor Joe Hummel, of Lake Forest College, some of the best practices for software development include these elements:

+ **Object-oriented programming** — This style of programming makes programs easier to understand and test.

+ **Components** — Software that's broken into components is easier to deploy. Later in this chapter, in the section "Components Defeat Monoliths," I expand on the benefits of using components.

+ **Testing** — *Integration testing,* or repeated automated testing, is important in order to see how components work together.

+ **Code reviews** — Standards are crucial for identifying how code should look. Having peers review each other's code (as they say, "Two heads are better than one") enforces standards and exposes developers to new styles.

✦ **Prototyping** — You should build your software frequently, to not only make sure that it works but also get it in front of end users early and often so that they can validate your progress.

✦ **Tools, tools, tools** — Use tools to help you manage your process and projects. See the next section for more about using tools.

Another best practice to keep in mind is that when it comes to developing software, less is more. A team of four to six developers can usually develop higher-quality software than larger teams can. As team size increases, so does the complexity of keeping everyone in the loop. Keep your team sizes small.

When you're using best practices, you have to keep things in context. The tools and processes you use for building commercial-quality software might not be the same tools and processes you should use to build software for an internal department that has a closed information technology environment.

Building a developer's toolbox

Just as plumbers and auto mechanics have toolboxes, software developers have toolboxes too. Your software development toolbox should include all the usual suspects:

✦ An integrated development environment, such as Visual Studio

✦ Third-party tools that you like to use for testing or logging

  Many developers take advantage of open source software, such as Nunit for unit testing and Log4Net for logging application errors.

✦ Project management software, such as Microsoft Project, or maybe even a simple spreadsheet program

✦ Collaboration software, such as Windows SharePoint Services, that you can use to store your project's artifacts

✦ Source code control software so you can keep all your source code safe and secure

You should build a toolbox of resources to which you can turn for advice about how to handle security, build secure Web sites, and face any other kind of software challenge. Sure, you could just "Google" whatever you're looking for. You have more success, though, if you turn to a common set of resources. Here's a start:

✦ **Software Engineering Institute (SEI)** — The SEI plays a huge role in defining software engineering. You can find SEI on the Web at `www.sei.cmu.edu/`.

✦ **Software Engineering Body of Knowledge (SWEBOK)** — The SWEBOK represents the consensus among academicians and practitioners for what the processes for software development should look like. If you have never thought about what it means to engineer software, the SWEBOK is a great place to start. You can download it at `www.swebok.org`.

✦ **Microsoft patterns and practices** — A few years ago Microsoft finally started sharing with the world how it thinks that software developed by using Microsoft tools *should* be developed. Microsoft patterns and practices is a combination of books, articles, software, and other resources that help you write software the way Microsoft believes it should be written. Find patterns and practices at `http://msdn.microsoft.com/practices/GettingStarted/`.

✦ **Rational Unified Process (RUP)** — RUP is one of the more popular development processes. Tons of books and articles have been written on the subject. Note that you can use the RUP without buying any of the tools that IBM makes to support the process. Read more about the RUP at `http://en.wikipedia.org/wiki/Rational_Unified_Process`.

✦ **Agile Manifesto** — The manifesto for agile software development can change the way you think about software development. Read the manifesto at `http://agilemanifesto.org/`.

✦ **MSDN Webcasts** — The Microsoft Developer Network, or MSDN, presents Webcasts on every kind of software subject imaginable. You can find Webcasts at `http://msdn.microsoft.com/events/`. Read more about MSDN in Book II, Chapter 3.

A Webcast that I find especially valuable is the series Modern Software Development in .NET, by Professor Joe Hummel. Dr. Hummel has a series on C# and on Visual Basic; you can download his Webcasts from `www.microsoft.com/events/series/modernsoftdev.mspx`.

Remember that much of the advice you find tells you how software *should* be developed, but not so much how it *is* developed. I suggest that you become familiar with how things are supposed to be done and still learn the techniques that other developers use to solve real-world problems.

Working with your partners in development

The most important lesson that software developers have learned is "It takes a village." Long gone are the days when hotshot programmers were expected, or allowed, to hole up in their offices for weeks while they created the next big application.

Now, software development is recognized as a team effort. Although some teams still place people in specialized roles, such as programmers, people are more commonly filling multiple roles on a project. The lines between analysts, designers, programmers, and testers are becoming more blurred.

The blurred roles are part of the reason that many developers objected to Microsoft's planned release of different versions of Visual Studio based on the roles of a development team. As roles blur, developers are expected to be more flexible. Many diehard programmers experienced the outsourcing of their jobs to India. Those programmers who were flexible enough to learn new languages or new roles found new jobs. Others weren't so fortunate.

Although I want to see programming jobs remain in the United States, the harsh reality is that most businesses' profit motives are much stronger than their loyalties to employees or even to the towns and cities where they get their start. The trend in development is for developers to think in higher levels of abstraction, which means being able to take on the role of a designer or analyst.

Not all developers work a 40-hour week, of course, although the length of that workweek is becoming the norm. My experience inside corporate information technology departments supports my theory that an increasing number of developers are maintaining reasonable hours. I've also observed that many consulting houses are becoming more reasonable about creating a work-life balance for their employees. I've heard that even developers at the company everyone loves to hate, Microsoft, are working regular hours.

Developers *are* sometimes expected to work extra hours, of course. Sometimes, during the software development life cycle, extra work is required, although it's becoming more of an exception than the norm.

Components Defeat Monoliths

Older software that was developed before the creation of modern software development techniques or that uses outdated practices or obsolete development tools is sometimes called *legacy software.* Almost all businesses support at least a few legacy applications. Sometimes, a company's legacy software is limited to a few non-essential utilities used by a single department. At other times, the legacy application is a mission-critical application that must be kept running. Either way, at some point, you'll be asked to support a legacy application.

I've supported my fair share of legacy applications, and here are some of the challenges I found:

✦ **Minimal, missing, or out-of-date documentation** — Although documentation usually isn't the strong suit of most developers, the complexity of some legacy applications can be overwhelming. Newer development techniques favor simplicity and allow the code to be self-documenting. At the same time, more intelligent tools, such as Visual Studio 2005, can update modeling documentation to reflect changes made in the source code.

✦ **Components that are tightly coupled** — A legacy application sometimes has dependencies on other software that can cause the application to crash. Components are considered *tightly coupled* when you can't separate them from each other. If the software is broken into pieces, those pieces, or *components,* can't be reused for other software. New applications must be created, which leads to the same logic being deployed in multiple applications.

✦ **The use of nonstandard protocols** — Software that was developed before the creation of standards such as XML often use proprietary file formats and communications protocols. This situation makes it difficult for the software to interoperate with other software.

✦ **"Spaghetti" source code** — The emphasis in coding hasn't always been on readability. As a result, programmers write programs that are cryptic and hard to understand.

✦ **General deployment and maintenance difficulties** — Many legacy applications were intended to be deployed in much simpler hardware configurations than the ones in use now. Software written in the mid- to late 1990s was probably never intended to be used over the Internet, for example.

You *can,* of course, find software developed by using all the latest tools and practices that have all these characteristics. However, developers who are paying attention to industry best practices and working with, rather than against, modern tools should find that they have to go out of their way to write bad software.

Software written with these drawbacks is *monolithic.* With a monolithic application, you can imagine the developer sitting down and writing one long piece of source code that does 25 different things. Although the software might work and be efficient, this approach is hard to maintain and scale.

Software developers now focus on

✦ **Readability** — Writing software shouldn't be a contest to see how cryptic you can be. Today's approach favors a programming style that avoids shortcuts and abbreviations and instead uses an implementation designed to be transparent to future developers. This technique makes the code self-documenting because you don't have to write documentation that explains what the code does.

✦ **Components** — Breaking down software into discrete, manageable components is favored over creating one huge application. Components can be reused in some cases and are easier to deploy.

One reason these changes have come about is that management has realized that hiring and retaining people is expensive. Even though modern tools and practices might be more verbose and require more processing power than legacy code, using modern tools and practices is acceptable because the power of hardware has increased relative to its price. Buying more hardware is cheaper than hiring additional developers.

Another reason that components have become more important is the expanded use of networking and the Internet. Developers found that by breaking applications into components that could be deployed across multiple servers and connected by a network, they could get around the monolithic applications that didn't run.

Architecture evolution

The 1990s approach to component-based design was most often implemented in a physical two-tier architecture: In this *client/server* architecture, some part of the application resides on the client, and another part resides on the server. A network connects the client to the server. In most cases, the data resided on the server while the program to access the data resided on the client.

As time went on, developers became more crafty at carving up their applications to run on multiple servers. This approach is generally referred to as *n-tier design* because an application can have any number, or *n* number, of tiers.

In reality, most applications stick with a two- or three-tier design. The standard for many applications is a logical three-tier design that looks like this:

✦ **Presentation layer** — The code for the graphical user interface

✦ **Business object layer** — The code that deals with the logic for your business domain, such as customers and orders

✦ **Data access layer** — The code that handles the process of moving data from the business objects into the data store, such as a database

One reason that this approach is popular is that it allows you to mix and match layers. Suppose that you create a business object layer that recognizes how your company manages its customers and orders. You can then create a Windows-based presentation layer and a Web-based presentation layer. Because all your business logic is specified only once in your business object layer, you have to maintain only one set of business objects. What's more, if you decide that users of smartphones need to be able to access your business object layer, you only have to create an additional presentation layer.

Contrast this approach with a monolithic application, in which you create separate applications for each user interface you need. You then have a Windows application, a Web-based application, and a third application for your smartphones. Each application has its own set of business logic for handling customers and orders. If you discover a bug or your business decides to changes its rules, you have to make changes in all three applications. Using a tiered approach, the change is limited to your business object layer.

You still have to test your application before you roll it out. For example, you might need to modify the user interfaces so that they can handle a new field. Still, this technique is much preferred to having three sets of business logic.

This logical three-tier design can be implemented in several ways in the physical world:

+ **Two tiers** — In this typical client/server model, the presentation and business object layers might reside on the client while the data access layer resides on the server.

+ **Three tiers** — In this model, each layer can be hosted on a different computer.

+ **More than three tiers** — If any of the layers is especially complex or requires significant processing power, each of the layers can further be divided and implemented on multiple computers.

+ **No tiers** — If all the code resides on a single computer, it can be said to have one tier or no tiers.

Component management in .NET

The unit of deployment in .NET is an *assembly*. In an application with three tiers (physical, business, and data access), as described in the preceding section, each tier would likely have its own assembly. Of course, that's not to say you can only have one assembly per tier. Each tier can have as many assemblies as necessary to adequately organize the source code. The application might look something like the image shown in Figure 3-1.

When an application is compiled, you can choose whether to compile it as an executable or a class library. In a three-tiered application, you might have the following assemblies:

+ **MyWindowsApp.exe** — The file you would execute on a client PC. The file contains all the code for the presentation layer. The presentation layer consumes code from the other two layers by creating a reference to that code.

✦ **MyBusinessObjects.dll** — The class library that contains all the code for your business logic.

✦ **MyDataAccess.dll** — Another class library that contains all the code for getting data to and from the data store.

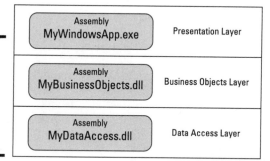

Figure 3-1: Each layer in a multi-tiered application is an assembly.

The reason that the business objects and data access layers are compiled as class libraries and not as executables is to prevent users from executing the files directly. Because no user interface is in those layers, users have no reason to execute them directly. The assemblies are just libraries of code that you can reference from other code.

To use the code that's in the business objects or data access class libraries, you create a reference in the executable file of the presentation layer, as shown in Figure 3-2.

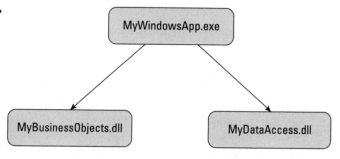

Figure 3-2: One assembly can use the code in another assembly by creating a reference.

After you create a reference to the assembly, you can access the code inside the assembly. Suppose that MyBusinessObjects.dll contains code to get a customer's address. To display the customer's address on-screen in your application, however, the presentation layer must reference the MyBusinessObjects.dll so that .NET knows where to get the code that gets the customer's address. See Chapter 3 in Book IV to read about referencing a class library.

After the reference is created, your presentation layer can access the code, which might look something this:

```
MyApp.MyBusinessObjects.Customer customer;
customer = new MyApp.MyBusinessObjects.Customer('Smith, John');
MyDataList.DataSource = customer.GetCustomerAddress();
```

The first line of this code asks that the Customer class in the MyBusinessObjects class library set aside some memory for the customer 'Smith, John'. The code that asks the data record for 'Smith, John' from the database is stored in the MyBusinessObjects class library. Herein lies the beauty of assemblies: You can use this logic to retrieve the customer information in any of the presentation layers you create. Figure 3-3 demonstrates how the presentation layer accesses the code in MyBusinessObjects.dll.

Figure 3-3:
The presentation layer assembly can access the code in the business objects layer.

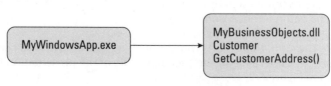

In the real world, you would probably use a customer identification number rather than the customer's name. What if the database had two 'Smith, John' entries? You would need, at least, some way to deal with the inevitability of having two or more different customers with the same name.

The second line of code tells .NET to use the customer name 'Smith, John' from the preceding line to call the code that retrieves the customer address. The code then assigns whatever value is returned to a data list, which presumably is used to display the customer's address on the screen.

What's in a namespace?

Notice that the code in the code sample is separated by dots, like this:

```
MyApp.MyBusinessObjects.
    Customer
```

Code is organized in .NET by using namespaces. *Namespaces* are a way to hierarchically organize code so that duplicate names can be used without creating confusion for .NET.

In this example, the top of the namespace hierarchy is named `MyApp`. Within the `MyApp` namespace is `MyBusinessObjects`. You might also find `MyWindowsApp` and `MyData Access` within the `MyApp` namespace. You access the code in those namespaces like this:

```
MyApp.MyWindowsApp
MyApp.MyWebApp
MyApp.MyDataAccess
```

Using namespaces this way allows someone else to have the same namespaces within a different namespace hierarchy. For example, if a co-worker has the namespace `TeamApp`, the namespace might look like this:

```
TeamApp.MyWindowsApp
TeamApp.MyMobileApp
TeamApp.MyBusinessObjects
```

In reality, you probably wouldn't prefix your namespaces with the word *My*. You'd most likely use your company's name or the name of the application. The namespace should allow you to easily identify the code contained within the namespace. Can you guess what kind of code you'd find in the Microsoft.Word or Microsoft.Excel namespaces?

All the software that makes up the .NET Framework Class Library is made up of assemblies. Microsoft created a special place to store all the assemblies for .NET called the Global Assembly Cache, or GAC. (Yes, it's pronounced "gack.") The GAC stores all versions of an assembly in a folder on your computer. You can store the assemblies you create in the GAC folder or in an application folder. See the section "Sharing Assemblies" in Book VI, Chapter 2 for more information on installing applications in the GAC.

Before the GAC came along, developers had no easy way to manage the versions of an application, so many people began to refer to the deployment of Windows applications as "DLL hell." This term reflected the fact that the files that contain the code libraries — DLL files — could quickly become your worst enemy if you realized that you didn't have the right version of the file you needed in order to make your application work.

Managed Code Execution

One hallmark of modern software development is the way software is executed on a computer. Previously, software deployment and execution worked like this:

The CLR virtual machine

Two big benefits of using the Common Language Runtime virtual machine are that code is easily portable to multiple hardware platforms and the CLR provides a safer, more stable execution environment.

The CLR provides these additional services for managed code:

✓ Automatic memory management

✓ Verification that code will be executed as intended and hasn't been tampered with

✓ Assurance that managed code can interact with unmanaged code (code running outside the CLR)

✓ Support for multiple versions of the code

See the nearby section "Taking Out the Garbage" for more information on automatic memory management.

1. A programmer wrote source code using some higher-level language, such as Visual Basic.

2. Before the computer could understand the source code, it had to be *compiled,* or converted to the native language that the machine understands.

3. Because each kind of computer has its own native language, the code had to be compiled each time the programmer wanted to use it on a different kind of machine. There wasn't much compatibility between machines, so the existing source code often had to be modified to address the subtleties of the new hardware environment, as shown in Figure 3-4.

4. Because the code was converted to the native language of the machine, the code, when it was executed, had direct access to the operating system and the machine's hardware. This access not only made programming complex, but also created an unstable operating environment.

Back in the 1990s, the folks over at Sun had the bright idea of creating a programming language that could work on any machine. The Java Virtual Machine that they built creates, on the hardware, a mini-environment that allows the software to be executed without touching the hardware, as shown in Figure 3-5. The Java Virtual Machine was smart enough to know how to make the software work with the hardware. Because of the resulting stable environment and simplified programming, Java was widely embraced.

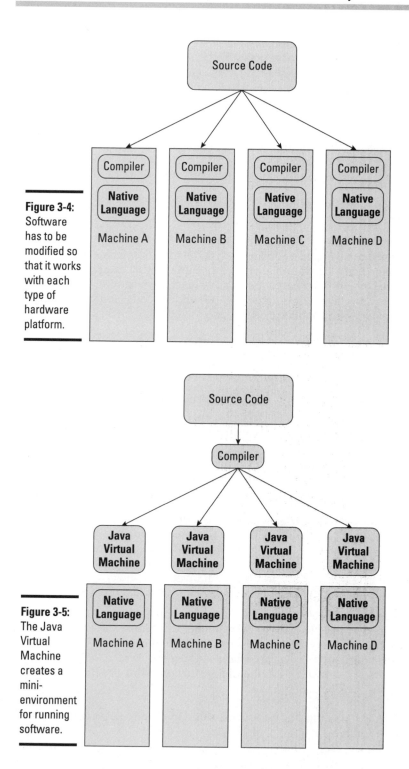

Figure 3-4:
Software has to be modified so that it works with each type of hardware platform.

Figure 3-5:
The Java Virtual Machine creates a mini-environment for running software.

Ever mindful of its competition, Microsoft sneaked a peek at Sun's Java Virtual Machine and liked what it saw. Over time, all the different Microsoft teams that were working on building development tools and languages started coalescing to work on their implementation of the virtual machine. Then the Microsoft .NET Framework was born.

The Microsoft version of the virtual machine is slightly different in implementation from Java, although they're similar conceptually. The virtual machine in .NET is the *Common Language Runtime (CLR)*. These steps show how using virtual machines changed the deployment and execution of software:

1. A programmer writes source code using a higher-level language, such as Visual Basic .NET.

2. The VB.NET compiler converts the source code into Microsoft Intermediate Language (MSIL). MSIL is the native language of the Common Language Runtime virtual machine. Rather than convert the source code into the hardware's native machine language, the compiler creates intermediate code that the CLR understands. Source code compiled into MSIL is *managed* code.

   All language compilers that target the .NET Common Language Runtime convert the source code into MSIL. Source code from multiple languages can then be used to create a single application.

3. The compiler also creates metadata about the source code. The metadata identifies to the CLR all the assemblies and other files that the source code needs in order to be executed properly. The CLR is responsible for resolving dependencies before the code is executed.

4. When the code's assembly is executed, it's compiled a second time from the MSIL into the native code for the hardware platform on which the code is being executed. This second compiler is the *just-in-time (JIT)* compiler because the MSIL code is compiled just before it's executed.

   When code is compiled using the just-in-time compiler, the compiled code is stored in memory. If the code is used again, it doesn't have to be compiled again. Rather, the copy of the code that's in memory is used. When the execution is complete, the code is removed from memory. If the code is called again after being removed from memory, it must be compiled into native machine code again by the JIT compiler.

5. Managed code (code that runs in the Common Language Runtime) is executed within the CLR virtual machine. As a result, the code doesn't have direct access to the hardware and operating system. The code is more stable and less likely to crash the system. To read more about the benefits of running code in the CLR virtual machine, see the preceding sidebar, "CLR virtual machine."

Figure 3-6 diagrams the way code is executed by using the Common Language Runtime.

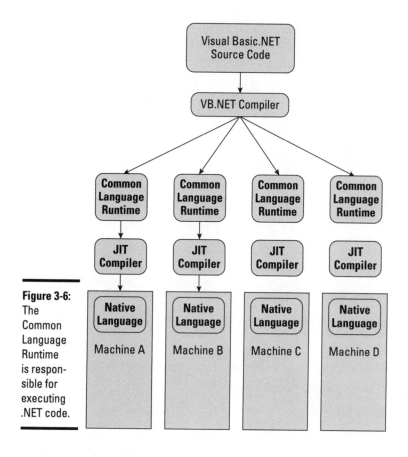

Figure 3-6:
The
Common
Language
Runtime
is respon-
sible for
executing
.NET code.

The architecture used by the Java Virtual Machine and Microsoft .NET are part of an international standard for how software execution should be managed. The languages of .NET are expected to conform to the Common Language Specification. The Common Language Runtime of .NET is the Microsoft implementation of the Common Language Infrastructure.

Taking Out the Garbage

One big service of the .NET Framework is automatic memory management, or *garbage collection*. Microsoft didn't make up this term — it's an authentic computer science term that applies to computer memory.

Before a computer program can use a resource, such as a database, the program must request that the computer set aside memory for the resource. After the program stops using the memory, the data stored in the memory is referred to as *garbage* because it's no longer useful. To reclaim the memory for another use, the programmer must remember to tell the computer that the garbage in the memory can be disposed of.

A garbage collector, such as the one in the .NET Framework, takes care of the business of asking for memory and then reclaiming it after the program is done using it. The garbage collector collects the garbage memory and then makes it available for use again.

Memory is used to store the resources a program needs to complete tasks, such as

✦ Store data, such as customer and order records.

✦ Display information on the screen or send it to a printer.

✦ Open network connections for sending data.

✦ Open a database connection.

✦ Open a text file.

The garbage collector frees the developer from having to perform these tasks:

✦ Track how much memory is available and how much is used.

✦ Assign memory to program resources.

✦ Release memory when resources are done using it.

The garbage collector allows developers who are creating a program to focus on customers and orders and other business domain entities rather than on memory management. Using a garbage collector eliminates two common errors that developers make when they have to manage their own memory:

✦ **They forget to free memory.** When a program doesn't release a computer's memory after the program's done using it, the memory is quickly filled with garbage and can't be used for useful tasks. This is often called a *memory leak*. When a program runs out of memory, it crashes. What's worse is that memory leaks can cause other programs — and even your whole computer — to crash.

✦ **They try to use memory that has already been freed.** Another common error that developers make is trying to access a resource that has already been removed from memory. This situation can also cause a program to crash unless the developer makes the program test whether the resource is still available. A developer who forgets that the resource is freed probably won't remember to test the resource before trying to use it.

Allocating memory

To prevent you from having to manage the memory yourself, the Common Language Runtime (CLR) allocates memory for program resources this way:

1. The CLR reserves a block of memory, which is the *managed heap*.

2. When you ask for resources, such as to open network connections or files, the CLR allocates memory for the resource from the managed heap.

3. The CLR notes that the block of memory is full so that it knows to use the next block of memory when you ask for a resource the next time.

Although you still have to tell the CLR that you need the resource, all the details of which memory addresses are occupied, and what they're occupied with, are handled by the CLR on your behalf.

Releasing memory

In this section, I describe how the CLR knows when to release the memory.

The CLR divides the memory in the managed heap logically into manageable pieces, or *generations*. The garbage collector (GC) uses three generations: 0, 1, and 2. The GC operates under the assumption that newly created objects will have shorter life spans than older objects.

Whenever you ask for a new resource, memory is allocated from the portion of the memory block designated as Generation 0. When Generation 0 runs out of memory, the GC starts a collection process that examines the resources in memory and frees anything it deems as garbage (anything that's unusable to the application). After freeing as much memory as possible, the GC compacts the memory so that all the remaining resources are placed next to each other in a neat stack. Compacting memory is something the developer doesn't have to do.

How do resources get into Generations 1 and 2? Well, if the GC cannot reclaim enough memory from Generation 0 to accommodate your new requests, it tries to move the resources from Generation 0 to Generation 1. If Generation 1 is full, the GC tries to move them to Generation 2. This process is how older resources that are still in use graduate through the generations.

Garbage collection isn't something you should try to control — it happens automatically.

The GC doesn't know what to do with certain kinds of resources after it realizes that you aren't using them any more — for example, resources from the operating system when you work with files, windows, or network connections. .NET provides you with special methods, named `Finalize` and `Dispose,` that you can use to tell the GC what to do with these resources.

The vast majority of resources you use in .NET don't require you to release them. The best practice is to implement the `Finalize` or `Dispose` methods any time you see that your resource has it available. See Book V, Chapter 3 to get the skinny on how to use methods such as `Finalize.`

Garbage collection isn't unique to .NET. Java also provides garbage-collection services to its developers. Read the article at `www.javaworld.com/ javaworld/jw-08-1996/jw-08-gc.html,` which describes how garbage collection works in Java. You'll find that the process is remarkably similar to garbage collection in .NET.

Chapter 4: The Languages of .NET

In This Chapter

✔ **Introducing the programming languages of .NET**

✔ **Finding the language that's right for you**

✔ **Figuring out the fundamentals of programming**

*P*art of the draw to Visual Studio 2005 is that it has many tools that make software development a breeze. You can fire up Visual Studio 2005 and, in no time flat, have a Windows or Web application that looks very professional.

Take a look at the application shown in Figure 4-1. It looks like any other Windows application you use. I created it in about five minutes using Visual Studio 2005. Even though I didn't write a single line of code, it looks like an element from a full-blown Windows application.

Figure 4-1:
You can create professional-looking Windows applications by using Visual Studio.

Visual Studio provided the Windows Form shown in Figure 4-1, and I just dragged and dropped the text boxes and buttons onto it. Behind the scenes, Visual Studio takes care of all the programming necessary to make this screen work by using *code generation,* which writes all the necessary code for you. All you have to do is use a designer (a graphical tool) to paint the screens and make them look the way you want. You can also use designers to generate code to build everything from DataSets to reports. Figure 4-2 shows a diagram of code generation.

Use Windows Designer to create Windows Form.

Drag and drop buttons, text boxes, and labels onto Windows Form.

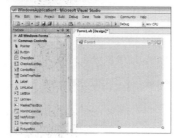

Visual Studio generates code.

Generated program displays window when executed.

Figure 4-2:
Visual
Studio
works
behind the
scenes to
generate
the code to
make an
application
work.

At some point, however, you need for your application to do more than just look pretty. When someone clicks a button or a menu item, your application should respond. This response takes place only when you write the code that tells the application what you want it to do, and that, my friend, requires programming. This chapter introduces the programming languages you're most likely to use.

Looking at the Languages of .NET

Even though Visual Studio can do a great deal for you, it can't write your program for you. When someone clicks a button, you have to provide code that carries out the desired action. The following list describes the kind of code you would have to create to perform a specific task:

✦ **Open a new window.** You have to write the code to open the new window.

✦ **Save a record to the database.** You have to write the code to save the record to the database.

✦ **Perform a calculation.** You have to — you guessed it — write the code to perform the calculation.

Programming languages have come a long way since they were first created. Modern programming languages are higher-level languages than their predecessors because each line of code that you write gets translated into multiple lines of instructions for the computer.

Before the introduction of higher-level languages, programmers wrote programs by using assembly language. *Assembly language* matches computer instructions line for line; in other words, each line of assembly language that you write is equal to one line of computer instructions. Writing programs in assembly languages was time-consuming and required extensive knowledge of how computers work.

The need for higher-level languages that allow programmers to write one line of code that's translated into multiple lines of computer instructions had to be addressed. These higher-level languages allow developers to be more productive. Also, programmers don't have to be as knowledgeable about the inner workings of computers.

The languages of .NET are all examples of higher-level languages. Microsoft has five languages for .NET:

✦ Visual Basic

✦ Visual C#

✦ Visual C++

✦ Visual J#

✦ JScript

Not all higher-level languages are created equally. Each of the languages of Microsoft .NET has its own set of advantages and disadvantages. In the next few sections, I describe each of these languages, starting with the old standby Visual Basic and working toward the exciting world of JScript.

Visual Basic

In the area of Windows programming, Visual Basic is as "old school" as it gets. This language has many devotees, and programmers love it because it's easy to learn, write, and debug. (Did I mention that Visual Basic is easy to learn?) You can easily begin writing workable software very quickly.

You can use Visual Basic to build these types of applications:

✦ Windows

✦ Web

✦ Mobile device

To make Visual Basic work with the Microsoft .NET Framework, the language had to be totally rewritten. In the process, many long-time Visual Basic programmers felt that Microsoft betrayed the defining characteristic of Visual Basic: It's easy to use.

Even though Visual Basic.NET was introduced in 2002, many new programs are still written in Visual Basic 6, the last version of VB before it was .NET-ized. Microsoft is aware that many developers still haven't made the move to Visual Basic.NET, so the company included a significant amount of documentation to help Visual Basic 6 developers take the plunge. Find more information at `http://msdn2.microsoft.com/kehz1dz1(en-US,VS.80).aspx`.

Even though the process of moving from Visual Basic 6 to VB.NET has been painful, it places Visual Basic on the same playing field as all the other .NET programming languages. Had Microsoft chosen not to rewrite Visual Basic, chances are that it would have been treated as a red-headed stepchild.

Rewriting Visual Basic made the language more powerful by turning it into a true object-oriented language. VB.NET allowed Microsoft to implement

✦ Customer-requested changes, such as inheritance and threading

✦ Complete access to all the features of .NET

✦ Interoperability between Visual Basic and the other .NET languages

✦ The removal of features such as `GoSub/Return` and `DefInt`

✦ Consistency between Visual Basic and other languages and language standards

This `Hello World` code sample from MSDN was written in Visual Basic.NET:

```
Module Hello
   Sub Main()
       MsgBox("Hello, World!") ' Display message
   End Sub
End Module
```

Notice how the syntax is simple. There aren't extra braces or punctuation required. For more information about this code sample, see MSDN at `http://msdn2.microsoft.com/3cf7t4xt.aspx`.

Visual C#

Released in 2002 with the first version of the Microsoft .NET Framework, Visual C# was created especially to take advantage of Microsoft .NET features.

C# has many characteristics in common with other languages in the C family of languages:

+ All statements end with a semicolon.

+ Blocks of code are enclosed in curly braces.

+ The language is case sensitive.

Check out the C# version of "Hello World":

```
using System;
// A "Hello World!" program in C#
namespace HelloWorld
{
    class Hello
    {
        static void Main()
        {
            System.Console.WriteLine("Hello World!");
        }
    }
}
```

The C# version of Hello World requires a few more lines than Visual Basic. I personally find the braces a nice visual cue for grouping code together. Other developers see them as a waste of space. For more information on this code sample, see the MSDN documentation at http://msdn2.microsoft.com/en-us/library/k1sx6ed2.aspx.

The C# language is useful for writing object-oriented applications. In addition to showcasing the .NET Framework, Microsoft created C# to compete with Java. Java syntax, like C#, has its roots in C. I don't know how many Java developers took the bait, but C# developers can hold their heads high and know that they too can use semicolons and curly braces with the best of them!

In its attempt to lure Java developers, Microsoft also created the Java Language Conversion Assistant, which converts Java source code into C#.

Visual C++

Visual C++, the most complex language in Microsoft's .NET offerings, is used to develop systems-level software, such as graphical user interfaces, device drivers, and mobile applications. Visual C++ is a development environment for creating Windows applications using the C++ programming language. Visual C++ can create applications that either work in .NET or run outside of it.

Here's a C++ version of "Hello World":

```
#include <iostream>
using  namespace std;

int main()
{
   cout << "Hello World! \n";
   return 0;
}
```

The C++ syntax is bit more cryptic than other high-level languages such as VB or C#. For example, cout is short for character output. C++ syntax isn't as intuitive as other languages. For an explanation of this code, see http://msdn.microsoft.com/library/default.asp?url=/library/en-us/dv_vstechart/html/vctoolkitcmd.asp.

Check out *C++ For Dummies,* by Stephen Randy Davis (Wiley Publishing), if you're interested in creating C++ applications. You have to get your mind around C++ before you can get any benefit from Visual C++.

You might think of Visual C++ as a development environment inside a development environment. Visual C++ allows you to use C++ syntax to write programs. Visual C++ provides several tools that shortcut the amount of effort required to create a standard C++ application, such as

✦ **Compilers** — Target the .NET Common Language Runtime (CLR) and the x86, x64, and Itanium hardware

✦ **Libraries** — Include Active Template Library (ATL), Microsoft Foundation Classes (MFC), standard C++, C Run-Time (CRT), and the C++ Support Library to support CLR programs

✦ **A development environment** — Supports project management and configuration; source code editing and browsing; and debugging

Visual C++ can be used as part of the Visual Studio IDE, or you can use its individual tools on the command line. Although C++ is a powerful language, it's also the most difficult of all the .NET languages to learn.

Visual J#

Visual J#, which is the Microsoft implementation of Java, allows Java programmers to write Java programs that run in .NET. However, J# programs don't run on the Java Virtual Machine (JVM), and J# isn't supported by Sun, the maker of Java.

Here's a J# code sample of "Hello World":

```
package HelloWorld;

// import java.lang.*;

class Program
{
    public static void main(String[] args)
    {
        System.out.println("Hello, World!");
    }
}
```

J# syntax uses curly braces and semicolons, like C# does. If you already know Java, then you shouldn't have any problems picking up C#. For a line-by-line explanation of this code, see http://msdn2.microsoft.com/ms240891. aspx.

Here's what you get with Visual J#:

+ **A compiler** — Compiles Java-language syntax to Microsoft Intermediate Language (MSIL), the language of the .NET Common Language Runtime

+ **A binary converter** — Allows you to convert Java programs, for which you don't have the source code, to .NET assemblies

+ **Class libraries** — Provide compatibility with Java Development Kit Level 1.1.4

Because J# syntax is Java syntax, you can use Visual Studio to debug Java applications.

One limitation of J# is that you can't access the features of the .NET Framework by using J# code. If your J# application needs to use the .NET Framework, you have to write an assembly by using another .NET language, such as C#.

For more information about whether to upgrade Java applications to J# or convert them to C#, see www.javaworld.com/javaworld/jw-01-2003/ jw-0103-migration.html.

JScript

JScript is the Microsoft implementation of ECMA 262, which is a standard for scripting languages. Because JavaScript is another implementation of ECMA 262, JScript and JavaScript are compatible.

JScript is the only scripting language offered by Microsoft for .NET. Scripting languages are different from object-oriented languages, such as C# and Visual Basic, because they're usually used to glue components together. The other languages of .NET are primarily intended for building components. JScript can manipulate those components.

Just Java slaying or freedom of choice?

You might be wondering why in the world Microsoft would create a language that emulates a competitor's language. The company has a few reasons:

✔ **To lure Java developers to .NET** — Although this reason seems obvious, it's probably not the primary reason for J#. In reality, most Java developers can easily learn C#, which is why Microsoft created the Java Language Conversion Assistant, which can convert Java source code to C#.

✔ **To leverage existing Java assets** — By migrating Java applications to J#, enterprises can continue to use their Java software while moving to .NET.

✔ **To provide a competitive teaching language** — Java is used as a teaching language in many universities. Schools now can choose between Java and J#.

The primary purpose for JScript and JavaScript has been to provide scripting programs in Web pages. JScript can manipulate Web pages. Scripting languages are different from languages you use to build components because scripting languages

✦ Are more flexible about declaring variables

✦ Allow for more ad hoc, on-the-fly code

Here's a "Hello World" code sample in JScript:

```
// A "Hello World!" program in JScript.
print("Hello World!");
```

Did I mention that JScript and scripting languages in general are more simple than other languages? If you eliminate the comment on the first line, it takes only one line of code to say `Hello World!` using JScript. What a wonderful world it would be if everything were so simple. For more explanation, see `http://msdn2.microsoft.com/9za221bh.aspx`.

As developers make scripts longer and make them do things that the other .NET languages do, the developers expect performance enhancements. As a result, Microsoft has made JScript more closely resemble the features of the other .NET languages, which makes scripts easier to maintain. Although JScript is a true object-oriented language, you don't have to use objects.

Other language contenders

Third parties provide more than 40 additional languages for .NET. Some of these languages are free, and others are commercially available for purchase.

For more information, see the GotDotNet Web site at `www.gotdotnet.com/team/lang/`.

Choosing the Right Language for the Job

One key feature of Microsoft .NET is that in order for a programming language to work with .NET, its compiler must be able to translate the language into Microsoft Intermediate Language (MSIL). Because all the languages can be converted to MSIL, all instructions that get executed by the computer should be similar, if not the same.

In other words, the computer doesn't care what programming language you choose when you're writing programs for .NET. MSIL equalizes all the languages as far as the computer is concerned.

Choosing a language should be motivated by human needs, not by the computer. Think about what you're trying to accomplish when you're making a decision. Your goal should be to write programs that do what you want them to do and that your teammates can read and maintain.

As you make your decision, keep these considerations in mind:

✦ **Microsoft has positioned Visual Basic as an easy entry point into Microsoft .NET.** If you're new to programming or new to .NET, Visual Basic is probably the way to go.

✦ **If you have experience with using Java, C, C++, or even one of the scripting languages, such as Perl or Python, you might appreciate Visual C#.** C# syntax is similar to these C-based languages.

Ajax attacks!

An exciting development for JScript is its new Web development methodology: Ajax (Asynchronous JavaScript And XML). It uses JScript and other technologies related to the Web to provide Windows-like user interfaces to Web pages. JScript is no longer just for accessing client-side content. Using Ajax, you can use JScript to interact with the server too.

Getting all the Ajax technologies to work together to create this rich Web experience is a daunting challenge. The Microsoft initiative named Atlas intends to provide a toolbox of Ajax controls. You can start using Atlas right now. Check out the Microsoft Atlas page for more information about Atlas and JScript: `www.asp.net/default.aspx?tabindex=9&tabid=47`.

+ **If you're primarily concerned about performance, you probably should choose C++.** Beware, however, that you pay a steep penalty in complexity. Also, to truly gain the performance edge, you can't take advantage of the services of .NET.

Unless you have the formal training and practical experience to write tight code (code that doesn't waste any memory or processor cycles), you probably won't gain any performance edge by using C++ without .NET. Don't buy the hype that you can write faster programs with C++. Although that's possible, most programmers don't have the experience to do it. Furthermore, in the amount of time you spend trying to figure it out, you could already have the program finished by using Visual Basic or C#.

+ **If you ever build Web applications with ASP.NET, you already use JScript.** Many of the ASP.NET server controls generate JScript to make them work. You should also try JScript whenever you need to get something done in a jiffy, such as when you parse a text file. You might find that you like the laid back style of JScript better than its more buttoned-up brethren.

For a Microsoft comparison of the languages of .NET, see `http://msdn2.microsoft.com/czz35az4(en-us,VS.80).aspx`.

Most people are choosing between Visual Basic and C#. Your historical use of one language over the other often dictates your choice. People who use Visual Basic tend to be less interested in aesthetics and more interested in getting the task done so that they can move on. C# programmers often speak of the purity and expressiveness of the language.

Having used both, I can give you these highlights:

+ Visual Basic is easy and fast to learn.

+ C# lends itself well to object-oriented development.

I like to use Visual Basic for all my ASP.NET code-behind files. I like to use C# for all my business objects.

Becoming a Good Programmer

Learning how to program is probably more important than choosing a language. By learning how to program, you can move fluidly among languages.

All programming languages share common themes, or *programming constructs*. You should find out how to perform some of these major common programming constructs:

✦ Declare variables.

✦ Understand variable types.

✦ Know when and how to use iterators to loop through variables.

✦ Control the flow of your program by using conditional if...then statements.

✦ Use arrays to store a series of data, such as the months in a year.

I suggest you start with the course catalog for the Computer Science department at your local college or university. You're more likely to find "what it means to program a computer" courses that cover programming fundamentals. Be careful about applied technology courses or books that teach a specific language, such as Visual Basic or Java. If possible, take a look at the syllabus or talk to the professor or lecturer before signing up. Explain that you want to get more out of the course than just language syntax.

Building software involves more than just writing code, and software development consists of several phases. This book shows you how to use Visual Studio 2005 in many of these different phases.

After the requirements gatherers gather and the analysts analyze and the designers design, at some point somebody has to write some code. If you want that person to be you, you need to learn language *syntax,* or the grammar of a programming language.

Learn the syntax

If you want to learn language syntax, consider *not* starting with Visual Studio. One useful feature of Visual Studio is that it allows you to develop software at a higher level of abstraction. As a result, Visual Studio generates a lot of code for you — code that you probably won't bother to take the time to understand. To be frank, the code that Visual Studio generates probably isn't the code you want to learn from.

Remember that writing cryptic code isn't the goal. The goal is to write code that's easy to read and maintain. The code generated by Visual Studio can be complex and abstract. It's good code because it's highly reusable, but it can be hard to understand.

Some people argue that you shouldn't bother trying to memorize syntax. As long as you know the basic programming constructs, you should be able to program in any language. Don't forget that companies want developers with high levels of productivity, which usually translates into using some kind of tool, such as Visual Studio.

Write your own code

When I was in college, the recommended order for taking courses was to start by using a text editor and manual compiler in a language like C, learn a C-derivative scripting language, such as JavaScript or Perl, and then learn Visual Basic .NET with Visual Studio.

Many of my classmates, however, chose instead to start with the VB.NET course and work their way backward. Unfortunately, they started with the easiest way to develop software. When they got to the harder courses, where you had to manage your own memory and create your own data structures, they were lost.

I had the same experience with Structured Query Language (SQL), which is the language of databases. When I first started working in information technology, I was doing a lot of report design. I mostly relied on report-design software to graphically build my database queries. Report designers, such as Crystal Reports, generate the SQL necessary to pull the data out of the database.

When I started doing application development, I realized quickly that my SQL skills were deficient. I immediately started making myself write out all my queries using a native SQL tool. After I stopped relying on code-generation tools and started writing my own SQL, I quickly learned the language. Now I get to choose whether using a code-generation tool is the best way to go, given the task that I need to accomplish.

Here's the bottom line: You need to know some language syntax if you expect to become more than a copy-and-paste coder. Here are some tasks you can undertake to become a better programmer:

+ Learn the principles of object-oriented design and programming.

+ Learn the basic programming constructs that are common across all programming languages.

+ Pick a language, and learn how that language implements object-oriented programming and basic programming constructs.

+ If you know that you will work with a specific technology, such as Windows Forms or Web services, commit yourself to learning as much as possible about that technology and its for best practices development.

+ Practice, practice, practice.

If you invest in these techniques, your code will be well written, no matter what.

Spend some time in other language studies

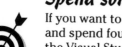

If you want to separate yourself from the development pack, pick a language and spend four consecutive weekends working with that language outside the Visual Studio environment. This technique is also a good way to teach yourself a new language, such as Java.

You might also need to familiarize yourself with some of these other languages and technologies:

✦ Standards for Web development — such as HTML, CSS, JavaScript, and Ajax — to help with troubleshooting

✦ File formats, such as XML and RSS, so that you can transfer data between disparate systems

✦ Query syntax of Structured Query Language (SQL) for writing stored procedures and queries for reading and updating databases

✦ Regular expressions for manipulating text

✦ Windows Active Directory and security

✦ Object models for Office applications, such as Word and Excel, and server applications, such as SharePoint and BizTalk

Chapter 5: The Many Editions of Visual Studio 2005

In This Chapter

✔ Sorting out multiple editions of Visual Studio

✔ Deciding which edition is right for you

✔ Choosing the right MSDN subscription

✔ Getting acquainted with Visual Studio Team System

✔ Looking at the future of Visual Studio

Sorting out all the different editions of Visual Studio is mind numbing. Microsoft provides a Visual Studio edition for developers at all levels of experience, from absolute beginners working on their own to large-scale development teams with thousands of members.

This chapter helps you make sense of the different editions of Visual Studio so that you can decide which one's right for you. I explain the features of Visual Studio Team System and discuss the future of Visual Studio.

Making Sense of the Visual Studio Editions

Although Microsoft still offers the old standbys Standard Edition and Professional Edition, the company expanded its offerings to reach out to everyone from novices all the way to high-end, large-scale development teams.

Visual Studio offers these editions, listed in order from the simplest to most complex features included in the edition:

✦ Visual Studio Express Editions

✦ Visual Studio Standard

✦ Visual Studio Tools for Office

✦ Visual Studio Professional

✦ Visual Studio Team System

One of Microsoft's major goals with Visual Studio is to enable personal productivity for all software developers. This list describes which edition you should use if you're in one of these groups:

+ **You're a hobbyist, student, or novice.** Check out the Express Editions.

+ **You do occasional development work by yourself.** You should appreciate the get-down-to-business features of Visual Studio Standard Edition.

+ **You create applications that use Office as their user interface.** Visual Studio Tools for Office makes creating Office applications dead simple.

+ **You're a professional software developer who works alone or on a small team.** Visual Studio Professional is geared toward you.

+ **You're part of a larger development team.** Your team should check out Visual Studio Team System.

Visual Studio Express Editions

The Express Editions of Visual Studio, which are less feature-rich than the other editions, are perfect for students, hobbyists, and folks just getting started. Rather than have one large, overwhelming soup-to-nuts software development tool, the Express Editions come in many flavors, depending on what type of development you want to do:

+ **Web** — Create Web applications and Web services by using Visual Web Developer 2005 Express. This edition allows you to write code by using C# or Visual Basic and provides editors for HTML and XML. It has a built-in Web development server that you can use to build and test your Web application. Numerous starter kits are provided to help you jumpstart your projects.

+ **Database** — Most applications are datacentric. SQL Server 2005 Express Edition is a fully functional database management system that integrates with Visual Studio. You can use Visual Studio to create databases, write stored procedures, and add data. Although database sizes are limited to 4GB, the databases are compatible with SQL Server 2005. So, the skills you acquire are transferable to SQL Server 2005.

+ **Windows** — Express Editions for Windows development includes editions for Visual Basic, C#, C++, and J#. Use Visual Basic, C#, and J# for building Windows applications, console applications, and reusable components. You can use C++ to create both managed and unmanaged code. To build Web applications, use the Web Developer Edition.

Most beginners will find that they make few compromises by using Visual Studio Express Editions. You get these benefits:

+ **Your developed applications are fully functional.** They aren't watered-down versions.

+ **As your needs grow, you can scale up to one of the higher editions.**

+ **Your skills are transferable to other Visual Studio editions.**

+ **The price is right.** You can download all the editions for Web and Windows development for free from the Microsoft Web site. Microsoft originally planned to charge $49 for the products after a period of being free for one year, but they decided to make the products free permanently. SQL Server 2005 Express Edition is also available at no charge.

Download these tools at `http://msdn.microsoft.com/vstudio/ express/default.aspx`.

The Express Editions of Visual Studio are an excellent choice for students or anyone wanting to learn how to program. When I was in college, these choices weren't available. As a result, students used tools like Microsoft Access. It's worlds away from enterprise-level database management tools, like SQL Server. Kudos to Microsoft for providing these tools and making them affordable.

Visual Studio Standard

Visual Studio Standard Edition is intended for developers working mostly on their own to develop departmental solutions. This edition is ideal for a smaller organization where someone does occasional development work, such as parse text files.

Visual Studio Standard provides these advantages:

+ Support for all .NET languages

+ The ability to build Windows, Web, and mobile device applications

+ Simplified menus

+ Productivity features, such as a code editor, IntelliSense, and code snippets

+ Visual designers for classes, databases, and stored procedures

+ Significantly less expense than the Professional Edition

Visual Studio Tools for Office

The Visual Studio Tools for Office (VSTO, pronounced "visto") edition is geared toward independent software vendors and systems integrators who build custom Windows and Web applications for the Microsoft Office system.

With VSTO, you get these features:

+ Visual Basic and C# programming languages

+ Integrated visual designers for working with databases

+ Advanced debugging tools

+ Designers geared toward building applications that use Word, Excel, and InfoPath as their user interfaces

Visual Studio Professional

Visual Studio Professional is geared toward professional .NET developers. This edition provides even more advanced visual designers and a tightly integrated toolset. If you develop software for a living, this edition is the one you're most likely to use.

Visual Studio Professional provides these features:

+ All the Microsoft .NET programming languages

+ Integrated visual database tools

+ Designers for XML schema design and XML style sheets

+ Advanced debugging and deployment tools

+ The ability to develop stored procedures, functions, and triggers for SQL Server 2005

+ Crystal Reports

Visual Studio Team System

The Visual Studio Team System (VSTS) has created a lot of buzz. VSTS is important because

+ It acknowledges the specialized roles that people play on large development teams.

+ It's Microsoft's attempt to move into the tools space of the software development life cycle.

The VSTS isn't a product; rather, it's composed of four client editions of Visual Studio:

+ Visual Studio for Architects

+ Visual Studio for Database Professionals

+ Visual Studio for Software Developers

+ Visual Studio for Testers

The Team System also includes a server component, the Team Foundation Server, that enables collaboration among the client editions of VSTS.

Because VSTS is a huge departure from the previous editions of Visual Studio, I dig into it in more detail later in this chapter, in the section "Developing When It's a Team Effort."

Choosing the Right Edition

With numerous editions of Visual Studio and numerous features strewn across these editions, finding an edition that's right for you can seem daunting. I found that the answer almost always comes down to money (somebody else's, you hope).

Because pricing can change, I don't quote specific prices here. However, I give you an idea of how much these editions cost:

+ **Express Editions** — Free

+ **Standard Edition** — Between $200 and $300

+ **Professional Edition and Visual Tools for Office** — Between $550 and $800

+ **Team Editions** — Between $2,300 and $5,500 (available only with an MSDN subscription)

+ **Team Foundation Server** — About $3,000 for the required separate server license

The price you pay depends on whether you're upgrading or paying full retail price.

Helping you decide whether to choose the Team System is beyond the scope of this book. Chances are that your employer will make the decision. Nevertheless, as a .NET developer, you have a responsibility to understand the role of the Visual Studio Team System. Check out the later section "Developing When It's a Team Effort" for more information.

Subscribing to the Microsoft Developer Network

Microsoft changed its licensing for MSDN (Microsoft Developer Network) with the release of Visual Studio 2005. MSDN provides you with access to Microsoft operating systems, server software, and productivity applications for development purposes.

You can choose a subscription from three levels of MSDN subscriptions:

✦ **Platform** — For about $700, you have access to all the Microsoft operating systems, such as Windows Server 2003 and Virtual PC.

✦ **Professional** — You get Visual Studio 2005 Professional Edition, SQL Server 2005, SQL Reporting Services Developer Editions, and Virtual PC, in addition to access to Microsoft operating systems for about $1,200.

✦ **Premium** — Provides you with the operating systems Virtual PC, SQL Server 2005 Developer Edition, and Visual SourceSafe; server products such as BizTalk and SharePoint; Office Professional Edition 2003; and Microsoft Business Solutions software, such as Great Plains and Microsoft CRM. You also get to choose an edition of Visual Studio. The price you pay for a subscription depends on the edition of Visual Studio you choose:

  • **Visual Studio Professional** — It costs about $2,500.

  • **Visual Studio Team Edition for Software Architects, Testers, or Software Developers** — Choose one of these editions for about $5,500.

  • **Visual Studio Team Suite** — For about $11,000, you get access to all three Team Edition editions of Visual Studio.

The Visual Studio Team Editions and Team Suite with MSDN Premium Subscriptions include the Team Foundation Server Workgroup Edition with five client-access licenses. The full-blown Team Foundation Server product requires an additional server license.

Check out the latest pricing at `http://msdn.microsoft.com/vstudio/howtobuy/Default.aspx`. For more details about what you get with each level of MSDN subscription, go to `http://msdn.microsoft.com/vstudio/products/subscriptions/`.

MSDN subscriptions provide you with development and testing licenses only. You can't use the software you download from MSDN in a production environment. In other words, you can't download an operating system and install it on a computer you intend to use for work. You can only test or develop.

A single MSDN subscription provides you with ten licenses for each product you download. You may install the software on ten computers one time or ten times on one computer. Only individuals with MSDN subscriptions may use the software. In other words, each member of your team needs an MSDN subscription if they plan to access software downloaded from MSDN. The licenses are valid forever, even if you choose not to renew your MSDN subscription. You may continue using the software for testing and development after your MSDN subscription expires.

Each developer requires a separate MSDN subscription. Just because a single MSDN subscription has ten licenses doesn't mean ten people can use it. Each person must have his own subscription.

Weighing your options

After you have an idea of what the pricing structure looks like and what you can get for your money, look at these scenarios I paint to help you with your decision-making process for selecting the edition of Visual Studio 2005 that's right for you:

✦ **If you want to save some money or mentor a young programmer:** Be sure to download all the Express Editions for free. Even if you think that you'll never need them, download them now at `http://msdn.microsoft.com/vstudio/express/default.aspx`. You never know when you might need a free edition of a relatively powerful development tool.

✦ **If you're a college student:** Check with your school bookstore or your department to see whether your school has an academic license with Microsoft. When I was in college, I picked up a copy of Visual Studio Professional for $25 — $5 per disc. Your school might have a similar license.

✦ **If you work in a small- to medium-size business or have your own consulting business:** Choose Professional Edition if you want to use the Crystal Reports Designer to create reports. The deal-breaker between the Express Editions and Visual Studio Standard is whether you need all tools integrated into one application. If you don't mind having separate tools for Web-based and Windows-based development, you can save a few bucks and go with the Express Editions. If you intend to do more development work, choose the Standard Edition. You benefit from using the Class Designer and being able to access remote databases.

✦ **If you're torn between the Standard and Professional Editions:** Before you choose Standard Edition over Professional Edition, ask yourself these questions:

   • How much work do I have with XML?

   • Do I need Crystal Reports?

   • How much database work do I have?

✦ **If you do extensive development work with Office:** Visual Tools for Office is a no-brainer — except, of course, that you get all the VSTO tools with the Visual Studio Team Editions. If you do only occasional Office work, stick with Professional.

Consider these scenarios as you decide whether to choose MSDN:

✦ **You're a professional developer or have developers working for you.** Spring for the MSDN subscriptions. Consider it part of the cost of doing business. Most developers expect to have access to these tools.

Evaluating your alternatives

Over the years, I have worked in a number of Microsoft shops. This type of shop tends to go with "all things Microsoft" and not even consider alternatives. Although Microsoft has many useful products, they're not always the right choices for all situations. They're often the easiest choices, though, especially if your infrastructure and development efforts are heavily invested in all things Microsoft.

Before you commit yourself and spend huge sums of money, ponder some alternatives:

✔ Supplement Visual Studio Professional with open source tools, such as Nunit for unit testing and FxCop for static code analysis.

✔ Consider using Project Mono, an open source version of C#.

✔ Explore alternative development environments, such as Eclipse and NetBeans.

Nothing about using Visual Studio is inherently bad. Just remember that when you frame solutions using Microsoft's tools, or any vendor's tools, you narrow your choices and lose perspective. By evaluating alternatives, you can see whether Visual Studio is the way for you to go.

✦ **You're a one-person show or you're on a budget, so maybe you can get around buying an MSDN subscription.** In that case, I suggest that you buy a copy of Virtual PC or VMWare and then install evaluation versions of whatever software you need to work with. You can save images of the evaluation versions if you need to reuse them for other projects.

As you make your decision about which tools to use, remember that Microsoft has a profit motive for selling Visual Studio. Why is it giving away the Express Editions? The answer is that all marketers know that a trial offer is the best way to sell something.

When you decide to go with Visual Studio, you're not only getting a productivity tool, but also joining a community. Using Visual Studio and Microsoft .NET will no doubt shape the way you approach solutions development.

Developing When It's a Team Effort

With Visual Studio 2005, Microsoft moves into the realm of software development life cycle tools in a big way. The products that comprise Visual Studio Team System were tested on thousands of user projects. Although your project might not be as big, you might still benefit from the team collaboration features.

In this section, I walk you through some of the features of Visual Studio Team System, starting with managing a project, defining its architecture, and building and testing the software. I expand on the features of Visual Studio Team System in Book VII, Chapter 2.

Managing projects with Team System

Although the Team System doesn't include a special edition for project managers, it allows project managers to use Visual Studio to

+ Create a project portfolio where all the project's artifacts can be accessed.
+ Select a development methodology from predefined templates.
+ Create a process-aware project portal complete with reports for evaluating progress.

A project manager views a project by using the Portfolio Explorer in Visual Studio or the project's portal. By using the Visual Studio Portfolio Explorer, you can

+ Maintain source code control.
+ Query work items, such as requirements, tasks, and bugs.
+ View progress reports.
+ View project documentation.
+ Review build information.

Because the project portal is SharePoint–driven, you can open artifacts (such as requirements checklists) in Excel and modify them. Multiple people can then work on these artifacts and check out, publish, synchronize, and enforce data-validation rules.

Visual Studio Team System allows other team members to perform these tasks:

+ Create and edit work items, associate work items with source code, and view work item queues.
+ Import work items into Microsoft Project and publish the updated project plan back to the project portal.
+ Sync updates from Project, Excel, and the portal to a team database, to allow developers to use Visual Studio to view and update work items.
+ Work with the tools and views that make them productive (analysts in spreadsheets, developers in Visual Studio, and project managers in Project). Other stakeholders can use the project portal to monitor progress.
+ View reports on scheduling, bug fixes, and requirements churning. Project managers can also drill into the reports to see underlying data.

✦ Collect data throughout the course of a project as developers work. You don't need to hold numerous status meetings and have people fill out and compile paperwork.

Architecting software

By using the designers in Visual Studio Team Edition for Software Architects, architects can

✦ Model applications and the target technology environment.

✦ Validate that the applications will run in the target environment.

These tools are geared primarily toward service-oriented architectures, such as Web services.

One incredible tool in Visual Studio Team Edition for Software Architects is the Application Designer. You can use it to

✦ Lay out applications that provide and consume new or existing Web services.

✦ Connect applications to build multi-tier applications.

✦ Show how to map applications to the logical datacenter design.

✦ Turn the diagram into code. The Application Designer creates projects and classes and stubs out methods.

 ✦ Keep code synchronized with design in both directions.

The Application Designer is beneficial for these reasons:

✦ Architects can see the visual structure of an application.

✦ You can lay out the design without committing to code, also known as *whiteboarding*.

✦ You don't have to abandon design tools when you move to code.

✦ You can validate designs long before anything gets built.

The Software Architect Edition also provides a Logical Datacenter designer, which allows architects to map the applications they design to a technology environment that will host them. The logical datacenter allows architects to

✦ Query their technology infrastructures.

✦ Define settings and constraints for the servers in their datacenters, such as what kind of authentication the server allows and whether the application needs scripting.

✦ Determine whether their applications will run in the target environment.

+ Use graphical tools to change the configurations of applications or host environments.

+ See communication pathways in the datacenter.

+ Drag, drop, and validate — the system does real-time validation to tell you what applications can be hosted on a given server.

+ Specify settings and constraints in the Application Designer for a component. Remember that models and validation work both ways.

The Application and Logical Datacenter designers open communications between designers, developers, and information technologists.

Developing software with Team System

The Software Developers Edition provides additional tools for testing and code analysis:

+ **FxCop** — Enable code analysis and receive warnings as part of the build process.

+ **Performance tools** — See which functions are called most often.

+ **Unit testing and code coverage** — Test your code and use visual tools to see how much of your code is tested.

Testing with tools

The testing tools in Visual Studio Team Edition for Testers allows users to

+ Record tests and generate scripts based on browser sessions.

+ Play back scripts.

+ Create validation rules to test for conditions on the Web pages.

+ Bind data to tests so that you can use data-driven tests (for example, to search for keywords in a database).

+ Use a load test wizard that groups counters and offers guidance so that you're not guessing what each counter does and which one to use.

Collaborating with Visual Studio Team Foundation

The Team Foundation Server (TFS) enables the collaboration features for the Team Editions of Visual Studio Team System. With Team Foundation Server, you get these features:

+ Source code control

+ Work-item tracking

+ Build automation

✦ Team communications

✦ Reporting

The integrated check-in procedure using TFS includes

✦ Channels for managing source code, work items, check-in notes, and policy warnings

✦ Check-in notes, which are fields the project manager creates that the developer is required to fill out before check-in

✦ The option to create a standard check-in process that can be reviewed

✦ Access to the compare feature so you can expedite code reviews by comparing two different versions of source code

✦ Policy warnings notification (for example, that check-in must be associated with a work item)

Taking a Visual Look Ahead

Microsoft's vision for the current editions of Visual Studio 2005 started culminating in 1999. While you're busy mastering the program's current set of tools, wisely look ahead at some technologies that will influence Visual Studio near and far:

✦ **Visual Studio code name Orcas** — The next version of Visual Studio, due sometime in 2007, will provide tools for targeting the latest Windows operating system, Windows Vista.

✦ **Office 2007** — The next version of Microsoft Office brings a new user interface, tighter integration, and more services.

✦ **Windows Vista** — The next Microsoft Windows operating system will have "new everything."

✦ **Atlas** — The Microsoft technology for implementing Ajax is already in beta.

✦ **The LINQ Project** — Future versions of Visual Studio will be much more datacentric.

✦ **Software factories, domain-specific languages, and dynamic services initiatives** — All these terms show Microsoft's direction for software development and information technology management.

✦ **Windows Live, Office Live, Visual Studio Live** — These services are Microsoft's latest move into subscription-based software.

See Book VII for more information on how you can start using preview editions of many of these technologies right now.

Book II

Getting Started with Visual Studio

The 5th Wave

By Rich Tennant

"Our automated response policy to a large company-wide data crash is to notify management, back up existing data, and sell 90 percent of my shares in the company."

Contents at a Glance

Chapter 1: Installing Visual Studio Professional

In This Chapter

✔ Using multiple versions of Visual Studio

✔ System requirements for Visual Studio

✔ Installing Visual Studio

✔ Launching Visual Studio

*A*s long as you have adequate hardware resources to run Visual Studio, getting it up and running is a straightforward process. You might spend all day waiting for the software to install, but then you can stay up all night playing around with all its cool new features. This chapter gives you all the details.

Installing Side by Side

You can use any release version of Visual Studio, from Visual Studio 6.0 through Visual Studio 2005, on a single computer. Of course, I don't recommend opening all the versions at one time. Here are the four versions:

✦ Visual Studio 6.0

✦ Visual Studio 2002

✦ Visual Studio 2003

✦ Visual Studio 2005

If you installed beta versions or any other prerelease version of Visual Studio 2005 on your computer, you must uninstall them completely before installing the final version of Visual Studio 2005. For more information, see `http://msdn.microsoft.com/vstudio/support/uninstall/default.aspx`.

As a rule, after you open an older version of a solution in the next version of Visual Studio, you can no longer open the solution in the previous version. For example, if you open a Visual Studio 2002 solution in Visual Studio 2003, you can no longer open the solution in Visual Studio 2002. Be sure to have backups of all your solutions before you start opening them in different versions.

Taking a look at all the .NETs

You can have multiple versions of the Microsoft .NET Framework installed on a single computer. Three versions of .NET have been released:

✦ Version 1.0, released with Visual Studio 2002

✦ Version 1.1, released with Visual Studio 2003

✦ Version 2.0, released with Visual Studio 2005

 Version 3.0 of the .NET Framework releases in early 2007 with Windows Vista. You'll be able to target version 3.0 with Visual Studio 2005. Book VII, Chapter 3 previews some of the features of Windows Vista and the next version of .NET.

Generally speaking, the version of .NET that's released with its corresponding version of Visual Studio can be used with only that version of Visual Studio.

 In reality, you can get around that rule. For example, you can use Visual Studio 2005 to write applications that target version 1.0 of the .NET Framework. I show you how to use previous versions of the .NET Framework with Visual Studio 2005 in Chapter 4 of this mini-book.

Getting help with the help collection manager

Each version of Visual Studio provides its own help collection. Because these collections can be quite large, you might want to combine them. You can use the Visual Studio 2005 Combined Help Collection to combine your help files. Combining them allows you to view all your help collections in the Visual Studio 2005 help viewer.

To use the help collection manager in Visual Studio 2005, follow these steps:

1. **Choose Help⇨Index.**

The Visual Studio 2005 Documentation window is displayed.

2. **In the Index work pane, enter the word help in the Look For field.**

The index automatically advances to the topics starting with the word *help.*

3. **Scroll down the index until you find the Collection Manager topic.**

4. **Click the Collection Manager topic.**

The help topic for the Visual Studio 2005 Combined Help Collection Manager is displayed, as shown in Figure 1-1.

5. **Follow the instructions in the help topic to combine your help collections.**

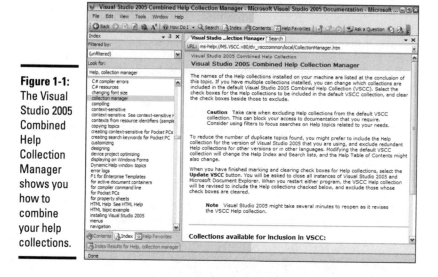

Figure 1-1:
The Visual
Studio 2005
Combined
Help
Collection
Manager
shows you
how to
combine
your help
collections.

Meeting System Requirements

Here are the minimum requirements for installing Visual Studio 2005
Professional Edition:

✦ A 600 MHz processor

✦ 256MB RAM

✦ 3GB disk space

✦ A CD-ROM or DVD-ROM drive

You also need one of these operating systems:

✦ Windows 2000 Service Pack 4

✦ Windows XP Professional Service Pack 2

✦ Windows Server 2003 Service Pack 1

As usual, the minimum requirements probably aren't where you want to be.
I'm sure Visual Studio will run on a computer using the minimum requirements, but you'll probably be able to drink a cup of coffee in between mouse
clicks, which defeats the purpose of using productivity software. In reality,
you probably want at least a 1 GHz processor with at least 1GB RAM. If you
don't think that you have enough hardware and you can't upgrade, consider
using one of the Express editions of Visual Studio.

If you're stuck running Visual Studio 2005 on an older machine that doesn't meet the requirements, I suggest adding more memory to the system. I personally run Visual Studio 2005, SQL Server 2005 Developer Edition, and all the other software you see in this book using a machine with dual Pentium III 450s and 756MB of memory. Sometimes it's slow, but it beats buying a new computer.

You must have Administrator rights to the computer on which you wish to install Visual Studio 2005. User rights are sufficient to *run* Visual Studio 2005.

Stepping Through the Installation

Installing Visual Studio is a fairly simple process. After you insert the DVD or CD, you see the Visual Studio 2005 Setup screen, as shown in Figure 1-2.

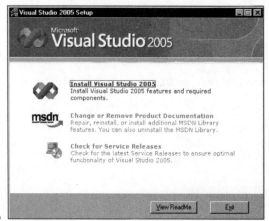

Figure 1-2:
The Visual Studio 2005 Setup screen walks you through the steps to install Visual Studio.

Installing Visual Studio is more involved than clicking setup.exe and walking through a wizard. Visual Studio requires a number of components to install in order to be fully functional. The installation process involves the following tasks:

1. Install Visual Studio and version 2.0 of the .NET Framework.

2. Install the help documentation.

3. Check for updates at Windows Update.

To start the Installation Wizard and install Visual Studio 2005, follow these steps:

1. **Click the Install Visual Studio 2005 option on the Visual Studio 2005 Setup screen (refer to Figure 1-2).**

Setup loads the installation components and displays the Welcome screen.

2. **After the setup components are loaded, click Next on the Welcome screen.**

The Microsoft Visual Studio 2005 Setup start page is displayed, as shown in Figure 1-3.

The start page displays a list of components that are already installed and a list of components to be installed.

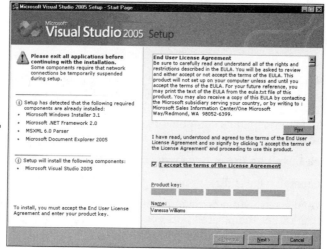

Figure 1-3:
The start
page lists
the com-
ponents that
Setup needs
to install.

3. **On the start page, select the check box labeled I Accept the Terms of the License Agreement, to indicate that you have read and agree to the license agreement displayed on the page.**

4. **Click Next.**

The options page is displayed.

5. **On the options page, shown in Figure 1-4, click the radio button indicating whether you want the Default, Full, or Custom installation, and then specify the installation path.**

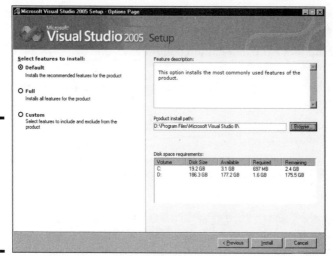

Figure 1-4:
Use the options page to indicate which features to install.

In the lower-right corner of Figure 1-4, note the table that displays disk space requirements. For this installation, I chose to install Visual Studio on the D drive. Notice that the C drive still has a disk space requirement. Visual Studio installs components on your system drive even if you choose to install Visual Studio on another hard drive.

6. **Click Install on the options page to start the installation.**

The install page is displayed.

If you chose Custom installation on the options page, you see the Next button rather than Install. After clicking Next, you can select all the individual components you want to install.

The install page displays the progress of the installation along with useful information about new features in Visual Studio 2005. After all the components are installed, the finish page is displayed.

If everything installs properly, the finish page displays a message stating that setup is complete. If any errors occur, they're displayed on this page.

7. **Click the Finish button to close the Installation Wizard.**

After the wizard closes, the Visual Studio 2005 Setup window is displayed again. You can click the link to install the product documentation. After the documentation is installed, the Setup window is displayed again. Click the link to check for service releases and install any service release that Windows Update displays for you.

Launching Visual Studio for the First Time

When you launch Visual Studio for the first time, you see the dialog box shown in Figure 1-5. You can choose a set of environment settings based on the kind of development work you do. Your choices for development settings are

✦ General

✦ Visual Basic

✦ Visual C#

✦ Visual C++

✦ Visual J#

✦ Web

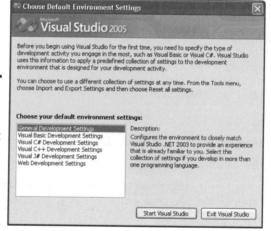

Figure 1-5:
Choose a
default
environment
setting the
first time
you launch
Visual
Studio.

The settings you choose determine the headlines you see on the start page and the kinds of project templates you see when you create a new project and set your default programming language. Development settings also let you customize menus, toolbars, and help documentation to suit the choice you made.

In this book, I use General Development Settings for all examples. In most cases, I try to give you the keyboard shortcut for a command when available. The keyboard shortcuts are pretty consistent across the development settings.

You can use the Import and Export Settings Wizard to change your development settings. To start the wizard, follow these steps:

1. Choose Tools⇨Import and Export Settings.

The Import and Export Settings Wizard is displayed, as shown in Figure 1-6.

Figure 1-6:
Use the
Import and
Export
Settings
Wizard to
change your
default
settings.

2. Click the Reset All Settings radio button, and click Next.

The Save Current Settings page is displayed.

3. If you want to save your settings so that you can reuse them later, click Yes and specify the filename and directory. To discard your settings, click No.

4. Click Next to save or discard your settings.

5. On the next page that's displayed, choose a default collection of settings from the list that's displayed, as shown in Figure 1-7.

6. Click Finish.

Visual Studio changes your settings.

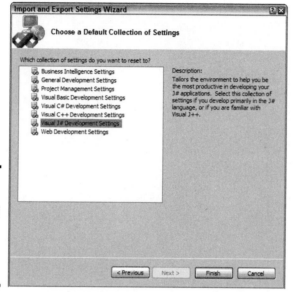

Figure 1-7:
Select a collection of settings to reset as your default settings.

You can also use the Import and Export Settings Wizard to import settings you saved from another machine or that a friend has sent you.

Chapter 2: Browsing Visual Studio

In This Chapter

- ✔ Becoming familiar with the development environment
- ✔ Understanding solutions and projects
- ✔ Browsing properties, servers, and code
- ✔ Painting forms with visual designers

*U*sing Visual Studio 2005, you have access to hundreds of commands, tools, and designers. The Visual Studio code editor and object browser put the more than 60,000 methods of the Microsoft .NET Framework at your fingertips. You have everything you need to build powerful, world-class Windows applications and Web sites — if only you knew where to begin.

Making Your Way Around

When you first open Visual Studio 2005, you see a screen similar to the one shown in Figure 2-1. This screen reflects a Visual Studio 2005 installation that uses the General Development settings. Note these features in Figure 2-1:

- ✦ **Start page** — This page is your dashboard for navigating Visual Studio 2005 and connecting to resources in the .NET community. The start page includes these features:

    - **Recent Projects** — A list of recently opened projects in Visual Studio 2005. Also includes links to open and create new projects and Web sites

    - **Getting Started** — A list of links to resources to help you get started using Visual Studio 2005

    - **Visual Studio Headlines** — A list of news relevant to Visual Studio 2005

    - **MSDN News** — A list of headlines from MSDN, the Microsoft Developer Network

- ✦ **Solution Explorer** — This task pane on the right side of the screen lists open solutions and the projects they contain.

- ✦ **Class View** — This tab on the task pane in the lower-right corner of the screen displays a tree view of classes contained in the open solution.

Server Explorer   Standard toolbar   MSDN News

Toolbox   Menu bar   Start Page   Solution Explorer

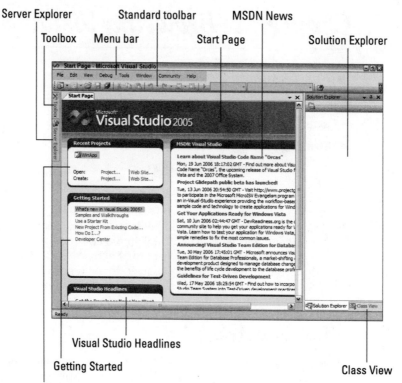

Figure 2-1:
Visual Studio
displays
a set of
tools that
are useful
to most
developers.

Visual Studio Headlines

Getting Started

Class View

Recent Projects

✦ **Server Explorer** — This task pane on the left side of the screen provides a tree view of the servers you're working with. The Server Explorer is automatically hidden by default. You can display it by hovering your mouse over it.

✦ **Toolbox** — This task pane on the left side of the screen provides groups of controls that you can drag and drop onto visual designers in Visual Studio 2005.

✦ **Menu bar and standard toolbar** — These two elements provide access to additional tools and windows.

Because most of the task panes, windows, and menus in Visual Studio 2005 are context sensitive, they display different options depending on what kind of application you're developing. For example, the toolbox displays text boxes and buttons that work in Windows applications when you open them.

Visual Studio provides many windows in addition to the ones displayed by default. You can display all the windows by using the View menu, as shown in Figure 2-2.

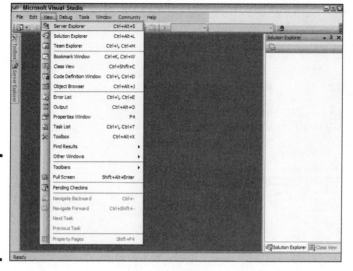

Figure 2-2:
Use the
View menu
to open
additional
windows.

Dealing with Windows Galore

Visual Studio 2005 displays content in two basic Window styles:

✦ Tabbed documents, such as the start page

✦ Task panes, such as the Solution Explorer

You can treat anything that opens as a tabbed document like a task pane
and vice versa. Here are your options for working with windows in Visual
Studio 2005:

✦ **Floating** — The window floats within the environment.

✦ **Dockable** — The window can be docked in a certain area of the screen.

✦ **Tabbed Document** — The window is placed in the tabbed-documents area.

✦ **Auto Hide** — The window is toggled between minimized and restored.

✦ **Hide** — The window is hidden from view.

To access the window options, follow these steps:

1. **Right-click the title bar of the window you want to manipulate.**

A context menu appears.

2. **Choose the window option from the context menu, as shown in
Figure 2-3.**

You can also access the window options by using the Window menu.

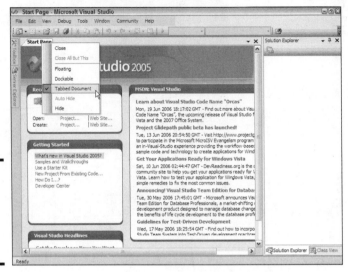

Figure 2-3:
Choose a
window
option from
the context
menu.

If you change your mind or make a mistake and want to restore all the windows to their original states, follow these steps:

1. **Choose Window⇨Reset Window Layout.**

   A confirmation box appears and asks you to confirm that you want the windows reset to the default layout.

2. **Click the Yes button.**

   All windows are restored.

Docking windows

When you make a window dockable, you can use positioning anchors to position it on the screen. To dock a tabbed document, follow these steps:

1. **Right-click the tabbed document and choose Dockable from the context menu.**

   The window appears as a floating window.

   If the Dockable option is already selected (a check mark appears next to it), the window is ready to be docked. Skip to Step 2.

2. Position your mouse over the title bar of the window and start dragging the window.

As you drag, position anchors appear on the screen.

3. Move the window toward a position anchor.

As you hover over a position anchor, a shadow is placed where the anchor will position the window, as shown in Figure 2-4.

4. Release the window over the position anchor.

The window is docked.

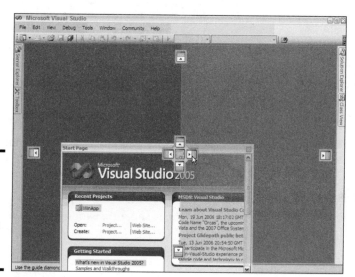

Figure 2-4:
Hover the window over one of the position anchors to dock it.

Working with tabbed documents

You can display any window as a tabbed document by simply right-clicking the window's title bar and choosing Tabbed Document from the context menu. When more than one document is displayed, you also have the option of creating horizontal and vertical groups of tabbed documents. To create a vertical tab group, follow these steps:

1. Right-click the tab of a tabbed document.

A context menu appears.

2. Choose New Vertical Tab Group from the context menu, as shown in Figure 2-5.

The documents are displayed side by side in the viewing area.

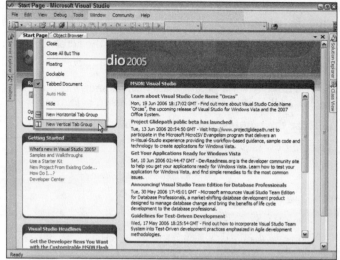

Figure 2-5:
Display tabbed documents vertically by using the New Vertical Tab Group option.

You can create horizontal groups by choosing New Horizontal Tab Group. To remove the groupings, right-click the tab of the tabbed document and choose Move to Previous Tab Group from the context menu.

Working with multiple documents

You can display tabbed documents as separate windows. To change this setting, follow these steps:

1. **Choose Tools⇨Options.**

   The Options dialog box appears.

2. **The General options in the Environment area are displayed by default. In the Window layout section, click the radio button next to Multiple documents, as shown in Figure 2-6.**

3. **Click OK to save your settings in the Options dialog box.**

Tabbed documents are now displayed as separate windows. You can right-click the title bar of a document window to view a context menu with display options.

Managing windows

Whether you choose to display content in tabbed documents, separate windows, or floating task panes, you can always use the Window menu to manage your open windows. Figure 2-7 shows the list of commands available on the Window menu.

Figure 2-6:
Click the
radio button
next to
Multiple
Documents
to display
documents
in separate
windows.

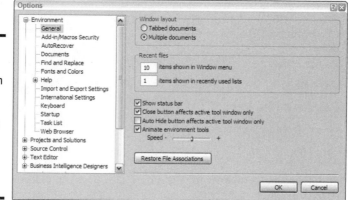

Figure 2-7:
Use the
Window
menu to
manage
your open
windows.

Building Solutions with Visual Studio 2005

Exploring Visual Studio without any files open is different from exploring it
when you have an application open for editing. Most windows and task
panes aren't populated with options until files are open. Although you can
use Visual Studio to open individual files, such as XML files, in most cases
you use Visual Studio to create new Windows and Web applications and edit
existing applications.

Applications you create with Visual Studio 2005 require many different kinds of files in order to work properly. The files that make up an application are *items*. Examples of items include

✦ Source code files

✦ References

✦ XML and HTML files

✦ Visual designer settings

✦ Data files

The items that make up an application are grouped into containers so that the items are easier to manage. Visual Studio 2005 provides two types of containers:

✦ **Project** — A group of items that combine to create a component of a solution, such as a Windows project

✦ **Solution** — A collection of projects and items that combine to create a deployable solution

You use the New Project dialog box, shown in Figure 2-8, to create new projects and solutions. You can invoke the New Project dialog box in one of several ways:

✦ Use the Recent Projects area of the start page.

✦ Choose the New⇨Project command from the File menu.

✦ Use the Solution Explorer to add a new project to an existing solution.

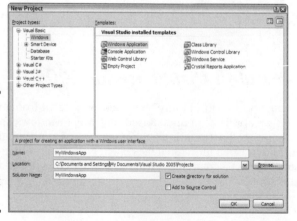

Figure 2-8:
Create new projects and solutions by using the New Project window.

Getting started with starter kits

Visual Studio 2005 provides a special kind of project template: a starter kit. A starter kit is special because, in addition to providing the files that Visual Studio needs in order to open, it provides sample code. Many starter kits are full-blown applications that you can start using right out of the box.

Here are a couple of starter kits included with Visual Studio 2005:

✔ Movie collection and screen saver samples for Visual Basic and C#

✔ A calculator sample for J#

You can open starter kits by using the New Project dialog box.

Exploring the New Project dialog box gives you some idea of the kinds of applications you can create using Visual Studio 2005. To open the New Project dialog box by using the Recent Projects area, follow these steps:

1. **Click the start page. If it isn't displayed, choose View➪Other Windows➪Start Page.**

2. **Locate the Recent Projects area of the start page in the upper-left corner of the screen.**

3. **Click the Project link, to the right of the Create option, as shown in Figure 2-9.**

The New Project dialog box appears.

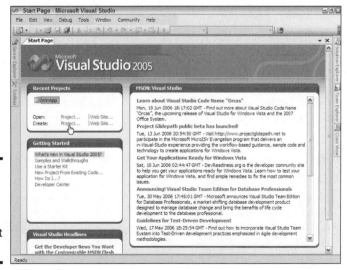

Figure 2-9:
Click the
Project link
to open the
New Project
window.

The New Project dialog box has three areas:

✦ **Project Types** — Displays the programming languages and kinds of projects you can create for each language.

✦ **Templates** — Displays the list of project templates available for each type of project.

Visual Studio uses project templates to know what files to create when you tell it to create a certain kind of application. For example, when you use the New Project dialog box to create a new Windows application, the Windows Application project template tells Visual Studio to create a Windows project with a new, blank Windows Form.

✦ **Project and solution details** — Allows you to name the project and tell Visual Studio where you want it saved. Allows you to specify whether you want a solution created and what to name it. By default, Visual Studio always creates a solution to contain your projects.

To create a new project by using the New Project window:

1. **In the Project Types tree, expand the Visual Basic project type category.**

A list of project types you can create by using the Visual Basic language appears.

2. **Click the Windows project type.**

A list of project templates that are available for Windows applications appears in the Templates window.

3. **Click the Windows Application template.**

4. **Enter a filename for your new Windows application in the Name text box.**

5. **Accept the default file location, or click the Browse button to select a new location.**

6. **Click OK to create the new project.**

A new Visual Basic project is created, and a blank Windows Form is displayed in the forms designer.

Using the Solution Explorer to manage solutions and projects

The *Solution Explorer* graphical tool helps you manage solutions and projects. When you open a solution or project, a graphical representation of the solution and the items within it are displayed in the Solution Explorer. In Figure 2-10, the Solution Explorer displays the new Windows application created in the preceding section.

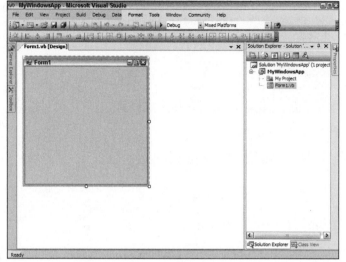

Figure 2-10:
Use the Solution Explorer to manage an open solution and its projects.

The Solution Explorer provides many commands you can use to manage your solution. To view a list of commands available for managing a solution, follow these steps:

1. **Right-click the solution in the Solution Explorer.**

   The solution is the topmost item in the tree. A context menu appears.

2. **Choose a command from the menu.**

You can also right-click a project in the Solution Explorer to view a context menu of project commands. Figure 2-11 shows the context menus for solutions and projects side by side.

Figure 2-11:
Right-click a solution (on the left) or project (on the right) to display a context menu.

On each of the context menus, the Add menu expands to display a list of items you can add to your solution or project. Items you can add to a solution include

+ New and existing projects
+ New and existing Web sites
+ New and existing items, such as XML files
+ Folders for organizing items

Items you can add to a Windows project include

+ New and existing items, such as Windows Forms, classes, and XML files
+ Folders for organizing items

The items you can add to other kinds of projects are specific to the type of project. For example, you can add Web Forms to Web sites.

You can right-click the items within a project to display context menus too. For example, when you right-click a Windows Form, you see a menu that displays the following commands to

+ View Code
+ View Designer
+ View Class Diagram

Working with solution and project menus

When you open a solution in Visual Studio 2005, the menu bar displays project-specific menus, including these three:

+ **Project or Website** — Manage Windows projects or Web sites.
+ **Build** — Build and deploy your solution.
+ **Debug** — Use the debugger.

Depending on the kind of project you open, you might also see menus for Data, Format, and Layout. When you're using Visual Studio 2005, don't forget to look up at the menu bar occasionally to see additional commands that you might not have known exist.

Using the Properties Window

Almost everything in Visual Studio — from controls to solutions — has properties. Properties can be quite simple, such as a few settings options, or composed of complex configuration wizards. The Properties window is displayed by default as a task pane on the right side of the screen.

You can view the properties of an item in several ways:

✦ Right-click an item and choose Properties from the context menu.

✦ Click an item and choose View⇨Properties Window.

✦ Click an item and press the F4 key.

Figure 2-12 shows the Properties window for a text box control for a Web site. To learn more about using properties, see Book III, about building applications with Visual Studio 2005.

Book II
Chapter 2

**Browsing
Visual Studio**

Figure 2-12:
Set the
properties
for an item
using the
Properties
window.

Browsing Servers

Use the Server Explorer to view server configuration details and connect to data sources. The Server Explorer is displayed by default as a task pane on the left side of the screen. You can use the Server Explorer for these tasks:

✦ Create and manage data connections.

✦ Drag and drop items, such as event logs and message queues, from a server to the design surface.

✦ View configuration details about services running on a server.

Figure 2-13 shows an example of the Server Explorer. See Book IV, Chapter 3 for more information about using the Server Explorer to manage data connections.

Figure 2-13: Use the Server Explorer to manage data connections and other server resources.

Writing Code with the Code Editor

Building applications requires writing code. For this purpose, Visual Studio 2005 provides a *code editor,* which is a special kind of word-processing program. Unlike the word processor that I used to write this book, a code editor is tuned to write programs. Although a regular word processor includes features like table formats and bullet points, the Visual Studio 2005 code editor has these features:

✦ **Autocomplete** — The code editor provides an intelligent authoring and editing autocomplete tool named IntelliSense. It provides you with a list of programming commands that are appropriate for the context in which you're writing. Figure 2-14 shows the code editor with IntelliSense in action.

✦ **Formatting** — Write consistent-looking code using features such as indenting, word wrapping, and tabifying blocks of code.

✦ **Outlining** — Collapse blocks of code so that they're out of view.

✦ **Macros** — Visual Studio 2005 provides helper tools, such as code snippets and comment and uncomment features.

Visual Studio 2005 provides intelligent code editors for

✦ .NET programming languages, such as Visual Basic, C#, and J#

✦ Web-based files, such as HTML, CSS, and XML

To open the code editor, use one of these methods:

✦ Open a file that uses any of the .NET languages I just mentioned.

✦ Double-click a code file in the Solution Explorer.

✦ Add a new programming file to a solution.

Book V shows you the code editor in action.

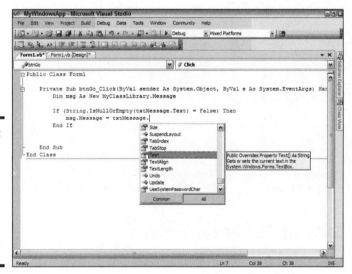

Figure 2-14:
The code
editor is a
special
word
processor
for writing
computer
programs.

Using the Forms Designer

One key feature of Visual Studio 2005 is that you can build a Windows application or Web site by dragging and dropping controls, like text boxes and labels, onto a design surface. The designer generates, behind the scenes, the code that's necessary to create the user interface you're painting with the designer. Visual Studio 2005 provides two distinct forms designers:

✦ Windows Forms Designer

✦ Web Forms Designer

The forms designers are displayed by default when you create a new Windows application or Web site.

Two windows that go hand in hand with the forms designers are the toolbox and the Properties window (see the section "Using the Properties Window," earlier in this chapter). The toolbox, displayed by default as a task pane on the left side of the screen, provides a list of the controls you can drag and drop onto the forms designer to create a Windows or Web Form. Figure 2-15 shows the Windows Forms Designer and the toolbox.

See Book III for examples of the visual forms designers.

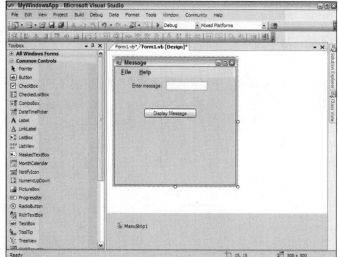

Figure 2-15: Use the toolbox to drag controls and drop them on the forms designer.

Taking a Look at Other Designers

Visual Studio provides many visual designers that are intended to increase your productivity. Here are a few:

✦ **Class Designer** — Model existing code or create new code by building models. Book V, Chapter 3 describes the class designer.

✦ **Dataset Designer** — Drag and drop tables from a database to create programmable DataSets. See Book IV, Chapter 3.

✦ **Crystal Reports** — Visually build reports for Windows or Web applications. Book VI, Chapter 4 demonstrates how to use the Crystal Reports designer.

✦ **Smart devices** — Create applications for smartphones and use emulators to see what the software does. Start building applications for smart devices in Book III.

Chapter 3: Making Connections with Visual Studio

In This Chapter

✔ Exploring the help features of Visual Studio 2005

✔ Reaching out to the .NET community

✔ Keeping up with certifications and Webcasts

*W*hen you use Visual Studio, you're not just using a development tool — you're joining a community. This statement is true no matter what development tool you use. The technologies people use often cluster them into communities, such as

✦ Java

✦ Linux and open source software

✦ Mac

✦ .NET

I'm not saying that people don't cross over, because they do. Many .NET developers are also closet Linux folks. Nevertheless, as a .NET developer, you're likely to run in the same circles as other .NET developers. In this chapter, I show you some of the ways that you can use Visual Studio to keep in touch.

Getting Help

When you install Visual Studio, help files are installed on your hard drive. The help documentation is a combination of local offline and online resources, including

✦ Online and offline MSDN (Microsoft Developer Network) documentation for Visual Studio and .NET

✦ Online content, such as community forums, from the Microsoft Web site

✦ Online content from third parties approved by Microsoft to provide content

MSDN includes a library full of documentation and a knowledge base. You can buy a subscription to MSDN that allows you to download software that you can use for development purposes. For more information about MSDN subscriptions, see Book I, Chapter 5.

You can view help content within Visual Studio or as a separate window. To set your options, follow these steps:

1. **Choose Tools⇨Options in Visual Studio 2005.**

   The Options dialog box is displayed.

2. **In the options tree on the left side of the dialog box, click the plus (+) sign next to the word *Environment*.**

   The list of environments is expanded.

3. **Click the Help option in the tree.**

   The general help settings are displayed.

4. **In the Show Help Using drop-down list, choose your preference for whether you want help content displayed in an integrated viewer within Visual Studio or in an external window, as shown in Figure 3-1.**

5. **Click OK to save your choices.**

You have to restart Visual Studio for your preferences to take effect.

I personally like to configure help to open in an external window. The Visual Studio 2005 interface is already cluttered with windows. By opening help in an external window, I can focus on the documentation.

Figure 3-1:
Set your preference for whether help is displayed within Visual Studio or in an external window.

You can access the Visual Studio help documentation in several ways, including the ones in this list:

✦ Use the Help menu in Visual Studio.

✦ Press F1 to view dynamic help topics based on the context in which you're working in Visual Studio.

✦ Use the features on the Community menu.

The Visual Studio help documentation is displayed in the Microsoft Document Explorer, which is a specialized Web browser. The Document Explorer has all the features you expect to see in help documentation:

✦ Contents

✦ Index

✦ Search

✦ Favorites

The Favorites feature creates a bookmark to your favorite help topics. To add a favorite help topic, right-click on the topic and choose Add to Help Favorites from the shortcut menu.

Your help favorites are saved when you exit Document Explorer. In the event your computer crashes, any favorites you create are lost. I suggest you periodically restart Document Explorer if you don't want to lose your favorites.

Another feature you'll definitely want to check out is the Sync with Table of Contents button. After you've located a topic using search or the index, you click the Sync with Table of Contents to display the topic in the Contents pane. Displaying the topic in this pane gives you the context in which the topic is used. Figure 3-2 shows the Sync with Table of Contents button.

Visual Studio's help documentation includes topics for .NET, Visual Studio, programming languages, and many other technologies. It's easy to get overwhelmed using the Index or Search features. By synchronizing a topic with the Table of Contents, you can quickly see the domain in which the topic belongs.

See the section "Discovering events" in Book V, Chapter 4 for an example of using help to locate a topic.

Book II
Chapter 3

**Making
Connections with
Visual Studio**

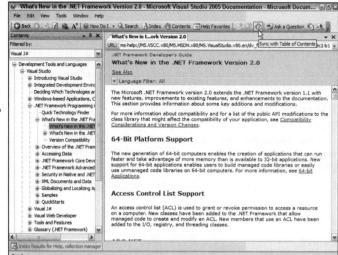

Figure 3-2:
Use the
Sync with
Table of
Contents
button to
place a help
topic in
context.

Visual Studio has some additional features that might surprise you in a help system:

✦ Filter the help contents and index by using categories such as .NET Framework, Web development, or a specific .NET language, as shown in Figure 3-3.

✦ Filter search results by language, technology, or content type.

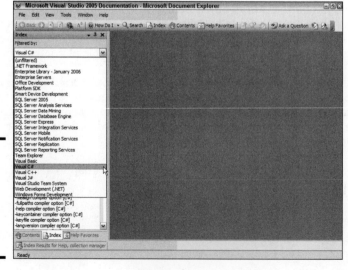

Figure 3-3:
Filter help
contents
and the
index to
narrow the
choices.

- ✦ Use special How Do I? topics covering everything from Crystal Reports to Visual Studio Tools for Office.

- ✦ Search the Microsoft online forums, ask questions, and check for answers.

- ✦ Submit suggestions or report bugs to Microsoft.

Figure 3-4 shows the Ask a Question feature where you can search public forms for answers. You can post questions to the forums if you can't find the information you need.

Book II
Chapter 3

Making
Connections with
Visual Studio

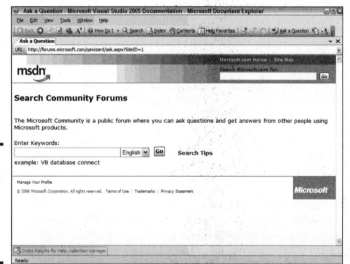

Figure 3-4:
Use the Ask a Question feature to search public forums.

Another useful help feature in Visual Studio is the start page (see Figure 3-5). When you open Visual Studio, the start page automatically displays head-lines from MSDN.

The news that's displayed on the start page uses a special technology, named RSS, for displaying news feeds. You can set the news feed on the start page to any RSS feed. For example, to set the start page to display the top stories from CNN, follow these steps:

1. **Choose Tools⇨Options in Visual Studio.**

2. **Expand the Environment options by clicking the plus (+) sign in the options tree.**

3. **Click the Startup option.**

4. **Type the URL for top CNN news stories in the Start Page News Channel field: http://rss.cnn.com/rss/cnn_topstories.rss.**

5. **Click OK to save your changes.**

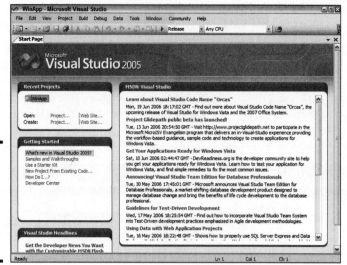

Figure 3-5:
The start page is displayed when you open Visual Studio.

Your start page is updated with the top stories from CNN, as shown in Figure 3-6.

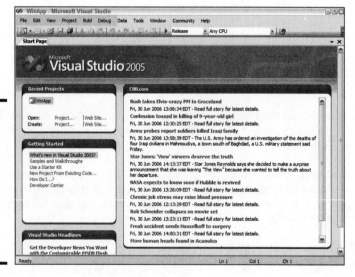

Figure 3-6:
You can update the RSS feed used to display headlines on Visual Studio's start page.

You can use the Search feature to search the Visual Studio documentation as well as online content from third-party Web sites. In the Search window, you can filter your results by these criteria:

✦ **Language** — Visual Basic or C#, for example

✦ **Technology** — Team System or Windows Forms, for example

✦ **Content type** — Controls or code snippets, for example

Four major providers are searched for results, as shown in Figure 3-7:

✦ MSDN Online

✦ Codezone Community

✦ Questions

✦ Local Help

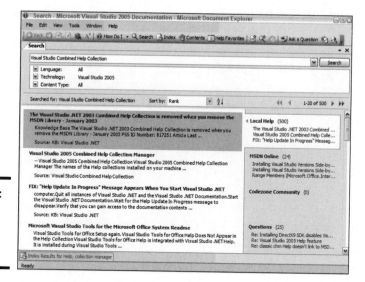

Figure 3-7:
Searches
use four
major
providers.

You can change the order in which the providers are displayed and remove providers by choosing the Tools⇨Options command.

As I mentioned earlier, the Document Explorer is a Web browser. Like most Web browsers, it has search and home pages that you can set to any Web page you wish. By changing the search and home pages, you can create shortcuts to resources on the Web that you use frequently while researching problems. For example, I set my home page to my My Yahoo! page and my search page to Microsoft's search page, which allows me to quickly access these resources from within the Document Explorer.

To change your Search and Home pages in the Document Explorer, follow these steps:

1. **Press F1 to open Visual Studio's help.**

2. **Click Tools⇨Options. The Options dialog box appears.**

3. **Click Web Browser.**

4. **Type the URLs you wish to use for your home page and search page, as shown in Figure 3-8.**

5. **Click the OK button.**

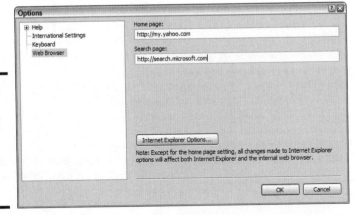

Figure 3-8:
Type URLs to use for Document Explorer's home and search pages.

To access the Search and Home pages in Document Explorer, on the View menu, click Web Browser⇨Search or Web Browser⇨Home, respectively.

The Document Explorer's Standard toolbar has a button to open the Search page. You can add a button to open the Home page by clicking Tools⇨ Customize. Drag and drop the Web Browser Home command in the View category onto the toolbar, as shown in Figure 3-9.

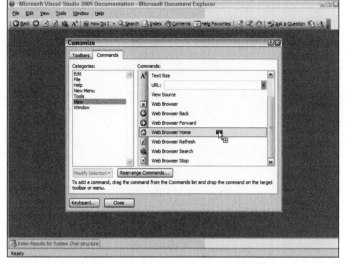

Figure 3-9:
Add the Web
Browser
Home com-
mand to the
toolbar.

Staying in Touch with the .NET Community

Visual Studio puts a major emphasis on using the online community. Part of
what makes .NET so valuable is the community that comes along with it. You
can use the .NET community to get

+ Help on a topic

+ Code samples and starter kits

+ Controls and add-ins that extend Visual Studio

The Visual Studio Community menu is another means for you to access the
.NET community. Use the Community menu in Visual Studio 2005 to

+ **Ask a question.** Search the Microsoft community forums for answers.
You can post questions to the forums if you can't find answers to your
questions.

+ **Check question status.** Check on the status of a question you asked in a
forum.

+ **Send feedback.** Make suggestions and report bugs to Microsoft.

+ **Check out the Developer Center.** Visit the developer center Web page
(on the Microsoft Web site), which provides access to additional Visual
Studio resources.

✦ **Hang out in the Codezone Community.** See links to additional online community Web sites where you can find code samples and tutorials.

✦ **Look at the partner-products catalog.** Search an online catalog for tools, components, add-ins, languages, and services that you can buy to extend or use with Visual Studio.

✦ **Do a community search.** Set the filter on the help search function to one of these five predefined filters:

- Template and Starter Kits

- IntelliSense Code Snippets

- Samples

- Controls

- Addins and Macros

When you access the features of the Community menu, shown in Figure 3-10, the content is displayed using the Microsoft Document Explorer, which also displays help for using Visual Studio.

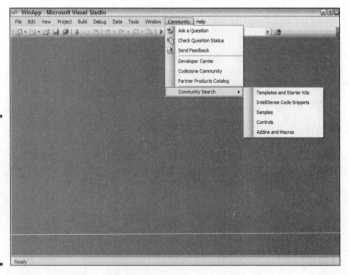

Figure 3-10: Access the .NET community by using the Community menu in Visual Studio.

Pursuing certification

As you make your way out and about in the .NET community, you likely want some way to show that you're not a poser. Microsoft provides a certification series designed to demonstrate, to all who care, that you know your stuff.

Microsoft offers three levels of certification:

+ **Technology** — These entry-level certifications demonstrate your proficiency in a specific Microsoft technology, such as.NET Framework, SQL Server, or BizTalk.

+ **Professional** — This more comprehensive set of certifications is geared toward professional software developers and information technology specialists.

+ **Architect** — This peer-reviewed certification requires at least ten years of advanced information technology experience.

Each level of certification accommodates specific certifications. For example, these certifications are available in the Professional series:

+ **Microsoft Certified Technology Specialist** — Tests your knowledge of developing software by using .NET and Visual Studio 2005

+ **Microsoft Certified Professional Developer** — Focuses more on specialized job roles, such as Web and Windows developers

+ **Microsoft Certified Applications Developer** — Geared toward people who develop applications by using .NET and Web services

+ **Microsoft Certified Solutions Developer** — Intended for people who build enterprise-level solutions

To read more about Microsoft certifications, go to `www.microsoft.com/learning/mcp/newgen`.

Viewing Webcasts

In the past few years, the quality of content on MSDN has improved substantially. Not only is the content more accurate, Microsoft has introduced more kinds of content in addition to plain old documentation. One area that I'm especially excited about is *Webcasts,* which are free Internet broadcasts of training, tutorials, and presentations.

You can participate in Webcasts live, while they're happening. Or, you can watch prerecorded Webcasts after the fact. An advantage of watching Webcasts live is that you can pose questions to presenters.

You can watch Webcasts about topics ranging from Windows Server 2003 to DotNetNuke to unit testing in Visual Studio 2005. Webcasts are a useful way to dig deeper into the core technologies you use every day or to get an overview of topics that are in your periphery.

Here are some Webcast resources you should check out:

✦ The MSDN Events and Webcasts page features Webcasts for Visual Studio and SQL Server: `http://msdn.microsoft.com/events`.

✦ The TechNet Events and Webcasts page helps you keep up with technical topics: `www.microsoft.com/technet/community/webcasts`.

✦ View Webcasts related to Visual Studio Team System: `http://msdn.microsoft.com/vstudio/teamsystem/community/webcasts`.

Chapter 4: Upgrading from .NET 1.1

In This Chapter

✔ **Deciding when to upgrade**

✔ **Converting Windows applications and class libraries**

✔ **Exploring conversion options for Web applications**

✔ **Using Visual Studio 2005 with previous versions of .NET**

What does it mean to upgrade to Visual Studio 2005? Two tasks are required for an upgrade:

✦ Move to the Visual Studio 2005 toolset.

✦ Use version 2.0 of the .NET Framework.

Depending on your situation, you might decide to

✦ Start using Visual Studio 2005 and .NET 2.0 right away for all new development.

✦ Upgrade all your existing Windows and Web applications to Visual Studio 2005 and .NET 2.0.

✦ Leave all or some of your existing applications in the versions of Visual Studio with which they were created.

✦ Upgrade your existing applications to Visual Studio 2005 while still using a previous version of the .NET Framework.

In this chapter, I talk about these scenarios and walk you through some conversion processes.

Making the Business Case for Upgrading

When you make the decision to upgrade to Visual Studio 2005, your existing applications must be converted to work with Visual Studio 2005 before they can be opened. In most cases, the conversion process doesn't change your code. Instead, it merely updates configuration files, such as project and solution files. The changes that are made depend on whether you're converting

✦ Windows applications

✦ Web applications

✦ Class libraries

Visual Studio 2005 uses version 2.0 of the .NET Framework by default. The syntax of programming languages such as C# and Visual Basic changes with each new version of the .NET Framework as new features are added and existing features are improved. The conversion process doesn't update your code to the latest syntax. Rather, the newer versions of .NET continue to support the syntax of previous versions. It's up to you to figure out if there's new and improved syntax and decide whether you want to change your code to use the new syntax.

When you make the decision to upgrade to Visual Studio 2005, you have lots of choices. As you think about whether you should upgrade, consider these issues:

✦ **Windows applications and class libraries aren't changed much by the conversion process.** Even though configuration settings are updated, your code stays the same.

✦ **Any code or controls that were deprecated in version 2.0 of the .NET framework still work.** You can't use the visual designers for deprecated controls, although you can use the code editor.

✦ **Your class libraries aren't optimized to take advantage of the latest features in .NET 2.0.** You have to figure out whether you should change your code.

After converting applications to Visual Studio 2005, analyze your code by using FxCop. It offers you suggestions for improving your code. See Book V, Chapter 5 for more information about FxCop.

✦ **Web applications require some finesse to get all their components converted properly.** You need to do some preparation work before you convert them.

✦ **Applications that are especially complex can be difficult to convert.** If you can't convert the entire solution, you might have to convert individual projects one at a time and then add them to your Visual Studio 2005 solution.

✦ **Clients running your applications must have the .NET 2.0 framework installed.** You can convert your applications to work with Visual Studio 2005 and deploy applications to work with previous versions of the .NET Framework. I show you how later in this chapter.

✦ **You can't "unconvert."** You can restore your backups, however, and discard the converted application if you don't like the results.

You have several alternatives to performing an outright upgrade of your application to Visual Studio 2005:

✦ **If it ain't broke. . . .** You might not have any compelling reason to upgrade your Visual Studio 2002 and 2003 applications to Visual Studio 2005. Unless you plan to take advantage of the new Visual Studio 2005 features in your Visual Studio 2002 and 2003 applications, you probably don't need to upgrade.

✦ **Go "side by side."** You can run all three versions of the .NET Framework and Visual Studio on a single computer. Your existing version 1.0 and 1.1 applications then work alongside any new version 2.0 applications you create.

✦ **Step up to the 2.0 framework.** Chances are that your .NET 1.0 and 1.1 applications will run on the 2.0 framework, even without converting them to work with Visual Studio 2005. You can take advantage of the new security and performance features of .NET 2.0 without touching your code.

✦ **Mix and match.** If you have relatively stable parts of your application that use previous versions of the .NET Framework and you want to do new development in Visual Studio 2005, you can mix and match. Just reference your older components in your new Visual Studio 2005 solution.

✦ **Take the brute force approach.** You can manually re-create your applications in Visual Studio 2005 by choosing to copy and paste your old code into newly created Visual Studio 2005 solutions.

✦ **Indulge in the best of both worlds.** You can target the .NET 1.1 runtime with your existing applications in Visual Studio 2005. I show you how later in this chapter.

All this assumes that you're converting from a previous version of the .NET Framework to the current version. If you're upgrading from a pre-.NET language such as Visual Basic 6, then you'll need to jump through a few hoops to get your application converted. Once converted, you'll still likely need to finesse the converted code to make it work.

**Book II
Chapter 4**

Upgrading
from .NET 1.1

You may able to reuse stable components created in Visual Basic 6.0 using a feature of the .NET Framework called COM Interop. With COM Interop, you can consume your Visual Basic 6 code from your .NET applications.

In the case of ASP.NET, you have additional considerations when you choose to upgrade to Visual Studio 2005 and ASP.NET 2.0:

✦ **ASP.NET uses a new, simplified model for managing resources, such as code and Web pages.** Project files are no longer needed because all the configuration settings are moved to web.config, an XML-based configuration file.

If you're really attached to using project files, you can use the Web Application Projects extension for Visual Studio 2005. Download the extension for free from Microsoft's Web site at `http://msdn. microsoft.com/asp.net/reference/infrastructure/wap`.

✦ **You can execute your Web sites on local development machines by using the new ASP.NET Developer Server.** Using the ASP.NET Developer Server requires less configuration and is more secure than using Internet Information Services as your local Web server.

✦ **ASP.NET 2.0 offers a new code-behind model, new controls for laying out Web pages and working with data, and improved deployment options.** Your productivity is greatly improved with ASP.NET 2.0.

See Book III for more information on creating Web applications with ASP.NET 2.0.

Considering Your Conversion Strategies

Visual Studio provides a conversion wizard for migrating projects from previous versions of .NET to the .NET 2.0 version. The conversion process itself is fairly straightforward: You just open your Visual Studio 2002 or 2003 solution in Visual Studio 2005, and the Conversion Wizard automatically opens and walks you through the conversion process.

Before you convert any applications, you need to do some preparation work on all of them:

✦ Make sure that you have good backups, in case you decide to rollback to the unconverted version.

✦ Make sure that all your source code compiles *before* you convert.

✦ Take the time to clean up any extraneous files that don't belong with the application.

✦ Make sure that the .NET 2.0 Framework is installed on all client machines that will run your application.

Converting Web applications requires more preparation than converting Windows applications because the conversion process is more involved. See "Converting Web applications," later in this chapter, for more details.

Converting Windows applications and class libraries

As a rule, you should try to convert an entire solution first rather than convert each of the projects in a solution individually. If the conversion process can't convert all the projects in your solution, you should

+ Allow the Visual Studio Conversion Wizard to convert the solution and as many projects as it can.

+ Open individual projects that don't convert in Visual Studio 2005. Walk through the Conversion Wizard for each project that doesn't convert with the solution.

+ Add the converted projects to the converted solution.

To convert Windows solutions and projects, follow these steps:

1. **In Visual Studio 2005, choose File⇨Open⇨Project/Solution.**

The Open Project window appears.

2. **Browse to your Visual Studio 2002 or 2003 Windows application and click the Open button. If you have a solution file, you should open it.**

The Visual Studio Conversion Wizard appears.

3. **Click Next to start the wizard.**

4. **Click the radio button next to Yes, Create a Backup before Converting, and specify a backup location. Click Next.**

A summary of the solution and projects to be converted is displayed.

5. **Click the Finish button to start the conversion.**

After the conversion is done, a completion window appears. Any errors that occur during the conversion process are listed.

6. **To display a conversion log, select the Show the Conversion Log When the Wizard Is Closed option, and click the Close button.**

The conversion log, shown in Figure 4-1, appears in Visual Studio 2005.

Follow these steps again to convert class libraries.

After the conversion, build your application in Visual Studio 2005 to make sure that all converted projects are compiled. If you have multiple projects in your solution, you should build your class libraries first and work your way through any dependencies until all your components are built.

**Book II
Chapter 4**

**Upgrading
from .NET 1.1**

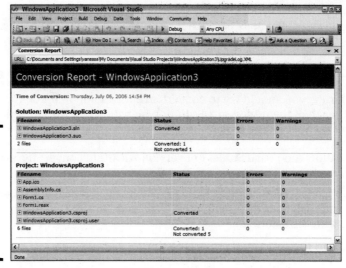

Figure 4-1:
View the conversion log for details about the conversion process.

Converting Web applications

The conversion process for Web applications is more involved than for Windows applications and class libraries. The Visual Studio Conversion Wizard performs several additional functions when converting Web applications, including these:

✦ Move project file configuration settings into the web.config file.

✦ Create new folders, such as App_Code, and move stand-alone class files.

✦ Update the code behind attributes to reflect new attributes.

Because the Web application conversion process is more involved, a few more preparation tasks are involved:

✦ Make sure that all files that need to be converted are included in the project. The Conversion Wizard converts only those files.

To include in a project any files that were previously excluded, open the project in Visual Studio 2002 or 2003, right-click the file, and choose Include in Project from the context menu.

✦ Remove any files from your project directory that aren't part of the project.

✦ When you convert multiple projects, make sure that no overlap occurs in the files that each project references.

✦ When you convert multiple solutions, make sure that no overlap occurs in the projects contained in the solutions.

✦ Remove references to other Web projects.

Microsoft released an update to the Conversion Wizard for Web projects in March 2006. You should download and install the update before converting your projects. You can read about the update and find a link to the download at `http://support.microsoft.com/kb/898904/EN-US/`.

To convert a Web application, follow these steps:

1. **Choose File⇨Open⇨Web Site.**

The Open Web Site window appears.

You must open your Web site using the Open Web Site window in order for the conversion wizard to work properly.

The Open Web Site window gives you several sources from which you may open your Web site. In most cases, you'll open your site from a local IIS site. You may also choose to open a site from an FTP site, remote Web server, or source control.

Don't select File System as your source. Converting a Web application from a file system causes the Web site to lose data about the site's structure.

2. **Select Local IIS from the list of sources in the left pane.**

A list of Web sites on the local computer appears.

3. **Navigate to the Web site you want to convert, select it (as shown in Figure 4-2), and click the Open button.**

The Visual Studio Conversion Wizard appears.

4. **Click Next to start the wizard.**

5. **Follow the steps in the Conversion Wizard to complete the conversion.**

Figure 4-2:
Open an existing Web site by using the Local IIS option.

If errors occur in the conversion, read the conversion log and determine which files weren't converted. Remember that class files aren't converted. They're copied to the solution directory "as is."

You may check the ConversionReport.webinfo file to view the steps taken to convert the application. The file is named ConversionReport.txt if you haven't installed the conversion wizard upgrade.

Build your applications by making sure that all dependent projects are built first. Always open your converted project by using the Local IIS option.

After the conversion, you have an ASP.NET 2.0 Web application that you can edit in Visual Studio 2005. The folder structure and code-behind model are updated to the new ASP.NET 2.0 model.

Running Web applications side-by-side

You can specify which version of the .NET framework you want a Web application to use. Version 2.0 of the framework is backward compatible with versions 1.0 and 1.1. You can then run your existing applications in version 2.0 and take advantage of improved security and performance features without recompiling.

Configuring your Web application to use version 2.0 of the .NET Framework requires that the .NET Framework version 2.0 be installed on the server where the application is hosted. If that version isn't installed, browse to the Windows Update site on the server and install it.

To configure a Web application to use version 2.0 of the .NET Framework, follow these steps:

1. **Launch the Internet Information Services Manger on the server.**

   In Windows Server 2003, you can find the IIS Manager by choosing Administrative Tools from the Start menu. If you can't find it there, look in the Control Panel.

2. **Expand the Web Sites folder and navigate to the Web site you want to configure.**

3. **Right-click the Web site and choose Properties from the context menu.**

4. **Click the ASP.NET tab.**

5. **Set the version by using the ASP.NET version drop-down list, as shown in Figure 4-3.**

6. **Click OK.**

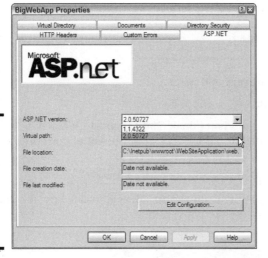

Figure 4-3:
Set the
version of
the .NET
framework
you want
the site
to use.

You can repeat these steps for all the Web sites hosted on the server to specify whether you want the site to use version 1.0, 1.1, or 2.0 of the framework.

Using copy and paste to control conversions

If you like to take control of your conversions, you can re-create your applications manually in Visual Studio 2005. Here's the overview:

1. Create new Windows or Web solutions.

2. Use the visual designers to manually re-create your forms, pages, user controls, and any other elements that are in your existing application. Make sure to keep your naming style consistent with your old application.

3. Copy any code that you want to bring over from your old solution. Your code should work as long as you re-created all your Windows and Web forms properly.

4. Build your applications and deal with errors.

Using the Visual Studio converters

Visual Studio 2005 provides two converters for converting Visual Basic 6.0 applications to Visual Basic.NET and for converting Java and Visual J++ 6.0 applications to C#:

✦ Visual Basic Upgrade Wizard

✦ Java Language Conversion Assistant

To open either of these converters, follow these steps:

1. **Choose File⇨Open.**

   The Open fly-away menu appears.

2. **Choose the Convert option.**

   The Convert dialog box appears.

3. **Choose either the Visual Basic 2005 Upgrade Wizard or the Java Language Conversion Assistant from the list of converters, as shown in Figure 4-4.**

4. **Click the Create New Solution radio button.**

5. **Click OK to start the Conversion Wizard, and follow the steps in the wizard to complete the conversion.**

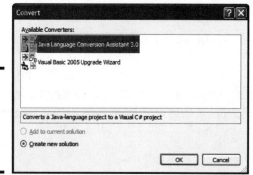

Figure 4-4: Choose a converter from the Convert dialog box.

Using Visual Studio 2005 with .NET 1.1

Suppose that you want the best of both worlds. You want to take advantage of the exciting new features in the Visual Studio 2005 development environment, such as the class designer and code snippets, and you still need to target the .NET 1.1 runtime environment. Well, my friend, that option is available to you.

Note that you can't use any of the features of the .NET 2.0 framework, such as generics and master pages. If you try, you receive an error message when you build your solution. Also, you can't use this trick with Web applications. ASP.NET uses a completely different build model than Windows applications and class libraries do. You can still get the lay of the Visual Studio 2005 land, though, while continuing to target previous versions of the .NET framework.

See Book III for more information about master pages and Book V for more information about working with generics.

To target .NET 1.1 with Visual Studio 2005, you need to

✦ Drop the references from the .NET 2.0 assemblies.

✦ Add references to .NET 1.1 assemblies.

✦ Use the .NET 1.1 compiler rather than the .NET 2.0 compiler.

Although you can do this process manually, tools are available to automate it. One of the most popular tools is Robert McLaws' MSBuild Toolkit. The MSBuild Toolkit extends the features of MSBuild. MSBuild (short for Microsoft Build Engine) is part of Visual Studio 2005. MSBuild is responsible for building your application when you choose Build Solution from the Build menu in Visual Studio 2005. MSBuild uses XML-based files to control how an application is built. MSBuild Toolkit provides replacement XML configuration files you can use to target the .NET 1.1 compiler.

**Book II
Chapter 4**

**Upgrading
from .NET 1.1**

To use the MSBuild Toolkit, follow these steps:

1. **Download the toolkit at `http://weblogs.asp.net/rmclaws/ archive/2005/06/04/410360.aspx`.**

2. **Follow the Installation Wizard instructions to install the toolkit.**

The toolkit installs two XML configuration files, or *targets* files — one for C# and another for Visual Basic — that you can use to tell Visual Studio to use a previous version of the .NET Framework. (The configuration files are called targets files because they end in the file extension .targets.) The toolkit also registers those XML files so that you can use them with Visual Studio without receiving a warning message.

To use the toolkit, the application's project files must already use the Visual Studio 2005 file format. If your application was created using a previous version of Visual Studio, you must open the application in Visual Studio 2005 to convert the project file format. See the section "Converting Windows applications and class libraries," earlier in this chapter, and follow the steps to convert your application to Visual Studio 2005.

Before you can target your Visual Studio 2005 application to a previous version of .NET, you must open the application's project file in a text editor and tell it to use the targets file installed by the toolkit. Visual Studio project files are also XML configuration files, so you can open them in any text editor. To modify the project file, follow these steps:

1. **Browse to the file directory where the application's project file is saved.**

Visual Basic project files have the file extension .vbproj, and C# project files use .csproj.

2. **Open the project file in a text editor, such as Notepad.**

3. **Locate this line in the file:**

```
<Import Project="$(MSBuildBinPath)\Microsoft.Csharp.
    targets" />
```

If your project is a Visual Basic project, the line references the Microsoft.VisualBasic.targets file.

The default file path for MSBuildBinPath is C:\WINDOWS\ Microsoft.NET\Framework\v2.0.50727.

4. **Change the line from Step 3 to use the targets file installed by the toolkit as shown in the following:**

```
<Import Project="$(MSBuildExtensionsPath)\Interscape\
    MSBuildToolkit\Interscape.MSBuildToolkit.CSharp.
    targets" />
```

The default file path for MSBuildExtensionsPath is C:\Program Files\ MSBuild.

5. **Save the project file.**

Repeat these steps in your application for every project that you want to target a previous version of .NET.

To target a previous version of .NET 1.1 with your application, follow these steps:

1. **Open your Visual Basic or C# application in Visual Studio 2005 by using the File menu.**

If you're opening an application created in a previous version of Visual Studio, you need to walk through the Conversion Wizard steps before you can open the application.

2. **Choose Build➪Configuration Manager.**

The Configuration Manager appears.

3. **Choose New from the Active Solution Platform drop-down list.**

The New Solution Platform appears.

4. **Choose .NET 1.1 from the Type drop-down list, as shown in Figure 4-5.**

5. **Click OK.**

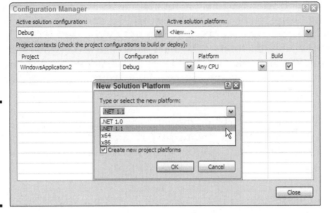

Figure 4-5:
Select
.NET 1.1
from the list
of available
platforms.

The platform for your project is updated to .NET 1.1 in the Configuration
Manager. When you build your application, Visual Studio 2005 targets
the .NET 1.1 version of the .NET Framework.

6. **Click the Close button to close the Configuration Manager.**

7. **Build your application by choosing Build⇨Build Solution.**

Verify that your application is compiled using the .NET 1.1 compiler by viewing the contents of the output window. You should see something similar to
Figure 4-6. Notice that Visual Studio used the Visual Basic and C# compilers
vbc.exe and csc.exe, respectively, for the version 1.1 framework.

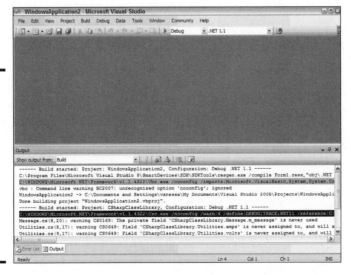

Figure 4-6:
Use the
output
window to
verify that
the build
process
used the
correct
version of
the .NET
compiler.

The Microsoft team responsible for MSBuild is also working on its own tool for using Visual Studio 2005 with the .NET 1.1 compiler. Its project is named MSBee, which stands for MSBuild Everett Environment. MSBee works similarly to the MSBuild Toolkit. The main difference is that you can't use MSBee using the Visual Studio 2005 Build menu. Instead, you have to manually build your applications using the command line. You can download MSBee for free at `www.codeplex.com/Wiki/View.aspx?ProjectName=MSBee`.

You aren't restricted to using these two applications. The .targets files are what makes it possible to create .NET 1.1 assemblies using Visual Studio 2005 and MSBuild. You can browse the Web for .targets files or even write your own.

Book III

Building Applications with Visual Studio 2005

The 5th Wave   By Rich Tennant

Of course it doesn't make any sense, but it's our only chance! Now hook your smartphone into the override and see if you can bring this baby in!!

Contents at a Glance

Chapter 1: Getting Smart About Smart Clients

In This Chapter

✔ Getting acquainted with Windows Forms

✔ Creating your first smart client application

✔ Working with controls

✔ Setting properties and responding to events

*V*isual Studio has all the tools you need to build everything from the simplest to the most complex Windows applications. Using the Microsoft .NET Framework, Visual Studio provides the visual designers that make building Windows applications a breeze. For example, Visual Studio gives you these elements to accomplish certain tasks:

✦ Project Templates — Set up your project.

✦ Visual designers — Lay out Windows Forms.

✦ The control toolbox — Add user interface elements to your Windows Forms.

✦ Wizards, property-setting windows, and shortcut task lists — Configure user interface elements.

This chapter walks you through some of the tools that Visual Studio provides for building managed Windows applications that are using either Visual Basic or C#.

Switching from Fat Clients to Smart Clients

The Windows operating system and applications that run on Windows have been around for more than 20 years. With ubiquity, early Windows applications became bloated and hard to deploy. In response, developers snubbed their noses at these newly dubbed fat clients and started using both client and server resources to create leaner applications.

Proving that the grass isn't always greener, folks quickly learned that thin clients had their problems too. Although thin clients were easier to deploy, they weren't all that feature rich, and they didn't work when the network went down. Then came the Internet, and the world went crazy for

Web-based applications. Many talented developers found innovative ways to twist and contort simple Web pages into full-blown desktop applications. Although developers had modest success in this arena, many diehard Windows programmers cringed at the lack of user interface sophistication in Web-based applications.

Thanks to cheap, fast hardware and the maturity of Windows application development, the Windows application is again being redefined, this time as the smart client. Although a smart client might look like any old Windows application, you can use its key differences to

✦ Create rich user experiences.

✦ Deploy and maintain applications with greater ease.

✦ Enjoy more security than in a traditional Windows application.

Smart clients still provide all the same features as earlier generations of Windows applications:

✦ You can build datacentric, interactive applications.

✦ You can access the local computer.

✦ They don't require a server in order to run.

Windows applications are all about creating an intuitive, visually appealing, and interactive user experiences. If user experience weren't important, we all would still be running good old-fashioned character-based applications in DOS.

Smart clients aren't the last word in Windows applications. The next wave of Microsoft products for Windows and Visual Studio will usher in even more opportunities for Windows developers to enhance the user experience. See Chapter 3 in Book VII to read more about the next generation of Windows applications.

Designing Windows Forms

The basic building block of a smart client Windows application is the Windows Form. Windows Forms, a key technology of the .NET framework, provide

✦ Libraries for creating the user interface

✦ Libraries for common tasks, such as reading and writing to the file system

✦ A set of controls that provide common user interface elements

The *Windows Forms Designer* is the Visual Studio visual design surface for working with Windows Forms. Use the Windows Forms Designer for these tasks:

✦ Visually lay out your user interface.

✦ Configure user interface attributes.

✦ Write custom code that's executed when users interact with your form.

Figure 1-1 displays the Windows Forms Designer in Visual Studio. The next section walks you through creating a new Windows application and using the forms designer.

Creating your first smart client project

Visual Studio uses Solutions and Projects containers to organize all the files necessary to build an application. When you create a new Windows application, Visual Studio creates all the files you need and prepares the development environment with the windows, designers, and editors you need in order to work with your new project.

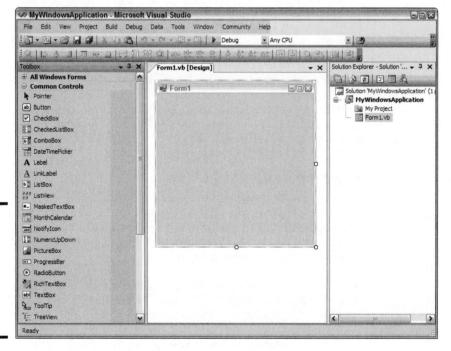

Figure 1-1: Use the Windows Forms Designer to lay out your user interface.

Book III Chapter 1

Getting Smart About Smart Clients

To create a new smart client project in Visual Studio, follow these steps:

1. **Choose File⇨New⇨ Project.**

   The New Project window appears.

   You can also open the New Project window by pressing the key combination Ctrl+Shift+N.

2. **In the Project Types hierarchy, click the programming language you want to use.**

   A list of project templates that are available for that programming language appears on the right.

   Windows applications created by using Visual Basic, C#, and J# use the .NET Framework. Although the examples in this chapter use Visual Basic, you can create Windows applications by using any language. See Chapter 3 in this mini-book for more details about creating Windows applications with C++.

3. **Click the Windows Application icon.**

4. **Enter a unique name for your application in the Name text box.**

   Although you can give your application any name you want, you probably should choose a name that describes your application. Many developers include the word *Windows* or the abbreviation Win in an application's name to distinguish it from other kinds of applications, such as Web or mobile applications.

5. **Click OK to create the application.**

Visual Studio creates a new solution with a Windows project. A new Windows Form is added to the project, and Visual Studio displays the form in the Windows Forms Designer.

Saying "Hello world!"

When you create a new Windows application, Visual Studio generates all the code necessary to display the Windows form on the screen when you run your application. To run your new Windows application, press Ctrl+F5. Visual Studio builds your Windows application and displays a blank Windows Form, as shown in Figure 1-2.

Most Windows applications use menus, text boxes, and buttons. These types of user interface elements are *controls*. Follow these steps to add controls to make your application say "Hello world!":

1. **Open the control toolbox by pressing Ctrl+Alt+X.**

2. **Drag and drop a label control from the toolbox onto the forms designer.**

3. **Drag and drop a button control onto the forms designer.**

4. **Double-click the button control.**

Visual Studio creates a block of code to handle the button's `Click` event. The code editor appears with the cursor flashing in the block of code.

5. **Type this line in the code editor:**

```
me.Label1.Text = "Hello world!"
```

6. **Press Ctrl+F5 to run your Windows Form.**

Figure 1-2:
Visual Studio generates the code to display a Windows form.

Book III
Chapter 1

Getting Smart About Smart Clients

When you click the button on your form, `Hello world!` appears on the label you add in Step 3, as shown in Figure 1-3.

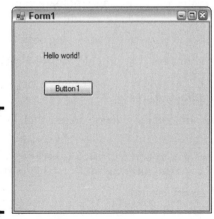

Figure 1-3:
"Hello world!" appears on the form's label.

Taking Command from Control Central

A Windows form is a blank canvas: It doesn't do much on its own. To bring your Windows form to life, you must add controls to it. *Controls* are user interface elements, such as buttons and text boxes, designed for interacting with your Windows form. Controls breathe life into your Windows forms. They

✦ Provide structure and navigation in the form of menus, toolbars, and status bars

✦ Allow users to interact with your forms by using buttons, labels, and text boxes

✦ Use dialog boxes to provide user feedback about your application's state

Visual Studio provides a toolbox chock full of controls. The control toolbox, shown in Figure 1-4, includes all the commonly used controls that even casual Windows users are familiar with, such as

✦ Labels, text boxes, and buttons

✦ Check boxes, list boxes, and combo boxes

✦ Calendars and date pickers

The toolbox displays controls in groups, or *tabs:*

✦ **All Windows Forms** — Contains an alphabetical list of controls

✦ **Common Controls** — Lists frequently used controls, such as labels and text boxes

✦ **Containers** — Used for laying out and grouping other controls on the form

✦ **Menus & Toolbars** — Creates the menus and toolbars your application uses

✦ **Data** — Contains controls and wizards for accessing data

✦ **Components** — Contains controls that provide back-end services, such as connecting to an event log

✦ **Printing** — Provides printing features

✦ **Dialogs** — Allows you to add common dialog boxes, such as those used for saving files

✦ **Crystal Reports** — Allows you to add a Crystal Report to your form. See Chapter VI, Chapter 4 to read more about Crystal Reports.

✦ **General** — Contains an empty group

This chapter demonstrates how to use frequently used controls, such as labels, text boxes, and buttons. More advanced controls, such as those in the containers and on the menus and toolbox tabs, are discussed in Chapter 2 of this mini-book. To read more about using data controls on Windows forms, see Book IV, Chapter 2.

Figure 1-4:
Add controls
to your form
from the
toolbox.

You can customize the toolbox by

+ Adding and removing tab groups

+ Moving tab groups up or down

+ Adding and removing controls to and from the tab groups

To customize the toolbox, follow these steps:

1. **Right-click an item, such as a specific control or tab, in the toolbox you want to customize.**

A shortcut menu appears, as shown in Figure 1-5.

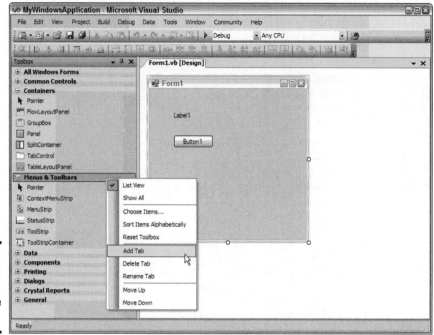

Figure 1-5:
Right-click a tab header to customize the tab.

2. From the shortcut menu, choose the action you want to take.

To add new controls to the toolbox, pick Choose Items from the shortcut menu.

Adding controls to your form

The easiest way to add a control to a form is to drag and drop it from the toolbox onto the Windows form. You can also draw a control to specify its exact size. To draw a text box on a Windows form, follow these steps:

1. Click the text box control in the toolbox.

If the toolbox is closed, press Ctrl+Alt+X to display it.

2. Move your mouse pointer to the Windows form.

Note that it isn't necessary to drag the text box.

The pointer changes to a plus (+) sign.

If you change your mind about drawing the control, click a different control or click the Pointer in the toolbox to reset your mouse pointer without adding a control to the form.

3. In the upper-left corner, click the mouse pointer wherever you want to start drawing the text box.

To draw a default-size text box, click and release your mouse button without dragging.

4. Drag the mouse pointer to the lower-left corner where you want the text box to end, as shown in Figure 1-6.

5. Release the mouse button.

The text box is drawn on the form.

Manipulating controls

Creating a user interface with controls involves more than dragging and dropping. To get the most from controls, you need to know how to position them on your form. This section covers some common tools for putting controls exactly where you want them.

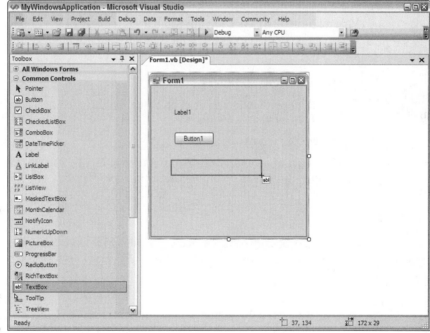

Figure 1-6: Release the mouse pointer in the lower-left corner of the text box.

Book III
Chapter 1

Getting Smart About Smart Clients

Formatting controls

Even the simplest Windows form can have dozens of controls on it. Developers often want to align controls in a way that's visually appealing to users. Although you can work with each control individually — drag, drop, resize, align — using the Visual Studio Format menu is much easier. After selecting two or more controls, use the Format menu to perform the following actions:

✦ **Align** — Position controls into alignment with one another.

✦ **Make Same Size** — Make controls the same width or height.

✦ **Horizontal Spacing** — Set the side-by-side spacing between controls.

✦ **Vertical Spacing** — Set the spacing above and below controls in a row.

✦ **Center in Form** — Position a control or group of controls in the center of the Windows form.

✦ **Order** — Set controls to appear in front of other controls.

✦ **Lock Controls** — Lock the position of a single control or group of controls so that the position can't be changed.

Visual Studio displays a Layout toolbar with many of the common formatting commands. To display the Layout toolbar if it's not already open, follow these steps:

1. **Choose View⇨Toolbars.**

A submenu displays a list of all Visual Studio toolbars, and check marks indicate all visible toolbars.

2. **Select the Layout option.**

The Layout toolbar appears, as shown in Figure 1-7. You can use this toolbar to access common formatting commands.

Figure 1-7:
The Layout toolbar.

To create a form with aligned labels and text boxes for accepting user input:

1. **Draw three labels on the form. Stack the labels vertically and try not to align them.**

2. **Draw three text boxes on the form — again, without aligning them.**

3. **Hold down the Shift key, and click the three text boxes.**

All three text boxes are now selected.

You have three options for selecting formatting controls:

- **Shift+click** — Format all controls to conform with the first control selected.

- **Ctrl+click** — Format all controls to conform with the last control selected.

- **Click and drag** — Click the form, and drag a selection rectangle around all the controls you want to select.

4. Click the Make Same Size icon on the Layout toolbar, as shown in Figure 1-8.

The text boxes are made the same size.

5. Click the Align Lefts icon on the Layout toolbar.

(Align Lefts is the second icon on the toolbar.) The text boxes are aligned to the left.

6. Position the mouse pointer over the right side of the text boxes. When the pointer turns to an arrow, drag your mouse to the right and left.

The boxes widen and narrow with the mouse movement.

7. Click the form to deselect the text boxes.

8. Hold down the Shift key while you select the three label controls.

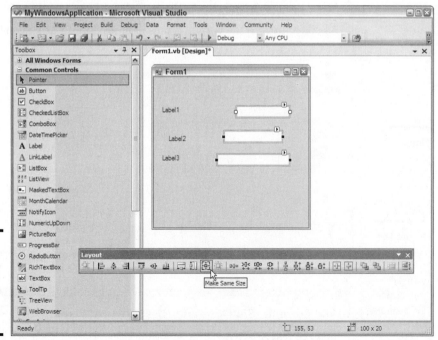

Figure 1-8:
Click the
Make Same
Size icon on
the Layout
toolbar.

9. **Choose Format⇨Align⇨Rights.**

The labels are aligned to the right.

10. **Position the pointer over the labels until it turns into a four-way arrow. Drag the labels to the left to create space between the labels and text boxes.**

You can use the arrow keys on your keyboard to move the labels around on the form.

When you add a control to a form, Visual Studio provides visual cues, or *snaplines*, for positioning the control. Snaplines recommend the best position for the controls in accordance with spacing recommendations set in the official Microsoft user interface guidelines.

The publication *Microsoft Official Guidelines for User Interface Developers and Designers* outlines the specifications for the placement and proper use of controls on Windows forms. You can view the guidelines online at `http://msdn.microsoft.com/library/default.asp?url=/library/en-us/dnwue/html/welcome.asp`.

To see snaplines in action, follow these steps:

1. **Drag a button control from the Visual Studio toolbox to the form design surface and don't release the button.**

2. **Move the mouse pointer to the lower-right corner of the form.**

As you approach the corner, blue snaplines appear, as shown in Figure 1-9.

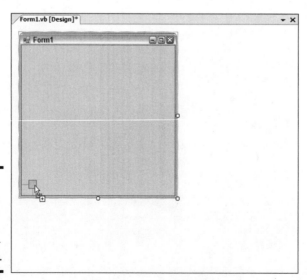

Figure 1-9: Snaplines provide visual cues for positioning controls.

3. **Drop the button on the form.**

4. **Drag a text box control to the form and don't release the text box.**

5. **Position the form above the button. When the snapline appears between the text box and the button, release the text box.**

Snaplines are visible any time you move controls on the design surface. The space between the button control and the edge of the form is the sum of the button's margin property and the form's padding property. Margins define the exterior space between controls, and padding designates space between a control's interior border and its contents. You can set these properties yourself or use snaplines to do it for you. See the section "Using the Properties Window," later in this chapter, for more information on setting control properties.

Locking controls

Getting the layout just right on a form can be a chore. You can keep your controls positioned where you want them by locking them in place. You have two options for locking controls:

✦ To lock all your controls and the form itself, choose Lock Controls from the Format menu.

✦ To lock an individual control, set the control's `Locked` property to True.

Setting the Tab order

Nothing's worse than when you press the Tab key in a Windows application and the cursor jumps to an unexpected field. The Tab order determines the order in which the Tab button moves from field to field on your form. To set the tab order, follow these steps:

1. **Choose View⇨Tab Order.**

The controls on the page display numbers representing their tab order.

2. **Click to select the controls in sequential order to set the tab order, as shown in Figure 1-10.**

3. **Repeat Step 1 to take the form out of tab-order selection mode.**

To designate that a control shouldn't be tabbed to, set the control's `TabStop` property to False. Controls with the `TabStop` property set to False are skipped when the user presses Tab. Controls that aren't visible or enabled are also skipped when the user presses Tab.

To set a control as invisible or disabled, set the control's Visible and Enabled properties to False.

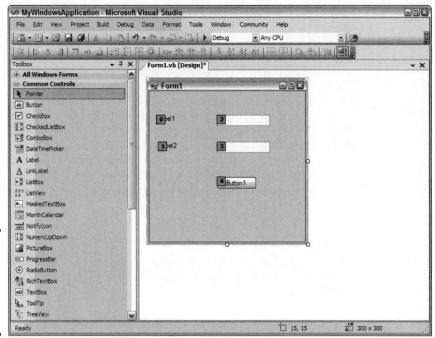

You can set a control's tab order by using the `TabIndex` property. (See the section "Using the Properties Window," later in this chapter, to see how to set a control's properties.)

Access a control's tasks with smart tags

Some of the controls you add to your form can walk you through simple task wizards by using *smart tags*. Smart-tag-enabled controls have a little arrow in the upper-right corner of the control. When you click the arrow, a list of common tasks associated with the control appears. To see a smart-tag-enabled control in action:

1. **Drag and drop a `CheckedListBox` control on the forms designer.**

2. **Click the smart-tag arrow to display a list of common tasks, as shown in Figure 1-11.**

3. **In the CheckedListBox Tasks window, click Edit Items.**

From the String Collection Editor that appears, you can add items to the `CheckedListBox` control.

The smart tags display a subset of tasks for the control. Use the control's Properties window to see all the tasks and properties available for the control.

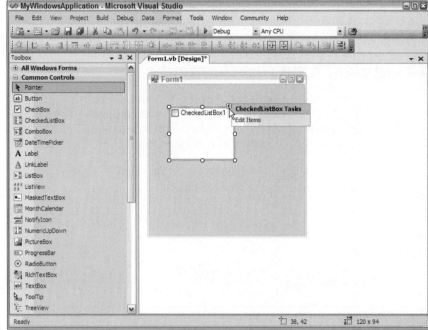

Figure 1-11:
Click the
control's
smart-tag
arrow to
display a list
of common
tasks.

Using more controls

Whenever possible, you should use the controls provided in Visual Studio.
Using them creates a consistent user experience because Windows users
are generally familiar with most Windows controls. Sometimes, however,
you might need a control that isn't available in the Visual Studio toolbox.
You have several options:

✦ **Build your own.** Because .NET is an object-oriented language, you can
extend an existing control or build your own.

✦ **Use ActiveX controls.** Windows Forms can host ActiveX controls, which
are built using the Component Object Model (COM) technology.

You add controls to the Visual Studio toolbox by choosing the Choose
Toolbox Items command from the Tools menu.

✦ **Buy the control.** Many third-party vendors sell controls. You could also
sell a control that you build.

✦ **Download the control.** Sometimes, you can find controls available for
free or as shareware on the Internet. Be sure to read the license before
you redistribute controls you find there.

> You can search for controls online by using the Community Search feature. See Book II, Chapter 3 for more information.

Using the Properties Window

Every control has a set of properties and events that define how the control acts when your application runs. For example, the button control's Text property specifies the text that's displayed on the button. The button control has a Click event that is executed each time a user clicks the button.

The Visual Studio Properties window displays a control's properties and events in a grid, as shown in Figure 1-12.

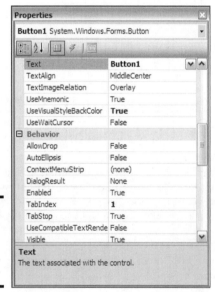

Figure 1-12: Setting a control's properties and events.

The Properties window is open by default. If you close the Properties window at some point, you have two options for opening it again:

✦ Choose View➪Properties Window.

✦ Press the F4 key.

The Properties window has the following elements:

✦ A drop-down list at the top displays the selected control. Use the list to select a control to view.

✦ A toolbar changes the view settings. Your view-setting choices are, from left to right:

- **Categorized** — Properties appear in groups.
- **Alphabetical** — Properties are sorted in alphabetical order.
- **Properties** — The control's properties are displayed.
- **Events** — The control's events are displayed.

✦ Two columns display the name-value pairs of the control's properties or events, depending on the view setting.

✦ A brief description of the selected property or event appears at the bottom of the window.

The Properties window is a visual tool that organizes and categorizes the thousands of properties and events available for manipulating controls. You use the Properties window for two tasks:

✦ Set a control's properties.

✦ Create event handlers for a control.

When you use the Properties window, Visual Studio generates the code to set the control's properties and create event handlers. You can do all this by using code, although it's much easier to use Visual Studio. To read about how to set properties and work with events in code, see Book V, Chapter 4.

You can access thousands of properties and events by using the Properties window. Visual Studio groups properties and events into categories so that they're easier to manage. The following list describes the properties and events categories:

✦ `Action` — Creates handlers for events such as `Click` and `Scroll`.

✦ `Accessibility` — Sets properties that make controls accessible to people with disabilities.

✦ `Appearance` — Contains properties related to font, color, border, and cursor style. The `Text` property and text-formatting properties are in this group.

✦ `Behavior` — Contains properties and events related to how a control acts. Examples include `Sorted`, `TabStop`, and `SelectedIndex Changed`.

✦ Data — Sets a control's data source, gets items selected in a control, and responds to changes in the data.

✦ Design — Contains design-time properties, such as whether controls are locked. The Name property is in here too.

✦ DragDrop — Responds to events related to dragging and dropping controls.

✦ Focus — Captures events related to how the control gains and loses focus.

✦ Key — Responds to keyboard-related events.

✦ Layout — Sets layout properties such as anchor, margin, and size.

✦ Mouse — Responds to mouse events, such as MouseUp.

✦ WindowStyle — Sets properties that define the Windows form itself.

Within each control are properties that you can set. Here are some common properties that many controls share:

✦ Name — Sets the identifier used to reference the control in code.

✦ Text — Sets the text displayed in the control.

To set the access key for a control, add an ampersand (&) in front of the letter to use as the access key in the text property. For example, to set the letter *P* in Print as the access key, set the text property for the control equal to &Print. A user can then press the Alt key in combination with the access key to execute the control.

Windows Forms are controls. You access the properties of a Windows Forms control the same way you access the properties for any control. Here are the common properties for Windows Forms:

✦ Text — Sets the text displayed on the form's title bar

✦ DefaultButton — Sets the button that responds to the Enter key by default

✦ CancelButton — Sets the button that responds to the Esc key by default

✦ MainMenuStrip — Sets the primary menu control for the form

In addition to the controls you use to customize your forms, you have events to consider. *Events* are actions that your application might handle or respond to. Examples of common events include

✦ Click

✦ KeyDown

✦ Load

✦ ValueChanged

You can get context-sensitive help for any property or event you see in the Properties window by positioning your cursor in the value field for the property or event and pressing the F1 key.

Setting properties

Properties are expressed as name-value pairs. A property's value isn't always as simple as color=black. Values can be complex. You can use the selectors, wizards, and ellipses on the Visual Studio Properties page to dynamically build complex property values.

Examples of complex properties include properties related to

✦ Setting data sources

✦ Editing collections of items

✦ Applying fonts and formatting

✦ Selecting images and files

To set properties for a control on a Windows form, follow these steps:

1. **Click the control in the forms designer.**

2. **Press the F4 key to display the Properties window.**

The control's name and type appear on the drop-down list at the top of the Properties window.

3. **Click the Properties button on the Properties window's toolbar to display a list of the control's properties.**

The Properties button is the third toolbar button from the left.

4. **Scroll down the properties list, and enter property values.**

You can type simple property values or select them from a drop-down list. Click the ellipsis button for more complex properties, such as collections to display a dialog box that builds the property, as shown in Figure 1-13. Click the plus (+) sign next to compound properties to set individual properties.

Book III
Chapter 1

Getting Smart About
Smart Clients

Figure 1-13:
Click the
ellipsis
button to
build
complex
properties.

Responding to events

The Visual Studio Properties window displays a control's events. For example, when a user clicks a button, the button's `Click` event occurs. You can use event handlers to write code that fires each time the event fires.

To set an event handler by using the Properties window, follow these steps:

1. **Select a form's control by clicking the control.**

2. **In the Properties window, click the Events button to display the control's events.**

To create an event handler by using a default name, either press Enter without typing a name or double-click the field for the name.

Double-click a control on the Windows Forms Designer to create the control's default event handler.

3. **Type a name for the event handler next to the event, and press Enter.**

Visual Studio creates the event handler and opens the code editor to the event handler.

See Book V, Chapter 4 for more details about responding to events.

Chapter 2: Building Smart Client User Interfaces

In This Chapter

✔ **Customizing Windows interfaces**

✔ **Using dialog boxes**

✔ **Adding menus and toolbars**

✔ **Inheriting from a base Windows Form**

✔ **Laying out controls in a Windows Form**

*U*sing Visual Studio to build Windows applications gives you a head start in your race against project deadlines. In this chapter, I show you tools and techniques to transform Visual Studio's out-of-the-box Windows projects into Windows applications that could make Bill Gates proud.

As I write this book, Windows applications are known as *smart clients*. Expect to see additional names crop up in reference to applications that target the new Aero interface in Windows Vista, the next version of the Windows operating system. Good old-fashioned smart clients will still work in Vista. See Book VII, Chapter 3 for more information about Aero and Vista.

Building the Windows Container

As the container that holds your controls, the Windows Form is one of the most important elements in building Windows applications. The Windows Form is your application's foundation, and it's highly customizable.

In this section, I explore some properties and controls you can use to modify the way your Windows Forms look and behave.

Setting common form properties

I'm sure that you can spot a typical Windows form from ten paces:

✦ It has the familiar little red close button in its upper-right corner.

✦ If it's like most windows, it has menus and toolbars.

✦ It's displayed on the taskbar along the bottom of the screen.

All these features of a typical window are determined by properties. Simply turning a property on or off can give a Windows form a complete makeover. The default Windows Form that Visual Studio creates in all new Windows projects has most of these typical properties. Some properties, such as menus, you have to set on your own.

Table 2-1 describes some common Windows Forms properties, sorted by property group:

Table 2-1	Common Windows Forms Properties
Property	*What It Does*
FormBorderStyle	Determines whether the window is resizable
Text	Sets the caption that appears on the form's title bar
ContextMenuStrip	Sets the shortcut menu that's displayed when a user right-clicks the form
Name	Sets the identifier used to access the form in code
StartPosition	Determines where the form appears when it's first opened
AcceptButton	Sets the default Enter button
CancelButton	Sets the default Esc button
ControlBox	Toggles the form's minimize, maximize, and close controls on and off
IsMdiContainer	Determines whether the form is a parent container in a Multiple Document Interface (MDI) application
Icon	Sets the icon displayed on the title bar and the taskbar when the form is minimized
ShowInTaskBar	Shows the form on the Windows taskbar
MainMenuStrip	Sets the form's menu control

You set these properties by using the Properties window. For more information on how to set a control's properties, see Chapter 1 in this mini-book.

Creating dialog boxes

A dialog box is a Windows Form with attitude. The dialog box pops up on top of forms that are already open and refuses to leave until the user responds. Many Windows applications use dialog boxes to get a user's attention.

Most dialog boxes are *modal,* which means that they must be closed or hidden before users can continue working with other windows. *Modeless* forms can remain open alongside other windows. Modeless dialog boxes are harder to manage because you have to keep track of the different windows a user works with. Visual Studio provides a modal dialog form that you can add to your application.

To add a modal dialog box to an existing Windows project, follow these steps:

1. **Press Ctrl+Shift+A to open the Add New Item window.**

2. **Select the Dialog template.**

3. **Enter a name for the dialog box, such as** MyDialog.

4. **Click the Add button.**

Visual Studio adds the dialog box to your project.

The dialog box is just a regular Windows Form with the modified properties shown in the following table:

Property	*Sets To*
AcceptButton	The form's OK button
CancelButton	The form's Cancel button
FormBorderStyle	FixedDialog
MinimizeBox	False
MaximizeBox	False
ShowInTaskbar	False
StartPosition	CenterParent

The dialog box also has an OK button and a Cancel button. The Cancel button's DialogResult property is set to Cancel. The DialogResult property returns the selected value to the parent form of the dialog box when the button is clicked.

To use the dialog box, follow these steps:

1. **Add a label and a text box to the dialog box you create in the preceding set of steps.**

2. **Set the OK button's DialogResult property to OK.**

When the user clicks the OK button in the dialog box, the value set in the DialogResult property is sent to the parent form.

3. **Add a label, text box, and button to the project's parent form. If no other forms exist in the project, press Ctrl+Shift+A to open the Add New Items window and add a Windows form.**

4. **Double-click the button to access the button's** `Click` **event.**

The code editor appears.

5. **In the button's** `Click` **event, type this code:**

```
Dim frmDialog As New MyDialog
frmDialog.ShowDialog()

If frmDialog.DialogResult = Windows.Forms.DialogResult.OK Then
    Me.TextBox1.Text = frmDialog.TextBox1.Text
End If
```

The first two lines of code open the dialog box you create in the pre-ceding set of steps. The remaining four lines test the `DialogResult` property of the dialog box and set the `Text` property on the text box of the parent form.

6. **Press Ctrl+F5 to run the application.**

To test the application, follow these steps:

1. **On the parent form, click the button that launches the dialog box.**

The dialog box appears.

2. **In the dialog box, type** hello **in the text box and click OK.**

The dialog box closes.

3. **The word** *hello* **appears in the text box in the parent form.**

Figure 2-1 shows you the parent form with the dialog box open.

Figure 2-1:
Text typed in the dialog box appears in the parent form.

Visual Studio has a number of preconfigured dialog box components that you can use in your applications. You work with the dialog box components in the Visual Studio toolbox by using code (unlike working with the dialog box you create in this section). The preconfigured dialog boxes create a con-sistent way for you to provide access to common features, such as printing and opening files. Table 2-2 lists the preconfigured dialog boxes.

Table 2-2		Preconfigured Dialog Boxes
Toolbox Tab	*Dialog Box*	*What It Does*
Dialogs	ColorDialog	Displays a color palette and controls for selecting a color
	FolderBrowserDialog	Prompts the user to select a folder
	FontDialog	Prompts the user to select a font
	OpenFileDialog	Prompts the user to open a file
	SaveFileDialog	Prompts the user to save a file
Printing	PrintDialog	Prompts user to select a printer and configure settings
	PageSetupDialog	Prompts user to change page-related settings
	PrintPreviewDialog	Previews the document to be printed

Use the preconfigured dialog boxes rather than create your own. The steps for using a preconfigured dialog box vary slightly because each dialog box has its own set of properties you must set.

To use the `ColorDialog` dialog box, follow these steps:

1. **Create a new Windows Form.**

2. **Drag and drop a text box and button onto the form.**

3. **Drag and drop a `ColorDialog` control from the Dialogs tab of the toolbox.**

   The `ColorDialog` appears at the bottom of the Windows Forms Designer rather than appear on the Windows Form.

4. **Set the `ColorDialog` control's `Name` property to MyColorDialog.**

5. **Double-click the button on the Windows Form.**

   The code editor appears.

6. **Type the following code in the code editor:**

```
If (MyColorDialog.ShowDialog() =
    Windows.Forms.DialogResult.OK) Then
  TextBox1.BackColor = MyColorDialog.Color
End If
```

Use the `ShowDialog()` method to display preconfigured dialog boxes.

7. **Press Ctrl+F5 to run the application.**

8. **Click the button on the form to launch the `ColorDialog` control.**

   The `ColorDialog` appears, as shown in Figure 2-2.

9. **Select a color and click OK.**

   The background color of the text box changes.

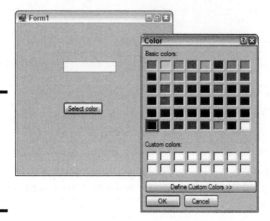

Figure 2-2:
The Color-
Dialog
control is
a precon-
figured
dialog box.

Adding menus and toolbars

Most Windows applications have menus and toolbars that give users access to commands. Visual Studio provides these two menu controls and three toolbar controls:

✦ ContextMenuStrip: The shortcut menu that appears when a user right-clicks

✦ MenuStrip: A standard menu that usually appears at the top of a form

✦ StatusStrip: A band that usually appears along the bottom of a form that displays status feedback information

✦ ToolStrip: A control that creates toolbars

✦ ToolStripContainer: A container for hosting menu and toolbar controls

The ToolStrip control, the granddaddy of all the menu and toolbars controls, has these features:

✦ Items that you can add to the menu and toolbar controls, such as ToolStripMenuItem

✦ Container controls that allow menus and toolbars to coexist in the same container

✦ Properties that allow you to set the look and feel of menus and toolbars

Because all menu and toolbar controls are related, they share the ToolStrip control's features. The procedure for adding items, working with containers, and setting properties is consistent across all menu and toolbar controls.

To add a menu to a form and configure the menu, follow these steps:

1. **Drag a MenuStrip control to a form and drop it.**

The menu docks itself to the top of the form.

2. Click the arrow in the upper-right corner of the `MenuStrip` control to display a list of tasks.

3. In the MenuStrip Tasks dialog box, click Insert Standard Items.

The `MenuStrip` control adds menu items for File, Edit, Tools, and Help, as shown in Figure 2-3.

4. Repeat Steps 1 through 3 to add a `ToolStrip` control to the form and insert standard items on the toolbar.

All the menu and toolbar controls are smart-tag-enabled. A smart-tag-enabled control has a little arrow in its upper-right corner. Click this arrow to access a task dialog box that displays common tasks for each control. The `MenuStrip` and `ToolStrip` controls display the same task dialog box. (Figure 2-3 shows the MenuStrip Tasks dialog box.) The available `MenuStrip` and `ToolStrip` tasks are shown in this list:

✦ **Embed in ToolStripContainer:** Moves the control inside a `ToolStripContainer` control

✦ **Insert Standard Items:** Adds standard command items to the control

✦ **RenderMode:** Sets a specific style for the control

✦ **Dock:** Sets the control's location to the top or bottom or the left or right side of the form

✦ **GripStyle:** Makes the control's move handle hidden or visible

✦ **Edit Items:** Opens the Items Collection Editor, which you use to edit the control's items

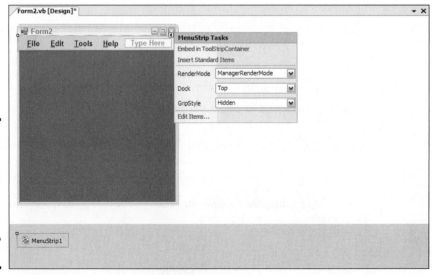

Figure 2-3:
Click Insert Standard Items to add standard menu items to the `MenuStrip` control.

Menus and toolbars display commands that users can execute. Each command is an item on the menu or toolbar control. A control's entire set of commands is the control's *items collection*. You can edit a control's items collection by using the Windows Forms Designer or the Items Collection Editor.

To edit items by using the Windows Forms Designer, follow these steps:

1. Drag and drop a StatusStrip control on the form.

The control docks itself to the bottom of the form by default.

2. Click the drop-down arrow in the control.

A list of available StatusStrip items appears, as shown in Figure 2-4.

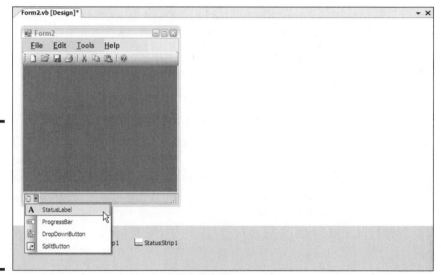

3. Select a StatusLabel control from the list.

The StatusLabel control is added to the StatusStrip control.

4. Repeat Step 3 to add a progress bar.

To add items to a MenuStrip control by using the Windows Forms Designer, follow these steps:

1. Click the MenuStrip control in the form.

A command placeholder named MenuItem appears, as shown in Figure 2-5.

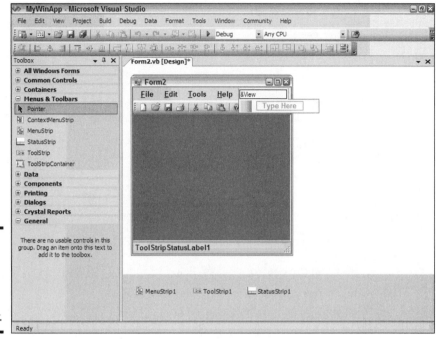

Figure 2-5:
Type a
command
in the
`MenuItem`
placeholder.

To insert a command between existing commands, right-click a command and choose Insert from the shortcut menu. Choose an item to insert from the list of available items.

2. **Type a command name, such as** View, **and press Enter.**

The placeholder expands for you to add more commands.

Table 2-3 lists the items you can add to the menu and toolbar controls.

Table 2-3	Items You Can Add to The `ToolStrip` Controls
Control Name	*Item You Can Add*
`MenuStrip`	`MenuItem`
	`ComboBox`
	`Separator`
	`TextBox`
`ToolStrip`	`Button`
	`Label`
	`SplitButton`

(continued)

Table 2-3 *(continued)*

Control Name	Item You Can Add
ToolStrip	DropDownButton
	Separator
	ComboBox
	TextBox
	ProgressBar
StatusStrip	StatusLabel
	ProgressBar
	DropDownButton
	SplitButton

You can start a control's Items Collection Editor in one of three ways:

✦ From the control's Tasks dialog box

✦ By using the control's Properties window

✦ From the control's shortcut menu

To use the Items Collection Editor from the control's shortcut menu:

1. **Right-click the form's StatusStrip control.**

The control's shortcut menu appears.

2. **Choose Edit Items.**

The Items Collection Editor appears.

3. **Click the drop-down list at the top of the editor to display a list of available items for the control.**

4. **Select DropDownButton from the list.**

5. **Click the Add button.**

A DropDownButton control is added to the members list, as shown in Figure 2-6.

6. **Click the up arrow to move the DropDownButton control to the top of the list.**

7. **Select the progress bar control from the Members list.**

The progress bar control is named ToolStripProgressBar1.

8. **Click the button with the X on it to delete the progress bar.**

9. **Click OK.**

The Items Collection Editor closes.

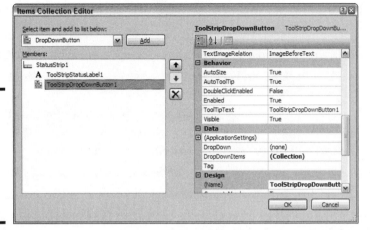

Figure 2-6:
Click the
Add button
to add an
item to the
control's
items
collection.

The properties of individual items on menu and toolbar controls are easier
to manage if you use the Items Collection Editor rather than the Properties
window.

Using a ToolStripContainer

The `ToolStripContainer` control makes it easy to host multiple menu and
toolbar controls on a single form. The `ToolStripContainer` control has
panels, as shown in Figure 2-7, where you place your menu and toolbar controls. The advantage of using `ToolStripContainer` is that your controls
automatically stack horizontally and vertically in the panel.

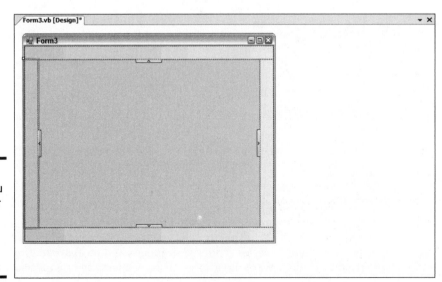

Figure 2-7:
Place menu
and toolbar
controls
in this
control's
panels.

To use a `ToolStripContainer` control in a Windows Form, follow these steps:

1. **Drag and drop a `ToolStripContainer` control on a Windows Form.**

2. **Click Dock Fill in Form in the `ToolStripContainer` control's Tasks dialog box.**

The control expands to fill the form. The control's top panel is visible by default.

3. **Drag and drop a `MenuStrip` control on the top panel.**

4. **Click the arrow tab on the ToolStripContainer control's top pane.**

The pane expands to accommodate another menu or toolbar.

5. **Drag and drop a `ToolStrip` control on the top panel, positioned below the `MenuStrip` control.**

6. **Click the tab on the bottom panel to make the panel visible.**

7. **Add a `StatusStrip` control to the bottom panel.**

Users can use the `ToolStripContainer` control to customize their work environments by moving toolbars and menus around within the panels of the `ToolStripContainer` control. Figure 2-8 shows you an example of a toolbar being moved.

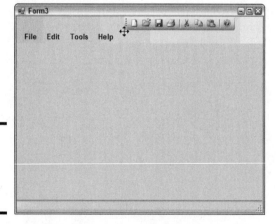

Figure 2-8:
Using a
control
to move
toolboxes.

Controlling styles

You can style the menu and toolbar controls by using the `RenderMode` property. You can use it to specify how you want the menu or toolbar rendered. The .NET built-in styles render your menus and toolbars to look like Office or Windows. You can set the `RenderMode` property to one of these four values:

✦ `Custom`: Sets the style to a custom renderer

✦ `ManagerRenderMode`: Uses the renderer specified in the `ToolStripManager`

✦ `Professional`: Uses a style that looks like Office 2003 and Windows XP

✦ `System`: Uses a flat Windows style

Figure 2-9 shows the same form with two different rendered styles. The form on the left uses system styling, and the form on the right uses professional styling. The professionally styled menus and toolbars are rounded and more elegant. You can set these styles by using the Tasks dialog box for each of the controls.

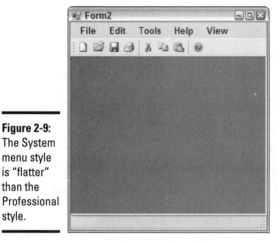
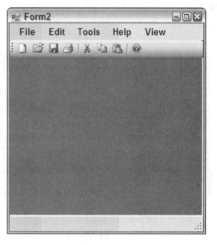

Figure 2-9:
The System menu style is "flatter" than the Professional style.

You use `ToolStripManager` to set a single style for all `ToolStrip` controls. For example, to set all the menus and toolbars to Professional, follow these steps:

1. **Set the `RenderMode` property for each menu and toolbar control to ManagerRenderMode.**

2. **Set the `RenderMode` property on `ToolStripManager` in the form's Load event by using this code:**

```
ToolStripManager.RenderMode =
    ToolStripManagerRenderMode.Professional
```

You access `ToolStripManager` in code. It's not a control that you can access from the toolbox, as on other menus and toolbars.

Creating a Multiple Document Interface

You might have used a Windows application where all the application windows are contained within a parent window. An application in which all child windows are contained within a parent window is a *Multiple Document Interface (MDI)*.

Creating an MDI application involves these high-level steps:

1. Create the parent container form.

2. Create child forms.

3. Write code that opens the child forms in the container.

To create the parent MDI form, follow these steps:

1. **Create a new Windows application in Visual Basic.**

Visual Studio creates a new Windows project with an empty Windows Form named Form1.

See Chapter 1 in this mini-book for more information about creating Windows applications.

2. **Set the Form1 `IsMdiContainer` property to True.**

3. **Add a `MenuStrip` control to the form.**

4. **Add the menu items Select and Window.**

5. **Add the menu items Open Form 2 and Open Form to the Select menu.**

Now that you have the parent form, create these child forms to open in the parent MDI form:

1. **Add a new form named Form2.**

2. **Add a label and a text box to the form.**

3. **Add a new form named Form3.**

4. **Add a `MonthCalendar` control to the form.**

In the parent MDI container Form1, follow these steps:

1. **Double-click the form to access the form's `Load` event.**

2. **In the `Load` event, type this line:**

```
Me.MenuStrip1.MdiWindowListItem = Me.WindowsToolStripMenuItem
```

This line sets the Windows menu item as the `MdiWindowListItem` control for the menu strip. As child windows are opened, the Windows menu displays the windows along with a check mark next to the active window.

3. **Below the `Load` event, type these lines:**

```
Private Sub GetChild(ByRef frmChild As Form)
    frmChild.MdiParent = Me
    frmChild.Show()
End Sub
```

This code sample creates a procedure named `GetChild` that accepts a child form as a parameter. When the child form is passed to `GetChild`, the procedure sets the child form's MDI parent container as the displayed form and displays the child form in the container.

4. In the Windows Forms Designer, double-click the Open Form 2 menu item.

The `Click` event is created.

5. Type this line in the `Click` event:

```
GetChild(New Form2)
```

This line passes `Form2` to the `GetChild` procedure.

6. Repeat Steps 4 and 5 for the Form 3 menu item, and substitute `Form3` for `Form2` in the code.

The entire code sample for Form1 is shown in this listing:

```
Public Class Form1

    Private Sub Window1ToolStripMenuItem_Click(ByVal sender
    As System.Object, ByVal e As System.EventArgs) Handles
    Window1ToolStripMenuItem.Click
        GetChild(New Form2)
    End Sub

    Private Sub Form1_Load(ByVal sender As System.Object,
    ByVal e As System.EventArgs) Handles MyBase.Load
        Me.MenuStrip1.MdiWindowListItem =
    Me.WindowsToolStripMenuItem
    End Sub

    Private Sub Window2ToolStripMenuItem_Click(ByVal sender
    As System.Object, ByVal e As System.EventArgs) Handles
    Window2ToolStripMenuItem.Click
        GetChild(New Form3)
    End Sub

    Private Sub GetChild(ByRef frmChild As Form)
        frmChild.MdiParent = Me
        frmChild.Show()
    End Sub
End Class
```

To test the MDI application, follow these steps:

1. **Press Ctrl+F5 to run the application.**

2. **Click the Select menu item.**

3. **Choose Open Form 2 from the Select menu.**

   Form2 opens and is contained within the parent form.

4. **Repeat Steps 1 and 2 to open Form3.**

5. **Click the Windows menu.**

   The Windows menu displays the open windows. A check mark appears next to the active window, as shown in Figure 2-10.

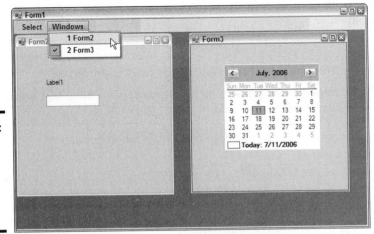

Figure 2-10:
Use the Windows menu to manage child windows.

Taking advantage of visual inheritance

Sometimes, you want to reuse forms. You can inherit from an existing form rather than create forms from scratch. You need two forms: the base form and one to inherit from the base form.

To create the base form, follow these steps:

1. **Press Ctrl+Shift+A to open the Add New Item window. Add a new Windows Form to the project.**

2. **Add a label and a text box to the form.**

3. **Choose Build⇨Build Solution.**

   You must build the base form in order to inherit from it.

To inherit from the base form, follow these steps:

1. **Choose Project⇨Add New Item.**

   The Add New Item window appears.

2. **Click the Inherited Form template.**

3. **Enter a name for the form.**

4. **Click the Add button.**

   The Inheritance Picker appears.

5. **Click the base form in the Inheritance Picker, as shown in Figure 2-11.**

6. **Click OK.**

   The inherited form displays the base form's controls.

You must build your solution whenever you make changes to the base form in order to make changes appear in the inherited form.

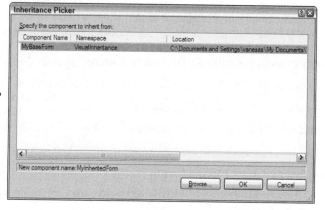

Figure 2-11:
Use the Inheritance Picker to inherit from a base form.

Book III
Chapter 2

**Building Smart
Client User
Interfaces**

Laying Out Your Controls

As user interface design becomes more sophisticated, users expect to have more control over the user experience. This means being able, at minimum, to resize windows. Resizing can wreak havoc on the controls that you spend lots of time nudging into their proper positions. Windows Forms provide several options for managing controls for resizing, including containers for grouping controls and properties for locking controls in place.

Grouping controls

The Visual Studio toolbox has a group of container controls. Use container controls whenever you need to

✦ Easily manipulate groups of controls in the Windows Forms Designer

✦ Create visible groupings of controls

✦ Make it easier to resize a form

The container controls are shown in this list:

✦ `FlowLayoutPanel`: Arranges controls in a horizontal or vertical flow

✦ `GroupBox`: Creates a visible grouping of controls with a caption

✦ `Panel`: Creates a scrollable grouping of controls

✦ `SplitContainer`: Arranges controls on two separate panels separated by a movable bar

✦ `TabControl`: Arranges controls on multiple tabs or pages, similar to a file folder

✦ `TableLayoutPanel`: Arranges controls in a tabular grid

You can position container controls inside other controls. The `FlowLayoutPanel` and `TableLayoutPanel` controls can dynamically reposition the child controls placed inside them when the Windows form is resized. To see `FlowLayoutPanel` in action, follow these steps:

1. **Add a `FlowLayoutPanel` control to a form.**

2. **Click the arrow in the upper-right corner of the control.**

The control's task dialog box appears.

3. **Click Dock in the parent container.**

The `FlowLayoutPanel` control expands to fill the form.

4. **Add two text boxes to the form.**

5. **Grab the second text box with your mouse and try to move the box below the first one.**

The text box "jumps" back because the controls placed in a `FlowLayoutPanel` flow either horizontally or vertically.

6. **Add a `GroupBox` control to the form.**

7. **Place a label and a text box inside the `GroupBox` control.**

As you add the controls, notice that snaplines appear inside the `GroupBox` control.

Although all the controls placed inside the `GroupBox` can be positioned exactly where you want them, `GroupBox` flows with the rest of the controls in the `FlowLayoutPanel` control.

8. **Add a `MonthCalendar` control to the form.**

9. **Press Ctrl+F5 to run the form.**

10. **Resize the form and notice that the controls move.**

Figure 2-12 shows the form in its default size and again resized. Notice that the controls are stacked in the form on the left because the form is narrow. As the form is resized, the controls move to fill the form.

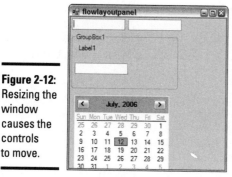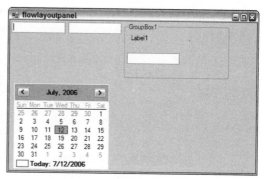

Figure 2-12:
Resizing the
window
causes the
controls
to move.

You have some options for controlling the flow in a `FlowLayoutPanel` control:

✦ To force a control to move to the next line, set the control's `FlowBreak` property to True.

✦ To change the direction of the `FlowLayoutPanel` control, set the `FlowDirection` property.

✦ To set `FlowLayoutPanel` so that child controls are clipped rather than wrapped to the next line, set the `WrapContents` property to False. Figure 2-13 shows a form that has `FlowLayoutPanel` with a clipped `MonthCalendar` control.

**Book III
Chapter 2**

**Building Smart
Client User
Interfaces**

Figure 2-13:
Setting a
property to
False to clip
controls
rather than
wrap them.

Setting layout properties

You might want to position controls in a way that they stay in place in the face of resizing. You can set many properties for controlling a control's layout:

✦ `Anchor`: Specifies an anchor position that the control maintains when the form is resized

✦ `Dock`: Positions the control so that one edge of the control is always touching the parent control's edge

✦ `AutoSize`: Allows a control to grow or shrink automatically

✦ `Margin`: Sets spacing outside a control's borders

✦ `Padding`: Adds spacing between a control's borders and its interior contents

The best way to picture these properties in action is to see them at work. The following sections walk you through using these properties.

Anchoring and docking

Anchoring and docking are two properties you can use to position a control when a form is resized. When you set a control's `Anchor` and `Dock` properties, you specify the edges of a form — top, bottom, left, right — to which you want to position your control. The `Dock` property accepts a `Fill` value, which forces the control to expand to touch all four sides of a form.

The primary difference between `Anchor` and `Dock` is that anchoring allows you to maintain a set distance between the edge of the control and the edge of the form. With docking, the control always maintains constant contact with the form's edge. There's no space between the control and the edge. Figure 2-14 shows a button that's anchored to the lower-left corner of the form and a status strip that's docked to the bottom.

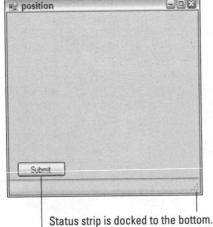

Figure 2-14:
`Anchor`
and `Dock`
properties
let you
position a
control.

Status strip is docked to the bottom.

Button is anchored to the bottom left.

Menus, toolbars, and status strips are always docked by default.

To anchor a Submit button to the lower-left corner of a form, follow these steps:

1. **Add a button to a form.**

For more information on adding a button to a form, see the section in Chapter 1 of this mini-book about adding controls to your form.

2. **Click the button and press F4 to open the Properties window.**

3. **Scroll to the** `Anchor` **property.**

The `Anchor` property is in the Layout category.

4. **Click the arrow on the drop-down list for the** `Anchor` **property.**

A visual positioning tool appears.

5. **Click the left and bottom bars to set the anchor.**

6. **Click the top bar to clear the anchor.**

Figure 2-15 shows you an example.

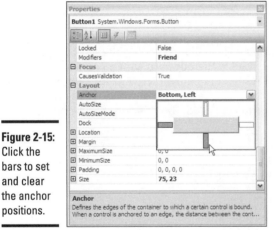

Figure 2-15:
Click the bars to set and clear the anchor positions.

Book III
Chapter 2

Building Smart
Client User
Interfaces

7. **Press Enter to set the property.**

8. **Press Ctrl+F5 to run the form.**

9. **Resize the form from the bottom, top, left, and right.**

Notice that the button maintains its distance from the bottom and the left.

You can use the `Anchor` property to expand a control as the form expands. To set a text box to grow as the sides of a form expand, follow these steps:

1. **Add a text box to the center of the form.**

2. **Set the text box's** `Anchor` **property to** `Left, Right`**.**

3. **Press Ctrl+F5 to run the form.**

4. **Resize the form to the left and the right.**

Figure 2-16 shows the form in its default size and resized. Notice how the text isn't completely displayed in the text box. After the form is resized, the text box expands and maintains equal distance from the left and right sides.

Figure 2-16:
The text box expands as its anchor sides expand.

Setting a control's Dock property is similar to setting the Anchor property. With the Dock property, you specify the edges to which you want to dock the control. The control always maintains contact with the edge you specify. Figure 2-17 shows a form with a StatusStrip control docked on the bottom of the form. As the form is resized, the StatusStrip control remains at the bottom.

Figure 2-17:
The control remains docked to the form's bottom edge as the form is resized.

Using automatic sizing

Two properties are related to setting automatic sizing:

✦ `AutoSize`: Specifies, by using a True/False value, whether the control should be automatically sized

✦ `AutoSizeMode`: Sets a control to `GrowAndShrink` or `GrowOnly`

The `AutoSizeMode` property works only if `AutoSize` is set to True. Although not all controls have an `AutoSizeMode` property, it provides more control than `AutoSize` when it's available. The size of a control grows rightward and downward.

To set the automatic sizing properties for a button, follow these steps:

1. **Add a button to a form.**

2. **Use the Properties window to set the button's Text property to** Please click this button.

Notice that the button displays only part of the text.

3. **Set the button's AutoSize property to True.**

The button expands to display the text, as shown in Figure 2-18.

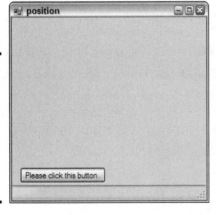

Figure 2-18:
The button expands to display the text when the `AutoSize` property is set to True.

Book III
Chapter 2

Building Smart Client User Interfaces

The `AutoSize` and `AutoSizeMode` properties honor the `MinimumSize` and `MaximumSize` property settings.

Setting margins and padding

Margins and padding set the space outside and within a control's borders, respectively. Because a control's border has four sides, the margins and padding properties comprise a set of properties. When you set the margins and padding properties, you can specify values for top, left, right, bottom, or all.

To set a control's margins and padding, follow these steps:

1. **Add a button to a form.**

For more information about adding a button to a form, see the section in Chapter 1 of this mini-book about adding controls to your form.

2. **Click the new button and press F4 to open the Properties window.**

3. **Scroll to the Margin property.**

4. **Click the plus (+) sign next to the Margin property to expand the property.**

5. **In the All property, type** 20.

All the button's margins are now set to 20.

6. **Drag another button to the form.**

As you approach the first button, notice that the snaplines are farther apart than usual because the first button's margin is higher.

The space between the two buttons when the snaplines are present is 23. The snapline's distance between controls is a sum of the two control's margins. The default margin for a button control is 3.

7. **Allow the second button to snap to the first button and drop the second button.**

8. **Change the padding property on the second button to** All = 10.

9. **Resize the second button so that you can see the button's text.**

Notice the padding that appears around the text now. Figure 2-19 shows you an example.

Figure 2-19:
The second button's text is padded in all directions.

Chapter 3: Building Visual C++ Applications

In This Chapter

✔ **Taking a fresh look at C++**

✔ **Peeking at the Visual C++ application wizards**

✔ **Creating managed and unmanaged applications**

*V*isual C++ is older than dirt. C++, the core language on which Visual C++ is based, is even older! Just because Visual C++ is, shall we say, *mature* doesn't mean that it can't hold its own against more modern programming languages. In this chapter, I give you the scoop on Visual C++ and show you how to create Visual C++ applications by using Visual Studio.

Getting to Know Visual C++

Visual C++ is one language in the suite of .NET languages. Unlike in the other .NET languages, the core syntax libraries in Visual C++ and its primary helper libraries aren't part of the .NET Framework. As a result, applications written in Visual C++ don't require the .NET Framework.

Creating a full-blown Windows application using just C++ syntax is quite challenging. If you're guessing that that's where Visual C++ comes in, you're right. Visual C++ is different from plain old C++ because it provides additional libraries, tools, and widgets that you can use to build sophisticated applications for Windows and the Web.

Visual C++ includes these elements:

✦ Standard libraries for building C++ applications: The C++ object-oriented language was created to extend the popular C language. The downside of using a low-level language like C++ is that you have to write more code to get something done than you do when you're using a higher-level language, such as Visual Basic or C#.

The result is that C++ programs are smaller and faster than higher-level languages because they can

- Run without the .NET common language runtime

- Interact directly with the operating system

- Manage their own memory and resources

C++ compilers exist for almost every operating system. If you write your application using only C++ syntax, you can compile your program to run in Unix even if you wrote it on a Windows computer.

✦ **Microsoft Foundation Classes (MFC), a library for building Windows applications:** The MFC library of classes wraps around the Windows application programming interface (API). The MFC library was written in C++ to provide object-oriented access to the features and commands of the Windows API. Before MFC was created, developers used the procedural language C to access the Windows API.

✦ **The Active Template Library (ATL) for building small, lightweight components:** The ATL library of C++ classes is designed for building components like ActiveX controls. Components built with ATL are usually consumed by another application. ATL Server is an extension of ATL for building powerful, high-performance Web applications and Web services.

ATL creates components known as COM objects. The *COM (Component Object Model) standard* defines the way components talk to each other. Components created with ATL conform to the COM standard and can use the COM services provided by Windows to communicate.

✦ **Support for accessing the services of the .NET Framework:** Wait a minute! Earlier in this section, I say that C++ applications don't require .NET. That's right: Although they don't require .NET, they *can* access the services of .NET when they want. As a result, code written in Visual C++ is either

- **Managed:** A Visual C++ program that uses the services of the .NET Framework. Any code that's executed in the .NET Common Language Runtime (CLR) is *managed.* Programs written in Visual Basic and C# are always managed because they can't be executed without the services of .NET, such as the CLR. You can read more about CLR and .NET in Book I, Chapter 2.

- **Unmanaged:** An application that doesn't require .NET. You create unmanaged Visual C++ applications by using the MFC library, the ATL library, or any of the standard C++ libraries.

The ability of managed and unmanaged code to coexist peacefully in Visual C++ is referred to as *interoperability,* or Interop. To read more about Interop, search the Visual Studio help index for *Interop.*

You can use Visual C++ to create all kinds of applications and components:

✦ Console applications

✦ Controls

✦ Dynamic link libraries

✦ Web services

✦ Windows applications

✦ Windows services

Because Visual C++ is a low-level language, you have to write more lines of code to do even simple tasks. Lots of code is involved in wiring up all the Visual C++ libraries in just the right way so that you can start building software. Thankfully, Visual Studio provides many templates and application wizards for building Visual C++ applications.

Visual Studio provides project templates for managed C++ applications. Because unmanaged applications require more code, Visual Studio uses application wizards to walk you through the process of setting up your application. Table 3-1 lists the project templates for managed applications, and Table 3-2 lists the Visual C++ application wizards.

Table 3-1	Visual Studio Project Templates for Creating Managed Visual C++ Applications
Project Template	*What It Does*
ASP.NET Web Service	Creates XML Web services by using ASP.NET
Class Library	Creates reusable class libraries and components that you can use in other projects
CLR Console Application	Creates a command-line application without a graphical user interface
CLR Empty Project	Creates an empty project to which you must add files manually
SQL Server Project	Creates a data access class library that you can deploy to SQL Server
Windows Forms Application	Creates a Windows application
Windows Forms Control Library	Creates custom controls for use in Windows Forms
Windows Service	Creates an application that runs as a Windows service

Table 3-2	Visual Studio Application Wizards for Creating Unmanaged Visual C++ Applications	
Project Template	*Application Wizard*	*What the Application Creates*
ATL Project	ATL Project Wizard	Dynamic link libraries (DLLs), applications, and services for creating components using ATL libraries
ATL Server Project	ATL Server Project Wizard	A Web application and ISAPI extension DLLs for responding to HTTP requests
ATL Server Web Service	ATL Server Project Wizard	An ATL server application configured to run as a Web service
ATL Smart Device Project	ATL Smart Device Project Wizard	A DLL or an application created by using ATL and designed to run on a smart device
Custom Wizard	Custom Application Wizard	A custom wizard
Makefile Project	Makefile Application Wizard	A project that sets build settings for a project built by using the command line
MFC ActiveX Control	MFC ActiveX Control Wizard	An ActiveX control using the MFC library
MFC Application	MFC Application Wizard	A Windows application using the MFC library
MFC DLL	MFC DLL Wizard	A DLL using the MFC library
Win32 Console Application	Win32 Application Wizard	A command-line application with or without MFC and ATL libraries
Win32 Project	Win32 Application Wizard	A Windows or console application, DLL, or class library with or without MFC and ATL libraries

The ATL, MFC, and Win32 application wizards include support for smart devices.

Visual C++ projects are organized into three folders:

+ **Header Files:** Holds source files that reference entities in the C++ libraries.

+ **Resource Files:** Holds resources such as bitmap files and cursors and the files that manage an application's resources.

+ **Source Files:** Holds source code files, including the main C++ source files that have the extension .cpp.

The Visual Studio project templates and application wizards generate the header, source, and resource files for the kind of application you create. For more information, search for *file types* in the Visual Studio help index.

Saying Hello, Visual C++

The Visual Studio project templates and application wizards make it easy to build managed and unmanaged Visual C++ applications. The steps for creating managed Visual C++ applications with project templates are virtually the same for building C# or Visual Basic applications. Whether you're using a project template or an application wizard, creating a Visual C++ project is similar to creating any other project in Visual Studio:

1. **Choose File➪New➪Project.**

The New Project dialog box appears.

2. **In the Project Types tree, click the plus (+) sign next to Visual C++ to expand the list of available project types.**

A list of available project types appears, as shown in Figure 3-1.

Figure 3-1 shows the New Project window using the C++ development environment settings. You don't have to use the C++ development environment settings to create C++ projects. See Book II, Chapter 1 for more information on changing your development environment settings.

**Book III
Chapter 3**

Building Visual C++
Applications

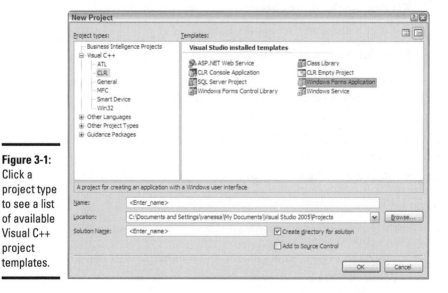

Figure 3-1:
Click a project type to see a list of available Visual C++ project templates.

3. Click the project type you want to create.

A list of available project templates for that project type appears in the Templates area of the screen.

4. Click a project template.

5. Enter a name for your project in the Name text box.

6. Click OK to create your project.

For unmanaged applications, Visual Studio starts the appropriate wizard. For managed applications, Visual Studio creates the project and adds header, resource, and source files.

Creating managed applications

Creating a managed Windows Forms application in Visual Studio is the same as creating a Windows Forms application in any other .NET language. To create a new managed Windows application by using the Visual C++ language, follow these steps:

1. Open the New Project window, as described in the preceding section.

2. In the Project Types tree, click the plus (+) sign next to Visual C++.

3. Click the CLR project type.

A list of project templates available for creating a CLR (Common Language Runtime) application appears.

4. Click the Windows Forms Application template.

5. Enter a name for the application.

6. Click OK to create the project.

Visual Studio creates the project and opens a blank Windows form in the Windows Forms Designer. The project created by Visual Studio includes these elements:

✦ **References:** Give your project access to the services of the .NET Framework.

✦ **Source files:** Jump-start your project.

✦ **Header files and resource files:** Support the project's source files.

To say "Hello world" in a managed Visual C++ application, follow these steps:

1. Drag and drop a label control and a button control on the Windows form.

2. Double-click the button control to access the control's `Click` event.

The code editor opens.

3. Type this code in the code editor:

```
this->label1->Text = "Hello world";
```

4. Press Ctrl+F5 to run your form.

When you click the button on the form, the text `Hello world` appears in the label.

Working with managed Windows Forms in the Windows Forms Designer is the same regardless of the underlying programming language. Refer to Chapters 1 and 2 in this mini-book for more information on using the Windows Forms Designer.

Creating unmanaged applications

The Visual Studio application wizards help you step through the creation of unmanaged Visual C++ applications. After you complete an application wizard, use Visual Studio resource editors and code wizards to complete your project.

Using a wizard to create an unmanaged application

Visual Studio has several wizards for creating Visual C++ projects. Use the Visual Studio application wizard to

✦ Generate source code to create the program's basic structure

✦ Include resources such as menus and toolbars

✦ Wire all the libraries to make the project work

To create a new Windows Forms application by using MFC, follow these steps:

1. Open the New Project window, as described at the beginning of this section.

2. Expand the list of Visual C++ project types and click MFC.

A list of available MFC application wizards appears.

3. In the Templates pane, click the MFC Application icon.

4. Give your project a name and click OK.

The MFC Application Wizard appears.

5. **Click the Next button to step through the wizard.**

6. **On the Application Type page, set the application type to Single Document, as shown in Figure 3-2.**

   Use the Application Type page to specify the kind of Windows form to create.

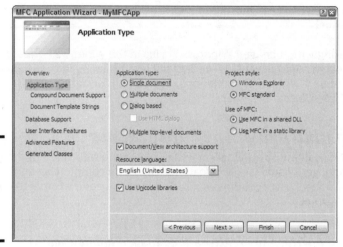

Figure 3-2:
Set the
application
type to
Single
Document.

7. **Continue stepping through the wizard to set options for database support and user interface features.**

8. **On the Generated Classes page, click the Base Class drop-down list. Select `CFormView`, as shown in Figure 3-3.**

   The Base class determines the kind of Windows form that the application creates.

9. **Click Finish.**

   Visual Studio adds the source, header, and resource files that are necessary to build the options you specify in the wizard.

The wizard generates a fully functioning Windows application. Press Ctrl+F5 to run it. You should see a window similar to the one shown in Figure 3-4.

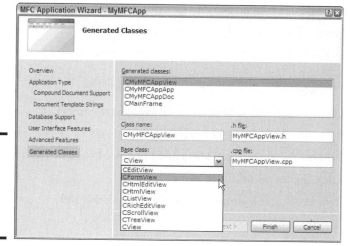

Figure 3-3:
Select this
Base class
to set the
Windows
form.

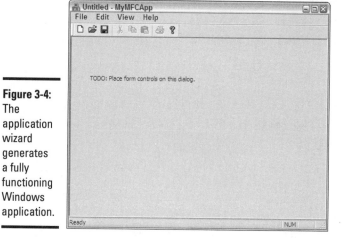

Figure 3-4:
The
application
wizard
generates
a fully
functioning
Windows
application.

**Book III
Chapter 3**

**Building Visual C++
Applications**

If your goal is to use C++ syntax, application wizards probably aren't the
route you want to take. Pick up a copy of *C++ For Dummies,* 5th Edition, by
Stephen Randy Davis (Wiley Publishing, Inc.) if you need to know about C++
syntax.

Managing resources

Visual Studio provides resource editors for working with a Visual C++ project's resources. Here are a few resource editors:

✦ **Dialog Editor:** Manages dialog boxes

✦ **Menu Editor:** Manages menus

✦ **String Editor:** Manages all your project's strings

To access a project's resources, follow these steps:

1. **Choose View⟹Resource View or press Ctrl+Shift+E.**

   A tree view of the project's resources appears.

2. **Expand the resource folders until you see the Menu folder.**

3. **Click the Menu folder to expand it.**

4. **Double-click the Menu resource IDR_MAINFRAME.**

   The Menu Editor opens, as shown in Figure 3-5.

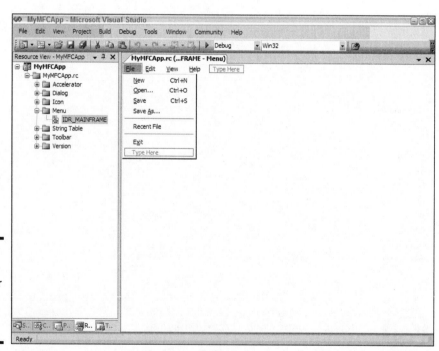

Figure 3-5:
Use the
Menu Editor
to edit the
project's
menus.

To add controls to your Windows form, follow these steps:

1. **Click the plus (+) sign next to the Dialog folder in your project's Resource View pane.**

A list of your project's forms appears.

2. **Double-click the form** `IDD_MYMFCWINAPP_FORM` **to open it.**

   The form opens in the Dialog Editor, as shown in Figure 3-6. Note that the name of the form is generated by using the project name you specify. If you used a project name other than MyMFCWinApp, insert your project's name between `IDD_` and `_FORM`.

3. **Drag and drop controls from the toolbox onto the Dialog Editor.**

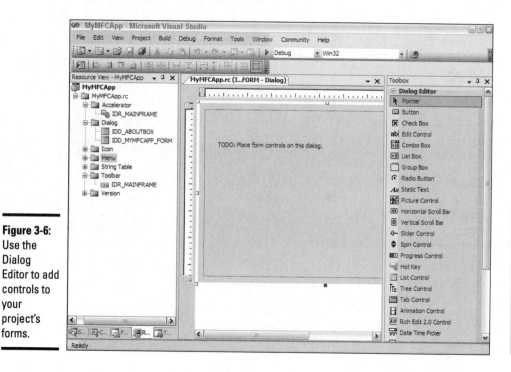

Figure 3-6:
Use the Dialog Editor to add controls to your project's forms.

Book III
Chapter 3

Building Visual C++
Applications

You can build event handlers for controls by choosing Add Event Handler from the control's shortcut menu.

To add a resource to a project, follow these steps:

1. **Click the Resource View pane.**

2. **Choose Project➪Add Resource.**

   The Add Resource dialog box appears.

3. **Choose a resource from the list of resource types.**

4. Click the New button, shown in Figure 3-7, to add the resource.

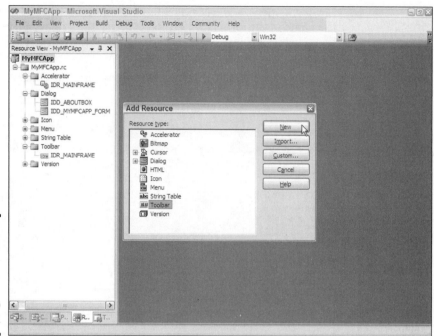

Figure 3-7:
Use the Add
Resource
window
to add
resources to
your project.

Chapter 4: Building Web Applications

In This Chapter

✔ Using Visual Web Developer

✔ Creating your first Web site

✔ Understanding server controls

✔ Getting comfortable with ASP.NET syntax

✔ Creating user controls

To help you build Web applications, Microsoft offers a wide array of products. In the past, it offered two products for Web development. You could build ASP.NET Web sites with Visual Studio 2003; Visual Studio and ASP.NET are used in the domain of building enterprise Web sites featuring e-commerce and full-blown Web-based applications. You could also build traditional HTML-based Web sites with FrontPage 2003, a powerful editor for building professional-looking Web sites.

The primary difference in these two approaches is that ASP.NET Web sites use server-side code to do everything from render dynamic content to access databases. Although FrontPage has some server-side elements, its emphasis is on helping users build good-looking Web sites quickly. Because the underlying technologies for these tools are different, they never worked well together.

In 2005, Microsoft started revealing its next wave of Web design and development tools. Not only do you get more choices, but these tools are also intended to provide better support for Web design standards, such as Cascading Style Sheets (CSS), and to work together seamlessly. The next wave of Microsoft tools includes these features:

✦ **Visual Web Developer** — The premiere Microsoft toolset for building ASP.NET Web sites is part of Visual Studio 2005.

✦ **Microsoft Expressions** — This set of three products (Graphic Designer, Interactive Designer, and Web Designer) targets professionals who design Web sites.

✦ **SharePoint Designer** — Because this new tool for designing SharePoint sites is built on FrontPage, it can create the file-based sites of FrontPage. SharePoint Designer supports the limited development of ASP.NET Web sites.

The new Microsoft Web design and development products recognize that building Web sites requires specialized skills. The person designing Web site graphics isn't usually the same person who's writing the site's data access procedures. Because the specialized tools "talk" to each other, Web designers, graphics designers, and developers can all work on different facets of the Web site without interfering with other areas or having to translate each other's work.

You can read more in Book VII about Microsoft Expression products and SharePoint Designer and how they work with Visual Studio.

Getting to Know the Visual Web Developer

Visual Web Developer is the Web development tool in Visual Studio 2005. You can use Visual Web Developer for these tasks:

✦ Create and edit Web sites by using ASP.NET.

✦ Design Web pages by using visual design tools.

✦ Test your Web sites on your choice of Web servers, including the lightweight ASP.NET Development Server.

✦ Use server-side ASP.NET controls for creating dynamic content.

✦ Publish your Web site to a host server.

✦ Use syntax-aware editors for HTML and server-side code.

✦ Access data by using server-based controls and wizards.

✦ Create a consistent "look and feel" for your Web sites by using themes and master pages.

✦ Build Web sites that have sophisticated features, such as personalization, membership, and site navigation.

Building better Web applications with ASP.NET

The *ASP* in ASP.NET stands for Active Server Pages. After people started realizing that using HTML to write Web pages by hand was a long and laborious chore, they started figuring out that they could replace static HTML content with server-side programs. For example, rather than write the same page header repeatedly, you can call a program on a server that magically spits out the page banner every time it's called.

An ASP.NET Web site uses its own kind of Web pages. ASP.NET Web pages are different from plain old Web pages in the following ways:

✦ Files end in .aspx rather than in the usual .htm or .html for Web pages.

✦ Directives in the form of <@ Page attribute="value"> set configuration attributes used by the compiler.

✦ A form element in the form of <form id="formname" runat="server"> is required on every ASP.NET Web page. The form control is responsible for intercepting a user's interaction with your Web page and sending it to the server for processing.

Microsoft didn't invent the form element. Rather, the form element is part of the HTML syntax and is often called a *server form.* Many server-side scripting languages, such as Perl and PHP, are used with the form element to respond to actions taken by someone using an HTML form. Microsoft invented the runat="server" attribute, which ASP.NET uses to build the form so that it can be sent to the browser.

ASP.NET Web pages are also called Web Forms because they use the HTML form element. The programming style for Web Forms is similar to Windows Forms, which may be another reason that the term *Web Forms* is used. Microsoft has mostly stopped using this term in favor of *Web page.* Interestingly, applications created to target the new Aero interface in Windows Vista employ a user interface control called a *page,* not *Windows Forms.*

✦ You can use Web server controls to invoke server-side programs. I discuss these special elements later in this chapter.

ASP.NET Web sites are hosted on the Microsoft Internet Information Services (IIS) Web server. The server intercepts all ASP.NET requests and passes the requests to ASP.NET for processing. The IIS Web server identifies an ASP.NET request from a plain old HTML request because ASP.NET Web pages use the .aspx file extension.

You use the visual design tools in Visual Web Developer to drag and drop Web server controls on an ASP.NET Web page. Visual Studio then generates the code to make the controls work, and you write your own, custom code that processes the controls when users interact with them in their browsers. Visual Studio packages all this code and creates a compiled computer program that's executed whenever a user requests the page.

When you use Visual Studio to run an ASP.NET Web site, Visual Studio compiles the pages. When you deploy your Web site to an IIS Web server, the files are copied "as is," and ASP.NET takes over the process of compiling the code for you. You can force Visual Studio to compile the code before you deploy it to IIS. See Book VI, Chapter 2 for more information about deploying ASP.NET Web sites.

Taking a trip with an ASP.NET Web page

Any time a user requests an ASP.NET Web page in her browser, a program runs on the Web server to deliver the page. When the user performs an action on the page, such as clicking a button to submit information, the page sends a request back to the server. The process of sending data back to the server is a *postback*.

The postback calls the same ASP.NET Web page that the user interacted with. The data the user entered into the browser is passed to the ASP.NET Web page's server-side code for processing. The server-side code customarily sends back a confirmation message to the user indicating whether the data was successfully processed.

A postback is also referred to as a *round trip* because data flows from the browser to the server and back to the browser each time the user performs an action on the page. For more information about writing the server-side code that responds to a postback in an ASP.NET Web page, see Book V, Chapter 4.

Creating Web sites

You can use the Visual Web Developer in Visual Studio to create different kinds of Web sites, depending on where you want to work with the site's content and the kind of Web server you want to use for testing. Here are the four kinds of sites you can create with Visual Studio:

✦ **File system** — Store your Web site's files in a folder on your local hard drive, and use the Visual Studio built-in Web server for testing.

✦ **Local IIS** — Create a Web site on your local machine by using Internet Information Services (IIS) as your Web server. Visual Studio creates the Web site in IIS for you.

✦ **Remote server** — Access an IIS Web server on a different computer by using the HTTP protocol.

✦ **FTP** — Access a Web server on a different computer by using the File Transfer Protocol (FTP). You typically use FTP when you access a site hosted on a third-party server.

Note that the kind of Web site you create doesn't determine how you choose to deploy it. That is, you can create a file system Web site and then later deploy it to an IIS server by using FTP. For more information on deployment options, see Book VI, Chapter 2.

Working with a file system Web site is generally much easier than working with any of the other configurations. If more than one developer is working on a single Web site, you might need to use one of the other approaches. For more information about team development and source code control, see Book VI, Chapter 3.

Saying "Hello, World Wide Web"

Creating a Web site in Visual Studio is the easy part of building a Web application. Choosing the content that goes into your Web application is a little trickier. When you create a Web site, Visual Studio does all the work for you. Visual Studio creates the folder structure and configuration files necessary to run the Web site. Here's what ASP.NET does when it creates a Web site:

✦ Creates a folder structure on your local computer for managing the Web site's files

✦ Provisions the project to the specified Web server

✦ Creates a new Web Forms page named `default.aspx`

✦ Creates a code-behind file for writing server-side code for the forms page named default.aspx.vb

✦ Adds an App_Data folder for storing data-related files

✦ Creates a web.config file for storing Web site configuration information

This book describes folder-based systems exclusively because they're easy to work with.

To create a new folder-based Web site, follow these steps:

1. **Choose File➪New Web Site.**

The New Web Site dialog box appears.

Goodbye, IIS; hello, ASP.NET Development Server

Because previous versions of Visual Studio didn't include a Web server, most developers used a local copy of IIS installed on their computers. Although IIS is no longer required for testing ASP.NET Web sites, it's still required for running ASP.NET Web sites in a production environment.

IIS adds a layer of complexity that you might not want to deal with. However, because IIS is the production Web server, you need to test your site with it anyway.

Because file-based Web sites use the ASP.NET Development Server, you don't need to do any configuration.

2. **Click the ASP.NET Web Site template.**

3. **The default location for a new Web site is the file system. Accept this location and enter a name, such as MyWebSite, after the pathname, as shown in Figure 4-1.**

   Leave the language set to Visual Basic.

4. **Click OK to create the ASP.NET Web site.**

   The default.aspx page opens in Design view.

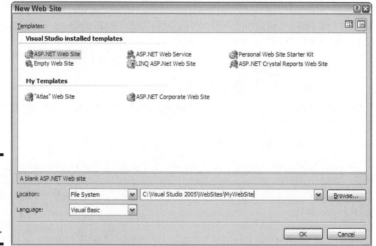

Figure 4-1: Append the name of the Web site to the file path.

Viewing ASP.NET syntax

An ASP.NET Web page is a combination of HTML markup elements and ASP.NET syntax. The `runat="server"` attribute is an example of ASP.NET syntax that tells the ASP.NET compiler to process that tag differently. Any plain-text or HTML tags are rendered to the browser exactly as they appear on the Web page. You use the Source view of an ASP.NET page to view its syntax. To view the `default.aspx` page in Source view, click the Source tab at the bottom of the Document Explorer, shown in Figure 4-2.

Notice the markup elements displayed in Source view:

✦ The `<%@ Page . . . %>` directive at the top of the page provides additional configuration information for the ASP.NET compiler.

✦ The `<!DOCTYPE . . . >` entry tells the client's Internet browser that the page complies with the XHTML standard. If you don't care about this standard, you can safely delete this line.

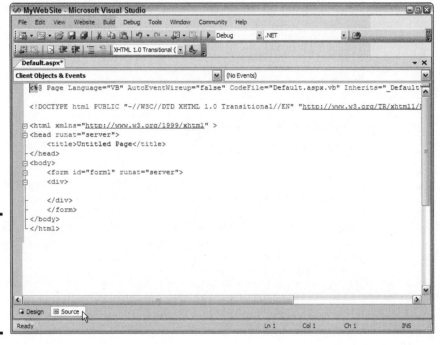

Figure 4-2:
Click the Source tab to display the page in Source view.

✦ Familiar HTML tags, such as `<html>` and `<head>`, are used.

✦ The `runat="server"` attribute is used on the `<head>` and `<form>` tags.

The syntax you see displayed in Figure 4-2 appears in every Web page you add to your project. You drag and drop controls from the toolbox onto the Web page's Design view, as described in the next section. As you add controls to the page, ASP.NET syntax appears in the page's Source view.

You can use the View menu to access the Web page's Source and Design views.

Adding content

The Web page that's added to a newly created ASP.NET Web site is blank. To make the page meaningful, you must fill it with content, such as

✦ Text boxes, labels, and buttons

✦ Plain text in paragraphs in lists

✦ Images and animations

✦ Tables displaying data and forms that allow users to enter and interact with data

You have several options for adding content to your Web page. If you know the ASP.NET syntax for building ASP.NET Web pages, you can just open any text editor and start adding content. Fortunately, you can use Design view in Visual Studio to add content.

Using the visual designer to add content in Visual Studio 2005 involves these three steps:

1. **Drag and drop the controls on the visual design surface.**

2. **Set the properties that determine attributes such as appearance and function.**

3. **Specify what happens when a user interacts with a control by either using a wizard to build the code or writing the code manually.**

Suppose that you want to create a simple Web form page that displays the text Hello world! when a user clicks a button. To add the content to the default.aspx Web page that I show you how to create in the preceding section, follow these steps:

1. **In Design view of the default.aspx page, drag and drop a Label control from the Toolbox task pane. If the toolbox isn't visible, press Ctrl+Alt+X.**

2. **Drag and drop a Button control on the designer surface.**

A button appears on the page.

3. **Press Ctrl+F5 to run the Web page.**

The Web page that appears has a label and a button. If you click the button, however, it doesn't do anything. To display Hello world, you have to finish setting the controls' properties and configuring the button to work.

To set the controls' properties, follow these steps:

1. **In Design view, press F4 to open the Properties window.**

2. **Click the Label control in the designer to display the label's properties in the Properties window.**

The Properties window lists properties on the left and their corresponding values on the right.

3. **Locate the Text property, and set the value to Blank by deleting the contents.**

Repeat these steps to set the button's Text property to Hit me. The Text property specifies the text that appears on the page.

Adding the code to make the button work requires you to work in Code view on the page. Although you can type the code directly in the code editor, it's easier to start in Design view and let Visual Studio write some of the setup code for you. Follow these steps:

1. In Design view, double-click the button you placed on the designer.

The code editor appears. Double-clicking any control in the designer creates a block of code that's linked to the default event handler for that control. In the case of a button, the default event handler is the `Click` event. The code that's typed in the code block is executed every time the button is clicked. For more information on event handlers, see Book V, Chapter 4.

2. In the code editor, type this line:

```
Me.Label1.Text = "Hello world!"
```

3. Press Ctrl+F5 to run the Web page.

4. When the Web page appears, click the button.

The statement `Hello world!` appears on the page, as shown in Figure 4-3.

Figure 4-3:
The ASP.NET Web page displays this message when you click the button.

Working with Web Sites

As I describe earlier in this chapter, creating a Web site using Visual Studio is easy. The hard part is figuring out what content to add. Luckily for you, Visual Studio lets you add all kinds of content to your Web pages and Web site, and you have a ton of different ways to view and edit your Web pages.

Adding new pages

Adding new pages involves more than just adding Web pages. You can use Visual Studio to add these elements:

✦ **Web pages** — ASP.NET Web forms, Web services, mobile Web forms, user controls, and plain old HTML files, for example

✦ **Web pages for mobile Web sites** — Mobile Web forms and user controls, for example

✦ **Files to control the look and feel of your Web site** — master pages, site maps, skin files, and Cascading Style Sheets, for example

✦ **Files for managing data** — XML files, class files, and data sets, for example

Use the Add New Item dialog box to add new content to your Web site. You can open this dialog box in two ways:

✦ Right-click the project folder in Solution Explorer and choose Add New Item.

✦ Choose Web Site⇨Add New Item.

You can add items that you already created by choosing the Add Existing Items option. Many of these items, such as the datasets, are displayed in their own designers. You don't have to write everything from scratch.

To add a new Web page to an existing Web site, follow these steps:

1. **Choose Website⇨Add New Item.**

The Add New Item dialog box appears.

2. **Click the Web Form template.**

3. **Enter the name** about.aspx **and leave the language as Visual Basic.**

Leave the Place Code in Separate File check box selected and the Select Master Page check boxes deselected.

The Place Code in Separate File option places all your program code in a separate, code-behind file. Master Pages are used to control the look and feel of your Web pages. See Chapter 5 in this mini-book for more information about using master pages.

4. Click the Add button, shown in Figure 4-4.

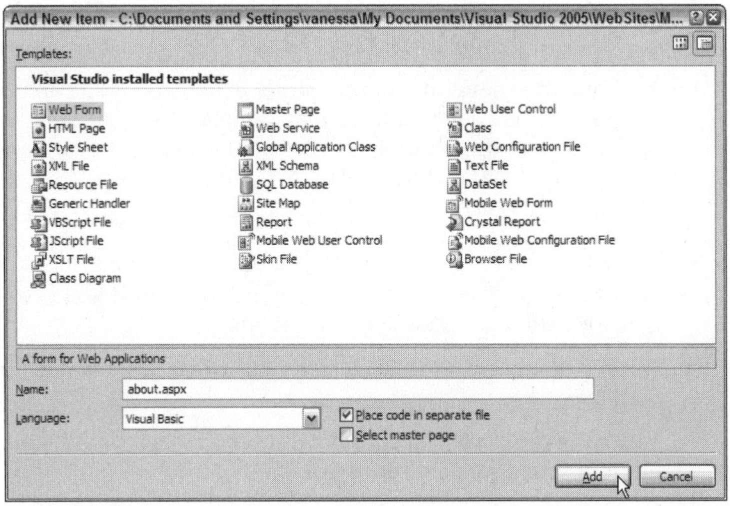

Figure 4-4:
Click the
Add button
to add a
new Web
page to your
Web site.

Book III
Chapter 4

Building Web
Applications

A new ASP.NET Web page is added to your Web site. The page opens in Design view so that you can add content. See Chapter 5 in this mini-book for more information on site navigation and linking to Web pages.

You can add empty folders for organizing your content. ASP.NET Web sites use several reserved folders, which you can add to your site at any time:

✦ `App_Browsers` — Stores browser definition files, which are used to tell ASP.NET how to render markup for certain kinds of browsers, such as on mobile devices

✦ `App_Code` — Contains source code for class libraries, helper utilities, and business objects

✦ `App_Data` — Stores data files, including a local database for managing Web site membership and roles

✦ `App_GlobalResources` and `App_LocalResources` — Contains resource files used for translating page content into other languages

✦ `App_Themes` — Stores all your skins, Cascading Style Sheets, images, and other "look and feel" files

✦ `App_WebReferences` — Contains files for Web services

✦ `Bin` — Stores compiled assemblies that you want to use in your Web site

You can add any of these folders by either choosing Website⇨Add ASP.NET Folder or right-clicking the project folder and then clicking Add ASP.NET Folder. You can also right-click any of these folders in Solution Explorer and choose Add New Item to display an abbreviated list of items you can add in that folder.

Benefiting from the battle of the server controls

ASP.NET provides several different kinds of controls you can use on your Web pages. You use *controls* to display dynamic content on your Web page. ASP.NET writes all the plumbing code that renders your content and passes a user's response back to the server for you to process.

ASP.NET provides these kinds of server controls:

✦ **Web server** — Simple controls, such as a label or text box, and complex controls, such as calendars and menus

✦ **HTML server** — Simple HTML elements that you expose for server-side coding

✦ **Validation** — A special kind of Web server control that validates the input of other Web server controls

✦ **User** — A custom control you create by using ASP.NET markup elements that can be embedded in a Web page

Server controls have many similarities. All of them

✦ Have the `runat="server"` attribute in their markup code.

✦ Must be placed inside an ASP.NET Web page in order to execute.

✦ Are accessible from server-side code, which means that you can write a program to manipulate the controls.

✦ Have events.

✦ Have properties that set their behavior at run-time.

✦ Must reside within the form control. (Each page can have only one.)

✦ Are rendered on the browser as a combination of plain HTML and JavaScript.

All these server controls, except user controls, are accessible from the toolbox. You add user controls by using Solution Explorer. You can place other kinds of controls in a user control to create a composite control.

A server-side control displays a little mark, or *glyph,* in its upper-left corner in Design view, as shown in Figure 4-5.

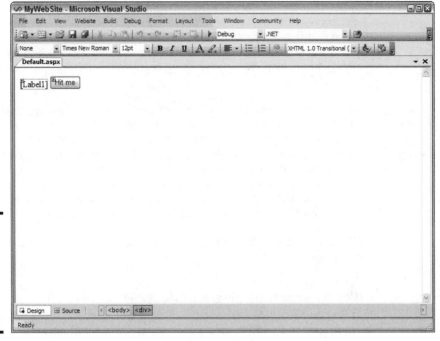

Figure 4-5:
A server-side control displays a glyph in its upper-left corner.

**Book III
Chapter 4**

**Building Web
Applications**

The syntax

The ASP.NET syntax for Web server controls looks similar to HTML markup syntax. As with HTML, ASP.NET syntax uses tags with attribute/value pairs. The markup for a Web server button control looks like this:

```
<asp:Button ID="Button1" runat="server" Text="Button" />
```

You can add attributes to the markup code by either typing them directly in Source view of the Web page or using the Properties window. The attributes specified in the markup code are properties of the Web server control, not HTML attributes. Some properties are mapped to HTML attributes. ASP.NET uses the collection of properties to determine how best to render the markup in a browser.

The markup code for an HTML server control looks like this:

```
<input id="Button2" type="button" value="button" runat="server" />
```

All server-side controls have these markup elements:

✦ **ID attribute** — Tells the server-side code how to access the control.

✦ **Runat attribute** — Flags the control as a server-side control.

Notice that the tags are a little different for Web server controls and HTML server controls. Web server control tags start with `asp:` and then the name of the control — for example, `asp:button` and `asp:textbox`. HTML server controls use HTML syntax, such as `<input>` and `<div>`. You can convert any HTML element to a server control by simply adding the `runat` attribute to the markup.

Server controls provided by ASP.NET use the tag prefix `asp`. Custom server controls created by you or a third party use the tag prefix defined for the custom server control. The tag prefix maps the control to the control's namespace. The namespace tells ASP.NET where the code that defines how the control works can be found. Tag prefixes are defined using a `Register` directive at the top of each Web page that uses the control. Alternatively, you can place the prefix information in the Web site's configuration file so that all pages in the site can use the custom server control.

All server controls must be contained within the `<form>` element on the Web page.

Web server controls versus HTML server controls

At first blush, HTML server controls and Web server controls look similar. They have some differences, however, as Table 4-1 illustrates.

Table 4-1	Comparison of HTML Server Controls and Web Server Controls
HTML Server Controls	*Web Server Controls*
Map almost one-to-one to HTML elements	Render to a single HTML element or a combination of elements
Are client-side by default	Server-side only
Properties mapped to HTML attributes	Properties aren't mapped directly to HTML attributes
Customized using CSS	Customized using CSS or templates
Don't support themes	Support themes

Here are some examples of Web server controls:

✦ `Label`, `TextBox`, and `Button`

✦ `LinkButton`, `ImageButton`, and `HyperLink`

✦ `TreeView` and `SiteMapPath`

To add an HTML control to a Web page and convert it to a server control, follow these steps:

1. **Click the plus sign (+) next to the HTML tab in the toolbox to expand the list of HTML controls.**

If the toolbox isn't displayed, press Ctrl+Alt+X to open it.

2. **Drag an Input(Button) control to the design surface and drop it.**

The image of a button appears.

3. **Right-click the button's image and choose Run As Server Control from the context menu.**

The button image is updated to show a little arrow in its upper-left corner.

The markup code for the button is changed to include this `runat` property:

```
<input id="Button2" runat="server" type="button" value="button" />
```

All the events captured for this control are now server-side. Double-click the button's image to display a server-side code block, where you can enter server-side code for the button's `Click` event.

To convert the HTML control back to a regular control, you can either

✦ Right-click the button's image and choose Run As Server Control.

✦ Remove the `runat` property from the control's markup in Source view.

Unless you plan to use server-side resources, you should always use plain HTML elements. Server-side controls use more resources than client-side controls. You should also consider whether you can deliver functionality in a client-side script rather than use server-side code. By using a client-side script, you eliminate a round trip back to the server.

For example, you can easily create a `Hello world` example by using a client-side script. Follow these steps:

1. **Add a paragraph element to your Web page by typing the following code in Source view on the Web page:**

```
<p id="output" style="color: Red; font-weight: bold"></p>
```

2. **Drag and drop an Input(Button) control in Design view on the page by using the HTML tab in the toolbox.**

3. **Enter Hit me in the Value property on the Properties window.**

If the Properties window isn't displayed, press F4.

4. **Double-click the image of the Input button.**

A JavaScript code block appears in Source view on the page. (JavaScript is a client-side scripting language.)

5. Type this code in the JavaScript code block:

```
document.getElementById("output").innerHTML = "Hello world!";
```

6. Press Ctrl+F5 to run the Web site.

The Web site appears in your browser.

7. Press the button.

The phrase Hello world! appears on the page.

This code sample uses the innerHTML property of the paragraph element. (I used this property for brevity.) The appropriate way to modify page content dynamically is to access the node and modify it by using the Document Object Model (DOM). The benefit of using innerHTML is that you can easily understand what this code is doing. The downside is that because the property isn't universal and doesn't provide a reference to the node in question, accessing the node again by using client-side code is impossible.

Earlier in this chapter, I use a Web server button control. How do you know when to choose an HTML input button and when to choose a Web server button control? Here are a couple of reasons to choose HTML input button controls over Web server button controls:

✦ HTML server controls provide more control over the HTML markup that's rendered in the browser. You can also control the markup of Web server controls by using a template, but it requires more work than using HTML server controls.

✦ HTML server controls are easier for non-Visual Studio users to understand. This information is especially valuable if you're working with Web designers who provide you with Cascading Style Sheets, because the designers might not understand how to provide styles for Web server controls.

On the other hand, here are some reasons that you might choose Web server button controls over HTML input button controls:

✦ Use Web server controls any time you want access to more properties than are available with a typical HTML element.

✦ Because Web server controls are server-side by default, you don't take the extra step of converting the controls to server-side, as you do with HTML server controls.

✦ Use Web server controls if you want to take advantage of device filters and browser definition files.

Visual Studio provides more visual design support for Web server controls than for HTML server controls. If you want to rely on HTML server controls, why use ASP.NET? I use Web server controls almost exclusively, except for the two generic HTML tags `div` and `span`. Any time I want to add dynamic text content to a page, such as a warning message, I use a server-side `div` or `span` tag to display the message programmatically.

You can also use a Label Web server control to display messages. Label controls are rendered as HTML `span` tags. The `span` tag is a generic inline container for use inside block-level containers, such as `div` tags and paragraph tags. Because messages are usually rendered at the block level, I prefer to use `div` tags. If I plan to display a message inside a block tag, such as a paragraph tag, I can choose a Label control. In reality, most browsers aren't affected if your `div` and `span` tags are improperly nested. It matters only if you're a purist, like me.

For an in-depth discussion of additional Web server controls, see Chapter 5 in this mini-book. It describes site navigation controls and hyperlinking mechanisms for transitioning between Web pages.

Login controls are covered in Chapter 6 of this mini-book, and data controls are covered in Book IV, Chapter 2.

User controls and custom controls

Sometimes, you want to create a reusable control that doesn't already exist in the Visual Studio toolbox. You can choose from two types:

✦ **User** — Create this type of control by using the same tools you use to build Web pages. Like other controls, user controls are contained within an ASP.NET Web page.

✦ **Custom** — Build your own, custom control and add it to the Visual Studio toolbox. Writing a custom control requires some programming expertise.

User controls are similar to ASP.NET Web pages because you can include HTML and server-side code in a single file. Unlike Web pages, user controls

✦ End in the file extension `.ascx`

✦ Use the `@ Control` directive rather than `@ Page`

✦ Must be hosted as part of an ASP.NET Web page

✦ Don't include host page elements, such as `html`, `body`, and `form`

**Book III
Chapter 4**

**Building Web
Applications**

In previous versions of Visual Studio 2005, user controls were used extensively as a means of providing page templates. For example, you would create header and footer user controls on each of your Web pages. That's no longer necessary with master pages.

I don't mean to imply that user controls are no longer valuable. You can use a user control any time you want to encapsulate a group of controls and make them reusable. For example, you could create a user control for displaying calendar controls.

To create this user control in an existing Web site, follow these steps:

1. **Right-click the Web site's project folder in Solution Explorer, and choose Add New Item from the context menu.**

The Add New Item dialog box appears.

2. **Click the Web User Control icon.**

3. **Give the user control the name calendar.ascx, and choose Visual Basic as the language.**

4. **Click the Add button to add the user control to your Web site.**

Visual Studio opens the user control in Design view.

To add your user control to an existing Web page, drag the `calendar.ascx` file from Solution Explorer and drop it on Design view of the Web page. Visual Studio adds the following markup to your Web page:

✦ At the top of the page:

```
<%@ Register Src="calendar.ascx" TagName="calendar" TagPrefix="uc1" %>
```

✦ In the page content:

```
<uc1:calendar ID="Calendar1" runat="server" />
```

This example shows a tag prefix being used for a custom control, as described in the section "The syntax," earlier in this chapter. The `Register` directive specifies the name of the control (`calendar`, in this case) and the tag prefix. To use the control on the page, the syntax references the custom control's tag prefix, `uc1`, and places the control's name after the colon. In this example, the control isn't mapped to a namespace. Instead, the control is mapped to the user control file using the attribute `Src="calendar.ascx"`. That's how ASP.NET knows where to find the control when it processes the control on the page.

In Design view of the Web page, the user control is displayed with a placeholder box until content is added to the user control. To open the user control for editing, follow these steps:

1. **In Design view of the Web page, click the smart tag arrow on the user control.**

The UserControl Tasks list appears.

2. **Click the Edit UserControl link, shown in Figure 4-6.**

The user control opens for editing.

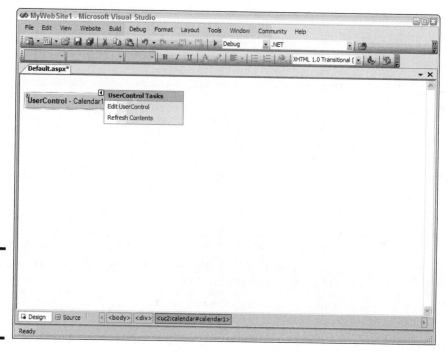

Figure 4-6:
Click this
link to open
the control
for editing.

A user control is blank when you first create it. You add controls to create a new control. Adding controls to a user control is similar to adding controls to a Web page. You simply drag and drop controls from the toolbox onto the design surface.

Because user controls are made up of other controls, they're often called *composite* controls.

One control that you can't use on a user control is the `<form>` server control. You might recall that user controls, like all server controls, are hosted in Web forms. You can't call a user control from the browser. Web forms can have only one `<form>` server control. You place your user control inside the `<form>` server control on the page where you want to display your user control.

Although you can place a `<form>` server control in a user control, you don't receive an error message until you execute the page where the user control is hosted.

The following example demonstrates how to create a user control. The example shows you how to create a specialized calendar control that displays the preceding, current, and following months. This user control encapsulates the controls and code that make the calendars work. The user control can be reused repeatedly without writing any code to make it work each time.

Follow these steps to create the calendar user control:

1. **Drag and drop a calendar control from the toolbox to Design view of the user control. Press Ctrl+Alt+X to display the toolbox.**

2. **Add two more calendar controls by repeating Step 1 or copying and pasting the markup code in Source view.**

You should have three calendar controls, named `Calendar1`, `Calendar2`, and `Calendar3`.

3. **Position your controls so that `Calendar2` is between `Calendar1` and `Calendar3`.**

4. **On `Calendar1` and `Calendar3`, use the Properties window to set the `ShowNextPrevMonth` property to false. Set the `SelectionMode` property to None. Press F4 to open the Properties window if it's closed.**

5. **With the user control displayed in Design view, double-click a blank area of the designer.**

Visual Studio opens the code editor and positions your cursor inside a code block for the `Page_Load` event.

The `Page_Load` event is called when the user control is loaded.

6. **In the `Page_Load` code block, enter this code:**

```
If (Not Page.IsPostBack = True) Then
    Me.Calendar2.VisibleDate = System.DateTime.Today
    Me.Calendar1.VisibleDate =    Me.Calendar1.TodaysDate.AddMonths(-1)
    Me.Calendar3.VisibleDate =    Me.Calendar1.TodaysDate.AddMonths(1)
End If
```

If you want to test whether your code is working, you can press Ctrl+F5 to run your Web site.

7. **In Design view of the user control, click `Calendar2` and press F4 to display the Properties window for that control.**

8. **Click the Events button on the Properties window toolbar.**

The Events button looks like a lightning bolt.

9. **Double-click the `VisibleMonthChanged` event.**

Visual Studio creates an event handler and opens the code editor for you.

10. **Type these two lines of code:**

```
Me.Calendar1.VisibleDate = Me.Calendar2.VisibleDate.AddMonths(-1)
Me.Calendar3.VisibleDate = Me.Calendar2.VisibleDate.AddMonths(1)
```

11. **Press Ctrl+F5 to run your Web site.**

Your Web page displays the user control with three calendars, as shown in Figure 4-7. As you navigate with the middle control, the other controls are updated too.

Book III
Chapter 4

**Building Web
Applications**

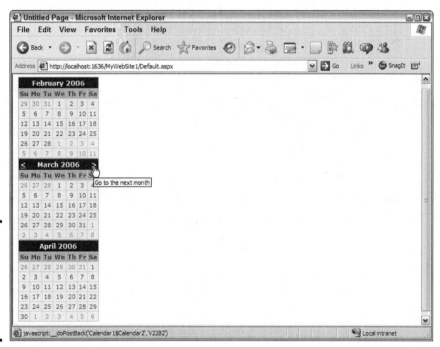

Figure 4-7:
Click the
middle
calendar
to update
all three
calendars.

Changing your view

You can use one of several views to edit ASP.NET Web pages in Visual Studio 2005:

✦ **Design view** — The `default.aspx` page is opened in Design view by default. Design view is a WYSIWYG visual designer in which you can build your Web page by typing content or dragging and dropping controls on the design surface.

✦ **Source view** — You can view and edit the underlying HTML markup that's used to build the Web page.

✦ **Code view** — Display the programming language editor associated with that Web page.

✦ **Component Designer view** — Create a visual design surface for nonvisual components.

Straight to the Source

Source view in Visual Web Developer displays the HTML markup and ASP.NET syntax used to create the Web page or user control. You use Source view to edit HTML markup and ASP.NET syntax.

You can display Source view of a Web page in one of three ways:

✦ Click the Source tab at the bottom of the Document Explorer on the Web page.

✦ Choose View➪Markup.

✦ Right-click the Web page in Solution Explorer and choose View Markup from the context menu.

Source view automatically displays the HTML Source Editing toolbar. It has several commands for formatting the markup and has these two additional validator commands:

✦ **Target Schema for Validation** — Use this drop-down list to specify whether Visual Studio should use XHTML 1.x, HTML 1.0, or a version of Internet Explorer in validating the Web page's markup.

✦ **Check Page for Accessibility** — The accessibility validator uses a number of accessibility standards to determine whether your page can be used by people with disabilities.

Run the validator commands if you want to ensure that your page conforms to industry standards.

When you run your ASP.NET Web page, the content that's sent to the browser isn't what you see in Source view in Visual Studio. Rather, the ASP.NET syntax is converted to HTML.

Figure 4-8 shows, on the left, Source view for the `default.aspx` page (created in the section "Saying 'Hello, World Wide Web,'" earlier in this chapter). The HTML that's rendered to the browser by ASP.NET is shown on the right.

Figure 4-8:
Check out this comparison of ASP.NET markup and the HTML rendered by ASP.NET.

In this example, the ASP.NET syntax is cleaner than the HTML. Part of the reason is the view state values you see in the HTML. The view state values are shown in the long sequence of characters and represent data stored on the page. View state is added by ASP.NET. In the case of simple HTML elements, such as labels and text boxes, ASP.NET syntax isn't much simpler than HTML. The real difference between HTML and ASP.NET shows up when you use more complex display structures, such as tables. For example, the GridView control requires a few lines of ASP.NET syntax and is rendered as a table created by using numerous lines of HTML.

See Chapter 6 in this mini-book for information about the view state.

Notice a couple of characteristics about the comparison:

✦ ASP.NET directives, such as @Page, aren't present in the output.

✦ Any HTML markup with the runat="server" attribute is converted to HTML.

For example, this line

```
<form id="form1" runat="server">
```

is converted to this one:

```
<form name="form1" method="post" action="default.aspx" id="form1">
```

The <form> tag is special because it designates which controls the users of your Web page can interact with. When you add controls to your Web page by using Design view, the markup necessary to build those controls is placed inside the <form> tag.

Source view is a syntax-aware editor that you can use to write or edit HTML and ASP.NET syntax. For example, to add a new hyperlink to your Web page, follow these steps:

**Book III
Chapter 4**

**Building Web
Applications**

1. **Type an opening tag bracket (<).**

A list of valid HTML and ASP tags appears.

2. **Press the down-arrow key to highlight the** a **tag, and press Tab.**

3. **Press the spacebar to display a drop-down list of valid attributes. Select the `href` attribute by pressing either the down-arrow key or the letter h. When the `href` attribute is displayed, press Tab to select it.**

4. **Type an equal sign (=). When the list of available Web pages appears, type** "http://www.cnn.com" **(with the double quotation marks).**

You can also use the Pick URL option to pick a URL.

5. **Type the closing tag bracket (>).**

Visual Studio fills in the closing tag for you.

You can also add new attribute/value pairs to existing HTML and ASP.NET tags by pressing the spacebar inside any of the tags.

Code editing

Visual Studio takes care of much of the task of writing code for you. ASP.NET has two coding styles:

✦ **Inline** — Code is written in Source view by using script tags.

✦ **Code-behind** — All code is maintained in a separate file.

The default approach uses the code-behind style. The code-behind file is divided into two files:

✦ One file, generated automatically by Visual Studio, contains all the code generated by Visual Studio to handle the controls you place on the screen and wires up the events you write code for.

✦ You view the other file when you click in Code view. This file contains all the code you write.

When you run your Web site, the code from these two files is combined.

Earlier versions of ASP.NET had only one code-behind file. This single code-behind file contained all the code generated by Visual Studio and the code written by the developer. Microsoft changed this model into two separate files to keep the code clean and prevent developers from being confused by the generated code. The feature that enables the code to be split into two files is *partial classes*. Together, the files create a class, which is a unit of a program. Partial classes make it possible to split a single class across two files. Partial classes are intended for use with code-generation tools. As a rule, you shouldn't create your own partial classes. You can read more about using classes to organize your code in Book V, Chapter 3.

You shouldn't change the code generated by Visual Studio. Any changes you make will likely be overwritten when the file is regenerated. It's okay to open the generated file from Solution Explorer and view its contents. But, you shouldn't add or edit the code.

Running your Web site

You need to run your Web site from time to time as you're developing to make sure that it's working properly. If you're working mostly with the visual Design view, you shouldn't have many problems. You can run your Web site in one of two modes:

✦ **Debug mode** — Provides detailed information about errors you might encounter in running your Web site. Most developers execute their Web sites in Debug mode while they're actively developing their sites.

✦ **Release mode** — After a site is ready to be deployed, its developer usually switches it from Debug mode to Release mode because the site runs faster in Release mode. However, the process halts when an error is encountered, and you don't get much useful feedback.

Most of the sample code in this book uses Release mode because it has less overhead. The downside is that you don't get good feedback when errors occur.

To start your Web site without debugging, press Ctrl+F5. To start it with debugging turned on, press F5. You can also use Debug menu commands for starting your Web site.

Debugging a Web site can be overwhelming — even professionals get hung up. For more information about using and configuring the debugger, see Book V, Chapter 7.

Using Starter Kits

A *starter kit* is a fully functional Web site that you can open and customize to suit your needs. Visual Studio 2005 includes a Personal Web Site starter kit. Starter kits are listed alongside other project templates in the New Web Site dialog box.

You can download additional starter kits from the Downloads page on the ASP.NET site: `www.asp.net/default.aspx?tabindex=5&tabid=41`. Here are some available starter kits:

✦ **Club Site** — A Web site for a club or organization

✦ **Time Tracker** — A Web site for tracking hours spent on a project

✦ **PayPal-enabled eCommerce** — A site for getting started with PayPal

✦ **DotNetNuke** — A good way to get started with DotNetNuke, a Web application framework for creating and deploying Web sites

Chapter 5: Laying Out Your Site

In This Chapter

✔ **Validating user input**

✔ **Adding navigation controls to your site**

✔ **Using themes and master pages**

✔ **Laying out Web pages with CSS**

*L*ook at any Web site and you're likely to see these common elements: validation feedback, navigational aids, and consistent headers and footers. In previous versions of Visual Studio, you had to be conversant in technologies as varied as JavaScript and XML in order to provide these features. Thanks to many of the new features in Visual Studio and ASP.NET, you can create high-quality Web sites while writing a minimal amount of code.

This chapter gets you acquainted with themes, skins, and master pages and introduces you to the benefits of using Cascading Style Sheets (CSS) to lay out your Web pages. I also show you how to use the ASP.NET validation controls to test user input and provide feedback to users.

Keeping Track of Input with Validation Controls

You have to create only a few Web forms before you realize that you need some way of ensuring that all your check boxes are checked and your text boxes are filled in with the right information. The collection of validation controls from ASP.NET help you do that.

The validation controls provide validation services for the controls you place on a Web page, to ensure that the data that's entered is correct. The validation controls also enable you to give users feedback about the correct data. For example, a Web page can include text boxes to capture this type of input from users:

✦ E-mail address

✦ Phone number

✦ Date of birth

How can you be sure that the values that are entered are in the proper formats? How can you ensure that values are even entered?

You have three options:

✦ Write server-side code that validates your text boxes after visitors click the Submit button. This process requires a round trip to the server.

✦ Write client-side script that validates your text boxes as users enter their data.

✦ Do nothing and hope for the best.

Using client-side script whenever possible is the preferred approach because it eliminates a trip to the server and provides immediate feedback to visitors. You can write all this client-side script yourself, or you can let the ASP.NET validation controls write it for you.

ASP.NET provides these validation controls:

✦ `RequiredFieldValidator` — Ensures that required fields contain a value

✦ `RangeValidator` — Checks whether entries fall within a specified range, such as between start and end dates

✦ `RegularExpressionValidator` — Tests whether entries match a certain pattern, such as ZIP + 4 or a telephone number

✦ `CompareValidator` — Compares an entry to a value

✦ `CustomValidator` — Lets you write your own control when none of the other controls provides the level of validation you need

✦ `ValidationSummary` — Displays a summary of all validation errors

Using validation controls is straightforward. To require that a user fill in a text box on an existing Web page, follow these steps:

1. **Open the Web page you want to add validation controls to, or create a new Web page.**

See Chapter 4 in this mini-book for more information about creating Web pages.

2. **Drag and drop a Label control and a Text Box control onto the Web page. Set the `Text` property on the label to `Enter name:` and set the text box `ID` property to `EnterName`.**

3. **Drag and drop a `RequiredFieldValidator` control from the Validation section of the toolbox.**

4. **Set the following properties for the `RequiredFieldValidator` control by using the Properties window:**

   - **ID** — Type **EnterNameRequired**.

   - **ControlToValidate** — Select `EnterName` from the drop-down list. It's the text box control you create in Step 1.

   - **Text** — Type **Name is a required field**.

5. **Add a button control and a label control to the page. Set the label's `ID` property to `Confirmation` and its `Text` property to `Confirmation Message`. Set the button control's `Text` property to `Submit`.**

6. **Double-click the button.**

   The button's `Click` event appears in the code editor.

7. **Type this code in the button's `Click` event:**

   ```
   If (Page.IsValid) Then
       Me.Confirmation.Text = "Page is valid!"
   End If
   ```

   This code snippet displays the message `Page is valid!` on the Confirmation label when the user clicks the button.

See Book V, Chapter 4 to read more about using events.

To test your validation control, follow these steps:

1. **Press Ctrl+F5 to run your site.**

2. **Click the Submit button on the page.**

   The page displays `Name is a required field.` next to the text box, as shown in Figure 5-1.

The `RequiredFieldValidator` control uses client-side scripting to test the contents of the text box. When you click the Submit button, the browser doesn't call the server. Instead, a client-side script validates the control. If the control passes the validation, data is sent to the server. Using client-side scripting is more efficient because you don't make wasted trips back to the server just to see whether the user has filled in a text box.

You should make a trip to the server whenever you need to validate sensitive information, such as a password. It isn't appropriate to use a validation control with client-side scripting because you would have to store the password in the client-side script. Client-side scripts are visible to users, so you would compromise your password. See Chapter 6 in this mini-book to see how to use the new ASP.NET `Login` controls to validate passwords.

Book III
Chapter 5

Laying Out Your Site

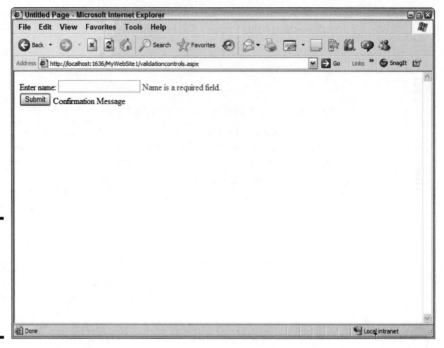

Figure 5-1:
The error
message is
displayed
next to the
required
text box.

---

3. **Type a name in the text box and press the Tab key.**

   The error message goes away.

4. **Delete the name from the text box and press the Tab key.**

   The message appears again.

5. **Type a name in the text box again and click the Submit button on the page.**

   The button's Click event is sent to the server for processing because the text box has a value in it, as required by the RequiredFieldValidator control.

6. **The page displays Page is valid! next to the button.**

   You may be wondering why the Page is valid! message wasn't displayed earlier, when you typed a name in the text box in Step 3 and the error message disappeared. For the message to appear, the data must be sent to the server. The data can be sent only if the validation control confirms that the data is valid when the button is clicked.

You can also mix and match validators. Often, multiple validations must be performed on a single control. For example, you may want to test whether a control has a value and whether the value conforms to a certain pattern, such as a phone number. In this case, you use a `RequiredFieldValidator` and a `RegularExpressionValidator`. The following example walks you through using the comparison and pattern validators to validate the same control:

1. **Drag and drop a label control and text box control to your Web page. Set the label's `Text` property to `Enter e-mail address`, and set the text box `ID` to `email1`.**

2. **Drag and drop another label control and text box control to your Web page. Set the label's `Text` property to `Re-enter e-mail address`, and set the text box `ID` to `email2`.**

3. **Add `RequiredFieldValidator` controls for each of the text boxes. Set the properties for the controls as described earlier in this section.**

4. **Add a `RegularExpressionValidator` control to the page.**

5. **Set the control's properties as follows:**

- `ValidationExpression` — Click the ellipsis and choose Internet E-mail Address.

- `Text` — Enter **E-mail address must be in the form user@company.com.**

- `ControlToValidate` — Select email1 from the drop-down list.

6. **Add a `CompareValidator` control to the page.**

7. **Set the control's properties:**

- `ControlToCompare` — Select email1.

- `ControlToValidate` — Select email2.

- `Text` — Type **Must match e-mail address above.**

8. **Press Ctrl+F5 to run your site and test the validators.**

Your page should look similar to the one shown in Figure 5-2.

Notice how the error message for the `RegularExpressionValidator` doesn't align next to the text box. That's because a placeholder for `RequiredFieldValidator` is sitting between the text box and the `RegularExpressionValidator` error message, as in this abbreviated code:

```
<asp:TextBox ID="email1" runat="server"></asp:TextBox>
<asp:RequiredFieldValidator>E-mail address is
    required.</asp:RequiredFieldValidator>
<asp:RegularExpressionValidator>Email address must be in the
    form user@company.com.</asp:RegularExpressionValidator>
```

**Book III
Chapter 5**

Laying Out Your Site

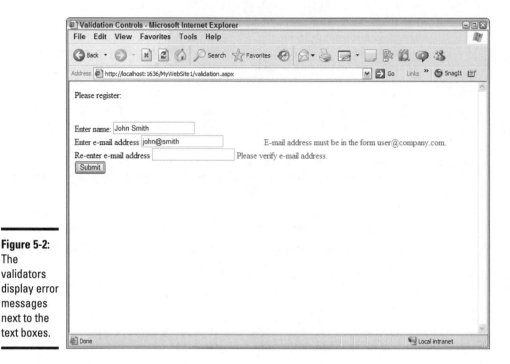

To eliminate the placeholder, change the `Display` property on `RequiredFieldValidator` from `Static` to `Dynamic`. Now your error message flows with the page layout.

Rather than display your messages next to text boxes, you can display them in a message box on the page. Follow these steps:

1. **Add a `ValidationSummary` control to the top of your page.**

2. **Type** Please correct these errors: **in the `HeaderText` property.**

3. **Set the `ErrorMessage` property on each of your validation controls to the message you want to display in the `ValidationSummary` control.**

4. **Put an asterisk in the `Text` property of each of your validation controls.**

5. **Press Ctrl+F5 to run your site and test it.**

The ValidationSummary control displays all error messages at the top of the page, as shown in Figure 5-3.

Now the user receives all error messages at the top of the screen after clicking the Submit button. An asterisk is displayed next to the text boxes, which makes an interesting demonstration of the `ErrorMessage` and `Text` properties:

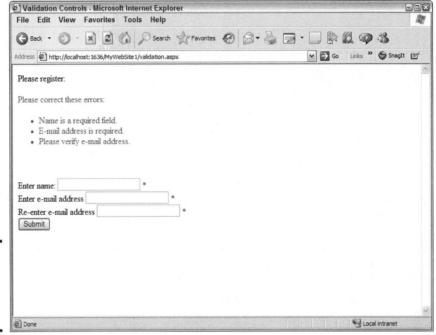

Figure 5-3:
Your site
should look
similar to
this one.

✦ Use the `ErrorMessage` property along with the `ValidationSummary` control when you want to display all feedback in a single place on the screen at one time.

✦ Use the `Text` property to display immediate feedback next to the control being validated.

Combining these approaches allows the user to see a visual cue next to the text box in question. These properties can accept text, HTML, or images.

You can group validation controls by using the `ValidationGroup` property. You can then use, for example, two `ValidationSummary` controls on a single page.

Mapping Out Your Site Navigation

ASP.NET provides built-in support for Web site navigation by using a combination of a site map and a set of navigation controls driven by the site map.

A *site map* is a logical description of the layout of a Web site. Visual Studio includes the following navigation controls:

✦ Menu

✦ SiteMapPath

✦ TreeView

Adding a site map

ASP.NET supports an XML-file-based site map by default. You can use a database-driven site map, if you choose. The syntax for the site map uses these two nodes:

✦ <sitemap> — The root node of the sitemap document contains all the <sitemapnode> nodes.

✦ <sitemapnode> — Each node represents a page on your Web site. Nodes can be nested.

The <sitemapnode> node has these attributes:

✦ Description — The page description

✦ Title — The page title

✦ URL — The URL for accessing the page

You can also specify a collection of roles that can access <sitemapnode> and a collection of custom attributes. These roles are likely to be used with a custom site map provider.

To create a new site map for an existing Web site, follow these steps:

1. **Right-click the Web site's project folder in Solution Explorer and choose Add New Item from the context menu.**

The Add New Item dialog box appears.

2. **Click the Site Map icon.**

Don't change the name of the site map.

3. **Click the Add button to add the site map to your Web site.**

Visual Studio opens a new site map file in Document Explorer.

4. **Type the URL, title, and description in the siteMapNode tags for each page in your Web site, as shown in Figure 5-4.**

You can add as many siteMapNode tags as required. SiteMapNodes can be nested to create a tree of nodes.

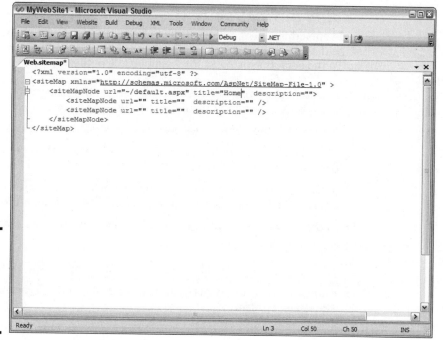

Figure 5-4:
Type your
page
information
in the site
map file.

Suppose that you have a Web site with the following four pages:

+ default.aspx

+ about.aspx

+ blogs.aspx

+ bookmarks.aspx

The following bit of code creates a site map you can use to describe access
to the four pages:

```
<siteMapNode url="~/default.aspx" title="Home">
   <siteMapNode url="~/about.aspx" title="About the site" />
   <siteMapNode url="" title="My Research Page">
     <siteMapNode url="~/blogs.aspx" title="Blogs I Read" />
     <siteMapNode url="~/bookmarks.aspx" title="Sites I
   Visit" />
   </siteMapNode>
</siteMapNode>
```

Adding navigation controls

To do something meaningful with the site map, you must include it with one of the navigation controls to display its contents. To add a `TreeView` control to the default.aspx page, for example, follow these steps:

1. Drag and drop the `TreeView` control from the Navigation tab of the toolbox into Design view of the default.aspx page.

An image of the `TreeView` control appears along with a list of tasks.

If the list of tasks isn't displayed, click the glyph in the upper-right corner of the `TreeView` control.

2. In the TreeView Tasks list, click the drop-down arrow for Choose Data Source. Click `<New Data Source>` from the drop-down list.

3. In the Data Source Configuration Wizard, click the Site Map icon.

4. Click OK.

The tree view is updated to reflect your site map, as shown in Figure 5-5.

5. Run your Web site by pressing Ctrl+F5 and test the hyperlinks in your `TreeView` control.

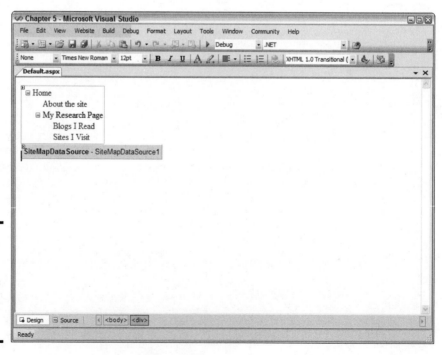

Figure 5-5:
The TreeView control gets it data from the site map.

Managing Your Site's Appearance with Themes and Master Pages

Visual Studio and ASP.NET provide two new tools for managing the "look and feel" of your Web sites:

+ **Themes and skins:** Easily separate the appearance attributes of controls from the controls themselves.

+ **Master pages:** Create a single page template to use with all your content pages.

Themes and master pages make administering your Web site easier. When you use themes and master pages, visitors can personalize their user experience on your Web site. For more information on personalization, see Chapter 6 of this mini-book.

Using themes and skins

A *theme* defines the look and feel of your Web site. Themes include these elements:

+ **Skins** — A set of properties that define a control's appearance

+ **Cascading style sheet (CSS)** — A standard for defining the appearance and layout attributes of HTML elements

See the section "Laying It Out with CSS," later in this chapter, for more information about creating cascading style sheets.

+ **Images** — Files that define the site's appearance, such as company logos

A theme has, at minimum, a skin file. Some overlap occurs between skins and CSS because both are used to control appearance. They have some crucial differences, however:

+ **Skins don't cascade.** Unlike with CSS, where you can create a hierarchy of styles, you define one skin for each type of control you use on your site. See the sidebar "Cascading styles" for more details on how CSS styles cascade.

+ **Skins define properties for ASP.NET Web server controls.** CSS styles apply to HTML elements.

+ **Skins apply to a single Web server control.** Styles can apply to a single HTML element or to collections of elements.

+ **Styles can be used to control the positioning of elements on a page.**

Cascading styles

A *CSS style* is a set of attributes that define the appearance and layout of an HTML element. For example, you can create a CSS style that sets a paragraph to use a specific font and font size. Think of a Web page as a container that holds containers of HTML elements. Paragraphs and div tags are examples of containers that hold content and other HTML elements.

You can define styles for each container (such as a Web page or a paragraph). As you define styles, the styles closest to the content are applied. For example, you may define a style

that sets the font color to black and the font family to Arial at the Web page level. If you define another style at the paragraph level that sets the font color to red, the content inside the paragraph is red. The font family is Arial, as defined for the Web page, unless you define a different font family for the paragraph.

In this way, styles cascade like a waterfall from higher-level containers to lower-level containers. The style elements defined closest to the content win over style elements defined in higher containers.

Here are some guidelines for choosing between skins and styles:

✦ Use skins to set properties specific to Web server controls.

✦ Use skins whenever you want to provide personalization features for your visitors.

✦ Use styles to set site-wide or page-wide properties, such as fonts.

✦ Use styles to control your page layout.

I recommend using skins to define general properties. If you need to define the appearance of a single element on a page, use styles.

Adding a theme to an existing site

You define themes for individual Web pages, an entire Web site, or all sites hosted on a Web server.

To add a theme to a Web site and associate the theme with the site, follow these steps:

1. **Right-click the Web site's project folder in Solution Explorer and choose Add ASP.NET Folder. Choose Theme from the submenu.**

A theme folder is added to the project.

2. **Enter a name, such as** MyTheme, **for the theme folder.**

You can rename themes by right-clicking and choosing Rename from the theme folder's context menu.

3. **Double-click the web.config file in Solution Explorer to open it.**

All your Web site configuration information is stored in the web.config file.

4. **Add the theme attribute to the page node in the web.config file so that the node looks like this:**

```
<pages theme="MyTheme">
```

5. **Close the web.config file and save the changes when you're prompted.**

All pages on your Web site now use the skins and the style sheet you add to the MyTheme folder.

Adding a theme as a style sheet

You can also apply a theme as a style sheet. A style sheet theme cascades like a style sheet, which means that local page settings take precedence over the theme. To set the Web site to use a style sheet theme, use this code rather than the code in Step 4 in the preceding set of steps:

```
<pages StyleSheetTheme="MyTheme">
```

To apply a theme to an individual page on your Web site, specify the proper attribute on the page's directive line, like this:

```
<%@ Page Theme="MyTheme" %>
<%@ Page StyleSheetTheme="MyTheme" %>
```

To apply a theme to all sites on a Web server, add a Themes folder to the path iisdefaultroot\aspnet_client\system_web\version\. Add your themes to the Themes folder. You can also add the Theme attribute to the pages element in the Web server's machine.config file.

Defining skins

Before you can start defining skins, think about the steps for creating your page layout and design:

1. Identify all common elements that you expect to use repeatedly throughout your site. You want to think in abstract terms about how many headings you want and how each one is different from the others. Picture your content in sections, such as sections for searches, What's New information, RSS feeds, and banner ads.

2. Decide which pages, if any, are unique. For example, a site commonly has a unique home page, and then individual pages reuse common elements.

3. Decide whether you want to use skins or styles to control the site's appearance. You can always change your mind later.

4. Implement your skins and styles.

5. Test your layout frequently. Don't be afraid to change your mind.

Try not to get hung up on whether you should implement a skin or a style. I've used styles for a long time, so I lean toward using them. Remember that your goal is to have working software. Don't fret over best-practices implementation. Go with what works, and don't be afraid to change your approach later.

The process of going through and changing your approach to solving a problem is *refactoring*. Although this process is often used in the context of building software libraries, it applies to any situation in which you have to make design choices. Choosing to use skins may make perfect sense today, but you may decide to implement style sheets later, when you're upgrading the site. The point of refactoring is to allow yourself the freedom to make a decision now with the understanding that you can change your mind in the future.

In this example, I assume that you're creating a Web site with these elements:

✦ A header to place elements such as your site's name and logo

✦ A sidebar on the left side for navigation

✦ A footer to place elements such as copyright information

✦ A main content area

The main content area is the part of the screen that changes dynamically. To define skins for both recurring content and one-off elements, suppose that you identify that you need these labels:

✦ A Web site title

✦ Sidebar content

✦ Header content

✦ A page content title

✦ Default content

The easiest way to build skins for controls is to add the control to a page, set the control's properties, copy the generated ASP.NET markup code to the skin file, and delete the ID property. To create a skin for the Web site title, follow these steps:

1. **Drag and drop a label control onto a page on your Web site.**

2. **Press F4 to display the label's properties.**

3. Set these properties:

- Bold = True
- Name = Verdana
- Size = X-Large
- ForeColor = DarkRed

You can set the properties however you like. I use these values only as an example.

4. Click the Source tab to display the page's source markup.

5. Copy the markup for the label you created and paste it in your skin file.

You add skin files the same way you add any new item: Right-click the App_Themes folder and choose Add New Item.

6. Delete the ID and Text attributes from your label's markup.

7. Add the attribute SkinID="siteTitle" to the label's markup.

8. Add a comment above your label, like this:

```
<%-- Web site title --%>
```

Repeat this process to add all your labels to the skin file.

To apply a skin to an individual control, you set the control's SkinID property to the SkinID you set in the skin file. For example, to apply the skin you create in the preceding set of steps to a label, follow these steps:

1. Add a label control to your Web page.

2. Set the label's SkinID property to siteTitle.

To test whether your skin is working, add text to your label and press Ctrl+F5 to run your Web site.

A skin that uses a SkinID is a *named* skin. You can also define a default skin that applies to all controls of the same type by not using a SkinID. For example, the following skin applies to all label controls that use the theme with this skin:

```
<asp:Label runat="server" cssclass="label" />
```

You can use skins with CSS styles. For example, the following label control uses a CSS style. Any skins defined for the page are applied also.

```
<asp:Label runat="server" cssclass="labelstyle" />
```

Mastering master pages

In the old days of development, developers used server-side includes and user controls to create a page template feel for their Web sites. Using the new ASP.NET master page feature, you no longer have to copy and paste repetitive code into your Web pages to create a template effect.

Although you could create page templates in previous versions of ASP.NET, you needed some coding expertise. The visual designer in Visual Studio didn't support custom page templates, either. Now, Visual Studio has visual designer support for master pages.

The master page looks and feels like any Web page, with two major differences:

✦ Master pages aren't called from the browser.

✦ The `ContentPlaceHolder` control on the master page is replaced with content from a content page.

Think of the master page as the template for your Web site. Any content that you want repeated on each of your Web sites is added to this page. For example, add the header and footer and any navigation element to your master page. After you associate your content pages with your master page, those elements appear on all your content pages.

To add a master page to an existing Web site:

1. **Right-click the Web site's project folder in Solution Explorer and click Add New Item.**

The Add New Item dialog box appears.

2. **Click the Master Page icon.**

3. **Click the Add button to add the master page to the Web site.**

Visual Studio creates the master page and adds it to the Web site.

Adding content to your master page

Adding content to a master page is similar to adding content to any Web page. If you use table layout, add a table and start adding your header, footer, and other elements. If you use CSS layout, add `div` tags or other placeholders you like to use. See the section "Laying It Out with CSS," later in this chapter, for more information on CSS layout.

You can also use ASP.NET expressions to add content to your master page. You can use expressions to add content to your page without typing the content in the page. For example, you can place information in a separate configuration file and then display that information on your master page. When you want to update the information, you only have to make a change in your configuration file.

Many people add configuration information to the AppSettings section in the web.config file. To add copyright information to the AppSettings section of an existing Web site, follow these steps:

1. **Choose Website⇨ASP.NET Configuration.**

The Web Site Administration Tool opens in your browser.

2. **Click the Application tab.**

3. **In the Application Settings section, click the Create Application Settings link.**

4. **In the Name text box, type** copyright.

5. **In the Value text box, type** &copy 2006 MySite, **as shown in Figure 5-6.**

6. **Click the Save button.**

The name/value pair is saved in the <appSettings> section of the web.config file.

7. **Click OK and close your browser.**

Any time you want to change the site's copyright information, use the Web Site Administration Tool.

The syntax for an ASP.NET expression is

```
<%$ expressionPrefix: expressionValue %>
```

ASP.NET expressions are often used for managing connection strings to database resources. For more information on managing connection strings, see Book IV, Chapter 5.

To use your new copyright on your Web site, follow these steps:

1. **Drag and drop a Literal server control from the toolbox to your master page.**

2. **Set the control's Text property equal to** <%$ AppSettings: copyright %>.

Your copyright is displayed in Design view on the master page, as shown in Figure 5-7.

The ContentPlaceHolder control you see in Figure 5-7 is where the content from your content pages appear. The control is added by default to the master page.

Book III
Chapter 5

Laying Out Your Site

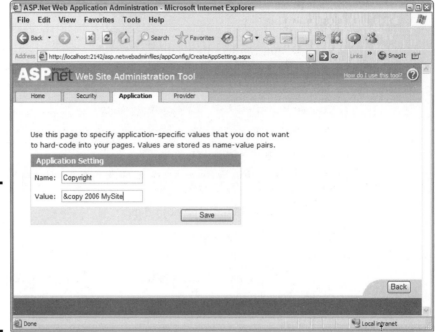

Figure 5-6:
Add
application
settings
with the
ASP.NET
Web Site
Administra-
tion Tool.

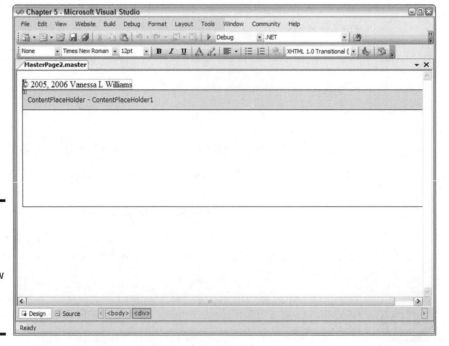

Figure 5-7:
The
copyright
appears in
Design view
of the
master
page.

Adding new content pages

Without content from your Web pages, a master page is nothing more than a shell. You must add new Web pages to your site and associate them with the master page.

To add new content pages to use with your master page, follow these steps:

1. **Right-click the Web site's project folder in Solution Explorer. Choose Add New Item from the context menu.**

   The Add New Item dialog box appears.

2. **Click the Web Form icon.**

3. **Enter a name for the Web form in the Name text box.**

4. **Select the Select Master Page check box.**

5. **Click the Add button.**

   The Select a Master Page dialog box appears.

6. **Click the master page that you want to associate with the Web form.**

7. **Click OK.**

The new Web form is different from a free-standing Web form in several ways:

✦ The attribute `MasterPageFile` is added to the `@Page` directive.

✦ A `ContentPlaceHolder` server control is added to the Web form.

✦ None of the usual HTML markup is present.

A page associated with a master page can't be executed on its own. As you add content to the page by using Design view, Visual Studio adds the content to the `ContentPlaceHolder` control on the page.

You can convert existing Web pages for use with master pages. I suggest that you walk through the steps in this section so that you can see the differences between a Web page that doesn't use a master page and one that does. Then you can modify your Web page to make it work with the master page.

Accessing the master page

You can make your content pages and master pages talk to each other. For example, you can store the content page's title in the content page and then display the title on the master page.

To use the best-practices guideline, display a title for each page on the browser's title bar by using the HTML element title. The problem is that

**Book III
Chapter 5**

Laying Out Your Site

when you use master pages, the title element is on the master page. You need to display the title from the content page using the title element on the master page.

To set the master page's title element by using content from the content page, follow these steps:

1. **Add this script to the master page Source view between the `<head></head>` tags:**

```
<script runat="server">
    Dim m_Title As String

    Public Property Title() As String
        Get
            Return m_Title
        End Get
        Set(ByVal value As String)
            m_Title = value
        End Set
    End Property

Sub Page_Load(ByVal sender As Object, ByVal e As
    EventArgs)
        If Not Page.IsPostBack Then
            Mytitle.DataBind()
        End If
End Sub
</script>
```

This Visual Basic code example creates a `Title` property for the master page. When the page loads, the master page's `DataBind` method is called on the `MyTitle` control, which tells the control to load data. For more information about data binding, see Book IV, Chapter 2.

2. **Add an `ID` attribute to the master page's title element:**

```
<title id="Mytitle">
```

The **ID** attribute makes it possible to access the title element with a script.

3. **Add the following ASP.NET expression between the opening and closing title tags:**

```
<%# me.Title %>
```

The title element appears this way:

```
<title id="Mytitle">
  <%# me.Title %>
</title>
```

The expression evaluates to the `Title` property you create in Step 1.

4. On the content page, add this directive below the `@Page` directive:

```
<%@ MasterType virtualpath="~/MasterPage.master" %>
```

The `@MasterType` directive creates a link between the content page and the master page so that you can access the master page's `Title` property.

5. Add this script to the content page just below the `@MasterType` directive you added in Step 4:

```
<script runat="server">
    Protected Sub Page_Load(ByVal sender As Object,
ByVal e As System.EventArgs) Handles Me.Load
        Master.Title = "My Page Title"
    End Sub
</script>
```

This Visual Basic code example sets the `Title` property of the master page to `My Page Title`.

6. Run your site by pressing Ctrl+F5.

Your Web page displays the title on the browser's title bar, as shown in Figure 5-8.

Book III
Chapter 5

Laying Out Your Site

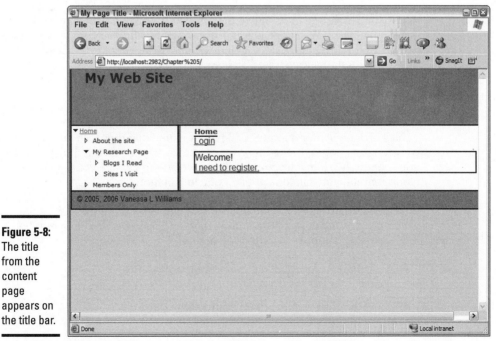

Figure 5-8:
The title from the content page appears on the title bar.

You aren't limited to using the title in the title element. You can use it with any server control. For example, to display the title in a label control, you use the following code:

```
<asp:Label ID="TitleLabel" runat="server">
  <%# me.Title %>
</asp:Label>
```

Just remember to call the control's `DataBind` method. In this case, you would call `TitleLabel.DataBind()`.

Laying It Out with CSS

You may be familiar with using Cascading Style Sheets (CSS) for setting fonts and background images. CSS also provides attributes for laying out and positioning elements on a Web page.

Regardless of whether you use master pages, you need a way to lay out your Web pages. Until the past few years, everyone used tables to lay out their Web pages. Using tables was a pain because of all the markup that was involved. The World Wide Web Consortium (W3C) intended for tables to be used for displaying tabular data, not for laying out Web pages. Without an alternative, many designers used tables to lay out their Web pages, too.

Microsoft is starting to acknowledge that Web design has been moving away from table-based Web page layout for a while. Finally, the company's next wave of Web design products includes visual designers for CSS layout, and it's committed to supporting CSS layout and positioning in its Internet Explorer Web browser.

Laying out a Web page by using table-based layout requires tables and sometimes nested tables. The large amount of HTML markup required to create tables obscures your content. CSS layout eliminates the table markup tags in your content pages. Using CSS, you can store all your layout information in a file separately from your content. If you decide to change your layout or your content, you can look at each one in isolation.

Visual Studio provides a style builder you can use for building CSS style rules. It helps if you're a little conversant in CSS syntax first. In a nutshell, CSS syntax is composed of these elements:

✦ **A selector** — An HTML element or custom-defined element that gets styled

✦ **A declaration** — A set of attribute/value pairs.

Here are some examples of selectors:

✦ **HTML elements** — Examples are h1, a, and input.

✦ **Classes that can be applied to any element** — Classes use the syntax .class.

✦ **IDs that can be applied to any element** — Only one style ID can be used per page. IDs use the syntax #id.

Here are a couple of examples of declarations:

✦ Single-value declarations, such as color: black;

✦ Multiple-value declarations, such as border: solid thick black;

Put together a selector and some declarations, and you have a style rule that looks like this:

✦ Applies to instances of the HTML element p:

```
p
{
    color: Black;
    font: arial;
}
```

✦ Applies to all HTML elements with the attribute class="container":

```
.container
{
    clear: both;
    border: solid thin red;
}
```

✦ Applies to the single HTML element on the page using the attribute id="header":

```
#header
{
    position: relative;
    width: 798px;
}
```

Here are some of the layout and positioning elements you should know about:

✦ **Top, Bottom** — Sets the top or bottom position of an element

✦ **Left, Right** — Sets the left or right position of an element

✦ **Height, Width** — Sets the height or width of an element

✦ **Z-index** — Sets the layer of an element where higher-order elements appear on top of lower-order elements

✦ **Position absolute** — Designates that an element is positioned according to the exact settings of the top, bottom, left, and right positions and the z-index

✦ **Position relative** — Designates that an element flows with the page layout and that any positioning attributes are relative to the flow of the page

Adding and creating CSS styles

You add CSS style rules to a style sheet. To add a style sheet to an existing Web site's theme folder, follow these steps:

1. **Right-click the Web site's App_Themes folder in Solution Explorer. Choose Add New Item from the context menu.**

The Add New Item dialog box appears.

2. **Click the Style Sheet icon.**

3. **Click the Add button.**

A style sheet is added to the folder.

Using Visual Studio to create styles is a two-step process:

1. **Add a style by choosing Styles⇨Add Style Rule.**

2. **Build the style by choosing Styles⇨Build Style.**

To create a style for all paragraphs on your Web site, follow these steps:

1. **Choose Styles⇨Add Style Rule.**

The Add Style Rule dialog box appears.

2. **From the Element drop-down list, select the HTML element for paragraph, P.**

3. **Click the arrow button in the center of the dialog box to move the P element into the Style Rule Hierarchy box on the right.**

Use the style rule hierarchy to create styles that select elements nested within elements, classes, or element IDs.

4. **Click OK to add the style to the style sheet.**

To build a style for the paragraph style, follow these steps:

1. **Choose Styles⇨Build Style.**

The Style Builder window appears.

2. **On the Font tab, click the Family ellipsis button. Use the Font Picker to select a font family, such as Arial.**

3. **Set additional attributes, such as font size and effects.**

4. **Click OK to build the style.**

The style builder builds the style declaration in the style sheet for you.

You can use the style builder to build the CSS layout for your Web page. To create a page template with a header, a left-side sidebar for navigation, a content placeholder, and a footer, use the style builder to create the styles. Follow these steps:

1. **Add style rules for each of these classes:**

   - `wrapper`
   - `header`
   - `leftnav`
   - `content`
   - `footer`

Although it's common practice to make classes lowercase, it isn't required.

2. **Using the style builder, set the styles for each of the rules created in Step 1 so that they look like this:**

```
#wrapper
{
    width: 798px;
    height: 100%;
    text-align: left;
    margin: 0 auto 0 auto;
    border-left: solid thin black;
    border-right: solid thin black;
    border-bottom: solid thin black;
    background-color: White;
}

#header
{
    width: 100%;
    position: relative;
    height: 100px;
    border-bottom: solid thin black;
    background-color: #66CC33;
    vertical-align: middle;
}

#leftnav
```

```
        {
            position: relative;
            float: left;
            width: 200px;
            border-right: groove thick #66CC33;
        }

        #content
        {
            float: left;
            width: 70%;
            position: relative;
            margin-left: 25px;
        }

        #footer
        {
            clear: both;
            width: 100%;
            background-color: #66CC33;
            border-top: solid thin black;
            font-size: smaller;
            padding-bottom: 10px;
        }
```

3. **Add the following style to the Body element:**

```
        text-align: center;
        margin: 0;
        background-color: #CCFF99;
        font-family: Arial;
```

Use div tags to apply your layout classes to the master page Source view, as shown here:

```
<body>
    <form id="form1" runat="server">
        <div id="wrapper">
        <div id="header">
        </div>
        <div id="leftnav">
        </div>
        <div id="content">
            <asp:contentplaceholder id="mainContent"
    runat="server">
            </asp:contentplaceholder>
        </div>
        <div id="footer">
        </div>
        </div>
    </form>
</body>
```

Now, add content to your master page:

1. **Add a `TreeView` control in your `leftnav` `div` tags.**

2. **Add a `Breadcrumb` control to the content `div` tag before the content placeholder.**

3. **Add header information, such as your site name and site logo, in the header `div` tags.**

4. **Add your copyright information to the page footer.**

The page should look similar to the one shown in Figure 5-9.

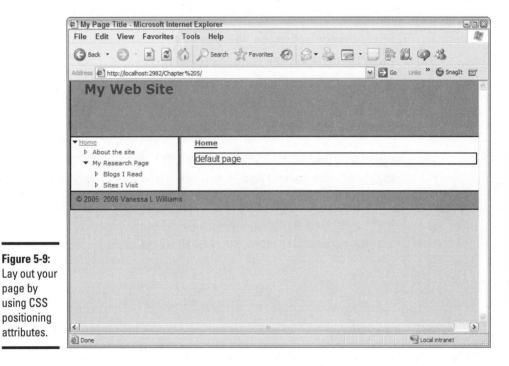

Figure 5-9:
Lay out your page by using CSS positioning attributes.

Learning to use CSS layout is no small feat. For more information, check out *CSS Web Design For Dummies,* by Richard Mansfield (Wiley Publishing, Inc.). Microsoft provides several design template starter kits that use CSS layout. You can download starter kits for free at `http://msdn.microsoft.com/asp.net/reference/design/templates`.

To apply your style sheet to an existing Web page, follow these steps:

1. **Drag your style sheet from Solution Explorer.**

2. **Drop the style sheet on the Web page.**

Visual Studio adds a `link` tag to your Web page, to associate it with the style sheet.

Applying styles to controls

You have a few options for applying styles to controls. For example, you can create CSS classes to store styles. To apply a CSS class to a server control, follow these steps:

1. **Select the control on the Web page.**

2. **Press F4 to display the control's properties.**

3. **Add your CSS class to the `CssClass` property.**

You can also use the style builder to create styles for individual controls. To use the style builder with a control, follow these steps:

1. **Add a control to a Web page or select an existing control.**

2. **Right-click the control and choose Style from the context menu.**

The Style Builder window appears.

3. **Build your style by using the style builder.**

The style is applied to the control by using the control's `Style` property.

Chapter 6: Exploring ASP.NET Services

In This Chapter

✔ **Introducing ASP.NET 2.0 services**

✔ **Managing state in your Web site**

✔ **Creating a membership-enabled site**

✔ **Personalizing your Web site**

*I*t has never been a better time to be an ASP.NET Web developer. After all those years of building tools for constructing Web sites, Microsoft finally realized that Web developers are trying to solve the same types of problems, such as registering people, logging in registered users, creating a personalized user experience, and monitoring the status of Web applications.

The latest version of ASP.NET provides the services developers need in order to build professional-quality Web sites without having to reinvent the wheel with each new Web site. This chapter introduces you to those new ASP.NET services and shows you how to use Visual Studio to leverage ASP.NET services in your next Web site project.

What a Wonderful Provider!

ASP.NET 2.0 offers many new services that provide common Web development features. These services include

+ **Membership** — Creates and manages user accounts for providing access to a secure Web site

+ **Role Manager** — Adds role-based management to your user accounts

+ **Personalization** — Gives visitors to your site a personalized experience by storing user profile information or allowing them to create their own user experience with Web parts

+ **Session State** — Manages user sessions and chooses the data store that's appropriate for your situation

✦ **Site Navigation** — Shows your site visitors how to move around in your site by using site maps and navigation controls

✦ **Web Events** — Monitors and stores your Web site's health

As you can imagine, writing all the code yourself to provide these services would be time consuming. Each of these ASP.NET services provides a combination of Web server controls, public properties and methods that implement the service, and access to a data store that all work well right out of the box.

ASP.NET services are made possible by the ASP.NET provider model. A *provider* is a type of software architecture that allows a framework, such as ASP.NET, to provide sophisticated services while hiding the implementation details of those services. The ASP.NET provider model has four layers:

✦ **Controls** — This set of Web server controls serves as the visible face of the service.

✦ **Services** — This public set of properties and methods, accessible by using Web server controls, provides the functionality of the service.

✦ **Providers** — All the implementation details that make the service "just work" happen by using these bits of code.

✦ **Data Stores** — This physical layer saves and retrieves the provider's data.

Table 6-1 shows the four layers of the ASP.NET provider model.

Table 6-1	Layers of the ASP.NET Provider Model
Layer	*Sample Technologies*
Controls	Login, TreeView
Services	Membership, site navigation
Providers	SqlProvider, XMLProvider, custom provider
Data Stores	SQL Server, XML document, custom data store

Why all these layers of abstraction? Why not just pass your data from the controls to the database? Creating distinct layers provides these benefits:

✦ You can customize any of the provider's layers without breaking the way the service works.

✦ The default implementation offers sophisticated services that work well out of the box.

Most ASP.NET services use a SQL Server database with a predefined database schema as the data store. If you decide that you want to change the data store's schema or use a completely different data store, you can create your own provider to access the data store. Any Web server controls that you use keep working because the implementation details are hidden away in lower layers of the service.

For example, the Membership service uses a SQL Server database by default to store membership data. To use a new data store, such as an XML file, with the service, you need to create a new provider. After you implement the details of accessing the XML data store in your new provider, telling the Membership service to use the new data store is a matter of changing the `SQLProvider` entry in the configuration file to `MyCustomXMLProvider`. Your membership-enabled Web site keeps working because the login controls are hidden from the details of the data store.

Using these ASP.NET services is a matter of using the controls associated with the service or setting configuration options in the Web site's `web.config` file.

Table 6-2 lists the ASP.NET services that use the provider model and the control or the `web.config` section that enables them.

Table 6-2	**ASP.NET Services and Their Controls**
Service	*Control or Type of Configuration Setting*
Membership	Login
Role management	`<roleManager>` section in web.config
Personalization	Web parts and `<profile>` section in web.config
Session state	Session object
Site navigation	Site map and navigation controls
Web events	`<healthMonitoring>` section in web.config

Book III
Chapter 6

Exploring ASP.NET
Services

This chapter walks you through the process of using membership, role management, personalization, and session state services. Chapter 5 in this mini-book covers site navigation.

If you're itching to get under the hood of the ASP.NET provider model so that you can create your own, custom providers, check out the ASP.NET Provider Toolkit: `http://msdn.microsoft.com/asp.net/downloads/providers/`.

Managing State

Web applications are different from other kinds of applications, such as Windows applications, because Web pages use the hypertext transport protocol

(HTTP) for communications between the browser client and the server. HTTP is a *stateless* protocol: After a Web page is rendered to the browser, the Web server severs its connection to the client. As a result, the Web server has no memory of anything your visitor clicks on the Web page.

To get around this limitation of HTTP, Web frameworks such as ASP.NET provide many services for storing and retrieving a Web page's data after a user performs some action, such as clicking a button, that requires processing on the server. Collectively, this process is known as *state management*.

You can use the ASP.NET state management features to develop your Web site without much consideration for how state is managed. ASP.NET takes care of all those details for you and hides their implementation. State management is one reason that frameworks such as ASP.NET are popular. Before ASP.NET, developers had to manage all state management details on their own. By using ASP.NET to handle the services of state management, you can focus on building your Web site.

The ASP.NET state-management offerings are client-side or server-side. Client-side state management stores state information on the client, and server-side stores state information on the server. Generally, you should use client-side state management for storing small amounts of short-lived information. Server-side state management is more secure and can store more state information over longer time intervals than client-side options can.

Your client-side choices are described in this list:

✦ **View state** — A property used by ASP.NET Web pages

✦ **Hidden-field** — A standard HTML hidden field

✦ **Cookies** — Files stored on the client's computer for saving key/value pairs

✦ **Query strings** — Key/value pairs appended to the end of a Web page URL

Here are the ASP.NET server-side offerings:

✦ **Application state** — Stores global values for the entire application to access

✦ **Session state** — Stores values for a user's session

✦ **Database** — Stores state information in a custom database

Regardless of whether you choose client-side or server-side management, ASP.NET uses these state-management features by default:

✦ View state stores all values associated with the Web server controls on a page.

✦ Application and session state are stored in server memory.

Understanding view state

Every time you add a Web server control to a Web page, you're using view state to capture any data associated with that control. For example, if you add a CheckBox server control to a Web page, the user's check box selection is stored in view state. ASP.NET removes the user's check from view state and sets the checked property on the check box equal to True. You don't have to know anything about view state to determine the check box's state. ASP.NET manages all that for you. You just query the check box's checked property.

You can use the view state to store your own data values independently of a Web server control. For example, to add a customer's identification number to a Web page's view state:

1. **Add a text box control and a button control to a Web page.**

2. **In Design view of the page, double-click a blank area of the design surface. Visual Studio creates a Page_Load event handler and opens the code editor.**

3. **Save the customer's identification number to the view state by using these lines of code:**

```
If Not Page.IsPostBack Then
    ViewState("CustID") = "123456"
End If
```

4. **In Design view of the page, double-click the button control. Visual Studio creates a Button Click event and opens the code editor.**

5. **To retrieve the customer's identification number from view state and display it in the text box, type this line:**

```
me.TextBox1.Text = ViewState("CustID").ToString()
```

6. **Press the Ctrl+F5 key combination to run your Web site.**

When you first run your Web site, the text box is empty. After you click the button, the value 123456 appears in the text box. Here's how it works:

1. When the page is first loaded in the browser, the Web page stores the value 123456 in its view state.

2. When you click the button, the browser sends the request to the Web server along with the view state. The Web server passes along the request with the view state data to ASP.NET.

3. ASP.NET picks apart the view state that the browser sent and provides state information to any controls. ASP.NET holds on to the 123456 value.

4. ASP.NET calls the `Page_Load` event. ASP.NET skips the code inside the `If` statement because the request is a postback.

A *postback* occurs when a request is sent from a Web page back to the Web server. See Chapter 4 in this mini-book for more information about postback.

5. The `Click` event is processed next, where `123456` is retrieved from the view state and placed in the text box.

The view state is a key/value dictionary. It acts like you would expect a dictionary to work. You add a key, such as `CustID`, and then a value, such as `123456`. You retrieve the value by using the key. Application state and session state are also key/value dictionaries. You add key/value pairs to application state and session state just as you do to view state:

```
Object("Key")  = "value"
```

Here's an example:

```
Application("AppStart") = Now
Session("CustID") = "123456"
```

Use view state whenever you need to

✦ Store small amounts of data, such as lookup keys for customer data or user identification data.

✦ Pass data from page to page and hide it from view.

Using session state

Whenever a user visits your Web site, a new session is created. ASP.NET creates a unique session identifier and associates it with the user's browsing session. You can store a collection of key/value pairs with the user's session. A collection of key/value pairs associated with a user's session is its *session state*.

Session state is enabled by default in ASP.NET. You can use session state to store information about a user's progress through your Web site on your Web server. Session state preserves the values across the lifetime of the user session as the user moves from page to page in your Web site.

Session state is stored in a dictionary and works similar to view state. You can use session state anywhere you would use view state. (See the preceding section for an example of how to use view state to store state information.)

Application state is similar to session state except that it stores values for the entire application, not just a single user's session.

Any time you need to store state, view state, session state, and application state are at your disposal, with no additional configuration required.

The Perks of Membership

One way to create a professional-looking Web site is to provide membership. Membership is the gateway to providing personalization features for your site, such as user profiles and Web parts. You can use membership to provide secure access to your Web site.

Before you can configure your Web site to use membership, you need to configure the default application services provider database. You must have SQL Server Express installed on your computer to set up the default provider database. After you do that, follow these steps:

1. **Launch the Aspnet_regsql.exe tool. (It's at *drive*:\WINDOWS\ Microsoft.NET\Framework*version number*).**

   The ASP.NET SQL Server Setup Wizard starts.

2. **Click the Next button to step through the wizard.**

3. **On the Select a Setup Option page, select Configure SQL Server for Application Services and click the Next button.**

4. **On the Select the Server and Database page, enter your database server's name and SQL Server instance, select Windows Authentication, and accept the `<default>` database. Click the Next button.**

   Be sure to enter your SQL Server instance, as shown in Figure 6-1. The default instance name for SQL Server Express is SQLExpress.

   Your settings are displayed on a summary page.

5. **Click the Next button to create the database.**

6. **Click the Finish button.**

You now have a default database that you can use for all ASP.NET services, including membership.

You need a Web site running on an IIS server in order to use the ASP.NET membership features. To create a Web site running on IIS, follow these steps:

1. **Choose File⇨New⇨Web Site.**

   The New Web Site dialog box appears.

2. **Click the ASP.NET Web Site template.**

3. **Select HTTP from the Location drop-down list.**

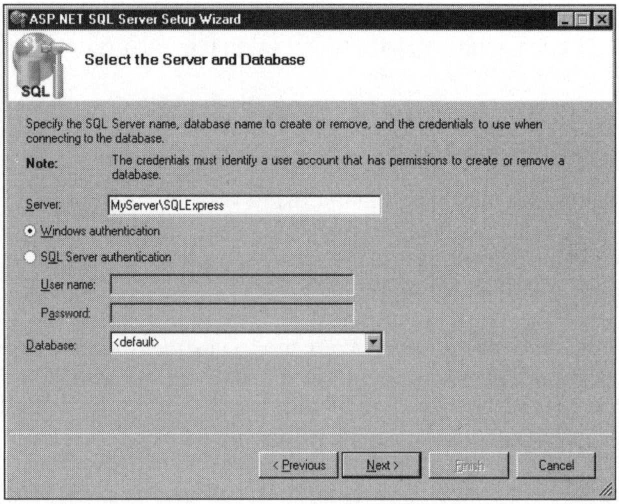

Figure 6-1:
Enter your
server name
and SQL
Server
instance
name.

4. **Click the Browse button.**

The Choose Location dialog box appears.

5. **Select Local IIS and then Default Web Site from the site hierarchy.**

6. **Click the Create New Web Application button, as shown in Figure 6-2.**

A new Web site is added to the site hierarchy.

7. **Enter a name, such as** MembershipWebSite, **and click the Open button.**

8. **Click OK.**

Visual Studio opens your new IIS Web site.

The easiest way to secure content is when it's organized into folders. Add folders named Members and Administrative to the Web site.

To configure membership for the Web site, follow these steps:

1. **Choose Website⇨ASP.NET Configuration.**

The ASP.NET Web Site Administration Tool is launched in a browser.

2. **Click the Security tab.**

3. **On the Security tab, click the link labeled Use the Security Setup Wizard to Configure Security Step By Step.**

The Security Setup Wizard starts.

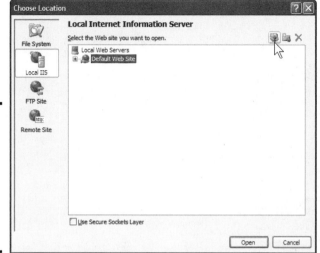

Figure 6-2:
Click the
Create
New Web
Application
button to
create a
new IIS
Web site.

4. **Click the Next button to step through the wizard.**

5. **In Step 2 of the wizard, select the From the Internet option. Then click the Next button.**

6. **Step 3 of the wizard confirms that you're using the default data store. Click the Next button to continue.**

7. **Use Step 4 of the wizard to define roles for your members. Select the Enable Roles for This Web Site check box and click the Next button.**

8. **Type a new role,** Administrators, **and then click the Add Role button. Repeat to add a Members role. Click the Next button to continue.**

9. **In Step 5 of the wizard, create a user account for yourself. Click the Next button.**

10. **In Step 6 of the wizard, click the plus (+) sign next to the MembershipWebSite directory hierarchy. Select the Administrative folder.**

11. **In the Rule Applies To section, select Administrators from the Role drop-down list.**

12. **Select the Allow option and click the Add This Rule button, in Figure 6-3.**

    The rule is added.

13. **Add a rule denying anonymous users access to the Members folder.**

14. **Click the Next button.**

    The wizard is complete.

**Book III
Chapter 6**

**Exploring ASP.NET
Services**

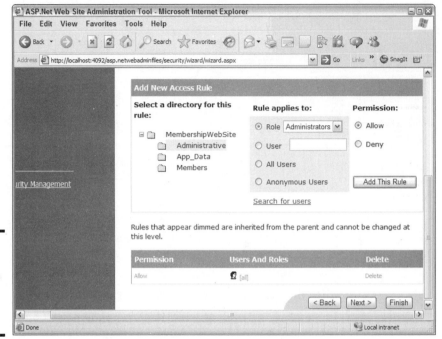

Figure 6-3:
Add an
access rule
for the
Adminis-
trator role.

15. **Click the Finish button to close the wizard and return to the Security tab.**

Use the Security tab to manage your users, roles, and access rules.

You need a way for people to log in to your Web site now that your site is set up for membership. Before ASP.NET 2.0, you had to create your own custom login pages. ASP.NET provides all the login controls you need in order to create a professional membership experience. The Login controls are shown in this list:

✦ Login — Provide the text boxes for username and password.

✦ LoginView — Create separate views for logged-in and anonymous users.

✦ LoginStatus — Tell users whether they're logged in to the site.

✦ LoginName — Display a user's login name.

✦ PasswordRecovery — Retrieve user passwords by using their e-mail addresses.

✦ CreateUserWizard — Provide controls for self-registration.

✦ ChangePassword — Allow users to change their passwords.

The Login controls are wired to work with the membership database. You don't have to write any code to make them work. The appearance of the Login controls is customizable using control templates.

Using the Login controls requires you to create a few Web pages. In your Web site, add these pages:

✦ `Login.aspx` — Your Web site's main login page must be named `Login.aspx` if you want to use the `LoginStatus` control.

✦ `Registration.aspx` — On this self-registration page, site visitors create their own usernames and passwords.

✦ `Members.aspx` — Add this page to your Members folder. A user must be logged in to your site in order to access the page.

Now that you have the membership set up, it's time to create your Web site's start page for logging in:

1. **Add a `LoginStatus` control from the Login group of the toolbox to default.aspx, the start page of your Web page.**

2. **Add a `LoginView` control to your start page.**

3. **In the `LoginView` control's AnonymousTemplate view, add a `Hyperlink` control from the Standard group in the toolbox.**

   The control has two view templates: Anonymous and Logged In. Access the view templates by clicking the arrow in the upper-right corner of the control.

4. **Press F4 to display the Properties window. Set these properties for the `Hyperlink` control:**

   • **Text: Type** I need to register.

   • **NavigateUrl:** Click the ellipsis and browse to registration.aspx.

5. **In the `LoginView` control's `LoggedInTemplate` view, type the text** Welcome, .

   Be sure to leave a space after the comma so that the user's name doesn't appear right next to the comma.

6. **Add the `LoginName` control to the `LoginView` control's `LoggedInTemplate` immediately following the text you entered in Step 5.**

7. **Press Ctrl+F5 to run your site.**

   Your page displays Anonymous Login view, as shown in Figure 6-4.

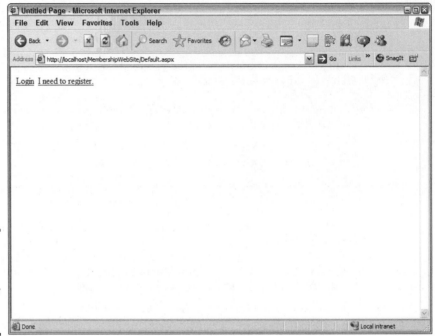

Figure 6-4:
The page
displays the
`LoginView`
anonymous
template.

Now you need to add login and user-registration capabilities to your site. To
set up the login page, Login.aspx, follow these steps:

1. **Add a Login control from the Login group of the toolbox.**

2. **Set the control's appearance by using the Auto Format feature.**

3. **Set the control's `DestinationPageUrl` property to the `default.`**
   `aspx` page in the Members folder.

To set up the registration page, `Registration.aspx`, follow these steps:

1. **Add the `CreateUserWizard` control from the toolbox's Login group.**

2. **Set the control's `ContinueDestinationPageURL` property to the**
   `default.aspx` page in the Members folder.

Run your Web site and test it. You should be able to log in and create a new
user account.

You can use membership and login controls in conjunction with master
pages. (Turn to Chapter 5 in this mini-book for more on master pages.)

Figure 6-5 shows you a master page using login controls in the Web site you create in Chapter 5 of this mini-book. I added, in the site's navigation, a Members Only link to the `default.aspx` page in the Members folder. Users who aren't logged in are directed to the login page.

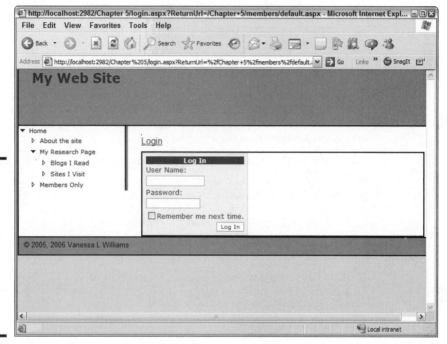

Figure 6-5: Member-ship and login controls go hand in hand with master pages and site navigation.

Book III Chapter 6

Exploring ASP.NET Services

Getting Personal

Even the simplest Web site now offers personalization features that allow a visitor to create a personalized user experience. This section introduces two ASP.NET personalization features: profiles and Web parts.

Profiling your visitors

A *profile* is used to store and retrieve user settings from a data source, such as a database. Examples of profile attributes include

✦ Contact information

✦ A favorite movie

✦ Preferences, such as themes

The ASP.NET profile service is easy to configure and use. It requires the application services default data store or another, custom data store of your choosing. (Refer to the earlier section, "The Perks of Membership," to see how to create the default data store.) If you already created the data store, the profile service uses it.

To enable profiles for your Web site, you must add the profile attributes to your Web site's web.config file. To add a favorite color attribute to your profile, follow these steps:

1. **Open the `web.config` file.**

The web.config file is an XML file that stores configuration settings for your Web site. To add a web.config file if your site doesn't have one yet, press Ctrl+Shift+A to open the Add New Item dialog box and select the Web Configuration File template.

2. **Between the `system.web` open and closing tags, add this code:**

```
<profile>
  <properties>
    <add name="FavoriteColor"
      type="System.String"  />
  </properties>
</profile>
```

It's that easy! You can start saving the favorite colors of all your logged-in users.

By default, only logged-in users can use properties. To allow anonymous users to use properties, follow these steps:

1. **Add this line to the web.config file:**

```
<anonymousIdentification enabled="true" />
```

2. **Add this line to the Properties section:**

```
<name="Property" allowAnonymous="true" />
```

To use the profile in your Web site, follow these steps:

1. **Add a `profiles.aspx` page to your Web site.**

2. **Add Label, Textbox, and Button server controls to the page.**

3. **Set the label's `Text` property to `Favorite Color:`.**

4. **Double-click the button to add code to its `Click` event. The code editor appears.**

5. **Type this line to set the profile attribute:**

```
Profile.FavoriteColor = Me.TextBox1.Text
```

6. **Double-click Design view of the page to access the page's Load event.**

The code editor appears.

7. **Type this line to load the profile's property:**

```
If Not Page.IsPostBack Then
    Me.TextBox1.Text = Profile.FavoriteColor
End If
```

To test your profile, run your site and log in. Enter a favorite color and click the button to save the profile.

Using Web parts

Web parts controls are the ultimate in personalization. What makes them powerful is that they allow users to customize their user experience. A visitor accessing a Web parts page can add and remove Web parts or change the layout of the page.

Web parts controls have three elements:

✦ **User interface controls** — These controls are the standard ASP.NET server controls, such as labels, text boxes, and buttons.

✦ **User interface structure components** — Structural components provide the layout and management features of Web parts. The two main structural components are the Web parts manager and the Web part zone.

✦ **Personalization layer** — This underlying infrastructure layer allows users to change the page layout by moving controls around or adding and removing controls from the page. Users' changes are saved permanently.

The Web parts controls are accessible from the WebParts group in the toolbox. You should be familiar with these Web parts:

✦ WebPartManager — Required by each page in order to manage the Web parts on the page.

✦ WebPartZone — Provides zones for laying out Web parts controls. A page can have multiple zones.

✦ CatalogZone — Provides a zone for creating a catalog of Web parts that a user can use to modify the page.

✦ EditorZone — Allows users to edit the Web parts on a page.

✦ ConnectionsZone — Enables you to create connections among Web parts.

Note that the zone-related controls are logical zones for working with Web parts. You're still responsible for laying out the page by using tables or CSS.

The main reason for using Web parts is their personalization features. Getting personalization up and running is no small feat. Use Web parts and Web parts pages for building portals that allow visitors to customize their views. A popular portal that uses Web parts is Microsoft SharePoint Portal Server 2003. SharePoint Portal Server's underlying infrastructure, Windows SharePoint Services, also uses Web parts.

Chapter 7: Building a Mobile Application

In This Chapter

✔ Exploring smart devices

✔ Creating applications for smart devices

✔ Building a mobile Web application

✔ Emulating smartphones

*O*ver the years, computers have insinuated their way into everyday life. Computers are used in machines from cars to refrigerators. All these computers need some kind of operating system to make them work. Sometimes, a company makes its own, proprietary operating system to go with a device, such as Palm personal digital assistants (PDAs). Other times, device manufacturers license their operating systems from companies such as Microsoft.

Microsoft provides several different flavors of operating systems for these devices. These versions of Windows, known as *smart devices,* are found in everything from ATMs and automobiles to cellular phones. Sometimes, these devices are mobile, in the case of cellular phones and PDAs. Other times, they're not, like the CD player or digital video recorder you may have connected to your living room television.

You can use Visual Studio 2005 to build software applications that run on smart devices. Visual Studio 2005 provides everything you need to connect to a smart device and test your application. If you don't have a physical smart device, you can use a device emulator for testing purposes.

As operating systems and hardware have become more robust, mobile devices now have the ability to move beyond being mere cell phone and personal information managers. More widespread adoption has users clamoring for everything from multimedia applications to business applications.

In this chapter, I explore two ways to use Visual Studio 2005 to create applications for smart devices:

✦ Build an application that runs on the device itself.

✦ Build a mobile Web site that users can access by using the Web browser on a smart device.

Developing Applications for Smart Devices

Building an application for a smart device by using Visual Studio 2005 is as simple as dragging and dropping. Unfortunately, a lot of forethought is required before you start developing mobile applications.

Mobile everything

Before you begin building applications for mobile devices, you have to identify the devices which you intend to work with. Mobile devices are in three general categories:

✦ **Smartphones** — These devices are used primarily as cellular phones. They have additional applications, such as calculators and note-taking tools, but don't include mobile versions of Office software, such as Word and Excel.

✦ **Pocket PCs** — These devices have touch screens and use mobile versions of Office applications, such as Word and Excel. Pocket PC Phone Edition uses cellular phone features.

✦ **Ubiquitous, embedded devices** — These devices aren't general-purpose computers, even though they have microchips embedded within them.

Microsoft groups its mobile strategy into these offerings:

✦ **Windows Mobile** — Includes smartphones and Pocket PCs

✦ **Windows CE Embedded** — Aren't device specific; embedded in everything from automobiles to industrial controllers

✦ **Tablet PC** — Uses a special version of Windows XP

✦ **Windows XP Embedded** — Used more in set-top boxes and points-of-sale where Windows XP security features are required

Any Windows XP application can run on a Tablet PC or a Windows XP Embedded device if the device is properly configured. The smart-device development options in Visual Studio 2005 don't apply to those devices.

Decisions, decisions

You have several options for building applications for smart devices. You have to decide whether to

✦ Target Windows Mobile or Windows CE or both

✦ Build managed applications using Visual Basic and C# or native code with C++

✦ Write server-side code

✦ Provide access to data

Some of these decisions are easier to make than others. For example, if you're not conversant in C++, writing an unmanaged application is challenging. I show you how to work through these decisions and go from there.

Pick your platform

Deciding which platforms to target is influenced by the problem you're trying to solve. For example, in a corporate environment, you probably have control over the kinds of devices employees are using, which makes the problem easier to solve. However, if you're trying to target multiple platforms, the problem is a bit trickier to solve.

Several flavors of Windows Mobile–based devices are on the market:

✦ Windows Mobile 5.0 (latest version code-named Magneto)

✦ Pocket PC 2003

✦ Smartphone 2003 and 2003 Second Edition

The distinction between Pocket PC and Smartphone is going away with the new version of Windows Mobile. Expect to see the Pocket PC platform merged with the Smartphone.

Windows Mobile-based devices already have the .NET Compact Framework installed on them. You can write managed applications using Visual Basic and C# to target the .NET Compact Framework on these devices.

If your device doesn't have the .NET Compact Framework installed, you have to install it.

Devices with Windows CE embedded may not already have .NET installed. Because these devices tend to be specialized models, you should consult the manufacturers' documentation before deciding to use them.

When you're picking your platform, you must also consider these issues:

✦ **Smartphones don't have touch screens.** Your application must be menu-driven (using the two soft keys on the number pad).

✦ **Pocket PCs have touch screens.** You aren't limited to developing a menu-driven application.

✦ **Windows CE devices are often embedded into all kinds of form factors.** The form factors may not use the Windows graphical user interface.

Know that the natives are restless

For the most part, smart device development has strictly been the domain of native code written in C++. Now that more memory and processing power can be packed into a smaller package, the arguments against using managed code are starting to fall away.

By using managed code, developers can use the rapid application development features of Visual Studio and create slicker user interfaces in less time.

One downside is that managed code requires the device to run the .NET Compact Framework, which increases the size of the application and the resources required to run it.

On the other hand, because unmanaged code doesn't require the .NET Compact Framework, applications run faster and require fewer resources. However, developers using unmanaged code must have significantly more technical skill, in order to develop applications by using C++.

Of course, some purists will always argue that unmanaged code runs faster than managed code. Although that may be true, the real question is whether it makes a difference to users. If they can't tell the difference, it becomes a matter of developer productivity. Similar arguments were made about the move from lower-level languages to higher-level languages. In most cases, developer productivity always wins out over hardware productivity.

Examples of applications created with C++ are utilities and games. You should use managed code for applications that have an intensive user interface and when developer productivity is required.

You can safely assume that any Windows Mobile-based device has adequate hardware to run managed code, although you should thoroughly stress-test your application before deploying it to production.

Go server-side

If the devices you need to target aren't running on a Windows Mobile-based platform or Windows CE, consider building a mobile Web application. Make sure that

✦ The devices have regular access to the Internet.

✦ You have enough bandwidth to accommodate your Web application.

✦ The user interface is device-friendly.

Access the data

Developing applications for smart devices that require data access is similar to working with data access in other kinds of Visual Studio projects. The special Microsoft database engine SQL Server Mobile is designed to work with smart device applications. You can use SQL Server Mobile to

✦ Keep a local copy of data stored on your smart device.

✦ Synchronize the local copy with a master copy.

SQL Server Mobile is the perfect approach to providing data access for smart devices that are occasionally connected to a network. For a detailed discussion on data access, see Book IV.

The next version of SQL Server to be designed for mobile devices is SQL Server 2005 Everywhere Edition. The software was released in a community technology preview (CTP) in June 2006. Like all CTPs, the software can be used in a testing environment. You can read more about SQL Server Everywhere, and download the CTP, at `www.microsoft.com/sql/ctp_ sqleverywhere.mspx`.

Differences in smart device development

When you develop smart device applications, you find that getting around in Visual Studio is similar to working with Windows applications. You can leverage everything you may already know about building applications with Visual Studio 2005. You create smart device applications in the same way as you create Windows applications — by dragging and dropping controls on the form — although a few conditions are different:

✦ You must choose a device or device emulator to connect to when you debug your application.

✦ Because smart devices use the .NET Compact Framework, you don't have access to the same things as you do in the .NET Framework.

✦ Testing is done on the device or device emulator, not on the development machine.

✦ Distributing applications requires a CAB file.

✦ You have to work with intermediary software, such as device emulators and ActiveSync, to connect to the device.

✦ You have to work within the constraints of the device itself (for example, the device has a small screen or lacks a touch screen).

A *CAB* file, or Microsoft Cabinet file, is used to compress many files into a single file. CAB files are often used with installation packages.

Saying "Hello, Smartphone!"

Visual Studio 2005 provides templates for creating device applications, class libraries, and console applications for Windows Mobile and Windows CE devices. You can also create control libraries for Pocket PC 2003 and Windows CE devices.

Getting your machine ready

Before you start building smart device applications, you have to take a few steps to get your machine ready. Visual Studio 2005 ships with project templates and device emulators for Pocket PC 2003 and SmartPhone 2003. The latest platform version for smart devices is Windows Mobile 5.0.

Before you start, download and install these programs:

✦ ActiveSync 4.1

✦ Windows Mobile 5.0 SDK for Pocket PC

✦ Windows Mobile 5.0 SDK for Smartphone

You need to download the software development kits (SDKs) for Windows Mobile 5.0 devices only if you plan to target those platforms with your application.

Microsoft provides a single tools page on its Mobile Developers Center portal, where you can download all these tools:

```
http://msdn.microsoft.com/mobility/windowsmobile/howto/
    windowsmobile5/install/default.aspx
```

Follow the installation instructions for each tool. You should be able to accept the defaults and install these tools without incident. If you have problems, go to the Windows Mobile support options page: http://msdn.microsoft.com/mobility/windowsmobile/howto/support/default.aspx.

Creating a smart device application

To create a new smart device application for a Smartphone 2003 model, follow these steps:

1. **Choose File⇨New⇨Project.**

   The New Project dialog box appears.

2. **In the Project Types tree, expand the Smart Device section.**

   A list of devices appears.

3. **Click to select Smartphone 2003.**

   A list of available project templates for this device is displayed.

4. **Click to select Device Application.**

5. **Type a name for the project, such as** MySmartPhoneApp, **shown in Figure 7-1.**

6. **Click OK to create the project.**

**Book III
Chapter 7**

**Building a Mobile
Application**

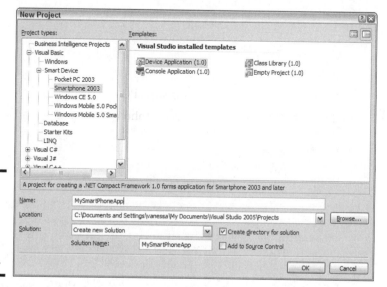

Figure 7-1:
Enter a
name for
the smart
device
application.

Visual Studio 2005 creates the smart device application and displays a forms designer. Rather than see a Windows form displayed, you see a device skin that looks like a smartphone. A main menu control is automatically added to the application because smartphone navigation is menu-driven.

To create the "Hello world!" application for the Smartphone 2003, follow these steps:

1. **Drag a label control from the toolbox and drop it on the device skin. If the toolbox isn't open, press Ctrl+Alt+X to open it.**

2. **Click the menu bar at the bottom of the device skin display. Type some menu text on the left and right menus.**

I typed `Main` on the left menu and `Hit Me!` on the right menu, as shown in Figure 7-2.

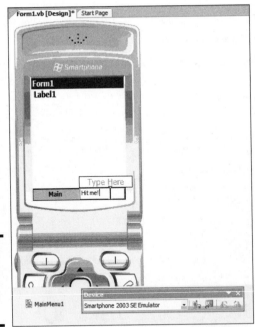

Figure 7-2:
Enter menu commands in the menu control.

On Smartphone devices, the left menu, or soft key 1, is used for affirmative actions (such as OK, Yes, and New), and the right menu, or soft key 2, is for Cancel or choosing menu options.

3. **Double-click the right menu to enter the code that's executed whenever a user selects the menu.**

A `Click` event is created, and the code editor appears.

4. Enter this line of code in the code editor:

```
Me.Label1.Text = "Hello world!"
```

5. Press Ctrl+F5 to run your device on the device emulator.

Visual Studio builds your application, and the Deploy dialog box appears.

6. Choose the Smartphone 2003 Emulator from the device list and click the Deploy button.

Your device application is executed on the emulator. Use your mouse to "press" the right soft key. The device application displays `Hello world!` on the screen, as shown in Figure 7-3.

Book III Chapter 7

Figure 7-3: Press the right soft key to execute your program.

Building a Mobile Application

You can also use the Device toolbar to select the specific device to connect to, connect to a device, and set device options. If the device toolbar isn't open, open it by choosing View➪Toolbars➪Device.

If you decide that you want your application to target a different platform such as the Pocket PC, making changes is simple. Follow these steps:

1. **Right-click the project name and choose Change Target Platform from the context menu.**

   The Change Target Platform dialog box appears.

2. **In the Change To field, change the platform to Pocket PC 2003, as shown in Figure 7-4.**

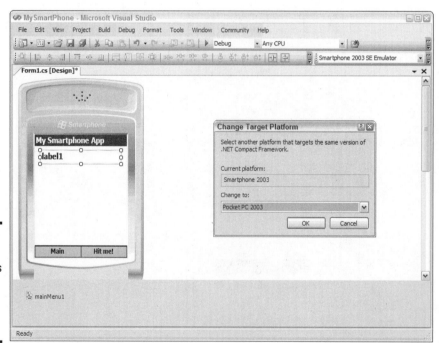

Figure 7-4:
Change the application's target platform to Pocket PC 2003.

3. **Click OK.**

   A confirmation window appears.

4. **Click Yes to confirm your choice.**

   Visual Studio closes and reopens the projects to reset the target platform.

To create a C++ smart device application, follow these steps:

1. **Choose File➪New➪Project.**

2. **In the New Project dialog box, expand the C++ project types.**

3. **Select Smart Device.**

4. **Select the MFC Smart Device Application template.**

5. **Name the project and click OK.**

   The MFC Smart Device Application Wizard appears.

6. **Click the Next button to start the wizard.**

7. **In the Platforms step, select the platforms you want to target and click the Next button.**

8. **Accept the defaults for the Application Type step, and click Finish to complete the wizard.**

The MFC application is created. The ReadMe.txt file offers a list and an explanation of the files created by the wizard. Open the MyMFCView.cpp file to add your code.

Building Mobile Web Applications

You can use Visual Studio 2005 to create Web sites specially designed for smart devices. You don't need to be a Web developer to do it.

You should be able to reuse your existing Web site development skills. Keep in mind, however, that building mobile Web sites requires you to do two things:

✦ Use mobile controls that can adapt to the device on which the Web site is being displayed.

✦ Display the Web site in a Web browser on the device itself, rather than in a Web browser on your local development computer.

Visual Studio uses mobile controls and device adapters to hide the complexity of building Web sites for multiple kinds of devices. As when you're building applications that run on smart devices, bear in mind that the user interface is restricted and some devices don't have touch screens. Also, your device must have network connectivity in order to access your Web server where the mobile Web site is hosted.

Setting up the mobile Web site

To create a Web site for a mobile Web application in Visual Studio 2005, follow these steps:

1. **Choose File⇨New⇨Web Site.**

The New Web Site dialog box appears.

2. **Select the ASP.NET Web Site template.**

3. **Select File System from the Location drop-down list.**

4. **Accept the default location to create the Web system. Type a name, such as** MobileWebSite, **at the end of the location.**

5. **Select Visual Basic from the Language drop-down list.**

6. **Click OK to create the Web site.**

The Web site is created, and Visual Studio opens the `default.aspx` page.

To turn the Web site into a mobile Web site, follow these steps:

1. **Delete the `default.aspx` page by right-clicking the page in Solution Explorer and choosing Delete from the context menu. Click OK in the confirmation window.**

The page is deleted.

`Default.aspx` is a regular ASP.NET Web Forms page.

2. **Add a Mobile Web Form page to the project by right-clicking the project in Solution Explorer and choosing Add New Item from the context menu.**

The Add New Item dialog box appears.

3. **Select the Mobile Web Form template.**

4. **Click the Add button.**

The page is added to the project.

You now have a fully functioning mobile Web site. You need to add your content to the Mobile Web Form you added in the preceding set of steps. For example, to create the "Hello world!" application, follow these steps:

1. **Press Shift+F7 to display the `default.aspx` page in the Visual Forms Designer.**

Alternatively, you can click the Design tab to display the page in Design view.

2. **In the toolbox, scroll down to the Mobile Web Forms section. Drag a label to the forms designer.**

   The Mobile Web Forms section is visible in the toolbox only when you have a Mobile Web Form open in the designer.

3. **In the Properties window, delete the word** *Label* **from the** `Text` **property.**

4. **Drag a Command button to the design surface and set the button's** `Text` **property to** `Hit me`.

5. **Double-click the Command button to display the Command's** `Click` **event.**

6. **Enter this line of code:**

   ```
   Me.Label1.Text = "Hello world!"
   ```

7. **Press Ctrl+F5 to run your Web site.**

Your mobile Web application is displayed in a Web browser. That's probably not what you want, though. Fire up your device emulator so that you can see what your mobile Web application looks like on your device.

Exploring device emulators

Before you can run your mobile Web site by using the Visual Studio Build command, you need to get your computer ready to work with the device emulator. Otherwise, your device can't communicate with the Web server on your local computer. To enable communication, you need to install ActiveSync, which you can download from Microsoft at `http://msdn.microsoft.com/mobility/windowsmobile/howto/windowsmobile5/install/default.aspx`. Follow the instructions on the Microsoft Web site to download and install ActiveSync. You should be able to follow all the default installation options without any problems.

After you install ActiveSync, the Get Connected Wizard appears. The wizard establishes a connection between ActiveSync and your device. If you're using a physical device, you should connect it now. Before you can connect to a device either physical or emulated, you must cradle it. To cradle a device emulator, follow these steps:

1. **Launch the Device Emulator Manager by choosing Tools⇨Device Emulator Manager in Visual Studio 2005.**

2. **Right-click one of the available emulators, such as the Pocket PC 2003 SE Emulator, and choose Connect from the context menu.**

   The emulator opens.

3. In the Device Emulator Manager, right-click the emulator name again. Choose Cradle from the context menu, shown in Figure 7-5.

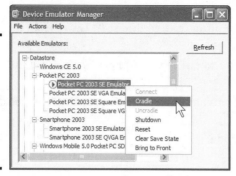

Figure 7-5:
Cradle the device emulator by using the Device Emulator Manager.

After the device is cradled, you can establish connectivity to it with ActiveSync. To connect to your cradled device or device emulator, follow these steps:

1. Click the Next button in the Get Connected Wizard.

The wizard searches all available ports for a cradled device.

2. When the device is found, the New Partnership step appears. Select the Guest Partnership option.

Guest partners don't synchronize data.

3. Click the Next button to advance the wizard.

ActiveSync connects to the device.

4. Minimize ActiveSync.

After your device or device emulator is connected to your PC using ActiveSync, you can view your mobile Web site on the device. Follow these steps to pull up the mobile Web site in the device emulator:

1. In the device emulator, click the Start button.

The Start menu appears.

2. Choose Internet Explorer.

3. On the Internet Explorer address bar, type the URL of the Web server where your mobile Web site is hosted.

The Web page is displayed in the device emulator, as shown in Figure 7-6.

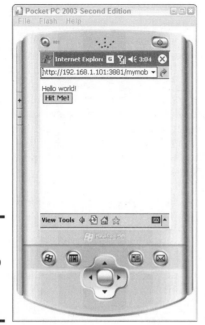

Figure 7-6:
Test your
mobile Web
site in a
device
emulator.

If you host your mobile Web site by using Microsoft Internet Information Services (IIS), you don't have to type the port number in the URL.

I suggest saving the state of your device emulator so that the next time you fire it up, Internet Explorer is already open. To save the state, choose File⇨ Save State and Exit. The next time you open that device emulator, it opens in the same state.

Automating your connection

Here are the high-level steps for using a device emulator to view your mobile Web application:

1. Connect to the device emulator.
2. Use the Device Emulator Manager to cradle the emulator.
3. Connect to the device by using ActiveSync.
4. Browse to your mobile Web application by using Internet Explorer on the device emulator.

You can automate a few of these steps, if you want. You can use the Visual Studio 2005 Browse With command to specify which browser you want to use for your Web site. You aren't restricted to just Web browsers — you can choose any kind of executable file, including batch files. That way, you can conveniently short-circuit all the steps involved in using an emulator.

A *batch file* is a text file with a series of commands in it. The commands you use in a batch file are the same ones you use on the command line or in the Run box that appears when you choose Run from the Windows XP Start menu. A batch file ends with the file extension .bat. When you execute a batch file, the commands in the file are executed just as though you were typing them on the command line.

To short-circuit all the steps involved in viewing your mobile Web site in a device emulator, use a batch file to open the device emulator and open the Device Emulator Manager.

The device emulator and Device Emulator Manager are installed by default in the file location C:\Program Files\Microsoft Device Emulator\1.0\. The device emulator needs to know the path to the saved state of the device you want to use. By default, state files are saved at C:\Documents and Settings\ *<username>*\Application Data\Microsoft\Device Emulator\. State files have the file extension .dess.

To create a batch file that opens these tools, follow these steps:

1. **Open Notepad or your favorite text editor.**

2. **In Notepad, type the command to open the device emulator:**

```
start /d "C:\Program Files\Microsoft Device Emulator\
    1.0\" deviceemulator.exe /s "C:\Documents and
    Settings\<username>\Application Data\Microsoft\
    Device Emulator\<GUID>.dess"
```

Replace *<username>* with your name. Your saved state filename should look something like {DE425A95-FBB8-46CB-8DFD-89867130F732}.dess.

3. **Type the command to open the Device Emulator Manager in Notepad:**

```
start /d "C:\Program Files\Microsoft Device Emulator\
    1.0\" dvcemumanager.exe
```

4. **Save your file and give it a name, such as** mydevice.bat.

To tell Visual Studio 2005 to use your batch file, follow these steps:

1. **Right-click on the project folder in Solution Explorer, and choose Browse With from the context menu.**

The Browse With dialog box appears.

2. **Click the Add button.**

The Add Program dialog box appears.

3. **Click the ellipsis button next to Program Name and browse to your `mydevice.bat` file.**

4. **Enter a name for the program in the Friendly Name text box. The friendly name appears in the Browse With dialog box.**

5. **Click OK.**

The Add Program dialog box closes, and your batch file is added to the Browse With dialog box.

6. **Click the Set As Default button to set your batch file as the default browser for this project.**

Figure 7-7 shows the Browse With dialog box after setting the default.

Figure 7-7:
Set your batch file as the default browser.

7. **Click the Browse button to launch your batch file.**

The device emulator you specified in the batch file opens. The Device Emulator Manager opens also. Use the device manager to cradle your device emulator. If the device emulator doesn't show that it's connected, press F5 to refresh the screen. After the device emulator is cradled, ActiveSync should automatically try to connect to it.

If your batch file fails, make sure that the commands are executed on a command line. If they don't work on the command line, they don't work in a batch file, either.

You can start multiple device emulators in a single batch file or create multiple batch files for each device emulator you want to run.

You need to execute your device emulator, cradle it, and connect to it only once. Afterward, you can build your Web site by using the Build menu and then refresh the browser in your device emulator.

Accommodating Special Considerations for Smart Device Applications

Even though Microsoft has made creating smart device applications super-easy, you must bear in mind that smart devices aren't just miniature Windows machines. Testing and deploying smart device applications is still a chore compared to testing and deploying regular Windows applications. Keep these considerations in mind as you start building smart device applications:

✦ A smartphone is designed to be used with one hand. Make sure that you emulate this one-handed experience when you test your application.

✦ ActiveSync doesn't always behave the way you expect. Be prepared to spend some time becoming comfortable with its idiosyncrasies.

✦ Be sure to read through the software development kit (SDK) for the device you're targeting. SDKs are quite informative.

✦ Security is a big concern with smart devices. Refer to the SDK for your device for more information on how to create security certificates for testing and deploying your application.

✦ In addition to the device's form factor, you must consider the battery life and memory constraints of the device you're targeting.

Book IV

Getting Acquainted with Data Access

"Now that we got Visual Studio, we should probably pimp our data storage system."

Contents at a Glance

Chapter 1: Accessing Data with Visual Studio

In This Chapter

✔ Taking a sneak peek at ADO.NET

✔ Getting acquainted with databases

✔ Adding data controls to Windows and Web Forms

*N*owadays, it's hard to find an application that isn't data-driven. Even if the application isn't centered around entering and viewing data, you may be surprised to find a tremendous amount of data access occurring behind the scenes — especially for Web sites. What may look like a static, boring Web site may be one that was built by using dynamic Web pages that get their content from a database.

Applications such as Windows SharePoint Services store all their information in databases. When a user uploads an Excel document to a SharePoint document library, for example, the file is stored in a database. Don't bother to traverse the file directory and look for the file, though, because it's not there.

Even when data isn't involved in an application, metadata may still be involved. *Metadata* is data about data, and it's showing up everywhere. For example, when you take a picture with a digital camera, the camera automatically stores the image resolution and thumb file format. This information, which is the image's metadata, can be used to determine how the image appears in an application.

Yes, the world has gone data crazy. Fear not, however, because Visual Studio has everything you need for accessing data, and metadata, and metadata about metadata in your applications. In this chapter, I show you how to use Visual Studio to create data-driven applications without getting bogged down in all the technology that makes data access possible.

Accessing Data with Visual Studio and .NET

Visual Studio provides many tools for accessing and manipulating data. The underlying technology that makes the tools in Visual Studio work is

ADO.NET. It provides all the commands and widgets you need in order to work with data in your application. With ADO.NET, you can

✦ Connect to data sources.

✦ Retrieve data from data sources.

✦ Display data in your application.

✦ Update data to reflect changes your users make.

Read on to see how ADO.NET works.

Meeting ADO.NET

ADO.NET is the technology in the Microsoft .NET Framework that makes it possible to work with data in your applications. You can work with ADO.NET by using wizards in Visual Studio or by writing your own code to access ADO.NET. Either way, it helps to understand conceptually how ADO.NET works.

ADO.NET is a part of the .NET Framework in the same way that ASP.NET and Windows Forms are part of the .NET Framework. The .NET Framework provides all the code that brings these technologies to life. Visual Studio 2005 provides wizards that generate code that let you use these technologies of the .NET Framework without digging into the details of how the technologies work.

Starting at the data source

Data access in ADO.NET begins with data sources. Starting with data sources makes sense: You can't display data until you know its source.

ADO.NET can access almost any data source imaginable. Using ADO.NET, you can access these data sources:

✦ **Databases, such as SQL Server and Oracle** — See Chapter 6 of this mini-book for an overview of Microsoft SQL Server.

✦ **XML files** — Chapter 5 of this mini-book shows you how to access XML files.

✦ **Objects** — Chapter 2 of this mini-book shows you how to connect to an object.

✦ **Web services** — Chapter 6 in Book V shows you how to work with Web services.

✦ **Local data stored in your project** — See Chapter 6 of this mini-book for more information on local data sources.

Visual Studio provides two tools for creating and managing data sources:

✦ The Data Source Configuration Wizard walks you through the steps of creating a new data source.

✦ The Data Sources window is a container for managing all your project's data sources. It's available only in Windows applications.

ASP.NET includes a set of data source controls for configuring data sources, and Windows has the new BindingSource component for wiring data sources to data-bound controls.

Retrieving data from data sources

Setting up data sources for your projects is the first step in retrieving data from the data sources. You have two options for telling ADO.NET which data to get from data sources:

✦ Write code using ADO.NET commands.

✦ Using the Visual Studio TableAdapter.

Before ADO.NET, an application stayed connected to the data source while getting data. You had to manage the process of walking through data records to reach the record you wanted. ADO.NET eliminates all that by using a disconnected model. With ADO.NET, you download your data from your data source and then disconnect from it. If you make changes to the data that you want to send to the data source, you have to connect to the data source again.

In a connected model, the data always remains in the data source. You connect to the data source, read data, and then display that data as you're reading it. You make changes to data while you're connected to the data source.

In the ADO.NET disconnected model, you don't have live access to the data to execute commands. Instead, you download a copy of the data, work with it offline, and then reconnect to the data source to pass back any changes. When you work with a disconnected model, you need a place to store the data you download from your data source. ADO.NET has two methods for executing offline downloads:

✦ **DataSet** — Stores the data you download from your data source. The DataSet is made up of tabular sets of data, similar to a database. A DataSet is essentially an offline database. You connect to the data source and download your data to the DataSet. The DataSet includes commands for accessing the data. Many controls can work with DataSets.

ADO.NET offers a *strongly typed* DataSet, which is a special type of DataSet. A regular DataSet uses generic names for its contents — for example, Table1, column1, or column2. In a strongly typed DataSet, generic placeholder names are replaced with meaningful names from the data source, such as replacing Table 1 with Customer table and column1 or column2 with CustID or CompanyName.

You can use the Visual Studio TableAdapter Configuration Wizard to work with tables in DataSets. The wizard builds all the commands to retrieve and update the table's underlying data source.

✦ **DataReader** — Downloads your data but doesn't have an offline storage mechanism. When you use a DataReader, ADO.NET expects you to have a place to store the data in your application and a means of accessing the data from that store. Although a DataReader is much faster than a DataSet, a DataSet is more convenient.

The wizards and controls in Visual Studio work with DataSets. See Chapter 5 in this mini-book for information on working with DataSets and DataReaders in your code.

The Data Source Configuration Wizard creates and configures the TableAdapter for retrieving data and filling a DataSet for storing the data offline. The section "Dragging and Dropping Data," later in this chapter, walks you through using the Data Source Configuration Wizard.

Displaying data

The user interfaces for Windows applications and Web applications are built by using controls, such as labels, text boxes, and buttons. ADO.NET provides an entire set of controls just for displaying data.

Different controls are used for the Web Forms and for Windows Forms, as listed in Table 1-1.

Table 1-1	Data Controls for Windows Forms and Web Forms	
Project Type	**Control**	**Description**
Windows	`DataGridView`	Displays data in a table
	`BindingSource`	Binds data to a control
	`BindingNavigator`	Provides navigation to records
	`ReportViewer`	Displays a reporting services report
Web	`GridView`	Displays data in a table
	`DataList`	Displays data using a customizable format
	`DetailsView`	Displays a single row of data; often used with a `GridView`

Project Type	Control	Description
	FormView	Displays a single record in a form
	Repeater	Displays data in a customizable list
	ReportViewer	Displays a reporting services report

ADO.NET data controls are designed to display data from a data source. *Data binding* connects a control to a data source. Any control can be data-bound, including everyday controls, such as labels, text boxes, and buttons.

Many of the Web data controls are customizable. Controls such as the Repeater control don't have any display properties. You define how your data appears by defining a template for the control. The template defines the HTML that is used to display the data. See Chapter 2 in this mini-book for an example.

Web controls are rendered as HTML markup. More data-specific controls are provided for Web Forms than for Windows Forms because rendering data using HTML is more challenging. Both Windows Forms and Web Forms can use any control to display data.

Chapter 2 in this mini-book demonstrates some of the ADO.NET data controls available for Windows Forms and Web Forms applications. Chapter 2 also shows you how to filter and sort by using data controls and how to bind data to regular controls, such as labels and text boxes.

Updating data

Most applications do more than just display data. Many times, users create new data or manipulate existing data. Updating and adding data is similar to viewing data: You have to store your changed data offline in your application by using either an ADO.NET DataSet or your own, custom data store; connect to your data source; and then execute commands against the data source that update it to reflect the changes made in the offline data store.

Visual Studio provides the TableAdapter Configuration Wizard for updating data. Chapter 3 in this mini-book shows the wizard in action.

Exploring the Visual Studio data toolbox

Working with data in your application requires many steps. Visual Studio provides a nice set of tools that "wrap around" ADO.NET and hide from you many of the complexities of how ADO.NET works. Table 1-2 lists the tools and what they help you do.

Table 1-2	Visual Studio Tools for Using ADO.NET	
Visual Studio Tool	*ADO.NET Feature*	*Where You Can See the Tool in Action*
Data controls	Display data	Chapter 2
Data Source Configuration Wizard	Manage data sources Retrieve data Store data in DataSets	Next section, Chapter 2, and Chapter 3
Data Sources window	Manage data sources Retrieve data	Next section and Chapter 2
TableAdapter Configuration Wizard	Retrieve data Update data	Chapter 3

Visual Studio also includes these tools:

+ **DataSet Designer** — Create and modify DataSets. See Chapter 3 in this mini-book for an extensive walkthrough.

+ **XML Designers** — Choose from several designers for working with XML data. See Chapter 4 in this mini-book for an extensive walkthrough.

+ **Server Explorer and Data Explorer** — Use Server Explorer and Data Explorer to manage database objects. See Chapter 6 in this mini-book for more information about working with databases.

Understanding Databases

To be able to work with data, you have to know a little something about how it's stored in a relational database, especially if you want to use DataSets. You often access databases — although Visual Studio can access more types of data sources than just databases. Even if data isn't stored in a database, you may decide to use a DataSet to store the data in your application's memory. A DataSet uses concepts that are similar to using a database.

A *database* is simply a place to store data. For example, you can store lists of information in a plain-text file, which is a database. Although plain-text files (often called *flat files*) may work fine for storing to-do lists, they don't' work well for storing business data. That's why modern database management programs, such as Microsoft SQL Server, were created.

The prehistoric flat file database

Believe it or not, before database management systems, business data was stored in flat files, which are hard to work with. They aren't fast, and gathering data from multiple files is difficult, especially when no standard exists for determining how data is stored in the files.

Programmers therefore needed a means of not only storing data but also accessing it again and associating it with other data in the database. The relational database management system was created to solve this problem. A *relational database management system,* or *RDBMS,* allows you to group common data records in a table. A table is made up of columns that represent fields in the records. Each record is a row in the table. For example, a database may have a Customer table and an Order table. Figure 1-1 shows an example of the Customer table.

Figure 1-1:
The
Customer
table is
made of up
rows and
columns.

CustomerID	TerritoryID	AccountNumber	CustomerType	rowguid	ModifiedDate
1	1	AW00000001	S	3f5ae95e-b87d-4...	10/13/2004 11:'
2	1	AW00000002	S	e552f657-a9af-4...	10/13/2004 11:'
3	4	AW00000003	S	130774b1-db21-...	10/13/2004 11:'
4	4	AW00000004	S	ff862851-1daa-4...	10/13/2004 11:'
5	4	AW00000005	S	83905bdc-6f5e-4...	10/13/2004 11:'
6	4	AW00000006	S	1a92df88-bfa2-4...	10/13/2004 11:'
7	1	AW00000007	S	03e9273e-b193-...	10/13/2004 11:'
8	5	AW00000008	S	801368b1-4323-...	10/13/2004 11:'

People who work with data commonly show how a record in one table relates to another record in another table. For example, someone in sales may want to know how many customers placed orders during the preceding quarter. By using a relational database management system, you can flag columns in your table so that you can answer this kind of question.

The flagged columns are primary keys and foreign keys. When a column in a table is marked as a *primary key,* each row in the table must have a unique value in its primary key column. For example, in a Customer table, the `CustomerID` column must be unique if the column is marked as the table's primary key. You use the primary key to look up values in the Customer table and know that you can find only one unique entry.

You can reference a table's primary key in another table. For example, in the Order table, you need to know who the customer is for the order. Rather than store the customer's name, which can change, you can store the customer's `CustomerID` value so that you can look up the customer's information by using the Customer table. In the Order table, the Customer table's primary key is a *foreign* key when you reference it in another table. Figure 1-2 shows an example of primary and foreign keys.

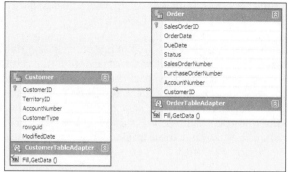

Figure 1-2:
Use primary and foreign keys to create associations between tables.

Understanding SQL

A relational database management system uses a standardized set of commands for creating tables and columns and for inserting, updating, and reading data. This set of commands is *Structured Query Language (SQL)*.

You can pronounce SQL either "es-cue-el" or "see-quel." I always spell out the acronym when I'm referring to the language. However, when I'm talking about Microsoft SQL Server, I always say "sequel." That way, I differentiate between the standard and the product.

To see some examples of SQL, see Chapter 6 in this mini-book.

Using Structured Query Language

I was first exposed to Structured Query Language while working at a little trucking shop in Indianapolis and designing reports for an application that ran on an AS/400. Later, I used SQL to build reports for a Windows-based application at another firm.

By the time I took a database course later on, I had already been working with SQL for several years. A major part of the database course was devoted to explaining Structured Query Language. Many of my classmates struggled to learn the language, and on the day of our final exam, I overheard some of them say that they were going to skip all the SQL questions because SQL was irrelevant and too difficult to learn.

I was amazed at the number of professional developers I encountered who shunned SQL. Like my classmates, they preferred to use graphical tools to build their queries. Although graphical tools are easy to use, you need to understand the basics of SQL. Using SQL is one of the first technical skills I learned, and it has never let me down.

Relational database management systems consist of more than just tables. Most RDBMSs include these elements:

✦ **Administrative tools** — Manage database objects, such as tables, queries, and users.

✦ **Wizards** — Add database objects, back up databases, and schedule administrative services.

✦ **Visual tools** — Build queries and diagrams of the database structure.

✦ **Rules** — Protect your data from being erroneously deleted.

Some popular RDBMSs are Microsoft SQL Server 2005 (see Chapter 6 in this mini-book), Oracle 10x, and Sybase SQL Anywhere.

Other kinds of database management systems exist in addition to relational database management systems. *Object* database management systems, for example, store data as objects rather than as tables. Object databases are becoming especially popular because many programs are written using object-oriented techniques. You can find more information about object databases at www.odbms.org/.

Dragging and Dropping Data

Visual Studio provides wizards you can use to add data to your Windows and Web applications. Adding data to an application is similar whether it's a Windows Form or a Web Form. Essentially, adding data is as simple as dragging and dropping a control onto your form. After you drop the control, use the Data Source Configuration Wizard to

✦ Connect to a data source.

✦ Select tables or build a query from the data source.

✦ Store data in an offline data store.

✦ Bind data sources to a control to display the data.

Preparing your computer to work with data

The examples in this section use the AdventureWorks sample database along with Microsoft SQL Server 2005 Express Edition. SQL Server Express is installed with Visual Studio 2005 Professional.

I chose to use the AdventureWorks sample database rather than the usual Northwind sample database because Microsoft recommends using Adventure-Works with SQL Server 2005. The AdventureWorks database has been tuned to work with SQL Server 2005 and show off some of the new features of SQL Server 2005.

If you didn't install SQL Server Express with Visual Studio 2005, see Chapter 6 for more information on installing SQL Server Express. The examples in this section also work with SQL Server 2005 Developer Edition.

To download the AdventureWorks database, go to wwwmicrosoft.com/downloads/details.aspx?FamilyID=e719ecf7-9f46-4312-af89-6ad8702e4e6e&DisplayLang=en. Download and install the Adventure-WorksDB.msi file. See Chapter 6 of this mini-book for more information about the SQL Server samples.

Adding data to Windows applications

To add data from the AdventureWorks database to a Windows Form, follow these steps:

1. **Create a new Windows application.**

   See Book III, Chapter 1 for more information on creating Windows applications.

2. **Drag and drop a `DataGridView` control from the Data section of the toolbox to a blank Windows Form.**

   If the toolbox is closed, press Ctrl+Alt+X to open it.

3. **Click the arrow in the upper-right corner of the `DataGridView` control to display the DataGridView Tasks dialog box.**

4. **Click the Choose Data Source drop-down list.**

   A list of the project's data sources appears. The list should be blank unless you already added data sources.

5. **Click the Add Project Data Source link, as shown in Figure 1-3.**

   The Data Source Configuration Wizard appears.

Before you can select data to display, you must configure the Data Source Configuration Wizard by following these steps:

1. **Click the Database icon on the Choose a Data Source Type page of the wizard. Click the Next button to go to the Choose Your Data Connection step.**

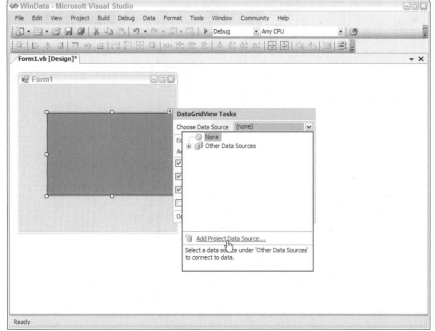

Figure 1-3:
Click the
Add Project
Data Source
link to start
the Data
Source
Configura-
tion Wizard.

2. Click the New Connection button to create a new database connection.

The Add Connection dialog box opens.

3. Make sure that the Data Source field is set to Microsoft SQL Server (SqlClient), as shown in Figure 1-4. Otherwise, click the Change button and set the data source to Microsoft SQL Server.

4. Click the Server Name drop-down list and select your computer's name from the list.

You can also type **(local)** or a period for the server name to indicate that you're using the local server.

5. Append \SQLExpress **to the server name you entered in Step 4, as shown in Figure 1-5.**

SQLExpress is the default name of the instance installed by SQL Server Express. (To read more about SQL Server instances, see Chapter 6 of this mini-book.) Even though the Visual Studio documentation says that you don't need to enter the SQL Server instance, you do. Otherwise, Visual Studio cannot connect to your database.

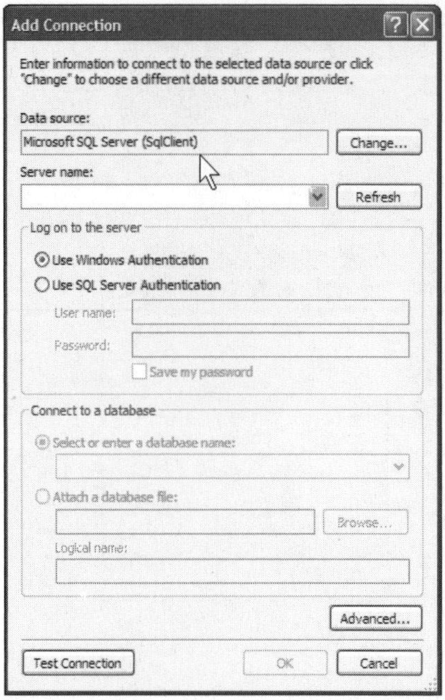

Figure 1-4:
Make sure
that the data
source is
set to
Microsoft
SQL Server.

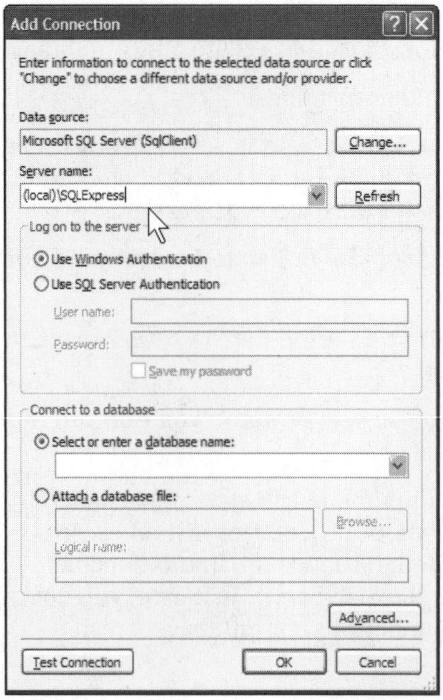

Figure 1-5:
Append the
default
name to the
server
name.

6. **Accept the Use Windows Authentication default option to log on to the server, unless you have something other than a default installation.**

   See Chapter 6 of this mini-book to read more about Windows and SQL Server authentication.

7. **Select the Attach a Database File option in the Connect to a Database section, and then click the Browse button to attach a database file.**

   The Select SQL Server Database File dialog box opens.

8. **Browse to the SQL Server database file directory where the Adventure Works sample is installed.**

   The default location for SQL Server databases is C:\Program Files\ Microsoft SQL Server\MSSQL.1\MSSQL\Data.

9. **Select the AdventureWorks_Data.mdf database file and click the Open button.**

   The path to the Adventure Works database file appears in the Add Connection dialog box.

10. **Click the Test Connection button.**

    If the connection is successful, you see the message `Test Connection Succeeded`. If the connection is unsuccessful, start troubleshooting your connection.

    See Chapter 6 of this mini-book for some tips on troubleshooting database connections.

11. **Click the OK button to close the test connection window.**

12. **Click the OK button to close the Add Connection dialog box.**

    The connection information appears in the Data Source Configuration Wizard.

13. **Click the Next button.**

    You're prompted to save the connection information.

14. **Leave the Save the Connection option selected and click the Next button.**

    The Choose Your Database Objects page appears.

15. **In the database objects pane, click the plus (+) sign next to Tables.**

    The list of database tables expands.

16. **Select the Department table, as shown in Figure 1-6, and then click the Finish button to add the data to the form.**

Visual Studio adds to your form the components that bind the `DataGridView` control to the Adventure Works data source.

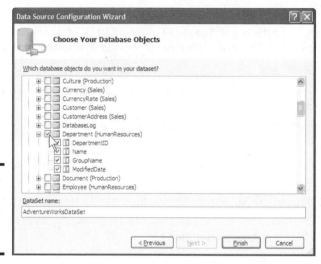

Figure 1-6:
Select a
table to add
it to your
form.

Run your form by pressing Ctrl+F5. Data from the Adventure Works' Department table appears in the `DataGridView` control, as shown in Figure 1-7.

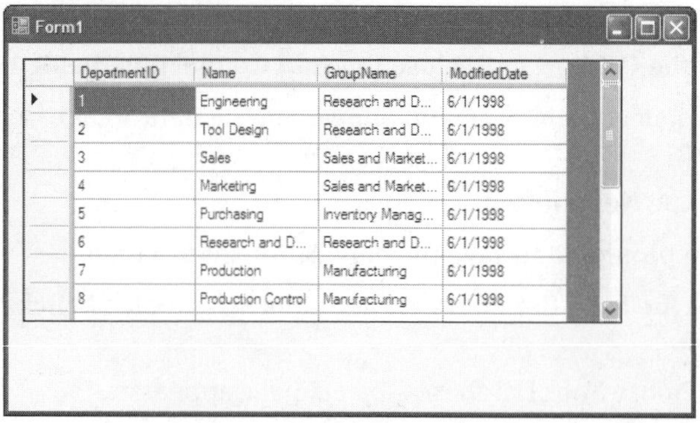

Figure 1-7:
Data
from the
Department
table
appears in
the control.

To read more details about using the Data Source Configuration Wizard, adding data source connections, and working with other data-bound controls, see Chapter 2 in this mini-book. The following section demonstrates how to use the Data Source Configuration Wizard to add data to a Web Form.

Adding data to Web Forms

You add data to Web Forms by using the Data Source Configuration Wizard. You can also use the wizard to add data to Windows Forms; however the process for selecting database objects such as tables varies slightly for Web Forms.

To add data to a Web Form using the Data Source Configuration Wizard, follow these steps:

1. **Create a new Web site.**

See Book III, Chapter 4 for more information on creating Web sites.

2. **Drag and drop a `GridView` control from the Data group in the Visual Studio toolbox to the Web Form.**

3. **Right-click the arrow in the upper-right corner of the `GridView` control to view the GridView Tasks dialog box.**

4. **Select New Data Source from the Choose Data Source drop-down list, as shown in Figure 1-8.**

The Data Source Configuration Wizard appears.

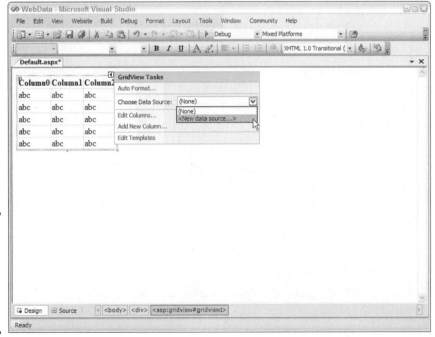

Figure 1-8: Add a new data source by using the GridView Tasks dialog box.

5. **Click the Database icon for the data source and click the OK button.**

6. **On the Choose Your Data Connection page, select your data connection. If you completed the steps for the Windows section, click the drop-down arrow to reuse that connection. Otherwise, follow steps 2–12 in the preceding section to create a new data connection to the Adventure Works database.**

7. **Click the Next button.**

   You're prompted to save the connection string.

8. **Click the Next button again.**

   The next page of the wizard, Configure the Select Statement, appears.

9. **Click the drop-down list of tables and choose Department.**

   The list of columns in the Department field appears.

10. **Select the asterisk to select all the columns, as shown in Figure 1-9.**

    The wizard builds the select statement.

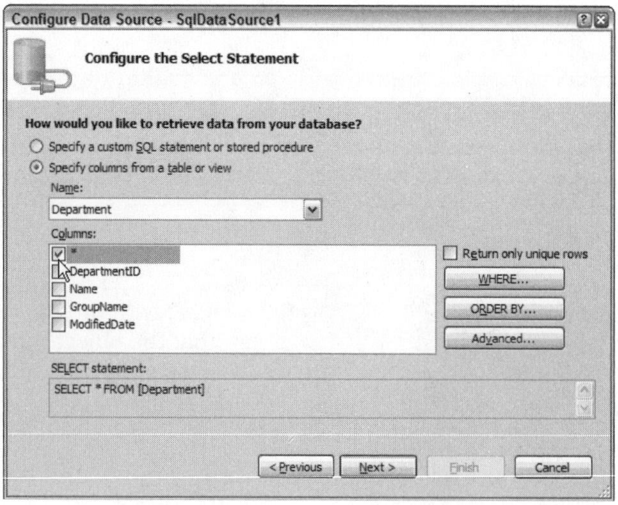

Figure 1-9: Select the columns you want to appear in the control.

11. **Click the Next button.**

    The Test Query page appears.

12. **Click the Test Query button to test the query.**

An error message may say that Department is an invalid object name. A bug in the Data Source Configuration Wizard makes it not work properly with databases that use schemas. To read more about configuring the Adventure Works database to work around the schemas, see Chapter 6 in this mini-book. You can work around this error after completing the wizard.

13. **Click the Finish button.**

The Data Source Configuration Wizard closes.

Visual Studio adds the following declarative syntax to the Web Form to make it display the data in the GridView control:

```
<asp:GridView ID="GridView1" runat="server" DataSourceID="SqlDataSource1">
</asp:GridView>
<asp:SqlDataSource ID="SqlDataSource1" runat="server" ConnectionString="<%$
    ConnectionStrings:AdventureWorksConnectionString %>"
    SelectCommand="SELECT * FROM [Department]">
</asp:SqlDataSource>
```

For the GridView control to access the Department table, the SelectCommand property must be more specific about how to reach the table. To make the SelectCommand property more specific, change it to

```
SelectCommand="SELECT * FROM [HumanResources].[Department]"
```

The HumanResources schema is associated with the Department table in the Adventure Works database. The [HumanResources].[Department] is the *fully qualified* name because it makes it clear how the table is accessed. Whenever you have trouble accessing a database table, make sure that you can access it by using its fully qualified name.

If you receive invalid-object errors while working with the Data Source Configuration Wizard in ASP.NET, make sure that the object's name is fully qualified and spelled correctly (including the use of upper-and lowercase).

Alternatively, you can use the Query Builder to build the select statement in Step 10 in the preceding set of steps. The Query Builder correctly builds the select statement.

Press Ctrl+F5 to run the Web Form. The data from the Department table appears, as shown in Figure 1-10.

**Book IV
Chapter 1**

**Accessing Data
with Visual Studio**

Untitled Page - Microsoft Internet Explorer

File   Edit   View   Favorites   Tools   Help

Address http://localhost:2133/WebData/Default.aspx

DepartmentID	Name	GroupName	ModifiedDate
1	Engineering	Research and Development	6/1/1998 12:00:00 AM
2	Tool Design	Research and Development	6/1/1998 12:00:00 AM
3	Sales	Sales and Marketing	6/1/1998 12:00:00 AM
4	Marketing	Sales and Marketing	6/1/1998 12:00:00 AM
5	Purchasing	Inventory Management	6/1/1998 12:00:00 AM
6	Research and Development	Research and Development	6/1/1998 12:00:00 AM
7	Production	Manufacturing	6/1/1998 12:00:00 AM
8	Production Control	Manufacturing	6/1/1998 12:00:00 AM
9	Human Resources	Executive General and Administration	6/1/1998 12:00:00 AM
10	Finance	Executive General and Administration	6/1/1998 12:00:00 AM
11	Information Services	Executive General and Administration	6/1/1998 12:00:00 AM
12	Document Control	Quality Assurance	6/1/1998 12:00:00 AM
13	Quality Assurance	Quality Assurance	6/1/1998 12:00:00 AM
14	Facilities and Maintenance	Executive General and Administration	6/1/1998 12:00:00 AM
15	Shipping and Receiving	Inventory Management	6/1/1998 12:00:00 AM
16	Executive	Executive General and Administration	6/1/1998 12:00:00 AM
18	Test	Test	4/3/2006 12:00:00 AM

Done   Local intranet

Chapter 2: Show Me the Data

In This Chapter

✔ Accessing data in a Windows application

✔ Taking a closer look at data binding

✔ Creating a data-centric Web site

Data is data is data, or so you would think. When you're working with data in Visual Studio, the approach you take for Windows Forms varies slightly from the one for Web applications. Although the Windows Forms Designer sports the Data Sources window, Visual Web Developer has no such jumping-off point for managing all your project's data sources.

Both designers share some tools, such as the Data Source Configuration Wizard, but the experience in Visual Web Developer is clunkier and less refined. The data tools in Windows Forms Designer integrate very well and flow seamlessly. Rest assured, whether you're building Windows applications or Web sites, Visual Studio has a data tool to get the job done. You just may have to tweak the Web tools until they mature.

In this chapter, I walk you through the procedure for working with the set of data tools in Visual Studio. Don't be surprised to see the same tools demonstrated once for Windows applications and again for Web sites. Despite having the same names, sometimes the tools behave completely differently.

Working with Data in Windows Applications

Visual Studio provides plenty of ways to access data in a Windows application. Here are the primary ways to add data access by using the Windows Forms Designer:

✦ Drag and drop a data control onto a form.

I show you how to access data by using the GridView control in Chapter 1 of this mini-book.

✦ Use the Data Source Configuration Wizard.

✦ Use the Data Sources pane.

Data sources are any source of data you wish to access in your application. Examples of data sources include databases, Web services, objects, and XML files. There's a Visual Studio wizard to access almost every form of data you can imagine.

You aren't restricted to just accessing Microsoft's data offerings such as SQL Server and Access. You can connect to any vendor's database management system by creating a data connection as described in the section "Connecting to databases" later in this chapter.

All the Visual Studio data tools are intertwined in such a way that even if you start out using one tool, you often end up finishing the task by using another wizard altogether.

Regardless of which tool you use, you always start by specifying a data source. After configuring the data source, you configure a control to use with the data source. Visual Studio generates the code to take care of everything that happens between those two points.

Of course, you can always write your own code to access data. (Sigh.) If you insist on doing things the hard way, see Chapter 5 for examples of using the code editor to access data with ADO.NET.

The Data Sources pane is a handy tool for managing all your project's data sources. The Data Sources pane works hand in hand with the Data Source Configuration Wizard to create new data sources and configure access to the data.

You can use the Data Sources pane to work with data source objects. Open the window in one of two ways:

✦ Choose Data⇨Show Data Sources.

✦ Press Shift+Alt+D.

Viewing data source objects

Use the Data Sources pane to add new data sources to your project and work with existing data sources. The Data Sources toolbar, shown in Figure 2-1, has these commands, from left to right:

✦ **Add New Data Source** — Start the Data Source Configuration Wizard.

✦ **Edit DataSet with Designer** — Open the DataSet Designer with the selected DataSet from the Data Sources tree. See Chapter 3 for more information about using the DataSet Designer.

✦ **Configure DataSet with Wizard** — Start the Data Source Configuration Wizard so that you can select database objects to add to the DataSet.

✦ **Refresh** — Refresh the data sources listed in the Data Sources tree.

Figure 2-1:
Use the
Data
Sources
toolbar to
work with
data
sources.

Add New Data Source

Configure DataSet with Wizard

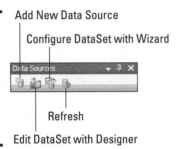

Refresh

Edit DataSet with Designer

Datasets are used to store data retrieved from data sources.

Data sources are listed in tree view in the Data Sources pane, as shown in Figure 2-2.

The Data Sources tree is a hierarchical view that shows these elements:

✦ **Expandable parent data sources** — A data source that uses DataSets, such as a database, shows the DataSet as the parent. Objects and Web services show a namespace.

✦ **Expandable child objects nested within the parent** — A DataSet expands to list the tables contained with it.

✦ **A set of child objects** — A table within a DataSet expands to list the table's columns.

Adding data sources

The Data Sources pane uses the Data Source Configuration Wizard to add new data sources. To start the Data Source Configuration Wizard from the Data Sources pane, follow these steps:

1. **Create a new Windows project.**

See Chapter 1 in Book III for more information on creating Windows projects.

2. **Choose Data⇨Show Data Sources.**

The Data Sources pane appears.

**Book IV
Chapter 2**

Show Me the Data

Figure 2-2:
The Data
Sources
pane
displays a
project's
data
sources in
tree view.

3. **Click the Add New Data Source button on the Data Sources toolbar.**

   The Data Source Configuration Wizard appears.

   Alternatively, you can choose Data⇨Add New Data Source to start the Data Source Configuration Wizard. Data sources created with the wizard appear in the Data Sources pane.

To add a new data source by using the Data Source Configuration Wizard, follow these steps:

1. **On the Choose a Data Source Type page in the wizard, select a data source, as shown in Figure 2-3.**

   Your data source choices in the wizard are Database, Web Service, and Object.

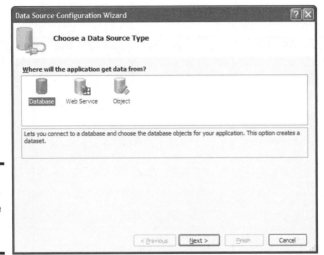

Figure 2-3:
Select the data source type in the wizard.

2. **Click Next. Depending on the data source you select in Step 1, the wizard displays one of the following pages to create your connection:**

   • **Databases** — The Choose Your Data Connection page appears. Select an existing database connection or select New Connection to add a new database connection. See the following section for more about managing database connections.

   • **Web Service** — Opens the Add Web Reference dialog box. Enter the URL for the Web service or browse for one. See Book V, Chapter 6 for more information about Web services.

   • **Object** — The Select the Object You Wish to Bind To page appears. It displays a tree view of the classes in your project. Click the Add Reference button to add a reference to another project.

   After you establish a connection to the data source, the wizard displays a list of the data source's objects.

   The generic term *object* refers to the contents of the data source. For example, the objects in a database are tables.

3. **Select from the data source the objects you want to use.**

4. **Click the Finish button.**

   The data source is added to the Data Sources pane. Figure 2-4 shows a Data Sources pane with a database, a Web service, and objects added to it.

**Book IV
Chapter 2**

Show Me the Data

Database

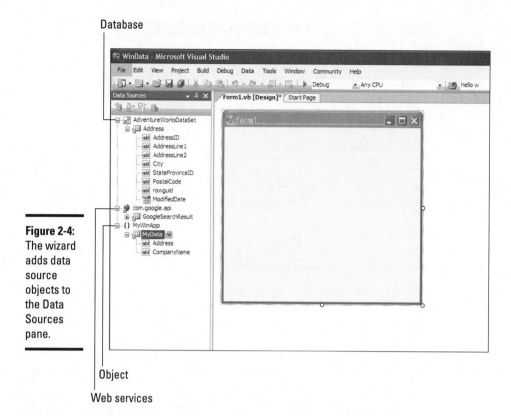

Figure 2-4:
The wizard
adds data
source
objects to
the Data
Sources
pane.

Object

Web services

Connecting to databases

A database is a kind of data source — probably the most popular. Because databases are such popular data sources, Visual Studio provides a special dialog box for creating connections to databases.

You can access the Connections dialog box in several ways, including the ones on this list:

✦ Choose Tools⇨Connect to Database.

✦ Using the Choose Your Data Connection page in the Data Source Configuration Wizard.

✦ Click the Connect to Database button on the Server Explorer toolbar.

Regardless of how you access the Connections dialog box, use it to make connections to all your project's databases.

Database connections are reusable. You don't have to create a new database connection each time you use the database as a data source.

Figure 2-5 shows the Add Connection dialog box for accessing a Microsoft SQL Server database. The choices available in the dialog box change to suit the selected database source.

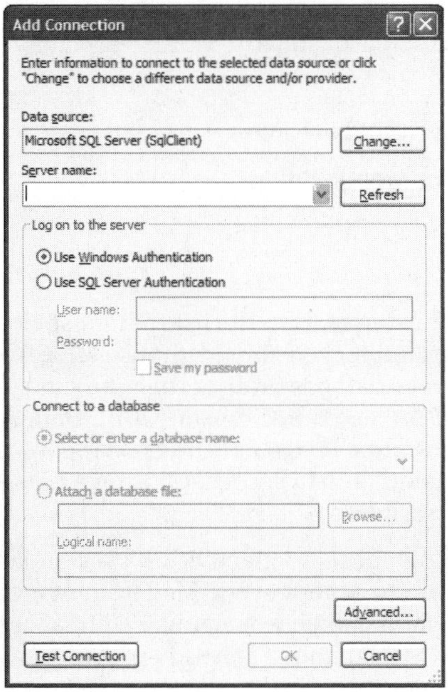

Figure 2-5:
Use the Add Connection dialog box to create database connections.

To change the database source in the Add Connection dialog box, follow these steps:

1. Choose Tools⇨Connect to Database.

The Add Connection dialog box appears.

2. Click the Change button to change the data source.

The Change Data Source dialog box appears, as shown in Figure 2-6.

The available data sources are

- Microsoft Access Database File
- Microsoft ODBC Data Source
- Microsoft SQL Server

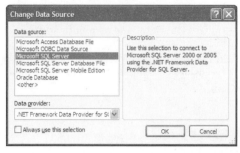

Figure 2-6:
Select a
new data
source in
the Change
Data Source
dialog box.

- Microsoft SQL Server Database File
- Microsoft SQL Server Mobile Edition
- Oracle Database
- Other

You should pick the data source from the list that most closely matches your data source. For example, you should choose Microsoft SQL Server to connect to a SQL Server database rather than the more generic ODBC Data Source. While you can use the Microsoft ODBC Data Source to access almost any data source imaginable, the other choices are tuned to work with a specific kind of data source. Click on a data source in the dialog box to view a description.

ODBC stands for Open Database Connectivity. It's a standard that has been used for many years to access everything from Access databases to text files. ODBC is a good choice when you need to access a data source for which Visual Studio doesn't already provide a way to access.

3. Choose a data source from the list.

When you click a data source, the Change Data Source dialog box displays the data source's default data provider and description.

A *data provider* is a component in ADO.NET, the data access technology in the Microsoft.NET framework. ADO.NET provides data providers for connecting to a database and executing commands against the database. The Add Connection dialog box configures the ADO.NET default data provider to work with the data source you select. For more information about data providers, see Chapter 5 in this mini-book.

Click the Data Provider drop-down box to select a different ADO.NET data provider to use with your data source. The data source's default data provider is selected automatically.

4. Click OK to close the Change Data Source dialog box. The Add Connection dialog box is updated to reflect the connection information required to connect to the data source.

5. Use the Add Connection dialog box to finish configuring the connection.

The information required from the Add Connection dialog box varies depending on the data source selected. All the data sources have these features:

+ **Advanced** — View and modify the data source's connection information in a property grid.

+ **Login information** — Specify the kind of login you want to use and a username and password to use if they're required.

+ **Test Connection** — Test the connection without closing the dialog box.

Any time you're having difficulties accessing a database, use the Add Connections dialog box to test your database connection. Without a working database connection, you can't access the database.

Use the Connections dialog box to create your connections, even if you plan to write code to access data. You can use the Connections dialog box to test your connection, which saves you from having to do a lot of troubleshooting time if your code isn't working properly.

The Connections dialog box creates a connection string that specifies how your application should access the data source. Connection strings store everything you type in the Connections dialog box, including server names, usernames, and passwords. You have to manage connection strings securely. To read more about managing connection strings, see Chapter 5 in this mini-book.

Adding controls from the Data Sources pane

The Data Sources pane is much more than a container for storing your project's data sources. You can drag and drop data from the Data Sources pane onto the Windows Forms Designer. Visual Studio adds a databound control to your form and "wires" it to your data source so that it magically works.

A control is *databound* if it retrieves data from a data source. A control's properties can also be databound. See the section "Binding by using the Binding property," later in this chapter, to see how to bind data to a control's property.

To add a databound control from the Data Sources pane, follow these steps:

1. Use the Data Source Configuration Wizard to add the Department table from the AdventureWorks database by following the steps described in the "Adding data sources" section, earlier in this chapter.

This example uses the AdventureWorks sample database from Microsoft. See Chapter 1 in this mini-book for information about downloading and installing the sample.

2. **Choose Data⇨Show Data Sources to display the Data Sources pane.**

3. **In the Data Sources pane, expand the AdventureWorks data source by clicking the plus (+) sign next to the data source.**

4. **Drag and drop the Department table on the Windows Form.**

   Visual Studio adds a `DataGridView` control and a `BindingNavigator` component to the form, as shown in Figure 2-7.

   Alternatively, you can expand the Department table and add columns individually to the form.

5. **Press Ctrl+F5 to run the form.**

BindingNavigator control

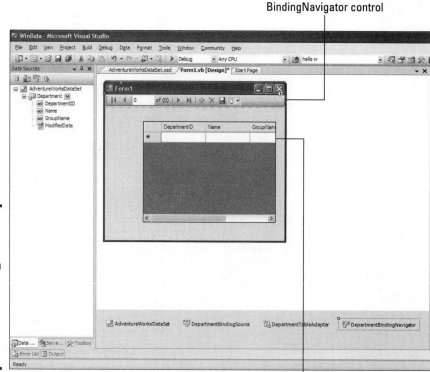

Figure 2-7:
Drag and drop data objects from the Data Sources pane to create databound controls.

DataGridView control

In addition to the `DataGridView` control, the Data Sources pane automatically adds several components to the Windows Form:

✦ **`BindingSource`** — Connects data sources to databound controls.

✦ **`BindingNavigator`** — Provides built-in record navigation, including buttons to add and delete records.

✦ **`TableAdapter`** — Builds the commands for retrieving and updating data from the data source.

These components are responsible for "wiring" your data source to your controls so that they "just work." You don't have to write any code to retrieve your data or update it. Simply drag and drop the data objects from the Data Sources pane onto the Windows Forms Designer. Visual Studio takes care of all the details, and you get all the credit!

You can view these components in the lower part of the designer screen.

Visual Studio adds a `DataGridView` control by default when you drop data from the Data Sources pane. You can specify the control you want to add to the Windows Form. To set controls for items in the Data Sources pane, follow these steps:

1. **Click the drop-down arrow for the data source in the Data Sources pane.**

A list of available controls appears.

You can work with a parent container, such as a database table, or you can set controls for individual columns in the table.

2. **Select a control from the drop-down list, as shown in Figure 2-8.**

When you drag the data object onto the form, the selected control appears.

Set the parent container's control to Details to drop the parent's child controls on the form.

The kinds of controls that are listed depend on the type of data in the data source. For example, a column that stores date-and-time data lists the `DateTimePicker` control. To use the shortcut menu to select a different control, right-click the data item in the Data Sources pane and then

✦ Choose None to display no control for the data.

✦ Choose Customize to add a control to the list.

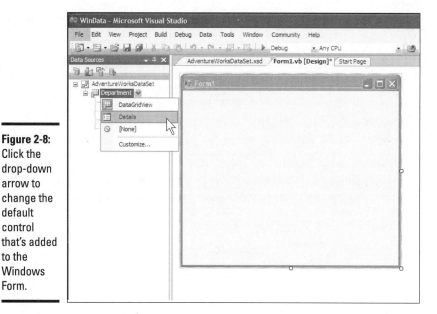

Figure 2-8:
Click the
drop-down
arrow to
change the
default
control
that's added
to the
Windows
Form.

Getting Your Data in a Bind

Binding is the process of "wiring" a data source to a data control. Visual
Studio provides several tools that make quick work of binding data sources
to data controls, thus making it possible to perform the following actions:

+ Navigate

+ Update

+ Delete

+ Sort

+ Filter

ADO.NET provides two components dedicated to providing binding services
that make databound controls "come alive" with little or no coding:

+ **BindingSource** — Links the data source and the databound control to
  make it possible to access and manipulate data.

+ **BindingNavigator** — Provides navigation to the data source linked to
  the BindingSource component.

Visual Studio creates the `BindingSource` and `BindingNavigator` components any time you drag and drop data from the Data Sources pane.

`BindingSource` is the recommended method for binding data in Windows applications regardless of the data source. No similar component exists for Web applications.

Using BindingSource to connect to other data

The `BindingSource` component, which is new to Visual Studio 2005, sits between your data source and the databound controls. The `BindingSource` component "wires" your data source to a control that displays the data. You can use `BindingSource` to

✦ Bind data to your controls without writing code.

✦ Change the data source without breaking the databound controls.

✦ Sort, filter, and add new data.

The `BindingSource` component simplifies working with data by exposing properties for common data-manipulation tasks, such as sorting and filtering data.

`BindingSource` is called a component rather than a control because there is no on-screen display associated with it. A control is a specific kind of component — one that you use to build your user interface.

The easiest way to work with the `BindingSource` component is to drag and drop data from the Data Sources window. The following examples show you how to use `BindingSource`'s sort and filter properties:

1. **Display the properties of a `BindingSource` component by selecting the component in the designer and pressing F4. The Properties window appears.**

For example, to use the `BindingSource` component `DepartmentBindingSource` created in the earlier section "Adding controls from the Data Sources pane," click the component and press F4.

2. **In the Filter property, type a value to use to filter the data source.**

For example, to filter the `GroupName` column in the `DepartmentBindingSource`, enter `GroupName like 'Executive%'`.

The `like` operator checks to see whether a value matches a pattern.

3. **In the** `Sort` **property, type the name of a column to sort by.**

   For example, enter `Name asc` to sort the Name column in ascending order.

   `asc` is short for ascending.

4. **Press Ctrl+F5 to run your form. The list of departments is filtered on the** `Group Name` **column and sorted in ascending order by name, as shown in Figure 2-9.**

Figure 2-9:
The data is filtered and sorted based on properties set in the `Binding-Source` component.

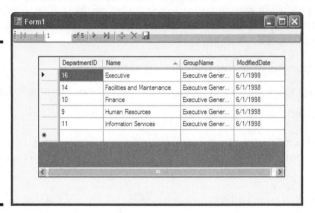

Two other important properties for the `BindingSource` component are

✦ `DataSource` — Specifies the data source used by `BindingSource`.

✦ `DataMember` — Specifies the table or object within the `DataSource` to use to get the data.

In the preceding example, `DataSource` is set to `AdventureWorksDataSet`. The `DataMember` property is Department. You can add another table to the DataSet and specify the `DataMember` property for the table.

You can use `BindingSource` features to step forward and backward through a set of records and add, update, and delete data. When a `BindingNavigator` component is used with `BindingSource`, its data-navigation and -manipulation features are automatically mapped to the `BindingNavigator` toolbar buttons.

Using BindingNavigator

The `BindingNavigator` component is a built-in menu control for navigating data. You can find the `BindingNavigator` control in the Data tab of

Visual Studio's Toolbox. The control, shown in Figure 2-10, includes the following buttons (from left to right) for navigating and manipulating data:

◆ Move First

◆ Move Previous

◆ Current Position

◆ Total Number of Items

◆ Move Next

◆ Move Last

◆ Add New

◆ Delete

◆ Save Data

Figure 2-10:
Use this control to navigate and manipulate data.

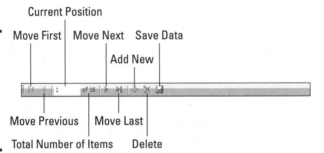

The `BindingNavigator` component is used in conjunction with `BindingSource`. The component has a `BindingSource` property that, when set to a `BindingSource` component, allows you to navigate and manipulate data.

Clicking a button on `BindingNavigator` triggers events in `BindingSource`. For example, when a user clicks the Add New button on `BindingNavigator`, the `AddNew` method in `BindingSource` is called. You don't have to worry about making it work. Just setting the `BindingSource` property for `BindingNavigator` "wires" the two components together. Better yet, just dragging and dropping objects from the Data Sources pane makes Visual Studio create and configure these two components for you.

To prevent users from adding data to the underlying data source, set the `AllowNew` property of `BindingSource` to `false`. The Add New button is automatically disabled in `BindingNavigator`.

Binding by using the Binding property

Any control's property can be bound to data. You don't always have to use special data controls to work with data. In the example in this section, I show you how to bind a department's name to a label control's `Text` property:

1. **Drag and drop a label control onto a Windows Form.**

2. **Open the label control's properties by pressing F4.**

   The Properties window appears.

3. **Click the plus (+) sign to expand the `DataBindings` property.**

4. **Click the down arrow for the `Text` property in the DataBindings section.**

   A list of data sources appears.

   To access additional properties you can create data binding for, click the ellipsis button in the `Advanced` property.

5. **Select a data source from the drop-down list or click the Add Project Data Source link to add a new data source.**

   If you add a new data source, the Data Source Configuration Wizard appears. You step through the wizard and add your data.

6. **Expand the data source and select the column you wish to bind the property to.**

   For example, select the Name column in the Department table to bind the `Text` property to it, as shown in Figure 2-11.

   The text `DepartmentBindingSource — Name` is added to the property's value.

7. **Press Ctrl+F5 to run the form.**

   The value of the first record in the data source appears in the label control's text property.

Using a `BindingSource` component as the data source in step 5 enables you to step through the records on your control with a `BindingNavigator`. By using the `BindingSource` as your data source for multiple controls, you can synchronize the data displayed by the controls. For example, if you add a `DataGridView` control to your form that uses the `DepartmentBindingSource` as described in the section "Adding controls using the Data Sources pane," then the `DataGridView` and the label control both display the same record. As you navigate through the records, both controls are updated to show the same data, as shown in Figure 2-12.

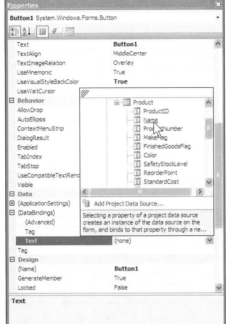

Figure 2-11:
Select the
Name
column from
the data
source.

Figure 2-12:
Both
controls
display data
for the
current
record.

Data binding to properties is useful any time you want to dynamically populate properties.

**Book IV
Chapter 2**

Show Me the Data

Accessing Data in Web Forms

Developing Web applications is challenging because you have to send information across a network. Of course, I'm not talking about just any network. Your Web pages are sent out by way of the world's network, the Internet.

Processing a Web page involves these stages:

1. A client's browser sends a request to a server for the Web page.

2. The server responds to the client and sends the contents of the Web page.

3. The client's browser receives the Web page and displays its content.

Repeat this process 100 bazillion times a day, and you have some idea of the amount of requests and responses bouncing around on the Internet.

The requests and responses of clients and servers are controlled by a set of rules named *HyperText Transfer Protocol* (HTTP). One characteristic of HTTP is that it's *stateless,* which means that after a request or response is processed, HTTP forgets that the response or request ever existed. If clients and servers on the Web suffer from amnesia with every click of the mouse, how is it possible to get data from servers to clients and back again?

When you want to make data work on the Web, three players do the heavy-duty lifting of making data-centric Web applications work:

✦ ASP.NET provides features that overcome HTTP's inability to maintain state.

✦ ADO.NET provides lots of widgets and commands for getting data from data sources, such as databases and XML files.

✦ Visual Studio provides the designer tools that make light work of using the high-tech gadgetry that makes Web applications work.

In this section, I show you how to use Visual Studio to access data on your Web pages. You can sleep better at night knowing that Visual Studio is protecting you from dealing with ASP.NET, ADO.NET, and HTTP, or you can have your own case of amnesia and happily get on with building data-centric Web applications with Visual Studio.

Meet the controls

The Visual Studio toolbox includes many data controls for displaying data and creating data sources. All the data controls are grouped on the toolbox's Data tab, as shown in Figure 2-13. To open the toolbox, choose View⇨ Toolbox or press Ctrl+Alt+X.

Figure 2-13:
Data
controls are
grouped on
the Data tab
of the Visual
Studio
toolbox.

Five controls display data on a Web page. They're often called *databound* controls because data is bound to them:

✦ **GridVew** — Displays a tabular view of data.

✦ **DataList** — Displays data in a list with a customizable format.

✦ **DetailsView** — Displays a single record at a time in a table row. This control is often used with GridView to create master/detail views.

✦ **FormView** — Displays a single record without specifying how the data is displayed. The display can be customized.

✦ **Repeater** — Displays data in a list that can be customized.

Each of these controls uses HTML markup to render your data to the client's Web browser. By default, the text is rendered by using table markup. All these controls can be customized, so you can specify the exact HTML markup you want ASP.NET to use when it sends the page to the browser.

Visual Studio provides a data source control for each kind of data source you can access in ASP.NET. The five controls for creating data sources are

✦ **SQLDataSource** — Accesses a database, such as Microsoft SQL Server or Oracle.

✦ **AccessDataSource** — Accesses a Microsoft Access database.

✦ **ObjectDataSource** — Accesses data in a business object.

✦ **XmlDataSource** — Accesses data in an XML file.

✦ **SiteMapDataSource** — Creates a data source to access a site map.

The data source controls are comparable to the BindingSource component used with Windows Forms. The obvious difference, of course, is that BindingSource works with multiple data sources where the ASP.NET data source controls are specialized to work specific data sources.

Going to the source

You use data source controls to configure access to a particular type of data source. Each control, except for the SiteMapDataSource control, has a configuration wizard that you use to configure the data source control. The SiteMapDataSource control doesn't need a wizard because it magically works with the site's site map. See Book III, Chapter 5 for more about site maps.

To launch the configuration wizard for any of the data source controls, follow these steps:

1. **Drag and drop one of the data source controls onto a Web Form.**

2. **Click the arrow in the upper-right corner of the control to display a task dialog box.**

3. **Click the Configure Data Source link in the Tasks dialog box, as shown in Figure 2-14.**

4. **Step through the wizard to configure the data source.**

Data source controls often store their results in DataSets. By using DataSets, you can easily sort and filter the data. You can also use parameters with data sources to specify criteria for which data should be retrieved, deleted, or updated. See the section "Updating data with the DataSet Designer," later in this chapter, for an introduction to working with DataSets.

You can configure data sources by using the databound controls.

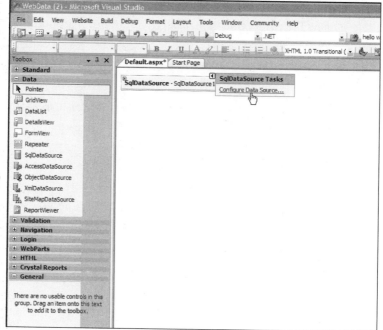

Figure 2-14:
Click the
Configure
Data Source
link to
launch a
config-
uration
wizard.

Using databound Web server controls

The ASP.NET databound controls are bound to a data source control. Visual Studio provides built-in designer support for configuring data sources to work with databound controls.

The steps for adding databound controls are similar for all the controls:

1. **Drag and drop a databound control, such as** `DataList`, **on the Web Form.**

Databound controls are grouped on the Data tab of the toolbox.

2. **Right-click the arrow in the upper-right corner of the control to display the control's Tasks dialog box.**

3. **Select New Data Source from the Choose Data Source drop-down list, as shown in Figure 2-15.**

The Data Source Configuration Wizard appears.

Alternatively, you can select an existing data source control. See the earlier section "Going to the source" for more information on creating data source controls.

Book IV Chapter 2

Show Me the Data

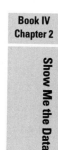

TIP

You associate an existing data source control with a databound control using the databound control's `DataSourceID` property.

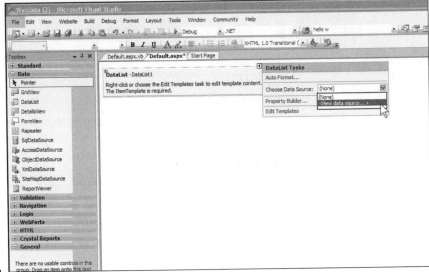

Figure 2-15:
Select New
Data Source
to add a
new data
source.

4. **Click a data source icon on the Choose a Data Source Type page.**

5. **Click the Next button.**

   Depending on the data source you choose, the wizard displays a dialog box for configuring the data source.

   This step displays the same wizard you see after completing Step 3.

   After you configure the data source, Visual Studio adds a data source control to match the type of data source you select on the first page of the Data Source Configuration Wizard.

6. **Step through the wizard to configure the data source.**

Customizing layout with templates

All Web server controls are converted to HTML markup so they can be displayed in a Web browser. Some controls, such as the `GridView` control and `DetailsView` control, are configured by default to render as HTML tables. Other controls, such as `FormView` and `Repeater`, allow you to specify the HTML markup you wish to use to display the control's contents.

You specify HTML markup for a control to use by setting the control's template properties. (The content you define in a template property is called a *template*.) There are several template properties you can define for a control, such as

✦ **HeaderTemplate** — Defines the HTML markup used to create the control's header.

✦ **ItemTemplate** — Defines the HTML markup used to display data items. There are several variations of the ItemTemplate that allow you to specify different HTML markup for alternating item rows or rows being edited. By specifying different markup, you provide visual cues to your user.

✦ **PagerTemplate** — Defines the HTML markup used for navigating between pages as data. For example, you might specify to use Next and Previous.

✦ **FooterTemplate** — Defines the HTML markup used to create the control's footer.

 Data controls aren't the only controls that use template properties. There are many Web server controls that allow you to define their layouts using templates. See the topic "ASP.NET Web Server Controls Templates" in the Visual Studio documentation for more information.

By using templates, you can explicitly define the HTML markup used to display your data in the Web browser. You can display data from a data source using controls, such as labels and text boxes that are databound to the data source. The following example shows you how to create an AlternatingItemTemplate property for a DataList control:

1. **Drag and drop a data source control, such as a SqlDataSource control, on a Web Forms page.**

2. **Configure the data source control to access a data source such as the Department table in the AdventureWorks sample database.**

   See the earlier section "Going to the source" for more information about adding data sources to your Web pages.

3. **Drag and drop a DataList control on a Web Forms page.**

4. **Choose the data source you create in steps 1 and 2 from the Choose Data Source drop-down list. The DataList's ItemTemplate property updates with the fields from the data source.**

5. **Click the EditTemplates link in the DataList Tasks window. The control appears in Template Editing Mode, as shown in Figure 2-16.**

Book IV
Chapter 2

Show Me the Data

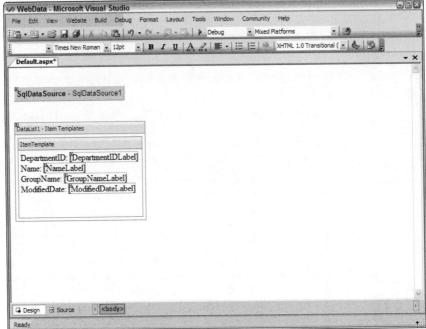

Figure 2-16:
Customize the template using Template Editing Mode.

6. Choose AlternatingItemTemplate from the Display drop-down list in the DataList's Tasks window.

The `AlternatingItemTemplate` appears in the control.

7. Drag and drop a `Label` control inside the `AlternatingItemTemplate` and click the EditDataBindings link in the Label Tasks window.

The DataBindings dialog box appears.

8. Click the Field binding option and choose a field from the Bound to drop-down list, as shown in Figure 2-17. Click OK.

If the Field binding option isn't available, click the Refresh Schema link. Once the schema is refreshed, you should be able to select the option. If the option doesn't become available, then there's a problem with your data source.

The Label control's text property is bound to the field you select. You can choose to bind the data to a different property in the DataBindings dialog box. When you run the page, data from the field appears in the Label.

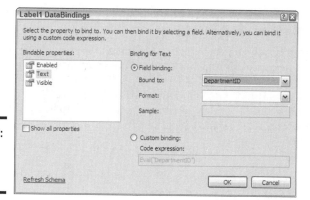

Figure 2-17:
Bind your
data to the
control.

An alternative approach to manually adding content to the
`AlternativeItemTemplate` property is to copy and paste the content
from the `ItemTemplate` property.

9. **Repeat steps 7 and 8 to add all the data you wish to display from your
data source.**

You now have a `DataList` control that has templates defined for the
`ItemTemplate` and `AlternatingItemTemplate` properties. In order to
provide a visual cue to the user for the alternating rows, you must define
the style properties for the template. Each template has its own set of style
properties. You use the style properties to create a custom look for displaying your data.

To set the style for a template in a Web server control:

1. **Click on the control in the Web Forms Designer to select it.**

For example, click on the `DataList` control used in the preceding
example.

2. **Press F4 to open the Properties window.**

3. **Scroll to the Styles properties.**

If you have properties grouped using the Categorized button in the
Properties window, all the style properties are grouped together in the
Styles category. All the style properties end in the word style, such as
`HeaderStyle` or `ItemStyle`. Each style corresponds to a template.

4. **Expand the style property you wish to set.**

For example, expand the `AlternatingItemStyle` property.

**Book IV
Chapter 2**

Show Me the Data

5. **Set the individual property items or specify a `CssClass` you wish to use from a Cascading Style Sheet.**

For example, select a `BackColor` for the `AlternatingItemStyle` property to set a different background color for alternating items.

Figure 2-18 shows the `DataList` control with the `BackColor` property set for the `AlternatingItemStyle` property. The data displayed in the alternating rows uses the `AlternatingItemTemplate` property defined earlier in this section.

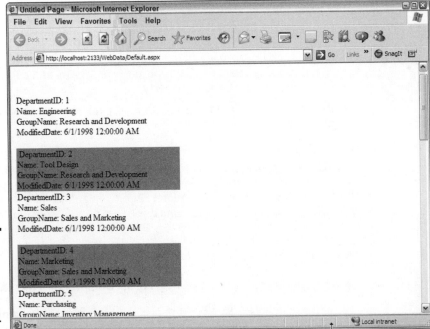

Figure 2-18:
Use styles to control the appearance of your data.

Working with tasks and properties

Databound Web server controls share many common tasks and properties. Table 2-1 lists some common tasks and properties. Tasks are accessed by using the control's Tasks dialog box, and properties are accessed by way of the Properties window.

Table 2-1	Common Data Web Server Control Tasks and Properties	
Feature	*How to Access It*	*Controls*
Choose Data Source	Tasks	All data Web server controls
Auto Format	Tasks	`DataList, GridView, DetailsView, FormView`
Edit Templates	Tasks	`DataList, GridView, DetailsView, FormView`
Edit Columns, Edit Fields	Tasks	`GridView, DetailsView`
Gridlines	Property	`DataList, GridView, DetailsView`
ShowHeader, ShowFooter	Property	`DataList, GridView`
Paging	Property	`GridView, DetailsView, FormView`

Use tasks and properties to specify style qualities, such as formatting and pagination. You can also determine whether a control allows data manipulation if the data source supports it.

Staying on the same page

Paging is a common property that "wires" a data display so that users can page through it. To change the paging properties for a `FormView` control, follow these steps:

1. **Add a `FormView` control to a Web page and configure it to access a data source such as the Department table in the AdventureWorks database.**

   See Chapter 1 in this mini-book for information about installing the AdventureWorks sample database from Microsoft.

2. **In the `FormView` Tasks dialog box, select the Enable Paging option.**

3. **In the Properties window, click the plus (+) sign next to `PagerSettings`.**

   The pager properties appear.

4. **Set these properties:**

   - For `Mode`, select NextPrevious.
   - For `NextPageText`, type **Next**.
   - For `PreviousPageText`, type **Previous**.

5. **Press Ctrl+F5 to run your site. The pager displays the words *Previous* and *Next,* as shown in Figure 2-19.**

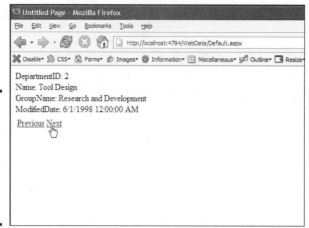

Figure 2-19:
Use the
`Pager`
`Settings`
property to
set custom
data paging
settings.

Auto Formatting

All the databound Web controls can be customized. The AutoFormat feature is an easy way to apply a custom style to databound controls. To apply AutoFormatting to a control, follow these steps:

1. **In the `FormView` Tasks dialog box, click the Auto Format option.**

The Auto Format dialog box appears.

2. **Select a format from the list of schemes.**

The selected format is previewed in the Preview pane.

3. **Click OK.**

The format is applied to the control.

To customize the Auto Format style, edit the control's `Style` properties in the Properties window or in the page's Source view, as shown in Figure 2-20.

Updating data with the DataSet Designer

Visual Studio provides the DataSet Designer as a means to add data to your Web site quickly and easily. The DataSet Designer makes light work of these tasks:

✦ Creating data sources

✦ Retrieving data from data sources

✦ Creating commands to update data in data sources

The DataSet stores an offline copy of the data retrieved from a data source.

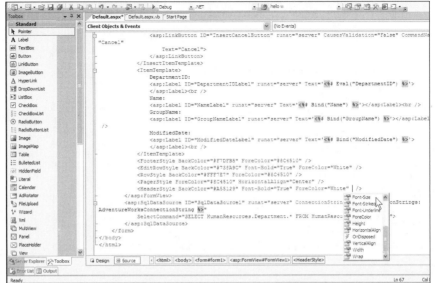

Figure 2-20:
Customize the Auto Format style by using the page's Source view.

To create a new DataSet, follow these steps:

1. **Click the Web site's project folder in Solution Explorer and choose Website⇨Add New Item.**

   The Add New Item dialog box appears.

2. **Click the DataSet icon and enter a name such as** AdventureWorks.xsd **in the Name text box. Click the Add button.**

   Visual Studio prompts you to add a new App_Code folder.

3. **Click the Yes button.**

   The TableAdapter Configuration Wizard appears.

4. **Select an existing database connection, or create a new connection on the Choose Your Data Connection page in the wizard.**

   If you already created a connection to the AdventureWorks database by following earlier examples, you can reuse that connection by choosing it from the drop-down list of connections. Figure 2-21 shows the wizard reusing an existing connection.

   Click the New Connection button to create a new connection to the AdventureWorks database. See the earlier section "Connecting to databases," to see how to configure a new database connection.

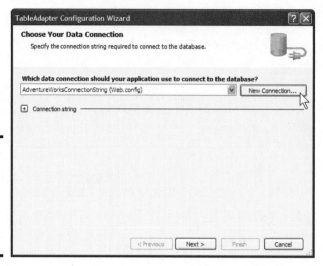

Figure 2-21:
Select an
existing
database
connection
or create a
new one.

5. **Click Next.**

   The Choose a Command Type page appears.

6. **Accept the default command choice, Use SQL Statements. Click Next.**

   You may use this page in the wizard to choose to use new or existing stored procedures instead of SQL statements.

7. **On the Enter a SQL Statement page, click the Query Builder button.**

   The Query Builder appears with the Add Table dialog box open.

8. **Select a table, such as the Department table, and click the Add button to add the table to the Query Builder.**

9. **Click the Close button to close the Add Table window.**

10. **Select each column in the Department table to add the columns to the query's output, as shown in Figure 2-22.**

    You can select the asterisk to select all columns in the table, but it's usually considered best practice to select columns individually. If you use the asterisk, then you run the risk of displaying additional columns if a new column is added to the table in the database.

11. **Click the Execute Query button to test your query, and then click OK to close the Query Builder.**

    Your SQL statement appears in the TableAdapter Configuration Wizard.

12. **Click Next.**

    The Choose Methods to Generate page appears.

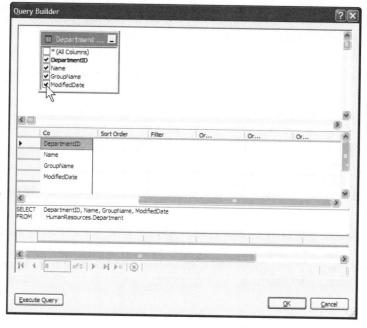

Figure 2-22:
Select all
the columns
in the
Department
table for
your query.

13. Accept the defaults and click Next.

The Wizard Results page appears.

14. Click the Finish button.

Visual Studio creates the DataSet and a TableAdapter for accessing and
updating the Department table. See Chapter 3 in this mini-book for more
information about DataSets and TableAdapters.

To use the DataSet as a data source for a data source Web control, follow
these steps:

1. Drag and drop an ObjectDataSource control on the Web Form.

**2. Right-click the arrow in the upper-right corner to display the control's
Tasks dialog box.**

3. Click the Configure Data Source link.

The Configure Data Source Wizard appears.

4. Select the TableAdapter from the Business Object drop-down list.

If you used the Department table from the AdventureWorks database,
then the name of the TableAdapter is DepartmentTableAdapter.

5. Click Next.

The Define Data Methods page appears. The methods created by the DataSet Designer appear in the SELECT, UPDATE, INSERT, and DELETE tabs. You may use the default methods or select different methods.

To create new methods, right-click on the TableAdapter in the DataSet Designer and choose Configure. The TableAdapter Configuration Wizard starts, and you can specify methods to generate.

6. **Click the Finish button.**

   You have a `DataSource` control that you can use as the data source for a databound control.

DataSets are reusable. To add an existing DataSet from another project to your project, right-click the project's folder and choose Add Existing Item.

Getting the view right with the GridView control

By far, the easiest data Web server controls to use are `GridView` and `DetailsView`. They have built-in support for sorting, paging, selecting, editing, and deleting.

Sorting and paging

To enable sorting and paging on a `GridView` control, follow these steps:

1. **Right-click the upper-right corner of the control to display the control's Tasks dialog box.**

2. **Select the Enable Paging and Enable Sorting options.**

3. **Press Ctrl+F5 to run your site.**

   The data appears in a table.

4. **To sort the table by the GroupName column, click the GroupName hyperlink.**

5. **To page forward, click the numeral 2 in the table's footer, as shown in Figure 2-23.**

Editing and deleting

When `GridView` uses an updatable data source, such as a DataSet, you can use the built-in functionality of `GridView` for editing and deleting records. To enable editing and updating in a `GridView` control, follow these steps:

1. **Drag and drop a `GridView` control on the form.**

2. **Set the `GridView` data source to an updatable data source, such as the `ObjectDataSource` control you create in the section "Updating data with the DataSet Designer," earlier in this chapter.**

The list of available tasks expands.

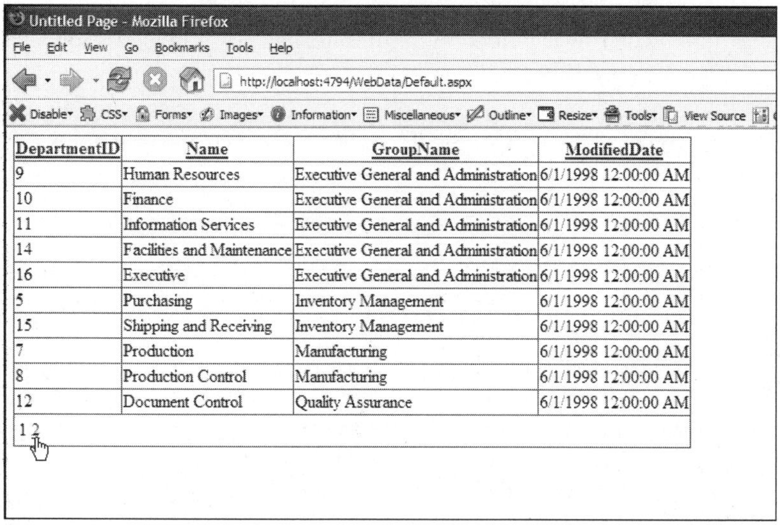

Figure 2-23:
Click the
hyperlink in
the table's
footer to
advance to
the table's
next page.

3. **Select the Enable Editing and Enable Deleting options, as shown in Figure 2-24.**

   The Edit and Delete commands are added to the `GridView` control.

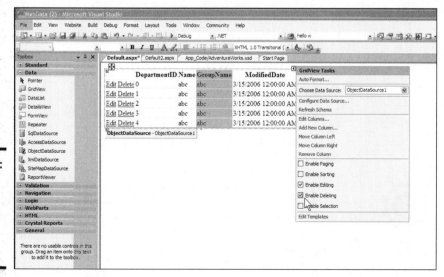

Figure 2-24:
Select the
Enable
Editing and
Enable
Deleting
options.

**Book IV
Chapter 2**

Show Me the Data

4. **Press Ctrl+F5 to run the site.**

5. **Click the Edit button on one of the rows.**

The row is placed in Edit mode, as shown in Figure 2-25.

	DepartmentID	Name	GroupName	ModifiedDate
Edit Delete	1	Engineering	Research and Development	6/1/1998 12:00:00 AM
Edit Delete	2	Tool Design	Research and Development	6/1/1998 12:00:00 AM
Edit Delete	3	Sales	Sales and Marketing	6/1/1998 12:00:00 AM
Edit Delete	4	Marketing	Sales and Marketing	6/1/1998 12:00:00 AM
Edit Delete	5	Purchasing	Inventory Management	6/1/1998 12:00:00 AM
Update Cancel	6	Research and Developi	Research and Developi	6/1/1998 12:00:00 AM
Edit Delete	7	Production	Manufacturing	6/1/1998 12:00:00 AM
Edit Delete	8	Production Control	Manufacturing	6/1/1998 12:00:00 AM
Edit Delete	9	Human Resources	Executive General and Administration	6/1/1998 12:00:00 AM
Edit Delete	10	Finance	Executive General and Administration	6/1/1998 12:00:00 AM
Edit Delete	11	Information Services	Executive General and Administration	6/1/1998 12:00:00 AM
Edit Delete	12	Document Control	Quality Assurance	6/1/1998 12:00:00 AM
Edit Delete	13	Quality Assurance	Quality Assurance	6/1/1998 12:00:00 AM
Edit Delete	14	Facilities and Maintenance	Executive General and Administration	6/1/1998 12:00:00 AM
Edit Delete	15	Shipping and Receiving	Inventory Management	6/1/1998 12:00:00 AM
Edit Delete	16	Executive	Executive General and Administration	6/1/1998 12:00:00 AM

Figure 2-25: Click the Edit button to place the row in Edit mode.

6. **Modify the record and click Update.**

The record is updated.

7. **Click the Delete button.**

You see an error message. The Delete button tries to delete the record, but the database doesn't let it. This example shows why you have to make sure that the data source can execute the commands that Visual Studio builds.

Generally speaking, *delete* is a bad word when you're working with data. You should mark records as inactive rather than delete them. This strategy preserves the integrity of the data.

Binding to expressions

Visual Studio allows you to bind a control's property to an expression. You can bind a property to these kinds of expressions:

+ `AppSettings`
+ `ConnectionStrings`
+ `Resources`

`AppSettings` and `ConnectionStrings` expressions are stored in the web.config file. *Resources* are resource files that store user interface information. To bind a control's property to an expression, you must first create something to which to bind. Book III, Chapter 5 walks you through how to add a name-value pair to the AppSettings section of the web.config file.

To bind to an `AppSetting` key named `AppName`, follow these steps:

1. **Select a control and view the control's properties.**

2. **In the Properties window, click the ellipsis button for the** `Expressions` **property.**

The Expressions dialog box appears.

3. **Select a property from the list of bindable properties.**

4. **Select AppSettings from the Expressions Type drop-down list.**

5. **Type AppName in the Expression Properties box, as shown in Figure 2-26.**

6. **Click OK.**

When you run the site, the property's value is replaced with the value that the `AppName` expression evaluates to.

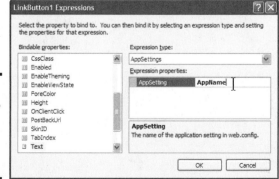

Figure 2-26:
Type an `App`
`Settings`
key in the
properties
box.

Chapter 3: Working with Strongly Typed DataSets

In This Chapter

✔ Creating DataSets in a class library

✔ Using the DataSet Designer

✔ Accessing data with TableAdapters

✔ Digging into the code of a typed DataSet

✔ Consuming typed DataSets

Programmers have always needed a way to work with data in their applications. Accessing data from files or databases every time you need data is impractical. To accommodate the need to have programs access data quickly, programmers store data in memory, using everything from arrays to integers to custom data structures.

Rather than make you spend lots of time thinking about how to store data in memory, Microsoft created the DataSet to provide a standardized means of storing data in memory for quick access.

A DataSet works like an in-memory database. The DataSet has tables with columns and rows, and you create relations between tables. You can load data into a DataSet from a database, or you can enter new data into the DataSet. You can insert, delete, and update records. Once you've made all the changes to records in your DataSet, you commit those changes to the actual database.

Visual Studio provides the DataSet Designer for creating and manipulating DataSets. In this chapter, I explain what a DataSet is and show you how to use the DataSet Designer to create a special kind of DataSet, the strongly typed DataSet.

Understanding the DataSet

A *DataSet* is a resource provided by the Microsoft .NET Framework for storing data in memory. Datasets store data in tables, and you can create relations between tables, similar to the way you create them in a database.

You use a DataSet to

✦ **Store an in-memory copy of data from a database or other data source.**

Data stored in a DataSet is disconnected from its original data source. The DataSet stores data in the computer's memory, where it can be quickly accessed by your program.

✦ **Store data modified by your program.**

As data stored in the DataSet is modified by your program or people using your program, the DataSet maintains copies of the original and modified records. You can specify constraints that prevent records from being modified or deleted in the DataSet. Because DataSets don't remain connected to the data source, you can provide feedback to your users without modifying the original data source.

✦ **Execute commands that retrieve data from the data source and send modified data back to the data source.**

Datasets accept a set of SQL statements specified by the programmer to select, insert, update, and delete records in the data source.

✦ **Act as a data source for databound controls, such as `GridView`.**

Datasets are a natural data source for databound controls. You assign your DataSet and a table in the DataSet to the control's `DataSource` and `DataMember` properties, and the control displays the data from the DataSet.

The .NET DataSet acts as an intermediary between your data source and a databound control, as shown in Figure 3-1.

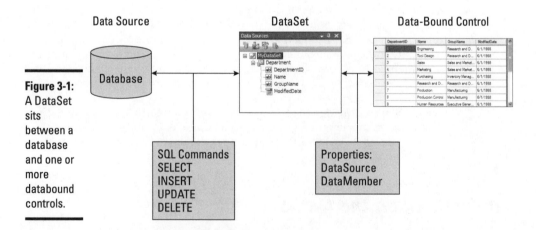

Figure 3-1: A DataSet sits between a database and one or more databound controls.

The .NET DataSet, which provides a basic structure for storing data, is composed of a set of these objects:

✦ **DataTable** — Contains a set of `DataColumn` and `DataRow` objects that represent a tabular set of data.

✦ **DataColumn** — Represents a column in a `DataTable` object.

✦ **Constraint** — Identifies `DataColumn` objects as unique or foreign keys.

✦ **DataRelation** — Creates a parent-child relationship between two `DataTable` objects.

✦ **DataRow** — Represents a row in a `DataTable` object.

A DataSet can contain one or more DataTables. A DataTable contains one or more `DataColumn` and `DataRow` objects. Figure 3-2 illustrates the relationship between the objects in a DataSet.

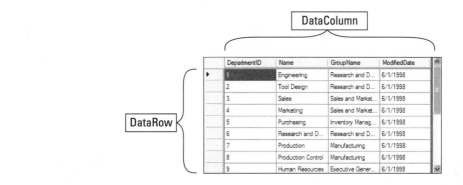

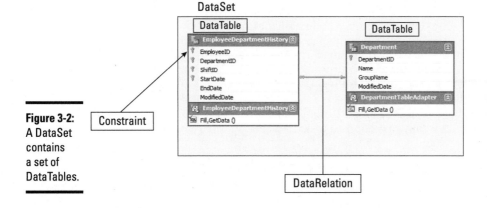

Figure 3-2:
A DataSet contains a set of DataTables.

Book IV
Chapter 3

**Working with
Strongly Typed
DataSets**

You can create two kinds of DataSets in .NET:

✦ **Typed** — This kind uses a schema from an existing data source to define the tables, columns, and constraints in the DataSet.

✦ **Untyped** — No schema is defined when the DataSet is created.

What's your type?

Typed and untyped DataSets are nothing new to .NET and Visual Studio. In previous versions of .NET, hardly anyone used typed DataSets. The code generated for typed DataSets by previous versions of Visual Studio had some quirks. People like me who saw how easy it was to use typed DataSets figured out ways to work around the flaws. With this release of Visual Studio 2005 and .NET, the bugs are worked out, and Microsoft is once again singing the praises of typed DataSets. Although, most of the articles you'll see about typed DataSets refer to them as strongly typed DataSets. Whether you choose to call them typed or strongly typed, they'll make your coding go a lot faster if you use them.

Because no schema is defined for untyped DataSets, you must create each DataTable you need along with the `DataColumn` objects. A typed DataSet is an intelligent DataSet because it's "aware" of an existing schema. Visual Studio provides the DataSet Designer visual tool for creating typed DataSets.

Typed DataSets force you to use the types defined in the DataSet's schema. For example, a typed DataSet that uses a schema to store customer data can't be used to store order data. You must modify the DataSet's schema so the DataSet knows how to store order data. An untyped DataSet, however, has no such restriction. You can store customer and order data in an untyped DataSet without explicitly defining how the data is stored.

While it may be tempting to think that using a DataSet is easier if you didn't have to explicitly define a schema, untyped DataSets allow you to get sloppy and can make your code difficult to read and follow. Using typed DataSets eliminates the ambiguity of not knowing for sure what data is stored in the DataSet. By referring to the DataSet's schema, you have no doubts about the typed DataSet's purpose in your code. The DataSet Designer makes it very simple to create typed DataSets.

Typed DataSets are often called strongly typed, while untyped DataSets are usually just referred to as DataSets.

Working with untyped DataSets

You create untyped DataSets by using the `DataSet` control on the Data tab of the control toolbox.

To create an untyped DataSet, follow these steps:

1. **Create a new Windows application.**

2. **Drag and drop a DataSet control from the Data tab of the toolbox onto the Windows Forms Designer.**

   The Add DataSet window appears.

3. **Select the Untyped dataset option.**

4. **Click the OK button.**

   Visual Studio adds the DataSet to your form.

You can create a DataSet in code. (See Chapter 5 of this mini-book.)

An untyped DataSet has no schema. A schema defines the structure of the DataSet. You must add the tables and columns to define the schema. To add tables and columns to your untyped DataSet, follow these steps:

1. **Click the DataSet you added to your form in the preceding set of steps.**

2. **Press F4 to display the Properties window.**

3. **Click the ellipsis button for the Tables property.**

   The Tables Collection Editor appears.

4. **Click the Add button to add a new table.**

   The table's properties appear on the right side of the editor.

5. **Type a name for your table in the TableName property, such as Customer.**

   The table's default name is Table1.

6. **Click the ellipsis button for the Columns property.**

   The Columns Collection Editor appears.

7. **Click the Add button to add a new column.**

8. **Type a name for the column in the ColumnName property, such as CustomerName.**

   You can set the column's properties, such as its default value and maximum length, in the Columns Collection Editor (see Figure 3-3).

9. **Repeat Steps 3–8 to add more tables and columns.**

You can use the DataSet's Properties window to access collection editors for relations between tables and constraints within a table.

Using the Properties window to add tables and columns doesn't change your DataSet from untyped to typed. In order to be a typed DataSet, the DataSet must have a schema file.

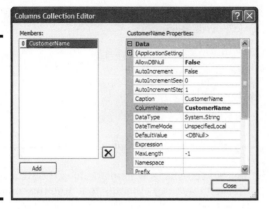

Figure 3-3:
Use the Columns Collection Editor to access the DataSet's properties and collections.

Flexing your strongly typed DataSets

Data types are used in programming languages to set the rules for how data is expected to behave. Examples of data types are integers and characters. When you declare a new variable, you specify the data type of the variable so that your program knows what to expect. A strongly typed DataSet creates a new data type for your application to use.

Strongly typed programming languages require you to specify a data type at the time you declare a variable. *Weakly typed* languages also use data types, but they aren't as strict about their usage. For example, a weakly typed language allows you to treat a string as an integer. Strongly typed languages are stricter about how type rules are enforced. Because strongly typed languages allow you to bend fewer rules, the language's compiler has more opportunities to prevent you from using types incorrectly. Many scripting languages, such as JavaScript and Perl, are weak typed. Visual Basic and C# are strongly typed languages.

For example, if you create the typed DataSet `CustomerDataSet` to store customer data, you create a new data type. Your new customer DataSet might include tables to store your customer's identity and contact data. You can declare a new `MyCustomer` variable that uses your customer DataSet type, like this:

```
Dim MyCustomer As New CustomerDataSet()
```

When you access your `MyCustomer` variable, it already knows how you want to define your customer's identity and contact data because it's of the type `CustomerDataSet`. For example, to add a new customer and set the caption for the account number column, you type

```
MyCustomer.Customer.AddCustomerRow("123456", "John", "Smith")
MyCustomer.Customer.AccountNumberColumn.Caption = "Accout Number"
```

DataSets versus business objects

Most professional software developers and architects agree that you should separate your data entity code from your presentation code. Most professionals create their own, custom code for defining the data entities used in their applications. This *business object layer* is often used in conjunction with another set of code, a data access layer. The *data access layer* defines methods of access to data. For example, you can have methods to access a SQL Server database and an XML file. Your business objects can use either of these access methods to populate itself.

In many cases, all these layers are way too much for the average programmer to set up. It's a lot of coding. For that reason, typed DataSets may be a good approach. DataSets aren't a cure-all. Although they're bloated and they're not always acceptable in Web applications, they work well in Windows applications.

I use typed DataSets rather than business objects in a few of my applications because the applications are easier to develop and maintain in the long run.

Using typed DataSets saves you from doing a lot of coding because Visual Studio generates the code for you. All you have to do is drag and drop tables from your database onto the DataSet Designer. To read more about the DataSet Designer, see the section "Creating Typed DataSets," a little later in this chapter.

Take another look at DataSets if you wrote them off in the past. In previous versions of Visual Studio, the code that was generated for typed DataSets was buggy and difficult to extend.

DataSets and XML, together at last

DataSets can use XML as their data source *and* be converted to XML. The XML language is used to create self-describing data files. For example, you can read an XML file into a DataSet, modify the data in the DataSet, and then produce the modified data as XML output. Or, you can open data from a database in a DataSet and produce the data as XML output.

You have to be able to write code to read and write XML to DataSets. There are no wizards to do it for you. See Chapter 5 in this mini-book to read more.

Typed DataSets use an XML schema to define their tables, columns, relations, and constraints. See the section "Viewing the source," later in this chapter, for more about viewing a typed DataSet's XML schema.

Creating Typed DataSets

Visual Studio provides the Dataset Designer for creating and working with strongly typed DataSets. A DataSet is *strongly typed* if it's generated from an existing data source schema that outlines the DataSet's structure. You don't have to create this schema yourself — you can drag and drop items from a database onto the DataSet Designer. The Designer builds the schema for you.

Whether you're using the DataSet Designer in a Windows application, Web site project, or smart device project, the Designer looks and acts the same.

Creating a DataSet in a class library

When you work with data, use the best practice of isolating your data code into separate projects so that you can reuse your data with other presentation layers. For example, if you create a data project that can be accessed by a Windows project and a Web site project, isolate your data in its own project so that you don't have to define it twice.

To use an existing DataSet in a Windows or Web project, see the section "Consuming a Typed DataSet," later in this chapter.

You create a data project by using a class library. To create a new class library, follow these steps:

1. **Choose File⇨New.**

2. **Choose Project from the submenu.**

The New Project dialog box appears.

3. **Expand the Visual Basic project type.**

You can create class libraries in other project types, such as C#, J#, and C++.

4. **Click the Class Library icon.**

5. **Type a name, such as** DataLibrary, **in the name text box.**

6. **Click the OK button. Visual Studio creates a new class library project.**

The class library project template creates an empty class file named class1.vb. You can safely delete this file for this example. To delete the file, right-click the file in Solution Explorer and choose the Delete command from the shortcut menu.

Visual Studio includes a project item named DataSet that you use to add a typed DataSet to your project.

To add a typed DataSet to your class library, follow these steps:

1. **Click the class library's project folder in Solution Explorer.**

   The project folder is under the solution.

2. **Choose Project⇨Add New Item.**

   The Add New Item dialog box appears.

3. **Click the DataSet icon.**

4. **Type a name, such as** MyDataSet.

   Typed DataSets end with the file extension .xsd, which is the extension for XML schemas. To read more about XML schemas, see Chapter 4 in this mini-book.

5. **Click the Add button.**

   Visual Studio opens the typed DataSet in the DataSet Designer, as shown in Figure 3-4.

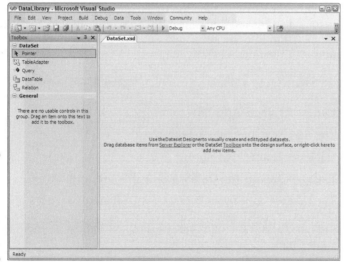

Figure 3-4:
Use the
DataSet
Designer to
create typed
DataSets.

Adding typed DataSets to existing projects

To access the DataSet Designer, you must create a new DataSet or open an existing one. The steps for these two tasks differ slightly, depending on whether you're opening a DataSet in a Web site project or a Windows project.

Follow these steps to add a strongly typed DataSet to a Web project:

1. **Right-click the Web site's project folder in Solution Explorer.**

2. Choose Add New Item from the shortcut menu.

The Add New Item dialog box appears.

3. Click the DataSet icon.

4. Type a name for the DataSet in the Name text box.

5. Click the Add button.

Visual Studio prompts you to add the DataSet to the App_Code folder.

The App_Code folder is part of the new Web site folder structure in ASP.NET 2.0. You can read more about the App_Code folder in Chapter 4 of Book III.

6. Click the Yes button to add the DataSet to the Web site's App_Code folder.

The DataSet appears in the DataSet Designer.

Visual Studio launches the TableAdapter Configuration Wizard. The wizard allows you to create a connection to a database and configure SQL statements for selecting and updating data. To see the TableAdapter Configuration Wizard in action, see the section in Chapter 2 of this mini-book about updating data with the DataSet Designer.

To add a DataSet to a Windows project, follow these steps:

1. Choose Project⇨Add New Item.

The Add New Item dialog box appears.

2. Click the DataSet icon.

3. Type a name for the DataSet and click the Add button.

The DataSet appears in the DataSet Designer.

To read more about the different ways to add DataSets to Windows applications, see Chapter 2 in this mini-book.

You can consume an existing DataSet in a Windows or Web application. See the section "Consuming a Typed DataSet," later in this chapter, for more information.

Exploring the DataSet Designer

Anytime you add a typed DataSet to your application, you'll use the DataSet Designer to create and modify its schema. A typed DataSet's schema is stored in an XML Schema file with the file extension .xsd. The DataSet Designer is essentially a visual schema designer where you define the tables and relations in the typed DataSet. Visual Studio uses the schema to generate the code to create your typed DataSet.

The DataSet Designer provides two features for creating typed DataSets:

+ **A toolbox** — Use the toolbox to build tables and relations.

+ **A design surface** — Drag and drop items from the toolbox or an existing database connection to the design surface.

Meet the players

The DataSet Designer uses a distinctive set of toolbox items for building typed DataSets. When you drag and drop database objects, such as tables, from an existing database connection, Visual Studio populates items from the DataSet Designer toolbox by using the schema information from your database connection.

This list describes the toolbox items used by the DataSet Designer:

+ **TableAdapter** — Retrieves data from the database and sends updates back for an associated DataTable.

+ **Query** — Retrieves data from the database, not associated with a specific DataTable.

+ **DataTable** — Provides a representation of a database table.

+ **Relation** — Creates links and constraints between DataTables.

The DataSet Designer's toolbox items are visual representations of technologies used in ADO.NET, the data access technology in the Microsoft .NET Framework. To read more about ADO.NET, see Chapter 5 in this mini-book.

You use the DataSet Designer to work with representations of your data visually. Behind the scenes, the Designer

+ Creates an XML schema that defines the tables and columns in your DataSet. The DataSet file itself is an XML schema file. The DataSet Designer adds annotations to the XML schema files to extend the XML schema syntax.

+ Generates the ADO.NET code that allows your program to access the data source.

See the section "Looking Under the Hood of a Strongly Typed DataSet," later in this chapter, to read more about viewing the code and XML markup generated by the DataSet Designer.

**Book IV
Chapter 3**

**Working with
Strongly Typed
DataSets**

Building a DataSet of your own

You can use the tools in the DataSet Designer's toolbox to manually create a typed DataSet.

Here are the steps you follow to add a new table to a typed DataSet:

1. **Create a new typed DataSet by following the steps in the section "Creating Typed DataSets," earlier in this chapter.**

2. **Drag and drop a DataTable from the toolbox onto the DataSet Designer. A DataTable with the name DataTable1 appears in the designer.**

   Press Ctrl+Alt+X to open the toolbox if it's closed.

3. **Click the DataTable's name and type a name, such as** Customer.

The DataTable needs columns. Add them by following these steps:

1. **Right-click the Customer DataTable.**

   A shortcut menu appears.

2. **Choose Add⇨Column.**

   A new column appears in the DataTable.

3. **Type name for the column, such as** CustID.

4. **Repeat Steps 1–3 to add FirstName and LastName columns to the DataTable.**

You can set properties for the DataTable's columns by using the Properties window. Examples of properties you can set are the column's `DataType` and `DefaultValue` properties. See the section "Going beyond database tables," later in this chapter, for an example of setting a column's property.

You add constraints to your Customer DataTable to specify whether a column is unique. To set the CustID column as the table's primary key, follow these steps:

1. **Right-click the Customer DataTable.**

   A shortcut menu appears.

2. **Choose Add⇨Key.**

   The Unique Constraint dialog box appears.

3. **Select the CustID column by placing a check mark next to it.**

4. **Select the primary key option.**

5. **Click the OK button.**

A little key icon appears next to the CustID column name, as shown in Figure 3-5.

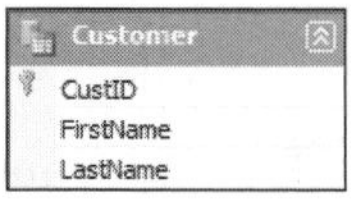

Figure 3-5:
A key appears next to the CustID column name.

You use the Relation item from the DataSet Designer toolbox to create a parent-child relationship between two tables. The Relation item creates a Relation which represents the relationship.

You can create a relationship between a table and itself. When a table is related to itself, the relationship is *reflexive*. See the next section for an example of a reflexive relationship.

There are three kinds of relations you can create using the Relation item:

✦ **Both Relation and Foreign Key Constraint** — Creates a parent-child relationship between two tables by using the columns selected in the Columns grid. A foreign key constraint is created that allows you to set rules for what happens when records are updated or deleted.

✦ **Foreign Key Constraint Only** — Identifies columns in the child table as foreign keys and allows you to set constraints for what happens when records are updated or deleted. You cannot access child records via their parent records because no parent-child relationship is established.

✦ **Relation Only** — Creates a parent-child relationship between the tables, but doesn't implement rules for what happens when records are updated or deleted.

Select the Relation Only option whenever you want to access a child table's records via its parent's records. Create a foreign key constraint whenever you want to specify rules for when parent or child records are updated or deleted. I generally setup both relation and foreign key constraints because it affords the highest amount of data integrity.

Follow these steps to create a Relation between two tables:

1. **Follow the first two step lists in this section to create a DataTable and columns. Then create a DataTable named CustomerAddress and add these columns:**

- CustID
- Address1
- Address2
- City
- State
- Zip

2. **Drag and drop a Relation item from the toolbox onto the designer. The Relation dialog box appears.**

   Use the Relation dialog box to specify a parent and child table and select the columns in each table that link the tables.

3. **Type a name for the Relation in the Name field. Relation names are usually some combination of the two tables' names, such as Customer_ CustomerAddress.**

4. **Select Customer as the parent table and CustomerAddress as the child table.**

   When your DataSet has only two tables, the Designer selects the parent-child tables for you.

5. **In the Columns grid, select the CustID column from each table.**

   The CustID column is the column that both columns share.

   Be sure to create columns before adding the Relation. You can't add new columns by using the Columns grid.

6. **Select the Both Relation and Foreign Key Constraint options.**

   Choosing the Both Relation and Foreign Key Constraint option or the Foreign Key Constraint Only option enables the constraint rule selectors, as shown in Figure 3-6.

7. **Use the constraint rule selectors to set the foreign key constraints:**
   - **Update Rule** — Cascade
   - **Delete Rule** — Cascade
   - **Accept/Reject Rule** — Cascade

   Constraint rules specify the action taken on a child record by the database when its parent record is updated or deleted. Your choices for Update Rule and Delete Rule are shown in this list:
   - **None** — Nothing happens to the child rows when a parent is updated or deleted.
   - **Cascade** — The child rows are deleted or updated.

Figure 3-6:
Choosing
to create
foreign key
constraints
enables the
constraint
rule
selectors.

- **SetNull** — The values in the child rows are set to `null`.

- **SetDefault** — The values in the child row are set to the default values.

The Accept/Reject Rule option specifies what happens to the child rows when a parent row either accepts or rejects changes. Your choices for Accept/Reject Rule are None and Cascade.

8. Leave the Nested Relation check box cleared.

Nesting the relation causes the child table to be nested inside the parent table.

9. Click the OK button.

You use the TableAdapter and Query items from the DataSet Designer toolbox to fill your DataSet with data. Using the TableAdapter item opens the TableAdapter Configuration Wizard, and the Query item opens the Table-Adapter Query Configuration Wizard. To see both wizards in action, see the section "Shepherding Data," later in this chapter.

Adding database objects

The easiest way to build a typed DataSet is to build it from an existing database. You use Server Explorer to drag and drop database objects onto the DataSet Designer surface. The designer presents a visual representation of the DataSet and creates a basic set of queries to select and update data. You then use a wizard to modify those queries or create new ones.

You use the set of Visual Database Tools, including Server Explorer, for manipulating database objects. See Chapter 6 in this mini-book for more information about the Visual Database Tools.

To connect to a database by using Server Explorer, follow these steps:

1. **Open Server Explorer by choosing View⇨Server Explorer.**

   You can open Server Explorer by clicking the Server Explorer link on the DataSet Designer design surface pane.

2. **Click the Connect to Database button on the Server Explorer toolbar.**

   The Add Connection dialog box appears.

   Alternatively, you can right-click the Data Connection icon and choose Add Connection from the shortcut menu.

3. **Create a new connection to the AdventureWorks database.**

   The connection appears in Server Explorer. (Chapter 2 in this mini-book walks you through the Add Connection dialog box.)

Adding database objects to the DataSet is a matter of dragging them from Server Explorer and dropping them on the design surface. Follow these steps to add new tables to the DataSet Designer:

1. **Click the plus (+) sign next to the data connection you created in the preceding set of steps.**

   The data connection expands.

   Server Explorer displays data connections as a hierarchical display of database objects. You view an object's contents by clicking the plus (+) sign to expand the container.

2. **Click the plus (+) sign next to the Tables folder.**

   A list of the data connection's tables appears.

3. **Drag the Department table to the design surface and drop the table.**

   A representation of the table and a TableAdapter appear on the Designer. The TableAdapter is responsible for creating commands to retrieve and update the data for the table it's associated with.

4. **Drag and drop the EmployeeDepartmentHistory table onto the Designer.**

   The table and a TableAdapter appear on the designer. Visual Studio creates links between the tables, as shown in Figure 3-7.

5. **Drag and drop the Employee table onto the designer.**

   The designer creates a link between the Employee table and the EmployeeDepartmentHistory table.

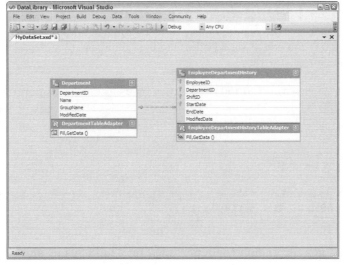

Figure 3-7:
The database tables appear on the designer with links between them.

6. Press Ctrl+S to save the DataSet.

Notice the link at the top of the Employee table that points back to itself, as shown in Figure 3-8. The Employee table has a record for each employee. Employees have a manager, and managers are employees, too. Rather than create a separate Manager table that duplicates information in the Employee table, the Employee table has a ManagerID column. The source of the ManagerID column is the Employee table, which creates a link. A column in a table using that table as its source is an example of a reflexive relationship.

Figure 3-8:
The Employee table has a link to itself.

Going beyond database tables

Tables aren't the only database objects you can add to your strongly typed DataSet. You can also add other kinds of database objects, such as stored procedures and views.

Access views and stored procedures by using Server Explorer. See the preceding section, "Adding database objects," for an example of using Server Explorer to access database objects.

To add a view from the AdventureWorks sample database to your DataSet, follow these steps:

1. **Drag and drop the vEmployeeDepartment view from Server Explorer onto the DataSet Designer.**

The view appears on the Designer. Views often start with the letter v.

2. **Click the vEmployeeDepartment DataTable name, and change it to** EmployeeDepartment.

3. **Right-click the FirstName column.**

4. **Click Properties from the shortcut menu that appears.**

The Properties window appears.

5. **Set the FirstName column's Caption property to First Name, as shown in Figure 3-9.**

Set the Caption property for a column to specify the text you want displayed in the column's header.

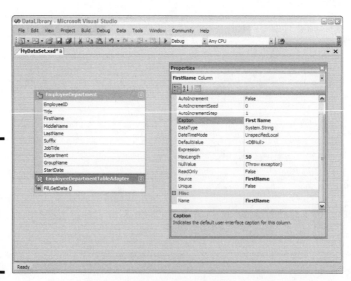

Figure 3-9:
Set the column's Caption property by using the Properties window.

The DataSet Designer cannot generate SQL commands to update your data when you use a view or stored procedure. You have to use the TableAdapter Configuration Wizard to write your own SQL statements or select stored procedures. (See the next section for more information about the wizard.)

Shepherding Data

You need some way to move data in and out of your DataSet. The new Microsoft .NET Framework technology, the TableAdapter, shepherds data between your data source and DataSet. Each table in your DataSet requires its own TableAdapter. The TableAdapter, located between your database and DataSet, performs these functions:

✦ Connects to your database

✦ Sends SQL statements to the database to retrieve and update data

When you add a database object from Server Explorer to a DataSet by using the DataSet Designer, the designer automatically creates a TableAdapter. The TableAdapter connects to the data source and generates a SQL statement to retrieve data to fill the table in the DataSet.

A single table in a DataSet doesn't have to correlate directly to a database table. A table in a DataSet can be filled with data from a view, stored procedure, or SQL statement you specify. See the preceding section, about going beyond database tables, for more information on adding views and stored procedures to a DataSet.

The DataSet Designer provides two wizards for creating TableAdapters:

✦ **TableAdapter Configuration Wizard** — Walks you through connecting to a database and creating SQL statements or stored procedures for accessing data.

✦ **TableAdapter Query Configuration Wizard** — Allows you to add queries for accessing data.

The TableAdapter wizards generate the code to make database connections and execute SQL commands by using ADO.NET to access the database. To read more about connections and SQL commands in ADO.NET, see Chapter 5 in this mini-book.

The TableAdapter wizards can generate SQL statements to retrieve and update data when the table's data source is a single table in a database.

If you use multiple tables in a database to fill a single table in a DataSet, you need to supply your own SQL statements or stored procedures to update the original data source.

Using the TableAdapter Configuration Wizard

The TableAdapter, the workhorse of the DataSet, is responsible for shepherding your data in and out of the database. The DataSet Designer configures a TableAdapter for each table you drop on the designer.

You use the TableAdapter Configuration Wizard to

✦ Generate stored procedures for a single table.

✦ Specify the exact SQL statements you want the wizard to use.

✦ Bind the TableAdapter to existing stored procedures.

It's common practice in data access to use stored procedures to retrieve and update data. A *stored procedure* is a program that's saved with your database. You can use SQL statements to write stored procedures to do anything you want to do to your data.

For example, you can write a stored procedure to retrieve data from your database. The SQL statement to retrieve an employee looks like this:

```
SELECT EmployeeID,FirstName, LastName
FROM Employee
WHERE EmployeeID = @EmployeeID
```

Rather than execute the preceding SQL statement every time you need to get an employee's data, you create a stored procedure named `GetEmployee`. The `GetEmployee` stored procedure has the SQL statement inside it. To execute the `GetEmployee` stored procedure, you type

```
EXEC GetEmployee @EmployeeID = 4
```

See the sidebar "The anatomy of a stored procedure" for more information on how to write a stored procedure.

You should use stored procedures over SQL statements because stored procedures are

✦ Stored centrally on the database server

✦ More secure than using SQL statements

✦ Reusable

✦ Easier to execute

The most commonly used stored procedures in data access are CRUD (Create, Read, Update, and Delete) procedures. The four letters in CRUD relate to each of the four SQL commands you use to retrieve and update data:

+ INSERT
+ SELECT
+ UPDATE
+ DELETE

Note that the C in CRUD stands for create, although the SQL command is INSERT. (I guess CRUD is easier to remember than ISUD.)

Generating stored procedures

You can use the TableAdapter Configuration Wizard to create new stored procedures for a single table. By default, the wizard creates SQL statements and uses them to access data.

Stored procedures are preferred because they provide a performance advantage over regular SQL statements.

The anatomy of a stored procedure

A *stored procedure* is a set of saved SQL statements. Stored procedures can

✔ Accept input parameters and return values as output parameters

✔ Return a status value to indicate whether the procedure succeeded or failed

When you create a new stored procedure, you have to do a few things, such as

✔ Use the CREATE PROCEDURE statement.

✔ Specify parameters.

✔ Use the SET statement to send information to the database about how you want the query executed.

✔ Type SQL statements that operate on data such as the SELECT, INSERT, UPDATE, or DELETE commands.

For example, to create a new stored procedure named GetEmployees with one input parameter, type the following lines:

```
CREATE PROCEDURE GetEmployee
    @EmployeeID int = 0
AS
BEGIN
    SET NOCOUNT ON;

    SELECT
    EmployeeID,FirstName,
    LastName
    FROM Employee
    WHERE EmployeeID =
    @EmployeeID

END
GO
```

After executing this block of SQL statements, SQL Server adds the stored procedure to the database. SQL Server changes the CREATE PROCEDURE statement to ALTER PROCEDURE after the procedure is created. The remaining lines in the procedure stay the same unless you modify them later.

**Book IV
Chapter 3**

**Working with
Strongly Typed
DataSets**

To generate new stored procedures for the department table, follow these steps:

1. Right-click the Department table in the DataSet Designer.

2. Choose Configure from the shortcut menu.

The TableAdapter Configuration Wizard opens with the Enter a SQL Statement page displayed.

Alternatively, you can choose Data⇨Configure.

3. Click the Previous button to step back to the preceding page in the wizard.

The Choose a Command Type page appears.

4. Select the Create New Stored Procedures option, as shown in Figure 3-10.

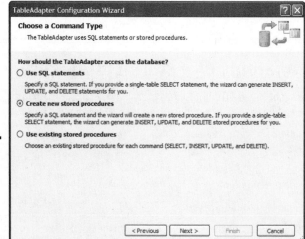

Figure 3-10: Select the option to create new stored procedures.

5. Click the Next button twice to advance to the Create the Stored Procedures page.

6. Type a name for each stored procedure in the appropriate text box, as shown in Figure 3-11.

See the later sidebar "Naming stored procedures" for more information on naming stored procedures.

Click the Preview SQL Script button to view the SQL script that Visual Studio uses to create the stored procedures. You can save the script and modify it to use with other tables.

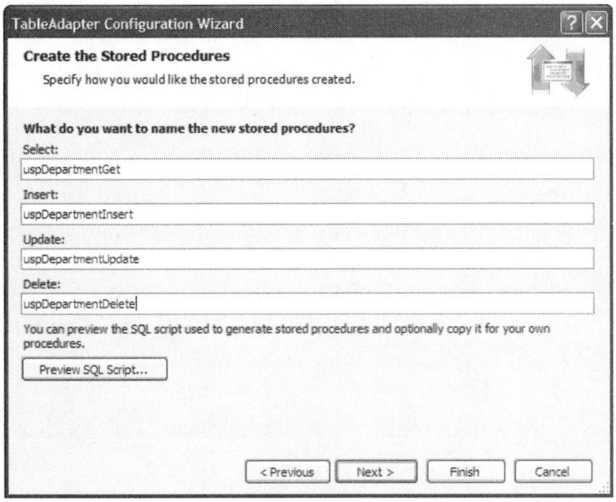

TableAdapter Configuration Wizard

Create the Stored Procedures
Specify how you would like the stored procedures created.

What do you want to name the new stored procedures?
Select:
uspDepartmentGet

Insert:
uspDepartmentInsert

Update:
uspDepartmentUpdate

Delete:
uspDepartmentDelete

You can preview the SQL script used to generate stored procedures and optionally copy it for your own procedures.

Preview SQL Script...

< Previous   Next >   Finish   Cancel

Figure 3-11:
Type a name
for each
stored
procedure.

7. Click the Finish button.

Visual Studio creates the four stored procedures in the database.

The TableAdapter uses the new stored procedures, rather than regular SQL statements, to access your data.

Expand the Stored Procedures folder in Server Explorer to view the new stored procedures, as shown in Figure 3-12.

Binding to existing stored procedures

You can tell the DataSet Designer to use an existing stored procedure to access data, usually whenever you already have stored procedures created. You're likely to use this feature often because DataSets rarely are simple enough to use only one table.

Follow these steps to bind a TableAdapter to an existing stored procedure:

1. Follow Steps 1–3 in the preceding section, "Generating stored procedures" to open the TableAdapter Configuration Wizard.

2. Select the Use Existing Stored Procedure option on the Choose a Command Type page.

3. Click the Next button.

The Bind Commands to Existing Stored Procedures page appears.

4. Click the drop-down arrow for each of the commands, and select the stored procedure to use, as shown in Figure 3-13.

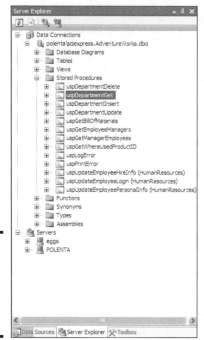

Figure 3-12:
View the new stored procedures in Server Explorer.

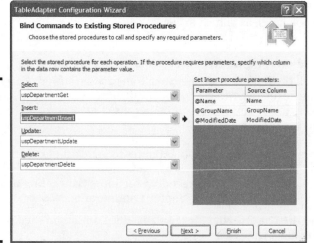

Figure 3-13:
Select existing stored procedures from the drop-down lists for each command.

5. **Verify that the source column matches the stored procedure's input parameters.**

   The DataSet Designer displays the stored procedure's input parameters and their corresponding source columns from the DataSet's table. To select a different source column, click the Source Column drop-down list and select a different column, as shown in Figure 3-14.

6. **Click the Finish button.**

Visual Studio generates the code to use the stored procedures.

Using the TableAdapter Query Configuration Wizard

You aren't stuck with the select statements that the DataSet Designer creates for you. You can specify additional statements for retrieving and updating data.

You use the TableAdapter Query Wizard to create additional queries. To start the wizard, follow these steps:

1. **Right-click the table in the DataSet Designer.**

2. **Choose Add from the shortcut menu.**

Naming stored procedures

You need a standard system for naming database objects, such as stored procedures. Most developers try to create a system that groups like procedures by using a combination of prefixes, table names, SQL commands, and clauses, such as:

- ✔ `prefixTableNameCommand`
- ✔ `prefixCommandTableName`
- ✔ `prefixTableNameCommandWhere`
- ✔ `prefixCommandTableNameWhere Sortby`

You can argue for and against each standard. When you're dreaming up your standard, remember that your database can easily contain thousands of stored procedures. Chances are that your scheme will break down as the quantity of stored procedures increases.

It's almost impossible to change your naming standard after the fact, so pick something and stay consistent. In my experience, naming conventions have little to do with helping you

actually find something. No matter what you dream up, you will struggle to find one stored procedure in a sea of stored procedures. Instead, your naming conventions should take the guesswork out of naming. It's one less issue you have to think about. When you're creating a stored procedure or using an existing one, the naming standard helps you know what to expect.

When you want to find stored procedures, I suggest getting into the habit of using the SQL Server Management Studio to view table dependencies. (See Chapter 6 in this mini-book.)

Whatever your standard system for naming stored procedures, never use the prefix `sp` (short for *system procedure*). Using that prefix on your own stored procedures creates a slight performance hit because SQL Server expects `sp`-prefixed stored procedures to reside in the master database. Microsoft uses the `usp` prefix (short for *user stored procedure*), in its AdventureWorks database.

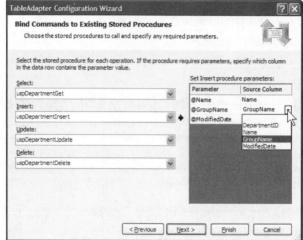

Figure 3-14:
Select a
different
source
column to
use as the
stored
procedure's
input
parameter.

A submenu appears.

3. Click Query.

The TableAdapter Query Configuration Wizard appears.

Alternatively, you can access the Add submenu from the Data menu.

You can use the TableAdapter Query Wizard to create CRUD statements in the following ways:

✦ **Use SQL statements to access data.** The wizard automatically generates the SQL statements for single-table data sources. Otherwise, you can use the Query Builder to build your statement.

✦ **Create new stored procedures.** For single-table data sources, the DataSet Designer generates the SQL statements for you. You can copy and paste your SQL statement into the wizard or use the Query Builder to build the SQL statement.

✦ **Use existing stored procedures.** The wizard displays input parameters and results columns for the stored procedure you select.

To create an additional query to sort your output, follow these steps:

1. Open the TableAdapter Query Wizard by following the preceding set of steps in this section.

2. Accept the default to use SQL statements.

Or, you can choose the option to create new stored procedures. Either way, the DataSet Designer generates the SQL statements for you.

3. **Click the Next button.**

   The Choose a Query Type page appears.

4. **Accept the SELECT default type, which returns rows.**

5. **Click the Next button.**

   The Specify a SQL SELECT statement page appears.

   The DataSet Designer generates the following SQL statement, which appears in the wizard:

   ```
   SELECT DepartmentID, Name, GroupName, ModifiedDate FROM
       HumanResources.Department
   ```

6. **Click the Query Builder button.**

   The Query Builder appears.

7. **Click the Sort Type drop-down list on the column grid.**

8. **Select Ascending from the Sort Type drop-down list, as shown in Figure 3-15.**

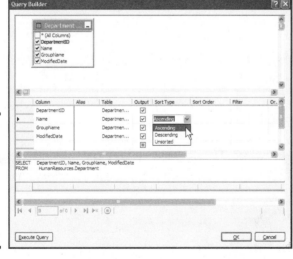

Figure 3-15:
Select
Ascending
from the
Sort Type
drop-down
list in the
column grid.

9. **Press Enter.**

   The Query Builder adds the following clause to the SQL statement:

   ```
   ORDER BY Name
   ```

10. **Click the OK button.**

    The updated SQL statement appears in the wizard.

11. **Click the Next button.**

The Choose Methods to Generate page appears.

12. **Type names that you want the wizard to use in generating methods, as shown in Figure 3-16.**

- **For the Fill a DataTable method, type** FillBySortByName.
- **For the Return a DataTable method, type** GetDataBySortByName.

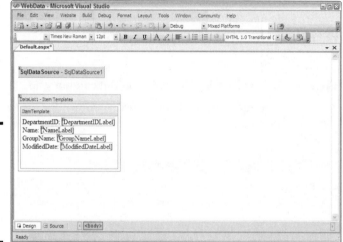

Figure 3-16: Type names you want the wizard to use in generating methods.

13. **Click the Finish button.**

The DataSet Designer generates the code using the SQL statement you enter in the wizard. The designer updates the TableAdapter to show the new query, as shown in Figure 3-17.

Figure 3-17: The Table-Adapter displays the new query.

Looking Under the Hood of a Strongly Typed DataSet

The DataSet Designer generates an XML schema and some ADO.NET code while you're creating a strongly typed DataSet. Creating a DataSet with only a few tables can generate thousands of lines of code. You may want to view that code so that you can understand how to build XML schemas or work with ADO.NET.

Viewing code

As you drop database objects on the design surface, Visual Studio generates code "behind the scenes." To view the code that Visual Studio generates, follow these steps:

1. **Click the Show All Files button on the Solution Explorer toolbar.**

2. **Click the plus (+) sign next to your .xsd file.**

3. **Double-click the file with the extension .Designer.vb file.**

   Visual Studio opens the file in the code editor.

Don't change the code generated by Visual Studio. You can't be sure that the program won't overwrite your changes.

Using partial classes

You can add your own code to extend the typed DataSet. The typed DataSet takes advantage of *partial classes,* a new feature in the .NET Framework. A class is a unit of code. In previous versions of .NET, all the code for a class had to be in a single file. Partial classes can span multiple files. As long as each partial class shares the same name and use the keyword `Partial`, Visual Studio smooshes them together when it compiles the class.

Partial classes are intended to separate Visual Studio's generated code from the code you write. As a rule, you don't need to create new partial classes.

For example, you can use a partial class to set the default value of a column or to set validation. Follow these steps to set a column's default value in a partial class for the Department table from the earlier section "Adding database objects":

1. **Open the typed DataSet you create in the section "Adding database object".**

   The typed DataSet contains a partial class generated by Visual Studio called DepartmentDataTable. When Visual Studio generates code for typed DataSets, it names the class by appending DataTable to the end of the table's name.

2. **Right-click the DataSet Designer.**

3. **Choose View Code from the shortcut menu.**

   The code editor appears.

4. **Position your cursor between the start and end statements for the `Partial` class in the code editor.**

**Book IV
Chapter 3**

**Working with
Strongly Typed
DataSets**

5. **Type the following line:**

```
Partial Class DepartmentDataTable
```

As you type, IntelliSense lists the available partial classes from the gen-erated typed DataSet code. IntelliSense is a feature of the code editor that helps you write code. Select or type **DepartmentDataTable**.

6. **Press Enter.**

Visual Studio generates the closing `End Class` statement.

7. **Select DepartmentDataTableEvents from the Class drop-down list in the upper-left corner of the code editor, as shown in Figure 3-18.**

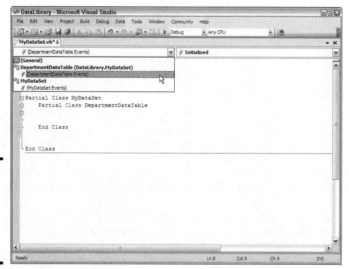

Figure 3-18: Select the event from the Class drop-down list.

8. **Select Initialized from the Methods drop-down list in the upper-right corner of the code editor.**

Visual Studio inserts the following event handler for the `Initialized` event in `DepartmentDataTable`:

```
Private Sub DepartmentDataTable_Initialized(ByVal
    sender As Object, ByVal e As System.EventArgs)
    Handles Me.Initialized

End Sub
```

The `Initialized` event is called after the data table completes its ini-tialization. The code for initializing the data table is generated by Visual Studio and is responsible for creating all the columns in the table.

9. Type the following line to set the ModifiedDate column's default value to the current date and time:

```
Me.columnModifiedDate.DefaultValue =
    System.DateTime.Now
```

The ModifiedDate column displays the current date and time when a new row is created.

Updating a ModifiedDate column when rows are inserted or updated in a table is a common practice. You can return the `ModifiedDate` value in the rows to test for optimistic concurrency violations. With optimistic concurrency, you don't lock rows when they're read them from a table. DataSets use optimistic concurrency.

Using the debugger to step through the code generated by Visual Studio is a valuable way to learn new coding techniques. See Book V, Chapter 7 for more information on debugging.

Viewing the source

You can view the XML Schema of a DataSet. To view the XML schema of a typed DataSet, follow these steps:

1. Right-click a DataSet in Solution Explorer.

For more information on adding DataSets to a project, see the section "Creating Typed DataSets," earlier in this chapter.

2. Choose Open With from the shortcut menu.

3. In the Open With dialog box, select the editor you want to use, as shown in Figure 3-19:

• Choose XML Schema Editor to open the DataSet in a visual XML schema designer.

• Choose XML Editor to view the XML source for the DataSet.

4. Click the OK button.

The schema opens in the editor of your choice.

You can open any XML schema file with the DataSet Designer. In the set of steps you just completed, substitute your XML schema file in Step 1 and choose the DataSet Designer in Step 3. To read more about creating XML schemas, see Chapter 4 in this mini-book.

The DataSet Designer marks up the standard syntax of an XML schema so that the schema can be used to generate ADO.NET code. The attribute designating that an XML schema should open in the DataSet Designer by default is `msdata:IsDataSet="true"`.

Figure 3-19:
Choose the editor you want to use to view the DataSet's schema.

Here's a good way to learn XML schema syntax: View a DataSet's XML schema in the XML Schema Editor as you use the DataSet Designer to manipulate the DataSet. Be sure to open the DataSet with the XML Schema Editor *after* you open the DataSet in the DataSet Designer.

Consuming a Typed DataSet

It's not enough to merely create a DataSet. You must configure your application to use or consume the DataSet in some way. Earlier in this chapter, I show you how to create a typed DataSet in a class library, in the section "Creating Typed DataSets." In this section, however, I show you how to consume a class library in a Windows project.

Typed DataSets are reusable. After you create a DataSet for one application, you can reuse the DataSet in another project. You may think that I'm referring to copying the DataSet file from one project to another. Although the copy-and-paste method is one means of "reusing," a more elegant approach is to create your DataSet in a class library, as I describe in the earlier section "Creating a DataSet in a class library," and consume that library in other projects.

You can use any .NET programming language you wish when you creating your class library in Visual Studio. The programming language of the class library and the project that uses the class library can be different.

To consume a class library in a Windows Form, follow these steps:

1. **Open or create your Windows project and Form wherever you want to display the DataSet.**

2. **Choose Data⇨Add New Data Source.**

The Data Source Configuration Wizard appears.

3. **Click the Object icon on the Choose a Data Source Type page.**

4. **Click the Next button.**

5. **On the Select the Object You Wish to Bind to page, click the Add Reference button.**

   The Add Reference dialog box appears.

   By adding a reference to the class library in your Window project, you can access the class library.

6. **Click the Browse tab and browse to the folder where your class library is saved.**

7. **Select the DLL file that was generated when you built your class file.**

   The class library appears in the wizard, and the DLL file is stored in the project's Bin folder.

8. **Select MyDataSet, as shown in Figure 3-20.**

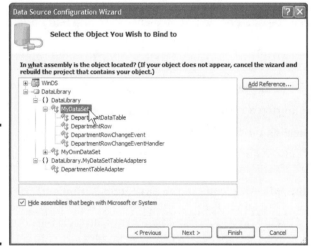

Figure 3-20: Select the DataSet after adding a reference to the class library.

9. **Click the Finish button.**

   The wizard adds the class library as a data source.

To use the data source with a databound control, follow these steps:

1. **Drag and drop the table from the DataSet in the Data Sources window onto the Windows Form.**

   The Windows Form Designer adds a `DataGridView` control that's bound to the DataSet to the form.

2. **Double-click the Windows Form.**

Book IV Chapter 3

Working with Strongly Typed DataSets

The designer creates an event handler for the form's `Load` event and displays the handler in the code editor.

3. Below the event handler, create a new variable to hold the table's TableAdapter by typing the following code:

```
Friend WithEvents MyTableAdapter As DataLibrary.
    MyDataSetTableAdapters.DepartmentTableAdapter
```

When you add the DataSet to the form, the Windows Form Designer generates the code to display the DataSet in the `DataGridView` control. Unfortunately, because the designer doesn't wire up the table adapter to automatically load data, the DataSet doesn't have any data.

4. In the form's `Load` event handler, type the following lines:

```
MyTableAdapter = New DataLibrary.MyDataSetTableAdapters.
    DepartmentTableAdapter
Me.MyTableAdapter.Fill(Me.MyDataSet.Department)
```

This code uses the TableAdapter you create in Step 3 to fill the DataSet.

Follow these steps to enable `DataGridView` to edit and update data:

1. On the window's Form, click the Save Item button on the `BindingNavigator` component.

2. Press F4 to display the button's properties.

3. Set the button's `Enabled` property to `true`.

4. Double-click the Save Item button.

The Windows Form Designer creates an event handler for the Save Item button's `Click` event.

5. Type the following code in the Save Item button's `Click` event:

```
Me.Validate()
Me.DepartmentBindingSource.EndEdit()
Me.MyTableAdapter.Update(Me.MyDataSet.Department)
```

Press Ctrl+F5 to run your Windows application. The Windows Form displays the data from the DataSet in the `DataGridView` control. As you use `Data GridView` to modify the data, the updates are saved in the DataSet. Click the Save Item button to save the data to the database.

Use the `ObjectDataSource` control in ASP.NET to connect a typed DataSet to databound controls in a Web site. See Chapter 2 in this mini-book for a walkthrough of using the `ObjectDataSource` control.

Chapter 4: Working with XML

In This Chapter

✓ **Creating and storing XML files in Visual Studio**

✓ **Using the XML Designer to create an XML schema**

✓ **Transforming XML with style sheets**

✓ **Using XML with the .NET Framework**

XML is the new gold standard for working with data in modern software application development. XML, short for eXtensible Markup Language, is a markup language like HTML, the language used to create Web pages. In HTML, you use a set of predefined markup tags, such as `<html>` and `<body>`. The tags use attributes to further define the markup, such as `<body background="white">`.

XML uses tags and attributes like HTML does. However, unlike in HTML, you define what tags and attributes to use. XML is used to describe data, so you make up your own tags and attributes to define the data. An XML file might use these tags to describe data about a book collection:

```
<Books>
<Book>
<Author></Author>
<Title></Title>
<Book>
</Books>
```

I say that the XML file *might* use these tags because no predefined rules specify the tags you use. You decide which ones to use. As long as you declare which tags you want to use and then use them consistently, anyone can understand how to read your XML file. As you can see, XML is a powerful language for describing data because XML files

✦ Are plain-text files that you can edit and read in any text editor

✦ Include a schema definition that identifies all the elements and attributes to use to describe data

✦ Transform into other languages, such as HTML

Microsoft has wholeheartedly embraced XML, and Visual Studio has several intelligent editors for creating and manipulating XML files. The .NET Framework has an entire namespace for reading and writing XML files, and Microsoft SQL Server supports XML as well. If you're a .NET developer, you have all the support you need for creating and consuming XML.

With Visual Studio, you can use XML without writing any code whatsoever. In this chapter, I show you how to use the tools Visual Studio provides for generating XML, including

✦ XML Editor with IntelliSense and validation

✦ XSLT Debugger

✦ XML Schema Designer

✦ XML snippets

The DataSet Designer generates an XML schema to support the creation of strongly typed DataSets. (See Chapter 3 in this mini-book to read more about the DataSet Designer.)

Having some understanding of XML technologies is helpful as you work with the Visual Studio tools. Don't worry: You don't have to be a whiz. I show you everything you need to know to get started using XML in Visual Studio. You can fill in the gaps in your XML knowledge as you go along.

Storing Data the XML Way

Ten years ago, developers had few options for transmitting data between disparate systems or storing configuration data. Everybody used comma- or tab-delimited plain-text files. Although XML is stored in a plain-text file, the power of XML lies in its ability to describe itself. Walk through the following scenario to see how XML has transformed data transmission.

Imagine that you need to send purchase order data to a supplier. Here's what the transaction might look like without XML:

1. You export the data from your database to a plain-text file, either comma- or tab-delimited.

2. You prepare a document that explains each of the columns in the output file, such as the data type and whether the data is required.

3. You send off the file and the document to your supplier.

4. Your supplier tells you that the file doesn't meet the specifications for his system and sends you the specifications.

5. You realize that you have to hire a programmer to transform your data to meet the supplier's specifications.

6. You decide that it's too much trouble and keep faxing your order forms.

I've seen this scenario play itself out it many variations over the years. Somebody gets the bright idea to submit data electronically. However, without agreed-on standards, the idea quickly gets abandoned because too much custom programming is usually required.

This scenario uses XML instead:

1. You create an XML Schema file that describes all the fields and attributes in your XML file.

2. You export your data to an XML file that conforms to the XML schema.

3. You send your XML file along with the schema to your suppliers.

4. Each supplier uses the schema to validate that your XML file contains all the required fields and attributes.

5. Each supplier uses a style sheet that transforms your XML file into the XML file that conforms to the schema for their corporate databases.

Of course, not everybody plays nice all the time. A handful of suppliers might reject your file and tell you that they don't use XML, or they might want to use a comma-delimited file. It's no big deal — just create a style sheet that transforms your XML file into a comma-delimited file that meets their requirements.

This example shows you the beauty of XML. You can accommodate the input and output requirements of multiple systems without having to write a new program every single time. As long as your program knows how to work with the XML, you can make all the changes you need.

Using XML to define your data is fairly straightforward, especially when you harness the power of Visual Studio. A little knowledge of XML, combined with the Visual Studio tools, goes a long way toward creating XML.

Use XML to describe data any time you need to

✦ Transmit data between disparate systems.

✦ Store configuration data for your application.

✦ Avoid the overhead of a relational database management system, such as SQL Server.

XML files can get really bulky when used to store large quantities of data, which doesn't make them appropriate for all data transmission scenarios. You should try to send the minimal amount of data required to complete a transaction when using XML.

Creating a new XML file

The first step in using the XML editors in Visual Studio is creating a new XML file. For example, Visual Studio supports creating these types of XML files:

✦ **XML document** — Stores self-describing data.

✦ **XML schema** — Defines the elements and attributes used in an XML document to describe data.

✦ **XSLT style sheet** — Transforms an XML document into another format, such as XML or HTML.

XML documents, XML schemas, and XSLT style sheets — they're all XML files. XML files use XML markup tags. XML schemas and XSLT style sheets use a set of predefined XML tags.

To create an XML file in Visual Studio, follow these steps:

1. **Choose File⇨New.**

A submenu appears.

2. **Choose File from the submenu.**

The New File dialog box appears.

You can press Ctrl+N on your keyboard to open the New File window.

3. **Click the icon for the type of XML file to create: XML File, XML Schema, or XSLT File.**

Clicking the XML File icon creates an XML document file.

4. **Click the Open button.**

Visual Studio displays the XML file in the appropriate editor. Figure 4-1 shows an XML document in the XML Editor.

All XML files require a declaration on the file's first line. Visual Studio adds the following XML declaration for you:

```
<?xml version="1.0" encoding="utf-8"?>
```

The declaration specifies which version of XML you're using and in which language the content is encoded. You don't need to change the declaration.

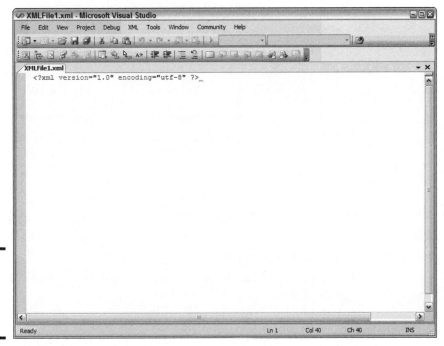

Figure 4-1:
A blank
XML file
appears in
the editor.

Describing data in an XML document

Suppose that you want to create a Web site to display your large set of recipes. You can easily store those recipes in an XML document and then transform them to HTML so that they can be displayed in a browser.

For each recipe, you need to store the following information:

✦ The recipe's name

✦ A list of ingredients, including quantities

✦ A list of step-by-step instructions

You can use the Visual Studio XML Editor to create an XML document that describes a set of recipes.

XML files contain markup tags to describe the data they store.

To create an XML document for storing data, such as the recipe in this example, follow these steps:

1. **Create a new XML document file by following the steps in the preceding section.**

Book IV
Chapter 4

Working with XML

2. **In a blank XML document file, type an opening root tag, such as** <recipes>.

   Visual Studio inserts the closing tag </recipes> for you, and then the XML Editor displays <recipes></recipes> in the XML document.

   XML uses opening and closing tags to describe data. The <recipes> tag is the XML document's root tag; in this case, it encloses a collection of recipes. A *root tag* is the outermost tag in an XML document.

3. **Between the recipes' tags, type** <recipe></recipe>. **Use the <recipe> tags to enclose a single recipe.**

4. **Inside the first <recipe> tag, type** name="".

   The tags appear as <recipe name=""></recipe>.

   name is an attribute of recipe. XML tags use attributes similar to HTML tags. Attributes allow you to describe properties for the tag.

5. **Between the <recipe> tags, type** <ingredients>.

   The <ingredients> tag stores a collection of individual <ingredient> elements.

6. **Between the <ingredients> tags, type** <ingredient>.

7. **Inside the <ingredient> tag, add tags for quantity and item.**

   Figure 4-2 shows an example of the XML file.

8. **Save your file as** recipe.xml.

All's well (and valid) that's formed well

When you create an XML document, you want your document to be well-formed and valid. An XML file is considered well-formed if all tags are

✓ Contained within a single document root tag, such as <recipes>

✓ Properly nested so that inner tags are closed

✓ Opened and closed properly

✓ Possess all the proper punctuation, such as quotation marks around attribute values

An XML file is valid if the document is

✓ Well-formed

✓ Consistent with the data schema defined for the document

You know whether your document is well-formed because the XML Editor displays squiggly lines under any syntax that's incorrect. I show you in the next section how to validate an XML document by using an XML schema.

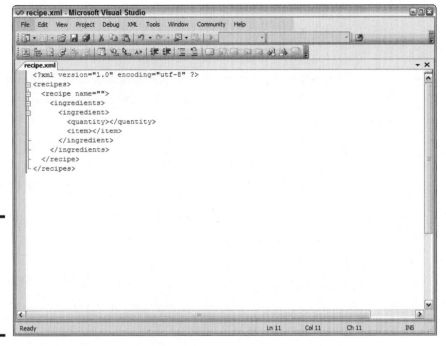

**Book IV
Chapter 4**

Working with XML

Figure 4-2:
Create
an XML
document
file to
describe
your data.

Using the data grid to add data

You add data to your XML document by typing values between the markup tags in the code editor. Visual Studio also provides a visual data grid that makes light work of adding data to XML files. You use the data grid to type your data into cells. To add data to an XML file by using the data grid, follow these steps:

1. **Open your XML file in Visual Studio. This example uses the recipe.xml file from the previous set of steps.**

2. **Choose View⇨Data Grid.**

The XML document appears in a grid view.

The Data Grid view displays a list of tables on the left. The data for each table appears in a grid on the right.

3. **Select the recipe table.**

The cursor appears in the Name column in the grid.

name is an attribute of recipe, as defined in Step 3 in the preceding section.

4. **In the Name column, type an ingredient, such as** Guacamole.

5. **Click the plus (+) sign next to Guacamole.**

A hyperlink to the recipe ingredients table appears.

6. **Click the recipe ingredients hyperlink, as shown in Figure 4-3.**

7. **Click the plus (+) sign in the data grid to expand the collection for the recipe.**

The ingredients ingredient hyperlink appears.

8. **Click the hyperlink.**

The ingredient appears in the grid with columns for quantity and item.

9. **Add the following ingredients in the grid:**

- 4 avocados
- 1 onion
- 1 lime

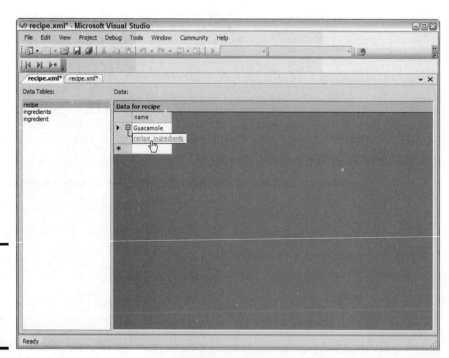

Figure 4-3:
Click the
hyperlink
to expand
the data
collection.

10. Choose View⇨Code to view the XML file.

The data you entered in the data grid appears in the XML file. Figure 4-4 shows the XML file with the recipe for guacamole.

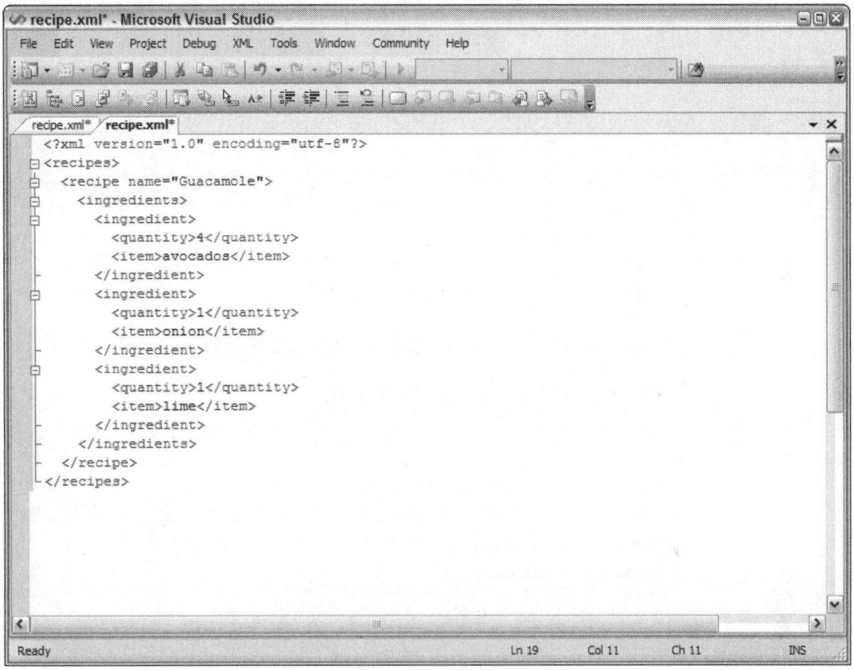

Figure 4-4:
Data entered in the data grid appears in the XML file.

```
<?xml version="1.0" encoding="utf-8"?>
<recipes>
  <recipe name="Guacamole">
    <ingredients>
      <ingredient>
        <quantity>4</quantity>
        <item>avocados</item>
      </ingredient>
      <ingredient>
        <quantity>1</quantity>
        <item>onion</item>
      </ingredient>
      <ingredient>
        <quantity>1</quantity>
        <item>lime</item>
      </ingredient>
    </ingredients>
  </recipe>
</recipes>
```

Creating an XML Schema

The value of XML lies in its self-describing documents. One technology that makes it possible for XML data to describe itself is the XML schema. If you ever work with databases, you probably recognize the word *schema*. A *schema* describes all the tables, columns, and data types in a database. An XML schema does the same thing.

A schema is used to verify an XML document's validity. XML files are opened by using a *processor*. A schema allows an XML file to respond to the processor's query "Tell me about yourself." The processor uses the schema's response about the XML document to determine whether the XML document is valid.

An XML file must be well-formed in order to be valid. The properties of a well-formed XML file are described in the earlier sidebar "All's well (and valid) that's formed well."

Building an XML schema

The syntax for creating an XML schema is straightforward to understand, but somewhat tedious to write. Never fear. Visual Studio provides a tool for generating an XML schema. Visual Studio generates the schema by inferring the schema from an existing XML document. Inferring a schema from an existing document and then tweaking it is much easier than building the schema from scratch.

Generating an XML schema from an existing XML document is more accurate when the document contains data. Having data in the file allows Visual Studio to make intelligent guesses about how the data is structured in the file. For more information on creating XML Schemas from scratch, see the W3 Schools tutorial at `www.w3schools.com/schema/`.

To infer the schema for an existing XML document, follow these steps:

1. **Open the XML document in Visual Studio.**

2. **Choose XML⇨Create Schema.**

   Visual Studio generates the schema file and displays it in the code editor.

   Figure 4-5 shows the schema that's inferred for the recipe.xml file you create in the earlier section "Describing data in an XML document." See the next section for more information on understanding the XML Schema syntax.

3. **Save the schema file.**

   XML Schema files use the .xsd file extension.

Visual Studio associates the schema file with the XML file by using the XML document file's `Schema` property. Press F4 to display the XML document's properties.

Associating the schema with your XML document does two things:

✦ Validates your XML document against the XML schema

✦ Allows you to use IntelliSense in the XML editor

See the section "Using IntelliSense" later in this section.

Using the XML Designer

Visual Studio provides a visual designer, the XML Designer, for creating, modifying, and viewing XML schemas. To view a schema in the XML Designer, open an existing schema file and choose View⇨Designer. The tables in the schema appear as grids and are linked to show the relationships between them.

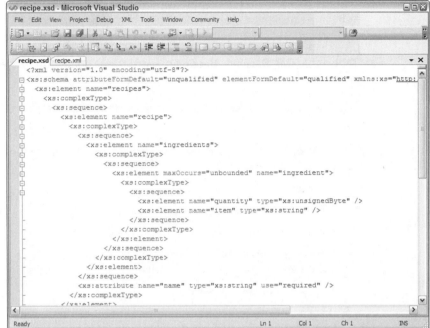

Figure 4-5:
Visual
Studio infers
the schema
from an
existing
XML file.

You use the XML Designer toolbox to drag and drop schema syntax onto a visual designer. Table 4-1 describes the contents of the toolbox.

Table 4-1	The XML Schema Toolbox
Toolbox Entity	*What It Does*
Element	Serves as a basic building block of a schema used to define the data contained in an XML document; can be nested
Attribute	Further describes the data enclosed within an element
attributeGroup	Defines a reusable group of attributes
complexType	Defines entities that can contain other elements, attributes, and simpleType entities
simpleType	Creates user-defined types that work in conjunction with facets to restrict the built-in data types such as string and integer
Group	Creates groups of elements
Any	Allows you to use elements from other schemas
anyAttribute	Allows you to use attributes from other schemas
Facet	Further defines or constrains a built-in type with simpleType
Key	Specifies that the element or attribute must be unique
Relation	Creates a reference to a key

The entities in the toolbox represent commonly used XML Schema syntax. You can access even more syntax options as you work on the Designer's grid surface and use the property pages.

To use the XML Designer to add an instructions collection to the Recipes document from the preceding section, follow these steps:

1. **Open the recipes.xsd document you created in the preceding section.**

Use the View menu to switch between Designer view and Code view.

2. **In Designer view, drag and drop an element from the toolbox onto the recipe element.**

The cursor appears in the grid.

3. **Type a name, such as** instructions, **and press Enter.**

An instructions element appears on the grid.

4. **Drag and drop an element onto the new instructions element. Type a name, such as** steps **in this example, and press Enter.**

The steps element appears.

5. **Drag and drop an element onto the steps element. Type a description, such as** text, **and set the data type to string.**

6. **Drag and drop an attribute onto the steps element.**

7. **Type** ordinal **for the attribute's name and select string as the data type.**

8. **Click the steps element and press F4 to display the Properties window.**

9. **Type** unbounded **in the maxOccurs property to allow multiple instances of the steps element.**

10. **Click the ordinal attribute on the Designer surface. Set the use property to required.**

Figure 4-6 shows the grid of the updated XML schema.

The easiest way to create an XML schema is to infer it from an existing XML document.

Sometimes, however, you need to use the XML Designer to further tweak the schema.

The neat thing about XML is that you can easily make changes to your data structure. In fact, after looking at your recipes a little more closely, you might realize that you forgot to capture the unit of measure for the ingredients. You decide that you want to have a separate equipment list. You can easily add these elements — and any others you discover — by using the XML Designer.

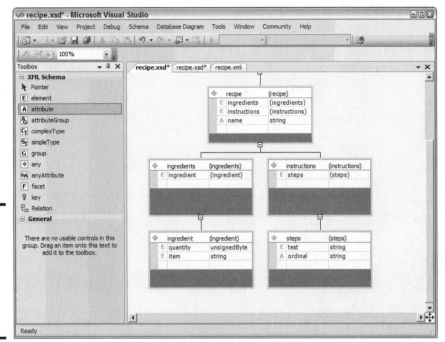

Figure 4-6:
The XML
Designer
reflects
added
elements
and
attributes.

To test your new schema, open the recipes.xml file from the section "Describing data in an XML document". You should see a squiggly, blue line under the closing `<recipe>` tag. If you hover your mouse over the closing `<recipe>` tag, a tooltip informs you that your document is incomplete, as shown in Figure 4-7.

You can use the XML Designer to open an XML schema, including strongly typed DataSets. Alternatively, you can use the DataSet Designer to open XML Schema files. For more information, see the section in Chapter 3 of this mini-book about viewing the source.

Using IntelliSense

Associating an XML document with an XML Schema file allows you to use IntelliSense in the XML Editor. IntelliSense provides XML syntax-checking as you use the XML Editor.

To see IntelliSense in action, open an XML document that uses an XML schema in the XML Editor. These steps show you how to use IntelliSense to add elements to an XML document:

1. **Open the recipe.xml file described in the earlier "Describing data in an XML document" section.**

**Book IV
Chapter 4**

Working with XML

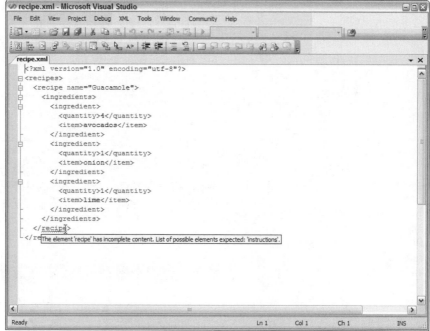

Figure 4-7:
Visual
Studio
informs you
that your
XML
document is
incomplete.

2. **Position your cursor between the `</ingredients>` and `</recipe>` closing tags.**

3. **Create an opening tag by typing a less-than (<) sign.**

IntelliSense displays a list of valid tags, including the instructions tag.

4. **Type the first few letters of the instructions tag to select it from the list. Press the Tab key to insert the tag into your XML document.**

5. **Close the tag by typing a greater than (>) sign.**

Visual Studio inserts the closing `</instruction>` tag for you.

6. **Repeat Steps 1–5 to continue adding the instruction steps to the XML document.**

Figure 4-8 shows you an example.

Using IntelliSense requires an XML schema. Inferring an XML schema requires an existing XML document. You can build an XML schema first and then use IntelliSense to build the XML document. Alternatively, you can create the XML document, infer the schema, and then use IntelliSense to finish adding data to the XML document. I prefer the latter approach because I don't have to dig out reference materials on creating XML schemas.

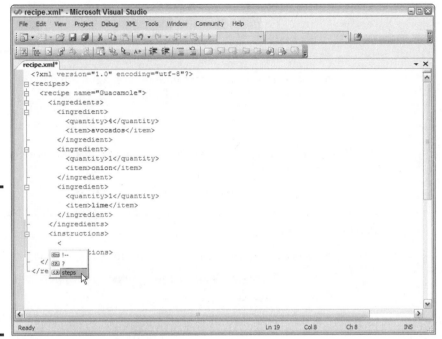

```xml
<?xml version="1.0" encoding="utf-8"?>
<recipes>
  <recipe name="Guacamole">
    <ingredients>
      <ingredient>
        <quantity>4</quantity>
        <item>avocados</item>
      </ingredient>
      <ingredient>
        <quantity>1</quantity>
        <item>onion</item>
      </ingredient>
      <ingredient>
        <quantity>1</quantity>
        <item>lime</item>
      </ingredient>
    </ingredients>
    <instructions>
      <
```

Figure 4-8:
IntelliSense uses your XML schema to help you complete the document.

Using XML snippets

The XML Editor uses XML snippets to insert commonly used XML tags. A snippet is a block of XML tags. You can create your own snippets, or you can quickly insert a snippet if your XML document is associated with a schema.

XML snippets are a kind of code snippet, which is an IntelliSense feature. You use code snippets to insert commonly used C# and Visual Basic code. See Chapter 5 in Book V for more details on using code snippets.

To use an XML snippet with the recipe.xml file described in the earlier "Describing data in an XML document" section:

1. **Position your cursor after the guacamole recipe.**

2. **Type an opening tag: <.**

   IntelliSense displays a list of available elements based on the document's schema.

3. **Press your down-arrow key to select the recipe element from the drop-down list and then press Enter.**

4. Press the Tab key.

Visual Studio inserts an XML snippet from the schema, as shown in Figure 4-9. The recipe tags and everything in between are inserted.

The areas that need to have text entered are highlighted in the code editor. Use the Tab key to move between the highlighted areas.

To create your own XML snippets from scratch, follow these steps:

1. Right-click the XML document and choose Insert Snippets from the shortcut menu.

2. Choose `Snippet` from the IntelliSense menu.

Visual Studio inserts a boilerplate template for creating XML snippets.

3. Replace the boilerplate content with your own XML tags.

See the Visual Studio help system for more information.

4. Save your file using the filename extension .snippet.

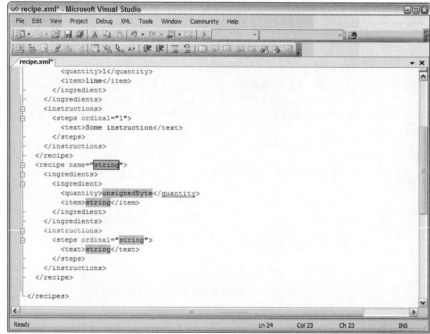

Figure 4-9:
Press the
Tab key to
insert an
XML snippet
based on
the
document's
schema.

Transforming XML with Extensible Stylesheet Language Transformations

The role of XML is to store self-describing data documents. At some point, that data needs to be displayed. You use a special kind of style sheet that uses Extensible Stylesheet Language Transformations (XSLT) to convert XML to another language, such as HTML, that you can use to display the file's contents.

You can use XSLT to transform XML documents into

✦ XML documents

✦ HTML documents

✦ XHTML documents

✦ Plain text documents

✦ Programming languages, such as C# or SQL

Visual Studio provides a file template and a code editor for creating XSLT files. Like all the code editors in Visual Studio, the XSLT Editor includes support for IntelliSense and code snippets.

Visual Studio can apply a style sheet to your XML file and display the output. An XSLT debugger is available to help you track down errors in your style sheet.

To create a new XSLT style sheet in Visual Studio, follow these steps:

1. **Press Ctrl+N to open the New File dialog box.**

2. **Click the XSLT File icon.**

3. **Click the Open button.**

An XSLT file appears in the code editor, as shown in Figure 4-10.

Unfortunately, no visual designer or code-generation tool in Visual Studio creates XSLT style sheets. Another glaring oversight is a lack of support for building the expressions you need for selecting nodes from your XML file.

The technology for selecting nodes from an XML document is XPath. I explain more about using it later in this section.

If you're having trouble building expressions, use InfoPath to dynamically build XPath expressions. InfoPath 2003 provides a visual tool for building XPath expressions. You can copy and paste the expressions from InfoPath into your style sheet.

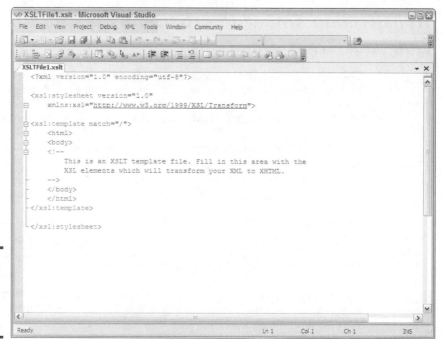

Figure 4-10:
An XSLT file
appears in
the code
editor.

Writing an XSLT style sheet

XSLT is written in XML. A style sheet consists of the following elements:

✦ **Declaration** — Identifies the file as an XSLT style sheet

✦ **Templates** — Define the style sheet's output

✦ **Supplementary content** — HTML tags, for example, that you want to present in the output

The "meat and potatoes" of an XSLT style sheet consists of the template (or templates) that defines the style sheet's output. The following example of an XSLT template uses the recipe.xml file you create earlier in this chapter. Notice that the template combines XSLT syntax with HTML:

```
<xsl:template match="/">
  <html>
    <body>
      <xsl:for-each select="recipes/recipe">
        <ul>
          <xsl:for-each select="ingredients/ingredient">
```

```
            <li>
              <xsl:value-of select="quantity" />
              <xsl:text> </xsl:text>
              <xsl:value-of select="item" />
            </li>
          </xsl:for-each>
        </ul>
      </xsl:for-each>
    </body>
  </html>
</xsl:template>
```

The output from this template looks like this:

```
<html>
  <body>
    <ul>
      <li>1 avocado</li>
      <li>1 onion</li>
      <li>2 tomatoes</li>
      <li>3 pepper</li>
    </ul>
    <ul>
      <li>2 tomatoes</li>
      <li>3 pepper</li>
    </ul>
    <ul></ul>
  </body>
</html>
```

The HTML tags are composed of output from the style sheet. The ingredients data is pulled from the recipe.xml document by using XPath expressions.

An XSLT template includes these items:

✦ Elements, such as `for-each` and `value-of`, that are used to operate on the data from the XML document

✦ XPath expressions used in the `select` attribute of a template's elements to navigate the XML document

✦ Functions, such as `last()` and `position()`, for evaluating whether to select a node or include text in the output

✦ Text, such as HTML markup tags, for inclusion in the output

Figure 4-11 shows an example of an XSLT style sheet used to transform the recipe.xml file from the "Describing data in an XML document" section into HTML.

**Book IV
Chapter 4**

Working with XML

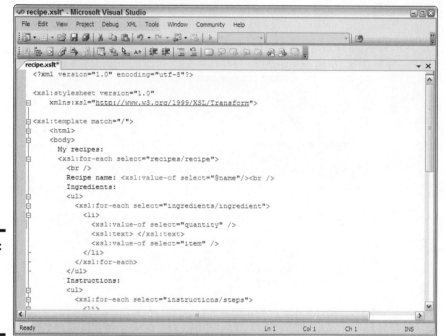

Figure 4-11:
XSLT
templates
transform
XML into
HTML.

Linking an XSLT file to another document

Once you create your XSLT style sheet, you must associate it with your XML document. Linking the XSLT file to the XML document makes it possible for you to view the output created by the XSLT style sheet.

To associate an XSLT file with an existing XML document in Visual Studio, follow these steps:

1. **Open the XSLT style sheet in Visual Studio.**

2. **Press F4 to display the Properties window.**

3. **Click the ellipses button for the Input property.**

4. **Browse to the XML document that you want to transform and select it.**

   The file's path appears in the Input property.

5. **Choose XML⇨Show XSLT Output.**

   The output appears in a separate window.

You can place, at the top of your XML document, a directive that links the style sheet to your document. When your XML document is displayed in an XML-aware browser, the output of the style sheet appears. To add a link for the recipe.xml document, type the following line at the top of the recipes.xml file:

```
<?xml-stylesheet type="text/xsl" href="recipe.xslt"?>
```

Figure 4-12 shows the XML document displayed in Internet Explorer.

Staying on the path with XPath

XPath is an important technology for XSLT templates. You use XPath to navigate an XML document and find the nodes, or sets of nodes, that you want to display in your output. Suppose that you have an XML document for storing recipes with a structure like this:

```
<recipes>
<recipe name="string">
    <ingredients>
      <ingredient>
        <qty>unsignedByte</qty>
        <item>string</item>
      </ingredient>
    </ingredients>
    <instructions>
      <steps ordinal="string">
        <text>string</text>
      </steps>
    </instructions>
  </recipe>
</recipes>
```

You can use an XPath expression, such as `/recipes/recipe`, to navigate to the recipe node in the XML document. Table 4-2 describes the XPath syntax.

Table 4-2		XPath Syntax
XPath Expression	*Syntax*	*What It Selects*
Nodename	instructions	The child nodes of the instructions node
/	/recipes	An absolute path to the root node
	/recipes/recipe	The child recipe nodes of the recipes node

(continued)

Table 4-2 *(continued)*

XPath Expression	Syntax	What It Selects
`//`	`//steps`	All `steps` nodes regardless of their recipe
`.`	`/recipes/recipe/ingredients/.`	The current node; the `qty` and `item` nodes in the example
`..`	`/recipes/recipe/..`	The parent node; all the nodes in the `recipes` node in the example
`@`	`/recipes/recipe/@name`	The `name` attribute of the recipe node

The easiest way to understand XPath is to use the `value-of` element in an XSLT style sheet and experiment with different expressions, like this:

```
<xsl:value-of select="recipes/recipe/@name" />
```

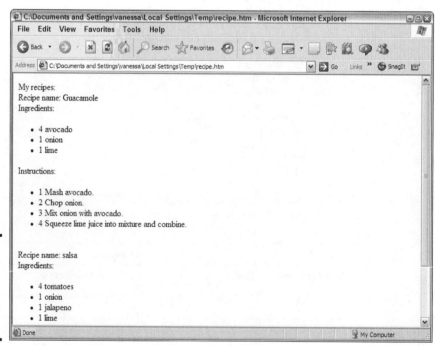

Figure 4-12:
The XSLT output appears in the browser window.

XML and .NET

The Microsoft .NET Framework provides many resources for working with XML in code. The XML-related classes in the .NET Framework have names that are similar to the XML technologies. For example, you use XPathNavigator in .NET to write code that navigates an XML document. The XML-related classes are in the System.XML namespace in .NET. Table 4-3 describes some of its common resources.

Table 4-3	System.XML Namespace in .NET
.NET Class	*What It Does*
XMLReader	Reads XML documents
XMLWriter	Writes to XML documents
XMLDocument	Represents an XML document
XPathNavigator	Navigates and edits XML documents
XMLSchema	Represents an XML schema

Each of the classes in the table includes numerous properties, methods, and additional classes for working with XML documents. For more information on using XML in code, see Chapter 5 in this mini-book.

Chapter 5: Under the Hood with ADO.NET

*V*isual Studio provides many controls, designers, editors, and wizards for accessing data in Windows and Web applications. These tools are made possible by ADO.NET, the data access technology of the .NET framework.

ADO.NET provides a common coding structure for accessing data regardless of the data source. The Visual Studio data access tools, such as the DataSet Designer, generate ADO.NET code behind the scenes for you. In this chapter, I show you how to "get under the hood" with ADO.NET and write your own ADO.NET code to access your data.

ADO is short for ActiveX Data Objects, the previous version of the data access technologies, before the .NET framework was introduced.

Meet the Players

The purpose of ADO.NET is to provide a simplified model for data access regardless of the underlying data source. By using a model like ADO.NET, developers can improve their productivity because they use one data access model — ADO.NET — to access many different kinds of data sources.

ADO.NET provides a set of common components for accessing data:

✦ **.NET Framework Data Provider** — Acts as a bridge between your application and a data source. Providers are available for many popular databases, including SQL Server and Oracle. When a native provider is unavailable for your data source, you use an ODBC or OLE DB provider to access your data source.

Each of the .NET Framework Data Providers provides a set of services for accessing data. See the following section for details on using data providers.

✦ **DataReader** — Provides forward-only access to a data source one row at a time by using one of the .NET Framework Data Providers. See the section "Reading Data with DataReaders," later in this chapter.

✦ **DataSet** — Provides an in-memory cache of data that's retrieved from a data source by way of one of the .NET Framework Data Providers. See the section "Caching Data with DataSets," later in this chapter.

Figure 5-1 shows the interplay of the .NET Framework Data Providers, DataReaders, and DataSets in ADO.NET.

DataReaders are a service of the .NET Framework Data Providers. I list the DataReader separately because it represents an important model for data access. DataSets are populated with DataReaders.

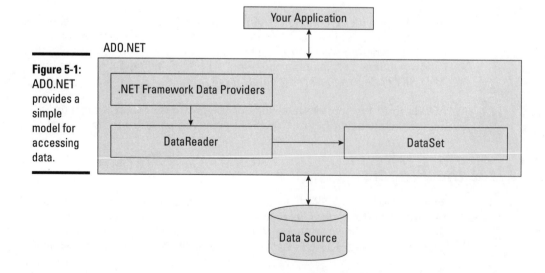

Figure 5-1: ADO.NET provides a simple model for accessing data.

You access the components of ADO.NET through the System.Data namespace in .NET.

The services of the .NET framework are organized into groups, or namespaces. To read more about namespaces, see Book V, Chapter 1.

Picking a Provider

ADO.NET uses data providers to provide access to many different kinds of data sources, such as SQL Server and Oracle databases. Table 5-1 summarizes the data providers available in the .NET Framework.

Table 5-1	.NET Framework Data Providers	
Data Source	*.NET Namespace*	*What It Accesses*
SQL Server	System.Data.SqlClient	SQL Server 7.0 databases and later
OLE DB	System.Data.OleDB	SQL Server 6.5, Oracle, and Microsoft Access databases by using OLE DB
ODBC	System.Data.Odbc	SQL Server, Oracle, and Microsoft Access databases by using ODBC
Oracle	System.Data.OracleClient	Oracle databases by using the Oracle client connectivity software

You should always use the provider that's tuned for your data source. For example, always use the SQL Server provider to access SQL Server 7.0 databases and later, and use the Oracle provider to access Oracle databases. Microsoft recommends the OLE DB provider for accessing Microsoft Access databases.

Never use a Microsoft Access database in a multi-tiered application. Access isn't an enterprise quality database and doesn't always perform well across a network. Consider using SQL Server Express Edition if you need a lightweight database.

**Book IV
Chapter 5**

Under the Hood with ADO.NET

The SQL Server provider uses its own communication channel for transmitting commands to SQL Server. As a result, the SQL Server provider is faster than the OLE DB and ODBC providers, both of which add their own layers of communication channels.

Always use the .NET Data Framework Provider for SQL Server to access SQL Server 7.0, SQL Server 2000, and SQL Server 2005 databases.

Accessing providers

You access the .NET Framework Data Providers through their .NET name-spaces. (Table 5-1 in the preceding section lists the namespaces for each of the .NET Framework Data Providers.) For example, to access the features of the SQL Server provider, type the following namespace in the code editor:

```
System.Data.SqlClient
```

Because of the way ADO.NET is constructed, you can access data without choosing a specific data provider. For example, you can write code that retrieves data from a data source without knowing in advance whether you want to use the SQL Server provider or the Oracle provider. Not choosing a data provider is useful when you need code to be flexible enough to choose your data source at runtime.

When you access data without using a data provider, you write *provider-independent* code. When you write it, you use the `System.Data.Common` namespace rather than one of the data provider namespaces listed in Table 5-1.

Writing provider independent data access code isn't for the faint of heart. To read more about what's involved in writing provider independent code, look for the topic **provider independent code** in the index of the Visual Studio 2005 documentation.

Objectifying the providers

Each .NET Framework Data Provider provides access to a common set of data access features and services. You use the following features and services of the providers to connect to your data source and retrieve data:

✦ **Connection** — Connects your application to a data source

✦ **Command** — Executes a SQL statement against a data source

✦ **DataReader** — Reads a forward-only stream of data one row at a time

✦ **DataAdapter** — Retrieves data for a DataSet and sends updates to the data source

Each .NET Framework Data Provider has its own flavor of the features and services in the preceding list. For example, the DataAdapter for the SQL Server data provider is the SqlDataAdapter.

Figure 5-2 illustrates the relationship among the data providers' features and services.

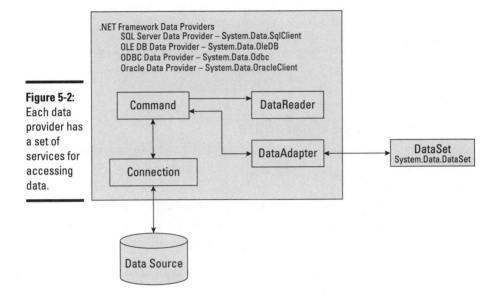

Figure 5-2:
Each data
provider has
a set of
services for
accessing
data.

You access the features and services of the data providers through the provider's namespace. For example, you access the Oracle data provider's DataReader, `OracleDataReader`, at `System.Data.OracleClient`. Table 5-1 lists the namespaces for each of the data providers.

The features and services in the preceding list are *objects* of the .NET Framework Data Providers. Before you can use any of these features, you must create a new *instance* of the object you want to use. To read more about creating object instances, see Book V, Chapter 3.

Making Connections

Each of the .NET Framework Data Providers has a connection object for establishing a connection to a data source. The *connection object* is the communication pipeline from the .NET Framework Data Providers and the underlying data source to your application. Table 5-2 lists the connection objects for each data provider.

**Book IV
Chapter 5**

**Under the Hood
with ADO.NET**

Table 5-2	.NET Framework Data Provider Connection Objects
Provider	*Connection Object*
SQL Server	`SqlConnection`
	`OleDbConnection`

(continued)

Table 5-2 *(continued)*

Provider	Connection Object
ODBC	OdbcConnection
Oracle	OracleConnection

Connecting to a database

You use the connection object for your data provider to connect to your data source. As you can imagine, connecting to a data source is a prerequisite for retrieving data from the data source. You use a connection object to

✦ **Pass a connection string to the connection object.** A connection string includes your username and password for accessing the data source. The connection object sends the connection string to the data source for validation.

✦ **Open the connection.** Opening a connection allows you to communicate with the data source.

✦ **Send commands by using the connection.** Send queries to retrieve and update the data source. See the section "Using Commands," later in this chapter.

✦ **Close the connection.** Each connection to the data source consumes resources on the server. Always close the connection as soon as you execute your commands.

ADO.NET uses a feature called connection pooling that groups together multiple database requests in a single connection. Connections that are exactly the same — same server, same database, same user credentials — are pooled by default with ADO.NET. Pooling connections together so they can be reused reduces the overhead required to open and close connections.

You should leave connection pooling enabled. You can disable connection pooling by using `pooling='false'` in your connection strings.

You follow the same sequence of events each time you want to access a data source. For example, to use a connection object to access a SQL Server 2005 database, follow these steps:

1. **Pick your .NET Framework Data Provider.**

You should always use the .NET Framework Data Provider for SQL Server to access SQL Server 7.0 databases and later. You access the SQL Server data provider by using the `System.Data.SqlClient` namespace.

2. **Create a new `SqlConnection` connection object.**

To create the new `SqlConnection` object `MyConnection`, type the following lines of code in the code editor:

```
Dim MyConnection As New System.Data.SqlClient.
    SqlConnection
```

3. **Create a new connection string to connect to a SQL Server 2005 database.**

   The connection string to connect to the AdventureWorks sample database installed on a local instance of SQL Server 2005 Express Edition using integrated security is

```
Data Source=(local)\sqlexpress;Initial Catalog=
    AdventureWorks;Integrated Security=True
```

   Visual Studio provides many tools for building connection strings. See the later section "Stringing up connections" for more information on creating and managing connection strings.

4. **Assign the connection string you create in Step 3 to the `ConnectionString` property of the `MyConnection` `SqlConnection` object, as shown in the following example:**

```
MyConnection.ConnectionString = ("Data Source=(local)\
    sqlexpress;Initial Catalog=AdventureWorks;Integrated
    Security=True")
```

5. **Call the `Open` method in `MyConnection` to open the database connection with the following line:**

```
MyConnection.Open()
```

   The data provider connects to the data source by using the connection string specified in Step 4.

6. **Send commands to the database to retrieve or update data.**

   See the section "Using Commands," later in this chapter, to see how to send commands to a data source.

7. **Call the `Close` method in `MyConnection` to close the database connection with the following line:**

```
MyConnection.Close()
```

Here's the entire code listing for the preceding code example:

```
Dim MyConnection As New System.Data.SqlClient.SqlConnection

MyConnection.ConnectionString = ("Data Source=(local)\
    sqlexpress;Initial Catalog=AdventureWorks;Integrated
    Security=True")

MyConnection.Open()
'send commands
MyConnection.Close()
```

**Book IV
Chapter 5**

**Under the Hood
with ADO.NET**

To use the connection object for any .NET Framework Data Providers, substitute the name of the provider's connection object listed in Table 5-2 where you see `SqlConnection` in the preceding code example.

For example, to work with an ODBC connection, type this line:

```
Dim MyConnection As New System.Data.Odbc.OdbcConnection
```

Always use structured exception handling every time you open a connection. (See Book V, Chapter 7.)

Closing your connection

You should always explicitly close your connection to your data source. Closing the connection releases resources. Opening your connections with a `Using` block is a good way to remember to always close your connections.

A *Using block* consists of starting and ending statements that create and dispose of the resource, respectively. The following code shows a `Using` block:

```
Using resource as New resourceType
.
.
.
End Using
```

You place, between the `Using ... End Using` statements, statements that access the resource. A database connection is an example of a resource you can use with a `Using` block, as shown in the following code sample:

```
Using MySqlConnection As New
    System.Data.SqlClient.SqlConnection()
  MySqlConnection.ConnectionString = ("Data
    Source=(local)\sqlexpress;Initial Catalog=
    AdventureWorks;Integrated Security=True")
  MySqlConnection.Open()
  'send commands
End Using
```

There's no need to explicitly call the connection object's `Close` method with the `Using` block. The `End Using` statement automatically closes the connection for you.

The comparable C# statement is

```
using (resourceType resource = new resourceType())
{
}
```

Rather than create a new, identical connection to a data source each time, ADO.NET reuses existing connections, in a process known as *connection pooling*. When you explicitly close your connection, the connection is returned to the connection pool, where it can be reused.

Stringing up connections

Nothing stops you in your tracks faster than an incorrect connection string. Without a valid connection string, your code can't establish a connection to the data source. If you're lucky enough to connect to the same data sources over and over, you have to build a working connection string only once. As long as the data source doesn't change, you can reuse your connection string.

Whether you work with the same data sources day in and day out or are always using different data sources, Visual Studio and .NET provide many tools to help you build and manage your connection strings. See the next section for more information.

A data provider's connection object uses the connection string to establish a connection to a data source when the connection object's Open method is called. A *connection string* is a set of name/value pairs *(keywords)* separated by semicolons, as shown in the following example:

```
Data Source=(local)\sqlexpress;Initial Catalog=
    AdventureWorks;Integrated Security=True
```

The set of keywords used to create a connection string are determined by the data source. Common name/value pairs used to connect to the SQL Server database are described in Table 5-3.

Table 5-3	Common SQL Server Connection-String Keywords	
Keyword	*What It Does*	*Usage*
Data Source or Server	Serves as name or network address of server	server=myserver, data source=myserver\server instance, server=(local)
Encrypt	Uses SSL encryption	encrypt=true
Initial Catalog or Database	Sets the name of the database to access	Initial Catalog= AdventureWorks
Integrated Security	Determines whether to use Windows security	integrated security=true
Password or Pwd	Sets the password to use when not using integrated security	password=mypassword
User ID	Sets the user ID to use when not using integrated security	user id=myuserid

Always use integrated security to access your data sources.

See the topic **Securing connection strings** in the Visual Studio 2005 documentation for more information. See the **Impersonation** topic in the Visual Studio 2005 documentation to read more about using integrated security with ASP.NET.

You set a connection string by using the `ConnectionString` property of the connection object.

ADO.NET uses the ConnectionString property to set the connection object's DataSource and DataBase properties.

Building connection strings

Visual Studio has many ways to help you build connection strings, including

+ Application settings in Windows applications
+ ASP.NET configuration settings
+ The Add Connection dialog box
+ .NET Framework Data Provider connection string builders

The .NET Framework makes extensive use of configuration setting files, such as application settings in Windows applications and configuration settings in ASP.NET, to store all kinds of information related to your application. Visual Studio provides tools for adding settings, such as connection strings, to .NET configuration files. For example, the ASP.NET Web Site Administration tool can be used to add several predefined and custom settings to your Web site. See Chapter 5 in Book III for more information on using the Web Site Administration tool.

Don't store connection strings in your source code. Your connection strings can be extracted from compiled code.

Adding connection strings to Windows projects

Windows projects store application settings, such as connection strings, in an XML configuration file named app.config.

To add connection strings to the application settings of a Windows project, follow these steps:

1. **Double-click the My Project folder in an existing Windows project to access the project's properties.**

2. **Click the Settings tab.**

   A grid appears where you enter application settings.

3. **Type** MyDbString **in the Name cell of the grid.**

4. **Select Connection String as the settings type.**

5. **Click the ellipsis button in the Value cell.**

   The Connection Properties dialog box appears.

6. **Connect to your data source by using the Connection Properties dialog box.**

   The dialog box returns a connection string to the Value cell from the Connection Properties dialog box, as shown in Figure 5-3.

   See the section in Chapter 2 of this mini-book about connecting to databases for more information on creating a connection string.

7. **Save the settings.**

   Visual Studio creates a new app.config file with your connection string.

You access the connection string by using the `My.Settings` expression. See the section "Using Commands," later in this chapter, to see an example of accessing a connection string from application settings.

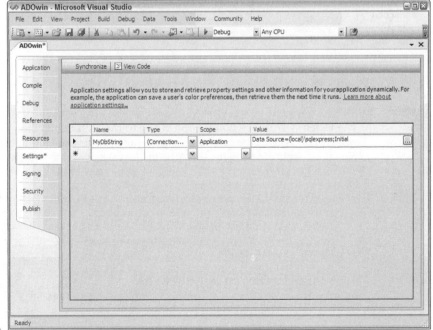

Figure 5-3:
Use the Connection Properties dialog box to build your connection string.

Book IV Chapter 5

Under the Hood with ADO.NET

Adding connection strings to Web projects

Web projects use the web.config file to store configuration settings, such as connection strings. The easiest way to add new connection strings to the web.config file is with the Data Source Configuration Wizard. I walk you through using the wizard in the section about adding data to Web Forms in Chapter 1 of this mini-book.

You can use the Data Source Configuration Wizard to configure many different kinds of data sources. Configuring a database with the wizard prompts you to select an existing data connection or configure a new connection. After creating the configuration string, the wizard prompts you to save the connection string in the web.config file, as shown in Figure 5-4.

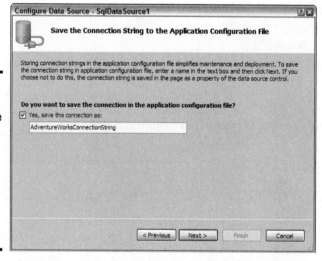

Figure 5-4: Use the Data Source Configuration Wizard to save connection strings in the web.config file.

The wizard writes the connection string to the web.config file. Alternatively, you can add the connection string manually to the web.config file. For example, a connection string for the AdventureWorks database might look like this:

```
<connectionStrings>
    <add name="AdventureWorksConnectionString"
    connectionString="Data Source=(local)\sqlexpress;Initial
    Catalog=AdventureWorks;Integrated Security=True"
            providerName="System.Data.SqlClient" />
</connectionStrings>
```

Add your connection string between the `<connectionStrings></connectionStrings>` **tags.**

Building connection strings manually

A common theme in building connection strings is the use of the Add Connection dialog box. It's used in both the application settings for Windows and the configuration settings for Web applications.

You access the Add Connection dialog box by choosing Tools⇨Connect to Database. The Add Connection dialog box creates a new connection in Server Explorer. Use Server Explorer to manage your connections to servers in your project.

You can grab the connection string from Server Explorer and reuse it elsewhere, in either code or a configuration-settings file. To copy a connection string from a data connection in Server Explorer, follow these steps:

1. **Create a new data connection by choosing Tools⇨Connect to Database.**

The Add Connection dialog box appears.

2. **Use the Add Connection dialog box to create a connection string.**

A new data connection appears in Server Explorer.

3. **Right-click the data connection in Server Explorer.**

You can open Server Explorer by clicking View⇨Server Explorer. The keyboard shortcut for Server Explorer is Ctrl+Alt+S.

4. **Choose Properties from the shortcut menu.**

The Properties window appears.

5. **Highlight the `Connection String` property, as shown in Figure 5-5.**

6. **Copy and paste the property.**

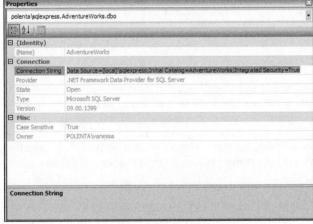

Figure 5-5: Copy and paste the `Connection String` property from Server Explorer.

Using the ADO.NET connection string builders

Each of the .NET Framework Data Providers includes a service for building and managing connection strings. The connection string builders provide the properties needed to build a connection string. The builder outputs a properly formatted connection string that you pass to the data provider's connection object. Table 5-4 lists the connection string builders for each data provider.

Table 5-4	Connection String Builders
Data Provider	*Object*
SQL Server	`SqlConnectionStringBuilder`
OLE DB	`OleDbConnectionStringBuilder`
ODBC	`OdbcConnectionStringBuilder`
Oracle	`OracleConnectionStringBuilder`

The following code uses the SQL Server data provider's connection string builder, `SqlConnectionStringBuilder`, to build a connection string for the AdventureWorks sample database:

```
Dim builder As New
    System.Data.SqlClient.SqlConnectionStringBuilder

builder.DataSource = "(local)\sqlexpress"
builder.InitialCatalog = "AdventureWorks"
builder.IntegratedSecurity = True
```

You pass the connection string from `SqlConnectionStringBuilder` to the connection object's `ConnectionString` property like this:

```
Dim MyConnection As New System.Data.SqlClient.SqlConnection
MyConnection.ConnectionString = builder.ConnectionString
```

Using Commands

You use a .NET Framework Data Provider's `Command` object to execute queries after connecting to a data source. Each of the data providers has a `Command` object. To use a `Command` object, follow these steps:

1. **Associate the `Command` object with a connection object. Use the `Connection` property to make the association, like this:**

```
MySqlCommand.Connection = MySqlConnection
```

The `Connection` object is the communication pipeline between the command and the data source.

2. **Specify a SQL statement. Use the** `Command` **object's** `CommandText` **property to set the SQL statement.**

   For example, to set the SQL statement for an ODBC data provider's `Command` object, type

   ```
   MyOdbcCommand.CommandText = "SELECT * FROM CUSTOMER"
   ```

3. **Call one of the** `Command` **object's** `Execute` **methods.**

   The `Execute` method runs the SQL statement specified in the `Command` object's `CommandText` property. The `Command` object has three `Execute` methods:

   - **ExecuteReader** — Returns a `DataReader` object. Use `ExecuteReader` any time you want fast access to a forward-only stream of data.

   - **ExecuteScalar** — Returns a single value. Use `ExecuteScalar` when you know that your query will return only one value, such as a `SELECT Count(*)` query.

   - **ExecuteNonQuery** — Doesn't return any rows. Use `ExecuteNonQuery` any time you need to execute a query, such as a `CreateTable` statement, that doesn't return any rows.

   You must call the `Open` method of the data provider's connection object before you call the `Command` object's `Execute` method.

Most data-centric applications make extensive use of stored procedures for data access. To use a stored procedure with a `Command` object, you must

✦ Set the `Command` object's `CommandType` property to `StoredProcedure`.

✦ Use the `Command` object's `Parameters` collection to define the stored procedure's input and output parameters.

To use the following stored procedure to access a SQL Server database by using the SQL Server data provider, follow these steps:

1. **Create the** `SqlConnection` **object and set the object's** `ConnectionString` **property, as shown in the following example:**

   ```
   Dim MySqlConnection As New System.Data.SqlClient.
       SqlConnection
   MySqlConnection.ConnectionString = My.Settings.
       MyDbString
   ```

   The `ConnectionString` property accesses the `MyDbString` connection string from the project's app.config file. See the earlier section "Adding connection strings to Windows projects" for more information about the app.config file.

2. **Create the `SqlCommand` object by entering the following lines:**

```
Dim MySqlCommand As New
    System.Data.SqlClient.SqlCommand
```

3. **To set the `SqlCommand` object's `Connection` property, enter this line:**

```
MySqlCommand.Connection = MySqlConnection
```

4. **Set the `CommandText` property of the `SqlCommand` object to the name of the stored procedure you wish to execute, as the following line shows:**

```
MySqlCommand.CommandText = "uspGetEmployeeManagers"
```

5. **Set the `CommandType` property to `StoredProcedure` by entering the following line:**

```
MySqlCommand.CommandType = CommandType.StoredProcedure
```

6. **Create a new `SqlParameter` object, like this:**

```
Dim MyParameter As New System.Data.SqlClient.
    SqlParameter
```

7. **To set the `ParameterName` and `Value` properties for the `SqlParameter`, assign values to the properties as shown below:**

```
MyParameter.ParameterName = "@EmployeeID"
MyParameter.Value = "6"
```

8. **Add the `SqlParameter` object to the `SqlCommand`'s `Parameters` collection, like this:**

```
MySqlCommand.Parameters.Add(MyParameter)
```

9. **Call the `Open` method of the `SqlConnection` object:**

```
MySqlConnection.Open()
```

10. **Call the `Command` object's `Execute` method with the following statement:**

```
MySqlDataReader = MySqlCommand.ExecuteReader()
```

The `Execute` method passes the stored procedure from the `Command` object to the database by using the connection object.

The `Command` object has a `CommandBuilder` you can use to automatically generate `Command` objects for single-table data access. See the topic **CommandBuilder object** in the Visual Studio 2005 documentation.

Reading Data with DataReaders

ADO.NET's DataReaders are old school data-access services. You use a DataReader any time you need fast, forward-only access to your data. Unlike a DataSet, which retrieves your data into an in-memory database model, there's no storage mechanism with a DataReader. When you retrieve data by using a DataReader, you had better have your "catcher's mitt" open to store the data.

A DataReader is often called a *firehose cursor*.

Each of the .NET Framework Data Providers provides a DataReader. Table 5-5 lists the DataReader objects for each provider.

Table 5-5	DataReader Objects
Provider	*DataReader Object*
SQL Server	SqlDataReader
OLE DB	OleDbDataReader
ODBC	OdbcDataReader
Oracle	OracleDataReader

You use the ExecuteReader method of the Command object to retrieve data for a DataReader.

Using a DataReader to retrieve data from a data source involves these steps:

1. **Call the Command object's ExecuteReader method.**

ExecuteReader builds the DataReader.

2. **Call the DataReader's Read method to advance to the next record.**

The first time you call Read, the next record is the first record because the DataReader is positioned in front of the first record.

3. **Use the DataReader's Get accessors to retrieve data from the row of data.**

The DataReader retrieves one row at a time.

See the section "Retrieving data with the Get accessors," later in this chapter, to see the DataReader's Get accessors in action.

4. **Advance to the next record by using the Read method.**

Because the DataReader retrieves one row at a time from the data source, use common practice to execute the Read method by using a loop.

See the following section to see the DataReader used with a while loop.

Even though you need only two methods to use the DataReader — ExecuteReader and Read — a lot of setup work is involved. The following steps walk you through using a DataReader to retrieve records:

1. **Select a .NET Framework Data Provider, as described in the section "Picking a Provider," earlier in this chapter.**

**Book IV
Chapter 5**

**Under the Hood
with ADO.NET**

2. **Create a new connection object for the data provider, as described in the section "Making Connections," earlier in this chapter.**

3. **Declare a new variable of the `DataReader` object type for your data provider.**

   For example, to declare a new DataReader variable for the ODBC data provider, you would type the following:

   ```
   Dim odbcReader As System.Data.Odbc.OdbcDataReader
   ```

   Notice that you aren't using the New keyword to create a new instance of the DataReader object. There are no constructors for DataReaders. Calling the Command object's ExecuteReader method builds the DataReader.

4. **Create a new `Command` object for your data provider to retrieve data for the object, as described in the preceding section.**

5. **Call the `Open` method of the connection object to establish a connection to the data source.**

6. **Call the `ExecuteReader` method of the `Command` object you create in Step 4 and pass the results to the `DataReader` object you create in Step 3.**

   For example, to call the ExecuteReader method on an OdbcCommand object and pass the results to an OdbcDataReader object you create in Step 3, type the following:

   ```
   odbcReader = odbcCommand.ExecuteReader()
   ```

   The OdbcCommand object executes the query against the OdbcConnection object when ExecuteReader is called and builds the OdbcDataReader object.

7. **Call the `Read` method of the `DataReader` object to retrieve one record from the data source. For example, to call the `Read` method for the `OdbcDataReader` you create in Step 3, type the following:**

   ```
   odbcReader.Read()
   ```

   The OdbcDataReader object advances to the next record.

   The default position of the DataReader is before the first row in the result set. The Reader method advances the DataReader to the next record.

8. **Retrieve values from the DataReader.**

   See the section "Retrieving data with the Get accessors," later in this chapter, for more information about using the DataReader's Get accessors to retrieve data.

9. **Close your connection object, as described in the section "Making Connections," earlier in this chapter.**

Close the `Connection` object by calling the `Close` method of the connection object or using a using block.

Here's the entire code listing:

```
Dim odbcConnection As New System.Data.Odbc.OdbcConnection
Dim odbcReader As System.Data.Odbc.OdbcDataReader
Dim odbcCommand As New System.Data.Odbc.OdbcCommand

odbcConnection.ConnectionString = My.Settings.
    MyOdbcConnectionString
odbcCommand.Connection = odbcConnection
odbcCommand.CommandText = "SELECT * FROM CUSTOMER"
odbcConnection.Open()

odbcReader = odbcCommand.ExecuteReader()
odbcReader.Read()
'do something here with the data in the row
odbcConnection.Close()
```

Stepping through data

The DataReader's `Read` method advances the DataReader to the next row in the result set. As long as more rows are present, the `Read` method returns the value `true`. The `Read` method is typically used to test the `Read` method's return value in a `while` loop.

A `while` loop loops through a set of statements as long as a test condition remains `true`. You can use a `while` loop to iterate through each row in a DataReader's result set and perform the same action on each row. For example, to use a `while` loop to step through a `SqlDataReader` object named `MySqlDataReader`, type the following lines:

```
While (MySqlDataReader.Read() = True)
    Me.lstDepartments.Items.Add(MySqlDataReader("Name"))
End While
```

The preceding example gets the value in column `"Name"` of the `MySqlDataReader` result set and adds the value to the items collection of a `lstDepartments` list box. The `while` loop performs the statement inside the loop as long as the `Read` method returns `true`. You end up with a list box full of items from the `SqlDataReader`. See the next section, about how to get data from a row.

Use the *HasRows* property of the DataReader to test whether the DataReader has more rows. The `HasRows` property returns the value `true` if more rows are present.

Retrieving data with the Get accessors

The `DataReader` object provides access to a forward-only result set which presents one row at a time. When you're deciding how to work with the data in row, you have to consider whether you want to work with the data

✦ In its native format or by using a typed accessor

✦ In a single column in the row or all the columns in the row

The DataReader provides several `Get` accessors for retrieving data. You should retrieve the data by using a typed accessor, such as `GetDateTime`.

The data types used in the underlying data source aren't the same as the data types used in the .NET Framework. The typed accessors convert the value from its native database type to a .NET Framework type.

The DataReader provides several options for retrieving data by using typed accessors. Each DataReader provides a set of common typed `Get` accessors, such as

✦ `GetChar` — Retrieves data as a `char` data type.

✦ `GetDateTime` — Retrieves data as a `DateTime` data type.

✦ `GetInt16` — Retrieves data as an `Int16` data type.

✦ `GetString` — Retrieves data as a `string` data type.

The `SqlDataReader` provides special types that work exclusively with SQL Server database types. Examples include

✦ `GetSqlChars`

✦ `GetSqlDateTime`

✦ `GetSqlInt16`

✦ `GetSqlString`

Use the `GetSql` typed accessors when you're using the `SqlDataReader`. The `GetSql` typed accessors are more precise than the .NET data types.

If you're unsure of the column's native data type, query the data source. The DataReaders provide the `GetFieldType` and `GetDataTypeName` methods you can use.

Of course, you can also retrieve data in its native format. The DataReader provides several methods, such as

✦ `GetValue` and `GetValues`

✦ `Item`

When you access the data in its native format, you must ensure that the data is converted to the appropriate .NET Framework data type. For example, the following statement retrieves a column by using the Item method and uses the `ToString` method to convert it to a string:

```
myString = MySqlDataReader.Item("Name").ToString()
```

To read more about converting data types, see Book V, Chapter 2. Additionally, see the topic **mapping data types** in the Visual Studio 2005 help documentation to see how native data types are mapped to .NET Framework data types.

Most `Get` accessors use a zero-based column index to retrieve a column. A zero-based index starts counting elements at zero rather than at one. For example, in a table with the columns CustID, FirstName, and LastName, the FirstName column might have the column index of one. To access the FirstName column by using the `GetSqlString` accessor, you type the following line:

```
MySqlDataReader.GetSqlString(1)
```

Using column indexes to retrieve values may be fast for the DataReader, but it's slow and confusing to a programmer. Fortunately, DataReaders have two methods for accessing columns by name:

✦ `Item` — Returns the column's value in its native format

✦ `GetOrdinal` — Returns the index number of the column

Each of these approaches has its drawbacks. If you use the `Item` method, you must explicitly convert the column to a .NET data type. Using `GetOrdinal` hits the data source twice — once to get the ordinal and again to retrieve the data by using the ordinal.

Here's an example of using `GetOrdinal` to access data:

```
Dim nameCol, groupNameCol As Integer
nameCol = MySqlDataReader.GetOrdinal("Name")
groupNameCol = MySqlDataReader.GetOrdinal("GroupName")

While (MySqlDataReader.Read() = True)
  myString = String.Format("{0} {1}",
    MySqlDataReader.GetString(nameCol),
    MySqlDataReader.GetString(groupNameCol))
  Me.lstDepartments.Items.Add(myString)
End While
```

**Book IV
Chapter 5**

**Under the Hood
with ADO.NET**

Use the `GetValues` method to retrieve all the columns in a row at one time. The `GetValues` method requires you to pass in an array that the method fills with the columns from the row.

Here's an example of using the `GetValues` method:

```
Dim MyArray(MySqlDataReader.FieldCount - 1) As Object
MySqlDataReader.GetValues(MyArray)
```

In the first line of this example, you use the DataReader's `FieldCount` property to set the size of the array. In the second line, you pass the array to the `GetValues` method. The array is filled with the values for the entire row.

The `GetValues` method retrieves values in their native data formats. The values must be converted to .NET data types.

With the values in the array, you can access them by using the properties and methods of arrays. To read more about using arrays, see Book V, Chapter 2.

The `GetValues` method, which is a fast way to grab an entire row, is typically used by `GetValues` to pass the array to the `ItemArray` method of the `DataRow` object.

DataRows are rows in a DataTable. You specify ahead of time which columns and data types exist in the DataTable. When you add a new row by using `ItemArray`, the data is plugged into the columns and converted to the column's data type. The following code fills an array and passes the array to a new DataRow in the `myTable` DataTable:

```
MySqlDataReader.GetValues(array)
row = myTable.NewRow()
row.ItemArray = array
```

The values in the array are converted to the appropriate data type for each column in the DataRow.

Retrieving schema info

The DataReader includes a `GetSchemaTable` method that you can use to retrieve the schema information about the result set. The `GetSchemaTable` method returns a DataTable, as shown in the following code:

```
Dim table As New DataTable
table = MySqlDataReader.GetSchemaTable()
```

You can use the DataRow's `ItemArray` method as described in the preceding section to add new rows to a table built with `GetSchemaTable`.

Caching Data with DataSets

DataSets are an important element in data access. ADO.NET provides the DataSet as a built-in memory cache for storing data retrieved from a data source. See the section about understanding DataSets in Chapter 3 of this mini-book.

The workhorse behind the DataSet is the `DataAdapter`. It provides the following services to the DataSet:

✦ Populates the DataSet with data from a data source by using the `Fill` method

✦ Updates a data source with changes made in the DataSet by using the `Update` method

Each of the .NET Framework Data Providers has a `DataAdapter` object. Table 5-6 lists the `DataAdapter` object for each data provider.

Table 5-6	DataAdapter Objects
Data Provider	*DataAdapter Object*
SQL Server	`SqlDataAdapter`
Ole DB	`OleDbDataAdapter`
ODBC	`OdbcDataAdapter`
Oracle	`OracleDataAdapter`

The `DataAdapter` object uses a set of `Command` objects to send SQL statements to a data source. The `DataAdapter` object exposes the `Command` objects by using the following set of properties:

✦ **SelectCommand**

You must specify a `SelectCommand` before you can call the `DataAdapter`'s `Fill` method.

✦ **InsertCommand**

✦ **UpdateCommand**

✦ **DeleteCommand**

See the section "Using Commands," earlier in this chapter, to read more about the properties of `Command` objects.

**Book IV
Chapter 5**

**Under the Hood
with ADO.NET**

Filling a DataSet

A DataAdapter acts as a bridge between the DataSet and the data source. Filling a DataSet involves these tasks:

✦ Create a DataAdapter and a DataSet.

✦ Create a Command object that holds the SELECT statement or stored procedure to retrieve data from the data source.

✦ Set the DataAdapter's SelectCommand property to the Command object.

✦ Call the DataAdapter's Fill method and pass in the DataSet.

As is the case with all the data access features of ADO.NET, filling a DataSet isn't as simple as creating a few objects and then calling the Fill method. You have to complete a number of prerequisite steps, such as creating a connection object.

The following example walks you through using a DataAdapter to fill a DataSet:

1. **Pick the .NET Framework Data Provider best suited for your data source, as described in the section "Picking a Provider," earlier in this chapter.**

This example uses the SQL Server data provider to fill a DataSet by using data from the AdventureWorks sample database in SQL Server 2005.

2. **Create a new connection and connection string, as described earlier in this chapter, in the section "Making Connections." Enter the following lines of code:**

```
Dim MySqlConnection As New System.Data.SqlClient.
    SqlConnection
MySqlConnection.ConnectionString = My.Settings.
    MyDbString
```

3. **Create a new DataAdapter and DataSet, as shown in the following example:**

```
Dim MySqlDataAdapter As New System.Data.SqlClient.
    SqlDataAdapter()
Dim MyDataSet As New System.Data.DataSet
```

4. **Create a new Command object, associate the Command object with your connection object, and set the CommandText property as described in the earlier section "Using Commands."**

For example, the following code sample creates a new SqlCommand object, associates the object with a SqlConnection object, and sets the SqlCommand object to a SQL statement:

```
Dim MySelectCommand As New System.Data.SqlClient.
    SqlCommand
```

```
MySelectCommand.Connection = MySqlConnection
MySelectCommand.CommandText = "SELECT * FROM
    HumanResources.Department"
```

5. **Set the `DataAdapter`'s `SelectCommand` property to the `Command` object you create in Step 4, as shown in the following:**

```
MySqlDataAdapter.SelectCommand = MySelectCommand
```

6. **Call the `DataAdapter`'s `Fill` method and pass in the DataSet as a parameter:**

```
MySqlDataAdapter.Fill(MyDataSet)
```

Behind the scenes, the `Fill` method does the following:

✦ Retrieves data from the data source by passing the SQL statement specified in the `SelectCommand` to a DataReader.

✦ Creates a DataTable by using the column information from the data source and adds the rows to the DataTable.

✦ Adds the DataTable to the specified DataSet.

Figure 5-6 shows the relationship among the objects of the SQL Server data provider used in the preceding example. The relationships are similar for other .NET Framework data providers.

Updating data with the Update method

You call the `DataAdapter`'s `Update` method to send data updates from the DataSet to the data source. The `Update` method uses `InsertCommand`, `UpdateCommand`, and `DeleteCommand` to update the data source.

Figure 5-6:
The SQL Data Adapter is the bridge between the data source and the DataSet.

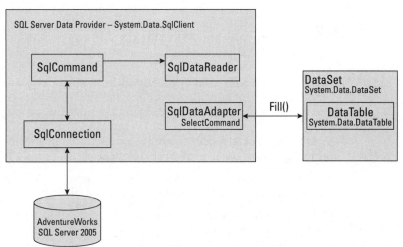

The `Update` method requires you to pass in a DataSet, a DataTable, or an array of DataRows, as shown in the following example:

```
MySqlDataAdapter.Update(MyDataSet)
```

The `DataAdapter` uses the `Command` objects specified in its properties to execute SQL statements against the data source.

Each of the .NET Framework Data Providers has a `CommandBuilder` object you can use to automatically generate commands against a single-table data source. `CommandBuilder` automatically builds the commands for a DataAdapter to use.

To use `SqlCommandBuilder` with the example from the preceding section, follow these steps:

1. **Create a new `SqlCommandBuilder` object after Step 5 in the preceding section.**

```
Dim builder As New System.Data.SqlClient.
    SqlCommandBuilder()
```

2. **Set the `SqlCommandBuilder`'s `DataAdapter` property:**

```
builder.DataAdapter = MySqlDataAdapter
```

The `SqlCommandBuilder` uses the DataAdapter's `SelectCommand` property to build the Insert, Update, and Delete commands.

3. **Call the `Update` method rather than the `Fill` method in Step 6 in the preceding section.**

Using TableAdapters

The TableAdapter, a new data access feature in ADO.NET, encapsulates all the retrieve and update commands and a connection object for a single table. Visual Studio provides extensive support for creating TableAdapters by using the TableAdapter Configuration Wizard in the DataSet Designer.

You can call the commands of a generated TableAdapter by using the standard "dot" notation of IntelliSense in the code editor. To access the properties and methods of a generated TableAdapter, follow these steps:

1. **Use the DataSet Designer to create a new DataSet with the Department table from the AdventureWorks database.**

See the section "Exploring the DataSet Designer" in Chapter 3 of this mini-book for more information on creating DataSets.

2. **Open a Windows Form and drag and drop the Department table from the Data Sources window.**

A `DepartmentTableAdapter` is created.

3. **Double-click the form to access the form's Load event.**

   The Code Editor appears.

4. **Type the following code in the code editor:**

   ```
   Me.DepartmentTableAdapter.
   ```

   The code editor displays a list of properties and methods available for `DepartmentTableAdapter`, as shown in Figure 5-7.

5. **Select a property or method from the list.**

Use the TableAdapter Configuration Wizard to generate TableAdapters.

Using transactions

SQL statements are executed by databases in transactions. A *transaction* is a group of statements executed against a database. You use statements such as `BEGIN TRANSACTION` and `COMMIT WORK` to mark the start and end of a transaction. In between the start and end are SQL statements that retrieve and modify data. The `ROLLBACK WORK` statement rolls back, or undoes, the statements executed in the transaction.

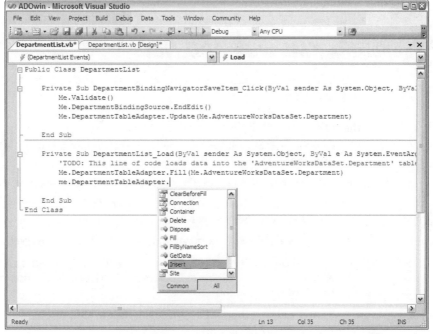

Figure 5-7: Use IntelliSense to access the methods and properties of Table Adapters generated by the designers in Visual Studio.

Book IV
Chapter 5

Under the Hood with ADO.NET

The .NET Framework provides a new model for transaction processing with the `System.Transactions` namespace. You use it to create two kinds of database transactions:

✦ **Implicit transactions** — Use the `TransactionScope` object to encapsulate a block of ADO.NET code in a transaction, as shown in this code:

```
Using scope As New System.Transactions.
    TransactionScope()
    .
    .
    .
End Using
```

✦ **Explicit transaction** — Create a `CommittableTransaction` object where you specifically call the object's `Commit` and `Rollback` methods. The following code creates a new `CommittableTransaction` object:

```
Dim tx As New System.Transactions.
    CommittableTransaction
```

You must add a reference to `System.Transactions` before you can access the objects in the namespace.

The `System.Transactions` namespace is the model for all kinds of transactions in .NET, not just database transactions. (See the Visual Studio 2005 documentation.)

Supporting XML with ADO.NET

ADO.NET provides extensive support for XML. You can use ADO.NET to do the following:

✦ **Fill a DataSet by using an XML document.**

Call the DataSet's `ReadXml` method to populate a DataSet with an XML document.

✦ **Create or infer a DataSet's schema from an XML schema definition.**

Call a DataSet's `ReadXmlSchema` or `InferXmlSchema` methods to create the DataSet's schema.

✦ **Create an XML document or XML schema from a DataSet.**

Call the DataSet's `GetXml` method to write the DataSet's content as an XML document. Call `GetXmlSchema` to write an XML schema file from the DataSet's schema.

✦ **Synchronize a DataSet's contents with an XML document.**

Use the `XmlDataDocument` object to create an XML document with the data from a DataSet.

The following sample code creates a DataSet and populates it with data from an XML document with the name recipes.xml:

```
Dim ds As New System.Data.DataSet
ds.ReadXml("recipe.xml", XmlReadMode.InferSchema)
```

Using the DataSet from the preceding code example, write an XML schema to the recipe.xsd file with this code:

```
ds.WriteXmlSchema("recipe.xsd")
```

You can combine the extensive ADO.NET support for XML with SQL Server 2005 support for XML. Using SQL Server 2005, you can

✦ Use the `xml` data type to store entire XML documents or fragments.

✦ Associate XML schemas with `xml` data types to create typed XML.

✦ Retrieve data stored in relational tables as XML markup using the `FOR XML` clause.

✦ Retrieve XML data as relational data by using the `OPENXML` function.

The AdventureWorks sample database provides several examples of using the `xml` data type. To read more about using XML with SQL Server 2005, see the topic "Using XML in SQL Server" in the SQL Server 2005 Books Online documentation.

Using ADO.NET in Your Applications

Using the features described in this chapter, you can use ADO.NET to access data seven ways from Sunday. Couple these features with all the designers in Visual Studio, and you have even more choices. Here are some recommendations for accessing data with ADO.NET:

✦ **Populate custom data entities with DataReaders.**

Many developers create their own custom data types for storing the data entities their application uses. For example, you can create a `Customer` data type and a `CustomerAddress` data type. Use a DataReader to populate your `Customer` and `CustomerAddress` data types. You can use this approach to separate the application from its underlying data source. (See Book V, Chapter 2.)

✦ **Use typed DataSets for prototyping or in conjunction with other data storage.**

Although typed DataSets are very fast to build, they perform slower than custom data entities in your application. They can be especially slow in Web applications. You don't have to use a typed DataSet for all your data access — you can use a combination of approaches. I like to use typed DataSets as a way to quickly build prototype applications. I create my own data entities after I get a better feel for what the data requirements are.

✦ **Create data access class libraries.**

Whatever approach you use, usually you should encapsulate your data access methods in a separate class file or class library. You create public methods or properties that return DataSets, DataTables, hashtables, arrays, or custom data entities that your data controls consume. See Chapter 2 in Book V for more information on hashtables and arrays.

For example, here's a method signature that returns a DataTable from the class DataAccess:

```
Public Function GetDepartments() As
    System.Data.DataTable
```

The `GetDepartments` method encapsulates all the data access code populating the DataTable.

To use the DataTable as a data source for a `BindingSource` component, enter these lines:

```
Dim data As New DataAccess
Me.MyBindingSource.DataSource = data.GetDepartments
```

Use the `BindingSource` component as the data source for a databound control.

✦ **Evaluate whether to use stored procedures or ad hoc SQL queries.**

People are on both sides of the camp on this issue. I personally have used ad hoc queries extensively without the sky falling on me.

✦ **Extend generated typed DataSets.**

Use partial classes to add features to typed DataSets. For example, you may decide to use a DataReader to populate a simple lookup table.

✦ **Create your own helper classes.**

A great deal of repetition occurs in building data access code. You can create your own helper classes, though, to cut down on all the repetition.

✦ **Use Enterprise Library.**

Another way to deal with all the repetition involved in coding data access is to use the Enterprise Library. It has all the best practices of using ADO.NET baked right in. (For more information about the Enterprise Library, see Book V, Chapter 9.)

Chapter 6: Using Visual Studio with SQL Server

In This Chapter

✔ Installing SQL Server 2005 Developer Edition

✔ Configuring the AdventureWorks sample database

✔ Creating scripts in database projects

✔ Creating stored procedures in SQL Server projects

✔ Using Visual Database Tools

*E*very program I've ever written has required some kind of data storage. In most cases, I used a database program like Microsoft SQL Server. SQL Server 2005, the latest release of the popular database program, works better than ever with Visual Studio 2005.

In this chapter, I show you how to install SQL Server 2005 and how to use Visual Studio to create and manage database objects.

Getting Acquainted with SQL Server 2005

SQL Server 2005 is the latest version of the popular Microsoft database management system. Each edition of Visual Studio includes a license for one of the editions of SQL Server 2005. Table 6-1 lists the editions of SQL Server and describes how to get the program.

Table 6-1	SQL Server Editions	
SQL Server Version	When to Use It	How to Get It
Enterprise Edition	In large companies	Purchase separately; retail price $24,999
Standard Edition	In small- and medium-size businesses	Purchase separately; retail price $5,999
Workgroup Edition	In departments or branch offices	Purchase separately; retail price $3,899
Express Edition	For prototypes or local development	Free download from Microsoft Web site; included with all Visual Studio Express Editions and Visual Studio Standard Edition

(continued)

Table 6-1 *(continued)*

SQL Server Version	When to Use It	How to Get It
Developer Edition	For prototypes or local development	Included with Professional, Tools for Office, and Team Editions of Visual Studio
Mobile Edition	In a database for mobile devices	Free download from Microsoft Web site

Get more information about each of the SQL Server 2005 editions, including pricing and product comparisons, on Microsoft's SQL Server portal at www. microsoft.com/sql/prodinfo/default.mspx. You can download SQL Server Express Edition and Mobile Edition from the portal.

Most developers use one of these two editions of SQL Server:

✦ **Express Edition** is free to use and redistribute. Express Edition replaces Microsoft SQL Server 2000 Desktop Engine (MSDE), the lightweight SQL Server 2000 database. You can include a local copy of a database in your application and freely distribute Express Edition with your application. You can easily use Express Edition as the database for a small Web site, for example. The size of Express Edition databases is limited to 4GB. Express Edition is also a good choice for developers who don't want or need the overhead of Developer Edition.

✦ **Developer Edition** is a fully functioning version of SQL Server 2005 Enterprise Edition. A Developer Edition license restricts you to using the product only in development and testing environments. Developer Edition is a good choice for consultants and corporate developers who may need to access complex databases.

Unless you know that you need the features of Developer Edition, I suggest starting out with Express Edition and then upgrading later, if you need it.

The examples in this book use SQL Server Express Edition; many developers always install Developer Edition. You may wonder why I chose to use SQL Server 2005 Express Edition for the examples in this book when Visual Studio 2005 Professional includes SQL Server 2005 Developer Edition. I use the Express Edition because I believe that less is more. SQL Server 2005 Express Edition is installed by default with Visual Studio 2005.

Installing SQL Server Developer Edition

SQL Server 2005 Developer Edition is installed separately from Visual Studio 2005. I recommend installing Visual Studio 2005 first and then installing SQL Server 2005 Developer Edition. Developer Edition requires version 2.0 of the .NET Framework, which is installed by Visual Studio 2005. Although Visual

Studio 2005 installs SQL Server 2005 Express Edition, installing the Developer Edition *upgrades* SQL Server.

Preparing your machine to install SQL Server requires many steps. Your installation steps depend on the services and components you choose to install.

Follow these steps to install SQL Server Developer Edition:

1. **Install Visual Studio 2005 or version 2.0 of the .NET Framework.**

See Book II, Chapter 1 for more information about installing Visual Studio 2005 Professional.

2. **Launch the SQL Server Developer Edition setup.**

The Start page appears.

If setup doesn't start when you place the disc in the drive, double-click the setup.hta file.

3. **Click the hyperlink for your operating system type.**

The Start page for your operating system appears.

4. **Before installing SQL Server, review the hardware and software requirements and read the release notes.**

The hardware and software requirements include instructions for accessing the Books Online documentation, where you can find complete installation instructions.

5. **After reviewing the installation documentation, click the link to install the server.**

The pre-setup wizard opens, and the end user license agreement appears.

6. **Read the license agreement and select the option if you agree to the terms and conditions of the license. Click the Next button.**

The wizard installs any prerequisites.

7. **Click the Next button again.**

The wizard scans your system's configuration and starts the installation wizard.

8. **Click the Next button one more time.**

The results of the system configuration check appear.

9. **Review the results and address any of the warnings or error messages, as shown in Figure 6-1. Click the Next button.**

The installation wizard prepares the installation files.

10. **Enter your registration information and click the Next button.**

Error message

Figure 6-1:
Review the
results of
the system
configura-
tion check.

11. **On the Components to Install page, select the components you want to install.**

The components you can choose to install include:

- **Database Services** — Installs the database engine which allows you to create and use databases

- **Analysis Services** — Installs tools to support data analysis and mining

- **Reporting Services** — Installs the Report Server and Report Builder for creating reports that run on SQL Server

- **Notification Services** — Installs services that enable users to subscribe to events and receive messages when those events occur

- **Integration Services** — Installs services that make it possible to merge data from multiple data sources

- **Workstation components, Books Online, and development tools** — Installs the client tools and documentation you need to administer SQL Server 2005 and develop database applications

At a minimum, you should choose to install Database Services and Workstation components, Books Online, and development tools. The remaining services allow you to create specialized database applications. You should install them as you need them. I show you how to use Reporting Services in Chapter 5 of Book VI. I suggest you go ahead and install Reporting Services now.

Reporting Services is available for SQL Server 2005 Express Edition. Unless you need the more advanced features of Developer Edition, you may find that Express Edition works fine. You can download SQL Server 2005 Express Edition with Advanced Services SP1 at `http://msdn.microsoft.com/vstudio/express/sql/download/`.

12. **Click the Advanced button.**

The Feature Selection dialog box appears.

13. **Click the plus (+) sign next to Documentation, Samples, and Sample Databases.**

14. **Select the Sample Databases and Sample Code and Applications options for installation, as shown in Figure 6-2, and then click the Next button.**

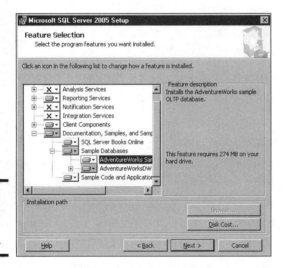

Figure 6-2:
Install the sample databases.

15. **Complete the steps to configure the services you selected to install in Step 11.**

The wizard displays a summary page before installation.

Refer to the SQL Server Books Online documentation for specific details on configuring services.

16. **Click the Install button, as shown in Figure 6-3, to start the installation.**

Use the Add/Remove Programs icon in the Windows Control Panel to add components to, or remove them from, your SQL Server installation.

Figure 6-3:
Click the
Install
button to
start the
installation.

Working with the SQL Server tools

SQL Server 2005 includes many helpful tools for working with databases. These tools include

✦ **SQL Server Management Studio** — Create and manage database objects.

✦ **Business Intelligence Development Studio** — Develop new projects that use Analysis, Reporting, and Integration Services.

✦ **Books Online** — Browse the comprehensive SQL Server documentation.

✦ **Sample databases and code** — Use samples to figure out how things are supposed to work.

The numerous wizards and designers in the Management and Business Intelligence Development Studios walk you through creating new objects. (The preceding section describes how to include the SQL Server tools during installation.)

If you decide to use SQL Server 2005 Express Edition, you need to install some additional tools to make your life easier. You should install the following tools:

✦ AdventureWorks sample database

✦ Books Online

✦ Management Studio Express

You can download these tools at the Microsoft TechCenter download page for SQL Server 2005 at www.microsoft.com/technet/prodtechnol/ sql/2005/downloads/default.mspx.

TIP

Run the SQL Server Surface Area Configuration Tool after installation. The tool helps you disable unused services and features of SQL Server so that you can minimize your security exposure.

You're likely to use the SQL Server Management Studio frequently for administering your databases. You can launch the Management Studio by choosing Start⇨All Programs⇨Microsoft SQL Server 2005. Figure 6-4 shows a Management Studio pane.

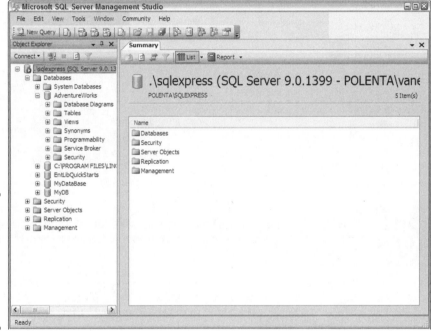

Figure 6-4:
Use the SQL Server Management Studio to administer your databases.

The Management Studio features Object Explorer, which is similar to Server Explorer in Visual Studio. As in Server Explorer, you right-click an object in Object Explorer to display a list of commands you can execute, as shown in Figure 6-5.

The Management Studio uses many of the same designers and explorers as Visual Studio. For example, the Query and View Designer is the same. See the section "Managing Your Database with Visual Database Tools," later in this chapter, to see the Query and View Designer in action.

One cool feature of the Management Studio is the Script As command: Right-click a table in Object Explorer and choose Script As from the shortcut menu. Select the kind of script you want to create, such as CREATE, and Management Studio generates the script.

**Book IV
Chapter 6**

Using Visual Studio with SQL Server

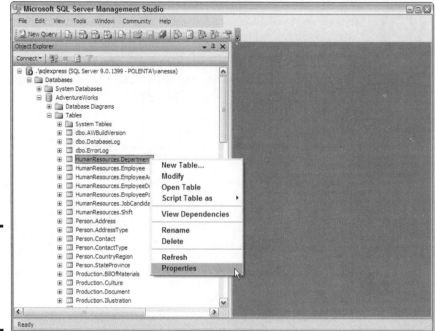

Figure 6-5:
Right-click
an object to
display a
list of
commands.

Use the Management Studio or Visual Studio for creating queries. SQL Server 2005 doesn't include a separate query tool, such as the SQL Server 2000 Query Analyzer.

The Management Studio for SQL Server Developer Edition includes support for solutions and projects. You use Solution Explorer similar to the way you use Visual Studio to work with database projects that store script items and database connections.

Using the AdventureWorks sample

The AdventureWorks sample database showcases many of the new features of SQL Server 2005. One feature that AdventureWorks uses extensively is *schemas,* which allow database objects to be grouped together. For example, the AdventureWorks database uses a schema named `HumanResources`. The tables Employee and Department are associated with the `HumanResources` schema.

One drawback of using schemas is that more typing is required when you use SQL statements to access data. For example, to access the Employee table, you must type HumanResources.Employee.

The code samples you install with SQL Server 2005 provide a set of scripts you can use to either remove the schemas or create synonyms for the schemas. The scripts are

+ AlterSchemaToDbo.sql
+ CreateSynonymsDbo.sql

Both of these scripts have the same net effect: You can access the tables without specifying a schema first. The main difference is that if you use the first script, AlterSchemaToDbo.sql, the code samples included with SQL Server don't work. If you don't care about using code samples, use whichever script you want.

You can reverse either script by using the scripts AlterSchemaFromDbo.sql or DropSynonymsDbo.sql.

The scripts are included with the SqlServerSamples.msi download, which you can find at `www.microsoft.com/downloads/details.aspx?FamilyId=9697AAAA-AD4B-416E-87A4-A8B154F92787&displaylang=en`.

The scripts are installed at C:\Program Files\Microsoft SQL Server\90\ Samples\Engine\Administration\AdventureWorks\Scripts.

The Data Source Configuration Wizard in ASP.NET doesn't properly qualify tables by using schemas. As a result, the queries you build by using the wizard don't execute.

Work around this problem by executing one of the scripts in this section. I show you how to work around the problem by manually editing the SQL statements; see the section about adding data to Web Forms in Chapter 1 of this mini-book.

Creating Database Projects

You can create two kinds of database projects in Visual Studio, and they are vastly different:

+ **Database Project** — Create and manage scripts by using SQL.
+ **SQL Server Project** — Create database objects and retrieve and update data from databases by using .NET programming languages such as Visual Basic and C#.

In a SQL Server Project, you use Visual Basic or C# to write complex data access procedures that take advantage of the features of the .NET Framework. Database projects are containers for storing SQL scripts.

**Book IV
Chapter 6**

**Using Visual Studio
with SQL Server**

Managing scripts with database projects

Visual Studio provides a project template for database projects. You use database projects to

+ Create SQL scripts.

+ Store database references.

+ Place scripts under source control.

+ Run and test scripts.

Storing scripts in a project keeps them together in a single container and allows you to place those scripts under source control. You can use the Visual Studio Visual Database Tools to generate scripts.

For more information about these tools, see the section "Managing Your Database with Visual Database Tools," later in this chapter. To read more about source control, see Book VI, Chapter 3.

You can add any kind of SQL script to a database project. Visual Studio provides templates and tools for generating certain kinds of scripts, such as

+ Change and Create scripts

+ Stored procedures

+ Triggers

+ Tables

+ Views

+ Database queries

To create a database project, follow these steps:

1. **Press Ctrl+Shift+N to open the New Project dialog box.**

2. **Click the plus (+) sign to expand the Other Project Types line.**

3. **Click the Database project type.**

A list of project templates appears.

4. **Click the Database Project icon.**

5. **Type a name and location for the project.**

6. **Click the OK button.**

Visual Studio prompts you to select a database reference.

The Add Database Reference dialog box appears if Visual Studio finds existing database connections in Server Explorer. The New Database Reference dialog box appears if no existing database connections are in Server Explorer.

7. Select an existing database reference or create a new one.

Visual Studio creates the database project and adds the database reference to Solution Explorer. Figure 6-6 shows a reference to the AdventureWorks database.

Adding a new database reference is similar to creating a new database connection. See the section "Connecting to databases" in Chapter 2 of this mini-book for more information.

See the next section for more information about working with database references.

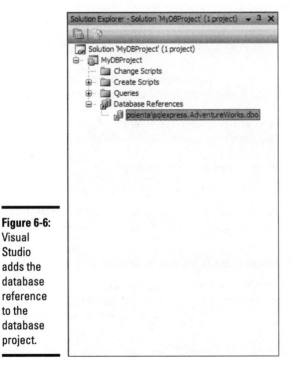

Figure 6-6:
Visual Studio adds the database reference to the database project.

Referencing databases

Database projects use database references to know which database to execute a SQL script against. Database references appear in Solution Explorer and are saved with the database project.

A SQL Server project uses a single database reference for the entire project. Other projects, such as Windows and Web projects, use database *connections* rather than database *references*. See the section about connecting to databases in Chapter 2 in this mini-book.

A database reference uses a database connection to know how to connect to the database. Database connections are visible in Server Explorer. You use Server Explorer to browse a database connection and view database objects, such as tables and views. You can't browse database objects by using a database reference in Solution Explorer. However, you can use Server Explorer to browse the database connection to which a database reference points.

When you add a new database reference to a database project, Visual Studio checks to see whether any existing database connections are in Server Explorer. If so, it prompts you to select those connections.

Otherwise, Visual Studio prompts you to add a new database reference. Adding a new one creates a new data connection in Server Explorer. The New Database Reference dialog box functions exactly the same as the Add Connection dialog box, which you use to add new data connections in Server Explorer.

See the section about connecting to databases in Chapter 2 of this mini-book for more information on creating database connections in Server Explorer.

A database project can have multiple database references. To add a database reference to an existing database project, follow these steps:

1. **Right-click Database References in Solution Explorer.**

2. **Choose New Database Reference from the shortcut menu.**

The Add Database Reference dialog box appears, or the New Database Reference dialog box appears if no database connections exist in Server Explorer for the project.

3. **Select an existing reference or create a new one.**

The Add Database Reference dialog box displays a list of all existing data connections in Server Explorer, as shown in Figure 6-7. If there are no existing data connections, the Add Database Reference dialog box doesn't appear.

4. **Click the Add New Reference button if you don't see the data connection you need.**

5. **Click the OK button.**

Visual Studio adds the database reference to the Solution Explorer.

Database references allow you to store references to multiple databases. For example, use a reference to a local database when you're working with a test database. Use another reference to a production database when you're ready to execute your scripts in a live environment.

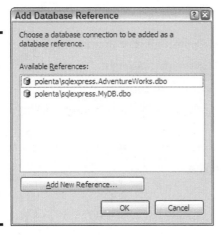

Set your test database as the default database reference. All your scripts are executed against the default database reference. To run your scripts against another database, you must explicitly select the database each time you execute the script. To set a database as the default database, right-click the database reference in Solution Explorer and choose Set As Project Default from the shortcut menu.

Creating scripts

Database projects include five project templates for creating SQL scripts. The available templates are

✦ Stored Procedure Script

✦ SQL Script

✦ Table Script

✦ Trigger Script

✦ View Script

The templates provide boilerplate SQL statements for creating scripts. For example, the table script template has a CREATE TABLE statement. The SQL Script template is a blank template.

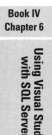

Create your own SQL script templates and save them as project item templates. See Book II, Chapter 2 for more information on creating project item templates.

To create a new script in a database project, follow these steps:

1. **Right-click the database project folder in Solution Explorer.**

2. **Choose Add SQL Script from the shortcut menu.**

   The Add New Item dialog box appears.

   Alternatively, choose Add Existing item from the shortcut menu to add an existing SQL script.

3. **Click the icon for the kind of SQL script you want to create.**

4. **Type a name for the script.**

5. **Click the Add button.**

   Visual Studio adds the script to the database project. The script appears in the Script Editor.

You can use the Visual Studio Visual Database Tools to generate scripts and queries. Scripts you can generate include:

✦ Change scripts

✦ Create scripts

✦ Database queries

See the section "Managing Your Database with Visual Database Tools," later in this chapter, to read more about using the Visual Database Tools to generate scripts.

Scripts created with Visual Studio use the file extension .sql. Because there are so many naming conventions for SQL scripts, Visual Studio recognizes more than just the .sql extension. An abbreviated list of file extensions appears in Table 6-2.

Table 6-2	File Extensions
File Extension	*File Type*
.tab	Table definition
.prc	Stored procedure
.viw	View
.trg	Trigger
.udt	User-defined data type

Using the script editor

Visual Studio includes a script editor for creating SQL scripts. The editor doesn't feature IntelliSense, like other Visual Studio editors, such as the code editor, do. However, you can use the Query Builder to generate SQL statements in the script editor.

To use the Query Builder with the script editor, follow these steps:

1. **Create a new script file by following the steps in the preceding section.**

2. **Right-click the area in the editor where you want to add a new SQL statement.**

   The Query Builder returns the SQL statement to the location where your cursor is positioned in the script editor.

3. **Choose Insert SQL from the shortcut menu.**

   The Query Builder appears.

4. **Use the Query Builder to build a SQL statement.**

   Visual Studio returns the SQL statement to the script editor.

   See the section "Managing Your Database with Visual Database Tools," later in this chapter, for more information on using the Query Builder.

The script editor places a blue line around SQL statements. You can invoke the Query Builder to edit the SQL statement inside that blue box. To edit an existing SQL statement, follow these steps:

1. **Create a script with at least one SQL statement, as the preceding set of steps describes.**

2. **Right-click the SQL statement inside the blue box, as shown in Figure 6-8.**

3. **From the shortcut menu that appears, choose Design SQL Block.**

4. **When the Query Builder appears, use it to modify the SQL statement.**

Executing scripts

You can execute an entire script or portions of a script, depending on what you want to accomplish. SQL scripts are often quite lengthy. If you don't need to run the whole script, you can simply highlight the portion of the syntax you need to run. Of course, you can always let the whole script from start to finish.

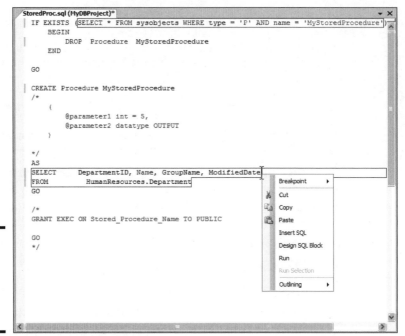

To execute a script by using a shortcut menu, follow these steps:

1. Right-click the script in the script editor or Solution Explorer.

2. Choose Run from the shortcut menu.

The SQL script executes against the default database. The output appears in the Database Output window.

Follow these steps to run a portion of a SQL script that's open in the script editor:

1. Highlight the SQL statement you want to execute in the script editor.

2. Right-click the selected text.

3. Choose Run Selection from the shortcut menu.

To execute a script against a specific database reference, follow these steps:

1. Right-click the script file in Solution Explorer.

2. Choose Run On from the shortcut menu.

The Run On window appears.

3. Select the database reference you want to use.

The script executes against the database reference.

The Run On dialog box gives you the option to create a temporary database reference. The reference is deleted after the script executes.

Drag and drop a script file onto the database reference you want to execute against in Solution Explorer.

Handling data with SQL Server projects

Previous versions of Visual Studio featured integration between the Visual Studio toolset and SQL Server. Integration was limited to using wizards and visual designers for manipulating database objects. Although that level of integration still exists, the Visual Studio SQL Server projects allow you to access SQL Server 2005 in a way that wasn't possible until now.

SQL Server projects are a new project type in Visual Studio designed to take advantage of integration between SQL Server 2005 and the .NET Framework. With SQL Server projects, you can do any of the following task:

✦ Write and debug .NET code that performs complex data operations by using the code editor.

✦ Deploy .NET assemblies as database objects to SQL Server 2005 databases.

✦ Execute .NET assemblies in SQL Server 2005.

Code written using the languages of .NET, such as C# and Visual Basic, is compiled into .NET assemblies. Code that takes advantages of the services of the Common Language Runtime (CLR) is *managed* code.

Using SQL Server projects, you write stored procedures, views, triggers, and other database objects by using .NET code. You execute your code using SQL statements to call the database objects.

Managed code that executes in SQL Server 2005 is a *CLR routine*. CLR routines are sometimes also described using the word *managed*, such as managed stored procedure or managed trigger.

To create and execute a managed stored procedure named `GetEmployees`, follow these steps :

1. Use .NET code to create a data access method named `GetEmployees`.

Assume that the method uses the namespace `MyDataProcedures.` `GetEmployeesProc.GetEmployees`.

It doesn't matter what the code inside `GetEmployees` actually does. Presumably the code accesses data, but it could just easily add 2 + 2.

2. Compile the code into the .NET assembly `GetEmployees.dll`.

Because .NET assemblies use the file extension .dll, they're often referred to as DLL files.

3. Deploy the `GetEmployees.dll` to a SQL Server 2005 database.

You can choose Build⇨Deploy Solution in Visual Studio to deploy assemblies to SQL Server 2005 databases in SQL Server projects.

Alternatively, connect to your SQL Server 2005 database by using the Management Studio and execute the following SQL statement in a new query:

```
CREATE ASSEMBLY GetEmployees from 'GetEmployee.dll'
    WITH PERMISSION_SET = SAFE
```

4. Create a stored procedure with the following SQL statement to execute the .NET assembly:

```
CREATE PROCEDURE uspGetEmployees
AS
EXTERNAL NAME MyDataProcedures.GetEmployeesProc.
    GetEmployees
```

Visual Studio performs this step for you when you use the Deploy Solution command.

5. Type the following SQL statement in a new query in SQL Server Management Studio to execute the stored procedure:

```
EXEC uspGetEmployees;
```

SQL Server 2005 executes the code in the .NET assembly `GetEmployees`.

You use a SQL Server project to create .NET assemblies that you can deploy to SQL Server 2005. To create a new SQL Server project, follow these steps:

1. Press Ctrl+Shift+N to open the New Project dialog box.

2. Click the plus (+) sign next to the Visual Basic project type.

3. Click the Database project type.

A list of database project templates appears.

4. Click the SQL Server Project icon.

5. Type a name and location for the project.

6. Click the OK button.

The Add Database Reference dialog box appears, or the New Database Reference dialog box appears if no data connections exist.

7. Select an existing database reference or create a new reference.

Visual Studio creates the new SQL Server project.

Unlike a database project, a SQL Server project can reference only a single database. See the earlier section "Managing scripts with database projects" for more information on creating database references.

To change the database that a SQL Server project references, follow these steps:

1. Double-click My Project in Solution Explorer.

The project's settings appear in the document window.

2. Click the Database tab.

The database reference appears.

3. Click the Browse button.

The Add Database Reference dialog box appears.

4. Select an existing database reference or create a new reference.

Enabling integration with SQL Server 2005

At the heart of SQL Server projects lies the integration of SQL Server 2005 with the Common Language Runtime (CLR) of the .NET Framework. SQL CLR integration allows you to deploy and execute .NET code to your SQL Server.

Before you can execute .NET code on your SQL Server, you must enable integration between SQL Server and the Common Language Runtime. To enable SQL CLR integration, execute the following SQL statement using the SQL Server Management Studio:

```
sp_configure 'clr enabled', 1
GO
RECONFIGURE
GO
```

Create a script file in a database project to execute the preceding statement, or use the SQL Server Management Studio.

Saying "Hello, SQL Server"

SQL Server projects provide templates for creating common database objects, such as

✦ Stored procedures

✦ Triggers

✦ User-defined functions

✦ User-defined types

✦ Aggregates

You add new items to the project by using the Add New Item dialog box. To create a stored procedure that outputs Hello SQL Server!, follow these steps:

***1.* Right-click the project in Solution Explorer.**

***2.* Choose Add⇨Stored Procedure from the shortcut menu.**

The Add New Item dialog box appears.

***3.* Type the name** hellosqlserver.vb.

***4.* Click the Add button.**

The stored procedure appears in the code editor.

***5.* Replace the line** `Add your code here` **with the following line:**

```
SqlContext.Pipe.Send("Hello SQL Server!")
```

Figure 6-9 shows you the code. Notice that you don't have to write any SQL statements to create the stored procedure. Visual Studio creates the stored procedure to access your .NET code when you deploy the project.

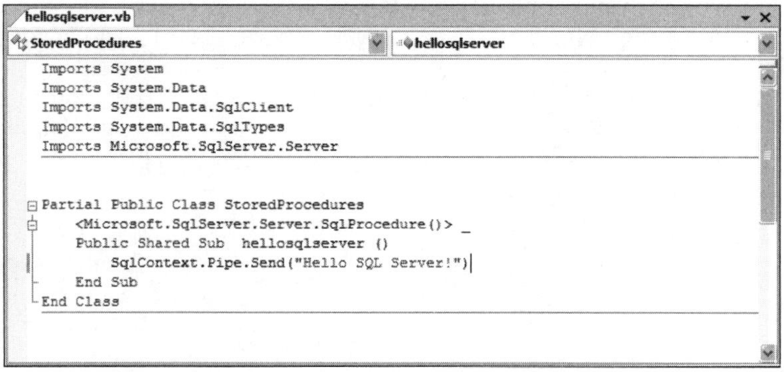

Figure 6-9:
Create a stored procedure in the Visual Studio code editor.

```
hellosqlserver.vb                                            ▾ ✕
StoredProcedures                    ⯆  hellosqlserver        ⯆
    Imports System
    Imports System.Data
    Imports System.Data.SqlClient
    Imports System.Data.SqlTypes
    Imports Microsoft.SqlServer.Server


  Partial Public Class StoredProcedures
      <Microsoft.SqlServer.Server.SqlProcedure()> _
      Public Shared Sub  hellosqlserver ()
          SqlContext.Pipe.Send("Hello SQL Server!")
      End Sub
  End Class
```

***6.* Choose Build⇨Build Solution.**

Visual Studio compiles the project.

***7.* Choose Build⇨Deploy Solution.**

Visual Studio deploys the stored procedure to the AdventureWorks database.

Deploying the stored procedure creates the stored procedure in SQL Server.

You can use Server Explorer in Visual Studio or the SQL Server in Management Studio to execute the stored procedure.

Executing CLR routines

You execute your managed CLR routines by using SQL statements. For example, to execute a managed stored procedure, type the following line:

```
EXEC mystoredprocedure
```

To use Server Explorer to execute the `hellosqlserver` stored procedure from the preceding section, follow these steps:

1. **Expand the Stored Procedures folder in Server Explorer.**

Press Ctrl+Alt+S to open the Server Explorer window if it's closed.

2. **Right-click the `hellosqlserver` stored procedure.**

You may need to refresh Server Explorer if you don't see the stored procedure. To refresh the Server Explorer contents, right-click the Stored Procedures folder and choose Refresh from the shortcut menu.

3. **Choose Execute from the shortcut menu.**

The output from the stored procedure appears in the Output window, as shown in Figure 6-10.

Figure 6-10:
The stored procedure's output appears in the output window.

If an error message tells you to enable CLR integration, see the earlier section "Enabling integration with SQL Server 2005."

Debugging SQL Server projects

Visual Studio provides support for debugging SQL Server projects. You must enable debugging before you can use the debugger. To enable debugging, right-click the database connection in Server Explorer and choose Allow SQL/CLR Debugging.

To debug the `hellosqlserver` stored procedure, follow these steps:

1. **Right-click the Test Scripts folder in Solution Explorer.**

2. **Choose Add Test Script from the shortcut menu.**

A new test script appears in the code editor.

3. **Type** exec hellosqlserver **in the script.**

4. **Insert a breakpoint by clicking the gray border to the right of the statement you type in Step 3.**

A red dot appears next to the statement.

5. **Right-click the test script in Solution Explorer and choose Set As Default Debug Script from the shortcut menu.**

6. **Press F5 to start debugging.**

The debugger stops at your breakpoint.

7. **Press F11 to step through each line in your stored procedure.**

To read more about using the debugger, see Book V, Chapter 7.

You can also start the debugger by right-clicking the stored procedure in Server Explorer and choosing Step into Stored Procedure.

Managing Your Database with Visual Database Tools

Visual Studio provides an extensive set of tools for creating and managing database objects. Almost any time you work with database objects or SQL Server projects, you're using one of the Visual Database Tools. Although the tools work with many kinds of databases, they're tightly integrated with SQL Server.

Visual Studio includes these tools for manipulating databases:

✦ **Server Explorer** — Connects to databases and access database objects

✦ **Database Diagram Designer** — Views or modifies a database's structure using a visual designer

✦ **Table Designer** — Creates and modifies tables

✦ **Query and View Designer** — Creates views and queries

Server Explorer is the key to accessing visual database tools. Database objects appear in a hierarchical tree view in Server Explorer. You invoke most tools by right-clicking a database object in Server Explorer and choosing a tool from the shortcut menu.

Change the hierarchical view of Server Explorer by right-clicking a data connection and choosing Change View from the shortcut menu.

Before you can work with a database in Server Explorer, you must create a connection to a database. For more information, see the section about connecting to a database in Chapter 2 of this mini-book.

You can use Server Explorer to create a new database in SQL Server. To create a new database, follow these steps:

1. **Choose View⇨Server Explorer to open Server Explorer.**

2. **Right-click the Data Connections folder.**

3. **Choose Create New SQL Server Database from the shortcut menu.**

The Create New SQL Server Database dialog box appears.

4. **Type your server's name or select a server from the server name drop-down list.**

Be sure to include the instance name. The default instance name for SQL Server 2005 Express is SQLExpress. The default instance name for SQL Server 2005 Developer Edition is MSSQLSERVER.

5. **Select the appropriate authentication type and enter your login credentials, if required.**

6. **Type a name for the database, such as** MyDataBase, **in the New Database Name field, as shown in Figure 6-11.**

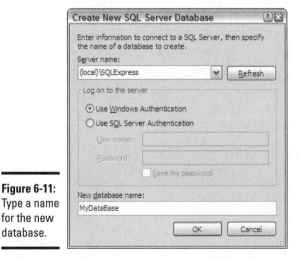

Figure 6-11:
Type a name
for the new
database.

Book IV
Chapter 6

Using Visual Studio
with SQL Server

7. Click OK.

A connection to the new database appears in Server Explorer.

Using a local database

In most cases, you create a database on a database server running SQL Server. Sometimes, however, you may wish to run the database on the local computer. A database that you deploy with your application is called a local database. You may choose to store your application's data in a local database rather than an XML file or a plain text file. Visual Studio supports using SQL Server and SQL Server Express .mdf database files and Access .mdb database files as local databases. All the Visual Database Tools work with local databases.

To create a new local database:

1. Create a new Windows application.

See Chapter 1 in Book III for more information on creating a Windows application.

2. Right-click the project folder in Solution Explorer.

3. Choose Add⇨New Item from the shortcut menu. The Add New Item window appears.

4. Click the SQL Database icon.

5. Type a name for the database in the Name textbox and click the Add button.

The database file is added to Solution Explorer. A data connection to the local database file appears in Server Explorer. The Data Source Configuration Wizard starts.

6. Click the Finish button to exit the wizard.

The Data Source Configuration Wizard creates a strongly typed DataSet. You use the Visual Database Tools to add tables, queries, and views to your local database as described in the next two sections. You access local databases using ADO.NET the same way you access remote databases.

You may also add an existing SQL Server or Access database to your project. To add an existing database file, right-click on the project folder and choose Add⇨Existing Item. You need to create a database connection to your local file in order to access the database. See Chapter 2 in Book IV to read about connecting to databases.

Follow steps 2 through 5 to add a local database to a Web site. The Data Source Configuration Wizard doesn't start. The default application services provider database used for Membership and other ASP.NET services is a local database. See Chapter 6 in Book III.

Deploying a local database

When you deploy a project that uses a local database, Visual Studio automatically includes SQL Server 2005 Express Edition. If the local client who installs your application doesn't already have SQL Server installed on their machine, it's installed with your application.

The first time you build your application, Visual Studio places a copy of the database file into your application's bin folder with all the rest of the application's output such as executable and DLL files. You have three choices for how Visual Studio manages the database file each time you build:

✔ **Copy if newer** — Copies the database file from your project to the bin folder if the project's file has been updated more recently than the copy in the bin folder.

✔ **Copy always** — Copies the file from your project to the bin folder every time. This is the default action.

✔ **Do not copy** — Never copies the file from your project to the bin folder.

You have to decide which approach is the most appropriate for your situation. In my experience, the copy always option works fine.

You set the copy option using the Copy to Output Directory property on the local database file. Access the property using the Properties window by right-clicking on the local database file and choosing Properties.

Adding tables with the Table Designer

Add tables to a database by using the Table Designer. To add a new table to the database you create in the preceding section, follow these steps:

1. **Click the plus (+) sign to expand the data connection in Server Explorer.**

2. **Right-click the Tables folder.**

3. **Choose Add New Table from the shortcut menu.**

The Table Designer displays a grid that you use to add new columns.

4. **Add these columns to the table by using the grid:**

- CustID, data type uniqueidentifier
- FirstName, data type varchar
- LastName, data type varchar

5. **Right-click the CustID column.**

6. **Choose Set Primary Key from the shortcut menu.**

A key appears next to the column name, as shown in Figure 6-12.

7. **Press F4 to display the table's Properties window.**

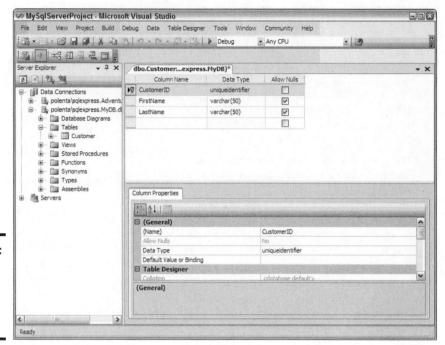

8. **Set the `Name` property to `Customer`.**

9. **Save the table.**

Visual Studio adds the table to the database, and it appears in Server Explorer.

The Table Designer is capable of doing much more than just adding columns. Click the Table Designer menu to see a list of commands that enable you to:

✦ Create foreign key relationships

✦ Create indexes

✦ Add check constraints

The Table Designer generates change scripts that execute the changes you make in the designer in SQL Server. You can harness the power of these scripts and reuse them, modify them, or execute them later.

To generate change scripts, follow these steps:

1. **Create a new table or modify an existing table in the Table Designer.**

Double-click an existing table object in Server Explorer to open it in the Table Designer.

2. **Choose Table Designer⇨Generate Change Script.**

The Save Change Script dialog box appears.

3. **Click the Yes button to save the script.**

To generate create scripts in database projects, right-click the table in Server Explorer and choose Generate Create Script to Project from the shortcut menu. In a database project, you can generate create scripts for any table in Server Explorer.

Adding queries and views

The Query and View Designer is a visual tool for creating queries and views. The tool is known as Query Designer when it's used for creating queries and View Designer when used to create views.

Query Designer is also known as *Query Builder.*

Use a query any time you need to execute a SQL statement against the database. Create a view when you want to save your query in the database.

You can save queries in a database project.

Examples of queries you can create with the Query and View Designer include

+ **Select** — Retrieves rows by using a SELECT statement
+ **Insert Results** — Copies rows from one table to another by using an INSERT INTO ... SELECT statement
+ **Insert Values** — Inserts a new row by using the INSERT INTO ... VALUES statement.
+ **Update** — Updates rows by using an UPDATE statement.
+ **Delete** — Deletes rows by using the DELETE statement.
+ **Make Table** — Copies results of a query into a new table by using the SELECT ... INTO statement.

To start the Query Designer, follow these steps:

1. **Right-click an existing data connection in Server Explorer.**

2. **Choose New Query from the shortcut menu.**

The Query Designer opens.

To start the View Designer, follow these steps:

1. **Right-click the Views folder in an existing data connection in Server Explorer.**

**Book IV
Chapter 6**

Using Visual Studio with SQL Server

2. Choose Add New View from the shortcut menu.

The View Designer opens.

The Query and View Designer has four panes that help you build SQL statements. Figure 6-13 shows you the Query Designer.

The four panes, from top to bottom, are

+ **Diagram pane** — Shows a visual representation of the query

+ **Grid pane** — Specifies which columns to display and how to sort, group by, and filter

+ **SQL pane** — Displays the SQL created by the Designer

+ **Results pane** — Displays the query's output

To see the Query Designer in action, check out the section about updating data with the data designer in Chapter 2 of this mini-book.

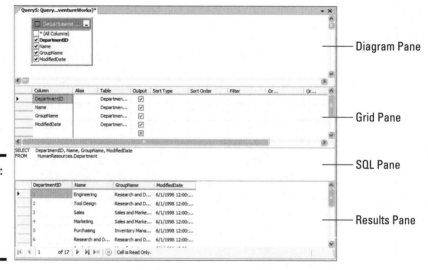

Figure 6-13: The Query and View Designer has four panes.

Book V

Coding

The 5th Wave   By Rich Tennant

"So should I look under handling, catching, or throwing exceptions? Throwing, right?"

Contents at a Glance

Chapter 1: Programming with Visual Studio 2005

In This Chapter

✔ **Performing common tasks in the code editor**

✔ **Organizing code in C# and Visual Basic**

✔ **Getting started with the basics of C# and Visual Basic**

Do you ever get the feeling that sometimes you're not alone? Well, if you've ever written a program using one of the Visual Studio code editors, you know what I mean. Writing code in Visual Studio is like having a word processor that knows what you want to say next.

As you start to type code in Visual Studio, helpers appear magically out of nowhere. Like the host at your favorite restaurant, they share with you a list of today's specials: "Might I suggest an Integer, or how about a DataSet, sir?"

Even if you have no clue about all the things listed for you, you just hover over one of them and a description appears. Like a museum tour guide, Visual Studio shares with you the intimate details of the programming artifacts you're inspecting.

In this chapter, I show you some of the magical helpers and guides that Visual Studio uses to help you write better code. I also give you a quick overview of how to write programs using two popular .NET languages: C#, and Visual Basic.

Using the Code Editor

Even though Visual Studio provides a great number of visual designers that allow you to generate code by dragging and dropping controls and components onto visual designers, at some point, you have to write some code. Visual Studio shines in the area of code writing by providing many editors for editing all kinds of files. The source code editor is especially feature rich. It has a number of productivity boosting features.

There are several ways to open source code files in the code editor, as follows:

+ Double-click a source code file in Solution Explorer.

+ Press F7 while viewing a form in the Windows or Web Forms designers.

+ Add a new source code file using the Add New Items window.

The code editor is more than just a plain text editor like Notepad. You can use the code editor to do many things, such as:

+ Enter code in the main Code Pane area.

+ Set breakpoints in the gray Indicator Margin along the left of the editor.

+ Select lines of code by clicking the space between the code pane and the Indicator Margin.

   You can optionally display line numbers in the Selection Margin.

+ Collapse code using the outline lines along the left margin of the code editor.

+ Jump to code using the Navigation Bar along the top of the code editor.

Figure 1-1 shows an example of the code editor.

Simplifying your common tasks

The code editor has many features similar to what you'd expect to find in a word processor. Some features, such as formatting, are slightly different. For example, you can't bold your code in the code editor. However, you can use familiar features such as copy and paste.

Managing indents

An important task when writing code is indentation. By properly indenting your code, you make it easier to read code on-screen. Visual Studio's code editor provides three indentation styles:

+ **None** — No indentation is applied to code.

+ **Block** — Indentation matches the preceding line of code.

+ **Smart** — Lines are indented according to the standards of the programming language.

By default, the code editor indents each code line based on the standards for the programming language, called *smart indenting*. As you type your code, the editor automatically indents the line. When smart indentation is enabled, you can't manually increase indentation using the Tab key.

Code Pane

Indicator Margin   Navigator Bar

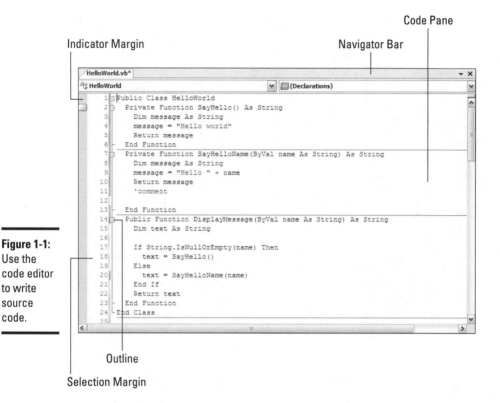

Figure 1-1:
Use the
code editor
to write
source
code.

Outline

Selection Margin

To change the indentation style used by the code editor, follow these steps:

1. **Click Options on the Tools menu.**

2. **Expand the Text Editor folder.**

3. **Expand a language to configure or click the All Languages folder to apply the setting to all programming languages.**

4. **Click Tabs.**

A list of tab settings appears.

5. **Set the Indenting style as Figure 1-2 shows.**

Accessing format commands

You can access formatting features to indent your code by choosing Edit➪Advanced. Table 1-1 lists the code editor's formatting commands and what they do. Note that not all commands are available for all languages.

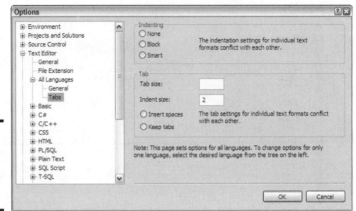

Figure 1-2:
Set the
indentation
style for the
code editor.

Table 1-1	Formatting Commands of the Code Editor
Menu Item	**Description**
Format Document	Applies indentation style to the entire document
Format Selection	Applies indentation style to the selected text
Tabify Selected Lines	Converts indentations to tab characters
Untabify Selected Lines	Converts indentations to white space
Make Uppercase	Changes the code of the selected text to uppercase
Make Lowercase	Changes the code of the selected text to lowercase
Delete Horizontal White Space	Deletes all white space on the line
View White Space	Displays character marks in the editor
Word Wrap	Toggles line wrapping on and off
Incremental Search	Activates a search of your document letter by letter as you type
Comment Selection	Places comment characters in front of the selected text
Uncomment Selection	Removes comment characters from selected text
Increase Line Indent	Increases indentation
Decrease Line Indent	Decreases indentation

Some indentation and comment commands are available on the Text Editor toolbar, as Figure 1-3 shows.

Most of these commands are useless if you're using smart indentation. Smart indentation automatically manages indentation for you. You might choose to turn smart indentation off if your company uses a different indentation standard. Also, you might decide that you want to use your own indentation standard, such as using white spaces instead of tabs.

Figure 1-3:
Use the Text
Editor
toolbar to
increase
indentation
or comment
out a
selection.

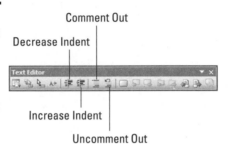

Comment Out

Decrease Indent

Increase Indent

Uncomment Out

Searching with Find and Replace

Visual Studio provides extensive Find and Replace capabilities that go way
beyond what you find in a standard text editor. Table 1-2 lists the Find and
Replace options. You access the Find and Replace commands by choosing
Edit⇨Find and Replace or by using keyboard shortcuts.

Table 1-2	Find and Replace Commands	
Command	*Keyboard Shortcut*	*Purpose*
Quick Find	Ctrl+F	Searches for text
Quick Replace	Ctrl+H	Replaces text
Find in Files	Ctrl+Shift+F	Includes options for searching for text in a set of files
Replace in Files	Ctrl+Shift+H	Includes options for replacing text in a set of files
Find Symbol	Alt+F12	Search scope restricted to symbols only

The Find and Replace commands all use the same dialog box, and most of
the commands use the same options. As Figure 1-4 shows, your Find and
Replace options are:

+ **Find What** — Text for which to search.

+ **Replace With** — Text that replaces the found text.

+ **Look In** — Specifies the scope of the search, such as Current Document
  or Entire Solution.

+ **Find Options** — Specifies options such as whether to match case or the
  whole word.

+ **Find Next** — Finds the next text match. The button toggles to say
  Replace Next when you are in replace mode.

+ **Replace All** — Replaces all matches. The button toggles to say **Find All**
  when you are in find mode.

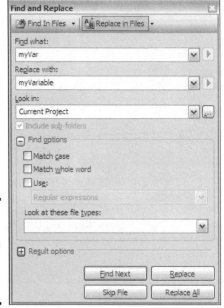

Figure 1-4:
Use Find
and Replace
commands
to search
your code.

To select a different kind of Find and Replace command, use the drop-down buttons displayed at the top of the Find and Replace dialog box.

Before you use Find and Replace, ask yourself whether one of Visual Studio's new refactoring features might work better. See Chapter 5 of this mini-book for an overview of refactoring in Visual Studio.

The Find Symbols command restricts your search only to symbols. *Symbols* are the methods and type definitions declared in source code. You can use the Find Symbols command to search your own code or external libraries for which you don't have source code. The results of the Find Symbols code appear in the Find Symbol Results window. Figure 1-5 shows the results from a search for "SayHello" in a set of source code. The results show me exactly where I used "SayHello" in source code. I can double-click any of the results to go to the source code.

Getting on task

Use the Visual Studio Task List to keep track of a simple list of to-do items. The Task List window displays two kinds of tasks.

✦ **User tasks** — Tasks entered directly into the Task List window.

✦ **Task comments** — Comments placed in your source code using special tags.

Figure 1-5:
The Find
Symbol
Results
window
displays
all the
instances
where the
text appears
in symbols.

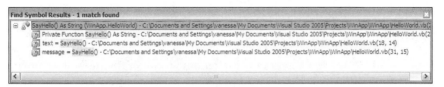

The Task List provides a consolidated list of tasks you enter directly into the Task List window and tagged comments you place inside your source code. The default set of tags you use to mark your comments is TODO, HACK, or UNDONE.

To tag a comment within your source code, you use the standard comment mark for your programming language followed by one of the task comment tags. For example, to add a task comment in Visual Basic, you type the following:

```
'todo Add method body
```

Tags may be entered in upper- or lowercase. By default, tags are in uppercase.

The Task List window consolidates all your task comments in a single view. You can double-click a comment in the Task List to jump to the location in the source code where the code appears. To open the Task List window, click Task List on the View window. Figure 1-6 shows an example of the Task List window.

Always check the Task List for code samples you download from Microsoft and other third parties. The samples usually include a list of tasks you need to complete in order to use the sample.

Figure 1-6:
Task
comments
from source
code
appear in
the Task List
window.

!	Description ▲	File ▲	Line ▲
	todo: Add method body	HelloWorld.vb	6
	refactor: Move to class library	HelloWorld.vb	18
	todo: Create unit test	HelloWorld.vb	30

Task List - 3 tasks
Comments

You can add your own task comment tags. Figure 1-6 uses a comment tag called `refactor`. To add your own task comment tags, do the following:

1. **Click Tools➪Options.**

2. **Expand the Environment folder.**

3. **Click Task List.**

4. **Type a name for the comment tag in the Name text box.**

5. **Click the Add button.**

   Your new comment tag appears in the token list.

6. **Click OK.**

Collapsing code

The code editor includes outlining features you can use to expand and collapse your source code. Use the Edit➪Outlining menu to access options to toggle outlining options.

The .NET programming languages provide syntax to create a named section of code you can collapse and expand. To use a `region` directive, you sandwich your code block between a `start` and `end` region directive. The syntax for the directive varies depending on the language you're using.

In Visual Basic, the directive looks like this:

```
#Region "Description of code block"
'source code here
#End Region
```

In C#, the directive appears as follows:

```
#region Description of code block
//source code here
#endregion
```

Note that C# doesn't require double quotes around the description. Figure 1-7 shows an example of a class using regions to organize the source code.

Using IntelliSense

Visual Studio's code editor has a special feature called IntelliSense that helps you complete syntax as you type. You might recognize IntelliSense as the feature that brings your dot notation to life. When you type a variable's name and then type a period or dot, you get a list of properties and methods you can use for that variable. The context-aware list of properties and methods is brought to you courtesy of IntelliSense.

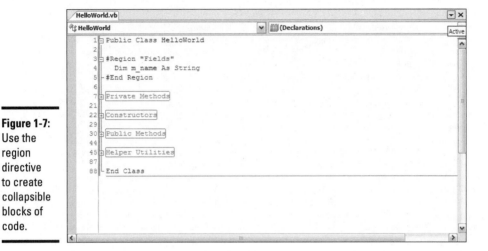

Figure 1-7:
Use the
region
directive
to create
collapsible
blocks of
code.

IntelliSense is capable of more than listing methods and properties. You can
see IntelliSense in action when you

✦ Hover your mouse over a property or method to view its signature.

✦ Open the parentheses on a method and receive feedback about acceptable parameter values.

The new IntelliSense features in Visual Studio 2005 take point-and-click
code generation to a whole new level. See Chapter 5 in this mini-book for
a demonstration.

Using visual cues

Visual Studio's code editor provides several visual cues you can use while
writing code. Examples include

✦ Colors are used to identify different kinds of code. For example, strings
are red and commented text is green.

✦ Bookmark and breakpoint symbols appear in the far-left margin.

✦ Coding errors have colored squigglies beneath them to indicate the kind
of error. For example, syntax errors appear with red squigglies beneath
them, while warnings use green squigglies beneath them.

Figure 1-8 shows an example of a squiggly underline on an undeclared variable.

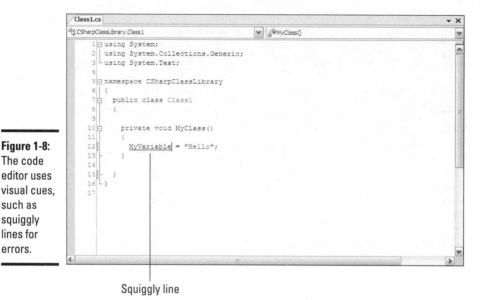

Figure 1-8:
The code editor uses visual cues, such as squiggly lines for errors.

Squiggly line

You can optionally turn on line numbers to help you with your code. To turn on line numbers, follow these steps:

1. **Choose Tools➪Options.**

2. **Expand Text Editor.**

3. **Click All Languages.**

4. **Place a check in the Line Numbers check box.**

Use the options in the Text Editor section to customize the code editor. You may wish to disable certain features in the code editor such as word wrap if you're working with especially large source code files. Disabling features when you're editing large files can make the editor less sluggish.

Browsing and navigating code

Often, you need to browse your own code or try to navigate your way through code someone else has written. Visual Studio provides two basic kinds of tools for browsing code:

✦ When you have the source code

✦ When you have a compiled assembly

The code editor has the following tools for browsing your own source code:

✦ **Navigation Bar** — Allows you to jump to the classes and methods defined in a source code file.

✦ **Bookmarks** — Allows you to place a bookmark in your code.

The Navigation Bar appears at the top of a source code file in the code editor. The left, drop-down box lists types or classes that you can find in the source code file. After selecting a type, you can view the type's members in the right, drop-down list. Selecting a member takes you to its declaration in source code. Figure 1-9 shows an example of selecting a type's member from the Navigation Bar.

Figure 1-9:
Use the
Navigation
Bar to
select the
types and
members
declared in
source
code.

A *bookmark* sets a place in code where you can jump to using the Bookmark window. To set a bookmark in source code:

1. **Position your cursor on the line where you want to set the bookmark.**

2. **Choose View⇨Bookmark Window to open the Bookmarks window.**

3. **Click the Toggle button on the far left of the Bookmark Window to set the bookmark.**

4. **Type a descriptive name for the bookmark.**

After you've set a bookmark, you can double-click the bookmark in the Bookmarks window to jump to that place in the code.

Visual Studio provides the Object Browser, Class View, and Code Definition for viewing assemblies. See the Browsing Types section in Chapter 2 of this mini-book for more information.

Exploring Visual Basic and C#

Visual Studio supports many programming languages. Visual Basic and C# are two popular .NET programming languages. In this section, I show you the highlights of using Visual Basic and C# with Visual Studio 2005.

Learning the basic syntax of programming languages such as Visual Basic and C# is the not the same as learning how to program. When you learn how to program, you learn about basic programming constructs such as conditionals and iterators. By learning the concepts of programming constructs, you can easily and quickly pick up any language syntax.

Organizing programs

An important element of using a new programming language is figuring out how you should organize your program. You might already know that you use the `Dim` statement to declare variables in Visual Basic and the `using` statement in C# to reference a namespace. That's all well and good, but if you don't know how to organize those statements in your source code file so they're in the proper order and nested, then your program won't compile.

Both Visual Basic and C# have similar approaches to program organization that use these elements:

✦ **Non-executable statements** — Lines of source code that provide setup and wrapper statements for grouping executable statements. Examples include:

  • **Imports (Visual Basic) or using (C#) statements** — The `Imports` and `using` statements allow you to use code elements from resources external to your project without fully qualifying the element's namespace each time you use it. These statements create a shortcut, in essence, to the namespace.

  • **Namespace and type declarations** — These statements create wrappers that organize your code.

    Namespace declarations create unique identifiers for the types you declare within the namespace.

    Data type declarations contain executable code. Examples of data types include classes and structures. See Chapter 2 in this mini-book for more details on types. Visual Basic includes a `Module` statement that allows you to write code without using types.

Visual Basic uses the Options statement to specify how and when syntax checking occurs. Options statements are set by default on the project's property pages, so you don't need to include Options statements in your source code.

✦ **Executable statements** — Lines of source code that provide the functionality of your program are *executable statements*. Executable statements are nested inside data type declarations and organized into members. Examples of members include:

- Methods
- Fields
- Properties
- Events

In C# programming, a *member* is defined as a method, field, property, or event based on the style of programming you use and how you intend to use the member. For example, a class could implement its color as a property member, in which case you would access it as

```
MyClass.Color
```

Implemented as a method, it might look like this:

```
MyClass.GetColor()
```

Coding standards dictate that using the property is preferred over using the method, however, both approaches work and can return the same value.

Visual Basic includes additional executable statements called *procedures* that can be used as class members or as part of a module. Examples of procedures in Visual Basic include:

- **Function** — A set of statements that returns a value.
- **Sub** — A set of statements that doesn't return a value.
- **Property** — Declares a property with Get and Set procedures.

The long and short of these organizing differences between Visual Basic and C# is that everything must be a data type in C#. In Visual Basic, you don't have to use types to organize your code, but it's recommended.

The most common data type used is a class. Classes are the fundamental building blocks of Object-Oriented Programming (OOP). You don't have to follow the principles of OOP to use classes in C# or Visual Basic. Some would have you believe that you always write object oriented code in C#, and it's easier to write old-style procedural code with Visual Basic. That simply isn't true. Yes, C# forces you to *use* classes and objects. That's not the same thing as writing object-oriented code. You can write procedural code using objects. See Chapter 3 to read more about classes and OOP.

Figure 1-10 shows two functions where you can see the differences between the coding styles in Visual Basic and C#. Notice, for example, that Visual Basic uses `Namespace...End Namespace` where C# uses `namespace {}`. Note also, that because C# is case sensitive, all its keywords are in lower-case, while Visual Basic's are in proper case.

Most development professionals adhere to a set of capitalization standards when it comes to naming variables, classes, and other units of code. The casing standards are consistent regardless of the programming language used. Chapter 5 in this mini-book covers these standards.

Figure 1-10:
The coding styles in Visual Basic and C# are similar, but their syntax differs slightly.

Lots of folks say that one or the other language is better: You can write good code in Visual Basic, and you can write horrible code in C#, and vice versa. What matters is how well you learn how to code, not which language you choose.

Getting started

In the following sections, I share with you a few syntax details for C# and Visual Basic. Refer to the Visual Studio documentation for more specifics on programming with either language.

Beginning at the beginning: The Main procedure

Every executable program requires a procedure called Main. The Main procedure is the entry point into your application. In Visual Basic Windows applications, the Visual Basic compiler creates a Main function for you when the Enable Application Framework check box is selected on the Application tab of the project's property pages.

Only executable programs such as Windows applications require a Main procedure. Class libraries don't require a Main procedure.

The Movie Collection Starter Kit for C# has a good example of a Main procedure. In the Program.cs source file, you'll find the following Main procedure:

```
static void Main()
{
  Application.EnableVisualStyles();
  Application.SetCompatibleTextRenderingDefault(false);
  Application.Run(new MainForm());
    }
```

Declaring variables and assignment

You must declare variables you wish to use and specify their data type. You can assign a value to the variable when you create it or assign a value in a separate assignment statement.

Visual Basic uses the keyword Dim to declare variables, like this:

```
Dim variablename as DataType
```

For example, to declare the variable i as the data type integer in Visual Basic, you type

```
Dim i As Integer
```

C# doesn't require any special keywords when declaring variables. You declare variables in C# using the following syntax:

```
DataType variablename;
int i;
```

You assign values to variables using the equal (=) operator. For example, to assign the value 7 to the variable i, you'd type this:

```
i = 7 '(VB)
i = 7; //(C#)
```

When you read an assignment statement, you say i "gets" 7, not i "equals" 7. In the case of variable assignment, the equal operator is not the same as equality.

You can declare a variable and assign a value in one statement. To combine declaration and assignment in Visual Basic, you type

```
Dim i As Integer = 7
```

And in C#:

```
int i = 7;
```

See Chapter 2 in this mini-book for more details on declaring variables and assigning values.

Creating classes and working with objects

The primary means of organizing code in Visual Basic and C# is class declarations. Your executable code is nested within a class declaration. The code below is an example of a class declaration in Visual Basic.

```
Public Class Customer
'executable code here
End Class
```

You use a class using the new keyword, which creates an instance of the class called an *object*. You use the object to access the executable code inside the class. For example, to create an object called newCust from the class Customer in Visual Basic, you'd type

```
Dim newCust As New Customer()
```

Here's the equivalent statement in C#:

```
Customer newCust = new Customer();
```

To call an executable procedure on the `newCust` object, you use dot notation, as shown here:

```
newCust.ValidateAddress()
```

You can consume objects in either language, regardless of what language the
object is written in. For example, you can consume a `Customer` object written in Visual Basic using C#, and vice versa.

See Chapter 3 in this mini-book for more details on declaring classes and creating objects.

Creating executable code

A single line of code is called a *statement*. Both Visual Basic and C# provide
syntax that allow you to write multiple statements as a block of code.

Examples where you need to use code blocks include `If...Then` statements
and `Try...Catch` statements.

C# uses curly braces to encapsulate multiple statements. Visual Basic uses
the syntax `Procedure...End Procedure`. Compare these two `If` statements for clarification:

```
'Visual Basic
If flag = True Then
  j = j + 1
  flag = False
End If

//C#
if (flag = true)
  {
    j = j + 1;
    flag = false;
  }
```

Members and procedures

Executable code is implemented as members of a data type, usually a class.
Basically, everything inside a class is a member of the class. A procedure
that adds two integers and returns a value is called a *method*. Variables
declared for use within the class are called *fields*.

Visual Basic also uses classes and members, but it uses keywords like Function and Sub to declare a procedure.

See Chapter 3 in this mini-book for more details on creating members and procedures in classes.

My Visual Basic

Visual Basic includes a new object called My, which you can use to access features related to your application and the .NET Framework. For example, you can use My.Settings to access your application's configuration settings.

You don't have to declare variables or create an instance to use My. You simply type My and a dot in the Visual Basic code editor, and a list of available objects appears. Three commonly used My objects are:

✦ My.Application — Sets properties of the current application such as setting a startup splash screen.

✦ My.Computer — Provides access to computer resources such as the clipboard and the file system.

✦ My.User — Provides information about the user account using the application.

Chapter 2: Understanding Data Types

In This Chapter

✔ **Declaring variables**

✔ **Seeing the differences between value types and reference types**

✔ **Understanding how data types are used in the .NET Framework**

✔ **Handling more than one variable**

✔ **Finding data types and using them in your code**

Data types are the fundamental organizing blocks of code in .NET. There's very little your program can do without using data types. If you've never programmed with .NET, you might be thinking data types in terms of integers and characters. Those are one kind of data type. But other data types are more flexible, sophisticated, and powerful than integers and characters. Examples include classes, structures, and enumerations.

Variables are used to access data that you place in your computer's memory. When you declare a variable, you specify its data type. This is how your computer program knows how to assign meaning to the ones and zeroes that you store in your computer's memory.

The data type you specify for the variable declaration determines everything about how that variable is treated throughout its entire lifecycle. In this chapter, I show you the data types available in the .NET Framework and how to create your own data types.

The Rules of Data Types

From the perspective of the computer, all data is just a set of ones and zeroes. Computer programs apply meaning to those ones and zeroes by using data types. A *data type* tells your computer how your program can interact with the data and what operations are legal.

Examples of data types are integers and characters. By telling your computer program that a given variable holds an integer data type, the computer knows that you can add and subtract the value. The same data type law tells your computer that you can't add and subtract characters. By using data types, you tell the computer the rules for interacting with your data.

These rules are to your benefit. The compiler for your program uses the rules for your data type to tell you in advance whether your program will break when you run it. Data types allow the compiler and Visual Studio to give you feedback about your code before you even execute it. Giving you feedback early in the process allows you to correct errors before your end users find them.

Of the many kinds of data types, there are simple data types like integers and characters, and there are complex data types like those provided by the .NET Framework. You can create your own data types by combining simple and complex data types.

Making a Declaration

Any time you want to use data in your program, you must first declare a variable to hold the value in memory. When you declare a variable, you do two things:

✦ **Name your variable** — You create an identifier that allows you to access the variable's value in memory and pass it around in your program.

✦ **Specify a data type** — You tell the computer how to allocate memory for the variable.

You'll most frequently declare variables in your programs. But you aren't limited to declaring only variables. You can declare constants, enumerations, and functions. You can declare namespaces and new data types as well.

Not all programming languages require you to specify a data type when you declare a variable. Languages, such as the languages of the .NET Framework, that require you to specify a data type are called strongly typed languages. Specifying a data type at the time of variable declaration

✦ Enables the code editor to use features such as IntelliSense.

✦ Allows the compiler to provide you feedback if you try to use data types improperly.

Declaring a variable is a straightforward process. For example, here's how you declare a variable in Visual Basic:

```
Dim myVariable as DataType
```

Once you declare a variable, you might assign a value to it. The first value assigned to a variable is its *initial value.* Assigning a value to a variable for the first time is called *initializing* the variable.

You don't have to initialize variables. The .NET Framework provides default initial values for you, depending on the data type; however, the initial values might not be what you expect. Certain kinds of data types are initialized to null, for example. You can't work with null in your program. You want to make sure that you assign a value to your variables before you start taking actions on those variables in your program.

You can initialize a variable when you declare it. For example, the following statement declares a variable of type integer and sets the variable's initial value to 7.

```
Dim i As Integer = 7
```

Alternatively, you can assign an initial or subsequent value using the equals operator (=), as shown in the following code:

```
i = 6
```

Complex data types called *classes* require you to use the new operator when you assign a value. For example, the following code declares a variable of the data type System.Data.DataSet. The second line of code uses the new operator to assign a value to the variable.

```
Dim ds as System.Data.DataSet
ds = new System.Data.DataSet
```

Using the new operator is called creating an *instance* of the class. The class is like a template that defines what values can be stored. When you assign an instance of a class to a variable, the variable is like a blank entry form based on the class template.

You can declare and initialize a class in one line, as shown here:

```
Dim ds as new System.Data.DataSet
```

The .NET Framework's Common Type System

One of the services provided by the .NET Framework is data type management in the form of the Common Type System (CTS). The CTS defines all the rules for how the programming language you use

✦ Declares types.

✦ Creates new types.

✦ Uses types in your source code.

The CTS ensures data type consistency among the programming languages of the .NET Framework.

Understanding the type hierarchy

The Common Type System has a type hierarchy that provides a base set of data types used by all the .NET programming languages. The root data type for all data types in the .NET Framework is `System.Object`.

The most common use of data types is declaring variables, as described in the preceding section. When you initialize a variable, either through assignment or the `new` operator, the computer uses the variable's data type to know how to allocate the memory for the variable. You can use two basic kinds of data types in .NET:

✦ **Value types** — Simple data types that are built into most programming languages, such as integer and Boolean.

The .NET Framework has a set of built-in value types that derive from the data type `System.ValueType`.

✦ **Reference types** — Complex data types that hold a memory address that points to data stored elsewhere in memory. Examples of reference types include classes, interfaces, strings, arrays, and delegates.

The easiest way to know the difference between value types and reference types is the way you declare and initialize variables of either type. Reference types use the `new` operator, while value types don't.

For example, the following code declares a variable of the value type integer using the C# keyword `int`:

```
int i = 1;
```

When you create a variable using a reference data type, you use the `new` operator. The code that follows creates a new variable `o` of the data type `System.Object`. Recall that `System.Object` is the root data type in the Common Type System.

```
System.Object o = new System.Object();
```

Throwing it on the stack or the heap

Value types and reference types are stored differently in memory, which contributes to why they're used differently. Value types are stored on the *stack,* while reference types are stored on the *managed heap.* The stack, or more specifically, the call stack, is an area of memory set aside for managing the execution of your program. You can visualize the stack as being one memory address stacked on top of another. The heap, however, is a large pool of memory where objects that require longer lifespans can live. By longer lifespan, I mean the object needs to live beyond the execution of a single function on the call stack.

The stack is more efficient to access than the heap. The stack discards a variable stored in memory as soon as your program stops using the variable.

Variables stored in the heap, however, are managed by the .NET garbage collector. The new operator requests storage to be allocated on the heap for the variable. The garbage collector clears the variable out of memory when it determines that the variable is no longer being used by your program, which might not correspond to the point in time when your program stops using the variable.

By being stored on the stack, value types are directly accessible. Reference type variables, however, return a reference to an address on the heap where the variable's value is actually stored. Figure 2-1 shows an example of value types and reference types in memory. The reference to a reference type is stored on the stack, which is how your program knows how to access the variable.

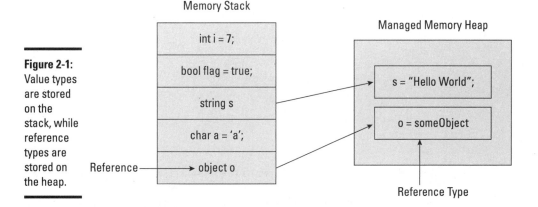

Figure 2-1:
Value types
are stored
on the
stack, while
reference
types are
stored on
the heap.

Completing your assignments

Another key difference between value types and reference types is how they're handled by assignments. When you assign a variable of a value type, the contents of the value type are copied. When you assign a reference type, only the reference is passed along.

The difference in how value types and reference types are assigned is attributable to how they're stored in memory. A reference type only stores a memory address that points to the actual value. When you copy a reference type, you are copying the memory address stored on the stack.

The following code sample uses value types, and the value for variable i is copied to the variable j:

```
private void TestValueTypes()
{
   int i;
   int j;

   i = 8;
   j = i;
   i = 5;
}
```

When this code executes, j has the value 8, and i has the value 5. j and i are independent variables. The value from i is copied to j.

Now look at how code using reference types does this. Note that the variables start out pointing to two separate values but wind up pointing to the same value:

```
private void TestReferenceTypes()
{
   System.Data.DataSet ds1 = new DataSet("DataSet 1");
   System.Data.DataSet ds2 = new DataSet("DataSet 2");

   ds2 = ds1;
   ds1.DataSetName = "My DataSet";

}
```

The statement ds2 = ds1; assigns the value referenced in the variable ds1 to the variable ds2. What happens to the value originally referenced by ds2? It's still there, but it can no longer be accessed because ds2 let go of it, as Figure 2-2 shows. Eventually, the garbage collector recognizes that the object is no longer in use and destroys it.

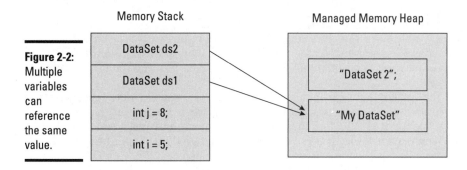

Figure 2-2:
Multiple
variables
can
reference
the same
value.

You might think it's silly that someone would create two variables and then assign one to the other. Once you start creating an application, you'd be surprised how easy it is to pass a variable by reference and not understand why your data isn't what you expected.

It's important to understand the differences between value types and reference types. Table 2-1 compares value types and reference types.

Table 2-1	Comparison of Value Types and Reference Types	
Category	*Value Types*	*Reference Types*
Data accessibility	Directly accessible	Accessed through a reference to the data
Memory allocation	Stack	Managed heap
When is memory freed?	When variable is destroyed	When garbage collection determines no longer in use
Garbage collection	Doesn't use	Uses garbage collection
Initialization	No special initialization required	Must use `new` operator
Default value	Initialized as zero	Initialized as null
Null values	Can never be null	Throws an exception when you try to use a null reference
Assignment	Assignment copies the value	Assignment passes a reference to the value
Base class	Derives from `System.ValueType`	Derives from `System.Object`
Conversion	Can be converted to reference type	Can be converted to value type in some cases

Popular value types

If you've done any programming at all, you're probably familiar with data types like char and integer. These are called *value types* in the .NET Framework. The Common Type System provides a set of built-in value types.

Your programming language provides a set of primitive data types that map to the built-in value type in the Common Type System. Table 2-2 lists the value types in .NET and their respective keywords in Visual Basic and C#. When you use one of these keywords as a data type in your program, it's compiled as the underlying .NET data type listed.

A *primitive data type* is a type that the programming language's compiler natively understands.

Table 2-2	Built-In Value Types and Their Language Keywords		
.NET Data Type	Visual Basic Keyword	C# Keyword	Description
System.Boolean	Boolean	bool	True or false
System.Byte	Byte	byte	Unsigned integer with values ranging from 0 to 255
System.Char	Char	char	Represents characters in the Unicode Standard, such as the letter 'a'
System.Decimal	Decimal	decimal	Decimal numbers ranging from −79,228,162,514,264,337,593,543,950,335 to +79,228,162,514,264,337,593,543,950,335
System.Double	Double	double	Fifteen decimal points of precision for binary floating-point arithmetic
System.Int16	Short	short	Signed integer with values ranging from −32,768 to +32,767
System.Int32	Integer	int	Signed integer with values ranging from −2,147,483,648 through +2,147,483,647
System.Int64	Long	long	Signed integer with values ranging from −9,223,372,036,854,775,808 through +9,223,372,036,854,775,807
System.SByte	Sbyte	sbyte	Signed integer with values ranging from −127 to +127
System.Single	Single	float	Seven decimal points of precision for binary floating-point arithmetic
System.UInt16	Ushort	ushort	Unsigned integer values ranging from 0 to 65,535

.NET Data Type	Visual Basic Keyword	C# Keyword	Description
System.UInt32	UInteger	uint	Unsigned integer values ranging from 0 to 4,294,967,295
System.UInt64	Ulong	ulong	Unsigned integer values ranging from 0 to 18,446,744,073,709,551,615

The data types `UInt16`, `UInt32`, and `UInt64` aren't compatible across programming languages. You should avoid using those data types if you plan for your code to be consumed by other .NET languages.

You might have noticed that many data types represent numbers. The amount of memory used by each of these data types corresponds to the range of values the data type can store.

Use the `System.Decimal` data type for financial calculations where rounding errors can't be tolerated.

Most of the .NET programming languages have a keyword for a data type that represents strings. Strings are not value types; however, they are reference types. See the next section to read more about strings.

In addition to the value types listed previously, the .NET Framework includes two other programming elements that define value types:

✦ **Structures** — A *structure* is a data type comprised of other data types. You use a structure to consolidate other data types into a single, named data type. Examples of two commonly used structures provided by the .NET Framework are `System.DateTime` and `System.Guid`.

The Visual Basic keyword that corresponds to `System.DateTime` is `Date`. C# doesn't have a keyword. `guid` is short for *globally unique identifier*. You use a `guid` any time you need a unique identifier. (guid rhymes with *squid*.)

You use structures to create your own data types. See the section "Creating Your Own Types" for examples of using structures.

✦ **Enumerations** — An *enumeration* defines a set of constants that can be accessed by the name applied. `System.DayOfWeek` is an example of an enumeration that enumerates the days of the week, as shown in Figure 2-3. Enumerations derive from `System.Enum`.

Popular reference types

All the classes in the .NET Framework are reference types. They're called *reference types* because the variable holds a reference to the value, not the actual value itself.

```
Form1.cs*                                                          ▾ ✕
CSharpDataTypes.Form1                    ▾   Form1_Load(object sender, EventArgs e)  ▾
     9 ⊟ namespace CSharpDataTypes
    10 | {
    11 ⊟   public partial class Form1 : Form
    12 |   {
    13 ⊟     public Form1()
    14 |     {
    15 |       InitializeComponent();
    16 ├     }
    17 |
    18 ⊟     private void Form1_Load(object sender, EventArgs e)
    19 |     {
    20 |       this.textBox1.Text = "Bible study is always on " + System.DayOfWeek.|
    21 ├     }                                                    ⚏ Friday
    22 |                                                          ⚏ Monday
    23 |                                                          ⚏ Saturday
    24 |                                                          ⚏ Sunday
    25 |                                                          ⚏ Thursday
    26 |                                                          ⚏ Tuesday
                                                                 ⚏ Wednesday
```

Figure 2-3:
Enumera-
tions define
a set of
constants.

All classes in the Common Type System derive from System.Object. You could say that makes System.Object the most popular reference type. Hopefully, however, you aren't actually declaring your variables using the System.Object type. While it's not incorrect, you should try to use the most specific data type possible.

C# provides the keyword object and Visual Basic uses Object to map to the System.Object type in CTS.

One of the most popular reference types is System.String. Many people think System.String is a value type, but it's actually an array of characters. That's probably because you don't have to use the new operator when you create a new string. You declare and use a string variable similar to how you use value types such as integer and Boolean.

Visual Basic and C# both provide a keyword to represent System.String. The following code declares and initializes a string variable in Visual Basic:

```
Dim s As String = "Hello"
```

Another popular reference type is System.Exception. Any time your program throws an exception, the exception you see is a reference type derived from System.Exception.

See the section "Browsing Types" later in this chapter to see how you can find more reference types in the .NET Framework.

Creating Your Own Types

Developers long ago figured out that describing a business domain strictly in terms of `ints` and `chars` is not easy to do. You can't bend the business to fit the limitations of a programming language. No, instead you must use a programming language that allows you to model whatever real-world problem you're trying to solve.

The .NET Framework allows you to create your own data types. You can use your own data types to

✦ Model your business in your software.

✦ Provide utility features.

✦ Customize existing types that don't quite fit your needs.

You can use the following kinds of data types to create your own data types:

✦ **Classes** — Classes are reference types that derive from `System.Object`. Class types define the data and behavior of a variable. In other words, classes define the data that a variable can store and provide procedures that act on that data. For example, a `Customer` class may store a customer's name and unique identifier. It may include an `AccountBalance()` procedure that returns the customer's current balance.

Visual Basic and C# provide the `Class` statement and `class` keyword, respectively, for creating your own class data types. See the next chapter for more information on creating classes.

✦ **Structures** — Structures are value types that derive from `System.ValueType`. Structures can store virtually all the same data and behaviors as a class.

You use the `Structure` statement in Visual Basic to create a structure. C# provides the `struct` keyword.

To create a `Customer` structure in Visual Basic, type the following code:

```
Structure Customer
  Dim m_firstName As String
  Dim m_lastName As String

  ReadOnly Property Name() As String
    Get
     Return m_firstName + " " + m_lastName
    End Get
  End Property
  WriteOnly Property FirstName()
    Set(ByVal value)
      m_firstName = value
```

```
        End Set
      End Property
      WriteOnly Property LastName()
        Set(ByVal value)
          m_lastName = value
        End Set
      End Property
    End Structure
```

To create a variable using the `Customer` data type, type the following code:

```
Dim cust As New Customer
```

To assign values to a variable, type the following code:

```
cust.FirstName = "John"
cust.LastName = "Smith"
```

The following line of code assigns the variable's `Name` property to a text box:

```
txtCustomerName.Text = cust.Name
```

Notice that the `cust` variable accesses only the structure's properties, not the variables declared at the beginning of the structure. The structure's properties, in turn, access the variable declared at the top of the structure. The variables and properties of the structure are called *members* of the structure. See the next chapter to read more about a data type's members.

✦ **Enumerations** — Enumerations are value types that derive from `System.ValueType`. You define a set of constants, such as the days of the week, in an enumeration. You can use the `System.Enum` data type to access additional features of enumerations.

Visual Basic provides the `Enum` statement, and C# uses the `enum` keyword for declaring enumerations. The following code shows an enumeration in C#:

```
enum Fiber
{8
   Angora,
   Mohair,
   Wool
}
```

Using object-oriented programming techniques, you can extend virtually all the types provided in the .NET Framework to meet your specific needs. See Chapter 3 in this mini-book for more information about object-oriented programming.

You often create user-defined types in a class library project. You can reference the class library in a Windows project or Web application when you need to use your user-defined types.

You can use your class and structure data types just like you do any other data type. You can declare them as variables, pass them as parameters, and return them from procedures. Use enumerations any time you need to reuse a set of values throughout your application.

At first blush, you might think there isn't much difference between structures and classes. Recall, however, that structures are value types and classes are reference types. As a result, structures often use less memory than classes. Each time a value type like a structure is passed around in a program, a copy of the structure is made. So what starts out using less memory could end up consuming quite a bit. For this reason, you'll often find that classes are used more than structures. Even though classes are initially more expensive to create, their memory usage is often more economical throughout their lifetime.

In general, you should create structures when the data type you're creating is small in size, like an integer, and you expect it to be short-lived.

When There's More than One

Quite often, you need to handle more than just one of something. Rarely does your business have just one customer or one product. You're usually dealing with sets of things. The .NET Framework provides many data types for dealing with situations when you have more than one item.

Data types that can handle sets of data are often referred to as data structures or collections.

The collection-related data types provided by the .NET Framework often allow you to

✦ Add, remove, and modify individual elements.

✦ Copy elements to another collection.

✦ Sort and index elements.

✦ Iterate through a set of elements.

The .NET Framework provides several data types you can use to manage collections. The two biggies are:

✦ **Array class** — An array is a set of data of all the same data type. You set the size of the array when you declare it. I like to picture an array as an Excel spreadsheet. A one-dimensional array is like a single row in the spreadsheet. A multidimensional array has more than one row. Arrays have been the staple data structure for a long time.

✦ **System.Collections namespace** — Other kinds of collections, such as lists and hash tables, are found in the System.Collections namespace.

A namespace references a set of data types. A namespace isn't a data type itself. There's no System.Collections data type in the .NET Framework. Rather, you use the System.Collections namespace to access data types used to manage collections.

Another kind of data structure provided by the .NET Framework is the ADO.NET DataSet. A *DataSet* is an in-memory representation of a database with tables, columns, and rows. For more on DataSets, turn to Book IV, Chapter 3.

Using arrays

The .NET Framework provides the System.Array class for creating arrays. An array defines a set of data that all have the same data type. You can define an array to use any kind of data type, such as a set of integers or a set of strings. You can even define an array using your own custom data types.

All items in an array must be of the same data type.

An array has the following properties:

✦ **Elements** — Each item that you add to an array is an element of the array. The data type of the element is called the *element type*.

✦ **Index** — The position of each element in the array. Arrays use zero-based indexes, so the first value in an array has an index of zero.

✦ **Length** — The total number of elements in the array.

✦ **Rank** — The number of dimensions in the array. A one-dimensional array has one row of data. A two-dimensional array has multiple rows.

✦ **Bounds** — The lower and upper bounds of an array define the starting and ending index for an array's elements. For example, an array with four elements has a lower bound of zero and an upper bound of three.

Declaring arrays is similar to declaring other types of data. In Visual Basic, you append parentheses to the variable's identifier, as shown in the following:

```
Dim dailyWeights() As Integer
```

To declare a multi-dimensional array in Visual Basic, you place a comma inside the parentheses for each additional dimension, such as

```
Dim dailyWeights(,) As Integer
```

In C#, you append brackets to the element's data type when you declare an array, as shown here:

```
int[] dailyWeights;
```

Similar to Visual Basic, you use commas to create multi-dimensional arrays, as shown in the following:

```
int[,] dailyWeights;
```

You can also create arrays of arrays, which are called *jagged arrays*. You add extra sets of parentheses or brackets for each nested array. A declaration for a jagged array in Visual Basic looks like this:

```
Dim dailyWeights()() As Integer.
```

Declaring an array doesn't actually create the array. Because arrays are reference types, you use the `new` operator to create the array and assign it to the variable you declare. For example, to create an array with five elements and assign it to the one-dimensional `dailyWeights` array using Visual Basic, you'd type:

```
dailyWeights = New Integer(4) {}
```

Recall that arrays have a zero-based index. Inside the parentheses, you place the array's upper bound, which is four in this example. The array's length is five because you start counting at zero.

Use the curly braces to place values into the array, as the following Visual Basic code shows:

```
dailyWeights = New Integer(4) { 155, 153, 154, 152, 150 }
```

Here's the equivalent statement in C#:

```
dailyWeights = new int[5] { 155, 153, 154, 152, 150 };
```

You might have noticed some subtle differences in syntax between Visual Basic and C#. Most notably, in the Visual Basic statement, you use the upper bound, while in C# you use the array's length. If you switch back and forth a lot between the two languages, maybe you can get a tattoo so you can keep it straight.

It isn't necessary to size an array when you're initializing the array in the same statement. Supplying five values automatically creates an array of `length = 5`. For example, the following statements are equivalent:

```
dailyWeights = new int[5] { 155, 153, 154, 152, 150 };
```

```
dailyWeights = new int[] { 155, 153, 154, 152, 150 };
```

There are three steps to using arrays:

1. Declare the array variable.
2. Create the array.
3. Initialize the array with values.

You can perform each step discretely or combine all three steps into one statement, as shown in the following C# statement:

```
int[] dailyWeights = new int[5] { 155, 153, 154, 152, 150 };
```

The equivalent statement in Visual Basic is

```
Dim dailyWeights() As Integer = New Integer(4) {155, 153,
    154, 152, 150}
```

You supply three pieces of information to declare and create an array:

✦ Element's data type

✦ Rank

✦ Upper bound or size of the array

To access the elements in an array, you use an indexer to specify the position of the element you wish to access. For example, the following C# code accesses the third element in an array of integers:

```
dailyWeights[2] = 175;
```

Arrays use a *zero-based index* (which means that you start counting from zero).

Using System.Collections

The .NET Framework provides many kinds of collections you can use when you need to handle more than one of something at a time. Table 2-3 lists the specialized collection types you can find in the `System.Collections` namespace.

Collection data types in the `System.Collections` namespace can be grouped based on the mechanism used to access elements in the collection:

✦ **Indexed** — Access elements using their position in the list of elements.

✦ **Keyed** — Access elements using the key in a key/value pair.

✦ **Neither indexed nor keyed** — Data types provide access methods other than an indexer or key.

Collections that use indexes are called *lists*. Keyed collections are called *dictionaries*.

Table 2-3		Data Types in the System.Collections Namespace		
Accessor	*Collection Type*	*Data Type*	*Description*	*Example*
Both	Dictionary	SortedList	A set of key/value pairs sorted by the key	A glossary of terms
Indexed	Collection	BitArray	An array of Boolean values	Whether your dog responds to the Come command given successively at the bark park
Indexed	List	ArrayList	An array of variable size	The number of debits to your bank account in the next 30 days
Keyed	Dictionary	Hashtable	A set of key/value pairs sorted by the key's hash number	The movies being shown at a theater
Neither	Collection	Stack	Last-in, first-out (LIFO) list	A pile of football players on a quarterback
Neither	Collection	Queue	First-in, first-out (FIFO) list	Line at the grocery store

The System.Collections namespace defines the DictionaryEntry structure, which represents a key/value pair in a dictionary collection type. See the section "Iterating through arrays and collections" later in this chapter to see a code sample using the DictionaryEntry structure.

The collection data types found in the System.Collection namespace are all classes. You use the new operator to create a new instance of a collection. The following code shows a Hashtable:

```
Dim ht As New Hashtable
```

Important actions you take on collections such as Hashtables include adding and removing elements. A Hashtable is a key-based collection, so you add elements using a key/value pair. The following code sample shows how to add elements to a `Hashtable`:

```
ht.Add("Screen 1", "Shane")
ht.Add("Screen 2", "My Friend Flicka")
```

Use the `Remove` method to remove an element from the hash table:

```
ht.Remove("Screen 1")
```

You supply the key when you want to remove the element.

Of course, you aren't limited to just using primitive types and strings in your collections. You can use any data type, including your user-defined data types. For example, instead of placing a movie title in the hash table, you could place a value created from a `Movie` class. The `Movie` class might store a movie's title, actors, release date, and show times. See the previous section "Creating Your Own Types" for more information.

The .NET Framework provides two other namespaces for using collection data types:

✦ **System.Collections.Generic** — Provides data types that allow you to create type-specific collections. In a type-specific or strongly typed collection, you specify in advance the type of data that can be placed into the collection.

Type-specific collections are called *generic collections*. All the collections listed in Table 2-3 have generic counterparts.

For example, the `Dictionary` data type is the generic version of the `Hashtable` data type. To create a keyed collection that accepts only the `Customer` data type, you'd use the `Dictionary` data type as shown here:

```
Dim invoiceCustomers As New Dictionary(Of String, Customer)
```

You add objects of the type `Customer` with a string key that represents their customer ID using the `Add` method, as shown in the following code:

```
invoiceCustomers.Add("1234", cust)
```

✦ **System.Collections.Specialized** — Contains a set of strongly typed or specialized collections. For example, the `StringDictionary` is a generic hash table that works only with the data type string. If you try to put some other data type, such as an integer, into a `StringDictionary`, you receive an exception.

Collections are used extensively throughout the .NET Framework. For example, Windows Forms and Web Forms have a set of control collections. You can iterate through a form's collection of controls to add controls or find a specific control you wish to use.

Iterating through arrays and collections

An important task in working with collections is to be able to step through the elements within the collection. C# and Visual Basic provide the foreach and For Each statements, respectively, for iterating through a collection.

For example, the following code shows iterating through an ArrayList using For Each in Visual Basic:

```
Dim list As New ArrayList
list.Add(1)
list.Add(2)
list.Add(3)

For Each i as Integer In list
  Dim j As Integer
  j = j + i
Next
```

The For Each statement in the preceding sample executes once for each element in the ArrayList for a total of three times. On third execution, j = 6 because 1 + 2 + 3 = 6.

The variable j is in scope only while execution is inside the For Each statement. Once execution moves off the Next statement the third time, you can no longer access j. If you want to use the variable j outside of the For Each statement, you need to declare it outside the For Each statement.

Keyed collections use the DictionaryEntry structure for iterating through values, as the following C# code sample shows:

```
Hashtable ht = new Hashtable();
ht.Add("Screen 1", "Shane");
ht.Add("Screen 2", "My Friend Flicka");

foreach (DictionaryEntry de in ht)
{
    lstMovies.Items.Add(de.Key + ": " + de.Value);
}
```

Figure 2-4 shows an example of the key/value pair from the hash table in a list box.

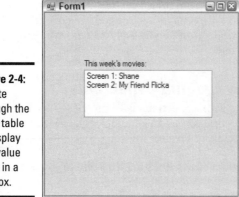

Figure 2-4:
Iterate
through the
hash table
to display
key/value
pairs in a
list box.

Collections in the real world

You have many choices for working with collections. Here are some guidelines to help you decide:

✦ **Choose arrays over collections** when the number of elements is known and not expected to grow.

✦ **Choose collections over arrays** any time you find yourself looking for methods like `Add`, `Remove`, `Item`, or `Count`.

✦ **Choose generic collections** when you know in advance the data type you want to store in the collection. Generic collections perform better than nongeneric collections.

Besides selecting the best type of collection for the job, you must also consider how you'll actually use the collection in your code. If you're creating your own data types, you need to consider how to manage multiples of your data types. You have a few options:

✦ Extend the collections classes provided by .NET.

✦ Wrap an existing collection.

In most cases, you'll probably wrap an existing collection when you want to provide your own custom collections. You have two approaches to wrapping an existing collection:

✦ **Create a new data type that wraps the collection.**

For example, you can create a data type called `MovieCollection` that allows you to handle a collection of movies without thinking about the underlying collection actually used.

✦ **Use a collection in an existing data type.**

An alternative approach to creating a separate wrapper collection is to include the collection in your data type. For example, you could create a generic collection of `Movie` types that you access from within your `Movie` type.

Converting Types

An important task when working with variables is converting a variable of one data type to another data type. For example, a variable with the Boolean value `True` is not the same as a variable with the string value `true`. They might look the same to you and me, but the computer sees the Boolean variable as either on or off and the string variable as an array of characters.

Recall that a variable's data type determines how much memory is allocated for the variable. When you convert from one data type to another, you're essentially asking the computer to give you more or less memory. There are two kinds of conversions you can perform:

✦ **Widening** — Going from a smaller data type to a larger data type

✦ **Narrowing** — Going from a larger data type to a smaller data

There is a risk of data loss with narrowing conversions. The syntax you use to widen or narrow depends on whether the conversion is either of the following:

✦ **Implicit** — Implicit conversions don't require any special syntax in order for the conversion to occur. For example, the following code implicitly converts a Boolean value to a string value:

```
Dim b As Boolean = True
Dim s As String = b
```

✦ **Explicit** — Any time you have to use special syntax to convert a variable, you're making an *explicit conversion.* Explicit conversions are often necessary when you perform a narrowing conversion.

The .NET Framework provides the `System.Convert` class, which you can use to explicitly convert from one type to another. For example, the following code converts a string to an integer in C#:

```
string s = "1000";
int i = System.Convert.ToInt32(s);
```

C# provides the `cast` operator for performing explicit conversions. The following code converts from an integer value to a byte, which is a *narrowing conversion:*

```
int i = 255;
byte b = (byte)i;
```

Recall that narrowing conversions can cause loss of data. For example, take a look at the following code sample:

```
int i = int.MaxValue;
byte b = (byte)i;
```

The maximum value of an integer data type is north of two million. So what's the value in the variable b after the conversion of integer i? It's 255. A byte holds values from only 0 to 255.

Visual Basic provides the Ctype function, which you can use for explicit conversions. You pass an expression to convert and the data type to convert to the Ctype function, as shown here:

```
Dim s As String = "255"
Dim b As Byte = CType(s, Byte)
```

Visual Basic has type conversion functions for each primitive data type and a function each for converting reference types and strings. For example, the following code is equivalent to using CType in the preceding sample:

```
Dim s As String = "255"
Dim b As Byte = CByte(s)
```

Any implicit conversion can be explicitly stated. The following code explicitly converts a Boolean value to a string value:

```
Dim b As Boolean = True
Dim s As String = Convert.ToString(b)
```

There's no harm in using an explicit conversion in place of an implicit conversion. You should use explicit conversion any time you want to make it clear to readers of your code that a conversion is occurring.

You aren't restricted to converting between primitive types and strings. You can convert any data type in the .NET Framework, your programming language, or your user-defined data types. System.Convert, Ctype, and the cast operator all allow any kind of data type for making conversions. The catch, of course, is that the data types you're converting must be compatible.

In order for a conversion to be successful, a conversion operator must be defined for the type you wish to go from to. See the Visual Studio documentation for a list of available conversions for your language.

The process of converting value types such as integers and Booleans to reference types such as strings and objects is called *boxing*. Boxing and its converse, `unboxing`, occur any time you use a value type when a reference type is expected. Passing value types as parameters when a reference type is expected is one example of when a value type is boxed.

All data types derive from `System.Object`; therefore, you can convert a variable of any data type to `System.Object`.

You can use the `System.Type` class to find out more information about a data type, such as the data type from which the data type is derived, and whether the data type is a value type or a reference type.

Meet the Newest Type: Nullable Types

It's often the case when working with values from databases that you encounter null values. A *null value* is an undefined value. A null value can make your program blow up when the program is expecting to see an integer or a Boolean or a string. To help you process and anticipate null values, the .NET Framework includes a new data type called `System.Nullable`.

You use `System.Nullable` to tell your program to accept a null value in your variable. `System.Nullable` provides the following properties:

+ **HasValue** — Returns a `true` or `false` value indicating whether the variable has a value or is null.

+ **Value** — Retrieves the variable's value. You use the `HasValue` property to test that the variable contains a value before using the `Value` property.

`System.Nullable` works with value types. Values types are primitive data types, such as `integer` and `char`. By definition, value types can't store null values. Reference types, such as strings, can store null values. As a result, it's not necessary for `System.Nullable` to work with reference types.

That's not to say that null reference types can't wreak the same kind of havoc in your program as trying to assign a null value to a value type. You should test your reference types for null values before you try to access the value.

When you declare a nullable value type, you tell `System.Nullable` which value type you wish to use. The following Visual Basic code sample creates a nullable of integer:

```
Dim i As System.Nullable(Of Integer)
```

The equivalent declaration in C# is:

```
System.Nullable<int> i;
```

C# provides the question mark (?) shortcut operator you can use when declaring nullables. The following statement is equivalent to the preceding statement:

```
int? i;
```

By declaring a variable as nullable, you can use the `HasValue` property to test for a null value. In the following code sample, if a nullable of integer `i` has a value, the value is returned. Otherwise, the procedure returns zero.

```
int checkValue(int? i)
{
  if (i.HasValue == true)
     return i.Value;
  else
     return 0;
}
```

Browsing Types

The .NET Framework has hundreds of data types. Your own code base might have dozens, and possibly even hundreds, of data types. Visual Studio provides the Object Browser for perusing the vast libraries of data types available to you.

You use the Object Browser any time you need to

+ Find a data type.

+ View the members of a data type, such as properties and methods.

+ View a description and get help for a data type.

You open the Object Browser using the View menu or the key combination Ctrl+Alt+J. It's not necessary to have a project open to use the Object Browser. Your open projects appear in the Object Browser.

Setting the scope

You'd be quickly overwhelmed if you had to look at all the data types in the Object Browser at once. Instead, the Object Browser allows you to limit the scope of the types you view at any one time to the following:

+ .NET Framework

+ Third-party components

+ Your own projects and components

To view only the components in the .NET Framework, follow these steps:

1. **Press Ctrl+Alt+J to open the Object Browser.**

2. **Click the Browse drop-down list in the Object Browser's toolbar.**

A list of browsing scopes appears.

The Object Browser displays data types from these browsing scopes:

- **All Components** — Displays the data types from the other options.

- **.NET Framework** — Displays data types found in the .NET Framework.

- **My Solution** — Displays data types created and referenced in the open solution.

- **Custom Component Set** — Displays data types from a third-party component.

3. **Click .NET Framework from the drop-down list.**

The assemblies in the .NET Framework appear in the Objects pane on the left, as shown in Figure 2-5.

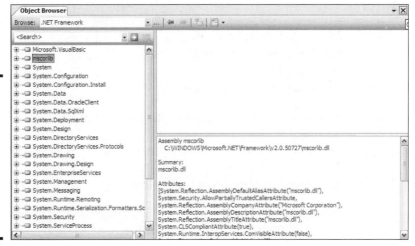

Figure 2-5:
The assemblies from the selected browsing scope appear in the Objects pane.

Use the My Solution browsing scope to view the assemblies referenced by your project.

Alternatively, you can use the Object Browser's Search drop-down list to search for a word. Search is limited to the browsing scope selected in the Browse drop-down list. See Chapter 7 of this mini-book for an example of using Search in the Object Browser.

Setting the view

The Object Browser displays data types of all kinds, including classes, enumerations, and interfaces. By default, data types appear in assembly containers; however, there are many different views, such as:

✦ **Assemblies** — The physical files in which the data type is defined.

✦ **Namespaces** — The logical namespace in which the data type is defined.

✦ **Object types** — The kind of data type, such as class, enumerator, or structure.

To view the data types by namespaces:

1. **Right-click inside the objects pane.**

A shortcut menu appears.

2. **Choose View Namespaces.**

The data types are grouped by their namespaces.

To group the data types by assembly, repeat Step 1 and choose View Containers from the shortcut menu.

Choose Group by Object Type from the shortcut menu to group the data types by the type of data type.

To view the physical assembly file where data is defined:

1. **Group the data types by assembly, as described in the preceding set of steps.**

2. **Click the assembly you wish to view.**

The assembly's name, path, and attributes appear in the Description pane. Figure 2-6 shows the assembly information for the System assembly.

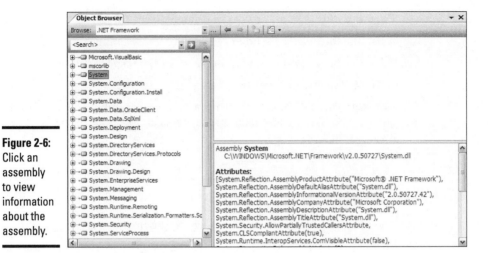

Figure 2-6:
Click an
assembly
to view
information
about the
assembly.

Viewing data types

You can use the Object Browser to view all kinds of information about data
types, including the following data types:

+ Assembly and namespace

+ Members such as properties and methods

+ Base data type and derived data types

To view a data type in the Object Browser:

1. **Set your browsing scope and view.**

2. **Click the plus sign (+) next to the container of data types.**

Depending on how you set up your view, you might also have to expand
the Namespaces and Object Type folders to access the actual data types.

3. **Click the data type to view its members and description.**

For example, to access the System.Enum data type with the data types
grouped by assemblies and object types, follow these steps:

1. **Click the plus sign (+) next to the mscorlib assembly.**

The Namespaces folder appears.

The mscorlib assembly contains the core namespaces of the .NET
Framework.

2. Click the plus sign (+) next to the Namespaces folder.

A list of namespaces found in the `mscorlib` assembly appears.

3. Click the plus sign (+) next to the System Namespace folder.

A list of Object Type folders appears.

Note that the .NET Framework has a `System` assembly and a `System` namespace. The System namespace spans across both the `mscorlib` and System assemblies.

4. Click the Structures folder.

A list of structure data types appears.

5. Click the `Enum` data type.

The members and description appear in the browser.

To view a member's description, click the member, as shown in Figure 2-7.

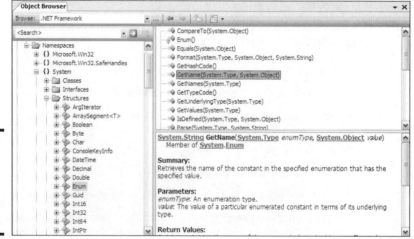

Figure 2-7:
Click a data type's member to view its description.

A data type's base data type can give you clues about whether the type is a value type or reference type. Viewing the type's derived data types shows you more specific implementations of the data type that might be more appropriate for you to use.

You can view a data type's base type and any derived types by expanding the data type. In the case of the `System.Enum` data type, its base type is `System.ValueType`. Many types are derived from `System.Enum`, as shown in Figure 2-8.

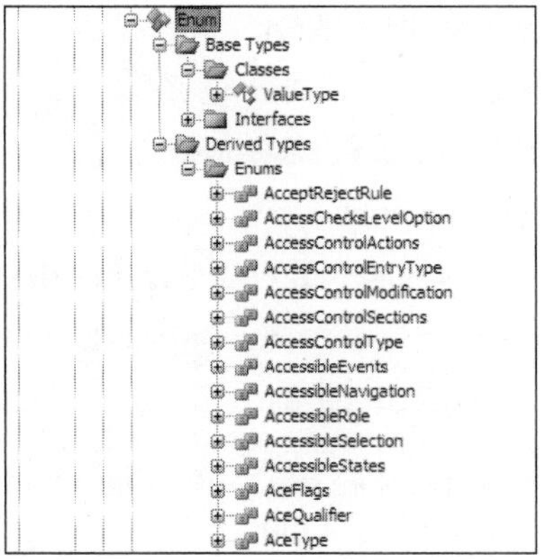

Figure 2-8:
Expand a
data type
to view its
base types
and derived
types.

You might have noticed that the data types, members, and other items in the
Object Browser have icons next to them. A different icon is used to represent each kind of data type, such as classes or structures. Search for the
topic "Class View and Object Browser Icons" in the Visual Studio help documentation for a summary of the icons used.

Viewing source code

Visual Studio provides several tools for browsing and navigating source code
including:

✦ **Class View** — Use the Class View to display a hierarchical view of the
solution you're developing.

✦ **Code Definition** — Displays a read-only view of the source code for the
selected object.

You use the Code Definition window in conjunction with the Class View or
Object Browser to view an object's source code. When viewing objects from
outside your project, the Code Definition window displays only the source
code's type and method declarations and comments. You can't actually view
the source code that implements the object.

The Code Definition window doesn't work in Visual Basic.

To use the Code Definition window with the Class View, follow these steps:

1. **Open a C# project in Visual Studio.**

If you don't have an existing C# project, you can open one of the C#
Starter Kits, such as the Movie Collection Starter Kit, from the New
Project window.

2. Press Ctrl+Shift+C to open the Class View.

The project appears in the Class View window.

3. Choose Code Definition Window on the View menu.

The Code Definition window appears.

4. Expand the classes in the Class View and click one of the objects.

The object's methods appear in the bottom pane of the Class View.

The Class View and the Object Browser use a number of icons to represent different kinds of objects. For example, the open and closing curly braces { } represent a namespace. See the topic "Class View and Object Browser Icons" in the Visual Studio documentation for a complete list of the icons used.

5. Click one of the public methods.

The method's source code appears in the Code Definition window, as Figure 2-9 shows.

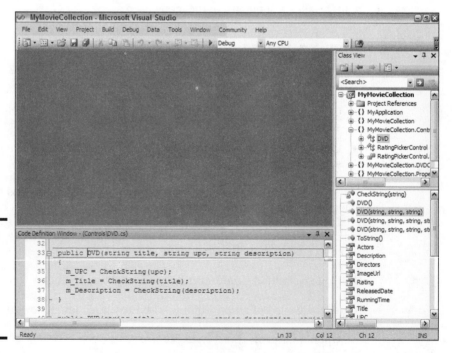

Figure 2-9: Source code appears in the Code Definition window.

The Code Definition window is a read-only view of the source code. To open the source code file in the code editor, right-click the item in the Class View window and choose Go to Definition from the shortcut menu.

To view the object in the Object Browser, right-click the object in the Class View window and choose Browse Definition from the shortcut menu.

Accessing Types in Your Source Code

Data types are logically organized into namespaces but physically organized into assemblies. *Assemblies* are the .dll files output when your source code is built. In order to consume types in your source code, you need to know how to access the physical and logical paths to data types.

✦ **References** provide access to the physical assembly files where the types can be found.

✦ **Namespaces** provide access to the logical path of the type within the referenced assembly.

You access the physical file where types are stored by adding a reference to the type. Visual Studio provides the ability to add new references and manage existing references in your project.

When you create a new project, Visual Studio automatically adds a number of references to common physical .dll files you might need to use in your project. You might remove any reference that you aren't using.

Once you've added a reference to the physical assembly where the type resides, you must also supply the logical namespace to access the type and its members. You can type the namespace in source code. If you have properly referenced the assembly, IntelliSense pops up to help you find the namespaces you need.

You can also include namespace directives at the top of your source code that provide a shortcut to namespaces you wish to use in your source code. The namespace directive in C# is `using`, and it's `Include` in Visual Basic. These directives allow you to access types within a namespace without fully qualifying the namespace every time.

For example, say you want to create a new DataSet in your source code. The `DataSet` type is found in the `System.Data` namespace. Using the fully qualified namespace looks like this in C#:

```
System.Data.DataSet ds = new System.Data.DataSet();
```

However, if you add the following `using` directive at the top of your source code file:

```
using System.Data;
```

Then, you can create a new DataSet like this:

```
DataSet ds = new DataSet();
```

Using namespace directives saves space in your code and makes your code easier to read in some cases. I say, "in some cases," because I can't tell just by looking at this code where this type lives. DataSet is a popular type, so I happen to know that it's not local to my source code.

Another approach is to create an alias for the namespace so that it quickly identifies that the type is being referenced from another namespace. To create an alias in C#, type the following:

```
using data = System.Data;
```

Now, you can qualify the type using the alias, as shown in the following code:

```
data.DataSet ds = new data.DataSet();
```

The same code in Visual Basic appears as:

```
Imports data = System.Data
Dim ds as new data.DataSet
```

Chapter 3: Get Some Class

In This Chapter

✔ **Using objects and classes**

✔ **Declaring classes and members**

✔ **Designing classes with the Class Designer**

*W*hen I first learned how to program computers, the style of programming was sequential. You wrote one line of code after another. Each line of code was numbered, and you thought about your program in terms of what happens first and what happens next.

When I went to college, I was taught a more sophisticated style of programming that uses functions to group statements of code. Functions are great because you can easily organize your code into reusable blocks.

When I started working as a programmer, I encountered yet a third style of programming that organizes code into classes. I found this curious because even though a program's basic building block is classes, the style of programming is called object-oriented programming (OOP).

Like most programmers' first encounters with OOP, it took me a while to figure out the relationship between objects and classes. If you think of software as a means of modeling a real-world scenario, the following points are worth remembering:

✦ **Objects represent the people, places, and things in your program.** For example, think about a business that sends an invoice to a customer. Invoice #100984 and Customer #60093 are objects your program needs to manipulate. The business, ABC Graphics, sending invoice #100984 to customer #60093 is an object, too.

✦ **Classes are the units of code you write to make objects come to life in your program.** For example, your program defines Invoice and Customer classes. Each class encapsulates the data and behaviors required to create objects that represent real-world invoices and customers.

You *write* classes, but you *think* in terms of objects, which is why programming with objects is called *object-oriented programming*. Table 3-1 compares OOP with procedural and sequential programming styles.

Table 3-1	Comparison of Programming Styles	
Programming Style	*Programmers' Approach*	*Basic Building Blocks*
Object-oriented	What objects am I modeling in my program?	Objects
Procedural	What functions do I need to tackle this problem?	Functions
Sequential	What's the next line of code to write?	Statements

Thinking in objects isn't limited to programmers. Objects are often found in the planning and design stages of a project, where object-oriented thinking is formally known as both of the following:

✦ **Object-oriented analysis** — Requirements analysts use objects to model problems in the business domain.

✦ **Object-oriented design** — Designers use analysis objects to model classes that programmers will write to create objects.

Programmers use object-oriented programming languages (OOPLs) such as Visual Basic, C#, C++, and Java to implement classes.

Even if you've never written an object-oriented program or know nothing about objects, chances are you're familiar with several of the characteristics of OO programming:

✦ Using the familiar dot notation to access the members of an object

✦ Using the new operator to initialize a reference type

✦ Setting an object's properties

Visual Studio provides many tools that support the activities of object-oriented design and programming. In this chapter, I cover some of the basics of working with objects and classes. I show you how to use the Class Designer to visually design and inspect classes and objects.

What's with Objects?

Classes and objects are the bedrock of object-oriented programming. *Classes* are special kinds of data types that you use to create objects in your code. Objects are placeholders in your code for the real people, places, and things upon which your program acts.

Classes are a complex data type. Simple data types store values such as integers and Booleans. Composite data types, such as structures that are capable of storing more than one value, aren't more sophisticated than integers and Booleans. The values you can store using classes, however, are beyond mere integers or sets of integers.

You might recognize simple data types as value types and complex data types as reference types. See Chapter 2 in this mini-book for a thorough discussion of the differences between value types and reference types.

A class is a data type capable of storing data and actions. When you declare and initialize a variable using a class data type, you create an object that stores data and action values defined by the class data type. Objects are used to accommodate the potential complexity of values stored for class data types. An object is often referred to as an *instance* of the class data type.

The term *object* is often interchanged for the term *class*. People often use the term *object* in a generic sense to mean "the class that defines the object." I seldom hear people use *class* when they mean *object*. You must consider the context in which the term is used to determine whether the author or speaker means class or object. I usually ask myself whether the author is writing about a data type or the value represented by the data type. If it's the former, then it's *class*. Otherwise, it's an *object*.

Classes act as a template for defining the data and actions of an object. You create objects using the class as a template. Each object created from the class is like a blank form into which you can place data. The source of that data may be a database, data typed on a screen by a user, or another object.

Some people find it helpful to think of classes as the blueprints for objects — or to think that classes are abstract and objects are concrete. I personally like to think of classes as a template for creating an object.

You're familiar with the concept of data, but you might not immediately understand what the potential actions of a class data type may be. Consider a class data type called `Customer`. You expect a `Customer` data type to store a customer's name and account number. If I asked you to tell me a customer's 30-days aging of their account, how might you approach solving this problem?

Given that an account's aging is based on the current date, you need to be able to calculate the value in real time. You can't query a database for the answer. Your `Customer` class needs a procedure that returns the account's aging.

It's usually considered bad form to store calculated values in a database. Classes often return calculated values for an object. For example, an `Employee` class may have a procedure that returns the employee's age.

Another example of actions is things that an object can do. For instance, a student registers for courses. Registering for courses is an action that a `student` object is capable of doing.

Classes are important to software development because they

+ Are a basic building block of programs
+ Group related code together in a unit
+ Control visibility and accessibility of your code
+ Encourage reuse
+ Are easy to extend
+ Can model real world scenarios
+ Map code to the real world

Code created using objects and classes and adhering to the principles of object-oriented programming display these characteristics:

+ **Abstraction** — Models a real-life thing using only the attributes relevant to solving the problem at hand.

  Creating user-defined classes is an example of an abstraction. When you approach a problem you're trying to solve, you identify the objects that are relevant to the problem. For example, you need a `Customer` object and an `Invoice` object to prepare invoices. You determine the level of detail required in your `Customer` and `Invoice` classes to adequately solve the problem of printing invoices.

+ **Encapsulation** — Wraps the data and actions of an entity into a single unit.

  Encapsulation isn't unique to object-oriented programming. Functions and subroutines are example of encapsulation as are classes.

+ **Inheritance** — Builds a hierarchy of related code by creating parent-child relationships between units of code.

  Inheritance allows you to create a supertype/subtype relationship between types. A simple example of inheritance is having a `Dog` class and a `Cat` class that inherits from an `Animal` class. The `Animal` class has all the data and actions common to both dogs and cats. Unique behaviors, such as a cat's purr, appear in the appropriate derived class.

+ **Polymorphism** — Allows child types to provide their own code to implement actions performed by their parent or sibling.

  Polymorphism makes it possible for a class hierarchy to share a common set of behaviors while each has its own implementation. For example, the `Animal` class has a reproductive cycle. The `Dog` and `Cat` classes each require their own implementation of a reproductive cycle. Polymorphism allows you to refer to the generic concept of a reproductive cycle in your code regardless of whether you mean a dog or a cat.

Another important characteristic of object-oriented design is information hiding. You should design your classes so that important design decisions are hidden. In other words, one should have to think about only initializing and accessing your classes, not understanding how you've written them. The classes in the .NET Framework are a good example of information hiding. You must explicitly think about information hiding as you design your application. It's possible to abstract, encapsulate, inherit, and polymorph without hiding information. Simply using object-oriented techniques doesn't ensure you're hiding information.

You use an object-oriented programming language such as Visual Basic, C#, or C++ to write object-oriented programs. The .NET Framework is an object-oriented library of classes.

In addition to the object-oriented programming languages, Visual Studio provides several tools to support OOP, including:

✦ Class Designer

✦ Class View

✦ Object Browser

✦ Object Test Bench

The only way to learn object-oriented design and programming is to do object-oriented design (OOD) and programming. Memorizing terms and definitions can help your vocabulary, but by themselves, they do very little to increase your understanding of OOD and OOP. So, instead of getting hung up on terminology, just start coding.

Anatomy of a Class in .NET

Classes and OOP have all-new terminology with which you might not be familiar and which might, at first, seem overwhelming. At its heart, classes are just ways to organize code similar to the modules, functions, and subroutines with which you might be familiar. Like modules, functions, and subroutines, you declare variables and procedures similar to how you do in modules.

Classes are templates that define an object's

✦ **Data** — Data is sometimes referred to as the object's *state,* which is the set of values an object holds at a given point in time.

✦ **Behavior** — Behaviors are the actions that the object takes.

The code that creates a new class is called a *class declaration*. A class declaration consists of the class header and body. The class header defines the following:

✦ **Attributes** — Optional keywords used by the compiler.

The .NET Framework provides several attributes for use in your class and method declarations. In Chapter 6 of this mini-book, I show you how to use the `WebService` and `WebMethod` attributes to turn ordinary classes and methods into Web services.

✦ **Modifiers** — Keywords that define how the class may be used.

For example, classes and members use access modifiers, such as public and private, to determine whether the class or member may be accessed by code outside the class or namespace.

✦ **Name** — Identity of the class.

✦ **Base class** — Data type from which the class is inheriting.

All classes implicitly inherit from `System.Object`.

✦ **Interfaces** — Comma-separated list of interfaces implemented by the class.

An *interface* is a set of member declarations with no source code to implement them. Interfaces make it possible to define a publicly consumable contract without writing the source code. Other developers can target the interface without fear of the interface changing. See Chapter 4 of this mini-book for more information on interfaces.

A class's body defines the class's data and behavior. The items declared inside a class are called its *members*. The members you can create inside a class body include:

✦ **Constants** — Values in the class that don't change.

✦ **Constructors** — Special procedures that are called to create an object using the class. An object is often referred to as an *instance* of the class.

✦ **Destructors** — Special procedures that are called before an object is discarded by your program.

✦ **Events** — Procedures that raise a notification when a certain action occurs.

✦ **Fields** — Variables declared for use within the class, often for storing data.

✦ **Indexers** — Procedures that index individual instances of the class.

✦ **Methods** — Procedures that provide the behaviors of the class.

✦ **Operators** — Procedures that define conversions for the class and extends built-in operators.

✦ **Properties** — Procedures that provide access to the class's data structure.

✦ **Types** — Nested data types, such as classes or structures, created within the class.

The combination of a class header and its body is called its *definition*.

You might have noticed that a class's body is made up of procedures and variables. If you've done any programming at all, you should be familiar with the concept of using variables and procedures to create your program.

In C#, a class's body is wrapped in opening and closing curly braces. Listed here is a class definition in C#:

```
public class Message
{
  private string m_message;

  public string Contents
  {
    get { return m_message; }
    set { m_message = value; }
  }

  public Message(string message)
  {
    this.m_message = message;
  }

  public string ReverseContents()
  {
    char[] c = this.m_message.ToCharArray();
    StringBuilder sb = new StringBuilder();

    for (int i = 1; i <= c.Length; i++)
    {
      sb.Append(c, c.Length - i, 1);
    }

    return sb.ToString();
  }
}
```

Can you tell which elements in this class are fields, properties, and methods? It's not immediately obvious just by looking at the code. To someone not familiar with OOP, this code looks like variable and procedure declarations. Table 3-2 summarizes the members in this class.

Table 3-2		Members Found in the Message Class
Member Type	*Quantity*	*Example*
Field	1	`m_message`
Property	1	`Contents`
Constructor	1	`Message(string message)`
Method	1	`ReverseContents()`

Take a look at the equivalent code sample in Visual Basic. Notice how the Visual Basic keywords `Property` and `New` provide clues as to the member's purpose.

```
Public Class Message
  Private m_message As String

  Public Property Contents() As String
    Get
      Return Me.m_message
    End Get
    Set(ByVal value As String)
      Me.m_message = value
    End Set
  End Property

  Public Sub New(ByVal message As String)
    Me.m_message = message
  End Sub

  Public Function ReverseContents() As String
    Dim c As Char() = Me.m_message.ToCharArray()
    Dim sb As New StringBuilder

    For i As Integer = 1 To c.Length
      sb.Append(c, c.Length - i, 1)
    Next

    Return sb.ToString()

  End Function
End Class
```

Classes are logically organized within namespaces. Your class code is stored in a physical file called an *assembly*. A single namespace can span multiple assembly files, but a single class can reside in only one assembly. To access classes, you must reference the assembly and the namespace within your project. See Chapter 2 of this mini-book for more information.

The C# keyword `this` and Visual Basic keyword `me` are used to reference the current instance of an object in your code.

Certain coding standards dictate how you name classes and members. See Chapter 5 of this mini-book for more information on using coding standards.

Inheriting the services of System.Object

All classes inherit from the .NET class `System.Object`. Inheriting from `System.Object` provides all the basic services your classes need to function as objects and get along with other objects.

`System.Object` is the base class of your class, and your class is a derived class of `System.Object`.

Any time your classes derive from a base class, you should check the documentation of the base class to determine if there any methods you should override. When you *override* a member, you write your own code to implement the member.

For example, the `System.Object` class has a method called `ToString` that you should override. By overriding `ToString` in the classes you define, you can get a string representation of objects created from your class. See Chapter 5 of this mini-book for more information on overriding.

There are several overridden methods for `System.Object`. Table 3-3 lists all the methods your class inherits from `System.Object` and identifies those that you should override.

It's considered good form to override a base class's methods when recommended. Overriding ensures that your derived class works as expected. Look for the section labeled "Note to Implementers" in the base class's type for information on overriding.

Table 3-3	Methods of System.Object	
Method	*Description*	*Override*
New	Constructor	Not required
Finalize	Destructor	Not recommended
Equals	Determines whether two object instances are equivalent	Yes
GetHashCode	Generates a hash code for use in hash tables	Not required

(continued)

Table 3-3 *(continued)*

Method	Description	Override
GetType	Returns the data type of the object instance	No
MemberwiseClone	Copies a value or an object reference	No
ReferenceEquals	Determines if two object instances are the same object	
ToString	Returns a human-readable representation of the object instance	Recommended

Using classes in your code

Recall that classes are data types. Therefore, you use them like you use any data type. They're reference types, so you use the new operator to create a new instance of a class.

The new operator calls the class's constructor method. A class may have more than one constructor. If no constructor method is defined in the class, the object is initialized using the default constructor. The default constructor is the New() method defined in the System.Object class. Recall that all classes derive from System.Object.

Classes are reference types, so everything I say in Chapter 2 of this minibook about how memory is allocated for reference types applies to classes. When you initialize a new instance of a class, the object itself is allocated on the heap. The reference to the object is allocated on the stack.

To create a new instance of the Message class created in the preceding section, you type the following:

```
Message m = new Message("Hello");
```

You use dot notation to access the members of the class. The member's visibility is determined by the modifier set on the member's declaration. You can always see public members but not private members. To call the ReverseContents member, type the following:

```
string s = m.ReverseContents();
```

Here's the equivalent code using Visual Basic syntax:

```
Dim m As New Message("Hello")
Dim s As String = m.ReverseContents()
```

There's no need to declare the `Message` class using Visual Basic and C# syntax. You can just as easily create the class in C# and then reference and instantiate it in Visual Basic.

Hopefully, this syntax looks familiar to you. If you've used any features in the .NET Framework, you've encountered this syntax.

You can use any of the classes in the .NET Framework or any third party library just by knowing the rules for declaring variables based on a class data type and creating instances of objects.

Using the Class Designer

Visual Studio provides a visual design tool called Class Designer that you can use to create class diagrams. Some common uses of the Class Designer are

+ Designing new classes

+ Visualizing existing classes

+ Refactoring classes

Another use of the Class Designer that might not be immediately evident is that of a training aid. You can use the Class Designer to familiarize yourself with the concepts of object-oriented programming. You can also use it to learn syntax.

You should use the Class Designer as an aid, not a crutch. If you rely too heavily on the tool, you risk being dependent on the tool. This is definitely not where you want to be if your company decides to migrate some projects to another object-oriented language such as Java.

Like most of the visual designers in Visual Studio, the Class Designer generates diagrams from code and code from diagrams. The diagrams and code are synchronized. The class diagram is a visual representation of source code.

The class diagrams created by the Class Designer are design diagrams, not analysis diagrams. Design diagrams usually show more implementation details than analysis diagrams. If you want a tool better suited to creating analysis diagrams, I suggest you use Visio for Enterprise Architects. You can easily generate classes from your Visio diagrams and then view those classes in the Class Designer.

Common tasks you can do in the Class Designer include the following:

✦ Create new classes and members

✦ Define relationships among classes

✦ View classes and relationships

✦ Refactor code

Exploring the Class Designer

The Class Designer is capable of designing more than just classes. You can use the Class Designer to design or view any kind of data type, including:

✦ Classes

✦ Delegates

✦ Enumerations

✦ Interfaces

✦ Structures

The Class Designer can also create Visual Basic modules. Modules are used to encapsulate your code. See the Visual Basic documentation for more information on the differences between classes and modules.

You add a new class diagram to your project using the Add New Item window. A project may have multiple class diagrams. To add a new class diagram:

1. **Right-click your project's folder in Solution Explorer.**

A shortcut menu appears.

2. **Choose Add⇨New Item on the shortcut menu.**

The Add New Item window appears.

3. **Click the Class Diagram icon.**

4. **Type a name for the class diagram.**

5. **Click the Add button.**

Visual Studio adds the class diagram file to Solution Explorer and opens it in the Class Designer.

Class diagrams use the .cd filename extensions. Like most files in Visual Studio, the class diagram file is an XML file.

Class diagrams are visual representations of classes in a project. The diagrams are similar to diagrams created using the Unified Modeling Language (UML) specification.

 UML is a modeling language that identifies 13 diagrams used for designing software. Many tools available on the market are capable of creating UML diagrams, including Microsoft Visio for Enterprise Architects. Visual Studio's class diagrams won't replace UML diagrams you're already using. Consider them another tool to add to your modeling arsenal.

The Class Designer consists of:

✦ Toolbox

✦ Designer surface

✦ Class Details pane

The designer provides a toolbar and shortcut menus to access additional features. The designer works with Solution Explorer, Class View, and Object Test Bench.

The Class Designer provides several commands you can use for working with your diagram. The commands you can use depend on what you have selected in the diagram. You have three levels of commands for working with class diagrams:

✦ **Diagram** — To work with the entire diagram, click a blank area of the diagram.

✦ **Type** — Click a shape to access commands that act on the data type.

✦ **Member** — Click a member within the type to view commands.

Figure 3-1 shows the Class Designer toolbar. The first column of Table 3-4 lists the commands of the Class Designer toolbar, as they appear on the toolbar from left to right.

Table 3-4	Commands Available on the Class Designer Toolbar	
Command Type	*Command*	*Description*
Arrangements of shapes	Group by Kind	Groups by kind of data type
	Group by Access	Groups by data type's access modifier
	Sort Alphabetically	Sorts by data type's names
Layout	Layout Diagram	Organizes diagram
	Adjust Shapes Width	Widens shapes

(continued)

Table 3-4 *(continued)*

Command Type	Command	Description
Member display options	Display Name	Displays members' names only
	Display Name and Type	Displays names and type
	Display Full Signature	Displays full declaration
Visual	Zoom In	Zooms in on diagram
	Zoom Out	Zooms out on diagram
	Zoom Percentage	Sets a zoom percentage
	Class Details Window	Opens the Class Details window

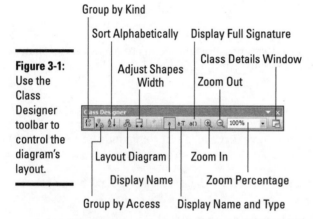

Figure 3-1: Use the Class Designer toolbar to control the diagram's layout.

The Class Designer menu provides you the opportunity to act upon the shapes that represent data types on the diagram. Table 3-5 lists the options available for data types you click in the class diagram.

Table 3-5   Type-Level Commands Available on the Class Designer Menu

Command	Description
Add	Selects a member to add to the type
Refactor	Accesses refactoring options for the type
IntelliSense	Generates code using IntelliSense
Show Base Class	Displays the type's base type on the diagram
Show Derived Class	Displays types derived from the type on the diagram
Collapse	Collapses members

Command	Description
Expand	Expands members
Show All Members	Displays any hidden members
Create Instance	Creates an object using the Object Test Bench
Invoke Static Method	Calls a static method using the Object Test Bench

You can access most of these commands from a shortcut menu when you right-click a shape in a class diagram. The shape's shortcut menu includes commands to delete the shape from the diagram and view the type's underlying source code.

Designing classes

One of the more exciting features of the Class Designer is the ability to design classes. You can drag and drop data types on the class diagram, and in the background, Visual Studio is generating the code to create the data type.

Creating a new class

The Class Designer is capable of creating all kinds of data types. The toolbox includes all the shapes you need to create data types and show relationships between data types.

To create a new class using the Class Designer:

1. **Add a new class diagram, following the steps in the previous section.**

2. **Press Ctrl+Alt+X to open the toolbox.**

   The Toolbox pane displays icons representing items you can add to the Class Designer.

3. **Drag and drop a Class icon from the Toolbox onto the Class Designer.**

   The New Class dialog box appears.

4. **Type a name for the class in the Name text box.**

5. **Select an access modifier from the Access drop-down list.**

   The public access modifier is accepted by default.

6. **Type a new filename for the class or select an existing file to add the class.**

7. **Click the OK button.**

   The Class shape appears on the Class Designer.

   Visual Studio generates the class declaration and places it in the file you created or selected in Step 6.

Figure 3-2 shows the Class Designer with a class called `Message`. You can see the `Message.cs` source code that Visual Studio created in the pane below the class diagram.

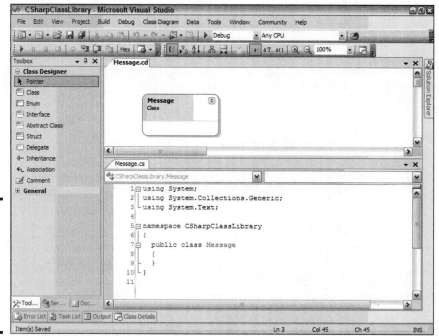

Figure 3-2:
Visual
Studio
generates
the class
declaration
for the new
class.

To add more types to the class diagram, drag the type from the Toolbox onto the design surface. A dialog box appears, similar to the one in Step 3.

Adding members to a class

You use the Class Designer to add members to your class. When you add a member using the designer, you specify the following information about a member:

✦ Name

✦ Data type

✦ Access modifier

You can, optionally, supply a descriptive comment and mark whether to hide the member on the class diagram.

Visual Studio uses the information you supply to create a member declaration in your source code. You have two options for adding members to your class with the Class Designer:

✦ **Type the members in the Class Details pane.** The Class Details pane shows the class's members grouped by methods, properties, fields, and events.

✦ **Add the members to the class in the class diagram.**

The class diagram and the source code are synchronized. Any members you declare directly in source code appear in the class diagram.

To add a new member using the Class Details pane:

1. **Click the section of the Class Details pane for the type of member you wish to add.**

If the Class Details pane is closed, choose View⇨Other Windows⇨Class Details to open the pane.

2. **Type the member's name in the line immediately below the section's header.**

For example, to add a new field, click the line below the Fields section where you see `<add field>`.

3. **Press the Tab key.**

The cursor stops in the Type cell.

4. **Type the member's data type.**

IntelliSense works in the Class Details pane.

5. **Press the Tab key and select the member's access modifier.**

6. **Press the Tab key and add a descriptive comment, if desired.**

7. **Click to place a check mark in the Hide column if you don't want the member to appear on the class diagram.**

Figure 3-3 shows a field and a property in the Class Details pane.

Visual Studio generates the member declarations for you in the class's source code file.

The Class Details pane features a toolbar button with shortcuts for adding members. To access the shortcut button, click the arrow on the button, as Figure 3-4 shows.

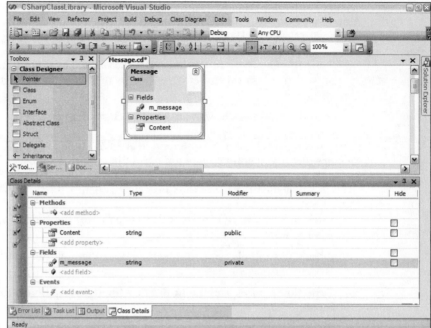

Figure 3-3:
Use the Class Details pane to add new members.

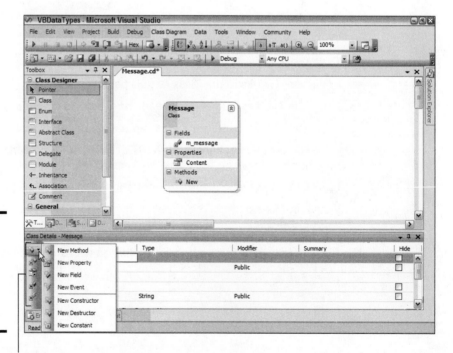

Figure 3-4:
Use the Class Details toolbar to add members.

The Class Designer toolbar

A method's declaration is a little more complex than a field or property declaration because a method may accept parameters. In addition, there are multiple kinds of methods, such as constructors and destructors. The Class Details pane has no problems adding methods to your class. To add a new constructor method, follow these simple steps:

1. **Click the shortcut button on the Class Details toolbar.**

2. **Chose New Constructor.**

A new constructor method appears in the Methods section of the Class Details pane.

Note that constructors use the same name as the class in C#. In Visual Basic, constructors are named New.

3. **Type the constructor's parameters in the lines below the constructor's declaration, as shown in Figure 3-5.**

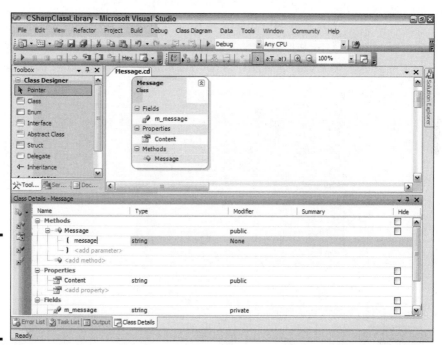

Figure 3-5:
Add parameters to the constructor method.

Visual Studio generates the member declarations and stubs out the member's bodies. Exceptions are placed inside the generated members to remind you that you need to add your code if you try to use the members. For example, the following code is the constructor generated for the preceding sample:

```
public Message(string message)
{
  throw new System.NotImplementedException();
}
```

The Class Designer is a good tool for designing a class domain. A designer can lay out the classes and then pass off their implementation to a programmer.

You can also create members using the class diagram. To create a member in the class diagram:

1. **Right-click the class in the class diagram.**

A shortcut menu appears.

2. **Choose Add on the shortcut menu.**

A list of members you can add to the class appears.

3. **Select the type of member you wish to add.**

The member appears in the diagram.

4. **Type the member's name in the diagram, as Figure 3-6 shows.**

Use the Class Details pane to complete the member's declaration.

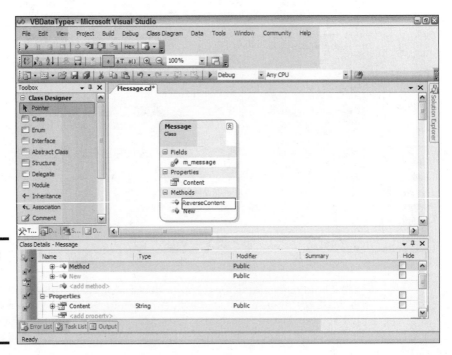

Figure 3-6:
Type the member's name in the class diagram.

Creating associations

The nature of OOP is that classes interact. You create an interaction between classes when you create member declarations in your class. For example, if you declare a field of the string type, you create an association between your class and the string class.

In the Class Designer, you show associations between only classes that are relevant to the model you're creating. You could show every association, but then your diagrams would be too crowded for people to understand. Instead, you should show only the associations that you want to draw attention to.

To create an association between two types:

1. **Create both types on the class diagram.**

2. **Click the Association icon in the toolbox.**

3. **Click the type where you want to draw the association.**

The cursor appears as a line, as shown in Figure 3-7.

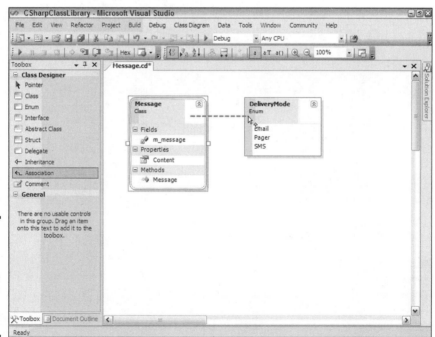

Figure 3-7:
Drag the cursor between the two classes to create an association.

4. Drag the line to the class.

An association between the classes appears. Visual Studio adds the association as a property.

You can show associations between classes and collections. To show an association between a class and a strongly typed collection follow these steps:

1. Add the member to your class that uses the strongly typed collection.

For example, add a field that uses a generic collection based on another data type in your diagram.

2. Right-click the member on the class diagram.

A shortcut menu appears.

3. Click Show as Collection Association, as shown in Figure 3-8.

An association between the classes appears.

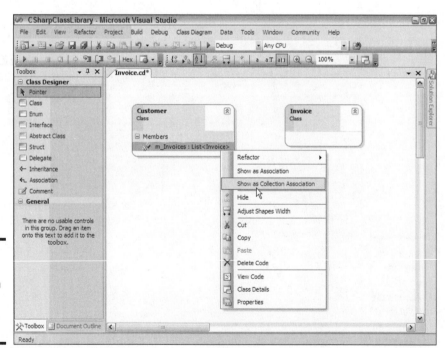

Figure 3-8: Create an association between a class and a collection.

Generating code

The Class Designer takes advantage of Visual Studio's code generation features. While using the Class Designer, you can access

✦ Advanced IntelliSense features, such as overriding type members and implementing abstract base classes.

✦ Refactoring commands, such as extracting interfaces from a type and renaming members.

Refactoring commands aren't available while designing classes using Visual Basic.

See Chapter 5 in this mini-book for more information on using IntelliSense and refactoring features of Visual Studio.

Viewing existing classes

The Class Designer is an excellent tool for viewing information about data types. You can view data types within your own project — or any types referenced by your project. This means that you can view types from the .NET Framework or a third party.

To view a type in your project, you simply drag and drop the source code file from Solution Explorer to the class diagram.

You use the Class View to drag referenced types from your project to the class diagram. For example, to add the type NullReferenceException to a class diagram, follow these steps:

1. **Add a new class diagram to your project.**

2. **Press Ctrl+Shift+C to open the Class View.**

3. **Type** System.NullReferenceException **in the Search box.**

   Alternatively, expand the Project Reference folders and navigate to the NullReferenceException type.

   The NullReferenceException type is in the System namespace in the mscorlib assembly. Your project references the mscorlib assembly by default.

4. **Press Enter.**

   The System.NullReferenceException appears in the search results.

5. **Drag and drop System.NullReferenceException on the class diagram.**

Admittedly, viewing a single type on a class diagram isn't very exciting. You can use the Class Details pane to view the type's members. You can also view a type's inheritance hierarchy. To view a type's base type, follow these steps:

1. Right-click the type and choose Show Base Class from the shortcut menu.

The base type appears on the class diagram.

2. Repeat Step 1 for each base type you display.

Show Base Class appears dimmed when you reach the top of the inheritance hierarchy.

Figure 3-9 shows the class diagram for the `NullReferenceException` type. Notice that `System.Object` is at the top of the hierarchy.

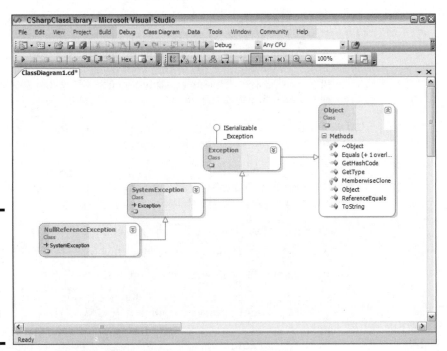

Figure 3-9:
Use the Class Designer to view a type's inheritance hierarchy.

To view the class diagram for an entire project, follow these steps:

1. Right-click the project folder in Solution Explorer.

A shortcut menu appears.

2. Choose View Class Diagram.

A class diagram of the project appears. Figure 3-10 shows the class diagram for a project created using the Movie Collection Starter Kit in Visual Basic.

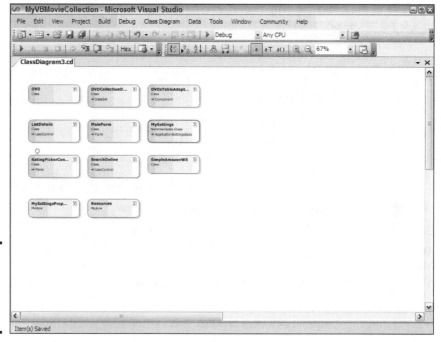

Figure 3-10:
Create
a class
diagram for
a project.

Working with objects

Earlier in this chapter, I describe how objects are the basis of everything we do in software. Programmers create classes to define the data and actions of objects in the real world, such as invoices and customers. Visual Studio provides the Object Test Bench as a means to create an object from a class in a visual environment.

The Object Test Bench (OTB) is a separate tool from the Class Designer, but you can access OTB from the designer. The Class Designer provides two commands for creating objects from the types on your class diagram:

✦ **Create Instance** — Calls the constructor method that you select.

✦ **Invoke Static Method** — Calls a static method that you select.

Static is a modifier that can be used on classes and methods. When a method or class is declared as static, you can use the class or method without first creating an instance of the class. In other words, you don't use the new operator when you use a static method or class.

See Chapter 8 of this mini-book to read more about the uses of Object Test Bench.

To create an instance of an object in the Object Test Bench with the Class Designer:

1. **Right-click the class that you want to use on the class diagram.**

A shortcut menu appears.

The type can't be a static class.

2. **Choose Create Instance.**

A list of the class's available constructors appears in a submenu.

3. **Choose the constructor you wish to use.**

The Create Instance window appears, which allows you to supply input parameters to the constructor and specify a name to use as the object's identifier.

4. **Type a variable name and supply parameter values, if required.**

5. **Click OK.**

The object appears in the Object Test Bench.

Invoking a static method is similar to creating an object instance. For example, to invoke a static method on a static class such as `System.Environment`:

1. **Drag and drop the static class onto the class diagram.**

The `System.Environment` type is in the `mscorlib` assembly. Drag the type from the Class View as described in the preceding section, "Viewing existing classes."

2. **Right-click the static class.**

A shortcut menu appears.

3. **Choose Invoke Static Method.**

A list of static methods appears.

4. **Select a static method from the list.**

The Invoke Method window appears.

5. **Enter parameter values, if required.**

6. **Click OK.**

The Method Call Result window appears.

If the method doesn't return a value, the method executes but no results appear.

The Method Call Result window displays the return value.

7. Type an identifier for the return value.

The identifier appears in the object's shape in the Object Test Bench.

8. Click OK.

The return value appears in the Object Test Bench. Figure 3-11 shows the return value for the GetLogicalDrives() static method on the System.Environment static class. Hover your mouse over the object to view the return value.

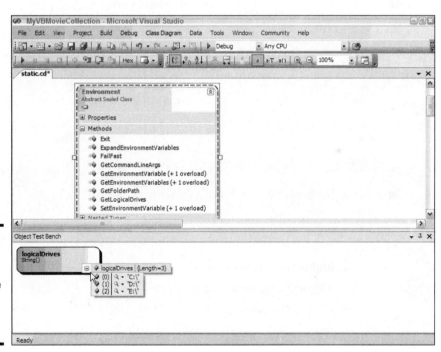

Figure 3-11:
The static method's return value appears in the Object Test Bench.

Chapter 4: Wiring Up Events in the User Interface

In This Chapter

✏ **Understanding events and event handlers**

✏ **Using Visual Studio to discover events**

✏ **Creating event handlers with Visual Studio**

✏ **Getting a grip on Windows and Web applications lifecycles**

*Y*ou create a Windows Form that requires a user to enter her username and password. You create a Web page with a drop-down list of state names that you want populated when the user browses to the page. You add a Print command to a menu that you want to execute the command to print a report. What do all these scenarios have in common?

All of these scenarios require some action to occur before your code can execute. A user must submit his credentials, a Web page loads, and a user clicks a menu command. The actions to which I am referring are called *events*.

You can probably think of several events off the top of your head: click, double-click, hover, and exit. You probably associate events with direct actions that a user takes to interact with your program. In reality, events go way beyond mere button clicking and mouse hovering. Events make it possible for your entire application and each form and control within the application to have its own lifecycle. From the moment your application fires up until the moment it shuts down, events are firing along the way.

As you already know, your code fires in response to events, such as button clicks. Taking advantage of the events in an application and control lifecycles make it possible for you to run code at a precise moment in an application's or control's lifecycle. Instead of waiting for a user to click a button, you can run code as soon as your application starts or even when a user's cursor leaves a text box.

Using Visual Studio, responding to events is as simple as a double-click, in many cases. Visual Studio generates codes behind the scenes that wire up your code to the event that fires it.

Handling Events

In most modern applications, the application responds to actions a user takes. Your application sits in a waiting state until a user comes along and clicks a button, a menu, or a drop-down list. When a user clicks a button, an action (the event) occurs, and the code that executes when an event fires is called an *event handler*.

An *event handler* is a procedure that runs when an event occurs. It's called an *event handler* because it handles events, but it's still a procedure like any procedure you write. You're responsible for writing event handlers to handle any events to which you wish to respond.

For instance, say you want a message box to pop up when a user clicks the OK button on your Windows Form. The following code sample uses Visual Basic syntax to make a message box appear:

```
MessageBox.Show("You clicked the OK button", "Handling
    Events", MessageBoxButtons.OK)
```

The question now is, where do you put that code? You know you want the message box to appear when the user clicks a button. You need to write an event handler for the button's `Click` event.

Right here is where you should stop me. How did I know that the code belongs in the button's `Click` event? Is it as simple as pulling the verb out of a sentence and calling it an event? Not quite.

Discovering events

Most of the documentation and articles that I read about events and event handling assume that the reader somehow magically knows what events they're supposed to write code for. Most people intuitively get the concept of click or double-click, but what about hover or paint?

In order for a button or some other component to have an event, someone must have written an event method for the component. The event method is the other side of the event handling story.

For example, the button you add to a Windows Form is actually the `Button` class in the `System.Windows.Forms` namespace. The button's `Click` event is the `Button` class's `Click` event method. An event method is a procedure in the same way that an event handler is a procedure. The difference is that the *event method* creates the event while the *event handler* responds to the event.

The class with the event method is called the *sender,* while the class with the event handler is called the *receiver.* When an event fires, it is said that the sender *raises* the event. The receiver *consumes* the event with an event handler.

By reducing events to methods in a class, all you have to do is refer to the class's documentation in order to figure out the set of events available to you. Of course, Visual Studio has a few tools you can use to help you in your quest:

+ **Properties window** — View the properties window of a component to see a list of the component's events.

+ **Code editor Navigation Bar** — Use the Navigation Bar at the top of the code editor to select an event.

+ **Help documentation** — Use the index or the Class Library Reference in the .NET Framework Software Development Kit (SDK) to locate documentation on a specific class.

The easiest way to discover events is to add a component to the Windows Forms Designer or the Web Forms Designer and view its properties. To do this:

1. **Create a new Windows or Web project or open an existing project.**

2. **Drag and drop a control or component from the Toolbox onto the form designer.**

The control or component appears in the designer.

Press Ctrl+Alt+X to open the toolbox if it's closed.

3. **Click the control or component to select it.**

4. **Press F4 to open the Properties window.**

The control or component's properties appear in the Properties window.

5. **Click the Events button on the Properties window toolbar to display a list of events available for the control or component.**

The Events button is the button with the lightning bolt.

The lightning bolt is the icon used to represent events in Visual Studio. You'll see the lightning bolt used in Object Browser, Class View, and the code editor's Navigation Bar.

Figure 4-1 shows an example of a button's properties in a Web site project. Notice that the button's class name appears in the drop-down list at the top of the Properties window. In this figure, the fully qualified class name for a Web button is `System.Web.UI.WebControls.Button`.

The class name is `Button`, and `System.Web.UI.WebControls` is the namespace used to access the `Button` class. You can use this information to look up the class documentation in Visual Studio's documentation.

Web projects and Windows projects use different controls. They might go by the same name, in the case of a button, but they're actually different classes. The fully qualified name for a Windows button is `System.Windows.Forms.Button`.

Figure 4-1:
A list of available events appears in the Properties window.

You can view list of events in the Visual Basic code editor's Navigation Bar. To view a list of events using the Navigation Bar, follow these steps:

1. **Repeat Steps 1 and 2 from the preceding step list.**

2. **Press F7 to open the code editor.**

3. **Click the Class Name drop-down list in the Navigation Bar.**

The Navigation Bar is at the top of the code editor.

4. **Select the control for which you wish to view events.**

5. **Click the Method Name drop-down list in the Navigation Bar.**

A list of events appears, as Figure 4-2 shows. Notice the lightning bolt icons next to the event names.

Having a list of event names is helpful, but it doesn't really tell you what the events do. You need to use the Visual Studio documentation to look up the class that creates the event. Before you can look up the event, you need to know the name of the class that creates the event. You can use the Properties window to get the fully qualified class name as shown in Figure 4-1.

Book V
Chapter 4

Wiring Up Events in
the User Interface

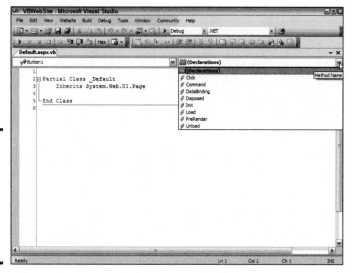

Figure 4-2:
A list of
events
appears in
the code
editor's
Navigation
Bar.

To look up event information in Visual Studio's help documentation:

1. **Choose Help⇨Index in Visual Studio.**

The index to the Visual Studio help documentation appears.

2. **Select .NET Framework in the Filtered By drop-down list.**

3. **Type the fully qualified class name in the Look For text box.**

The index jumps to the topic as you're typing.

4. **Click the index entry that corresponds to the class.**

The documentation appears in the document pane.

A list of hyperlinks to topics within the help documentation appears across the top of the pane.

5. **Click the Events hyperlink.**

A list of events for the class appears, as shown in Figure 4-3.

A description appears for each event. Click an event to view details documentation about the event method. You'll often find examples of how to write event handlers for the event method.

Your help documentation might look different if you have Visual Studio configured to view help integrated inside Visual Studio. Figure 4-3 shows the external help viewer. You can change your help settings by choosing Tools⇨ Options.

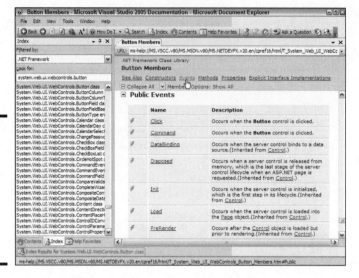

Figure 4-3:
View a class's event details in the Visual Studio documentation.

Wiring up events and event handlers

In order for your code to execute when an event fires, the event must have some way to know your event handler exists. You create a link between the event and the event handler that essentially says "When this event occurs, call me."

There are several ways to create a link between an event and an event handler. Well, really, there's only one way. You have to register your event handler with the event method, which means writing code. But hardly anyone bothers to register their own event handlers because you can use Visual Studio to generate the code for you.

The process of creating a link between an event and an event handler is called *wiring up the event handler*.

There are two steps to registering an event handler:

1. **Create the event handler.**

You place the code you want to execute when the event fires inside the event handler.

2. **Wire up the event handler to the event.**

Visual Studio takes care of both of these steps for you. There are two approaches you can take to register an event handler, depending on whether you're accessing default or nondefault events.

Every control or component designates a default event. The default event is usually the event most frequently fired for the control. For example, the Click event is the default event for a button on a Windows Form. It makes sense when you consider that buttons are clicked far more often than any other action.

Visual Studio makes it really easy to register an event handler for a default event. All you have to do is double-click a control in the Windows or Web Forms Designers. For example, if you double-click a button control in the Windows Forms Designer using C#, Visual Studio generates the following code:

✦ **Event handler**

```
private void button1_Click(object sender, EventArgs e)
{
}
```

The code block for the event handler appears in the code file for the Windows or Web Form.

Event handlers accept two arguments: a reference to the sender object that raised the event and any data associated with the event in the form of event arguments. Events that don't have any data use the EventArgs event data class provided by the .NET Framework. Any time you see a custom event data class such as MouseEventArgs e, you know there's probably data available that your event handler can use. Otherwise, it's safe to assume that the event doesn't have any data.

✦ **Wiring up the event handler to the event**

```
this.button1.Click += new System.EventHandler(this.button1_Click);
```

The preceding code isn't readily visible to the programmer. In the case of Windows applications, the code appears in the partial class with the file extension designer.cs or designer.vb. In Web sites, the code is generated when the page is run.

System.EventHandler is a delegate data type provided by the .NET Framework for wiring up event handlers to events. System.EventHandler is not actually an event handler. Rather, System.EventHandler acts as the go-between for the event handler and the event. The event has no knowledge of the event handlers sitting out there waiting to handle the event. The event does have knowledge of the System.EventHandler delegate. System.EventHandler holds a reference to your event handler, which it passes along to the event.

You can use Visual Studio to generate event handlers and wire them to events for nondefault events, too. To create event handlers for nondefault events, follow these steps:

1. **Open the Properties window for the control or component for which you wish to handle an event.**

See the preceding sections for an example of using the Properties window to view events.

2. **Locate the event for which you wish to create an event handler.**

3. **In the property grid, type the name of the event handler you want to create, as shown in Figure 4-4.**

Alternatively, you can select an existing event handler from the drop-down list. You can also double-click the grid to create an event handler with a default name.

The default name used by Visual Studio for event handlers is *variableName_Event*. For example, the Click event for button1 is button1_Click.

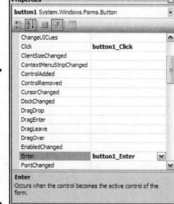

Figure 4-4: Use the Properties window to add event handlers for nondefault events.

Of course, an alternative approach to using the Properties window or the forms designer is to write your own event handler and wire the handler to the event. I've already shown you the syntax for C#. What follows is the syntax for Visual Basic:

```
Friend WithEvents Button1 As System.Windows.Forms.Button

Private Sub Button1_Click(ByVal sender As System.Object,
    ByVal e As System.EventArgs) Handles Button1.Click

End Sub
```

Get a Lifecycle

When I started developing ASP.NET applications, I was overwhelmed by the number and order of events that fired every time a user browsed to a Web page. Once I took the time to understand the lifecycle of ASP.NET applications and their resources, such as Web pages and Web services, figuring out when I wanted my code to execute was a snap.

Each kind of application has its own lifecycle events with which you should be familiar. ASP.NET applications, Windows applications, and mobile applications all have their own sets of controls and application lifecycles. If you specialize in one of these kinds of applications, you need to understand what happens when a user fires up your application.

Understanding lifecycles in Windows applications

Sometimes, waiting for an end user to click a button before your code executes is too late. For example, it's common to want to retrieve data from a database to populate a drop-down list. If you want the drop-down list populated before the user clicks a button, you need to find a different event to handle.

When your application starts up, a series of events fire off. These events call the main form in your application, which in turn adds controls such as the text boxes, menus, and buttons you dragged onto the form. Each control fires its own series of events as it goes about the business of drawing itself on the screen. The events of the application, main form, and controls describe a lifecycle that you can use to insert your own code via event handlers.

When your application starts, the main form and controls in your application go through the following events:

✦ **HandleCreated** — Provisions resources from Windows for the control.

✦ **Load** — Occurs before the form or control appears for the first time.

✦ **Layout** — Occurs when child controls are added.

✦ **Activated** — Occurs when the form is active.

✦ **Shown** — Occurs the first time a form is displayed.

The events listed previously do not include every event that fires. There are even more events. As you can see, you have a lot of opportunities to control what happens as forms and controls are appearing. For example, it's fairly common to use the Load event to provision resources for controls on the form. You might hit a database and populate a drop-down list during a form's Load event.

Events aren't limited just to startup. Several events occur during shutdown, such as:

✦ **FormClosing** — Occurs as the form is closing.

✦ **FormClosed** — Occurs once the form has closed.

✦ **Deactivate** — Occurs when the form loses focus and is no longer active.

Events don't occur sequentially for parent and child controls. That is, you don't step through the form's events and then through the controls on the form. Rather, the events are nested. For example, imagine you have a form with a button and a text box. The HandleCreated event occurs three times — once for each control. The form's HandleCreated event occurs first, and then the button's and then the text box's. The form goes through its load, layout, activated, and shown events.

Forms are derived from the control class. So forms are controls like buttons and text boxes. Forms share a lot of events with other kinds of controls.

One final event, ApplicationExit, occurs before your application shuts down. You can use the ApplicationExit of the Application class to perform any cleanup tasks before your application shuts down.

Visual Basic provides its own set of language-specific events for application startup and shutdown, called MyApplication. To use MyApplication, follow these steps:

1. **Right-click your project in Solution Explorer.**

2. **Choose Properties from the shortcut menu.**

   The Project Designer appears.

3. **Click View Application Events on the Application tab.**

   Visual Basic's MyApplication class appears in the code editor.

4. **Add an event using the code editor's Navigation Bar, as shown in Figure 4-5.**

Between startup and shutdown, any number of events might occur on forms and controls. Examples include Paint, Lostfocus, and Leave. Many seemingly simple activities have several events that make it happen. For example, consider a button click. Before the button's Click event occurs, the MouseEnter, MouseDown, and MouseClick events occur. After the click happens, the MouseUp event fires.

As you can see, you have plenty of opportunities to jump in and execute code without waiting on an end user to come along and interact with your program.

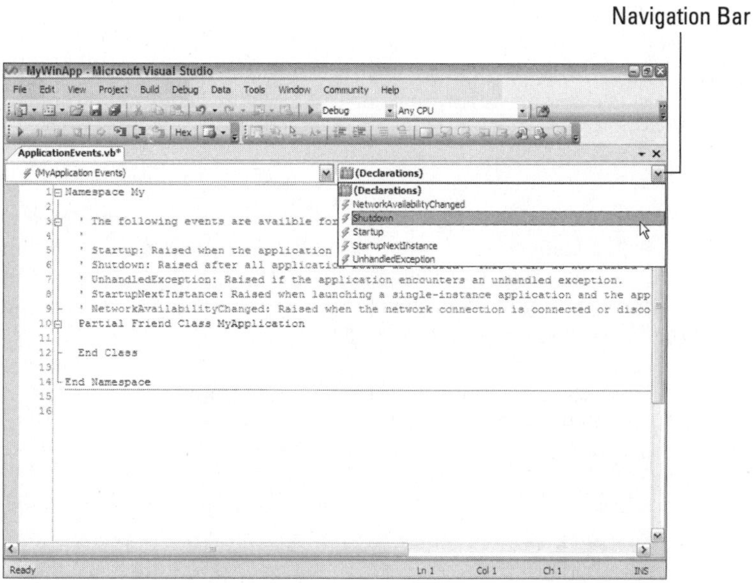

Navigation Bar

Figure 4-5:
Use Visual
Basic's
MyAppli-
cation
events to
access
application
startup and
shutdown.

You might be asking yourself which events to use and in which order they should occur. Sometimes, you can figure it out just by reading a class's documentation, as described in the earlier section "Discovering events." Other options are to

✦ **Add event handlers for the events you're trying to discover.** You can use the debugger to step through the event handlers as code executes, write output to a file when the handler fires, or display text on a form.

✦ **Use reflection to discover events.** *Reflection* is a feature of the .NET Framework that essentially asks your code to look in a mirror and describe itself.

Sample code on the GotDotNet Web site uses reflection to write event information to a file. The code sample is called `EventSpy`, and you can find it at `www.gotdotnet.com/community/usersamples/Default.aspx?query=eventspy`.

Understanding Web page lifecycles

You're sitting at your home in Denver, Colorado, where you browse to a Web page created using ASP.NET. Your request for a Web page must travel from your browser to a Web server in Kansas. The challenge in ASP.NET Web pages is getting the event from the client in Colorado to the server in Kansas. Thankfully, ASP.NET handles most of the details of making this work for you.

Nevertheless, it's important to understand some concepts related to events in ASP.NET. At first blush, the event model seems similar to Windows applications. You double-click a control in the Web Forms Designer, and Visual Studio creates an event handler in your source code. In reality, it's more complicated than that. Many people get confused when their code doesn't execute as they expect it to.

Web pages are *stateless,* which means that ASP.NET forgets what it's processed from page to page. Each request for a Web page is independent from previous requests. Of course, this isn't the experience that you have as an end user. You must understand a few concepts as a developer to keep this process transparent to your end users.

✦ **View state** — This is a hidden field in your Web page that stores data associated with a Web page's controls, such as the value in a text box.

ASP.NET 2.0 introduces a new view state feature called *control state.* Control state stores a limited set of a control's property data.

✦ **Postback** — This refers to an action that occurs when a Web page sends data back to the server for processing. Clicking a submit button on a form is an example of a postback.

✦ **Render** — Web browsers don't understand the declarative syntax of ASP.NET or server-side code written using C# or Visual Basic. As a result, Web pages must be converted to, or *rendered,* as HTML.

The ASP.NET lifecycle starts when someone uses a Web browser to request a Web page. The ASP.NET lifecycle includes three players:

✦ **Application** — The Web page request is sandwiched in a set of `Application` events that set up and tear down an environment to host and fulfill the client's request.

✦ **Page** — The Web page has its own lifecycle where it builds itself and prepares the HTML that makes its way to the browser.

✦ **Controls** — Each server control has a lifecycle that creates the control on the page.

Unlike Windows applications, Web pages live and die in one sitting. That is, the lifecycles for the application, page, and controls last a matter of seconds. Each time a page is requested, the application, page, and controls are built, sent to the browser, and then discarded.

Let's examine these lifecycles a little more closely so we can know what's going on. The very first request for a resource such as a Web page for an ASP.NET Web site results in the `ApplicationManager` being created for the entire Web site. The `ApplicationManager` sets up a hosting environment in which all subsequent requests are processed. This hosting environment is called an *application domain*. Each ASP.NET Web site operates in its own exclusive application domain.

Each request is handled within its own application inside the application domain. The application steps through a number of events that set up the execution environment to process the request, such as:

✦ **BeginRequest** — Occurs before any other event during the processing of a request.

✦ **AuthenticateRequest** — Establishes the identity of the user.

✦ **AuthorizeRequest** — Ensures that the user has permission to process the request.

✦ **PreRequestHandlerExecute** — Occurs before an event handler is called to process the request.

At this point, the request is processed. For example, a request to a Web page calls the Web page's constructor, or a request to a Web service calls the Web service's constructor.

If the page has already been called once, it might be stored in the ASP.NET cache. As a result, the request might be fulfilled from the cache rather than calling the resource each and every time a request is made.

An ASP.NET Web page has its own lifecycle that it uses to fulfill the request. Here it is:

✦ **Page_PreInit** — Determines whether this is a new request or a postback request.

✦ **Page_Init** — Controls are available and accessible via each control's `UniqueID` property.

✦ **Page_Load** — Control properties are populated from view state and control state if the request is a postback.

✦ **Execute control events** — If the request is a postback, controls which postback events, such as a button click, are fired.

✦ **Page_PreRender** — Last chance to make final changes to the page before its view state is saved.

✦ **Page_Render** — View state is added to the page and each control renders itself to HTML.

✦ **Page_Unload** — The page has been sent to the Web browser and is ready to be discarded.

After the page is discarded, the application wraps up the request processing by saving state data if required and updating the cache. The final event is the EndRequest event.

You'll interact with three kinds of events the most:

+ **Postback events** — When users interact with your Web page by selecting items in drop-down lists and clicking buttons, it causes your Web page to post back to the server.

+ **Page setup events** — You use page setup events such as Page_Load to perform tasks such as populate controls with data from databases respond to postbacks.

+ **Application events** — You use application-level events to perform initial startup and shutdown tasks and handle errors.

Handling postback events

When a user interacts with your Web page and sends data back to the server, it's called a *postback*. Postback events fire after the Web page's Page_Load event. Handling postback events is similar to handling events in Windows Forms.

Postback events, such as a button click, occur after the Web page's Page_Load event.

To create an event handler for a default event, you double-click the control in the Web Form's designer. You use the Properties window to event handlers for nondefault events. See the section, "Wiring up events and event handlers" for more details on creating event handlers with Visual Studio.

One thing that Visual Studio does that's different for ASP.NET Web page event handlers is that it adds the event handler to the Web server control's declaration in the ASP.NET page. For example, assume you double-click a button in the Web Forms Designer. Visual Studio creates an event handler called Button1_Click. Visual Studio ties the event handler to the Web server's declaration using the OnClick attribute, as shown in the following snippet:

```
<asp:Button ID="Button1" runat="server" OnClick="Button1_
    Click" Text="Button" />
```

It's not necessary to designate an event handler for a button's Click event. The default behavior of a button that is clicked is to post back to the server. If you want code to execute in response to the Click event, you place it inside the button's Click event handler. Other postback events fire after the button's Click event handler.

You aren't restricted to processing just button clicks. You can respond to other events, such as when an item is selected from a drop-down list. The default event for a drop-down list is `SelectedIndexChanged`. This event allows you to capture the value a user selects from a drop-down list. For example, the following code uses the `SelectedValue` property of a drop-down list to place the selected value in a text box:

```
protected void DropDownList1_SelectedIndexChanged(object
    sender, EventArgs e)
{

    this.TextBox1.Text = this.DropDownList1.SelectedValue;

}
```

When the user selects a value from the drop-down list, it appears in the text box, as Figure 4-6 shows. The user must click the Submit button first in order to cause the page to postback.

Figure 4-6:
This event fires when the page posts back to the server.

The value appears after the page does a postback.

An important concept in handling postbacks and postback events is to query the Web page's `IsPostback` property. The property returns `true` if the request is the result of a postback. It's common to check the `IsPostBack` property during the `Page_Load` event.

For example, assume you need to load items into a drop-down list. You create a procedure called `LoadItems`, as shown in the following code:

```
private void LoadItems()
{
  this.DropDownList1.Items.Add("Hello World");
  this.DropDownList1.Items.Add("Goodbye");
}
```

You assume you can call `LoadItems()` in the `Page_Load` event. Unfortunately, when you do that, your `LoadItems()` procedure is called every time the page posts back. This results in your drop-down list being loaded every time. The `IsPostBack` property allows you to test whether the page is posting back. The `IsPostBack` is a Boolean property, which means it returns one of two values:

✦ **True** — If you want your code to execute every time after the page's first load, you use this statement.

In C#, it looks like this:-

```
If (Page.IsPostback == true)
```

In Visual Basic, it looks like this:

```
If Page.IsPostBack = True Then
End If
```

✦ **False** — If you want your code to run only the first time the user accesses it, you test the `IsPostBack` property for false.

Alternatively, you can use C#'s not operator `!`, as shown here:

```
If(!Page.IsPostBack)
```

Using the Visual Basic keyword `Not` looks like this:

```
If Not Page.IsPostBack Then
End If
```

You just include your code inside the `If` clause, as the following code shows:

```
protected void Page_Load(object sender, EventArgs e)
{
  if (Page.IsPostBack == false)
    LoadItems();
}
```

Many controls have an `AutoPostBack` property you can enable. When this property is enabled, the control causes a postback without requiring the user to click a button.

Handling application events

Sometimes you need to capture an event that's related to the application. For example, you might want to log the first time an application starts or when errors occur. ASP.NET provides application-level events for which you can write event handlers.

You write event handlers in the global application class file. The global application class file is named global.asax. To add the global.asax file to your Web site:

1. **Right-click on your Web site folder in Solution Explorer.**

2. **Click Add New Item from the shortcut menu.**

   The Add New Item window appears.

3. **Click the Global Application Class icon.**

   Leave the name of the file as global.asax.

4. **Click the Add button.**

   The file opens in the Documents pane, as Figure 4-7 shows.

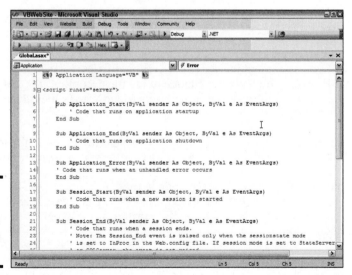

Figure 4-7:
Place application-level events in this file.

There are several application-level events you can add to the global.asax file, including the following:

✦ **Application_Start** — Fires only the very first time a Web site is accessed.

✦ `Application_End` — Fires only once before the entire Web site is shut down.

✦ `Application_Error` — Fires any time an unhandled exception occurs.

Global.asax derives from the `HttpApplication` class. As a result, Global. asax supports all the events of the `HttpApplication` class. `Application_ Start` and `Application_End` are special events that aren't part of the `HttpApplication` class. ASP.NET knows to fire these two events at the very beginning and the very end of a Web site's lifecycle.

`Application_Error` is your last opportunity to catch unhandled exceptions in your ASP.NET applications. It's common practice to use `Application_ Error` as the event handler to place code that you want executed every single time an execution is thrown.

For example, assume you have a `Try/Catch` block in your Web page. In your `Catch` clause, you simply use the `throw` statement, as shown here:

```
Try
 'some code here
Catch ex As Exception
 'attempt to handle the exception
 Throw
End Try
```

The `throw` statement passes the exception to `Application_Error` event handler where you have the chance to log the exception. `Application_ Error` allows you to pass your user to a friendly error message page, if appropriate.

Be sure to use `Server.ClearError()` to clear the exception before you pass the caller from `Application_Error` to another page in your application.

Global.asax allows you to place code in the `Session_Start` and `Session_End` event handlers. `Session_Start` is a very reliable event you can use to log that a new session has started. You can use `Session_End` to clean up resources.

There are many additional events available to you in the application lifecycle. Unfortunately, not all these events fire consistently. The only event that's guaranteed to fire, besides the three application events mentioned earlier, is `Application_EndRequest`.

Chapter 5: Getting Productive with Visual Studio 2005

In This Chapter

✔ Analyzing your code with FxCop

✔ Digging into the new IntelliSense features

✔ Creating XML documentation from code comments

✔ Refactoring C# code

*T*he promise of the latest suite of Visual Studio products is personal productivity. The features covered in this chapter show you how to take your productivity with Visual Studio 2005 to the next level.

I show you how to use Visual Studio 2005 Professional to analyze your code with FxCop. I show you the new code snippets and refactoring features. If you're new to object-oriented programming, Visual Studio 2005 has several new IntelliSense features that make light work of turning your code into objects.

Sending Your Code to Boot Camp

Have you ever wondered how some developers know what to name their variables and custom data types? Is there some secret society where all the in-the-know developers get memos on when to use a field instead of a property? Actually, there is — sort of.

Attending the naming convention

The .NET Framework Software Developer Kit (SDK) contains a document called the Design Guidelines for Class Library Developers. Even though the design guidelines are for class library developers, you can take advantage of the recommendations in the guidelines when writing your own code. Some of the topics covered in the guidelines include:

✦ Naming conventions

✦ Using data types and class members

✦ Handling errors and raising exceptions

If nothing else, the naming conventions outlined in the design guidelines are very helpful. I find that using naming conventions makes it very easy to quickly identify the purpose of a block of code just by looking at how it's named. It also reinforces the concepts in object-oriented programming because you associate certain naming conventions with specific OOP constructs.

The following two case standards are used the most in naming conventions:

+ **Camel casing** — First letter is lowercase and first letter of a concatenated word is uppercase, as in `dogBark`.

+ **Pascal casing** — First letter is uppercase and first letter of a concatenated word is uppercase, as in `DogBark`.

Table 5-1 shows some of the naming guidelines that use camel and pascal casing.

Table 5-1		Naming Guidelines
Case	*Identifier*	*Example*
Camel	Fields	`customerName`
	Local variables	`employeeID`
	Parameters	`updateSql`
Pascal	Class	`Customer`
	Method	`ValidateAddress()`
	Property	`CompanyName`

Other examples of conventions include prefixing the letter `I` to interfaces such as `IEnumerable` and appending the word `Exception` to derived exceptions such as `NullReferenceException`.

You should use the keywords `Me` (in Visual Basic) and `this` (in C#) to distinguish between fields and local variables. For example, the following code uses a local string variable named `text` and a field named `greetingName` in a method, as shown here:

```
Public Function DisplayMessage() As String
  Dim text As String

  If String.IsNullOrEmpty(Me.greetingName) Then
     text = SayHello()
  Else
     text = SayHelloName()
  End If
```

```
    Return text
End Function
```

One convention not covered in the design guidelines is how to name controls. Many developers still use Hungarian notation-style prefixes in front of their controls — such as `txt` for *text box* or `btn` for *button*. If you want to do that, you can, as long as you're consistent. I like to use a single prefix for all controls, such as `UI` for *user interface*. I've seen developers start to use `UX` for *user experience*. Either way, all your controls are grouped together, as shown in Figure 5-1.

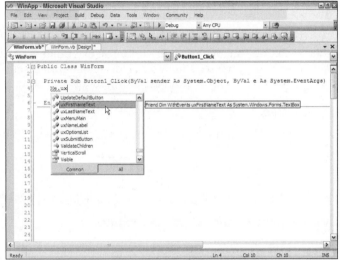

Figure 5-1:
Using a single prefix on all user interface controls groups them together.

You can find a list of Hungarian naming conventions for Visual Basic in Microsoft's knowledge base at `http://support.microsoft.com/kb/q173738`. Charles Simonyi created the concept of using prefixes to identify variables. He's originally from Hungary, which is why this style of notation is called Hungarian notation. See Chapter 1 in Book VII to read more about what Charles is up to now and what it has to do with Visual Studio.

Search for the topic "Class Library Design Guidelines" in the Visual Studio documentation to access the complete guidelines.

Calling all cars! FxCop to the rescue!

I know what you're thinking: You don't have time to read a bunch of rules. You have deadlines. You get paid to bang out code, not read rulebooks. And you certainly don't have the discipline it takes to review your code for compliance to rules.

What you need is a cop — someone who can police your code and tell you when you violate the rules. FxCop is a code analysis tool that you can download free from the GotDotNet Web site. FxCop analyzes your code for conformance to the .NET Design Guidelines for Class Library Developers.

You can download the software at `www.gotdotnet.com/team/fxcop`. Be sure to download the version that targets version 2.0 of the .NET Framework.

Visual Studio Team System has integrated support for code analysis using FxCop.

FxCop analyzes compiled assemblies. You need to build your project at least once before FxCop can analyze your code. You can build your project using the Build menu. See Chapter 1 in Book VI for an in-depth discussion of builds. To use FxCop to analyze an assembly, follow these steps:

1. **Open FxCop.**

Access FxCop from the All Programs menu of your Start button.

2. **From the Project menu, click Add Targets.**

The Open window appears.

The assemblies you want to analyze are called *targets* in FxCop.

3. **Browse to the location of your assemblies.**

Note that assemblies are located in the Bin folder in your solution's directory.

4. **Select the assembly you wish to analyze and click the Open button.**

The assembly appears in FxCop. (Press the Shift key to select multiple assemblies.)

5. **Choose Analyze from the Project menu.**

The FxCop engine analyzes your assemblies. The results appear in FxCop.

6. **Browse through the list of warnings and select one to view its details.**

The first time you use FxCop, you'll likely be overwhelmed by the volume of messages. I like to sort the list by the Rules column while I step through and examine the messages.

When you click a message in FxCop, a description of the message appears. The description provides you with:

✦ Member under inspection

✦ Hyperlink to the source code

✦ Problem description and suggestion resolutions

✦ Hyperlink to an online help description of the problem and resolution

Figure 5-2 shows a warning triggered by a violation of the Test for empty strings using string length rule in the Movie Collection Starter Kit.

Figure 5-2:
FxCop
provides
detailed
descriptions
of the
problems
discovered
and
suggests
resolutions.

When you click the source code hyperlink, the offending code opens in Visual Studio. Sure enough, the code tests for an empty string instead of using `String.IsNullOrEmpty`, as shown in the following code:

```
if (singleString == "")
{
  singleString = part;
}
```

By changing the code to the following, the warning goes away:

```
if (string.IsNullOrEmpty(singleString))
{
  singleString = part;
}
```

If you decide there's a certain rule you don't care about enforcing, you can choose to exclude the rule. To exclude the rule, right-click the message and choose Exclude, as Figure 5-3 shows.

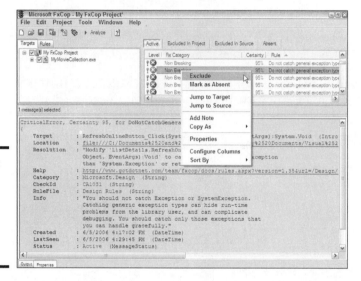

Figure 5-3: Exclude rules that aren't relevant for your situation.

> **TIP**
>
> If you don't like the rules included with FxCop, you can create your own. See the documentation for FxCop for more information.

Setting up FxCop as an external tool

FxCop features a command-line version that you can include in build scripts or integrate into Visual Studio as an external tool. To integrate FxCop as an external tool in Visual Studio, just follow these steps:

1. **Click External Tools from the Tools menu.**

   The External Tools window appears.

2. **Click the Add button.**

3. **Type** Run FxCop **in the Title field.**

4. **Browse to the FxCop command-line executable for the Command field.**

   The default value is C:\Program Files\Microsoft FxCop 1.35\FxCopCmd.exe.

5. **Type arguments that you normally use on the command line.**

   For example, to analyze files using the solution's build directory, use the argument variable $(TargetDir). You can click the arrow next to the Arguments field to select an argument variable, as shown in Figure 5-4.

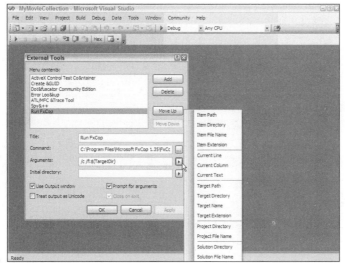

Figure 5-4:
Add FxCop
as an
external tool
in Visual
Studio.

6. **Enable the Use Output Window and Prompt for Arguments check boxes.**

7. **Click the OK button.**

   Run FxCop appears from the Tools menu.

You can run FxCop by clicking RunFxCop from the Tools menu. The output appears in the Output window, as Figure 5-5 shows. You can double-click an entry to view the source code.

It's Not Your Father's IntelliSense Any More

For years, developers have been using homegrown tools and utilities such as CodeSmith to generate repetitive code. The IntelliSense features in Visual Studio 2005 do way more than generate repetitive code. IntelliSense supports coding styles such as test-driven development (TDD) and object-oriented programming (OOP). If your style is copy and paste, IntelliSense has a tool for you, too.

Figure 5-5:
With FxCop as an external tool, you can view analysis output in the Output window.

Using code snippets

A major goal for almost all development projects is to increase code reuse. IntelliSense code snippets are a perfect example of reuse in its simplest form.

Code snippets are like copy and paste on steroids. Using shortcut keywords or a menu, you can browse a library containing hundreds of code samples that you can insert into your code. Best of all, the code samples work like templates that highlight the fields where you need to insert code specific to your application.

For example, I always forget the syntax for Select statements. I can use a code snippet to refresh my memory. To insert a Select code snippet in Visual Basic, simply follow these steps:

1. **Position your cursor where you want the code inserted.**

2. **Type** select **and press the Tab key.**

A code snippet appears in the code editor, as Figure 5-6 shows.

The blocks highlighted in green indicate where you place your values.

3. **Type your values.**

Press Tab to maneuver between the highlighted blocks.

In the preceding example, I use the code snippet's shortcut to access the snippet. If you don't know the shortcut, you can select a snippet using the following options:

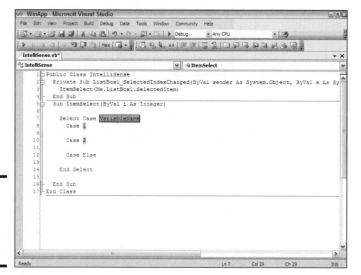

Figure 5-6:
The code
snippet
appears as
a template.

✦ Choose Edit➪IntelliSense➪Insert Snippet.

✦ Right-click the code editor and select Insert Snippet from the shortcut menu.

✦ In Visual Basic, type a question mark (**?**) and then press the Tab key.

It's important to position your cursor where you want the snippet to appear in the code editor. If you just want to browse snippets without selecting a snippet, use the Code Snippets Manager. You access the manager by choosing Code Snippets Manager from the Tools menu.

The Code Snippets Manager allows you to access snippets for many programming languages in one screen. The manager displays a snippet's location, description, and shortcut. *Snippet files* use XML syntax and end in the file extension .snippet. You can add snippet files you create or download from the Web using the Code Snippets Manager, as shown in Figure 5-7.

When you access code snippets via a menu, you use the Code Snippets Picker. Snippets are organized into folders in Visual Basic. C# provides a list of snippets. To access a snippet via the Code Snippets Picker, do the following:

1. **Position your cursor where you want to insert the code snippet.**

2. **Right-click the code editor.**

A shortcut menu appears.

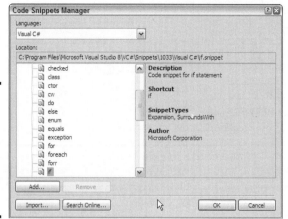

Figure 5-7:
Use the
Code
Snippets
Manager to
browse and
add code
snippets.

3. **Choose Insert Snippets.**

    The Code Snippet Picker appears.

4. **Select a snippet from the list.**

    The snippet appears in the code editor.

    In Visual Basic, use the Tab key to navigate the folders until you find the snippet you need.

    If you hover your mouse over the snippet, you'll see the snippet's shortcut, for future reference, as Figure 5-8 shows.

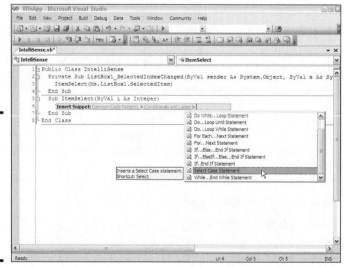

Figure 5-8:
Use the
Code
Snippet
Picker to
find a
snippet and
view its
shortcut.

Visual Basic provides a broader range of snippets for everything from basic language constructs to accessing resources in Windows. The C# snippets are limited to flow control and data type and member declaration snippets. C# has a folder of refactoring snippets that you see demonstrated in the section "Factoring in the Refactoring" later in this chapter.

Stub it out with method stubs

One of the complaints about development environments like Visual Studio is that it requires you to define everything from the bottom up. Some people complain that this style requires you to dig into the minutiae before you've had a chance to see the big picture of how your program should be laid out. A new IntelliSense feature that allows you to generate method stubs from a method call makes it easy to stay focused.

A *code stub* is a placeholder for an unimplemented piece of code.

Generating method stubs is common in test-driven development (TDD). Adherents to TDD believe you should write tests first. You can use Intelli-Sense to generate method stubs from unit tests.

In essence, the Generate Method Stub feature allows you to use a method call before you write it. You invoke the Generate Method Stub feature to generate the method's declaration from the method call.

To create a new method stub from a method call, perform the following steps:

1. **Create a method call in your code.**

Be sure to specify any parameters. If you want the method stub to return a value, assign the method call to a variable of the correct data type.

For example, the following method call accepts a string parameter and returns a string:

```
string s = DisplayWelcomeMessage("John");
```

2. **Right-click the method call and choose Generate Method Stub from the shortcut menu.**

IntelliSense generates the method stub, as Figure 5-9 shows.

Note that the method body throws an exception if the method is called.

Adding using statements

If you're like me, you start typing away in the code editor and forget to reference all the namespaces you need with a `using` statement.

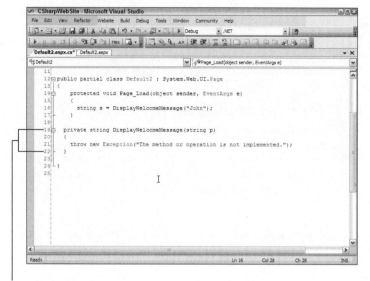

Figure 5-9:
IntelliSense can generate a method stub from a method call.

The method stub

IntelliSense has a feature that adds `using` statements for data types that aren't fully qualified. This can be helpful when you access a type without adding the `using` statement or copy code from another resource, such as a sample on the Web.

To add a `using` statement:

1. **Add an unbound data type to your code.**

   For example, the following code uses the `SqlCommand` without fully qualifying the namespace:

   ```
   SqlCommand cmd = new SqlCommand();
   ```

2. **Position your cursor on the last letter of the data type.**

3. **Hover your mouse over the last letter of the data type.**

   A smart tag appears.

4. **Click the smart tag and select the `using` statement, as shown in Figure 5-10.**

   Visual Studio adds the `using` statement to the top of the source code file.

   For example, the following statement is added for the `SqlCommand` type:

   ```
   using System.Data.SqlClient;
   ```

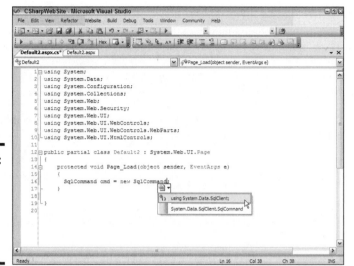

Figure 5-10:
Add a
`using`
statement
for an
unbound
data type.

This feature works for only C# `using` statements. You can't use it with Visual Basic `Imports` statements.

Objectifying your code

IntelliSense provides several features that make quick work of common, object-oriented tasks. In OOP, a number of abstract elements are defined. Developers are responsible for writing the code that implements the abstract elements. The concrete implementations are said to *inherit,* or *implement,* the abstract elements.

Abstract classes and interfaces are two abstract elements used in object-oriented programming. You inherit from an abstract class and implement an interface.

The process of inheriting or implementing from abstract elements requires a lot of typing. For example, assume you want to inherit from an abstract class that has ten members. You have to re-create all ten members in your derived class.

IntelliSense provides features that copy abstract methods to your concrete classes. You can access these features from a shortcut menu in the code editor or the Class Designer.

Implementing abstract classes

An abstract class defines a class that is used for inheritance only. You can't create an instance of an abstract class. Rather, you must create a new class that inherits from or implements the abstract class. The class you implement is called a *concrete class* because you can create an instance of the class.

IntelliSense provides a feature that makes quick work of inheriting from an abstract base class. To inherit from an abstract class:

1. **Create a new concrete class.**

2. **Type a colon (:) after the class name declaration.**

   For example, assume you want to create a new class called RssReader that inherits from the abstract class XmlReader. Type the following:

   ```
   public class RssReader: System.Xml.XmlReader
   ```

3. **Right-click the abstract class and choose Implement Abstract Class from the shortcut menu.**

   IntelliSense creates method stubs for all the members of the abstract class.

   Figure 5-11 shows the concrete class RssReader in the Object Browser. The class inherits from XmlReader and has all the same methods.

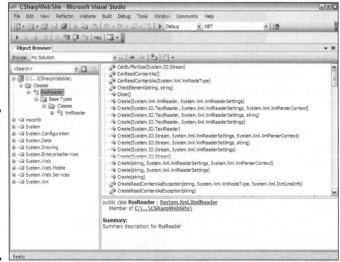

Figure 5-11: IntelliSense adds the methods from the abstract class to the concrete class.

Implementing interfaces

An *interface* is a data type that lists a set of methods. The interface doesn't actually provide the code for the methods. The implementation of the interface occurs within a class you create. Many classes can implement a single interface, and any class can implement multiple interfaces. The interface creates a contract that defines what the methods look like in a class.

To implement interfaces using IntelliSense:

1. **Create a new class.**

2. **Type a colon (:) after the class name declaration.**

3. **Type the name of the interfaces you wish to implement.**

   For example, the following class header implements the `IFormatProvider` and `ICustomFormatter` interfaces:

   ```
   public class RssReader: IFormatProvider,
       ICustomFormatter
   ```

4. **Right-click the interface's name in the header.**

   A shortcut menu appears.

5. **Choose Implement Interface from the shortcut menu.**

   IntelliSense adds stubs for the methods from the interface.

   Figure 5-12 shows a class that implements the `IFormatProvider` and `ICustomFormatter` interfaces.

Overriding members

At times, you want to provide a different implementation of a method in your new class than what's provided in the base class. For example, assume you create a new class `Dog` that inherits from the base class `Animal`. `Animal` class provides a `Vocalize` method that defines what it means for an animal to "speak." You want to change the implementation of `Vocalize` in your `Dog` class so that you can make the dog bark.

Providing another implementation of a method requires two elements:

✦ **In the base class,** the method must use the keyword `virtual`.

   For example, the following code creates a `virtual` method in the `Animal` class:

   ```
   public virtual void Vocalize()
   {
       //some code here
   }
   ```

The class header

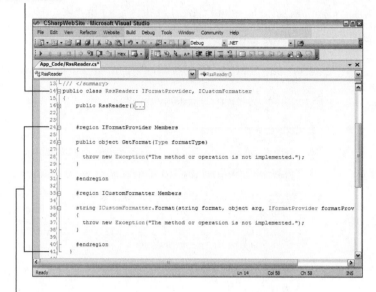

Figure 5-12:
IntelliSense
stubs out
methods
when you
implement
an interface.

The method stubs

✦ **In the derived class,** the method must use the keyword `override`.

The following code creates a new implementation of the base class's
`virtual` method created in the derived class `Dog`:

```
public override void Vocalize()
{
   base.Vocalize();
}
```

You can use IntelliSense to display a list of methods that can be overridden
and create method stubs for you. To use IntelliSense to override methods,
follow these steps:

1. **Create a new class.**

Note that all classes implicitly derive from `System.Object`. As a result,
your class can override methods of `System.Object`.

See Chapter 3 in this mini-book for recommendations on overriding
`System.Object`.

2. **Position your cursor in the code editor where you want to insert the
new method.**

3. **Type the keyword** `override` **and press the spacebar.**

   A list of methods that can be overridden appears, as shown in Figure 5-13.

4. **Select a method to override.**

   The method stub appears in the code editor.

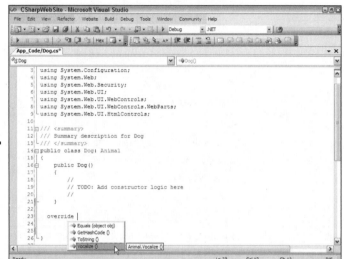

Figure 5-13:
Use
IntelliSense
to select a
virtual
method to
override.

Creating XML Documentation

You probably know that you're supposed to comment and document your code. If you're like most developers, you probably don't take the time to actually do it. IntelliSense and the .NET language compilers make it easy for you to turn your lowly code comments into documentation.

Creating documentation for your code requires you to use the following:

✦ **Comment markers** — Each language has its own comment marker for creating documentation. The comment marker in Visual Basic is three, single-quotation marks (' ' '). The C# comment marker is three forward slashes (///).

✦ **XML tags** — Each language defines a set of recommended XML tags you should use to define your comments, but you can use any well-formed XML tag you wish. Table 5-2 lists some of the recommended XML tags for Visual Basic and C#.

Table 5-2	Code Documentation XML Tags
XML Tag	**Description**
`<c>`	Marks comment as code.
`<code>`	Marks multiple lines of comments as code.
`<example>`	Identifies comment as an example of how to use the documented code.
`<exception>`	Shows exceptions that can be thrown.
`<include>`	Refers to another file containing documentation.
`<list>`	Creates a bulleted or numbered list or table in your documentation.
`<para>`	Denotes a paragraph.
`<param>`	Describes a parameter used in a method declaration.
`<paramref>`	Creates a reference in your documentation to a parameter.
`<permission>`	Grants document access permissions to a member.
`<remarks>`	Adds supplementation information.
`<returns>`	Describes a return value.
`<see>`	Creates a hyperlink to another type or member.
`<seealso>`	Specifies text to appear in a See Also section.
`<summary>`	Provides a brief description of the type or member.
`<typeparam>`	Describes a type parameter for a generic type.
`<typeparamref>`	Refers to a type parameter for a generic type.
`<value>`	Describes the value a property represents.

Like all XML tags, you place your text inside opening and closing tags. For example, the code that follows shows a code comment in Visual Basic and the class header it describes:

```
''' <summary>
''' This class provides a Hello World greeting.
''' </summary>
''' <remarks>Created as an example.</remarks>
Public Class HelloWorld
```

The code editor provides a documentation template when you add comment markers. To add documentation comments to your source code, do this:

1. **Position your cursor above the type or member you wish to document.**

2. **Type the comment marker for your programming language.**

   A documentation template appears in your source code, as Figure 5-14 shows.

Figure 5-14:
The code editor adds a document template when you type code comment markers.

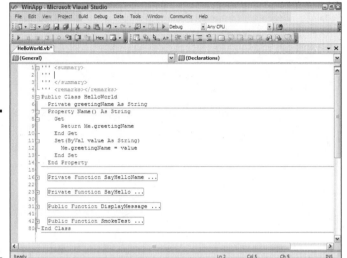

3. Type your comments in between the opening and closing XML tags.

The documentation template provided depends on whether you're documenting a type or a member. For example, Visual Basic supplies the following template for a method:

```
'''  <summary>
'''
'''  </summary>
'''  <returns></returns>
'''  <remarks></remarks>
```

The code comments you add appear in IntelliSense, or you can output the comments as XML documentation. Figure 5-15 shows an example of a code comment in the IntelliSense List Members feature.

Outputting your code comments as XML documentation is a feature of your language's compiler. You can turn on XML documentation in the Visual Studio Project Designer. To enable XML documentation using the Project Designer, do the following:

1. Right-click your project in Solution Explorer.

A shortcut menu appears.

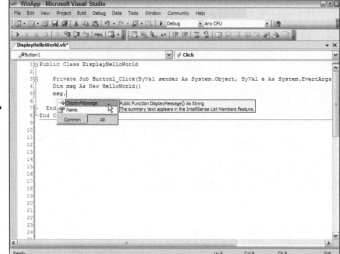

Figure 5-15:
Code
comments
appear
in the
IntelliSense
List
Members
feature.

2. **Choose Properties.**

   The Project Designer appears.

3. **Click the Compile tab in a Visual Basic project. In a C# project, click the Build tab.**

4. **In Visual Basic, enable the Generate XML Documentation File check box. In C#, enable the XML Documentation File and Specify a Filename check boxes.**

   By default, the XML documentation file is saved to the bin folder for the build configuration selected.

5. **Click the X in the upper-right corner of the Project Designer to close the window.**

The preceding set of steps tells the compiler to use the /doc switch. You can add the /doc switch to any batch files or build scripts you use to automatically generate output.

The preceding set of steps doesn't work for ASP.NET Web sites because Web sites don't use the project model. You have a few options, which include:

✦ **Precompile your site** — ASP.NET Web sites are compiled as resources on the site and accessed by users. You can, however, precompile the site, which would allow you to the /doc option on the compiler.

✦ **Use Web Application Projects** — Microsoft has released an extension to Visual Studio 2005 that allows you to use projects with your ASP.NET Web sites.

To create XML documentation for your project, build your project. Any code decorated with comment markers is output to an XML file. Figure 5-16 shows a sample of XML documentation.

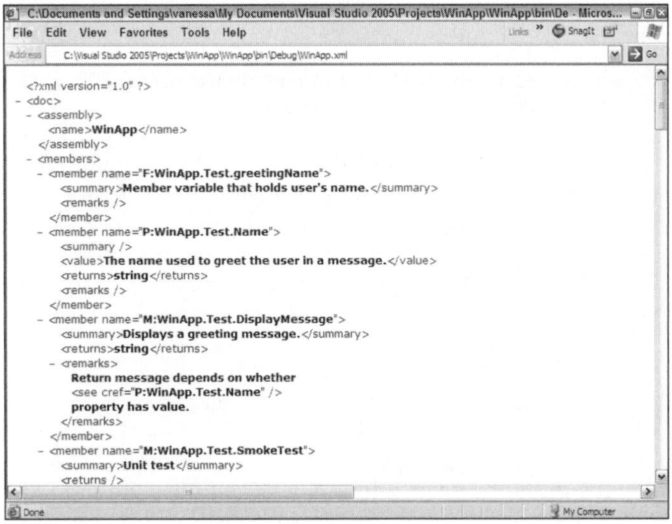

Figure 5-16:
The compiler creates an XML documentation file based on your code comments.

```
C:\Documents and Settings\vanessa\My Documents\Visual Studio 2005\Projects\WinApp\WinApp\bin\De - Micros...
File  Edit  View  Favorites  Tools  Help                        Links  »  SnagIt
Address  C:\Visual Studio 2005\Projects\WinApp\WinApp\bin\Debug\WinApp.xml                    Go

  <?xml version="1.0" ?>
- <doc>
  - <assembly>
      <name>WinApp</name>
    </assembly>
  - <members>
    - <member name="F:WinApp.Test.greetingName">
        <summary>Member variable that holds user's name.</summary>
        <remarks />
      </member>
    - <member name="P:WinApp.Test.Name">
        <summary />
        <value>The name used to greet the user in a message.</value>
        <returns>string</returns>
        <remarks />
      </member>
    - <member name="M:WinApp.Test.DisplayMessage">
        <summary>Displays a greeting message.</summary>
        <returns>string</returns>
      - <remarks>
          Return message depends on whether
          <see cref="P:WinApp.Test.Name" />
          property has value.
        </remarks>
      </member>
    - <member name="M:WinApp.Test.SmokeTest">
        <summary>Unit test</summary>
        <returns>
Done                                                My Computer
```

Because the documentation files use XML output, you can use XSLT style sheets to transform your XML into any format you want, including HTML or plain text.

You can create MSDN-style documentation from the XML documentation files created by your language's compiler. NDoc is a tool that creates documentation for C# projects. You can download NDoc for free at `http://ndoc.sourceforge.net`. VBCommenter creates documents for Visual Basic projects. Download VBCommenter from GotDotNet at `www.gotdotnet.com/workspaces/directory.aspx?ST=vbcommenter`.

Factoring in the Refactoring

Refactoring is the process of changing source code from its current form to another. Even if you think you've never refactored code, chances are you have. You refactor any time you make a decision about how to implement something. Assume you need to write a program that processes data from a file. You start jotting down some ideas for procedures and variables you know you need. As you commit your ideas to code, you invariably break your code into smaller, reusable bits of code. That's refactoring.

Refactoring is often necessary when you must add a feature or fix a bug in an existing code base. You refactor code any time you ask yourself whether you should

✦ Copy and paste code or extract common code to a reusable procedure.

✦ Use a lengthy conditional statement or create separate procedures.

✦ Write a single procedure that performs three tasks or write one procedure that calls three other procedures.

Refactoring is quite common in object-oriented programming. Before OOP, programs were often brittle. It was difficult for a developer to make a change to an existing code base without fear of triggering a cascade of bugs throughout the rest of the program. OOP provides many constructs that make it easier to break units of code into smaller, reusable pieces that are loosely coupled to one another, which makes refactoring possible.

Of course, I'm describing the goal of OOP techniques. In reality, most of us don't start out implementing our perfect, object-oriented designs using OOP. Nor should we strive to do so. The beauty of refactoring using OOP is that it gives you permission to let go of perfection. Letting go of your visions of building the perfect system allows you to get busy building the best system you can in the here and now. You can always refactor your code later when you have more knowledge.

In the past, refactoring often meant using a combination of Copy, Paste, and Find and Replace to rename parameters or change return values. Visual Studio 2005 provides support for many kinds of refactorings. Table 5-3 provides a list of common refactoring techniques and where you can find them.

Table 5-3	Refactoring Options in Visual Studio 2005		
Technique	*Description*	*Tool*	*Language*
Encapsulate field	Creates a property from a public field	Refactor menu	C#
Extract interface	Creates a new interface from an existing method	Refactor menu, Class Designer	C#
Extract method	Creates a new method from a code fragment	Refactor menu	C#
Implement an abstract class	Creates a derived class from an abstract class	Class Designer, IntelliSense	C#, VB
Implement an interface	Creates method stubs in a class that inherits from an interface	Class Designer, IntelliSense	C#, VB

Technique	Description	Tool	Language
Move a type member	Moves a type member from one type to another type	Class Designer	C#, VB
Override	Creates a method stub for a member being overridden	Class Designer, IntelliSense	C#, VB
Promote local variable to parameter	Changes a local variable to a method parameter	Refactor menu	C#
Remove parameters	Removes parameters from a method's declaration	Refactor menu	C#
Rename identifiers	Renames a type or a member of a type	Class Designer	C#, VB
Reorder parameters	Changes the order of a method's parameters	Class Designer, Refactor menu	C#

Visual Studio 2005 updates all the places in source code where the refactored code is called. There's no need to use Find and Replace to update method calls.

The refactoring techniques implement abstract classes, implement an interface, and override features of IntelliSense. See the "It's Not Your Father's IntelliSense Any More," section earlier in this chapter for examples of how to use it.

C# provides more refactoring opportunities than Visual Basic. Your choices for Visual Basic are mostly limited to those features available in IntelliSense and the Class Designer.

Refactoring with the Class Designer

The Class Designer provides access to the IntelliSense refactoring features via the Class Designer menu. The Class Designer menu adds a Refactoring menu that you can use to access refactoring features specific to C#.

You aren't restricted to using the menu items to refactor in the Class Designer. For example, to implement an interface, follow these steps:

1. **Add a class that you want to implement the interface.**

2. **Add the interface you want to implement.**

3. **Click the Inheritance icon in the toolbox.**

4. **Drag the line from the class to the interface.**

The interface's members are stubbed out in the class, as Figure 5-17 shows.

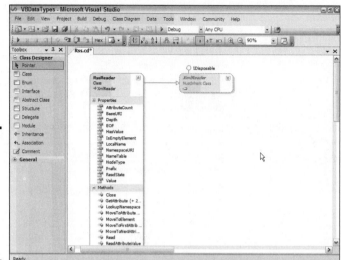

Figure 5-17:
Drag an inheritance line to implement an interface in the Class Designer.

Moving a type member to another type in the Class Designer is as simple as cut and paste. For example, assume you create a `Customer` class. As you're adding the properties `FirstName`, `LastName`, and `CompanyName`, you realize that none of your customers have both a `CompanyName` and a `FirstName` and `LastName`. You decide to create two new classes that inherit from the `Customer` class. You want to move the `FirstName` and `LastName` properties to a `ResidentialCustomer` class and the `CompanyName` property to a `CommercialCustomer` class. To move the types, you do the following:

1. **Right-click the property in the class you want to move.**

A shortcut menu appears.

2. **Choose Cut, as shown in Figure 5-18.**

The property disappears from the class.

3. **Right-click the class where you want to move the property.**

A shortcut menu appears.

4. **Choose Paste.**

The property appears in the class.

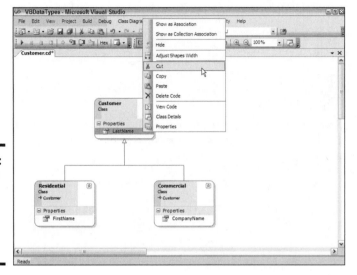

Figure 5-18:
Click Cut to
move a
property
from one
type to
another.

Refactoring C#

Visual Studio provides extensive support for refactoring in the C# programming language. You can access all the C# refactoring commands by clicking the Refactor menu while in the code editor. A limited set of commands is available in the Class Designer.

In most cases, the C# refactoring commands work like this:

1. **Position your cursor on the source code that you wish to refactor.**

On commands that change methods such as Remove Parameters, you can place your cursor on the method declaration or the method call.

2. **Choose the refactoring command you wish to execute from the Refactor menu.**

A dialog box appears.

3. **Complete the dialog box for the refactoring command.**

Some commands, such as the Reorder Parameters command, display a preview dialog box where you can review changes before you commit.

For example, to reorder a method's parameters:

1. **Position your cursor on the method declaration or the method call.**

2. **Choose Reorder Parameters from the Refactor menu.**

The Reorder Parameters dialog box appears.

3. Click the arrows to reorder the parameters.

A preview of the new method signature appears in the dialog box.

4. Enable the Preview Reference Changes check box.

5. Click the OK button.

The Preview Changes window appears, as shown in Figure 5-19.

The Preview Changes window displays the method signature and each method call. The changed code appears in the lower pane.

6. Click the method's references to review code changes.

7. Click the Apply button to save the refactored code.

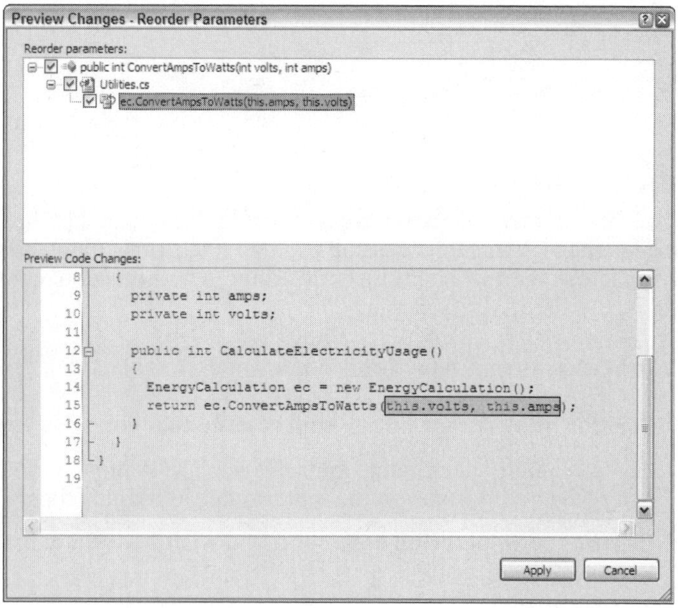

Figure 5-19: Preview your refactored code in the Preview Changes window.

Chapter 6: Exploring Web Services

In This Chapter

✔ Creating a new Web service

✔ Testing Web services with GET, POST, and SOAP

✔ Using WSDL and UDDI to find Web services

✔ Consuming Web services in server-side code

✔ Accessing Web services with client-side code

A Web service is a kind of Web application. Unlike regular Web applications, however, a Web service has no user interface. Generally, Web services aren't intended to be accessed by end users directly. Rather, Web services are *consumed* by other applications. For example, a Web service that returns the current temperature for a given city could be called by or consumed by a town's Web page.

Web services have two basic uses:

✦ **Interface between systems** — Many different kinds of systems run on different hardware and platforms. Trying to write software that allows all these disparate systems to talk to each other has been challenging. Many of the interfaces quickly become brittle. Web services use standards that overcome the difficulties of creating system interfaces.

✦ **Reusable components** — Rather than copy and paste code or deal with distributing components, you can make the features of your code available as a Web service.

Don't be fooled by the term *Web service*. It's called a *Web service* because it uses the technologies of the Web, namely HTTP and XML. But you aren't restricted to publishing your Web services over the Internet. Many companies use Web services within their companies. For example, your public relations department can publish their press releases via a Web service method called `GetPressReleases(date)`. Your Web site development staff can consume those services and display them on a public Web site, corporate portal, or an RSS feed.

Never created a Web service before? Never fear. In this chapter, I show you how to use Visual Studio 2005 to create a Web service, test it, and call it from another application.

Saying Hello to Web Services

Web services make extensive use of Web-based technologies such as HTTP and XML. Thankfully, you don't need to dig into how Web services use these technologies because Visual Studio and ASP.NET take care of all that for you.

To create a new Web service, follow these steps:

1. **From the File menu, choose New⇨Web Site.**

The New Web Site window appears.

2. **Click the ASP.NET Web Service template.**

3. **Type a name for your Web service.**

You should give your Web service a meaningful name.

4. **Click the OK button.**

Visual Studio creates the Web service project.

The Web service created by Visual Studio is fully functional. To run the Web service, press Ctrl+F5. Visual Studio launches the service in your Web browser.

Recall that Web services don't have user interfaces. ASP.NET uses a template to generate the service.asmx page. The page lists a single method, `HelloWorld`, created by Visual Studio.

To test the `HelloWorld` method:

1. **Click the HelloWorld hyperlink on the services.asmx page.**

A test page appears, as Figure 6-1 shows.

The page includes a button to invoke the test method. It also shows the sample SOAP headers that ASP.NET uses to communicate with the Web service using SOAP. You don't need to know SOAP in order to use Web services because Visual Studio and ASP.NET take care of all that for you. I explain SOAP in more detail in the section "Testing Web services" later in this chapter.

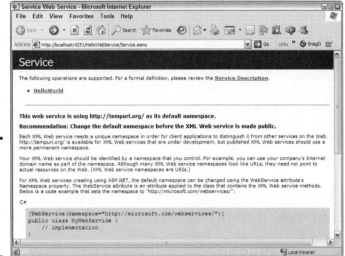

Figure 6-1:
ASP.NET
generates a
page to test
the Web
service's
methods.

The default test page generator is located at C:\WINDOWS\Microsoft.
NET\Framework\v2.0.50727\CONFIG\ DefaultWsdlHelpGenerator.aspx.
You can modify the page to better suit your needs if you want.

2. **Click the Invoke button. An XML file appears with the value** `"Hello`
`World"` **in a single string node.**

Understanding ASP.NET Web services

A Web service project consists of two main components: an entry point to
access the service and a class that contains the code for the Web service.
Because Web services don't have user interfaces like Web sites, Web services are accessed via an .asmx page, which serves as the entry point to the
Web service. The .asmx page has a `WebService` processing directive at the
top of the page that defines the programming language of the Web service, the
code-behind file, and the class name that provides the Web service's functionality. The features of a Web service are implemented in a class. The class
uses attributes to identify which methods are publicly accessible via the Web
service. Using attributes allows you to use private methods in your class.

While many Web services are accessed via .asmx pages, ASP.NET Web sites
are typically accessed via .aspx pages.

Figure 6-2 shows an example of a simple HelloWorld Web service created
with Visual Studio.

http://localhost/MyWebService/Service.asmx

Entry point into
Web service.

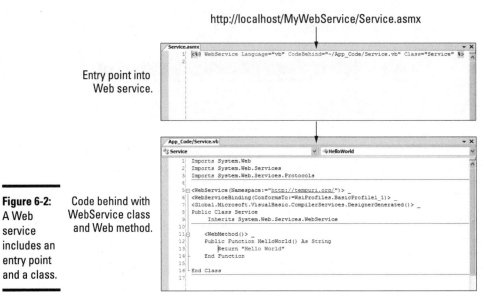

Figure 6-2:
A Web
service
includes an
entry point
and a class.

Code behind with
WebService class
and Web method.

Visual Studio automatically wires up the Web service's class with the attributes it needs to function as a Web service. The class that Visual Studio creates for the Web service uses two attributes:

✦ **WebService** — A Web service has one `WebService` attribute that identifies the Web service's namespace. The attribute can also include a description.

✦ **WebMethod** — Each method that's accessible from the Web service must have the `WebMethod` attribute above it.

To change the name of the service and the class created by Visual Studio, follow these steps:

1. **Right-click the .asmx file in Solution Explorer.**

2. **Choose Rename from the shortcut menu.**

3. **Type a new name for the .asmx file — such as** HelloWebService.asmx.

The name you use for the .asmx file is the name you use to access the Web service via its URL.

4. **Repeat Steps 1 through 3 to rename the** `Service.vb` **or** `Service.cs` **class created by Visual Studio. The class is located in the App_Code folder.**

The file's extension depends on whether you're using Visual Basic or C# as the programming language.

5. **Open the class file and change the class's name from `Service` to its new name, such as `HelloWebService`.**

6. **Open the .asmx file and change the `WebService` processing directive so it points to the new class file and name, as shown in the following code:**

```
<%@ WebService Language="vb"
    CodeBehind="~/App_Code/HelloWebService.vb"
    Class="HelloWebService" %>
```

An .asmx file can point to more than just a class file. It can also point to a precompiled assembly, or you can include your code inside the .asmx file.

7. **Press Ctrl+F5 to run the Web service. Notice the Web service's name and URL are updated, as shown in Figure 6-3.**

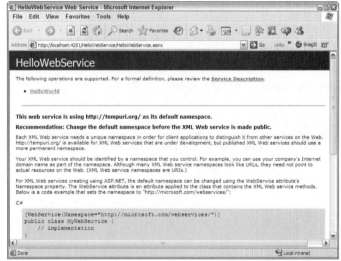

Figure 6-3: Change the name of the Web service to make it more descriptive.

Each Web service must have a unique namespace. The namespace qualifies the Web service's methods so that each method is unique. Visual Studio automatically assigns the namespace `http://tempuri.org/` to Web services. You should change the namespace. It's not necessary for the namespace to point to an actual working URL. Rather, it should be unique.

The default namespace `http://tempuri.org` is pronounced *TEMP-you-are-eye* and is short for *temporary URI*. URI stands for Uniform Resource Identifier, and it's used to provide a name or location for a resource.

To change the namespace and add a description to the Web service, follow these steps:

1. Open the class file used by your service. The class file is in the App_Code folder.

2. Type a new namespace in place of the default namespace and add a description for the Web service, as shown in the following:

```
<WebService(Namespace:="http://mycompany.com/
    webservices", Description:="A web service that
    returns a Hello World message")>
```

You use the colon and equal sign combination (:=) after a property to designate that you're using the property out of order.

The WebMethod attribute supports the Description property. Use it to add a description to the methods exposed by your Web service.

3. Press Ctrl+F5 to run the Web service.

The Web service's description appears on the ASP.NET generated page, as shown in Figure 6-4. Notice also that a description for the HelloWorld method appears.

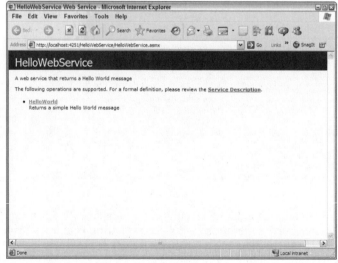

Figure 6-4:
Use the Description property to add descriptions to your Web service and methods.

Adding a method

The methods you add to your Web service class aren't automatically accessible via your Web service. You must explicitly mark them as Web service methods.

You mark Web service methods with a `WebMethod` attribute. Figure 6-5 shows a code sample with a single public method that uses two private methods. The public method is marked with the `WebMethod` attribute on line 11. Note that the private methods aren't accessible.

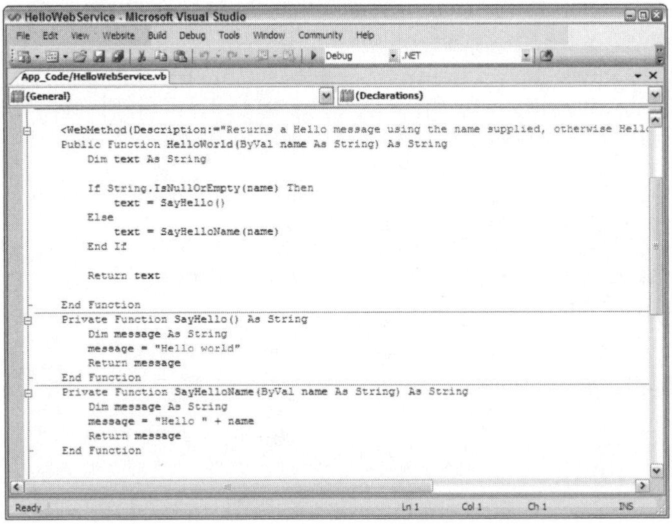

Figure 6-5:
Use the
WebMethod
attribute
to make
a public
method
accessible
via a Web
service.

Testing Web services

There are several ways to test your Web services short of building a full-blown application. The easiest way to test your Web services is to press F5 while in Visual Studio. You can also access your Web services via URL or using an HTTP form. In most cases, you communicate with Web services using HTTP, the communication protocol of the Internet.

Whichever method you choose, you must be aware of your three communication choices when working with Web services:

✦ **GET** — Uses HTTP with an encoded URL to call the Web service. The basic syntax for accessing a Web service with GET is to use a URL like the following:

```
http://<servername>/<projectname>/service.asmx/
    methodname?parameter1=value&parameter2=value
```

✦ **POST** — Uses HTTP to pass the method's parameters without displaying them in the URL. The POST approach is more secure.

✦ **SOAP** — Uses an XML dialect called SOAP to enclose the request to and response from the Web service. SOAP is often used in conjunction with HTTP, although it isn't required. SOAP is the standard for Web services message encapsulation.

The testing services provided by ASP.NET use POST by default. The following section shows you how to enable testing with GET. ASP.NET doesn't provide a facility for testing SOAP messages. You must create your own. To read more about using SOAP, see the section "Communicating with a Web service," later in this chapter.

Sending a GET request

A GET request passes the Web services parameters with the URL. For example, the following URL calls the `HelloWorld` method on the `HelloWebService` and passes the value `John` to the `name` parameter:

```
http://localhost:4251/HelloWebService/HelloWebService.asmx/
    HelloWorld?name=John
```

The Web service returns an XML document with the value `Hello John`, as Figure 6-6 shows.

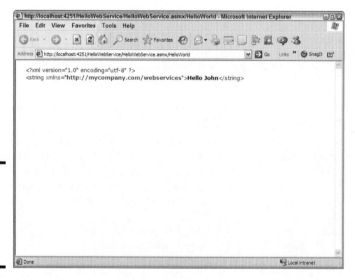

Figure 6-6:
The Web service returns an XML document.

Passing in parameters at the end of a URL is called *encoding*. Any time you see a URL with parameters appended, your browser sends an HTTP GET request to the Web server. GET requests are considered more risky than POST requests because the parameter values are in plain sight. The alternative is to use an HTTP POST request, which sends the parameter values in the message body.

If you receive an error message when you try to access your Web service using HTTP GET, it's likely because you need to enable the GET protocol in your project's web.config file. To add the protocol, paste the following code in between the opening and closing <system.web> tags in web.config:

```
<webServices>
   <protocols>
      <add name="HttpGet"/>
   </protocols>
</webServices>
```

Sending a POST request

You can use an HTML form to test your Web service using a POST request. With a POST request, the Web service's parameters aren't visible in the URL.

To test a Web service with a HTTP form, do this:

1. **Click the Web service in Solution Explorer.**

   Press Ctrl+Alt+L to open Solution Explorer if it's closed.

2. **From the Website menu, choose Add New Item.**

   The Add New Item window appears.

3. **Click the HTML Page icon.**

4. **Type a name for the HTML page and click the Add button.**

   The HTML page appears in the code editor.

5. **Type the following HTML to create a form:**

   ```
   <form method="POST" action='http://<servername>/
      <projectname>/Service.asmx/HelloWorld'>
   </form>
   ```

   The action attribute specifies where the form should post. Type the URL of your Web service. Append a forward slash and the name of the method to execute. In the preceding example, the form executes the HelloWorld method on the Web service.

6. **Drag and drop input elements for text from the toolbox onto the HTML page.**

7. **Drag and drop a Submit button.**

   Make sure the elements appear in between the form tags.

8. **Set the name attribute for your input elements to the parameter for your method.**

For example, the following HTML form posts to the `HelloWorld` method of the `HelloWebService`:

```
<form method="POST"
      action='http://localhost:4251/HelloWebService/
      HelloWebService.asmx/HelloWorld'>

    <input id="Text1" type="text" name="name"/>
    <input id="Button1" type="submit" value="button" />
</form>
```

9. **Press Ctrl+F5 to run your Web page. The page appears.**

Make sure you have the HTML page open when you press Ctrl+F5 or set the HTML page as the startup page for the site.

10. **Type the parameter values in the page, as Figure 6-7 shows.**

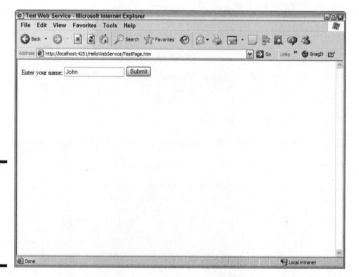

Figure 6-7: Type the parameter values into the test page.

11. **Click the Submit button.**

When you click the Submit button, the HTML page sends the parameters in the form `parameter=value` to the Web service method. Using the example in Figure 6-7, the browser submits `name=John` to the Web service.

The Web service responds with an XML document containing the value `Hello John`, as shown in Figure 6-6.

See later the section "Consuming a Web Service" for more information on what to do with the XML document returned by the Web service.

Testing with SOAP

You might also want to test the SOAP messages generated by your Web service. The test page generated for your Web service shows a sample SOAP message that ASP.NET generates, as shown in Figure 6-8.

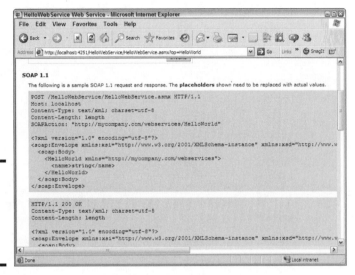

Figure 6-8:
ASP.NET
generates
sample
SOAP
messages.

Because SOAP messages are XML-based, you can use standard Web technologies to test the messages. The following example uses JScript and MSXML to submit a SOAP request and display the response. MSXML is the Microsoft XML Parser. You use it to process the XML you send and receive. JScript is a client-side scripting language that you use to display values on the Web page. The following example shows you how to use MSXML and JScript to test SOAP messages without assuming you have any knowledge of these technologies.

To create a test for SOAP:

1. **Add a new HTML Page to your project.**

2. **Add a script tag to the page in between the head tags, as shown in the following:**

```
<head>
<script type="text\jscript">
</script>
</head>
```

3. **Create a new object to hold an XML document.**

```
var xmlDoc = new ActiveXObject("Msxml2.DOMDocument");
```

4. **Create a new object to communicate with a Web server.**

```
var xmlHTTP = new ActiveXObject("Msxml2.XMLHTTP");
```

5. **Create a new function that creates the SOAP message and loads it into
the XML document you create in Step 3.**

```
function createXmlDoc(name)
{
    var soapXml  = "<?xml version=\"1.0\" ?>" ;
    soapXml += "<soap12:Envelope "
    soapXml +=
    "xmlns:xsi=\"http://www.w3.org/2001/XMLSchema-
    instance\" " ;
    soapXml +=
    "xmlns:xsd=\"http://www.w3.org/2001/XMLSchema\" " ;
    soapXml +=
    "xmlns:soap12=\"http://www.w3.org/2003/05/soap-
    envelope\">" ;
    soapXml += "<soap12:Body>" ;
    soapXml += "<HelloWorld
    xmlns=\"http://mycompany.com/webservices\">" ;
            soapXml = soapXml + "<name>" + name.value   +
    "</name>" ;
     soapXml += "</HelloWorld>";
     soapXml += "</soap12:Body></soap12:Envelope>"

     xmlDoc.loadXML(soapXml) ;
}
```

You can find an example of the SOAP request on the Web service's test
page. Be sure to pass in any parameter values to the request. For example, here's the SOAP request generated by ASP.NET for the Web service
shown in Figure 6-5:

```
<?xml version="1.0" encoding="utf-8"?>
<soap12:Envelope
    xmlns:xsi="http://www.w3.org/2001/XMLSchema-
    instance"
    xmlns:xsd="http://www.w3.org/2001/XMLSchema"
    xmlns:soap12="http://www.w3.org/2003/05/soap-
    envelope">
   <soap12:Body>
    <HelloWorld
    xmlns="http://mycompany.com/webservices">
      <name>string</name>
    </HelloWorld>
   </soap12:Body>
</soap12:Envelope>
```

6. **Create a function that sends the SOAP request to the Web server.**

The following is an example of how to create a function:

```
function sendXml()
{
    xmlHTTP.Open ( "Post",
    "http://localhost:4251/HelloWebService/HelloWebServi
    ce.asmx", false);
    xmlHTTP.setRequestHeader("Content-Type",
    "application/soap+xml; charset=utf-8" );
    xmlHTTP.setRequestHeader("Content-Length",
    xmlDoc.xml.length);
    xmlHTTP.Send(xmlDoc.xml);
}
```

The sendXML function uses the XMLHTTP object to send the SOAP request to the Web service. You can find the header information for the request on the Web service's test page. Here's the SOAP request generated for the Web service shown in Figure 6-5:

```
POST /HelloWebService/HelloWebService.asmx HTTP/1.1
Host: localhost
Content-Type: application/soap+xml; charset=utf-8
Content-Length: length
```

7. **Create a function that outputs the SOAP request and response to the Web page.**

```
function writeResponses()
{
    SoapRequest.innerText =  xmlDoc.xml;
    SoapResponse.innerText =  xmlHTTP.responseText;
}
```

8. **Create a function that calls all three functions.**

```
function getSoap(name)
{
    createXmlDoc(name);
    sendXml();
    writeResponses();
}
```

9. **Add an HTML form that wires everything up.**

```
<form>
    <p>Enter name:<input id="inputName"></input></p>
    <p><input type="button" id="btn"  value="Enter"
                onclick="getSoap(inputName)"></input>
    </p>
    <p>Request:</p>
    <div id="SoapRequest"></div>
    <p>Response:</p>
    <div id="SoapResponse"></div>
</form>
```

10. **Display the page in the browser.**

Figure 6-9 shows an example.

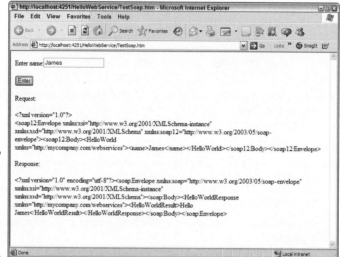

Figure 6-9:
Use a Web page to test your SOAP requests and responses.

I modified this script from the script at www.codeproject.com/webservices/aspwebsvr.asp.

You can also use the testing facilities in Visual Studio Team System to create a Web test to test your Web services. See the topic, "How to: Create a Web Service Test," in the Visual Studio documentation for more information.

You can test soap requests online at www.perfectxml.com/SOAPTestClient.asp.

Consuming a Web Service

Web services return XML documents. An XML document is just a string, so you can use any programming language to modify an XML document. In fact, people use all kinds of languages — from Python and PHP to JavaScript — to work with XML.

Of course, the .NET Framework provides extensive support for consuming XML and Web services, including:

✦ Visual Studio generates proxy classes that allow you to use any Web service like a local class.

✦ ASP.NET generates the communication infrastructure necessary for accessing Web services.

Communicating with a Web service

Web services typically use a special message format called SOAP that allows you to send and receive Web service requests over HTTP, which is the protocol of the Internet. SOAP stands for Simple Object Access Protocol, and it's important because it's independent of both language and platform.

You aren't limited to sending SOAP messages over HTTP. You can use SOAP with any transport protocol.

SOAP encapsulates the messages you send to and from your Web service in a SOAP envelope. The SOAP request and response travels via a transport protocol, such as HTTP. As long as you have access to HTTP, you can use Web services. Think of SOAP as a delivery truck and HTTP as the highway. The contents of the SOAP delivery truck is your XML document.

SOAP's platform and language independence makes Web services great choices for creating interfaces between disparate systems. For example, a Linux-based application can offer data access via a Web service that's consumed by an ASP.NET Web application.

ASP.NET takes care of writing SOAP requests and responses and creating the XML messages for you. You don't need to learn any new technical skills to start using Web services right away. To see an example of the SOAP responses and requests generated by ASP.NET, just run your Web service. Figure 6-8 shows an example of the SOAP messages generated for the `HelloWorld` method of the `HelloWebService`.

Web services aren't limited to using just SOAP messages. They can also use GET and POST requests, as explained in the previous section, "Testing Web services." GET and POST requests are part of the HTTP protocol. ASP.NET uses POST or SOAP, depending on which protocol it thinks works best. To ensure that your messages are always sent using SOAP, add the following code to your Web service's web.config file:

```
<webservices>
    <protocols>
        <remove name="HttpPost" />
        <remove name="HttpGet" />
    </protocols>
</webservices>
```

Finding Web services

You might not always be consuming your own Web services. There are plenty of Web services on the Web. Web services, including the ones you create with ASP.NET, use two technologies to announce themselves to the world:

✦ Web Services Description Language (WSDL)

✦ Universal Discovery Description and Integration (UDDI)

WSDL is an XML document that describes the Web service, while UDDI is like the Web services yellow pages. You don't have to list your Web service with a UDDI directory, but you can if you want.

The WSDL tells the world, or another developer at least, what they need to know to use your Web service. Among other things, the WSDL provides information about the following elements:

✦ **Namespaces** — Lists the services available in the namespace. The namespace encapsulates the Web service's details using the tags shown in the following:

```
<wsdl:definitions
    targetNamespace="http://mycompany.com/webservices">
<wsdl:documentation>A web service that returns a Hello
    World message</wsdl:documentation>
</wsdl:definitions>
```

✦ **Operations** — Uses the `<portType>` element to define the Web methods available in the service. The `<message>` element defines the Web methods parameters.

```
<wsdl:portType name="HelloWebServiceHttpGet">
    <wsdl:operation name="HelloWorld">
    <wsdl:documentation>
Returns a Hello message using the name supplied,
    otherwise Hello World if name is null.
</wsdl:documentation>
<wsdl:input message="tns:HelloWorldHttpGetIn"/>
<wsdl:output message="tns:HelloWorldHttpGetOut"/>
</wsdl:operation>
</wsdl:portType>
<wsdl:message name="HelloWorldHttpGetIn">
<wsdl:part name="name" type="s:string"/>
</wsdl:message>
    <wsdl:message name="HelloWorldHttpGetOut">
<wsdl:part name="Body" element="tns:string"/>
</wsdl:message>
```

✦ **Types** — Identifies the data types used by the Web service with the `<types>` element, as shown in the following:

```
<wsdl:types>
   <s:schema elementFormDefault="qualified"
     targetNamespace="http://mycompany.com/webservices">
   <s:element name="HelloWorld">
   <s:complexType>
   <s:sequence>
<s:element minOccurs="0" maxOccurs="1" name="name"
     type="s:string"/>
</s:sequence>
</s:complexType>
</s:element>
   <s:element name="HelloWorldResponse">
   <s:complexType>
   <s:sequence>
<s:element minOccurs="0" maxOccurs="1" name=
     "HelloWorldResult" type="s:string"/>
</s:sequence>
</s:complexType>
</s:element>
<s:element name="string" nillable="true" type=
     "s:string"/>
</s:schema>
</wsdl:types>
```

+ **Protocols** — Uses the `<binding>` element to define the message format, such as SOAP, and set details for the port.

```
<wsdl:binding name="HelloWebServiceHttpGet" type=
     "tns:HelloWebServiceHttpGet">
<http:binding verb="GET"/>
   <wsdl:operation name="HelloWorld">
<http:operation location="/HelloWorld"/>
   <wsdl:input>
<http:urlEncoded/>
</wsdl:input>
   <wsdl:output>
<mime:mimeXml part="Body"/>
</wsdl:output>
</wsdl:operation>
</wsdl:binding>
```

+ **Services** — Identifies the collection of protocols available for use with the service.

```
<wsdl:service name="HelloWebService">
<wsdl:documentation>A web service that returns a Hello
     World message</wsdl:documentation>
   <wsdl:port name="HelloWebServiceSoap" binding=
     "tns:HelloWebServiceSoap">
<soap:address location="http://localhost:4251/
     HelloWebService/HelloWebService.asmx"/>
</wsdl:port>
   <wsdl:port name="HelloWebServiceSoap12" binding=
     "tns:HelloWebServiceSoap12">
```

```
<soap12:address location="http://localhost:4251/
    HelloWebService/HelloWebService.asmx"/>
</wsdl:port>
    <wsdl:port name="HelloWebServiceHttpGet" binding=
    "tns:HelloWebServiceHttpGet">
<http:address location="http://localhost:4251/
    HelloWebService/HelloWebService.asmx"/>
</wsdl:port>
</wsdl:service>
```

ASP.NET automatically creates a WSDL document for your Web service. To view the WSDL for your Web service, click Service Description on your Web service's test page, as Figure 6-10 shows.

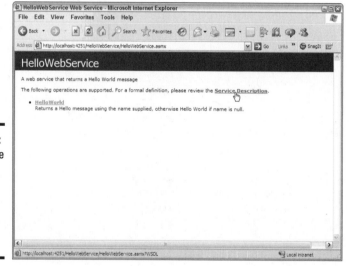

Figure 6-10: Click Service Description to view the WSDL document for your Web service.

UDDI provides a directory listing for your Web service. There are three UDDI directories:

✦ **Green Pages** — Lists services offered by the registrant.

✦ **White Pages** — Lists basic address information.

✦ **Yellow Pages** — Categorizes business based on standard industrial classifications.

Many companies set up UDDI directories within their organizations for internal consumption only. This allows developers and other consumers of Web services to easily see what services are available. Using Web services within your organization is a great way to reuse code.

You can access a public UDDI directory at `http://soapclient.com/uddisearch.html`.

Using a Web service in your application

Visual Studio provides excellent support for using a Web service in your application. It doesn't matter what language was used to create the Web service. When you reference the Web service in your application, Visual Studio places a wrapper, called a *proxy class,* around the Web service that allows you to access the Web service like it was your own code.

Adding a Web reference

In order to access a Web service in your projects, you must add a Web Reference. When you add a Web reference, Visual Studio generates code, called a proxy class, that you can use to access the Web Reference.

To add a Web reference to a Web service, follow these steps:

1. **Right-click the project and click Add Web Reference.**

The Add Web Reference window appears.

2. **Type or paste the URL for a Web service in the URL text box.**

3. **Click the Go button.**

The Web service appears in the window, as shown in Figure 6-11.

4. **Click the Add Reference button.**

The reference appears in Solution Explorer.

Figure 6-11:
Use the
Add Web
Reference
window to
add a Web
service to
your project.

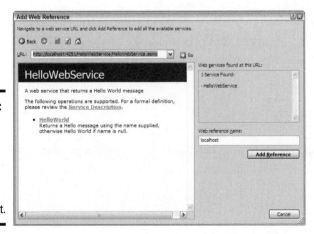

Binding with BindingSource

`BindingSource` is the preferred way to data bind in Windows applications. You can use a Web service as a data source for a `BindingSource` component.

Here's how to use a Web service with a `BindingSource`:

1. Add a Web Reference to your Web service in your Windows project.

2. Create a new instance of your Web service.

For example, to create a new instance of the `HelloWebService`:

```
Dim ws As New localhost.HelloWebService
```

3. Drag and drop a `BindingSource` component from the Data tab in the Toolbox onto your Windows Form.

4. Add your Web service as a data source for the `BindingSource` component using the component's `Add` method.

For example, the following code adds the `HelloWebService` to a `BindingSource` component:

```
BindingSource1.Add(ws.HelloWorld(Me.txtEnterName.Text))
```

5. Set the `BindingSource` component as the source for a control's data binding.

For example, the following code data binds the `BindingSource` component to a label control's `text` property:

```
Me.lblDisplayMessage.DataBindings.Add("Text",
    Me.BindingSource1, "")
```

You can use the preceding code in a button's `Click` event to call the Web service. Here's the entire code sample in a button's `Click` event:

```
Private Sub Button1_Click(ByVal sender As System.Object,
    ByVal e As System.EventArgs) Handles Button1.Click
  Dim ws As New localhost.HelloWebService

  BindingSource1.Add(ws.HelloWorld(Me.txtEnterName.Text))
  Me.lblDisplayMessage.DataBindings.Add("Text",
    Me.BindingSource1, "")
End Sub
```

When a user clicks the button, the code calls the `HelloWorld` method of the `HelloWebService`. The name parameter is passed in using the value entered by a user in the `txtEnterName` text box. The return value appears in a label control called `lblDisplayMessage`.

Consuming a public Web service

Of course, not all Web services are created with Visual Studio and ASP.NET. You can connect to many publicly available Web services.

Here's an example of how to connect to a public Web service from the National Weather Service:

1. **Add a Web reference to the National Weather Service Web service using the following URL:**

```
www.weather.gov/forecasts/xml/DWMLgen/wsdl/ndfdXML.wsdl
```

Note the ending file extension of the URL is wsdl. WSDL is the service description file for the Web service. Visual Studio uses the wsdl file to generate a proxy class.

2. **Create a new subroutine called `getWeather`.**

```
Private Sub getWeather()
End Sub
```

3. **Create a new instance of the Web service.**

```
Dim ws As New gov.weather.www.ndfdXML()
```

4. **Create a new instance of an XML document.**

```
Dim xml As New System.Xml.XmlDocument
```

5. **Call a Web method on the Web service and load the value into an XML document.**

```
xml.LoadXml(ws.NDFDgenByDay(39.77, -86.16,
    System.DateTime.Now(), "1",
    gov.weather.www.formatType.Item12hourly))
```

The Web method `NDFgenByDay` returns an XML document with basic weather information such as high and low temperature for today's date at the latitude and longitude supplied. You can do anything you want with the XML document, such as parse it to return the values you want to display.

6. **Save the XML document to a file.**

Figure 6-12 shows the results.

```
xml.Save("weather.xml")
```

Here's the entire code sample:

```
Private Sub getWeather()
  Dim xml As New System.Xml.XmlDocument

  Dim ws As New gov.weather.www.ndfdXML()
  xml.LoadXml(ws.NDFDgenByDay(39.77, -86.16,
    System.DateTime.Now(), "1",
    gov.weather.www.formatType.Item12hourly))

  xml.Save("weather.xml")
End Sub
```

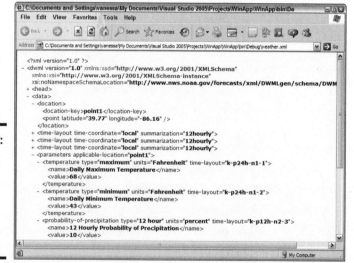

Figure 6-12:
The Web service returns an XML document that you can parse.

Before you can call the `getWeather()` method you create in the previous set of steps, you must make a slight modification to the proxy class generated by Visual Studio. In step 1, when you add the Web reference, Visual Studio generates code — called a proxy class — that essentially turns the Web service into a data type. In this example, ASP.NET flakes out waiting for the National Weather Service to return its SOAP message. The next set of steps show you a workaround you can use.

Even if you never plan to use the National Weather Service's Web service, you may still find this workaround useful. From what I've read on the Web, there are plenty of public Web services that give ASP.NET grief.

To workaround the problem:

1. **Add a class file to your project.**

Use the Add New Item window to add a class file.

2. **Type the namespace from the Web service in your new class file.**

You can find the namespace in the Reference.vb or Reference.cs file generated by Visual Studio for the Web service. In the case of the National Web Service, the namespace is `gov.weather.www`.

3. **Add a partial class to the class file for the Web service's class generated by Visual Studio.**

For example, a partial class for the National Weather Service looks like:

```
Namespace gov.weather.www
    Partial Class ndfdXML
    End Class
End Namespace
```

Creating a partial class allows you to modify the generated class without actually changing the generated code. As a rule, you should avoid changing generated code.

4. **Add a function to the partial class that overrides the `GetWebRequest` method.**

The following function sets the request's `KeepAlive` property to false so ASP.NET doesn't timeout while communicating with the Web service:

```
Protected Overrides Function GetWebRequest(ByVal uri As
    Uri) As System.Net.WebRequest
  Dim webRequest As System.Net.HttpWebRequest =
    MyBase.GetWebRequest(uri)
  webRequest.KeepAlive = False
  Return webRequest
End Function
```

Here's the equivalent function in C#:

```
protected override System.Net.WebRequest
    GetWebRequest(Uri uri)
{
  System.Net.HttpWebRequest webRequest =
    (System.Net.HttpWebRequest) base.GetWebRequest(uri);
  webRequest.KeepAlive = false;
  return webRequest;
}
```

When you build your application, the partial class you create is combined with the partial class generated by Visual Studio.

What should you do with your new weather Web service? Should you create a widget that calls the service and displays the results on a Web page? I suggest not, because it creates a lot of overhead. Instead, you might call the Web service a few times a day and store the results in an XML file or database. You can then parse the results and create a record in a database table. Your widget can then query the database without being dependent on the Web service.

Putting your Web service in a Web application

You can use Web services in a Web application. Because ASP.NET creates a proxy class, you can call your Web service like you'd call any other bit of code.

To use a Web service in a Web application, follow these steps:

1. **Add a Web reference to the Web service you wish to consume.**

2. **Create an instance of your Web service.**

```
Dim ws As New localhost.HelloWebService
```

3. **Call your Web service.**

For example, the following code calls the `HelloWebService` and returns the results to a text box.

```
Me.TextBox1.Text = ws.HelloWorld("John")
```

Getting on the client side

You aren't limited to just accessing Web services via server-side code. You can also use client-side scripting languages such as JScript to call Web services.

Web services return an XML document, for which JScript provides excellent support. Here's a simple script and HTML page that tests the `HelloWebService`:

```
<html>
<head>
    <title>Test Web Service</title>
    <script type="text/jscript">
    function callService()
    {
        var xmlDoc;
        var url;

        xmlDoc = new ActiveXObject("Msxml2.DOMDocument");
        xmlDoc.onreadystatechange = function ()
            {
```

```
                    if (xmlDoc.readyState == 4)
                        {
                            displayText(xmlDoc);
                        }
                }

            url =
    "http://<servername>/HelloWebService/HelloWebService.asmx/
    HelloWorld?name=" +
                    document.getElementById("text1").value;

            xmlDoc.load(url);

        }

        function displayText(xmlDoc)
        {

            var currentNode;
            currentNode = xmlDoc.selectSingleNode("string");

            document.getElementById("displayMessage").innerHTML
    = currentNode.text;

        }

        </script>

</head>
<body>
    <form>
        Enter your name:
        <input id="Text1" type="text" name="name" />
        <input id="Button1" type="button" value="button"
    onclick="callService()" />
        <div id="displayMessage"></div>
    </form>
</body>
</html>
```

The script works only in Internet Explorer because it uses an ActiveX control which other browsers don't support. You can find lots of scripts on the Web for manipulating XML with JScript.

You should definitely take a closer look at the XMLHTTPRequest object. This object allows you to send GET and POST requests to a Web server. Best of all, it works without causing the browser to refresh. The XMLHTTPRequest object is at the heart of the new Web development methodology called AJAX.

Chapter 7: Handling Exceptions and Debugging

In This Chapter

✔ **Using** `Try...Catch...Finally` **blocks**

✔ **Throwing exceptions**

✔ **Viewing exceptions in the Exception Assistant**

✔ **Setting breakpoints and stepping through code**

✔ **Using the Watch window to view data**

✔ **Debugging code generated by Visual Studio**

*A*nyone who has done even a little coding has been deflated by seeing the Visual Studio Debugger open instead of their beautiful masterpiece. Sometimes you spend more time with the Visual Studio Debugger than you do writing code. Of course, you might see less of the debugger if you start using structured excepting handling to capture exceptions when they do occur. And this chapter shows you how to do just that.

Structured Exception Handling to the Rescue

Whether you're writing code as a professional or a hobbyist, you want your code to perform as advertised. When a user clicks a button to load information from a file, you want to make sure that file is there. If the file isn't there, you want to have some way to deal with the error.

In .NET-speak, errors are called *exceptions*. Code you write to address the exception is called an *exception handler*. When exceptions occur that you haven't written code for, the exception is called an *unhandled exception*. Unhandled exceptions are usually fatal and cause your application to fail.

Visual Studio doesn't really provide exception-handling features. Rather, you deal with exceptions by writing exception handlers in the language of your choice. You can use Visual Studio to do the following:

✦ Step through error-producing code using the Visual Studio Debugger.

✦ Use the Exception Assistant to view details about an exception.

✦ Use code snippets to add exception handlers to your code.

An *exception* is just what it sounds like — anything that occurs in your code that's exceptional or out of the ordinary. For example, if your code opens a file and the file server goes down while you're accessing the file, that's an exception. Not being able to access the file server or find the file in the first place isn't an exception. Your code should test to see whether the file exists before it tries to open the file.

The .NET Framework provides a model for managing exceptions that includes:

✦ Structured exception handling

✦ Common exception framework

✦ Ability to create your own custom exceptions

Handling exceptions

In the good old days, it was every man for himself when it came to handling exceptions. You could return a value when an exception occurred or do nothing at all. While there are plenty of ways you can handle exceptions, you *should* handle exceptions using structured exception handling.

Structured exception handling involves using the following code blocks:

✦ **Try** — Executes statements that might cause an exception, such as opening database connections.

✦ **Catch** — Specifies the exception to catch and executes code to deal with the exception.

✦ **Finally** — Executes every time whether exceptions generate.

Another important feature in structured exception handling is the throw statement, which lets you create a new exception or pass an existing exception to the calling function.

Here's an example of a Try..Catch..Finally block for opening and closing a database connection with ADO.NET:

```
Private Sub AccessData()

  Dim MyConnection As New System.Data.SqlClient.SqlConnection
  MyConnection.ConnectionString = My.Settings.MyDbString

  Try
      MyConnection.Open()
      'send commands

  Catch ex As Exception
```

```
    'handle exception

Finally
    MyConnection.Close()
End Try

End Sub
```

The statements executed in the `Try` block are wired to the `Catch` block. If any statement in the `Try` block throws an exception, the `Catch` block gives you a chance to

✦ Attempt to recover from the exception.

✦ Log the exception.

✦ Provide feedback to the user.

Any code in the optional `Finally` block executes, regardless of whether an exception occurred. Place your cleanup code, such as closing database connections, in the `Finally` block.

Catching exceptions

The .NET Framework provides an extensive catalog of exceptions that starts with the generic `System.Exception`. All exceptions inherit from `System.Exception`. You use a `Catch` block to capture exceptions and handle them. Table 7-1 lists examples of exceptions found in the .NET Framework.

Table 7-1	Example Exceptions Found in the .NET Framework
Exception	*Usage*
`System.Exception`	A generic exception.
`System.NullReferenceException`	Occurs when you attempt to access the value of an object that doesn't exist.
`System.ArgumentNullReference Exception`	Occurs when an unexpected null reference is passed as an argument.
`System.Data.SqlClient. SqlException`	An exception thrown when SQL Server returns a warning or error.
`System.IndexOutofRangeException`	Thrown when you attempt to access beyond an array's index.
`System.InvalidCastException`	Thrown when an attempt to cast from one data type to another is invalid.

You can handle any of the exceptions listed in Table 7-1 using a `Catch` block.

`Catch` blocks use the following syntax:

✦ The keyword `catch`

✦ An optional argument that specifies the kind of exception to catch

Here is a `Catch` block that catches a `SQLException`:

```
Catch ex As System.Data.SqlClient.SqlException
```

You should use multiple `Catch` blocks to catch different kinds of exceptions. You should always try to catch the most specific exception first. The least specific exception is `System.Exception`.

For example, the following code shows two `Catch` blocks:

```
Catch ex As System.Data.SqlClient.SqlException
    'do something with the exception
Catch ex As System.Exception
    'do something with the exception
```

Only one of these `Catch` blocks executes. It's important to list your `Catch` blocks in order of most specific to least specific. As your code executes, it starts at the first `Catch` block and steps through each until it finds a match. If `System.Exception` is the first `Catch` block, no other `Catch` blocks execute.

Figuring out which exceptions you should use can be difficult. One option is to add the exception to the Watch window while debugging. That allows you to see the specific exception captured. Figure 7-1 shows an example of a `System.Exception` caught in the Watch window. See the section "Understanding Debugging," later in this chapter, for more information about using Watch windows.

Figure 7-1:
Use the
Watch
window to
puzzle out
information
about
exceptions.

As Figure 7-1 shows, exceptions provide a lot of information. Some useful properties of exceptions include:

✦ **Data** — Gets a set of key/value pairs that provide optional, additional information about the exception.

✦ **GetBaseException** — Gets the root exception, called the *base exception*, that causes a chain of exceptions to start.

✦ **InnerException** — Gets the exception that causes the current exception. The base exception's `InnerException` is null because the base exception is the first exception in the chain.

✦ **Message** — Gets the exception's description.

✦ **Source** — Is used to get or set the name of the application or object that causes the exception. You can set the `Source` property before you pass an exception to another method to process.

✦ **StackTrace** — Provides a list of all the methods called before the exception occurs.

✦ **TargetSite** — Gets the method that causes the exception. The method provided by the `TargetSite` is the same method listed at the top of the `StackTrace`.

It's important to capture information about exceptions. Exceptions don't always occur while you're sitting in front of your laptop with a cup of joe and your debugger fired up. Exceptions occur when you're two weeks past your deadline on a new project and the last thing you have time for is something you haven't thought about in six months to start malfunctioning. You can use an exception's properties to puzzle out what caused the exception.

Many people log their exceptions to a database or a log file. A popular logging tool for .NET is called log4net. You can download log4net for free at `http://logging.apache.org/log4net`.

Throwing exceptions

When an exception occurs, it is said that the exception is *thrown*. The source of this term is the keyword `throw`, which is used to raise an exception when an error occurs.

There are two uses of the `throw` statement:

✦ **To cause an exception in your program** — The syntax to throw an exception is `throw someException`.

For example, to throw an exception when a null value is passed to a method, you would use the `System.ArgumentNullException` as the following code demonstrates:

```
Private Function SayHello(ByVal name As String) As
    String
If name = Nothing Then
  Throw New System.ArgumentNullException
End If
Return "Hello world, " + name
End Function
```

✦ **To pass an exception to a calling function** — You use the `throw` statement within a `Catch` block to pass an existing exception to a calling function, as the following code shows:

```
Try
    'do something that causes an exception
Catch ex as System.Exception
    Throw
End Try
```

The `Catch` block captures the exception. The `throw` statement passes the captured exception to the calling function. Figure 7-2 shows an example of the `throw` statement in action.

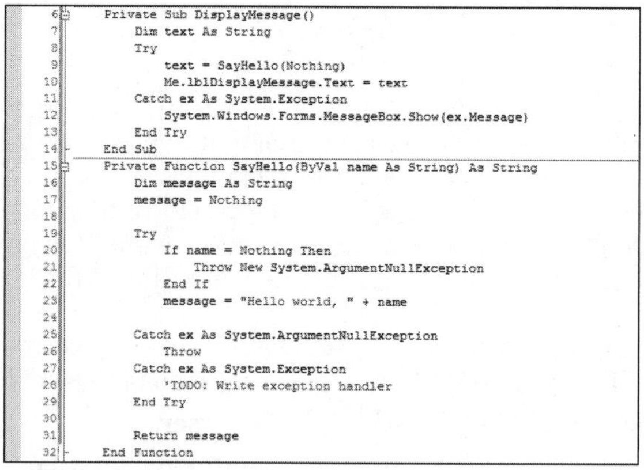

Figure 7-2:
Use the throw statement to pass an exception message to a calling function.

```
 6   Private Sub DisplayMessage()
 7       Dim text As String
 8       Try
 9           text = SayHello(Nothing)
10           Me.lblDisplayMessage.Text = text
11       Catch ex As System.Exception
12           System.Windows.Forms.MessageBox.Show(ex.Message)
13       End Try
14   End Sub
15   Private Function SayHello(ByVal name As String) As String
16       Dim message As String
17       message = Nothing
18
19       Try
20           If name = Nothing Then
21               Throw New System.ArgumentNullException
22           End If
23           message = "Hello world, " + name
24
25       Catch ex As System.ArgumentNullException
26           Throw
27       Catch ex As System.Exception
28           'TODO: Write exception handler
29       End Try
30
31       Return message
32   End Function
```

Note the following in the code sample shown in Figure 7-2:

✦ The subroutine `DisplayMessage()` calls the function `SayHello()` on line 9.

✦ On line 21, `SayHello()` throws an exception of the type `System.ArgumentNullException` because a null value was passed in as a parameter.

✦ Code execution jumps to line 25, where the `Catch` block captures the exception.

✦ Line 26 throws the exception to the caller, `DisplayMessage()`.

✦ Execution returns to line 11, the `Catch` block in `DisplayMessage()`, which captures the exception thrown to it by line 26.

✦ Line 12 displays a message box that displays the exception's `Message` property, which is `Value cannot be null`.

Other times when you might want to use the `throw` statement include:

✦ **To test your exception handlers** — You might find it helpful to have your unit test or other testing harness throw exceptions to test your exception handlers and logging utilities.

✦ **When you use an exception-handling framework** — There are many patterns for how you should handle exceptions. For example, in ASP.NET Web sites, it's typical to have a common exception handler in the Globals.aspx page. All your code's exception handlers simply use the `throw` statement. Any exceptions are automatically handled by an application-wide handler in Globals.aspx.

Using a centralized exception handler makes it easier to ensure that all your exceptions are logged properly. You can also make sure your users are sent to a consistent error page.

Using Visual Studio to manage exceptions

The Microsoft .NET Framework provides an extensive set of exceptions that you can catch and throw. While it's possible to create your own exceptions, in most cases, it isn't necessary. Instead, use the Object Browser to view the list of exceptions available in the .NET Framework.

To use the Object Browser, follow these steps:

1. **Press Ctrl+Alt+J to open the Object Browser.**

2. **In the Browse drop-down list, choose .NET Framework.**

3. **Type** exception **in the Search box and press Enter.**

   A list of objects with the word *exception* in their names appears.

   The .NET Framework uses a naming standard whereby all exceptions end with the word *exception,* such as `System.FormatException`.

4. **Right-click one of the entries listed in the Object Browser and choose Group by Object Type from the shortcut menu.**

   The objects are grouped together by type.

By default, the list of objects is sorted alphabetically. By grouping the objects by type, you see all the exception objects grouped together in the Classes folder.

To view more information about an exception, click the plus (+) sign to expand the exception. Click the exception's name to view the exception's properties and methods. A summary pane lists summary information about the exception. Figure 7-3 shows the exceptions derived from the `System.ArithmeticException` object.

To learn more about an exception, click the exception in the Object Browser and press the F1 key to display help about the exception.

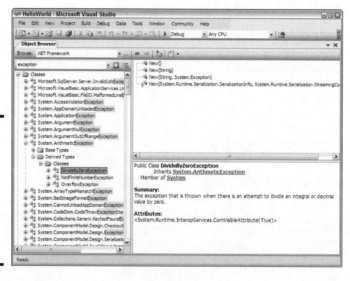

Figure 7-3:
Use the Object Browser to explore the exceptions available in the .NET Framework.

You should always use the most specific exception type available. For example, `System.DivideByZeroException` is more specific than `System.ArithmeticException`.

All exceptions inherit from `System.Exception`. As a result, all exceptions have the same properties of `System.Exception`.

Visual Studio provides the Exception Assistant for viewing information about exceptions while using the Visual Studio Debugger. Visual Studio displays the Exception Assistant any time exceptions are either of the following:

✦ **Unhandled** — Any time Visual Studio encounters an exception while executing your code, the Exception Assistant appears.

✦ **Caught** — While using the Visual Studio Debugger, you can open the Exception Assistant if the debugger breaks at the point where the exception is caught. Press Shift+Alt+F10 to open the Exception Assistant.

Figure 7-4 shows an example of the Exception Assistant for an unhandled exception. The Exception Assistant provides you with

✦ The exception's message.

✦ Tips for troubleshooting the exception message.

✦ The exception's properties. Click View Detail to view the exception's properties.

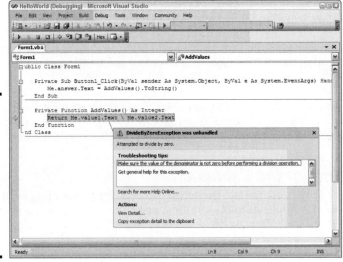

Figure 7-4:
The Exception Assistant appears when an unhandled exception is encountered.

Understanding Debugging

Debugging allows you to stop your code during execution and inspect it. Visual Studio provides a sophisticated debugger that allows you to

✦ Control the execution of your code so you can peek inside your code while it's running.

✦ Test your code while you're designing it.

✦ View the data used by your code.

✦ Get detailed information about exceptions that occur.

Enabling debugging

In order to use the Visual Studio Debugger with your code, you must build your code using the Debug build configuration. The Debug build configuration tells the compiler to create a program database (PDB) file for your code. The PDB file stores the data about your source code, such as

✦ Source code line numbers

✦ Variable names

✦ Method names

The Visual Studio Debugger uses the PDB file to know how to access your source code as it's being executed.

The data stored in the program database file are called *symbols*.

You should generate PDB files for all builds, including release builds. Generating a PDB file allows you to debug the build even if you didn't build it as a debug build.

To set your application to use the Debug build configuration, choose Debug from the Solution Configurations drop-down list on the Standard toolbar. To create or modify build configurations, see Book VI, Chapter 1.

Firing up the debugger

Your application has two modes in the debugger: executing or breaking. While your application is executing, everything's A-okay. Once your application stops executing, or breaks, then you get busy with the debugger.

Your application executes until it encounters either of the following:

✦ **Breakpoint** — A marker you set in the code that tells the debugger to stop execution

✦ **Exception** — An unhandled error generated by your code that causes program execution to stop

While your code is in break mode, you have the features of the debugger at your disposal for examining your code.

Controlling execution

One of the primary features of the Visual Studio Debugger is the ability to control your program's execution. Controlling execution allows you to walk through your code as well as check the values of variables and data.

The debugger provides the following code execution options:

Understanding Debugging **609**

Book V
Chapter 7

Handling
Exceptions and
Debugging

✦ **Starting** — Starts your code. You must use the Debug build configuration for the debugger to fire up.

✦ **Stepping** — Allows you to step through your code.

✦ **Breaking** — You can break the code's execution by setting a breakpoint or manually breaking. Your code breaks automatically when an unhandled exception occurs.

✦ **Stopping** — Execution stops when your program completes execution or you manually stop it.

There are several ways to start the debugger:

✦ **Debug menu** — Use the commands Start Debug, Step Into, or Step Over to execute your code.

✦ **Run to Cursor** — Right-click an executable line of code and choose Run to Cursor from the shortcut menu. The debugger starts your code and breaks at the line where your cursor sits.

✦ **Keyboard shortcuts** — Table 7-2 lists common keyboard shortcuts you can use to control the debugger.

I use the keyboard shortcuts almost exclusively to step through code.

✦ **Debug toolbar** — The Debug toolbar acts like VCR buttons for controlling your code's execution. Figure 7-5 shows the Debug toolbar.

Table 7-2	Common Debugging Keyboard Shortcuts
Keyboard Shortcut	*Command*
F5	Start Debugging
Ctrl+F5	Start without Debugging
F11	Step Into
F10	Step Over
Shift+F11	Step Out

Figure 7-5:
Use the Debug toolbar to control your code's execution.

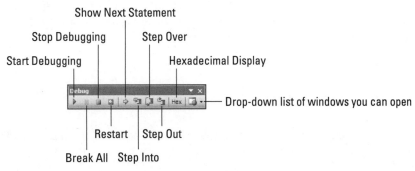

Breaking execution

The first step in using the debugger is breaking your code during execution. To break your code during execution, you can do any one of the following:

✦ Click the Break All button on the Debug toolbar.

✦ Choose Break All from the Debug menu.

✦ Press Ctrl+Alt+Break.

In most cases, you'll likely set a breakpoint in your code before you start execution. By setting a breakpoint, your code stops executing at the line of code where the breakpoint is set. You can then step through the code and watch your variables as the code executes.

Here's how to set a breakpoint:

1. Go to the line of source code in the code editor where you want code execution to break.

2. From the Debug menu, choose Toggle Breakpoint.

A solid glyph appears in the code editor's left gutter. The breakpoint appears in the Breakpoints window. Figure 7-6 shows the breakpoint.

The solid glyph

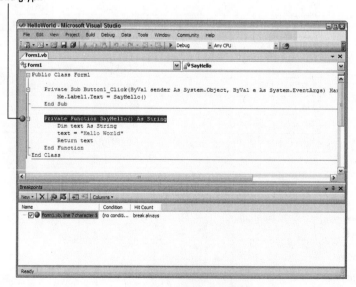

Figure 7-6:
Set a break-
point in the
code editor.

You can use alternative ways to set breakpoints, such as the following:

✦ Click the left gutter in the code editor to toggle a breakpoint for an executable line of code.

✦ Right-click a line of code and choose Breakpoint from the shortcut menu.

✦ Press F9.

You can use the Breakpoints window to manage your breakpoints. The Breakpoints window allows you to

✦ Create new breakpoints.

✦ Enable or disable breakpoints.

✦ Set conditions on when the breakpoint occurs.

✦ Filter the breakpoint for specific machines, processes, and threads.

✦ Specify how many times the code should execute before execution breaks.

To create a new breakpoint using the Breakpoints window:

1. **Press Ctrl+Alt+B to display the Breakpoints window.**

2. **Choose New⇨Break at Function.**

The New Breakpoint window appears.

3. **Type the name of the function where you want to create the breakpoint in the Function text box.**

For example, type **SayHello()** to create a breakpoint at a function called `SayHello()`.

4. **Click the OK button.**

The function appears in the Breakpoints window, as Figure 7-7 shows.

Stepping through code

Visual Studio provides several options for controlling the execution of your code. Besides just starting, pausing, and stopping code execution, you can step through your code one statement at a time. The three, step options are:

✦ **Step Into** — Breaks on each line of code.

✦ **Step Over** — Breaks on each line of code except functions. The function executes and code execution breaks at the first line outside of the function.

✦ **Step Out** — Resumes execution on a function and then breaks at the first line of code outside the function.

Step Into and Step Over start the debugger at the next line of code. Step Out allows you to stop debugging a function but then break execution as soon as the function exits.

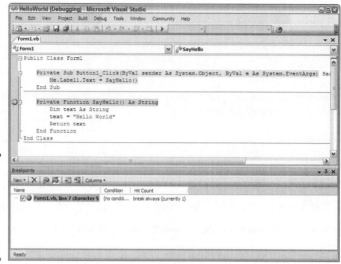

Figure 7-7:
Use the
Breakpoints
window to
add new
breakpoints.

To step through your code, follow these steps:

1. Set breakpoints in your code.

For example, create a form with a button and add a Click event for the button. Set the breakpoint on the button's Click event to break the code's execution when you click the button.

2. Press F5 to start the debugger.

Visual Studio builds your code and starts execution. The code executes until it encounters a breakpoint. Figure 7-8 shows an example of the debugger hitting a breakpoint. The code editor highlights the code in yellow.

3. Press F11 to step into the next line of execution.

4. Continue to press F11 until you encounter a function.

To follow the execution into the function, press F11 to step into the function.

To execute the function without stepping through it, press F10 to step over the function.

To step out of the function once you enter it, press Shift+F11 to step out.

Figure 7-9 shows an example of the debugger stepping into a function. The debugger hit the breakpoint in line 3 in Figure 7-9. I pressed the F11 key to step through each line. At line 7, I encountered the function SayHello(). I stepped into the function, and the debugger jumped to line 14 where the function starts. The arrow in the code editor's left gutter shows the current line being executed.

Execution breaks where you set the breakpoint.

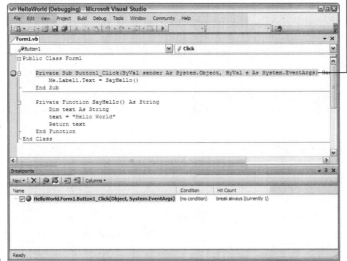

Figure 7-8:
The debugger highlights the code statement when it hits a breakpoint.

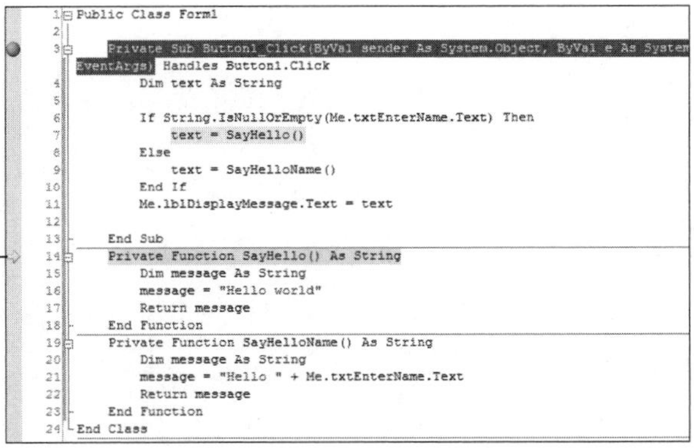

Figure 7-9:
Use the debugger to step through your code.

The arrow indicates the line being executed.

5. **Press Shift+F11 to step out of the function.**

   The debugger executes the function and returns to the calling line of code.

   In the case of the code in Figure 7-9, pressing F11 returns you to line 7 and breaks execution.

6. **Resume stepping through the code using the F11 key.**

   F5 is the shortcut key for the Continue command. Press F5 at any time to resume execution until the code terminates or hits another breakpoint.

The Debug toolbar has three buttons that correspond to the Step Into, Step Over, and Step Out commands, respectively.

You can use the Run to Cursor command to execute your code to the cursor. Right-click a line of code in the code editor and choose Run to Cursor from the shortcut menu. Code execution breaks at the line where your cursor is positioned.

To know whether your code is running or debugging, you'll see the word *(Running)* or *(Debugging)* in the title bar. Figure 7-10 shows an example.

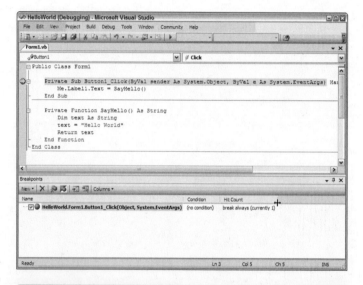

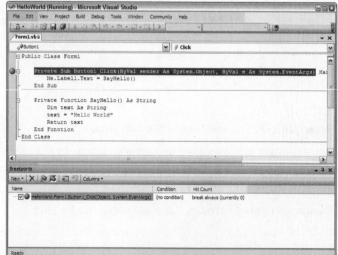

Figure 7-10: The title bar displays the execution status of your program.

Viewing data with the debugger

The Visual Studio Debugger provides several windows for managing the debugging process. These windows automatically appear in the bottom of the screen by default while you're debugging. You can access and open debugging windows by choosing the Debug⇨Windows menu selection. Table 7-3 lists the debugging windows and their functions.

Table 7-3		Debugging Windows and Their Functions		
Window	*Type*	*Access*	*Shortcut Key*	*Function*
Breakpoints	Execution control	Debug menu	Ctrl+Alt+B	Creates a new breakpoint or edits an existing breakpoint.
Output	Feedback	Debug menu		Displays results or feedback.
Script Explorer		Debug menu	Ctrl+Alt+N	Lists scripts used by your program.
Watch	Variable	Debug menu	Ctrl+Alt+W, 1	Displays variables and expressions you add to the window.
Autos	Variable	Debug menu	Ctrl+Alt+V, A	Displays variables used in the current and preceding lines of code.
Locals	Variable	Debug menu	Ctrl+Alt+V, L	Displays all variables in scope.
Immediate	Variable	Debug menu	Ctrl+Alt+I	Executes commands and sets variable values.
Call Stack	Memory	Debug menu	Ctrl+Alt+C	Displays functions in memory.
Threads	CPU	Debug menu	Ctrl+Alt+H	Displays a set of instructions being executed by your program.
Modules	Memory	Debug menu	Ctrl+Alt+U	Lists the software modules used by your program.
Processes	Memory	Debug menu	Ctrl+Alt+Z	Displays processes which your program has launched or attached to.
Memory	Memory	Debug menu	Ctrl+Alt+M, 1	Displays contents of memory.
Disassembly	CPU	Debug menu	Ctrl+Alt+D	Displays assembly code of your program.
Registers	CPU	Debug menu	Ctrl+Alt+G	Displays registers' contents.
QuickWatch	Variable	Debug menu in break mode	Ctrl+Alt+Q	Displays values of current value or expression.
Exception Assistant	Feedback			Displays information about an exception when an exception occurs.
DataTips	Variable	Hover mouse over variable		Displays value of variable in scope.

Figure 7-11 shows the tabs of the debugging windows at the bottom of a screen. Click a tab to access the window.

Figure 7-11:
Use the debugging windows at the bottom of the screen to debug your code.

Many of the debugging windows allow you to observe the contents of your variables and data structures.

Visual Studio has a feature called DataTips that lets you view the contents of a variable. Simply hover your mouse over a variable that's active, and a DataTip appears that displays the variable's value. Figure 7-12 shows a DataTip.

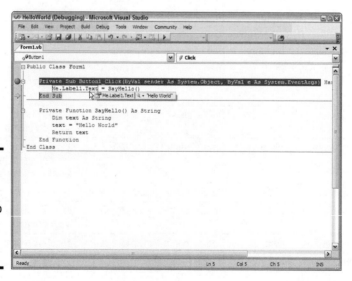

Figure 7-12:
Hover your mouse over a variable to display its value in a DataTip.

The variable in Figure 7-12 is a string variable. You can use DataTips to display complex variables such as DataSets.

Visual Studio also provides the Autos, Locals, and Watch windows for viewing variable values. The Autos and Locals windows populate automatically. You use the Watch window to identify a specific variable you want to monitor.

To use the Watch window to monitor a DataSet, follow these steps:

1. **Set a breakpoint in your code where you wish to monitor a variable.**

2. **Press F5 to start the debugger.**

3. **When code execution breaks, choose Debug⇨Windows ⇨Watch 1.**

The Watch window appears.

The debugger must be in break mode to open the Watch window. There are a total of four Watch windows. Each window has a number from 1 to 4 appended to it.

4. **Right-click the object you wish to add to the Watch window.**

5. **Choose Add Watch from the shortcut menu.**

The object appears in the Watch window.

Be sure to click the object and not a property of the object.

6. **Press F5 to resume execution.**

The code executes until it hits a breakpoint.

When the variable or object is in scope, its values appear in the Watch window, as Figure 7-13 shows.

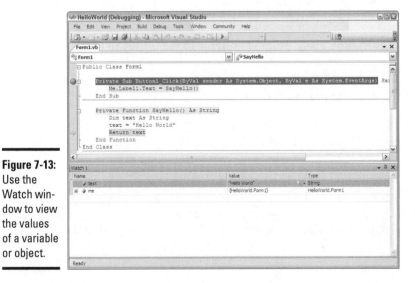

Figure 7-13:
Use the Watch window to view the values of a variable or object.

You can add objects to the Watch window by typing their names in the Name field. For example, to add a Watch using a DataSet with the name `DataSet1`:

1. **Open the Watch window using the preceding steps.**

2. **Type** DataSet1 **in the Name field.**

IntelliSense lists the properties and methods you can select.

3. **Select a member of the DataSet to watch.**

Figure 7-14 shows the Watch window with DataSet members added.

Figure 7-14:
Use
IntelliSense
to add
members to
the Watch
window.

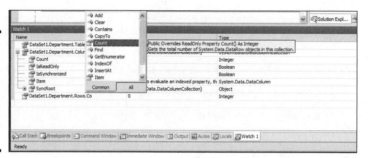

Debugging for those special circumstances

The Visual Studio Debugger is sophisticated, and you can use it to debug very complex scenarios. Using the debugger in a single tier Windows application is about as easy as it gets. In the real world, however, applications aren't quite that simple.

You can use the Visual Studio Debugger to debug any of these:

✦ ASP.NET Web sites

✦ Managed stored procedures

✦ Scripts

✦ Code on remote servers

Going through the setup processes for each of these is beyond the scope of this book. See the Visual Studio documentation for more information.

Once you get the debugger set up to work in your scenario, the business of controlling execution and watching variables is basically the same.

Debugging ASP.NET Web sites

When you debug an ASP.NET application, you must set `debug=true` in the compilation section of the web.config file. The first time you run the debugger on an ASP.NET Web site, Visual Studio displays a dialog box that prompts you to enable debugging. Figure 7-15 shows an example.

Figure 7-15:
You must
enable
debugging
on ASP.NET
Web sites.

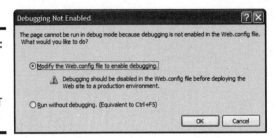

Before you deploy your site to a production server, you must open the web.config file and set `debug=false`, as the following code shows:

```
<compilation debug="false">
```

Debugging generated code

Visual Studio generates a lot of code for you. There might be times when you want to step through that code with the debugger so you can see how the code works. To step into code that is not yours, you must disable the debugger's Just My Code feature.

To disable the feature, follow these steps:

1. **Choose Tools⇨Options.**

   The Options window appears.

2. **Click Debugging.**

3. **Disable the Enable Just My Code check box.**

4. **Click OK.**

Now you can hit breakpoints inside generated code. To see generated code, click the Show All Files button on Solution Explorer's toolbar.

Chapter 8: Testing Code with Visual Studio

In This Chapter

✓ **Understanding different kinds of software testing**

✓ **Creating and running unit tests**

✓ **Introducing stubs and mocks**

✓ **Using the Object Test Bench**

✓ **Exploring unit testing frameworks**

So you're plugging along coding like crazy. You'll have this set of requirements knocked out in no time. But how do you know when you're done? If you're unit testing your code as you go, the answer is when your code passes all your tests. If you're not unit testing as you go, you'll probably code until you feel like you're done and then pass the code off for somebody else to test.

I did an internship as a software tester with a consulting house. There was one developer in particular who never tested his code. Of course, he said he tested code, but it always went kablooey as soon as I got it. If he ever bothered to look at the requirements, I'll never know. I had to refer him to the requirements documents over and over again until his code finally fit the bill.

Testing is an important part of the software development life cycle. Many kinds of tests are performed to ensure an application fulfills its requirements. Developers are usually responsible for writing tests called *unit tests* (see the next section for more information) to test the code they write. In Visual Studio 2005 Professional Edition, testing is more of a coding practice than a feature. Microsoft provides upgraded editions of Visual Studio that provide extensive support for all kinds of testing.

In this chapter, I discuss the importance of testing, show you how to write simple unit tests, and show you some of the Visual Studio tools you can use to support your testing efforts.

What Is Unit Testing?

Testing means different things depending on the context in which it's used. Developers are usually responsible for testing the code they write, which is called *unit testing*. After code passes unit tests, it's usually checked into a source code control repository. At some point, the entire system under development is compiled, and quality assurance testers perform even more testing.

The kinds of tests you might encounter include:

✦ **Unit tests** — These are programs written by developers to test the code they write.

✦ **Integration tests** — These are tests that test units of code once they've been integrated with each other.

✦ **System tests** — During system tests, the entire integrated system is tested. Depending on the kind of software being tested, system tests might include user interface testing, regression testing, and load testing.

✦ **Acceptance tests** — During acceptance tests, any or all of the system's stakeholders might participate in testing the software in a lab.

As the software progresses through testing, the tests become less focused on the inner workings of the code. As a result, testing becomes less automated and requires more user interaction. In the case of acceptance testing, it's common to set up a test lab where end users come in and bang away at the system for weeks at a time, uncovering bugs and functional shortcomings.

As a developer, you're actively involved in writing and running unit tests. Your interaction with the testing process beyond unit testing depends on several factors, including the extent to which your code provides any of the system's core functionality.

Of course, use of unit testing doesn't mean there are no bugs. Rather, the implicit understanding is that when you check in your code, you're telling other developers that the code works at some basic level of functionality. If your code breaks every time it's called by another developer, it's a pretty good indication that you're either not unit testing or not doing enough unit testing.

When I've worked as a tester in the past, I could always spot developers who never ran unit tests. Not only did their code usually not conform to the requirements, it usually blew up as soon I tried to test it. Other developers, however, were very conscientious about unit testing their code. As a result, I didn't need to interact with those developers as much. In other words, if you don't want quality assurance and your fellow developers on your back, unit test your code.

By definition, unit testing is about writing code. When you write a unit test, you're writing code to test code. You write a unit test to test a single unit of your code. For example, assume your project includes code for a `Customer` object and an `Address` object. You should have one unit test for each object. The unit test contains multiple tests to test the various methods and properties of your object. Figure 8-1 shows an example.

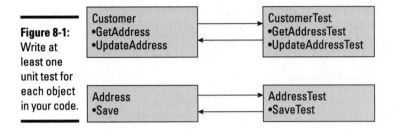

Figure 8-1:
Write at least one unit test for each object in your code.

There are tons of rules about how you should write your tests. They're not really rules; they're more like opinions. And everybody has an opinion on what it means to unit test. Some of these opinions are that

✦ All tests should be automated and run as part of a suite.

✦ All your code should be tested.

✦ You should write your tests before you write your code.

Getting started with unit testing can be quite overwhelming. While these approaches are valid and ones to which you should aspire, remember that it's better to

✦ Write imperfect tests than to write no tests at all.

✦ Run tests manually before you check in your code than run no tests at all. Test the riskiest parts of your code first until you get the hang of unit testing.

Unit Testing in Visual Studio

Unit testing is an important good coding practice. While you're coding, you should write tests that make sure your code works as you expect. Unit tests aren't supposed to test every aspect of the system. Rather, unit tests are sanity checks you use to make sure your code works. For example, if your requirement states that the function should return an integer, you might create a unit test to test that the value returned by your function is indeed an integer.

When used properly, unit tests help you achieve the following important goals:

✦ Write better code.

✦ Have a starting point for testing code.

✦ Keep the development process flowing.

✦ Increase your confidence in your code.

There are lots of patterns and frameworks for writing unit tests. At its simplest, a unit test simply tests that your code does what it says it does. Unit tests either pass or fail. There's no in-between.

Creating unit tests

Before you can write a unit test, you need code to test. In this section, I use a very simple Hello World example with the following methods:

✦ `DisplayMessage()` — Displays a `Hello World` message, depending on whether the user supplies a name.

✦ `SayHello()` — Returns the message `Hello World`.

✦ `SayHelloName(name)` — Returns the message `Hello` plus the name provided as an argument.

These methods are used in a Windows Form that displays a `Hello World` message. If the user enters a name in a text box on the form, the user's name appears in the message.

Listed below is the code to be unit tested. Notice there are three methods to test:

```
Public Sub DisplayMessage()
    Dim text, name As String
    name = Me.txtEnterName.Text

    If String.IsNullOrEmpty(name) Then
        text = SayHello()
    Else
        text = SayHelloName(name)
    End If

    Me.lblDisplayMessage.Text = text
End Sub

Private Function SayHello() As String
    Dim message As String
    message = "Hello World"
    Return message
End Function

Private Function SayHelloName(ByVal name As String) As String
    Dim message As String
    message = "Hello " + name
    Return message
End Function
```

To test this code, you write a set of tests that makes sure the output is as expected. For example, the `SayHello()` method is supposed to return `Hello World`. The unit test should test the return value. Listed here is a function that tests `SayHello()`:

```
Dim message As String
Dim results As New Hashtable

message = SayHello()

If Not message = "Hello World" Then
  results.Add("Form1.SayHello", "Failed")
End If
```

The test uses a hash table to store a key/value pair that consists of the name of the test case and the case's result. You can add the results of all your tests to a hash table and then output the hash table to a file or screen.

Each test you create is called a *test case*. Some functions might require multiple test cases. For example, DisplayMessage can return two different messages, so two test cases are appropriate. Following is the entire code sample that tests the set of code.

```
Public Function SmokeTest() As Hashtable
    Dim message As String
    Dim results As New Hashtable

    'test sayhello
    message = SayHello()

    If Not message = "Hello World" Then
        results.Add("Form1.SayHello", "Failed")
    End If

    'reset variable
    message = Nothing

    'test sayhelloname
    message = SayHelloName("John")
    If Not message = "Hello Jim" Then
        results.Add("Form1.SayHelloName", "Failed")
    End If

    'test displaymessage
    Me.txtEnterName.Text = Nothing
    Me.lblDisplayMessage.Text = Nothing
    DisplayMessage()
    If Not Me.lblDisplayMessage.Text = "Hello World" Then
        results.Add("Form1.DisplayMessageNoName", "Failed")
    End If

    'test displaymessage
    Me.txtEnterName.Text = "John"
    Me.lblDisplayMessage.Text = Nothing
    DisplayMessage()
    If Not Me.lblDisplayMessage.Text = "Hello John" Then
        results.Add("Form1.DisplayMessageWithName", "Failed")
```

```
        End If

        Return results

End Function
```

Before you start criticizing me for having too much repetitious code or doing too many things in one procedure, take into consideration the point of this demonstration. My point is that you don't have to write fancy code in order to unit test. There are several ways to improve this code. As a developer, I may choose to improve the code or leave it a little rough around the edges. Either way, it gets the job done. At the end of the day, I know exactly whether my procedures work or don't.

I intentionally named this procedure SmokeTest to indicate that this is a first test just to make sure the code works. In electronics, a new circuit will smoke when it's powered up if it has been wired incorrectly. Attaching power to a circuit for the first time is often called a smoke test. If no smoke appears, then it's assumed the circuit has been wired properly. In software development, the term smoke test is often applied to any initial tests that are run to ensure that a component has basic functionality. Though a smoke test isn't usually comprehensive in itself, a smoke test is usually refined into a more comprehensive unit test.

Running a battery of tests

It's important that you be able to run your tests with the click of a mouse or by entering a single command. In this section, I show you how to create a simple Windows Form that runs your unit tests and outputs the results to the screen.

To create a Windows Form to display the results of your unit tests, follow these steps:

1. **Create a new Windows Form.**

   See Chapter 1 in Book III to see how to add a Windows Form to a project.

2. **Drag a button and a list box onto the form.**

3. **Use the Properties window to set the button's name to btnRunTests and the list box's name to lstResults.**

4. **Double-click the button to access the button's Click event handler.**

   The code editor appears.

5. **Create a new instance of the class where the unit test is.**

   Typically, unit tests are created as separate units of code. For example, you might create a test for a Customer object called CustomerTest. To create a new instance of the CustomerTest object so you can access the object's tests, you'd type the following:

```
Dim myTest as New CustomerTest
```

The unit test from the preceding example isn't in a separate unit of code. Rather, the test itself is embedded in a Windows Form called `DisplayHelloWorld`. You might choose to embed your tests in your forms when you first start unit testing, although it isn't considered a best practice to do so.

Type the following code to create a new instance of `DisplayHelloWorld`:

```
Dim myTest As New DisplayHelloWorld
```

This code allows you to access the unit test in the Windows Form.

6. Create a new instance of a Hashtable and a key/value pair to represent each entry in the Hashtable.

```
Dim htResults As New System.Collections.Hashtable
Dim testcase As System.Collections.DictionaryEntry
```

This code assumes that the results of your unit tests are stored in a Hashtable.

7. Call the unit test and pass the results to the local Hashtable.

For example, type the following code to access a test method called `SmokeTest()` and pass the results to the local Hashtable.

```
htResults = myTest.SmokeTest()
```

Simple tests that are run to make sure code works are often called *smoke tests*. I've used the method name `SmokeTest()` to signify that this is an informal test. For example, it might be a first attempt at creating a set of tests for a unit of code.

8. Use a For Each statement to loop through each entry in the Hashtable and display the results in the list box.

```
For Each testcase In htResults
    Me.lstResults.Items.Add(testcase.Key + ": " +
    testcase.Value)
Next
```

9. Press F5 to run your test form.

10. Click the button to run your tests.

The results appear in the list box, as shown in Figure 8-2.

You might wonder why I didn't output the results of my successful unit tests. The whole point of unit tests is that they should be fast. If they aren't fast, you won't run them. I don't care about the tests that pass. I only care about the ones that don't. In Figure 8-2, I immediately see that one of my tests failed. I need to go take care of that.

Figure 8-2:
Display the
results of
your failed
unit tests.

Writing better code

One of the positive side effects of unit tests is that you write better code. For example, while writing the test for DisplayMessage(), I realize that the subroutine is tightly coupled to the Windows Form, which makes the unit test harder to write. So I decide to rewrite the DisplayMessage subroutine as a function so it's easier to test. The new function looks like this:

```
Private Function DisplayMessage(ByVal name As String) As
    String
    Dim text As String

    If String.IsNullOrEmpty(name) Then
        text = SayHello()
    Else
        text = SayHelloName(name)
    End If

    Return text

End Function
```

The unit test for DisplayMessage changes so that it's more consistent with my other unit tests:

```
'test displaymessage
message = Nothing
message = DisplayMessage(Nothing)
If Not message = "Hello World" Then
  results.Add("DisplayHelloWorld.DisplayMessageNoName",
    "Failed")
End If

'test displaymessage
message = Nothing
message = DisplayMessage("John")
If Not message = "Hello John" Then
```

```
results.Add("DisplayHelloWorld.DisplayMessageWithName",
    "Failed")
End If
```

Rewriting code is called *refactoring*. See Book V, Chapter 5 for more information on refactoring.

Approaches to Unit Testing

Within the past few years, unit testing has taken on a life of its own. It's not cool not to unit test. One of the hardest choices when creating unit tests is deciding what to test. When you examine code you want to test, you'll find the following issues to consider:

✦ **Public methods** — *Public methods* are the features of your code that are exposed to the outside world. Pretty much everyone agrees you should unit test your public methods. After all, a public method is sitting there saying, "Call me."

✦ **Private and protected methods** — The private and protected methods in your code do the work of your public methods. As a result, some people believe it's wasteful to test private and protected methods. They believe that unit testing public methods implicitly tests private and protected methods. Plus, testing private and protected methods is harder. By their nature, private and protected methods are, well, private and protected. Unlike public methods, they aren't saying, "Call me." Just the opposite is true, so you need to go out of your way to test them.

✦ **Interactions with other code** — Unless you're writing all your application's features in a single function, chances are high your code needs to interact with other code. The very nature of unit testing, however, is that you want to test only a single unit of code. How can you do that if you have to interact with other code?

Public methods are easily tested because, by definition, you can call a public method from anywhere in your code. You can use Visual Studio's Object Test Bench to call public methods in your code. See the section, "Using the Object Test Bench," later in this chapter.

People take all kinds of approaches to solve the problems of testing private methods or code that interacts with other code. One popular approach is to use software that specializes in unit testing, usually called *unit testing frameworks*. See the section "Automating tests with testing frameworks," later in this chapter.

There are two approaches to testing code that interacts with other code: stubs and mocks. Keep reading for information on those approaches.

Letting stubs do the tough testing

By definition, a unit test is only supposed to test one unit of code. No unit of code lives in isolation, however. Most developers work around this pesky paradox by using code stubs. The code stub acts as a placeholder for units of code that the unit being tested needs to interact with. The code stub placeholder is better than interacting with the actual units of code, because each unit of code introduces a new set of variables. Instead, the code stub can be programmed to return a consistent set of values against which the unit can interact. Returning a consistent set of values creates predictability, which makes it easier to create tests that you can repeat over and over again.

In reality, developers who use stubs usually go ahead and test the real units of code that interact with the unit their testing, as long as it's simple to do so. For example, say you create a `Customer` object that has a public method called `GetAddress`. `GetAddress` returns an `Address` object. The `Customer` and `Address` objects are each units of code that have their own set of unit tests. Many developers will create a test that allows their `Customer` object to interact with the `Address` object, even though the test extends beyond the unit they wish to test.

When the developer encounters a set of code that would be too complicated or messy with which to interact in a simple unit test, the developer usually creates a stub. The stub returns a set of canned values that the developer expects to get from the code. For example, say your `Customer` object has a method called `UpdateAddress`. `UpdateAddress` accepts a new address for a customer and passes that data off to an `Address` object. The `Address` object calls a service that validates the address against a valid zip code database. You don't want to have to deal with all that when you're testing your `Customer` object. Instead of using the `Address` object, you create a stub that returns two possible values. If you pass in a valid address, it returns the value `ValidAddress`. If you pass an invalid address, it returns the value `InvalidAddress`. How does the stub know what's a valid address and what's an invalid address? You specify in the stub that `123 Main Street`, for example, is a valid address. Everything else is invalid. Figure 8-3 shows an example of a stub.

Simplifying testing with mocking objects

Other developers believe that creating a bunch of objects and stubs is too much work. These developers use a special library to create mock objects. With mock objects, or mocks, you tell the object which methods you expect it to run, how many times the methods will run, and what values to return.

For example, assume you use a mock `Address` object to interact with your `Customer` address. For your `UpdateAddress` test, you tell the mock `Address` object to call the `Address` object's `Save` method. Your test tells the mock object that you're going to send a value of `123 Main Street` to the `Save` method and you expect it to return a value of `true`. Your test also tells the mock object you're going to send the value `123 Nowhere Boulevard` and you expect the `Save` method to return the value `false`. Figure 8-4 shows an example of a mock object.

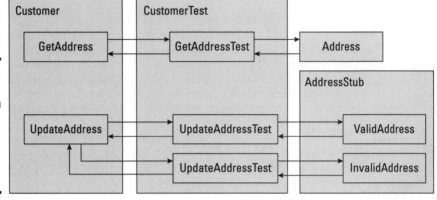

Figure 8-3:
Use stubs any time you want to avoid messy code interactions in your testing.

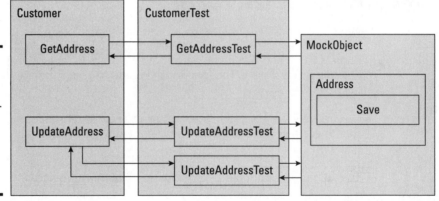

Figure 8-4:
Use mock objects to set expectations about methods called and values returned.

The stubbies versus the mockers

Deciding which method to use can be a little difficult at first glance, but there are several key differences between using mocks and stubs, based on what you want to test for. Here are some of them:

✦ You tell your mock objects which methods to call, how many times they'll be called by your test, and what return values you expect.

✦ Stubs usually return only values.

✦ You create mocks for all objects with which your code interacts.

✦ You only create stubs when necessary.

✦ Mocks require a library of code to create the mock objects.

I call those who use stubs "stubbies," and those who use mock objects "mockers." Stubbies and mockers usually have totally different approaches to unit testing that go beyond the mere use of stubs and mocks. Stubbies tend to test clusters of interacting objects together. For example, stubbies might test all the code related to customers and orders together because those units of code interact.

Mockers, on the other hand, are more likely to take a top-down approach. They might start testing at the user interface level first and use mock objects to mimic the behavior of business rules or data access code. Mockers are likely to test first and code second. In other words, they use testing as a way to discover what code they still need to write to make their system work.

The use of mock objects is very popular in a style of development called test-driven development (TDD). With TDD, you test first and code second. For more information, see the Test Driven Web site at http://www. testdriven.com.

Using the Object Test Bench

In the Microsoft .NET Framework, everything's an object. When you write code, you're writing code to create your own objects. For example, a Windows Form is an object. When you add a new Windows Form to a project, you're creating a new object. The functions you add to your form are the object's methods.

Objects must be created before you can use them. Visual Studio provides the Object Test Bench as a test environment where you can interact with your objects.

To read more about objects, see Chapter 3 of this mini-book.

You use the Object Test Bench to perform the following tasks:

✦ Create a new instance of an object.

✦ Create multiple instances of the same object.

✦ Call an object's public methods.

✦ Evaluate the results of the method.

The Object Test Bench is a good way to explore your own code, somebody else's, or the .NET Framework.

You access the Object Test Bench from the Class Designer, Class View, or Object Browser. To create a new instance of an object using Class View, follow these steps:

1. **Open a solution where you want to use the Object Test Bench.**

2. **Press Ctrl+Shift+C to open the Class View window.**

The namespace for your projects appears in the Class View.

3. **Expand the namespace until you find the object you want to view in the Object Test Bench, as shown in Figure 8-5.**

The project displayed in Figure 8-5 is a refactored version of the `HelloWorld` example used in the preceding section.

Figure 8-5:
Use the
Class View
to create
a new
instance of
an object in
the Object
Test Bench.

4. **Right-click the object.**

A shortcut menu appears.

5. **Choose Create Instance.**

A submenu appears with a list of the constructors you can use to create the object.

A constructor is a special kind of method that creates instances of objects.

6. **Choose the constructor from the menu.**

The Create Instance window appears.

7. Type the name you want to use for the instance in the Object Test Bench.

A default name is provided.

For example, to create an instance of the `HelloWorld` class, open the Create Instance window and type the name **helloWorldExample** in the Create Instance window, as Figure 8-6 shows.

Using the Create Instance window is the same thing as typing the following code:

```
Dim helloWorldExample as New HelloWorld()
```

Figure 8-6:
Type a name
for the
object
instance in
the Create
Instance
form.

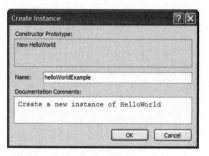

8. Click OK.

The object appears in the Object Test Bench.

Visual Studio builds your project before it creates an instance of your object. You must resolve any build errors before you can use the Object Test Bench.

You can call an object's public methods from the Object Test Bench. To call a public method, follow these steps:

1. Right-click an object instance in the Object Test Bench.

A shortcut menu appears.

2. Choose Invoke Method.

A submenu appears. All the object's public methods appear in the list.

3. Click the method you wish to invoke. The Invoke Method window appears.

For example, to call the `DisplayMessage()` method on the `helloWorldExample` object from the preceding set of steps, choose Invoke Method⇨DisplayMessage(ByVal as String).

The Invoke Method window displays a parameters grid where you can enter values to pass to the method, if required.

4. **Type parameter values in the Invoke Method window, as shown in Figure 8-7.**

For example, the `DisplayMessage()` method accepts a string parameter. Type a value for the parameter such as `"John"`.

Figure 8-7:
Type parameter values in the Invoke Method window.

5. **Click OK.**

The Method Call Result window appears, displaying the results of the method call. To save the returned value to the Object Test Bench, enable the `Save return value` check box.

6. **Click OK.**

An object representing the value appears in the Object Test Bench. Figure 8-8 shows the Object Test Bench with the results from two method calls.

 Everything in the .NET Framework is an object. I mean everything, including Windows Forms. If you're struggling with getting your mind around object-oriented programming or you want to learn more about the .NET Framework, use the Object Test Bench to explore.

Figure 8-8:
Use the Object Test Bench to invoke public methods on your objects and view the results.

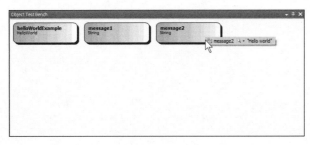

Automating tests with testing frameworks

Unit tests are often grouped together so they can be executed by a testing framework. A framework isn't necessary, but using a framework allows you to do these things:

✦ Formalize unit testing.

✦ Create consistency among unit tests.

✦ Make it easier to automate testing.

✦ Execute groups of tests at one time.

Frameworks are a necessity for most systems. Because unit tests are so granular, even a simple system has lots of tests. In most cases, it makes sense to use a framework to administer the tests. Unit testing frameworks exist for nearly every programming language under the sun. Two popular unit testing frameworks for the .NET Framework include:

✦ **NUnit** — By far, NUnit is the most popular testing framework around. NUnit is an open source framework. Because NUnit is open source, it's available for free. One of the drawbacks of NUnit is that it isn't integrated into Visual Studio. Still, many folks use NUnit to manage their unit tests.

✦ **Visual Studio Team System** — The newest edition of Visual Studio, Visual Studio Team System (or VSTS), provides a unit testing framework that's integrated into Visual Studio. Using the framework is as simple as right-clicking the code you want to test and choosing Create Tests from the shortcut menu. Your tests are stored in Test Projects. VSTS provides support for many different kinds of tests, including the ability to record Web tests. For more on Visual Studio Team System, turn to Book VII, Chapter 2.

Two other popular unit-testing tools for the .NET Framework include:

✦ **NMock** — Creates mock objects for use with unit tests.

✦ **TestDriven.NET** — Integrates testing frameworks, such as NUnit, into the Visual Studio development environment. TestDriven.NET gives you the ability to access testing commands from a shortcut menu in the code editor.

Chapter 9: Using Enterprise Library

In This Chapter

✔ **Getting started with Enterprise Library**

✔ **Integrating Enterprise Library in your applications**

✔ **Using the Data Access Application Block**

*B*uilding good software is tough. You know your applications need to have consistent data access and user authorization features. You know you'd like your applications to be able to tell you when something's broken. But where do you start? If you're like most developers, you don't have time to think about anything but the problem you're trying to solve.

What's worse is that most of the examples that you see in books and on the Internet are not production quality. That is, they give you a sense for how the code works at some basic level, but you can't really take the code and run with it. In order to cut to the chase and show you an example, most code samples skip the best practices like using structured exception handling. So, even when you take the time to find examples, chances are they still have big, fat holes in them.

Enter the Enterprise Library from Microsoft's patterns and practices group. Enterprise Library is a library of code that provides your applications with everything from data access to exception management. The library includes fully functional code blocks that you can easily integrate into your projects. Best of all, Enterprise Library makes it easy to include enterprise-quality security, logging, data access, and other nonfunctional features without sacrificing your focus on solving your business problem.

Exploring Enterprise Library

Enterprise Library is comprised of a set of application blocks. Each application block provides a set of services that solves problems common to typical development projects. The library includes five, general-purpose application blocks that consume a set of core functions.

The five, general-purpose application blocks are as follows:

✦ **Caching** — Creates a local cache for storing data your application needs to access frequently.

✦ **Cryptography** — Encrypts and decrypts data in your application.

✦ **Data Access** — Accesses databases using simplified commands.

✦ **Exception Handling** — Creates reusable exception handlers for common tasks such as logging exceptions.

✦ **Logging** — Outputs messages from your application to the destination of your choice.

✦ **Security** — Authorizes users of your application in a consistent manner.

Each application block uses properties saved to your application's configuration file to define how the block works. Enterprise Library includes a tool called the Enterprise Library Configuration Console that you use to edit configuration properties.

Windows applications use the app.config configuration file. Web sites use the web.config configuration file.

The application blocks are designed to work out of the box. For example, most applications need some kind of logging functionality. You can use the Logging Application Block to log messages of low severity to an event log while sending messages of a higher severity to your e-mail inbox.

Using Enterprise Library allows you to

✦ **Increase developer productivity.** By using the blocks in Enterprise Library, your developers save time by not having to develop everything from scratch. Many of the application blocks simplify using existing features of the .NET Framework which improves productivity.

✦ **Leverage best practices.** The library represents Microsoft's recommendations for how you should implement features of the .NET Framework.

✦ **Implement consistent techniques.** Deciding to use the library on a single project or throughout an entire enterprise creates consistency among developers and across projects. Developers aren't faced with architectural decisions when they should be thinking about implementing business logic.

✦ **Make it your own.** All the source code for the blocks is included in the Enterprise Library. You can customize and extend the blocks to exactly fit your needs.

Where to start?

Before the Enterprise Library was a library, each application block stood on its own. For example, the Data Access Application Block (DAAB) was pretty popular when it first came out. You could download DAAB without installing the full-blown library. In the January 2006 version of the Enterprise Library, all the application blocks work together as part of a unified library. You can pick and choose which blocks you wish to use, but you have to download and install the entire library. Installing the entire library is quite simple, but figuring out exactly which features you want to use can be challenging.

Every time I download a new version of the Enterprise Library I'm always overwhelmed with figuring out where to start. This chapter walks you through the technical details of how to get started using the library. Before you dive in, however, I also make the following suggestions for getting started with the Enterprise Library:

✦ **Decide on one or two application blocks to implement.** You should identify your needs before you start trying to use the blocks.

✦ **Provide extra time in your project for learning how to use the blocks.** Don't assume the blocks will save you time right out of the box. As with any new tool, you should allot extra time for getting up to speed.

✦ **Invest time in learning the features of the blocks before you plan to start using them.** You should read up on the blocks before you start executing code.

Each application block uses the best practices recommended by Microsoft for .NET development. You should consider using the blocks as a way to learn more about these best practices. At the same time, the blocks might have more overhead than you need in your application. I've often used the blocks as a way to understand how to use a certain technology and then stopped using the block once I understood enough about how to do it on my own.

One of the easier blocks to hit the ground running with is the Data Access Application Block. You can start using the DAAB without a huge investment in time. You can add additional blocks such as the logging and exception handling blocks as time permits. I walk you through using the DAAB in the section "Accessing data with the Data Access Application Block" later in this chapter.

Microsoft continues to release new and updated application blocks all the time. Another new resource that often includes application blocks are software factories. A software factory is a development tool that helps you rapidly build applications. In June 2006, Microsoft released the Mobile Client Software Factory, which helps you build Windows Mobile applications and the Smart Client Software Factory which, you guessed it, helps you build smart client Windows applications. Each of these software factories includes application blocks specific to creating the kinds of applications featured in the software factory. You can download the software factories at Microsoft's patterns and practices Web site at `http://msdn.microsoft.com/practices/`.

Getting help

Enterprise Library includes several resources for getting help. There's an entire online community using and supporting Enterprise Library. Some places to go for help include:

✦ **Enterprise Library Documentation** — The documentation included with the library provides extensive explanations for how to use each of the application blocks.

✦ **QuickStart Applications** — The library includes a set of tutorials and walkthroughs for using each of the application blocks.

✦ **Microsoft patterns and practices home** — Enterprise Library exists as part of Microsoft's patterns and practices initiative. Check out the p&p home page for more information at `http://msdn.microsoft.com/practices`.

The patterns and practices home page is an excellent resource for guidance on building software with Microsoft .NET. I suggest you browse their catalog of resources.

Getting Started with Enterprise Library

The latest release of Enterprise Library for version 2.0 of the .NET Framework is January 2006. Enterprise Library is available as a free download from Microsoft's Web site. You can download the January 2006 release of the Enterprise Library, view additional information about the library, and find additional application blocks at the Microsoft patterns and practices home page at `http://msdn.microsoft.com/practices`.

Be sure to check out the patterns and practices home page. In the past, I found most of the documentation there to be a bit over the top and hard to understand. Now that the site has matured, it's starting to offer some really practical resources.

You have to register in order to download the library from Microsoft's Web site. The installation process is pretty straightforward. You have the option to select which application blocks you wish to install. You also can choose to compile the library immediately following the installation, which I suggest you do. Otherwise, you'll have to run a batch file manually afterwards to compile the library.

The Enterprise Library installation wizard installs the following:

✦ **Source code** for all the application blocks and supporting tools.

✦ **Unit tests** that were used to test the application blocks while they were being developed.

✦ **QuickStarts** for each application block that demonstrates the block's use.

✦ **Documentation** that shows you how to use the library.

✦ **Batch files** to build the library.

✦ **Configuration console** that allows you to manage the library's configuration files.

The default installation location for the Enterprise Library is C:\Program Files\Microsoft Enterprise Library January 2006. You access the Enterprise Library via the Start menu at All Programs⇨Microsoft Patterns and Practices⇨ Enterprise Library January 2006 as Figure 9-1 shows. Table 9-1 lists all the items accessible from the Enterprise Library on the Start menu.

Figure 9-1:
Access the Enterprise Library from the Start menu.

Table 9-1	Installed Items with Enterprise Library
Menu Item	*Purpose*
Application Blocks for .NET	Source code for each of the application blocks including unit tests for NUnit and Visual Studio Team System.
QuickStart Applications	Tutorials that demonstrate how to use each of the application blocks.
Build Enterprise Library	Batch file that builds the Enterprise Library into deployable assemblies.
Copy Assemblies to Bin Folder	Batch file that copies the Enterprise Library's assemblies to a common destination folder.
Enterprise Library Blogs	Hyperlink to the blog community on Microsoft's Web site.
Enterprise Library Community	Hyperlink to online community on GotDotNet.
Enterprise Library Configuration	Application for managing configuration information for the application blocks.
Enterprise Library Documentation	Help files.
Enterprise Library Release Notes	Release documentation.
Enterprise Library Solution	Solution containing source code.
Enterprise Library Solution (NUnit Tests)	Source code with unit tests using NUnit.
Enterprise Library Solution (VSTS Tests)	Source code with unit tests using Visual Studio Team System.
Install Instrumentation	Batch file that enables monitoring services for the application blocks.
Uninstall Instrumentation	Batch file that removes monitoring services.

Building the library

When you install Enterprise Library, the source code for all the application blocks is placed in a folder named src in the library's default installation folder. In order to use those applications, you must first compile them into assemblies. Once compiled into assemblies, you can reference the assemblies in your source code and use them.

You have two options for launching the build process that compiles the Enterprise Library's source code:

✦ Execute the Build Enterprise Library batch file.

✦ Build the Enterprise Library using Visual Studio.

Enterprise Library includes two batch files that you can use to easily build the Enterprise Library. The Enterprise Library is made up of multiple projects, so you use the second batch file to copy all the assemblies to a common destination folder. To build the library using the Build Enterprise Library batch file, follow these steps:

1. **Choose Build Enterprise Library from the Start menu.**

   A command window appears.

   The Build Enterprise Library menu item runs the BuildLibrary.bat batch file. The file builds each of the projects found in the Enterprise Library's src folder. There are a number of projects to build, so be patient as the batch file executes.

   Upon completion, the batch file pauses so that you can view the batch file's output. The batch file displays the message Press any key to continue.

2. **Press a key on your keyboard to complete execution of the batch file.**

3. **Choose Copy Assemblies to Bin Folder from the Start menu.**

   A command window appears.

   The Copy Assemblies menu item runs CopyAssemblies.bat. The batch file copies all the assemblies found in the bin folders of each project in the Enterprise Library's src folder to a common bin folder in the default Enterprise Library folder.

Figure 9-2 shows an example of the build process using batch files.

To build the Enterprise Library using Visual Studio, follow these steps:

1. **Choose Enterprise Library Solution from the Start menu.**

   Visual Studio opens.

2. **Select a build configuration from the Standard toolbar.**

   Enterprise Library includes a Debug and Release build configuration.

3. **Choose Build Solution from the Build menu.**

   Visual Studio builds the projects.

   To delete all the assemblies before building, choose Clean Solution from the Build menu before building.

You need to run the CopyAssemblies.bat file if you want all the assemblies in a common folder.

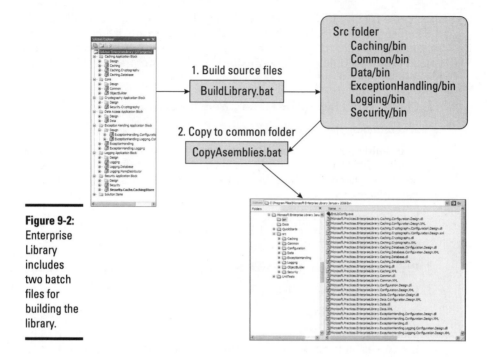

Figure 9-2:
Enterprise
Library
includes
two batch
files for
building the
library.

By default, Enterprise Library is built using the Debug build configuration. To build a release build, you might use Visual Studio or specify the release parameter on the BuildLibary.bat file, as Figure 9-3 shows.

Figure 9-3:
Use the
release
parameter
to create a
release
build.

When you build the library, the build process places the assemblies in the bin folder for each project. Most of the application blocks generate .dll files that you reference in your project. The library also creates the executable file EntLibConfig.exe used to run the Enterprise Library Configuration application.

Using the library

Enterprise Library consists of application blocks you can use to provide services to your application such as logging and caching. In order to call those services, you must first reference any assemblies you plan to use and configure the services.

Referencing assemblies

Each application block has its own set of assemblies that you must reference in your source code.

To add references to an application block:

1. Open your project in Visual Studio.

2. Right-click your project in Solution Explorer.

A shortcut menu appears.

3. Choose Add Reference.

The Add Reference window appears.

4. Click the Browse tab.

5. Navigate to the location where the Enterprise Library assemblies are located.

If you've run CopyAssemblies.bat, all the assemblies are located at C:\ Program Files\Microsoft Enterprise Library January 2006\bin.

6. Press the Ctrl button while clicking the assemblies you wish to reference.

At a minimum, you need to reference the core assemblies of Microsoft.Practices.EnterpriseLibrary.Common.dll and Microsoft.Practices.EnterpriseLibrary.ObjectBuilder.dll.

You should add references to any application block's assemblies you plan to use. For example, to access the data access assembly, add `Microsoft.Practices.EnterpriseLibrary.Data`.

Refer to the Enterprise Library documentation for more information about which assemblies you need to add.

7. Click OK.

The references are added to the project. Figure 9-4 shows the references in the Project Designer for a Windows application.

When you build your application, Visual Studio places a copy of the Enterprise Library assemblies you reference in your application's bin folder.

Figure 9-4:
You must
add
references
to the
Enterprise
Library's
assemblies.

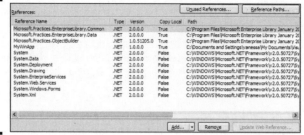

In the preceding example, I reference the assemblies from the default installation folder. In a production environment, you should check the Enterprise Library's source code into your source code control database. Developers should download a local working copy to reference. See Book VI, Chapter 3 for more information on source code control.

Setting namespaces

Once you've referenced the Enterprise Library's assemblies, you can access the features of the application blocks you've referenced. Like all .NET code, the Enterprise Library is organized into namespaces. The topmost namespace is `Microsoft.Practices.EnterpriseLibrary`. Each application block uses its own namespace, such as `Microsoft.Practices.EnterpriseLibrary.Data`.

To access code in the Enterprise Library without fully qualifying the namespace, you can add an `Imports` or `using` statement at the top of your class. For example, to use a `using` statement in a C# source code file to qualify the data access application block, type this:

```
using Microsoft.Practices.EnterpriseLibrary.Data;
```

Configuring the blocks

Each of the application blocks uses configuration settings. The Enterprise Library includes a tool called the Enterprise Library Configuration console that you can use to configure the blocks. The console outputs XML into a configuration file your application uses. Windows applications use the app.config file and Web sites use web.config. Note these are the standard configuration files used by these projects.

To configure Enterprise Library, follow these steps:

1. **Choose Enterprise Library Configuration from the Start menu.**

The Enterprise Library Configuration application opens.

You must build the Enterprise Library before you can access the configuration console. If you haven't built the library, you're prompted to build the library. After the library builds, the console opens.

2. **Click the New Application button to create a new configuration file.**

   An Application Configuration folder appears in the configuration hierarchy.

   You can also open an existing configuration file. To open an existing configuration file, browse to an existing app.config file in a Windows project or web.config file in a Web site. The configuration console adds configuration items to your existing file without overwriting your file's contents.

3. **Right-click the Application Configuration folder.**

4. **Choose New from the shortcut menu.**

   A list of application blocks appears.

5. **Select the application block you wish to add to your application.**

   The block appears in the configuration hierarchy.

   For example, to add the data access application block choose Data Access Application Block from the menu.

   The configuration console lists name/value pairs required to configure the block.

6. **Add configuration items for the application block.**

   Refer to the Enterprise Library documentation to read more about required configuration items for each application block.

   Figure 9-5 shows the connection string configuration item for the Data Access Application Block.

Figure 9-5:
Manage config-
uration
settings for
application
blocks
with the
Enterprise
Library
Config-
uration tool.

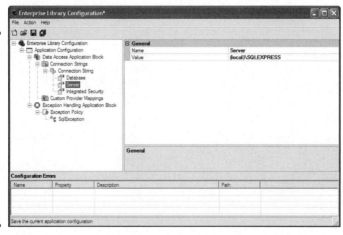

7. **Repeat Steps 3 through 6 to add each application block you want to use with your application.**

8. **Choose Save Application on the File menu to save your configuration file.**

   Save the file as app.config for a Windows application or web.config for a Web application.

   The configuration console outputs your configuration as XML. The XML that follows shows the connection string created for the Data Access Application Block.

```
<configSections>
 <section name="dataConfiguration"
   type="Microsoft.Practices.EnterpriseLibrary.Data.
   Configuration.DatabaseSettings, Microsoft.Practices.
   EnterpriseLibrary.Data, Version=2.0.0.0,
   Culture=neutral, PublicKeyToken=null" />
</configSections>
<dataConfiguration defaultDatabase="Connection String"
   />
 <connectionStrings>
   <add name="Connection String"
   connectionString="Database=AdventureWorks;Server=
   (local)\SQLEXPRESS;Integrated Security=SSPI;"
   providerName="System.Data.SqlClient" />
 </connectionStrings>
```

You aren't limited to storing your configuration information in app.config or web.config files. You can use your own file and reference it within your application's configuration file. To reference a configuration file called my.config, add it to your app.config or web.config file like this:

```
<enterpriseLibrary.ConfigurationSource selectedSource="File
   Configuration Source">
  <sources>
    <add name="File Configuration Source"
  type="Microsoft.Practices.EnterpriseLibrary.Common.
  Configuration.FileConfigurationSource, Microsoft.
  Practices.EnterpriseLibrary.Common, Version=2.0.0.0,
  Culture=neutral, PublicKeyToken=null"
      filePath="my.config" />
    <add name="System Configuration Source"
  type="Microsoft.Practices.EnterpriseLibrary.Common.
  Configuration.SystemConfigurationSource, Microsoft.
  Practices.EnterpriseLibrary.Common, Version=2.0.0.0,
  Culture=neutral, PublicKeyToken=null" />
  </sources>
 </enterpriseLibrary.ConfigurationSource>
```

Accessing data with the Data Access Application Block

The Data Access Application Block is a popular block that wraps around ADO.NET, which provides the data access features of the .NET Framework. The block accesses data using three key elements:

✦ **Connection strings** — You enter connection strings for your databases in your application's configuration settings. You can specify one default database which you don't have to reference by name when accessing. I suggest you use a name so to avoid any confusion.

✦ **Database object** — DAAB uses a `Database` object to create an in-memory representation of your database connection. You specify the kind of database to which you're connecting in your connection string so you can work with a generic `Database` object in your code.

By using a generic `Database` object, you can change your underlying database connection without modifying your data access code. Figure 9-6 shows how the DAAB sits between your source code and the database.

✦ **Execute commands** — The Database object includes a set of six commands you can execute against the database. Table 9-2 lists the commands and their functions.

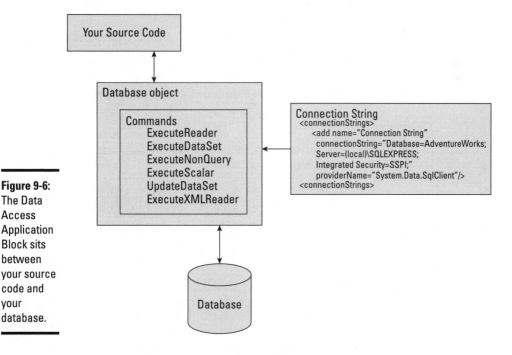

Figure 9-6:
The Data Access Application Block sits between your source code and your database.

Table 9-2	Database Object Commands and Their Functions
Command	*Purpose*
ExecuteReader	Uses an ADO.NET DataReader to retrieve data from a database.
ExecuteDataSet	Fills an ADO.NET DataSet with data retrieved from a database.
ExecuteNonQuery	Retrieves multiple values from output parameters or executes any SQL command against a database, including update statements.
ExecuteScalar	Retrieves a single return value.
UpdateDataSet	Uses a DataSet to update a database.
ExecuteXMLReader	Returns values from the database as XML.

Refer to the Enterprise Library Documentation and the Data Access QuickStart Applications for specifics on using the Database object.

To use the Data Access Application Block to fill a DataSet, follow these steps:

1. **Use the Enterprise Library Configuration console to create a connection string for your database.**

2. **Add references to the Enterprise Library assemblies as described in the previous section "Referencing Assemblies."**

3. **Add an Imports statement at the top of your source code like this:**

   ```
   Imports Microsoft.Practices.EnterpriseLibrary.Data
   Imports System.Data
   ```

4. **Create a subroutine called GetData to hold the data access code.**

   ```
   Private Sub GetData()
   End Sub
   ```

5. **Create the Data Access Application Block's database object inside the GetData subroutine.**

   ```
   Dim db As Database
   ```

   All commands are executed against the Database object. The Database object is in the Microsoft.Practices.EnterpriseLibrary.Data namespace.

6. **Call the CreateDatabase method of the DatabaseFactory object.**

   ```
   db = DatabaseFactory.CreateDatabase()
   ```

   The CreateDatabase method creates an in-memory representation of the default database specified in the configuration. To access a specific database, pass in the name of the connection string, such as the following:

   ```
   db = DatabaseFactory.CreateDatabase("MyDB")
   ```

The `CreateDatabase` method uses the data provider specified in the configuration to create the proper kind of database, such as SQL or Oracle, for example.

To access a database without using the `DatabaseFactory`, you can use the following code:

```
Dim db As SqlDatabase
db = New SqlDatabase(myConnectionString)
```

`SqlDatabase` expects a connection string. `SqlDatabase` is an object in the `Microsoft.Practices.EnterpriseLibrary.Data.Sql` namespace.

7. Create an ADO.NET DataSet.

```
Dim ds As DataSet = Nothing
```

8. Call the `Database` object's `ExecuteDataSet` method.

For example, to execute a SQL string against the database, pass in a command type of text and the SQL string, as shown in the following:

```
ds = db.ExecuteDataSet(CommandType.Text, "Select * from
    HumanResources.Department")
```

The Data Access Application Block executes the SQL statement and returns a DataSet.

Getting a head start with QuickStarts

Enterprise Library includes eight tutorials called QuickStart applications. Each application is a stand alone tutorial that demonstrates features of the application blocks. The QuickStarts are Visual Studio solutions. Most of the QuickStarts include C# and Visual Basic versions of the source code. You access the QuickStarts from the Start menu. Table 9-3 lists the QuickStarts.

Table 9-3	Exploring the QuickStart Applications	
QuickStart Application	*Source Code*	*Description*
Caching	C# and VB	Demonstrates Caching Application Block.
Configuration Migration	C# and VB	Provides guidance on how to migrate from the Configuration Application Block in previous versions of Enterprise Library to the new configuration model.
Cryptography	C# and VB	Demonstrates using the Cryptography Application Block.
Data Access	C# and VB	Demonstrates using the Data Access Application Block; includes a sample database.

(continued)

Table 9-3 *(continued)*

QuickStart Application	Source Code	Description
Exception Handling	C# and VB	Demonstrates using the Exception Handling with or without using the Logging Application Block.
Logging	C# and VB	Demonstrates using the Logging Application Block.
Security	C# and VB	Demonstrates using the Security Application Block.
SQL Configuration Store	C#, Unit tests	Provides an extension of the Enterprise Library that uses a SQL Server database to store configuration data.

Each of the QuickStarts includes a QuickStart form that demonstrates a series of scenarios for using the application block being demonstrated. To use a QuickStart application:

1. **Launch the QuickStart application you wish to use.**

The application opens in Visual Studio.

All the QuickStart applications can be found in the QuickStart Applications folder in Start⇨All Programs⇨Microsoft Patterns and Practices⇨Enterprise Library January 2006.

2. **Execute any prerequisite batch files for the QuickStart application.**

Some of the QuickStarts, such as the Data Access Application Block QuickStart, include batch files that prepare your local environment to use the QuickStart.

3. **Press F5 in Visual Studio to run the QuickStart application.**

The QuickStartForm opens.

Each of the QuickStarts provides a set of scenarios that demonstrates the application block's features.

The SQL Configuration Store QuickStart doesn't include a user interface. You'll need NUnit or Visual Studio Team System to execute the unit tests provided. To view a class diagram of the SQL Configuration Configuration Store, open the SqlConfigSource.cd file in the SQLConfigurationSource project.

4. **Click the buttons along the side of the QuickStartForm to view scenarios.**

Figure 9-7 shows the QuickStartForm for the Caching QuickStart.

5. **Click the View Walkthrough button to open the corresponding help text that explains the demonstration scenarios.**

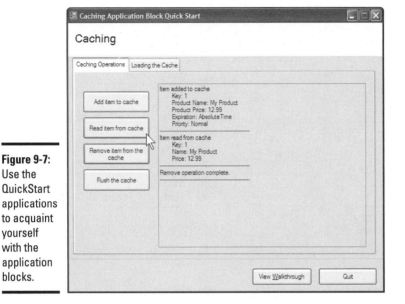

Figure 9-7:
Use the
QuickStart
applications
to acquaint
yourself
with the
application
blocks.

It might also be helpful to view the underlying code being demonstrated. To view the source code, double-click any of the scenario buttons in the Windows Forms Designer. The code editor opens at that button's `Click` event.

All of the QuickStarts include a default set of configuration items in the app.config file. You can use the Enterprise Library Configuration console to view the app.config file for any of the QuickStart applications. You can find all the source code including app.config files in the QuickStarts folder at C:\ Program Files\Microsoft Enterprise Library January 2006.

Book VI

Going the Extra Mile

The 5th Wave   By Rich Tennant

"Okay, well, I think we all get the gist of where Jerry was going with the site map."

Contents at a Glance

Chapter 1: Building Solutions and Projects

In This Chapter

✔ **Understanding the build process**

✔ **Creating build configurations**

✔ **Viewing build feedback**

✔ **Automating daily builds**

A software application is composed of many pieces — presentation code, data-access libraries, unit tests, configuration files, installation programs, and more. Visual Studio organizes these pieces into *projects*. The entire application is called a *solution*.

As you're creating the interfaces and writing the data access code for your solution, you need to stop periodically and test your application. In order to test your application, you need to run a compiler that converts the human-readable source code in your projects to machine-readable binary files. Visual Studio provides a set of build commands you use to compile your projects and solutions.

By its nature, the build process is tightly coupled to deployment. In the simplest deployment case, you create a Release build and distribute the output files. Very rarely is real life so simple. Some types of applications — such as multiple-tier Windows applications, ASP.NET Web sites, and mobile applications — are inherently more difficult to deploy. There are many variables to take into consideration when creating release builds.

In this chapter, I show you how to build your solutions and projects for use on a local development computer. (See Chapter 2 in this mini-book to read about deploying release builds.)

Understanding Solutions and Projects

Visual Studio uses logical containers called *projects* and *solutions* for grouping together all the code and resources associated with an application. A solution contains all the projects necessary to build an application. Projects include all the source code and support files necessary to create the application. For example, a solution may contain one project each for the following:

+ Windows forms
+ Data-access code
+ Database code
+ Testing code
+ Installer

The process of converting all the code found in a set of projects to an application is called *building* or *creating a build*. Builds have settings that define where the output files are located and whether debug information is included. A group of settings is called a build configuration. Visual Studio solutions and projects include two default build configurations:

+ **Debug** — Code compiles with information for debugging and no optimization. The nature of the build is to enable you to test your code.

+ **Release** — Code compiles with optimizations and no debugging information. The release configuration is intended for production deployment.

Builds can target a specific hardware platform, such as the x86 or x64 architectures. The Debug and Release build configurations provided by Visual Studio target the x86 architecture.

The anatomy of a build

Building software is the process of taking a set of inputs and creating a set of outputs. The inputs include the following:

+ Source-code files
+ Resource files
+ Configuration files
+ Local database files

The build process takes these files and converts them to a set of outputs that include:

+ Binary files, such as application executables and dynamic link libraries (DLLs). Binary files are called *assemblies*.
+ Debugging information.

    Debugging information is stored in a program database (PDB) file. (See Chapter 7 in Book V for more information about debugging.)
+ Feedback messages such as compiler warnings and errors.

The build process uses a compiler to convert your human-readable input files into machine-readable binary files. Each programming language uses its own compiler.

You use the outputs from a build to accomplish the following:

✦ Test an application you're developing.

✦ Deploy an application to a test or production environment.

✦ Determine whether you can check in your source code to form part of your source-code repository.

   The inputs to the build process — the source code — are *checked in* (established as source code) after you have a successful build.

Figure 1-1 shows the build process; note that the outputs are deployed, but usually they're not checked into source code control.

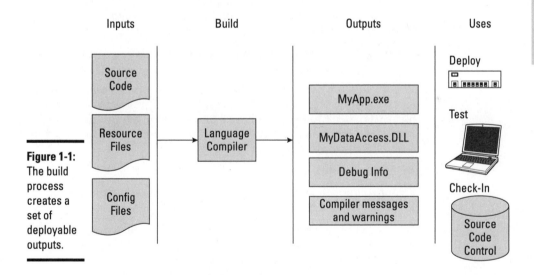

Figure 1-1:
The build process creates a set of deployable outputs.

Using the Build menu

Visual Studio provides a Build menu you can use to launch different build commands for your solution or project. The options on the Build menu are

✦ **Build:** Compiles any source code that hasn't yet been compiled. The Build command doesn't delete any existing output files. Instead, the Build command performs an incremental build of any files not yet compiled.

✦ **Rebuild:** Deletes or *cleans* any existing output files and compiles all source code into binary files.

✦ **Clean:** Deletes all the output files generated by previous builds.

✦ **Publish:** Calls the publishing wizard to build and deploy the solution. (See Chapter 2 in this mini-book for more information on using the Publishing Wizard.)

✦ **Batch Build:** Compiles multiple build configurations as a batch.

Deployable projects such as SQL Server Reporting Projects display the Deploy command on the Build menu. If you have the Web Deployment Project Add-In installed, you also have the option Add Web Deployment Project on the Build menu. (See Chapter 2 in this mini-book for more information about Web Deployment Projects.)

You execute build commands against solutions or individual projects. Here are some scenarios for how you may use the Build menu:

✦ **Building projects individually when a solution has many projects.**

Compiling large solutions and projects is time-consuming. For that reason, you may choose to build individual projects as you need them rather than building the entire solution. Using the Build command to incrementally compile source files can also save time.

✦ **Building each project in a solution individually when a dependent project is generating compile errors.**

When a solution has many projects that are dependent upon one another, an error in one project cascades to the dependent projects — which makes it difficult to find the original error. Instead of plowing through a long list of errors and warnings, compile each project individually and deal with any errors you find.

✦ **Building an entire solution.**

If your solution builds lightning-fast, then you can use either the Build or Rebuild Solution command.

You may choose to use the Rebuild option (rather than Build) if you're getting strange errors that you don't think you should be getting. Rebuild wipes out all the previous build's outputs.

✦ **Building individual projects as changes are made to them.**

When you have large projects and solutions, building is faster than rebuilding the entire solution.

Using the Start command on the Debug menu calls the Build command and executes your application. During development, many developers press the F5 key with the expectation that their code is going to build and execute. Only after they see that long list of compiler errors do they start using the Build menu.

The commands on the Build menu correspond to targets files used by the Microsoft Build Engine (MSBuild). To read more about MSBuild, see the section "Automating builds" later in this chapter.

Selecting the active build and platform

When you build a solution or a project, you select a named build configuration you wish to build, such as Debug or Release. Each build configuration has specific properties that determine how the project is built. Visual Studio 2005 automatically creates the Debug and Release build configurations for each project and solution you create.

The build process creates code for a specific hardware platform (such as Intel's x86 or x64 architectures). You pick a hardware platform at the time you build your solution or project.

To set a build configuration and a hardware platform for a build, you use the Solution Configuration and Solution Platform drop-down lists on the Standard toolbar, as Figure 1-2 shows.

**Book VI
Chapter 1**

**Building Solutions
and Projects**

Figure 1-2:
Use the
Standard
toolbar to
set the
active build's
Solution
Configura-
tion and
Platform.

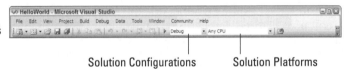

Solution Configurations   Solution Platforms

Dealing with compiler output

The major function of the build process is to *compile* your source code into binary files. The build process provides output that shows the list of commands executed, along with any feedback from those commands. In the event the compiler is unable to compile your code, error messages appear in the Errors window.

If you execute your build using the Start command on the Debug menu, a dialog box warns you that the build was unsuccessful. If you use the Build menu, then the Error window appears. Figure 1-3 shows an error message that cropped up when I tried to use a variable that I hadn't yet declared.

Each programming language uses its own compiler. The message displayed in Figure 1-3 is from the Visual Basic compiler. The C# compiler displays the following message for the same error:

```
The name 'myVariable' does not exist in the current context.
```

Error List
1 Error
0 Warnings
0 Messages
Description
File
Line
Column
Project
1 Name 'myVariable' is not declared.
DisplayHelloWorld.vb
4
9
WinApp
Error List
Output

Figure 1-3: Error and warning messages from the compiler appear in the Errors window.

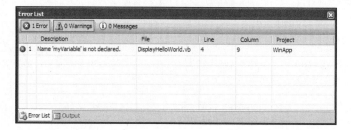

Among other things, you can use the Errors window to

- ✦ **Go to the source code where the error occurred** — Double-click an error and Visual Studio opens the source-code file — and positions the cursor right where the error occurred.
- ✦ **Get help on an error** — Right-click an error and choose Show Error Help from the shortcut menu.

Hover your mouse pointer over an error in source code to display the error in a tooltip, as Figure 1-4 shows.

Public Class DisplayHelloWorld
Private Sub Button1_Click(ByVal sender As System.Object, ByVal e As System.EventArgs) Handles Button1.Click
myVariable.Text = "Hello"
Name 'myVariable' is not declared.
End Sub
End Class

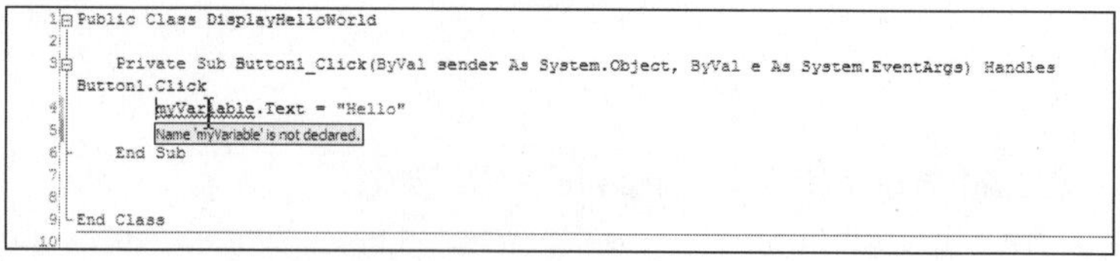

Figure 1-4: Hover your mouse pointer over an error to view the error in a tooltip.

Use the Output window to view the commands executed by the build process. The Output window displays the following information:

- ✦ Build configuration
- ✦ Compiler and switches used
- ✦ Output from the compiler
- ✦ Build status

Messages appear for each project compiled in the build. Figure 1-5 shows a successful build for a single project using the Debug build configuration.

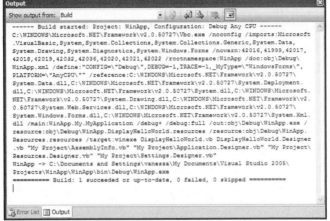

Figure 1-5:
The Output window displays the compiler command used to build your project.

The long line that appears in Figure 1-5 between the first and last lines is a single command that executes the compiler. To create this command, the Build command pulls together all the project settings, references, and properties you set using Visual Studio.

You can copy and paste the compiler command from the Output window to reuse on the command line or in a batch file. Batch files are a good way to automate builds. You'll probably need to qualify the path names to your project's resources. To open a Visual Studio command prompt, click Start⇨ All Programs⇨Microsoft Visual Studio 2005⇨Visual Studio Tools⇨Visual Studio 2005 Command Prompt.

To specify whether a file should be compiled with a project, use the Properties window to set the file's `BuildAction` property.

Using Configuration Manager

You use the Configuration Manager to create new build configurations and manage existing configurations for solutions and projects. You use Project Designer to associate a project's properties with its build configuration.

To create a new build configuration using the Configuration Manager, follow these steps:

1. **Click Configuration Manager on the Build menu.**

The Configuration Manager appears, displaying the configuration settings for the configuration and platform selected at the top.

2. **Select New from the Active solution configuration drop-down list.**

The New Solution Configuration window appears.

3. **Type** Staging **in the Name field.**

4. **Select Debug from the Copy settings from drop-down list.**

5. **Leave the check in the Create new project configurations check box.**

6. **Click OK.**

The new configuration appears in the Configuration Manager as Figure 1-6 shows.

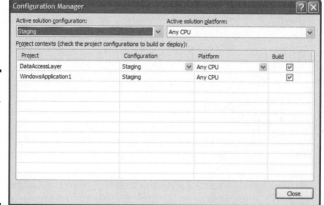

Figure 1-6:
Use the Configuration Manager to create a new build configuration.

A solution's build configuration is composed of two main elements:

✦ **Project configurations:** A *project configuration* is a set of build-and-debug properties defined for a given project.

✦ **Platforms:** This setting specifies what hardware platform the build targets.

For each project in the solution, you select a project configuration and a platform. You create new project configurations and hardware platforms if necessary. You use the Project Designer to set the properties for each project configuration. You include the project in the build by placing a check in the Build column. Figure 1-7 shows an example of selecting a project configuration for a solution configuration.

Visual Studio writes the build configurations you create in Configuration Manager to the appropriate solution or project file. When you build your solution or project, the Microsoft Build Engine uses the solution or project files as a script. For example, the following lines are added to the solution file for the staging build configuration:

```
Staging|Any CPU = Staging|Any CPU
```

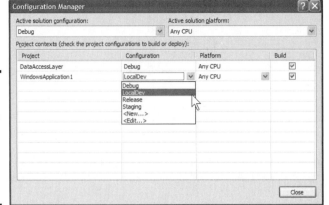

Figure 1-7:
Select the
project con-
figurations
for the
solution
configura-
tion to use.

Open your solution file or project file in any text editor to view the changes
made by the Configuration Manager. (See the section "Automating builds,"
later in this chapter, to read more about the Microsoft Build Engine.)

If you have a specific hardware platform in mind, you can use the Configuration
Manager to specify that a build target that platform. For example, to create a
new Debug solution configuration that targets the x64 platform, follow these
steps:

1. **Open the Configuration Manager.**

2. **Click Debug from the Active solution configuration drop-down list.**

3. **Click New from the Active solution platform drop-down list.**

   The New Solution Platform window appears.

4. **Select x64 as the new hardware platform.**

5. **Click OK.**

   A new Debug solution configuration for the x64 platform is created.

If you're using the MSBuild Toolkit, you can select a version of the .NET
Framework to target using the Platform. (See Chapter 4 in Book II for more
information about using the MSBuild Toolkit to target a specific version of
the .NET Framework.)

Setting project configurations

Visual Studio solutions and projects have many settings that define the solution or project. These settings are called *properties* and they define attributes such as

✦ Other code referenced by the project

✦ Where to place the project's compiled output

✦ Which debugger to use

You access the properties for a solution or project by choosing Properties from the solution's or project's shortcut menu. There are two views for properties:

✦ **Project Designer:** Displays properties for a project in the Document Explorer. All Visual Studio projects use the Project Designer to manage their properties.

✦ **Property Pages:** Displays properties in a dialog box. Solutions and ASP.NET Web sites use the Property Pages window to manage their properties.

ASP.NET Web sites don't use projects, so they don't use the Project Designer. Microsoft has released a new project type (Web Application Projects) that allows you to have ASP.NET projects.

Using the Project Designer

Visual Studio 2005 includes a new feature called the Project Designer that lets you access your project's configuration settings in a single designer.

To access the Project Designer, follow these steps:

1. **Right-click your project in Solution Explorer.**

A shortcut menu appears.

2. **Click Properties.**

The Project Designer appears in the Document Explorer, showing a set of tabs along the left that group together common properties. To access a set of properties, click its tab. Figure 1-8 shows the Project Designer for a C# class library project type.

You can also open the Project Designer through the Project menu.

Some tabs in the Project Designer feature properties that you can configure to match your build configuration type (for example, you can set build properties for a Debug build). To set the build properties for a C# or J# project type, follow these steps:

1. **Open the Project Designer.**

2. **Click on the Build tab.**

The project's build properties appear.

3. **Select a build configuration from the Configuration drop-down list.**

The properties for the selected build configuration appear. If you want to manage properties for all your build configurations, you can choose All Configurations.

4. **Select a build platform from the Platform drop-down list.**

5. **Set properties in the Project Designer.**

The properties you choose depend largely on whether you intend to debug or release the output. The properties for Visual Basic projects are slightly different because the compilers are different.

There's no OK or Save button for the Project Designer. The properties are saved immediately.

The Project Designer for Visual Basic project types has a Compile tab instead of a Build tab. You can access build properties from the Compile tab.

You can set unique build configuration settings for properties in the Build and Debug tabs in C# and J# project types and Build and Compile tabs in Visual Basic project types.

**Book VI
Chapter 1**

**Building Solutions
and Projects**

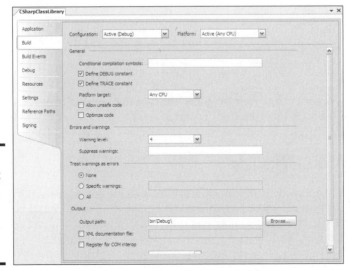

Figure 1-8:
The Project Designer groups common properties in tabs.

Using the Property Pages

Solutions and ASP.NET Web sites use the Property Pages dialog box to manage properties. Here's how to use a solution's Property Pages to set project dependencies:

1. **Right-click the solution in Solution Explorer.**

A shortcut menu appears.

2. **Expand Common Properties.**

A list of properties appears.

3. **Click Project Dependencies.**

4. **Select a project from the Project drop-down list.**

Your project must have more than one project to set project dependencies.

5. **Check the project dependencies, as Figure 1-9 shows.**

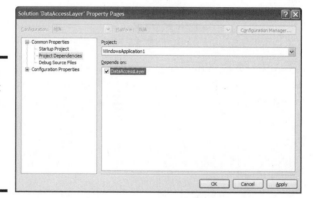

Figure 1-9:
Set project dependencies in the Solution Property Pages window.

6. **To verify that your projects build in the correct order, click Project Build Order from the Project menu.**

Managing Your Builds

Building software for your own use on a single computer is fairly straightforward. However, most software is developed in teams. Even if you don't plan to release the build, managing builds while a project is being developed is a challenge.

Visual Studio 2005 Professional Edition doesn't provide much support for managing team builds. Microsoft has, however, released a new product called Team Foundation Server that targets team-based development. In this section, I share with you some of the best practices for managing builds — and a few tools that can help manage your build process.

Handling Lone Ranger builds

Most builds that occur on an individual developer's workstation are part of the code/build/test cycle. You code a little. You build. You test. You code a little more.

At some point, however, the code must be integrated with the larger code base (*checking in* the new code). Many professionals use source code control software to help manage the code base. Even without source code control, the goal is the same: You need to integrate your changes without breaking your existing code.

Even hobbyists and casual developers can benefit from using source code control. (Chapter 3 in this mini-book tells you more about that process and its advantages.)

The integration process for an individual developer, whether that developer is working solo or as part of a team, should go something like this, in this order:

1. Get the latest source code from the source-code repository before starting any new task.

2. Write new code or change existing code.

3. Write unit tests for the new code.

4. Build the code on the developer's local computer.

5. Address any issues with the compiler and run unit tests.

6. Get the latest version of source code from the source code repository if other developers are adding code to the repository.

7. Build the code again using the updated code from the repository.

8. Run unit tests again.

9. If the tests pass, check the code into source code control.

At some point — ideally daily — a master build should be made from the integrated source code. If you're working alone, then you can fire up the master build any time you want. If the master build breaks, then the developer who broke the build needs to figure out why — and get the code working again. Figure 1-10 illustrates the daily integration and build process from the perspective of a single developer.

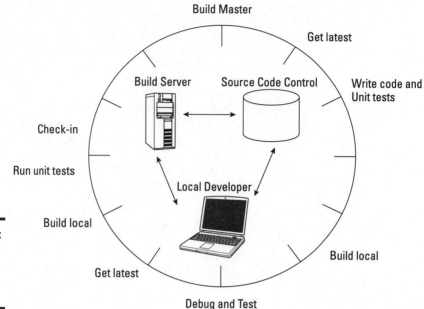

Figure 1-10:
Each
developer
integrates
code daily.

Not much time elapses between the point where a new task is started and the new code is integrated into the master source code. Code is integrated when the master source code compiles successfully and passes all unit tests.

Code kept on a developer's local workstation doesn't count for anything. Code isn't useful unless it's integrated.

Creating master builds

The build created from an integrated set of source code is called a *master build*. The accepted standard is that master builds should be built daily. There are tools available that create master builds continuously so developers have instant feedback about whether their code integrates successfully.

Master builds use the latest version of the code from source code control to create the build. Every morning, the first thing a developer does is check the status of the build. If the master build is broken, then the developer can't work. Fixing the master build is the number-one priority. The developer responsible for breaking the build is usually the one responsible for fixing it.

If the master build is successful, then all developers pull down the latest version of code. Each developer integrates continuously throughout the day. Figure 1-11 shows an example of multiple developers and a build server using source code control.

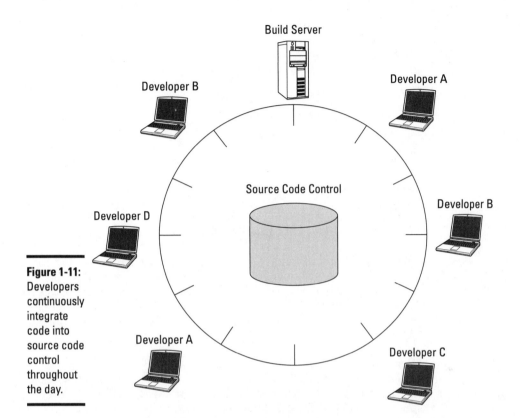

Figure 1-11:
Developers
continuously
integrate
code into
source code
control
throughout
the day.

It may be necessary to distribute the build's output to customers, testers,
and developers. Ideally, the master build's output should be kept in a
common repository; folks who need access should be able to download
from there.

Automating builds

Regardless of how frequent you build your master build, your build process
should be automatic and easy to execute. Ideally, you should just have to
click one button or execute one command to start the process. For daily
builds, you can add your build command to the server's scheduler.

If your build process requires more than just the click of a button, then
chances are you won't be able to repeat your build process. Repeatable
build processes make it possible to re-create a specific build when beta
testers call and complain that their versions aren't working.

Daily builds are usually part of a larger process that may also involve some other tasks:

✦ Executing automated unit and regression tests.

✦ Running static code analysis.

✦ Creating backups of source code.

✦ Logging the steps of the build.

✦ Sending e-mails to all interested parties when the build is complete.

The most important feature of any build is the *smoke test* — a thorough preferably automated, test of your software's major features after the build. You know you have a good build when you pass the smoke test. If your application doesn't pass the smoke test, it's time to debug and rebuild.

Your master build process should be separate from Visual Studio. Remember that your build process should be doable in one click. It's not a one-click process if you have to open Visual Studio, open a solution, and then click the Build command. For master builds, you should use a *build engine* — a program that allows you to automate your build process. Two popular build engines are the following:

✦ **Microsoft Build Engine (MSBuild):** When you use the Build menu in Visual Studio 2005, you're actually sending commands to Microsoft's new build engine, Microsoft Build Engine (MSBuild). MSBuild is a separate tool that specializes in building .NET projects. You can run MSBuild from the command line and build your projects without having Visual Studio installed.

MSBuild uses XML configuration files to define how projects are built. Visual Studio's project files include the XML syntax that MSBuild uses to build the project. You can create your own MSBuild XML configuration files — helpful if you want to completely automate your build and run it on a dedicated build machine.

✦ **NAnt:** This is a popular open-source tool for creating builds from the command line. Like MSBuild, NAnt uses XML files to script the build process. NAnt's build files end with the file extension `.build`.

You can download NAnt for free at `http://nant.so.net/`.

Chapter 2: Deployment Options

In This Chapter

✔ **Deploying Windows and Web applications using ClickOnce**

✔ **Digitally signing your code and strong naming assemblies**

✔ **Creating an installer**

✔ **Precompiling Web sites**

*D*eploying an application can be as simple as copying a single file or as complex as installing multiple components with dependencies on each other. Deploying needs to be done not just once, but throughout the life of your application. For example, you often need to deploy the following:

✦ Prerelease versions of your application for testing

✦ Major releases

✦ Updates to your application

Even though I talk about deployment near the end of this book, it's one of the first things you start thinking about for your application. (Don't forget that you can skip around to different chapters to find information as necessary in this book.) You should test your deployment strategy with your daily build.

I worked on more than my fair share of projects where deployment consisted of following a list of 25 steps that required you to do the following:

✦ Copy file X from this server.

✦ Copy file Y from that server.

✦ Execute file X on the client's computer.

✦ Create six ODBC connections.

✦ Register component Z on the client's computer.

✦ Create shortcuts on the desktop and on the Start menu.

Requiring your customers or internal IT staff to jump through these hoops every time a client installation is required isn't only brutal — it's unprofessional. People will invariably make mistakes when they dread installing your application. Nothing is worse than discovering that you forgot to install a required component *after* the computer is deployed 20 miles away.

Complicated installation processes can quickly overwhelm even the smallest companies. Many IT shops use ghosting software that allows them to make an image of a client computer's hard drive and copy that image onto other machines. When a technician skips a step in manual deployment, the mistake multiplies exponentially as the ghosted image is used to build new machines.

The time to think about the ease or difficulty of installing software is *before* the software is ever built or acquired. If you're acquiring software, ask what is required in order to install the software. If you're building commercial software, treat simplified deployment as a competitive advantage.

Some software development houses make a lot of extra revenue by having sloppy deployment procedures. I'm not talking about paying to have a consultant help you configure new software — I'm talking about jumping through a bunch of hoops just to get the software *installed*.

Visual Studio provides two strategies for deploying your applications and components:

✦ **ClickOnce** — Publish your application or component to a common repository, where users can download the application.

✦ **Windows Installer** — Create an executable setup file that walks users through the steps in an installation wizard.

The strategy you choose depends on many factors, such as

✦ The complexity of your application

✦ The frequency of updates and releases

✦ Whether your application needs to run locally

✦ Whether users have network access

✦ Whether your application is all managed code

In this chapter, I discuss the deployment options available in Visual Studio 2005, tell you when you should use each one, and share some third-party alternatives you should consider.

Deploying Smart Client Applications

In the late 1990s, the development world went crazy for Web applications. Part of the draw was capturing some of the ease of administration that comes along with Web sites. Rather than install a single Windows application on a thousand computers, why not have a thousand computers access a single Web application? It sounds great in theory; however, many folks quickly realized that using Windows applications sometimes just make the most sense.

Microsoft listened and created a hybrid deployment model that allows you to deploy your Windows application to a Web server. Using the new ClickOnce feature, Visual Studio 2005 copies the files needed to deploy your Windows application to a Web server. Your Windows clients then install, or even just run, the application from the Web server.

Of course, sometimes your application needs to exercise more control over the target installation machine than you can with a Web server. When you need more control over your application's installation, you may want to use the *Windows Installer,* a component in Windows operating systems that manages software installation. Visual Studio 2005 provides several project templates you can use to target the services of the Windows Installer.

From No Touch to ClickOnce

Microsoft started introducing the concept of Web-based installation in previous versions of the .NET Framework. The technology was improved and the name changed from No Touch to ClickOnce.

You use ClickOnce to

✦ Copy application files to a central Web site

✦ Deploy updates to a Web site

✦ Install applications on client machines from the Web site

You aren't restricted to deploying to a Web site; you can also deploy to an FTP server or CD. You can configure an application to automatically check a Web site for updates. Alternatively, you can use the `System.Deployment` namespace to write custom code that targets ClickOnce.

You can choose for your clients to run an application locally or only from the Web server. Either way, the application is downloaded to a local cache. You can find the cache at Documents and Settings\[username]\Local Settings\Apps.

The user is supplied with a link to the Web server or file server. For example, a user can click a link that you send by e-mail so that the application is downloaded to a local cache and executed. The user doesn't need administration privileges because the application runs in a secure mode and can't access the machine.

A ClickOnce process using Visual Studio may work like this:

✦ The developer publishes a Windows application to a deployment server.

Visual Studio 2005 creates a Web site to act as a deployment server. All files needed to run the application are copied to the Web site.

✦ The client clicks a hyperlink that deploys the Windows application on the local machine.

The hyperlink is a link to a setup file on the deployment server. The setup file downloads the application's files to the local computer and executes the application.

You have two options for deploying the application on the client:

✦ **Online** — The user must click the hyperlink every time she wants to run the application. The application is always installed in the local cache. When the user clicks the link, the deployment server downloads any updated components before executing the application from the local cache.

✦ **Offline** — The user can choose a shortcut from the Start menu to open the application. An uninstaller is provided on the Control Panel.

The good news is that you don't have to do anything special to use ClickOnce. The features are part of the .NET Framework. The bad news is that not all applications can be installed using ClickOnce. For example, you can't access the Registry or add assemblies to the Global Assembly Cache (GAC) by using ClickOnce. Use Windows Installer instead.

ClickOnce is intended for scenarios where your applications use a rich user interface to provide access to resources such as database servers and Web services. Many corporate applications fit into this scenario, which makes ClickOnce helpful from an administration standpoint. You don't have to physically deploy or update applications on every machine.

Visual Studio 2005 provides the Publishing Wizard for taking advantage of the .NET Framework's ClickOnce technology. You have two options for accessing the Publishing Wizard:

✦ Choose Build⇨Publish.

✦ Use the Publish tab in the Project Designer.

Applications published using the Publishing Wizard are *ClickOnce applications.*

To publish a Windows application to a Web site by using the Publishing Wizard, follow these steps:

1. **Open the Windows application in Visual Studio.**

2. **Choose Build⇨Publish <projectname>.**

Your project name appears after the Publish command on the Build menu. The Publishing Wizard appears.

The default choice is to publish to a Web site, as shown in Figure 2-1, and the wizard lists a location to create the Web site. If you want to use a different URL, type the pathname in the wizard.

Alternatively, you can type or browse to a file share, FTP server, or disk location.

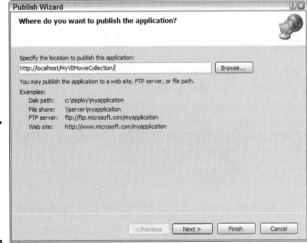

Figure 2-1:
The Publishing Wizard publishes to a Web site by default.

3. **Click the Next button.**

4. **At the prompt, choose whether to run the application online or offline.**

5. **Click the Next button.**

The Ready to Publish summary page appears.

6. **Verify your choices and click the Finish button.**

The wizard builds your project and publishes it to the Web server. Figure 2-2 shows the output from the wizard.

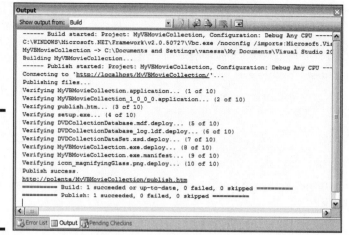

Figure 2-2:
The wizard builds the project and copies files to the Web site.

The output window displays a hyperlink to the Web site where you can install the application.

Accessing the published application

When you publish the application to a Web server, ClickOnce creates a Web site with a publish.htm file you can use to deploy the application to the local client. Accessing a published application is often referred to as *consuming* the application.

To access the published application locally, follow these steps:

1. **Browse to the URL where the application was published.**

You can find the URL in the output window, as described in the preceding section. You can also use the Publish tab in the Project Designer to determine where the application is published.

If you publish your application to a file share, use the UNC path to access the publish.htm file. If you publish to a CD, run the setup.exe file.

2. **Click the Install button on publish.htm, as shown in Figure 2-3.**

The Install button runs the setup.exe file.

ClickOnce downloads local copies of the application to a cache and launches the application. A security warning appears if the application isn't properly signed, as shown in Figure 2-4. See the later section "Signing your code" for more information on removing this security warning.

**Book VI
Chapter 2**

Deployment Options

Figure 2-3:
Click the
Install
button to
install and
launch the
application.

3. **Click the Install button to complete the installation. The files are copied, and the application is launched.**

Figure 2-4:
A security
warning
appears if
the applica-
tion isn't
properly
signed.

If you chose to publish your application so that it runs offline, the installation process creates, on the Start menu, a shortcut to the cached copy of the application. Otherwise, the application can be run only by using the URL to the deployment server. The application can be removed or configured by using the Add/Remove Programs applet in the Control Panel.

To remove an installed application by using the Control Panel, follow these steps:

1. **Open the Windows Control Panel.**

2. **Double-click the Add or Remove Programs icon.**

3. **Navigate to the program you want to remove in the Add or Remove Programs window.**

4. **Click the Change/Remove button.**

A maintenance window appears, as shown in Figure 2-5.

5. **Click the radio button to remove the application, and then click OK.**

The application is removed from the local computer.

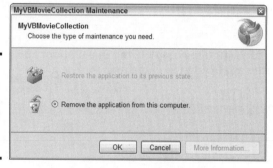

Figure 2-5:
Remove the
application
by using the
Control
Panel.

Checking out your publishing options

Visual Studio provides several options for deploying applications with ClickOnce. You access these options by using the Publish tab in the Project Designer. To access the Publish tab, follow these steps:

1. **Right-click the project in Solution Explorer.**

2. **Choose Properties from the shortcut menu.**

The Project Designer appears.

3. **Click the Publish tab, shown in Figure 2-6.**

You can use the Publish tab to do the following:

✦ **Set the publishing location.** Specify the path to a Web server, FTP server, network file share, or local file path where you want to publish files.

✦ **Designate the installation as online or offline.**

✦ **Specify which application files to include in the deployment.**

✦ **Select prerequisite components to install on the client machine.**
By default, version 2.0 of the .NET Framework is required. You can choose to require your own custom components or components from third parties, such as Crystal Reports.

✦ **Schedule application updates and provide an alternative location for retrieving updated files.**

✦ **Set options, such as a URL for support, or make an application deployed to a CD automatically start when the CD is inserted.**

✦ **Specify that the Publishing Wizard automatically increments version numbers each time the application publishes.**

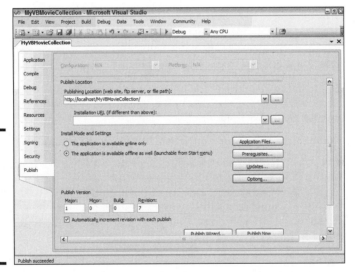

Figure 2-6:
Use the Project Designer's Publish tab to set publishing options.

Signing your code

For a ClickOnce application to run on a local computer, the computer needs to know that the application is safe to run. ClickOnce accomplishes this by digitally signing the application, also known as *code signing*. Digitally signed applications bind an application's publisher to the application and ensure that the application hasn't been tampered with en route to the consumer.

A digitally signed application uses a digital certificate to store all the information required to validate an application and its publisher. When you use the Publishing Wizard, Visual Studio automatically creates a certificate you can use for testing. Use the common practice of using a separate certificate for testing and releasing software, to prevent someone from obtaining test code with a release certificate.

Code signing is a fairly common requirement. You should create a single test certificate and reuse it rather than allow Visual Studio to create a new certificate every time. To sign a ClickOnce application, follow these steps:

1. **Right-click the project in Solution Explorer.**

2. **Choose Properties from the shortcut menu.**

The Project Designer appears.

3. **Click the Signing tab.**

The Signing tab has two purposes:

- Sign ClickOnce files.

- Sign assembly files.

See the section "Sharing assemblies," later in this chapter, for more information on signing assembly files.

4. **Select the Sign the ClickOnce manifests option.**

If you already ran the ClickOnce wizard once, Visual Studio automatically creates a test certificate. You see a check mark and the certificate's details, as shown in Figure 2-7.

5. **Click Select from Store or Select from File to select a certificate to use.**

If you need to create a new test certificate, click the Create Test Certificate button. You're prompted for a password to use for the certificate. Visual Studio creates the certificate and adds it to the project. The certificate is installed in your computer's personal store of certificates. Copy the .pfx file to a central location so that you can reuse it. Next time, you can choose Select from File and select the test certificate.

Figure 2-7:
The certificate's details appear on the Signing tab.

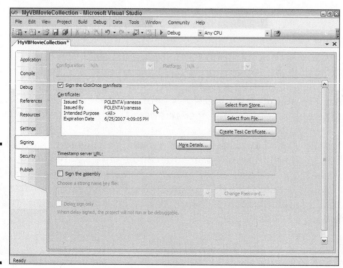

Alternatively, you can use the makecert.exe command in the .NET Software Development Kit to create certificates.

6. Click the More Details button.

The Certificate window appears.

The text in the certificate states that the certificate isn't trusted. At this point, a certificate in your personal store doesn't come from a trusted certificate authority (CA). You must install the certificate in the Trusted Root Certificate Authorities store.

7. Click the Install Certificate button, as shown in Figure 2-8.

The Certificate Import Wizard appears.

8. Click the Next button to step through the wizard.

The Certificate Store page appears.

9. Select the Place All Certificates in the Following Store option.

10. Click the Browse button.

The Select Certificate Store window appears.

11. Select Trusted Root Certificate Authorities and click OK.

The store appears in the wizard.

12. Click the Next button.

13. On the Completion page, click the Finish button.

A security warning informs you that you're about to install a new trusted certificate authority. The danger is that someone can sign software with your test certificate and run the software on your computer.

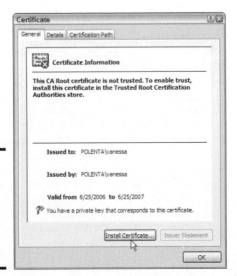

Figure 2-8:
Click the
Install
Certificate
button to
install the
certificate.

14. **Click Yes to accept the security warning.**

The certificate is installed in the Trusted Root Certificate Authorities store.

15. **Repeat Steps 7 through 13 to install the certificate in the Trusted Publishers store.**

Figure 2-9 shows a certificate published in the Trusted Publishers store.

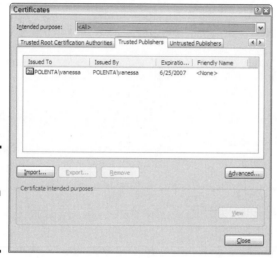

Figure 2-9:
Install your
certificate in
the Trusted
Publishers
store.

Now, whenever you install the application, you aren't prompted to install it.

Obviously, you don't want to deploy your test certificate into production. You need to acquire a release certificate from a certification authority (CA). A *certification authority* is an entity whose identity has been verified and who can validate your identity. For example, VeriSign is a certification authority from whom you can buy a certificate. Read more about the VeriSign code-signing products on its Web site: www.verisign.com/ products-services/security-services/code-signing/.

If you're distributing software only within your internal organization, you may not want to purchase a certification from a third party. In that case, your organization can make itself a CA for within your organization and issue certifications.

Whichever route you take, you need some way to distribute the certificates to the Trusted Publishers store on all your clients. Additionally, if your company is issuing its own certificates, it needs to register itself on each client machine in the Trusted Root Certification Authorities store.

I'm fairly certain that you don't want to run around to each client machine and install code signing certificates. That defeats the purpose of using ClickOnce. Instead, use Windows Installer to create an installer package that installs the certificates. You can use other tools too, such as the Windows certificate-management console (certmgr.exe).

If you want to learn more about code signing, check out the Microsoft white paper on code-signing best practices at www.microsoft.com/whdc/winlogo/drvsign/best_practices.mspx.

Updating your applications

You have several options for updating your ClickOnce applications. When you need to publish updates, you just update your software in Visual Studio and publish it again by using the Publishing Wizard. Old versions of the software are retained, and new versions are pushed out.

When and how frequently a user's application checks for updates depends on how you configure the Publishing Wizard. You access update options by using the Updates button on the Publish tab of the Project Designer. See the section "Publishing options," earlier in this chapter, for more information on using the Publish tab.

These update choices are available to you:

✦ **After the application starts** — Speeds up start time because the application checks for updates after it opens. Any new updates are downloaded and installed the next time the application runs.

✦ **Before the application starts** — Updates are installed when a user launches the application.

✦ **Scheduled updates** — Indicates how frequently the application should check for updates, as shown in Figure 2-10.

✦ **Required update to a minimum version** — Forces a client to update by requiring the use of at least a minimum version of the application.

You can use the Application Updates window to specify an update location that's different from a publish location. For example, you can publish to a CD and update to a Web server.

Each time you run the Publishing Wizard, Visual Studio automatically updates the application's version number. The version number is part of the application's digital signature, which .NET uses to ensure that the application is valid. If you haven't made any changes to the application, the build process doesn't build the application. As a result, the wizard uses a new version number when it publishes a copy of the application from the previous version. As a result, the application doesn't run on the client machine. If you want to force Visual Studio to publish an update when you haven't made any changes to the code, be sure to use the Build⇨Clean command first. The Publishing Wizard is then forced to build the application.

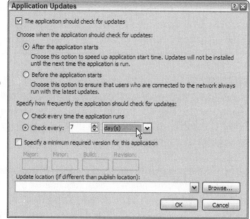

Figure 2-10:
Use the Application Updates window to configure and schedule updates.

Making a Windows Installer

Visual Studio 2005 provides setup projects you can use to deploy your applications. Setup projects create a Windows Installer file with the extension .msi.

These setup projects are available in Visual Studio:

✦ Setup projects create an installer file that can be used to deploy a program on a target machine or to a virtual directory on a Web site. Visual Studio provides a wizard to walk you through creating setup projects.

✦ Merge module projects create reusable setup components for consumption by setup projects.

✦ A Cab project creates a .cab file from the items added to Solution Explorer. Cab files are often used to distribute components such as ActiveX controls. The .cab file format (short for Microsoft Cabinet) is used for compressing files.

You can distribute the resulting MSI (Microsoft Installer) files by using CDs or DVDs or a file share for installation across a network. The MSI files can install an application on a target machine in a Windows application, or on a Web site in a Web application.

The installation projects provided by Visual Studio take advantage of Windows Installer, which is an installation framework available on Windows operating systems. The installer takes care of how everything gets installed; you just focus on what you need to install. For example, the installer can create Registry entries, shortcuts, and ODBC connections for you. You use a Visual Studio setup project to tell the Windows Installer what to install. You don't have to write the code to make any of this installation happen. The Windows Installer gets it installed for you.

Applications installed by using Windows Installer can

✦ Self-repair if the program is damaged

✦ Roll back if the installation can't be completed

Windows Installer is sophisticated — there's nothing you can't install with it.

Creating a setup project for an existing application

Although you can create stand-alone setup projects, you usually add setup projects to an existing solution that you want to deploy. To create a setup project for an existing application, follow these steps:

1. **Open a solution that includes a project you want to deploy.**

2. **Right-click the solution in Solution Explorer.**

   A shortcut menu appears.

3. **Choose Add➪New Project.**

4. **In the Add New Project Window, expand the Other Project Types category and select Setup and Deployment.**

   A list of project templates appears.

5. **Select Setup Wizard.**

6. **Type a name for the project, and click OK.**

   The Setup Wizard appears.

7. **Click the Next button.**

   The Choose a Project Type page appears.

8. **Select the Create a Setup for a Windows Application option.**

   You can use the wizard to create a Web setup project, merge module, or .cab file.

9. **Click the Next button.**

The Choose Project Outputs page appears. The project output from the other projects in the solution appears on this page. If no other projects are in the solution, this page doesn't appear. You have to add files to the setup project manually.

10. **Select the project output groups you want to deploy with your setup project.**

You want, at a minimum, content files and the primary output, which is the assembly created by your project.

Specify that a file should be included as a content file by accessing the file's properties in Solution Explorer.

11. **Click the Next button.**

12. **Add any files you want to deploy with your setup project.**

13. **Click the Next button.**

The Create Project page appears.

14. **Click the Finish button.**

The project is created, and the content is added to Solution Explorer, as shown in Figure 2-11.

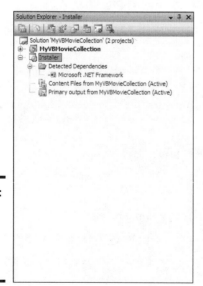

Figure 2-11:
The Setup
Project
appears in
Solution
Explorer.

Setup projects have a number of editors you can use to build your installer, including the ones in this list:

◆ **File System** — Identifies which files and shortcuts are created on the file system of the target machine

◆ **Registry** — Creates Registry entries

◆ **File Types** — Associates file extensions with applications

◆ **User Interface** — Customizes the installation wizard

◆ **Custom Actions** — Customizes the installation process

◆ **Launch Conditions** — Creates conditional installation steps

These editors are fairly straightforward to use after you realize that you're taking the perspective of the target computer. You have to start out by asking yourself what you want the target machine to look like when the installer is complete and then figure out how to make that happen by using these editors.

Putting the Installer to work

To install a simple application and create shortcuts on the user's desktop and Start menu, use the File System Editor as described here:

1. Create a new setup project, as described in the preceding set of steps.

The File System Editor opens by default.

You can open any of the editors by using the View menu or the icons on the Solution Explorer toolbar.

The File System Editor displays the file system of the target machine. You can elect to install files or shortcuts to special folders that are common to all Windows computers, such as a User's Desktop or Favorites folder.

By default, the Application Folder, User's Desktop, and User's Program Menu folders are added to the editor. Right-click the option File System on Target Machine to add more folders.

2. Select Application Folder.

The folder's contents appear in the pane on the right.

If you added your setup project to a solution with an existing project, the projects' output selected in the wizard appears. Right-click Application Folder and choose from the menu to add more files.

Use the Properties window to set an installation folder for Application Folder.

3. **Right-click Primary Output in the Application folder.**

   A shortcut menu appears.

4. **Choose Create Shortcut.**

   A new shortcut appears, as shown in Figure 2-12.

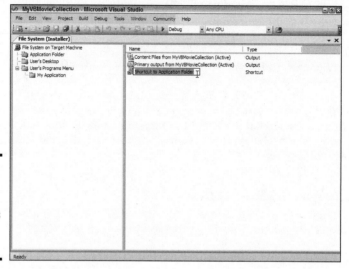

Figure 2-12:
Add a new
shortcut to
the project's
primary
output.

5. **Type a name for the shortcut because you want the shortcut to appear on the target computer.**

6. **Right-click the shortcut and choose Cut.**

7. **Right-click User's Desktop and choose Paste.**

   The shortcut appears in the folder.

8. **Right-click the User's Programs Menu folder.**

9. **Choose Add⇨Folder from the shortcut menu.**

10. **Type a name for the folder because you want the folder to appear on the user's Program menu.**

11. **Repeat Steps 3 through 7 to add a shortcut to the new folder.**

You now have an installer that installs your application and creates shortcuts on the user's desktop and then adds a folder with a shortcut to the Program menu.

Here's how to test the installer:

1. **Right-click the setup project in Solution Explorer.**

2. **Choose Build from the shortcut menu.**

The project builds and packages the files.

If you choose to build the entire solution, the setup project isn't included in the solution's build configuration in the Configuration Manager. Either enable it to be built or build the project by using the Build menu.

3. **Repeat Step 1 and choose Install from the shortcut menu.**

The installer wizard appears.

4. **Step through the wizard to install your application.**

Sharing assemblies

Most of the time you want your assemblies to be private. Private assemblies are accessed only by your application. If you want to share your assemblies with other applications, you need to place them in the Global Assembly Cache. Examples of assemblies you may find in the GAC are the assemblies of the .NET Framework. When you place the assemblies in the GAC, all applications have access to them.

To publish an assembly to the GAC, it must use a strong name, which guarantees that all assemblies in the GAC have a unique name. A *strong name* is made up of the assembly's name, version number, public key, and digital signature. Suppose that your company creates an assembly named `OrderEntry`. Another company could feasibly create an assembly with the same name. A strongly named assembly creates a unique assembly even if the assembly names are identical.

If you attempt to publish to the GAC an assembly that isn't strongly named, you receive an error message, as shown in Figure 2-13.

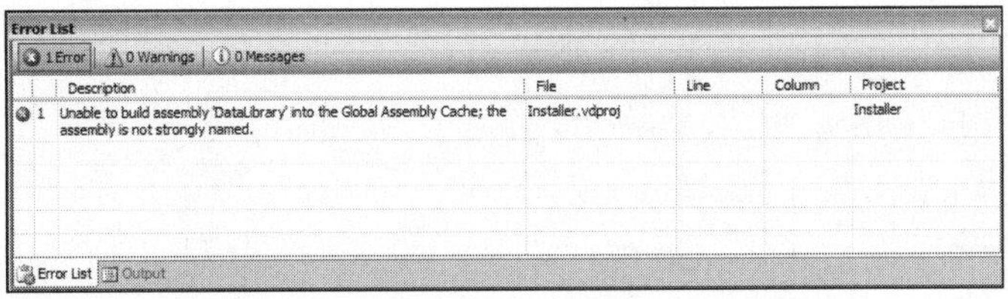

Figure 2-13:
Assemblies must be strongly named before you can install them into the Global Assembly Cache.

Visual Studio 2005 provides a way to strong name assemblies and publish them to the GAC. To strong name an assembly, follow these steps:

1. **Go to the Signing tab of the Project Designer for the assembly you want to sign.**

2. **Select the Sign the Assembly option.**

3. **Click the Choose a Strong Name Key File drop-down list.**

4. **Click Browse to reuse an existing key file, or click New to create a new key file.**

   If you click New, the Create Strong Name Key window appears. Type a name for the key file and a password to protect the file.

   The key file appears on the tab, as shown in Figure 2-14.

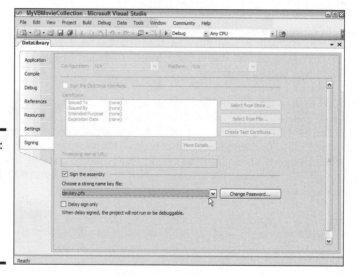

Figure 2-14:
Use the Signing tab to strong name the assembly with a key file.

To install the assembly in the GAC by using a setup project, follow these steps:

1. **Open the File System Editor in the setup project.**

2. **Right-click File System on Target Machine.**

   A shortcut menu appears.

3. **Choose Add Special Folder⇨Global Assembly Cache Folder.**

   A GAC folder appears in the editor.

4. **Right-click Global Assembly Cache Folder in the editor.**

5. **Choose Add➪Project Output.**

   The Project Output Group window appears.

6. **Select the project from the Project drop-down list and select Primary Output, as shown in Figure 2-15.**

7. **Click OK.**

   The primary output appears in the editor.

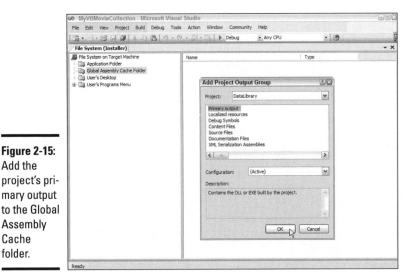

Figure 2-15:
Add the project's primary output to the Global Assembly Cache folder.

Build the setup project, and install it on a test machine. To view the GAC to ensure that the assembly was installed, take these steps:

1. **Open Administrative Tools in the Control Panel.**

2. **Double-click Microsoft .NET 2.0 Configuration.**

   The configuration management console appears.

3. **Select Manage the Assembly Cache.**

4. **Select the View List of Assemblies in the Assembly Cache option.**

   A list of assemblies appears.

5. **Locate your assembly, as shown in Figure 2-16.**

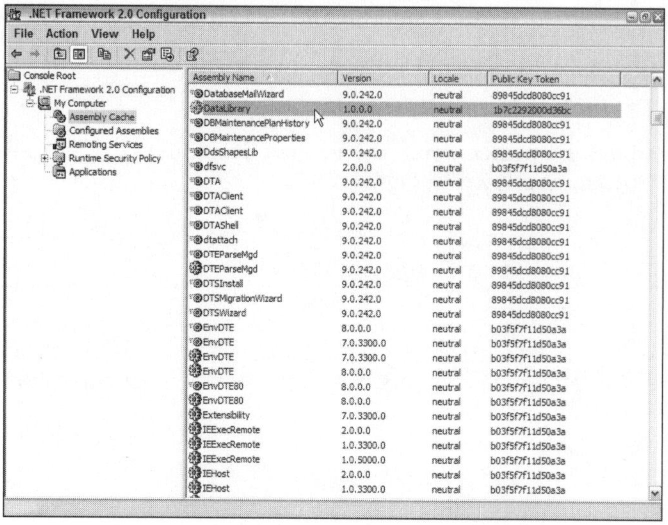

Figure 2-16:
View the
Global
Assembly
Cache to
verify that
the assem-
bly is
installed.

Deploying Web Applications

Deploying Web applications is more complicated than deploying Windows applications. One key difference is what occurs during the build process. Windows applications are compiled into assemblies. You can distribute those assemblies by any means you want. Visual Studio provides a number of tools to assist with the distribution of Windows assemblies, as described in the preceding section.

Web sites are different. When you use the Build command with a Web site, Visual Studio compiles the page only for testing. You can't deploy the output created from the Build command — and you don't need to. Because ASP.NET Web sites are compiled on demand when users access the Web site, you can just copy and paste your Web site, if you want.

You may want to compile your Web sites before you deploy them, which is often called *precompiling*. Precompiled Web sites have these benefits:

✦ They start faster because no performance hit occurs while the requested page compiles.

✦ Source code isn't deployed to the Web server; only assemblies and static files are.

✦ You get feedback from compiler errors before the Web site is deployed.

Next, the deployment begins. Web sites often have two stages of deployment:

✦ **Test server** — When a Web site is first created, it may be initially deployed to a test server. Several developers and testers can access the test site. The test site usually remains up after the site is deployed to production. The test site provides a working copy of the production Web site, where changes can be made.

✦ **Production server** — After a site is ready to go live, it's published to a production Web server.

In reality, several versions of the Web site can be running on different test servers. Developers can also have local copies of the site running on their development machines. They may deploy their local copies to the test server.

Because of the nature of Web sites, they're often changed more frequently than Windows applications. Changes are usually made to a single page or a set of pages, and then only those changes are deployed. In other cases, the entire Web site may be deployed.

Making frequent changes to the structure, layout, and design of a Web site can be disruptive to your site's visitors. As a result, more firms are starting to limit the number of changes they make to the site. Rather than change the site, firms are creating fluid sites that use content databases and configuration files to control the site's content and flow. Rather than change the Web site when you want to change content or the site flow, changes are made to content databases or configuration files.

Whether you're deploying to a test server or a production Web server, Visual Studio provides several options for deploying Web sites:

✦ **Web setup project** — Packages your Web site by using an installer that you then execute on the Web server

✦ **Copy Web Site tool** — Copies and synchronizes sites between a local store and a server

✦ **Publish Web Site** — Precompiles the Web site and copies it to the target of your choice

✦ **Web Deployment Projects** — Gives you the most flexibility (because it's an add-in) in precompiling your Web site

You can also just copy and paste your files from your test server to production. The major drawback of copy-and-paste strategies is that you can easily make mistakes.

To use the Publish Web Site utility in Visual Studio, follow these steps:

1. **Open your Web site in Visual Studio.**

2. **Choose Build⇨Publish Web Site.**

   The Publish Web Site window appears.

3. **Specify a target location where the Web site should be copied.**

   You can enter or browse to a URL, UNC, or local file path.

4. **Select the option labeled Allow This Precompiled Site to Be Updateable.**

   This feature copies your .aspx files as is to the Web site. You can update these pages later without having to recompile and deploy the entire site.

5. **Click OK, as shown in Figure 2-17.**

   All code-behind files are compiled into a single assembly. The assembly, aspx files, and static files, such as images, are copied to the target location specified in Step 3.

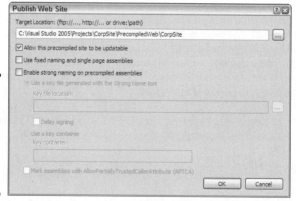

Figure 2-17:
Use the Publish Web Site utility to precompile your Web site.

Make a backup of your production Web site before deploying a new Web site. If the new site doesn't work, you can quickly roll back.

A common challenge when you're deploying Web sites is not overwriting the web.config file. The web.config file on a test server usually has different settings than on a production server. For example, the test server may have connection strings that point to test databases. The Microsoft add-in Web Deployment Projects gives you more control over precompilation and web.config files.

You can download the Web Deployment Project add-in at `http://msdn.microsoft.com/asp.net/reference/infrastructure/wdp/default.aspx`.

The Web Deployment Project add-in adds an Add Web Deployment Project command to the Build menu. You can't add a new project from the Add New Project window.

To add a new Web Deployment Project to a Web site, follow these steps:

1. **Download and install the Web Deployment Project add-in.**

2. **Open an ASP.NET Web site project in Visual Studio.**

3. **Choose Build⇨Add Web Deployment Project.**

The Add Web Deployment Project window appears.

4. **Type a name for the project and click OK.**

The Web Deployment Project appears in Solution Explorer.

You access the features of the Web Deployment Project by using its property pages. Use them to do the following:

✦ Set compilation settings.

✦ Determine how assemblies are generated.

✦ Sign assemblies.

✦ Configure how the site is deployed.

You configure a group of property page settings for each build configuration. For example, you likely don't want to use the deployment project with your debug build configuration. You can create different deployment settings for staging and Release build configurations.

For example, to change the web.config file for deployment by using a Release build, follow these steps:

1. **Right-click the deployment project in Solution Explorer and choose Property Pages.**

2. **Select Release from the Configuration drop-down list.**

All settings you create in the property pages apply only to the Release build configuration.

3. **Select the Deployment tab.**

4. **Select the Enable Web.config File Section Replacement option.**

5. **In the Web.config File Section Replacements text box, type**
connectionStrings=releaseconnectStrings.config, **as shown in**
Figure 2-18.

   The Web.config section to replace is connectionStrings. It's replaced
   by the contents of the file releaseconnectStrings.config, which is a text
   file that holds the connectionStrings section. You can name your
   .config file anything you like.

6. **Click OK.**

   The settings are saved.

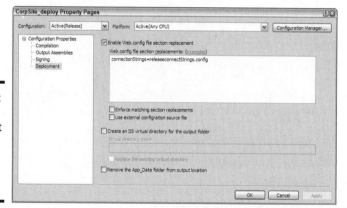

Figure 2-18:
Use Web
Deployment
Projects to
merge
web.config
files.

Build your site by using the Release configuration. The web.config file is
merged with the config file. And you have a Release version of your Web
site that you can deploy to your production server using whatever method
suits you.

Chapter 3: Checking Out Source Control

In This Chapter

✔ **Setting up source control**

✔ **Adding and retrieving source code**

✔ **Performing daily integration tasks**

✔ **Using source control on a team project**

*W*hether you're on a team of hundreds or a team of one, you need some way to manage your source code. You use source code control software for these tasks:

+ Provide a central repository for storing source code.

+ Create a new version of source code every time changes are made.

+ Track the history of your source code.

Visual Studio doesn't provide source code control features. However, it provides menus and windows you can use to access some third-party source code control products, such as Microsoft's Visual SourceSafe. Any source code control software that implements the Visual Studio Integration Protocol can provide source control services to Visual Studio.

Using Source Code Control with Visual Studio

Visual Studio provides menu commands you can use to drive the features of your integrated source code control provider. Visual Studio acts as a gateway to third-party source control providers, which are referred to as *plug-ins* in Visual Studio.

A source code control environment includes these elements:

+ **A centralized database** — Stores master copies of source code

+ **Local working folders** — Holds source code that's downloaded on each developer's computer for editing

A team can use a dedicated build server that downloads source code from the database to a local working folder.

How source code control works

Any developer who needs to use source code downloads a working copy of the source code to a local folder. To edit the source code files, the developer must check out the source code files. After the editing is finished, the developer checks the files back into the source code control database.

The process of checking a file into source code is often referred to as *integration*. Presumably, the developer has unit-tested the code before integrating it into the master source code. Unit testing your code before checking it into source code helps maintain the integrity of the master source code. Integrated code, even when it's tested, can cause the master source code not to compile. See Book V, Chapter 8 for more information on unit testing.

Automated build processes usually download the latest version of source code and execute a build script to build the master source code. The build server may create in the database a new version of the code, labeled with the build number. The development team can then re-create the build at any time. See Chapter 1 in this mini-book for more information on build automation.

Getting ready for source control

Before you can integrate source code control with Visual Studio, you must do a couple of things first:

+ **Set up and configure your source code control provider's server environment.** Setting up the server usually involves installing administration tools, adding users, and creating new databases.

+ **Install your source code control provider on each client who needs access to the source control database.** Even though you access source code control via menu commands in Visual Studio, your source control provider's client software must be installed on each client computer.

After you install your source code control client, Visual Studio displays additional menus and commands you can use to access your source code control repository. Here are some common source code controls tasks you can complete:

+ Adding a new or existing project to source control.

+ Opening an existing project from source control.

+ Check out or check in source code.

+ Get the latest version of source code.

+ Remove a project from source control.

One of the first tasks you need to do before you start using source code control is to set your local working folder. The local working folder is the local repository on the client's machine where source code files are downloaded.

When you edit source code files, you edit them by using files in the local working folder.

Your source code control provider allows you to set a local working folder. If you don't set a local working folder, Visual Studio downloads files to your default projects folder. You can change the default projects folder in Visual Studio or set the local working folder in your source control provider.

To change the default projects folder in Visual Studio, follow these steps:

1. **Choose Tools⇨Options.**

The Options window appears.

2. **Select Projects and Solutions.**

A list of settings for projects and solutions appears.

3. **Set the default folder location by using the Visual Studio projects location field, as shown in Figure 3-1.**

4. **Click OK.**

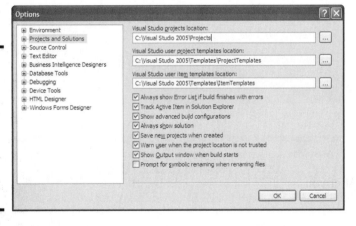

Figure 3-1:
Visual
Studio
downloads
files from
source
control to
the default
projects
folder.

To set the local working folder by using Visual SourceSafe, follow these steps:

1. **Choose File⇨Source Control in Visual Studio.**

A submenu appears. You must have Visual SourceSafe installed on the client in order to use the Source Control menu in Visual Studio.

2. **Choose Launch Microsoft Visual SourceSafe.**

Visual SourceSafe opens.

3. **Provide your login credentials, if you're prompted.**

4. **Click the dollar sign ($) at the top of the folder hierarchy.**

5. **Choose File➪Set Working Folder.**

   The Browse for Folder window appears.

6. **Select a folder to use as the working folder.**

7. **Click OK.**

   The working folder appears in Visual SourceSafe, as shown in Figure 3-2.

Figure 3-2:
Local files are saved to the working folder set in Visual SourceSafe.

Going outside the box

You aren't limited to using a source control provider that integrates with Visual Studio. You can use any source control provider as long as it supports a developer's daily tasks of getting the latest version of source code, checking out items for editing, and checking items back in.

Integrated source control can boost productivity. However, using a solution that isn't integrated can be just as productive, depending on the sophistication level of your developers in using the source control tool. Making sure that

your developers have at least two monitors on their desktops so that they don't have to switch between source control and Visual Studio can help also.

The popular open-source source code control solution WinCVS isn't integrated with Visual Studio. You should use a tool like WinCVS even if you aren't required to use source control. You can download WinCVS for free at www.wincvs.org/.

If you don't set your local working folder in your source control provider, Visual Studio uses the default projects location to download source code. Use the local working folder if you want to download controlled source code to a different location than your default projects folder in Visual Studio.

Binding to a source control provider

After you install your source code control provider, you can access the source code control features in Visual Studio. Promptly add your new or existing solutions and projects to your source code control database. The *binding* process creates a link between a local copy of source code and the source control database.

Visual Studio adds files to your source code control database in this way:

1. Creates a parent folder in your database named `<solution>.root` where `<solution>` is the solution's name in Visual Studio.

2. Adds a folder to the `*.root` folder for your solution.

3. Adds folders for each project to the solution folder.

Microsoft recommends that you use solutions to organize your source code. You should add your solutions to source code control. When you add a solution, all its projects are added too. If you add a new project to a solution, you can easily add that project to source code. Follow these rules for working with solutions and projects with source code control:

✦ Create a blank solution first.

✦ Always add projects to solutions.

✦ Name your solutions so that they identify the system under development.

To create a blank solution, follow these steps:

1. **Press Ctrl+Shift+N to open the New Project window.**

2. **Click the plus (+) sign next to Other Project Types.**

3. **Select Visual Studio Solutions.**

   A list of solution types appears in the templates pane.

4. **Select Blank Solution.**

5. **Type a name for the solution and click OK.**

   Select the Add to Source Control option to add the solution to source control when it's created.

Here's how to add a solution to a Visual SourceSafe source code control database by using Visual Studio:

1. **Open or create the solution in Visual Studio.**

2. **Choose File⇨Source Control.**

   A submenu appears.

3. **Select Add Solution to Source Control.**

   The Visual SourceSafe login appears. At this step, Visual Studio passes off your request to your source code control provider.

4. **Type your login credentials to access the Visual SourceSafe database, and click OK.**

   The Add to SourceSafe window appears.

5. **Select a location for your solution to be added to the database and enter a name.**

   Visual Studio provides the default name <solutionname>.root. You should generally accept the default name, as shown in Figure 3-3.

Figure 3-3:
Visual Studio appends the .root extension to solutions added to source control.

Ideally, you want your solution's name to describe the system you're developing. If the solution name is the same as the project name, distinguishing between the solution and project folders can be confusing.

6. **Click OK.**

   Visual SourceSafe prompts you to create the root entry.

7. **Click the Yes button to create the parent folder.**

   Visual SourceSafe adds your solution's projects and files to the database.

Don't spend a lot of energy organizing your source control folders in your source control provider. In reality, you don't spend much time using the source control view of your solutions and projects. You mostly interact with Solution Explorer in Visual Studio. Instead, focus on using meaningful names in Solution Explorer and accept the defaults in your source control database.

To add a project to an existing solution already in the source code control database:

1. **Add the project to the source-controlled solution.**

2. **Choose File➪Source Control.**

A submenu appears.

3. **Choose Add Selected Projects to Source Control.**

A dialog box prompts you to confirm your choice.

4. **Click the Yes button.**

Visual SourceSafe adds your project to the database under the existing solution's root folder.

There may be times when you want to unbind source code from the source code control database. To unbind your local copy from the database, follow these steps:

1. **Open the solution or project under source control in Visual Studio.**

2. **Choose File➪Source Control.**

A submenu appears.

3. **Choose Change Source Control.**

Use the Change Source Control window to view the binding properties, such as server name, database, and local working folder. Click the Columns button, shown in Figure 3-4, to add columns to the view.

Columns button

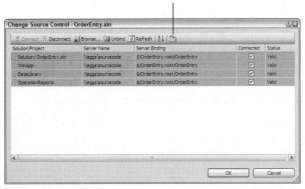

Figure 3-4:
Use the Columns button to view additional binding properties in the Change Source Control window.

4. **Click the solution or project to unbind, and click the Unbind button.**

   Visual Studio prompts you to confirm your choice.

5. **Click the Unbind button in the dialog box.**

   The binding is removed.

   The source code remains in the database. Only the link between the local copy and the database is severed.

You can use the Change Source Control to connect and disconnect from the source control database. A *connection* is a live data link to the database. Disconnecting allows you to work offline from the database. You can connect to the database when you have a network connection again.

Performing common source control tasks

Source control bound to a source control database is locked. To edit a source code file that's under source code control, you need to check it out first. After you complete your edit, you check the file back into the source control database. Any time you work with source code, you should always synchronize your local copy of the source code with the master copy in the source control database.

The number of source control tasks you use daily is usually limited to three:

✦ Get the latest version of source code.

✦ Check the source code into the database.

✦ Check the source code out of the database.

In Visual Studio, you access your source control provider by choosing File⇨ Source Control. You're likely to manage your source code in Visual Studio in three other ways:

✦ Right-click an item in Solution Explorer to access source control commands.

✦ Use the Source Control toolbar.

   Choose View⇨Toolbars⇨Source Control to open the Source Control toolbar, shown in Figure 3-5.

✦ Use the Pending Check-Ins window to manage checked-out source control.

Table 3-1 describes the common source control commands.

Figure 3-5:
Use the
Source
Control
toolbar to
access com-
mon source
control
commands.

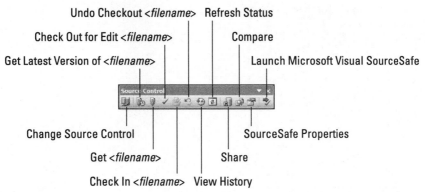

Undo Checkout *<filename>*   Refresh Status

Check Out for Edit *<filename>*   Compare

Get Latest Version of *<filename>*   Launch Microsoft Visual SourceSafe

Change Source Control   SourceSafe Properties

Get *<filename>*   Share

Check In *<filename>*   View History

Table 3-1	Common Source Control Commands
Command	*What It Does*
Check In	Checks a file into the source control database
Check Out for Edit	Checks out a file from the source control database so that it can be edited
Compare	Shows the differences between two files
Get	Creates a read-only copy of the file in the local working folder
Get Latest	Gets the latest version of the file
Undo Checkout	Discards the last checkout
View History	Displays a file's history

Visual Studio provides visual clues about a file's status — whether it's checked in or checked out or not source controlled. A visual cue is displayed next to certain items in Solution Explorer:

✦ **Checked-in items** — A lock

✦ **Checked-out items** — A check mark

✦ **Items not in source control** — A plus (+) sign

Figure 3-6 shows the visual cues in Solution Explorer.

Retrieving files from source control

The Visual Studio commands Get and Get Latest Version retrieve files from source control. You use these commands with a solution or project that's already under source control. See the earlier section "Binding to a source control provider" to see how to add a solution or project to source control.

Figure 3-6:
Solutions
under
source
control
provide
visual cues
in Solution
Explorer.

Source control providers "version" your source control files each time you perform a check-in. In most cases, you use the Get Latest Version command to retrieve the most recently checked-in version of a file. You use the Get command if you want to specify additional options, such as whether to make the file writable when it's retrieved.

You use the View History command along with Get to access previous versions of projects and files. To open a previous version of a file, follow these steps:

1. **Right-click the file for which you want to retrieve a previous version.**

2. **Choose View History from the shortcut menu.**

   The History Options window appears.

3. **Type a label or date range to filter the history, if you want.**

4. **Click OK.**

   The History window appears.

5. **Select the version you want to retrieve and click the Get button, shown in Figure 3-7.**

   The Get window appears.

6. **Specify Get options, such as whether to make the file writable.**

7. **Click OK.**

   Visual Studio retrieves the file.

Editing source-controlled files

You must check out source-controlled files before you can edit them. You can check out a single file or an entire project. Visual Studio provides a Check Out for Edit command that instructs your source control provider to

✦ Download the latest version of the source-controlled file

✦ Mark the file as writable

Figure 3-7:
Use the Get command in a file's history to retrieve previous versions of the file.

To check out a file by using the Visual SourceSafe plug-in, follow these steps:

1. **Right-click the file in Solution Explorer.**

2. **Choose Check Out for Edit from the shortcut menu.**

The Check Out for Edit window displays a tree view of all the files that must be checked out. For example, the project file is automatically checked out when you check out a code file, as shown in Figure 3-8.

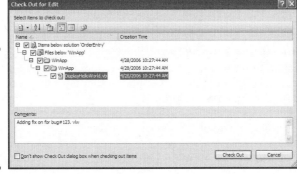

Figure 3-8:
The Check Out for Edit window displays the files being checked out.

3. **Type a comment to describe the reason for the checkout, if you want.**

4. **Click the Check Out button.**

Visual SourceSafe downloads the latest version of the files to your local working folder and marks them as writable. A check mark appears next to the filenames in Solution Explorer.

There may be times when you want to check out a previous version of a source-controlled file. To check out a previous version, follow these steps:

1. **Download the version of the file you want from the source control database by following the steps in the preceding section.**

2. **Execute the Check Out for Edit command.**

The Check Out for Edit window appears.

3. **Click the Options button (the first button) on the toolbar.**

4. **Select Check Out Local Version.**

If the Check Out Local Version command is unavailable, click Advanced and select the Don't Get Local Copy option.

5. **Click the Check Out button.**

Visual SourceSafe checks out the local copy of the file.

You can undo a checkout by using the Undo Checkout command. Any changes to the local file are lost.

Depending on how Visual SourceSafe is deployed, it may place an exclusive lock on your file when it's checked out. This lock prevents anyone else from checking out the file from the database. If your database is configured to use multiple checkouts, other users can check out the file. All changes are merged in the database. Check with your database administrator to determine how your source control provider is configured.

Multiple checkouts are often used with ASP.NET Web sites. Multiple developers, therefore, can check out the entire Web site. Because developers aren't usually working on exactly the same source file, merge issues are infrequent.

Checking files into source control

You can check in files by using the Check In command. You can use the Pending Check-Ins window in Visual Studio to display a list of all files that are checked out for the open solution.

To use the Pending Check-Ins window, follow these steps:

1. **Right-click any file in Solution Explorer.**

2. **Choose View Pending Checkins from the shortcut menu.**

The Pending Checkins window appears, and by default displays checked-out files in tree view. Click the Flat View button to display a flat list of files, as shown in Figure 3-9.

3. **Clear the check boxes for any files you don't want to check in now.**

4. **Click the Comments button to add a check-in comment to all the files.**

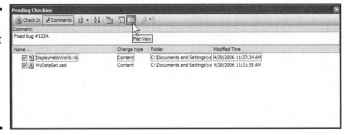

Figure 3-9:
Click the Flat View button to display a flat list of checked-out files.

**Book VI
Chapter 3**

**Checking Out
Source Control**

5. **Click the Check In button.**

The files are checked in to source control and marked as Read-Only in the local working folder.

Retrieving a solution or project from source control

After a new solution or project is added to source code control, you must download the solution or project from source code control before you can use it. For example, if you're working in a team environment, you may need to retrieve a solution or project that another team member creates and adds to source control.

To open a project from the source control database, follow these steps:

1. **Press Ctrl+Shift+O to open the Open Project window.**

2. **Click the icon for your source control provider along the left side of the window.**

A list of source control databases appears in the file explorer. Figure 3-10 shows an example of accessing a Visual SourceSafe database.

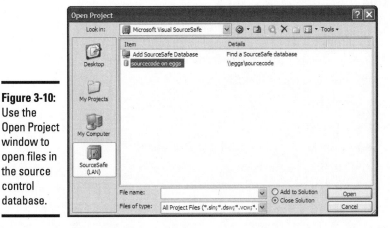

Figure 3-10:
Use the Open Project window to open files in the source control database.

3. **Navigate to your solution or project file and click the Open button.**

Visual Studio downloads the files from the source control database to the local working folder.

See the earlier section "Getting ready for source control" for information on how to set the local working folder.

You can open a Web site from the source control database by using the Open Web Site window in Visual Studio.

Source Code Control in the Real World

Source code control is an activity that falls under a larger area of the software development life cycle known as software configuration management (SCM). SCM is often referred to as change management because managing the changes to software is one of SCM's primary goals.

Software configuration management encompasses many activities, such as

✦ Identifying items, such as source code, subject to change management

✦ Defining a change control process for managing changes

✦ Controlling software builds and releases

In practical terms, source code control is a key element in managing changes, builds, and releases. Here are some other tools that enable SCM:

✦ Requirements-tracking software

✦ Bug-tracking software

✦ Scripts for creating builds

By using source code control software in conjunction with other SCM tools, you can

✦ Trace software features to requirements

✦ Trace code changes to bug-fix requests

✦ Track versions

✦ Reproduce builds

✦ Create a traceable history of who did what and when

✦ Identify differences among releases

You can read about software configuration management in the Software Engineering Body of Knowledge (SWEBOK). The SWEBOK represents the latest thinking on how to engineer good software. Even if you don't believe that software should be engineered, you can get plenty of good information from the SWEBOK. You can download it at www.swebok.org/.

A software project has many items, in addition to source code, that need to be controlled. Here are some examples, which are often referred to as *artifacts* or *work products:*

✦ Requirements specifications

✦ Architecture diagrams

✦ Build scripts

✦ Installer programs

✦ Compilers

Some people choose to place these artifacts in a source control tool, such as Visual SourceSafe. Because some items, such as requirements documents, aren't source-controlled, many teams use document management systems, such as Microsoft Windows SharePoint Services.

The new Microsoft product Team Foundation Server (TFS) helps teams manage a project's artifacts and the SCM process. TFS works hand in hand with Visual Studio to create an integrated change-management process.

Regardless of which tools you use, be sure to follow these best practices when you use source control:

✦ Get the latest version of source code frequently.

✦ Check in your changes to source code frequently.

✦ Build your software from the master source code daily.

✦ Back up your master source code.

✦ Implement bug-tracking software that links to your source code changes.

✦ Include everything you need to reproduce a build, including build scripts, installers, and compilers.

Going Beyond Integration

The daily integration of each developer's changes to source code is only one piece of the source control puzzle. Source code control providers, such as Microsoft Visual SourceSafe, support additional commands related to managing version control of your software, such as

+ **Share** — Shares source code between two projects without using copy and paste.

+ **Branch** — Splits off a file or project as a separate file or project. For example, if you branch a file at version 3, you have two independent copies of version 3.

+ **Merge** — Combines the contents of two files and creates a new, merged version. You still have two files, but the contents are merged.

+ **Diff** — Compares two versions of a file. You can use the Merge command to create a new merged version.

+ **Label** — Associates a lookup tag with the source-controlled item. Labels are often used at the project level for version control. For example, the daily build process may use a label to associate a build number with a project. Team members can use the build number to retrieve the source code used to create the build from the database.

+ **Rollback** — Erases all successive versions after a chosen version.

+ **Pin** — Marks a version of a file that can't be changed until the pin is removed.

Visual Studio 2005 has menu access to many of these commands. However, in most shops, a source control administrator performs these tasks using whichever tool is most appropriate, which is often a batch file.

Visual SourceSafe 2005 (VSS) has a command-line feature you can use to execute source control commands on the command line or in a batch file. The VSS administrator should use these commands. Your developers shouldn't use the command line for day-to-day source control activities. See the VSS help system for more information about using the SS.exe command-line utility.

Visual SourceSafe integrates with SQL Server 2005. You can either create projects in SQL Server Management Studio or use a Visual Studio database project. Note, however, that the two project types aren't interchangeable. Therefore, you may just want to check in your script files rather than check in the entire project.

A popular tool for managing changes in SQL Server databases is DBGhost. You can learn more about it at www.innovartis.co.uk.

Chapter 4: Building Professional Reports with Crystal Reports

In This Chapter

✔ Creating new reports

✔ Using formulas, SQL expressions, and parameters to customize reports

✔ Accessing ADO.NET DataSets as report data sources

✔ Passing parameters to reports in code

✔ Deploying reports

I believe that reports are the lifeblood of any good software. Without good reports, users abandon your software. One of the best reporting tools available is Crystal Reports, a product included with Visual Studio 2005. Crystal Reports isn't a Microsoft product; it's owned by a company named Business Objects.

In this chapter, I show you how to design reports using the embedded Crystal Reports Designer. You'll see how to connect to your data sources, including ADO.NET DataSets. Of course, creating the report is only half the battle. You need to know how to integrate the report in your application. I show you how to display your reports in Windows and Web applications. While I'm at it, I give you a few pointers on grouping, filtering, and creating formulas.

Choosing the Right Crystal Edition

Business Objects sells many editions of Crystal Reports. The latest version is version 11, which is sold in these editions:

✦ **Developer** — Integrate reports into custom applications and includes license to redistribute reporting components.

✦ **Standard Edition** — Create reports based on data stored on a local computer.

✦ **Professional Edition** — Create reports by using more than 35 data drivers, access custom in-memory data, or write custom SQL commands.

✦ **Integrated Developer Environment (IDE)** — Several editions of Crystal Reports that are created by Business Objects are embedded directly into popular IDEs, including these:

- Visual Studio 2005

- Visual Studio .NET

- Delphi

- Borland

- Java

The official name of the edition of Crystal Reports embedded in Visual Studio is Crystal Reports for Visual Studio 2005. All editions of Crystal Reports, except for IDE, are separate, stand-alone software. The IDE editions are embedded within a specific IDE and can't be executed outside the hosting IDE. Developers who need advanced report design features in a separate, stand-alone package can upgrade to Crystal Reports Developer Edition. All editions of Crystal Reports include these features:

✦ **Report Designer** — Create professional reports by using a visual designer.

The report designer features drag-and-drop controls, guided experts, and extensive formatting options.

✦ **Data Access** — Access data from dozens of sources, including databases such as Oracle and SQL Server.

Crystal Reports has truly impressive data access features. I use Crystal Reports to access everything from Access databases to my local file system to Exchange Server databases.

✦ **Report Viewing** — View and export reports in every format imaginable.

The Crystal Reports report viewer provides built-in navigation and drill-down capabilities.

Business Objects offers a server product for Crystal Reports: The Crystal Reports Server includes a common, centralized repository for storing enterprise reports, a scheduler, and a framework for publishing reports to a Web server.

Creating Reports with Crystal Reports

The first step in creating any report is knowing which information you want your report to display. Before you start using any report design tool, you should put some thought into these issues:

✦ Who your audience is and how you expect the report to be used

✦ What your data source is and whether it must be transformed or cleansed

✦ How records should be filtered, sorted, or grouped

✦ Whether to prompt your users for parameters

If you're using Crystal Reports with Visual Studio 2005, chances are that you're creating reports for a software application, such as an order-entry system. After you give some thought to how you want to build your report, follow the steps in this outline:

1. Add a Crystal Reports file to your project.

2. Select a data source for your report.

3. Design the report by using the embedded Crystal Reports Designer.

4. Integrate the report with your application.

5. Deploy your application and reports.

Crystal Reports provides tools to walk you through creating your report, selecting a data source, and designing the report. You rely on a combination of tools from Crystal Reports and Visual Studio 2005 to integrate and deploy your report.

To add a new Crystal Reports file to an existing project and use the Report Wizard to create a new report, follow these steps:

1. **Use the Add New Item window to add a new Crystal Reports file.**

If this is the first time you're accessing Crystal Reports, an end-user license window appears. Read the license and choose whether to accept the terms.

The Crystal Reports Gallery appears, as shown in Figure 4-1.

2. **Select Using the Report Wizard to create a new report.**

The Crystal Reports Gallery gives you three options for creating reports:

• Using the Report Wizard

• As a Blank Report

• From an Existing Report

I suggest using the Report Wizard unless you have a specific need to use one of the other two options.

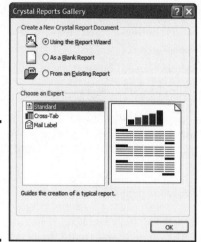

Figure 4-1:
Use the
Crystal
Reports
Gallery to
create a
new report.

3. **Select the Standard Report Expert.**

The Crystal Reports Gallery provides three experts for creating reports when you use the Report Wizard:

- **Standard** — Creates a regular report
- **Cross-tab** — Creates a matrix report similar to an Excel pivot table
- **Mail label** — Creates a report with multiple columns, like the kind used to print address labels

4. **Click OK.**

The Standard Report Creation Wizard appears.

5. **Create a new data source.**

To connect to the AdventureWorks sample database in SQL Server 2005, use the OLE DB connection:

a. **Expand the Create New Connection folder.**

b. **Double-click the OLE DB folder.**

c. **In the OLE DB dialog box, select Microsoft OLE DB Provider for SQL Server and click the Next button.**

d. **On the Connection Information page, enter your connection information and select the AdventureWorks database.**

e. **Click the Finish button. (The connection appears in the wizard.)**

6. **Expand the AdventureWorks data source.**

7. Expand the **HumanResources** schema and move the **Department** and **EmployeeDepartmentHistory** tables to the Selected Tables pane.

8. Click the Next button.

The Link page appears.

9. Confirm that the links between the two tables are correct.

The wizard automatically creates the links for you.

10. Click the Next button.

The Fields page appears.

11. Select the following fields for the report:

- Department.Name
- Department.GroupName
- EmployeeDepartmentHistory.EmployeeID
- EmployeeDepartmentHistory.StartDate
- EmployeeDepartmentHistory.EndDate

12. Click the Next button.

The Grouping page appears.

13. Select the **Department.GroupName** and **Department.Name** fields to group by, as shown in Figure 4-2.

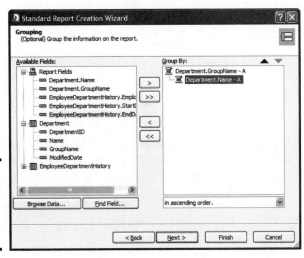

Figure 4-2:
Select fields to group by in the report.

You aren't restricted to grouping by the report's fields. You can group by any field in the list of available fields.

14. **Click the Next button.**

    The Summaries page appears.

15. **Change the function for each of the summarized fields from Sum to Count.**

16. **Continue clicking next until you see the Report Style page.**

17. **Choose a Report Style from the list of styles and click the Finish button.**

    The report appears in the Crystal Reports Designer, shown in Figure 4-3.

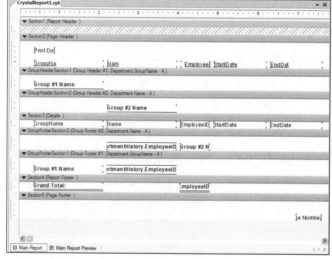

Figure 4-3:
The Report Wizard creates the report and displays it in the Crystal Reports Designer.

Click the Main Report Preview button, at the bottom of the designer, to view the report's data.

Crystal Reports files use the file extension .rpt. This type of file uses a proprietary file format. Visual Studio supports creating reports by using Report Definition Language (RDL). See Chapter 5 in this mini-book to read more about creating RDL reports.

Connecting to Data Sources

I believe that the most important aspect of report creation and design is the data source. All too often I see developers and power users get frustrated with Crystal Reports because they aren't producing the reports they expect. The reason is usually that they don't start with the right data source. Crystal Reports provides access to almost every data source under the sun. As a .NET developer, you're likely to be most concerned with accessing these kinds of data sources:

+ Databases, such as SQL Server and Oracle

+ ADO.NET typed DataSets

+ Custom data entities

In the preceding section, Steps 5 through 11 walk you through accessing data by using the Report Wizard. In most cases, you use the Report Wizard when you create a new report. However, you can access the Database menu and the Database Expert any time you need to manage your report's data sources.

You can use the Crystal Reports object model to pass data sources from your application, such as an ADO.NET typed DataSet, to a Crystal Report.

See the section "Integrating Reports," later in this chapter, for more information on using ADO.NET typed DataSets and the Crystal Reports object model.

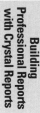

Getting to know your databases

The Crystal Reports Database menu is one of the most important menus for first creating a report. You access the menu from the Crystal Reports menu in Visual Studio or by right-clicking Database Fields in the Field Explorer and choosing one of these commands:

+ **Database Expert** — Launches the Database Expert, which you can use to configure your report's data source

+ **Set Database Location** — Sets the location, which is useful if you want to change from a test database to a production database

+ **Log on or off server** — Lets you test to see whether the database is running

+ **Verify Database** — Confirms the tables and columns in your data sources and synchronizes your report's fields with the data source

+ **Verify on Every Print** — Verifies the data source's schema on every print

+ **Show SQL Query** — Lets you view the query that Crystal Reports is using to retrieve data

Use the Show SQL Query command every time you make a modification to your report's record selection. You can then see the SQL statements generated by Crystal Reports to access your data.

Using the Database Expert

The Database Expert walks you through visually creating data source connections and linking tables. Note that you aren't limited to connecting to just databases. Crystal Reports supports many kinds of data sources.

Crystal Reports uses a database metaphor to represent data sources. For example, an Excel file with three spreadsheet tabs is represented as a single database with three tables. The columns in the spreadsheet tabs are the columns in each of the tables.

Before you fire up the Database Expert, you should decide first which data source you're using. For example, if you want to use an ADO.NET typed DataSet as your data source, you need to create the DataSet before you can select it.

You can access the Database Expert in two ways:

✦ **When you create a new report with the Report Wizard** — Step 5 in the earlier section "Creating Reports with Crystal Reports" walks you through using the Database Expert in the Report Wizard.

✦ **In an existing report via the Database menu** — You can access the Database menu from these menus:

- The Crystal Reports menu

- A shortcut menu on the report

- A shortcut menu on Database Fields in the Field Explorer

To use the Database Expert to access data, follow these steps:

1. **Access the Database Expert from the Database menu (via the Crystal Reports menu or the shortcut menus on either the Report or Database fields in the Field Explorer).**

   The Database Expert lists data sources in the Available Data Sources pane on the left and a list of selected tables on the right. Use the arrow buttons in the middle to move data sources between the panes.

2. **Select a data source from the list of available data sources.**

   Data sources are grouped into these folders:

   - **Project Data** — Lists sources from the current project and to which you're already connected

   - **Current Connections** — Lists sources to which you're already connected

   - **Favorites** — Provides a list of sources that have been marked as favorites

- **History** — Shows sources to which you were recently connected

- **Create New Connection** — Shows data sources to which you can create new connections

To connect to an existing data source, expand any folder except for Create New Connection.

To create a new connection, follow these steps:

a. **Click the plus sign (+) next to Create New Connection.**

   A list presents the kinds of data sources to which you can connect.

b. **Select the type of data source you want to create.**

   For most data sources, the Database Expert opens a dialog box or connection window for you to establish your connection.

c. **In the dialog box, complete your connection to your data source.**

   The data source appears on the list of Available Data Sources in the Database Expert. Figure 4-4 shows the Database Expert with a connection to the AdventureWorks sample database. See the earlier section "Creating Reports with Crystal Reports" for an example of creating a connection to the AdventureWorks SQL Server database.

Book VI
Chapter 4

Building
Professional Reports
with Crystal Reports

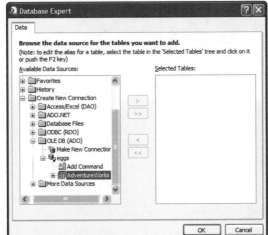

Figure 4-4:
New connections appear in the data sources hierarchy.

3. **Expand your data source to reveal the resources you can access.**

   You can access more than just tables in a database. You can also access stored procedures and views. When you access resources, such as Excel files, the Database Expert treats each worksheet as a table.

4. **Select the table you want to add to your report.**

5. **Click the topmost arrow button to move the table to the Selected Tables pane.**

6. **Repeat Steps 3–5 to add tables to your report.**

   When you add more than one table, the Link tab appears.

   To use the Link tab to establish links between multiple tables, follow these steps:

   a. **Select the Links tab.**

      If the tables share a common field, such as `CustomerID` in both a `Customer` table and an `Order` table, a link appears between the tables. If not, you can create your own links. If the links are incorrect, click the Clear Links button.

   b. **Drag and drop the column from one table onto the linked column on the table to create a link between the tables.**

      Figure 4-5 shows two tables linked on the DepartmentName and Name columns.

      To modify the kind of link between the tables, right-click the link or click the Link Options button.

Figure 4-5:
Drag
and drop
columns
from one
table to
another
to create
a link.

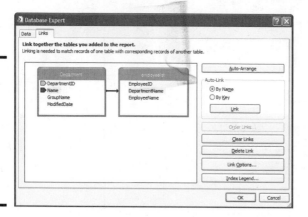

7. **Click OK after you add all your tables and create links between them.**

   If you discover that you forgot to add a table or your links are incorrect, you can always open the Database Expert again.

REMEMBER

Don't do it just because you can

Although you *can* use the Database Expert to add individual tables to your report and create links between them, in practice, that's not how most people access data in Crystal Reports. Most developers use stored procedures because they usually provide better performance. However, server performance isn't everything. Sometimes, human performance is more important.

Crystal Reports can build sophisticated SQL statements by using a graphical tool. Don't fool yourself into thinking that every single report

must use a stored procedure created by a Microsoft Certified Database Administrator. If you do, you're imposing a requirement that's likely to create a huge reporting backlog.

Instead, let junior developers use tools such as Crystal Reports to build reports. Teach them best practices for evaluating when to use server-side or client-side calculations. Reserve fancy stored procedures for reports that truly need them and let junior developers build the other 80 percent that don't.

Book VI
Chapter 4

**Building
Professional Reports
with Crystal Reports**

A good compromise between using tables and stored procedures is the virtual table. Crystal Reports has an Add Command feature, which allows you to provide your own SQL statements to execute against the data source. To use a command to create a virtual table, follow these steps:

1. **Open the Database Expert and select or create a data source, as described in the preceding steps.**

2. **Double-click Add Command, as shown in Figure 4-6.**

The Add Command to Report window appears.

Figure 4-6:
Use Add
Command
to build a
virtual table
from a SQL
statement.

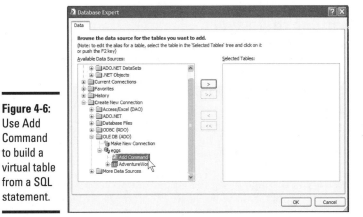

3. **Type your SQL statement in the query box.**

4. **Click the Create button to add parameters used by your query.**

5. **Click OK.**

The command appears in the Selected Tables pane.

To change the name of the command from the default name `command` to something meaningful, first click the command and press F2.

The commands you build can be as sophisticated as stored procedures. Remember that you can't reuse commands among reports, like you can among stored procedures. However, Business Objects, the maker of Crystal Reports, has upgraded products you can buy that allow you to store commands in a central repository.

Using the Crystal Reports Designer

Visual Studio 2005 includes an embedded version of the Crystal Reports Designer. You use the designer to visually lay out your reports. The designer includes a set of the following elements:

✦ **Experts** (similar to wizards) that walk you through building a report

✦ **Report objects,** such as report fields and charts, that you drag and drop onto the designer surface

✦ **Report sections,** to which you add report objects

To design a report, you add report objects to the section of the report where you want the object to appear. For example, you can add a title in the report's Report Header section.

Adding content to a report

Crystal Reports provides a sophisticated set of tools for adding report content. Your report's content can come from several sources, such as

✦ Plain text you enter in a text object

✦ Database fields

✦ Formulas you create

✦ Lines, boxes, and images

This section walks you through using the embedded Crystal Reports Designer to lay out a report. Follow these steps to create a report to use throughout the section:

1. **Create a new report that connects to the AdventureWorks sample database.**

   See the earlier section "Creating Reports with Crystal Reports" to see how to create a report that connects to the AdventureWorks sample database.

2. **Add the following tables to the report:**

   - `Person.Contact`
   - `Person.ContactType`
   - `Sales.StoreContact`

3. **Set the following relationships between the tables:**

   - `Contact.ContactID = StoreContact.ContactID`
   - `StoreContact.ContactTypeID = ContactType.ContactTypeID`

4. **Add the following data fields from the list of available fields:**

   - `Contact.FirstName`
   - `Contact.LastName`
   - `Contact.EmailAddress`
   - `Contact.Phone`

5. **Click the Finish button.**

6. **Click the Main Report Preview button, at the bottom of the designer, to preview the report.**

   Figure 4-7 shows the report in the Crystal Reports Designer.

7. **Save the report as StoreContacts.rpt.**

Exploring the Field Explorer

The Field Explorer in the Crystal Reports Designer appears on the left side of the screen. You can use the objects in the Field Explorer to customize your report. The Field Explorer includes the following report objects:

✦ **Database Fields** — Explore the list of fields available from the data source. Right-click Database Fields to access the Database menu.

✦ **Formula Fields** — Create simple or complex calculations.

✦ **Parameter Fields** — Create parameters that prompt a user for input to run the report.

✦ **Group Name Fields** — Insert and manage groups.

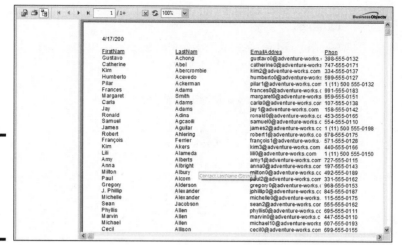

Figure 4-7:
The report
appears in
the Crystal
Reports
Designer.

✦ **Running Total Fields** — Create a running total based on a field in your report.

✦ **SQL Expression Fields** — Create a field that uses SQL expressions. SQL expression fields are executed on the SQL server.

✦ **Special Fields** — Add predefined fields, such as Print Date and Page Number.

✦ **Unbound Fields** — Create predefined formula fields based on native data types.

Figure 4-8 shows the Field Explorer. Press Ctrl+Alt+T to open it.

You can mix and match fields to create sophisticated report scenarios. For example, you can create a new formula field that references a database field and a parameter field. You use fields for these tasks:

✦ Display values.

✦ Calculate values.

✦ Query users for input.

✦ Filter records.

✦ Group records.

✦ Sort records.

✦ Set formatting properties.

Reports are divided into sections, to which you add fields. A report can have all, some, or none of the following sections:

✦ Report Header and Footers

✦ Page Header and Footers

✦ Group Headers and Footers

✦ Details

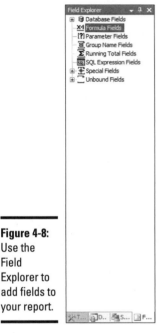

Figure 4-8:
Use the
Field
Explorer to
add fields to
your report.

**Book VI
Chapter 4**

**Building
Professional Reports
with Crystal Reports**

You format report sections by using the Section Expert. See the section "Meet the Experts," later in this chapter, to read more.

After you add a field to a section in the report, it becomes a report field. Follow these steps to create a new report field that displays the contact's name in the format lastname, firstname in the StoreContacts report you create in the preceding section:

1. **Choose Insert➪Text Object from the Crystal Reports menu.**

The mouse pointer turns into the shape of a text box.

2. **Drop the text object next to the Phone field in the report's Details section.**

The cursor blinks inside the text box.

3. **Expand Database Fields in the Field Explorer.**

4. **Drag and drop the `Contact.LastName` field inside the text object where the cursor is flashing.**

   The text {LastName} appears.

5. **Type a comma in the text object.**

6. **Drag and drop the `Contact.FirstName` field inside the text object.**

7. **Click somewhere off the text object.**

8. **Use your mouse to position the report fields so that they appear in the order lastname, firstname, text object, e-mail address, and phone.**

   To remove a report field, click the field and press the Delete key.

9. **Add a text object to the Page Header section above the text object you create in Step 2.**

10. **Type a column header in the text object, such as** Contact Name.

11. **Expand the e-mail address and phone fields so that they display their values without truncating data.**

    Periodically click the Main Report Preview button to check your field formatting. Figure 4-9 shows a preview of the report.

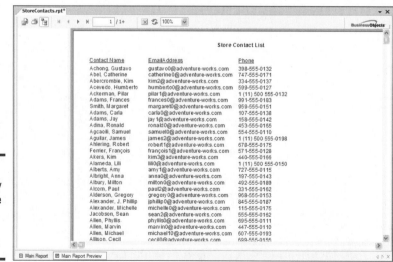

Figure 4-9: Periodically preview the report to check formatting.

Accessing commands with toolbars

The Crystal Reports Designer has two toolbars, shown in Figure 4-10, that provide quick access to commonly used commands for formatting and adding content:

✦ **Insert toolbar** — Choose commands for inserting summaries, charts, and subreports. (See the top toolbar in Figure 4-10.)

✦ **Main toolbar** — Choose formatting commands (such as bold and font), experts, and object properties. (See the bottom toolbar in Figure 4-10.)

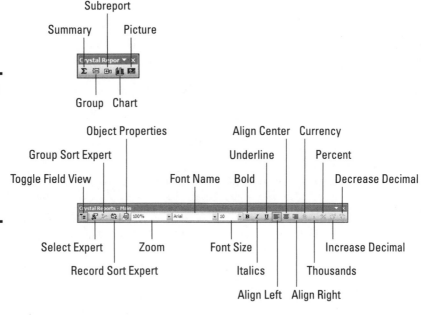

Figure 4-10:
Use the
Crystal
Reports
toolbars to
access
commonly
used
commands.

Formatting objects

Use the sophisticated Crystal Reports format editors and experts to completely customize the appearance and behavior of the fields and sections that appear in your reports. The formatting tools are shown in this list:

✦ **Format Editor** — To access the format editor, right-click any field in your report and choose Format Object from the shortcut menu. The tabs visible in the Format Editor depend on the type of object you're formatting. For example, a field that displays a `true/false` value has a Boolean tab. Figure 4-11 shows the Format Editor for a text object; Table 4-1 describes some common uses of the Format Editor.

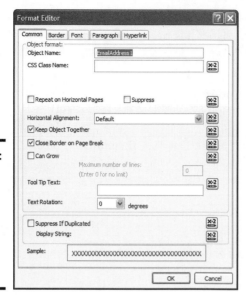

Figure 4-11:
Use the
Format
Editor to
apply
formatting
to the
report's
objects.

✦ **Chart Expert** — Right-click a chart to access the Chart Expert. Use it to specify the chart's type and data source and to format its axes.

✦ **Highlight Expert** — Right-click an object in a report's Details section to access the Highlight Expert. Use it to apply conditional formatting to an object based on the value of the field or another field.

✦ **Section Expert** — Access the Section Expert from the Report menu. The Section Expert allows you to insert, delete, and format sections. See the next section to see the Section Expert in action.

Table 4-1		Common Uses of the Format Editor
Tab	*Command*	*What It Does*
Common	CSS Class Name	Sets the CSS class that the object should use
	Repeat on Horizontal Pages	Repeats object on additional horizontal pages
	Suppress	Disables the field so that it doesn't appear
	Keep Object Together	Keeps grouped objects on the same page
	Can Grow	Allows the object to expand to display values
	Suppress If Duplicated	Prevents the object from being printed multiple times if the same value is repeated

Tab	Command	What It Does
Border		Places a border around an object
Date	Style	Allows you to choose a date style from a list or create your own
Font		Sets font properties
Hyperlink	Type	Allows you to choose whether the hyperlink links to a Web site, e-mail address, or file and then set the URL

Most formatting options allow you to select a discrete value or apply a formula to calculate the formatting value or determine whether the formatting should appear. In the next section, I show you how to suppress a group based on the value a user provides in a parameter. You can enter a formula for a format anywhere that you see the X+2 formatting button, shown in Figure 4-12.

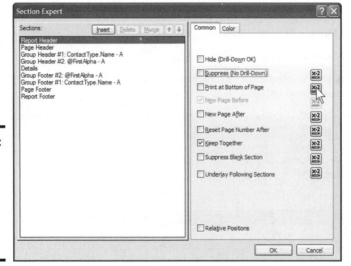

Figure 4-12: Click the Formula button to calculate formatting based on a formula.

You can format report objects by using your mouse to resize and move objects.

Meet the Experts

The Crystal Reports Designer provides a sophisticated set of tools, or *Experts,* that group similar commands. You can find Experts for everything from conditional highlighting to managing grouping.

Most Experts use a combination of fields and formulas to provide their features. In Crystal Reports, a field is more than just a database field. Each parameter, formula, and expression you add to your report is a field that becomes available for use in an Expert. In this section, I show you how to use fields, formulas, and Experts to customize your report.

Getting your group on

You often group records based on one or more fields in your data source. You use the Group Expert or the Section Expert to manage groups. Each group is a section in the report with its own header and footer. You can choose to display or suppress group headers and footers. To group the records in the StoreContacts report from the earlier section "Adding content to a report" on the contact type, follow these steps:

1. **Choose Report⇨Group Expert from the Crystal Reports menu.**

   The Group Expert appears.

2. **In the list of available fields, expand the ContactType table.**

   The list of fields appears.

3. **Click the Name field to select it.**

4. **Click the topmost-arrow button in the center of the Expert to move the Name column to the Group By pane.**

   The field appears in the Group By pane, as shown in Figure 4-13.

5. **Click OK.**

   A `GroupHeaderSection` and `GroupFooterSection` appear in your report.

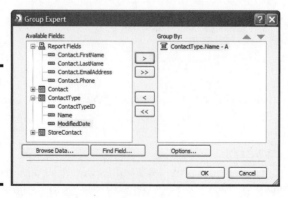

Figure 4-13: Use the Group Expert to group data in your report.

Sometimes, you want your report's groups based on a calculated value. You create a formula field that outputs the value you want to use and then group on that formula field. To create a formula field that displays the first letter of a contact's last name, follow these steps:

1. **Right-click Formula Fields in the Field Explorer.**

2. **Choose New from the shortcut menu.**

The Formula Name window appears.

3. **Type a name for the formula, such as** FirstAlpha.

4. **Click the Use Editor button.**

The Formula Editor appears. The Formula Editor has three panes that list the report's fields, functions, and operators. Use the objects in these panes to build formulas.

5. **In the Functions pane, expand the String functions.**

6. **Locate the** `Mid (str, start, length)` **function.**

The `Mid` function extracts characters from a string based on the starting position and length provided in the formula.

7. **Double-click the function to add it to the Formula Editor.**

The text `Mid (, , )` appears in the editor.

8. **Drag and drop the** `Contact.LastName` **field from the list of report fields onto the** `Mid` **formula between the left parenthesis and the first comma.**

The formula appears as `Mid ({Contact.LastName}, , )`.

9. **Type the number 1 as the starting position and the number 1 as the length.**

The formula appears as `Mid ({Contact.LastName},1 ,1 )`.

10. **Press Alt+C to check your formula for errors.**

A dialog box appears, as shown in Figure 4-14.

11. **Click OK to close the dialog box.**

12. **Click the Save and Close button.**

The formula appears in the Field Explorer.

To group by the formula you created, repeat the steps to create a group; this time, however, select the `FirstAlpha` field in Step 3.

An alternative approach to using a formula field is to use a SQL expression. SQL expressions use SQL syntax and are calculated on the SQL server, which can boost performance in some instances. The values used in formula fields are calculated on the client.

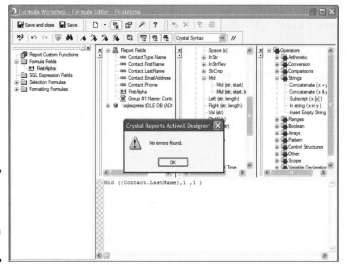

Figure 4-14:
Press Alt+C
to check
your formula
for errors.

Don't assume that performing calculations on the server is better than the client. Client computers are now usually fast enough to handle client-side report processing. I always do client-side processing first and then test the report on my slowest client computer. Always test your reports on the actual machines your users are running because development computers are usually more powerful. If I see the client computer choking on the report, I look at whether I should offload calculations to the server. I would rather bring the client computer to its knees in a testing situation than obliviously bring down a production server.

To create a SQL expression, follow these steps:

1. **Right-click SQL Expression Fields in the Field Explorer.**

2. **Choose New from the shortcut menu.**

3. **Type a name for the field and click OK.**

The SQL Expression Editor appears.

4. **Expand the list of string functions, and locate the SUBSTRING function.**

5. **Double-click the SUBSTRING function.**

The SUBSTRING function is the SQL equivalent of the Crystal Reports Mid function.

6. **Build or type the expression so that it appears like this**
```
{fn SUBSTRING("Contact"."LastName",1 ,1 )}.
```

7. **Press Alt+C to check your syntax.**

8. **Click Save and Close to close the editor.**

Use the Group Expert to group by the SQL expression.

View the SQL statement generated by Crystal Reports to see whether your calculations occur on the server or the client. To view the SQL statement, choose Database⇨Show SQL Query from the Crystal Reports menu.

Recognizing that filtered is better

Most reports need to have some kind of filter on the data source. You usually allow users to provide the filtered value based on parameters. To create a new parameter, follow these steps:

1. **Right-click Parameter Fields in the Field Explorer.**

2. **Choose New from the shortcut menu.**

The Create Parameter field appears.

3. **Type a name for the field.**

4. **Type the text that you want to display when the user is prompted.**

5. **Select the type of values that are accepted in the parameter.**

6. **Click the Default Values button to specify the values that appear in the parameter.**

7. **Click OK to create the parameter.**

The parameter appears in the Field Explorer.

To use the parameter to select records, follow these steps:

1. **Choose Report⇨Select Expert from the Crystal Reports menu.**

The Choose Field window appears.

2. **Select the field you want filtered and click OK.**

The Select Expert appears.

3. **Select Is Equal To from the drop-down list.**

4. **Select your parameter from the list of available values.**

The parameter has a question mark in front of it, as shown in Figure 4-15.

5. **Click the New button to add another filter, or click OK to close the window.**

The filter is added to the report.

Figure 4-15:
Select the
parameter
as the
filtered
value.

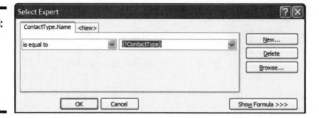

When you preview your report, you're prompted for the parameter values, as shown in Figure 4-16.

Figure 4-16:
Crystal
Reports
prompts you
for the
parameter's
value when
you run the
report.

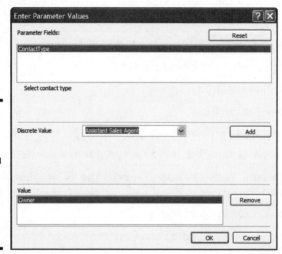

You can pass parameter values to your report from your application. See the section "Integrating Reports," later in this chapter.

Always try to minimize the record selection you use in the Crystal Reports Designer. Quite frequently, the report has to retrieve the entire set of data and then apply the filter. For example, you may have a table with 2,000 records but need to display only 10 of those records. The Select Expert usually has to retrieve all 2,000 records and then apply the filter on the client. For that reason, I always try to supply filtered records as the data source. I suggest using these items when you need to filter data:

✦ Prefiltered stored procedures

✦ Views

♦ Crystal Reports command objects

♦ ADO.NET DataSets

♦ Custom data entity collections

Mixing it up with parameters and formulas

Parameters can be used for more than record selection. Use parameters any time you want to give users control over a report's layout. For example, you can use parameters to control the way subreports are sorted, grouped, and displayed.

To use a parameter to turn formatting on and off for the StoreContacts report created in the earlier section "Meet the Experts," follow these steps:

1. **Create a new parameter field.**

2. **Set Boolean as the value type, and type a name for the parameter such as** DisplayAlphaGroup.

3. **Choose Report⇨Section Expert from the Crystal Reports menu.**

The Section Expert appears.

4. **Select the Group Header for the** `FirstAlpha` **group.**

5. **Click the Formula button next to Suppress.**

6. **Type the following lines in the Formula Editor:**

```
if {?DisplayAlphaGroup} = false
then true
```

The preceding formula tests the value of the `DisplayAlphaGroup` parameter you create in Step 2. If the value of the parameter is `false`, the group header is suppressed.

7. **Click the Save and close button.**

8. **Click OK.**

9. **Click the Main Report Preview button.**

If you aren't prompted for the parameter, click the report's Refresh button. The Refresh button has two arrows in a circle on it.

When you set `DisplayAlphaGroup` as `true`, the group header appears in the report. When the parameter's value is `false`, the group header is suppressed. Figure 4-17 shows the report with the headers turned on (on the top in the figure) and off (on the bottom).

Book VI Chapter 4

Building Professional Reports with Crystal Reports

Store Contact List

Contact Name	EmailAddress	Phone
Purchasing Agent		
A		
Alpuerto, Oscar	oscar0@adventure-works.com	855-555-0174
Alvaro, Emilio	emilio0@adventure-works.com	178-555-0129
Amland, Maxwell	maxwell0@adventure-works.com	614-555-0134
Anderson, Mae	mae0@adventure-works.com	1 (11) 500 555-0181
Antrim, Ramona	ramona0@adventure-works.com	327-555-0148
Ashton, Chris	chris3@adventure-works.com	556-555-0145
Atkinson, Teresa	teresa0@adventure-works.com	129-555-0110
Appelbaum, Sabria	sabria0@adventure-works.com	922-555-0193
Adams, Jay	jay1@adventure-works.com	158-555-0142
Adina, Ronald	ronald0@adventure-works.com	453-555-0165
Agcaoili, Samuel	samuel0@adventure-works.com	554-555-0110
Aguilar, James	james2@adventure-works.com	1 (11) 500 555-0198
Albury, Milton	milton0@adventure-works.com	492-555-0189
Alcorn, Paul	paul2@adventure-works.com	331-555-0162
Allen, Phyllis	phyllis0@adventure-works.com	695-555-0111
Allison, Cecil	cecil0@adventure-works.com	699-555-0155
B		
Bremer, Ted	ted0@adventure-works.com	962-555-0166
Brewer, Alan	alan1@adventure-works.com	494-555-0134
Brian, Walter	walter0@adventure-works.com	163-555-0155
Bernacchi, Robert	robert4@adventure-works.com	449-555-0176
Berndt, Matthias	matthias1@adventure-works.com	384-555-0169
Berry, John	john11@adventure-works.com	471-555-0181
Burnett, Timothy	timothy0@adventure-works.com	251-555-0172
Burton, Stephen	stephen2@adventure-works.com	1 (11) 500 555-0129

Store Contact List

Contact Name	EmailAddress	Phone
Purchasing Agent		
Alpuerto, Oscar	oscar0@adventure-works.com	855-555-0174
Alvaro, Emilio	emilio0@adventure-works.com	178-555-0129
Amland, Maxwell	maxwell0@adventure-works.com	614-555-0134
Anderson, Mae	mae0@adventure-works.com	1 (11) 500 555-0181
Antrim, Ramona	ramona0@adventure-works.com	327-555-0148
Ashton, Chris	chris3@adventure-works.com	556-555-0145
Atkinson, Teresa	teresa0@adventure-works.com	129-555-0110
Appelbaum, Sabria	sabria0@adventure-works.com	922-555-0193
Adams, Jay	jay1@adventure-works.com	158-555-0142
Adina, Ronald	ronald0@adventure-works.com	453-555-0165
Agcaoili, Samuel	samuel0@adventure-works.com	554-555-0110
Aguilar, James	james2@adventure-works.com	1 (11) 500 555-0198
Albury, Milton	milton0@adventure-works.com	492-555-0189
Alcorn, Paul	paul2@adventure-works.com	331-555-0162
Allen, Phyllis	phyllis0@adventure-works.com	695-555-0111
Allison, Cecil	cecil0@adventure-works.com	699-555-0155
Bremer, Ted	ted0@adventure-works.com	962-555-0166
Brewer, Alan	alan1@adventure-works.com	494-555-0134
Brian, Walter	walter0@adventure-works.com	163-555-0155
Bernacchi, Robert	robert4@adventure-works.com	449-555-0176
Berndt, Matthias	matthias1@adventure-works.com	384-555-0169
Berry, John	john11@adventure-works.com	471-555-0181
Burnett, Timothy	timothy0@adventure-works.com	251-555-0172
Burton, Stephen	stephen2@adventure-works.com	1 (11) 500 555-0129
Buskirk, Deanna	deanna0@adventure-works.com	131-555-0171
Brown, Carolee	carolee0@adventure-works.com	1 (11) 500 555-0146

Figure 4-17:
Use
parameters
to control a
report
object's
formatting.

Integrating Reports

Crystal Reports provides many ways to integrate reports into your applications. The first choice you have to make is where your reports will reside. Crystal Reports has two options for report locations:

✦ **Embedded** — Embedded reports are stored in your project. The code that Visual Studio generates for an embedded report creates a strongly typed version of the report. Embedded reports are the default storage choice for reports in Visual Studio projects. Because embedded reports are strongly typed, you can access your embedded report in code by using IntelliSense, which makes writing code simpler. However, because embedded reports are compiled with your application, you have to redeploy your application if you update a report.

✦ **Non-embedded** — Reports that aren't embedded reside elsewhere, usually in a central repository on a file server. Non-embedded reports are more complicated to access in code, but you can deploy updated reports without compiling your application.

After you decide where to store your files, you have to decide how to serve them up to your users. Again, you have several choices:

✦ `ReportDocument` — The `ReportDocument` object model provides an in-memory representation of a report. Embedded reports are kinds of `ReportDocument` objects. You use the `ReportDocument` object model to load reports and pass parameters and use the entire report as the source for the `CrystalReportViewer` control.

✦ `CrystalReportViewer` — `CrystalReportViewer` is both a control and an object model. As an object model, it's more limited than `ReportDocument`. In most cases, you should use the `CrystalReportViewer` control to display your report loaded into a `ReportDocument` object. In addition to using `ReportDocument`, you can use `CrystalReportViewer` to display reports from the following:

- CrystalReportSource
- File path
- Web service

✦ `CrystalReportPartsViewer` — Use it to display all or part of a report as a Web part in the ASP.NET Web parts framework.

✦ `CrystalReportSource` — ASP.NET Web sites use this control as a wrapper report source control; it wraps around your report. You use `CrystalReportSource` as the report source for the `CrystalReportViewer` control.

✦ `Crystal Reports Server` — You can purchase the separate product Crystal Reports Server from Business Objects to serve up your report objects.

You can mix and match these choices to find the optimum setting for your application. For example, when you're prototyping a report, you can bypass the object model altogether and load embedded or non-embedded report files directly into the `CrystalReportViewer` control. You can use `CrystalReportPartsViewer` to display a report on a Web portal and display the same report by using `CrystalReportViewer` in a Windows application.

How not to use Crystal Reports

I worked in a shop once where the IT staff mistakenly believed that each user who ran a Crystal Reports report required the Crystal Reports Designer installed on the client. Every time a new user needed a report, IT installed the full-blown stand-alone version of Crystal Reports on the client's machine. This practice was not only expensive and time consuming — it also severely limited the scope of report distribution.

Although most companies plan on having report designers throughout their organization, in most cases report design is something that few people have a knack for. If your users can and will design reports, by all means buy them Crystal Reports. Most people want it only to *run* reports, though, not design them. And, you can run reports all day long from within your custom application. If you don't want to build a custom application to distribute reports, consider buying Crystal Reports Server.

Using the ReportDocument object model

The experts, wizards, and embedded Crystal Reports Designer are great tools for designing reports. When the times comes to integrate your reports, however, you probably will take advantage of the Crystal Reports object model to access your reports via code. Crystal Reports for Visual Studio 2005 provides two object models that you should be familiar with:

✦ `CrystalReportViewer` — Used to display your report

✦ `ReportDocument` — Represents your report in memory

You should use the object model to access your reports because of these benefits:

✦ You gain greater control over your reports and their appearance.

✦ You can populate DataSets and custom data entities.

✦ You can separate your reporting from your presentation layer.

The `ReportDocument` object model allows you to create abstract representations of your reports, which encourages code reuse. For example, if your application has ten reports, all of which access the same data source, do you really want to write code to access each report? What happens when you add an eleventh report? Do yourself a favor and invest in learning the object model.

Rather than copy and paste code from the tenth report to the eleventh, consider this alternative approach, which uses the `ReportDocument` object model:

✦ Provide users with a list of reports from which they can select a report.

✦ Create a single Windows or Web Form named `DisplayReports`.

✦ Add a `CrystalReportsViewer` control to the `DisplayReports` Form.

✦ Set the `CrystalReportsViewer` control's `ReportSource` property to an abstract `ReportDocument` object named `MyReport`.

✦ Create a new instance of the report selected by the user, and assign the report to the `MyReport` object.

Each time your user selects a report, the `DisplayReports` Form is reused to display the report. Adding a new report is as simple as adding the report to your list of reports. You don't have to write a bunch of repetitive code every time you add a new report.

Using an ADO.NET DataSet

If you want to use ADO.NET DataSets as the source for your report, you must use the `ReportDocument` object model. In the same way that Crystal Reports expects your database to already have data, it expects your DataSet to be filled before data can be displayed.

Keep it simple, Dummy

Manually adding reports to an application that's already deployed is no picnic. As a corporate developer, I see this situation play itself out over and over again. Adding reports to the software is considered trivial, so no feature for adding new reports exists. As a result, each time a business user requests a report, a developer finds it easier to create an ad hoc report and either print it for the user or e-mail an exported version of the report. Before long, developers spend all their time running reports for business users.

When you're managing reports, here's the bottom line: If it isn't easy to add reports to your application after it's in production, reports don't get added. I know a lot of developers who detest using reporting tools such as Crystal Reports. If they already feel that way, you're giving them all the excuses they need to put it off indefinitely.

Adding reports to your application should be as simple as adding the report to a list of existing reports. You shouldn't have to copy and paste a bunch of code, create new windows, and otherwise jump through hoops.

To use an ADO.NET DataSet with the ReportDocument object model:

1. **Create a strongly typed DataSet by using the Department table from the AdventureWorks sample database.**

   See Book IV, Chapter 3 for more information on creating strongly typed DataSets.

2. **Create a new Crystal Reports report named DepartmentList.**

3. **Add the Department table from the AdventureWorks DataSet, as shown in Figure 4-18.**

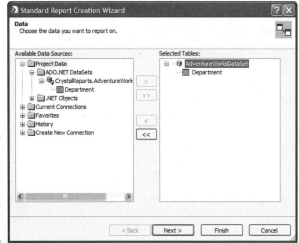

Figure 4-18:
Add the Department table from the ADO.NET DataSet.

4. **Add fields and design the report by using the embedded Crystal Reports Designer.**

5. **Drag and drop the CrystalReportViewer control from the Crystal Reports tab in the toolbox.**

   Press Ctrl+Alt+X to open the toolbox.

6. **Drag and drop a ReportDocument control onto the CrystalReportViewer control.**

   The Choose a ReportDocument window appears.

7. **Select the CrystalReports.DepartmentList report from the Name drop-down list.**

   Adding the ReportDocument control to the form does the following three things:

- Creates a new `ReportDocument` object.

- Creates a new instance of the embedded report. In this case, `ReportDocument` creates a new instance of the `DepartmentList` report.

- Assigns the `DepartmentList` instance to the `ReportDocument` control.

Using the `ReportDocument` control wires up your report to the abstract ReportDocument object so that you can pass in the populated DataSet to the report. If you don't want to use the `ReportDocument` control, you need to use this bit of code:

```
Dim report As New DepartmentList()
Me.CrystalReportViewer1.ReportSource = report
```

8. Click the OK button.

The `ReportDocument` component appears in the designer.

9. Set the `CrystalReportViewer` control's `ReportSource` property to the `ReportDocument` object you create in Step 8.

To set the `ReportSource` property by using the control's smart tag, follow these steps:

a. Click the arrow in the control's upper-right corner.

b. In the `CrystalReportViewer` Tasks window, select Choose a Crystal Report.

c. In the Choose a Crystal Reports window, select the `ReportDocument` object.

Be sure to select the object and not the .rpt file, as shown in Figure 4-19.

d. Click OK.

Alternatively, use the following code to set the `ReportSource` property in code:

```
Me.CrystalReportViewer1.ReportSource = Me.departmentList1
```

10. Double-click the form's title bar to open the form's `Load` event in the code editor.

11. Add the following code to create a new instance of the typed DataSet and populate the DataSet by using a TableAdapter:

```
Dim ads As New AdventureWorksDataSet
Dim ta As New AdventureWorksDataSetTableAdapters.
   DepartmentTableAdapter()
ta.Fill(ads.Department)
```

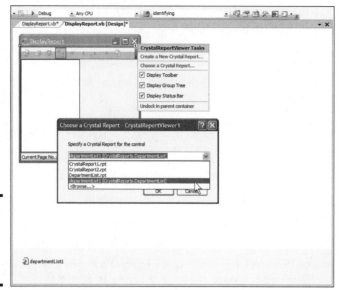

Figure 4-19:
Select the
`Report`
`Document`
object.

12. **Add the following line to set the `ReportDocument` object's data source:**

```
Me.departmentList1.SetDataSource(ads)
```

13. **Press Ctrl+F5 to run the form.**

Your report appears, as shown in Figure 4-20.

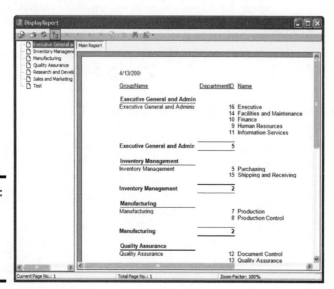

Figure 4-20:
The report
appears in
the Crystal
Reports
Viewer.

The `SetDataSource` method of the `ReportDocument` object accepts more than just DataSets. You can also use these elements:

✦ A DataTable

✦ A DataReader

✦ A collection of custom-defined entities

The Crystal Reports documentation has tutorials for using the `SetDataSource` method.

You may be wondering why you have to jump through all these hoops to get data into your report. Although it would be simpler to access the Adventure-Works database by using the Database Expert, your report is now coupled to the AdventureWorks database. If you decide down the road that you want to populate your Department table from a different data source, you have to crack open every report that accesses that data source. By using objects, such as strongly typed DataSets and custom-defined entities, you create a layer of abstraction between your report and its underlying data source. A layer of abstraction affords you the luxury of being able to make changes to your data sources later.

Why not just pass in the data source straight to the report viewer? For all the Visual Studio controls, you just assign the DataSet to the control's `DataSource` property. The report viewer doesn't have a `DataSource` property — it has a `ReportSource` property. You assign reports, not data sources, to the `ReportSource` property. Access to the data source is encapsulated in the report, as shown in Figure 4-21.

The `CrystalReportViewer` control uses a `ReportSource` property.

Book VI
Chapter 4

**Building
Professional Reports
with Crystal Reports**

Figure 4-21:
Access to the data source is encapsulated in the report.

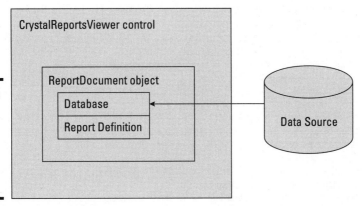

TIP

Design your report with a database connection so that you can preview the data. Choose Database⇨Set Datasource Location to change the report's data source from the database connection to a DataSet.

Using parameters

When you work with reports, you have to be able to discover a report's parameters and pass parameter values to the report. In most cases, you want to encapsulate the parameters in your own application. Suppose that your report requires start and end date parameters. Rather than allow Crystal Reports to prompt the user for the parameters, you will probably create a Windows or Web Form that uses two date-picker controls. The user can then click a Load Report button that calls the report and passes to it the date parameters selected by the user.

Figure 4-22 shows a Windows Form that allows the user to enter start and end dates and click a button to run the report.

Figure 4-22:
The
Windows
Form
prompts
the user
to enter
the report's
parameters.

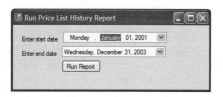

The following code is executed when the user clicks the Run Report button:

```
Dim startDateParam, endDateParam As CrystalDecisions.Shared.
    ParameterDiscreteValue
startDateParam = New CrystalDecisions.Shared.
    ParameterDiscreteValue()
endDateParam = New CrystalDecisions.Shared.
    ParameterDiscreteValue()

startDateParam.Value = Me.startDate.Value
endDateParam.Value = Me.endDate.Value

Me.listPrice1.ParameterFields("StartDate").CurrentValues.
    Add(startDateParam)
Me.listPrice1.ParameterFields("EndDate").CurrentValues.
    Add(endDateParam)
```

```
Me.CrystalReportViewer1.ReportSource = Me.listPrice1
```

The first three lines of code create two new `ParameterDiscreteValue` variables, to which you pass the values of the form's date-picker controls in the next two lines of code.

The next two lines add each of the `ParameterDiscreteValue` objects to the embedded report's `ParameterFields` collection.

In the last line, the embedded report is set as the `CrystalReportViewerControl` report source.

This simple example shows the use of parameters in code. You're likely to want to create helper utilities that allow you to discover parameters and add values dynamically.

Using the CrystalReportSource control

Displaying reports in ASP.NET Web sites requires the use of the `CrystalReportSource` control. It encapsulates the report and acts as a report source for the `CrystalReportViewer` control.

Reports aren't embedded in ASP.NET Web sites, so you can't access them by using code. Instead, you use the `CrystalReportSource` control to load the report.

To use the `CrystalReportSource` control to add a new report source, follow these steps:

1. **Create a new Web site.**

2. **Create a new Crystal Reports report.**

3. **Drag and drop a `CrystalReportSource` control on the default.aspx page.**

4. **Click the arrow in the upper-right corner of the `CrystalReportSource` control to display the control's task list.**

5. **Select Configure Report Source.**

   The Configure Report Source window appears.

6. **Select the report you create in Step 2 as the report source.**

   You can also create a new report from this window.

   The `CrystalReportSource` control uses a Report tag to specify the file path to the report. Because reports aren't embedded in ASP.NET Web sites, the report is accessed by using the file path. The following code shows the source for a report file added to a `CrystalReportSource` control:

```
<CR:CrystalReportSource ID="CrystalReportSource1"
    runat="server">
  <Report FileName="Reports\CrystalReport.rpt">
  </Report>
</CR:CrystalReportSource>
```

The path is relative to the Web site.

7. Click OK.

The Configure Report Source window closes.

8. Set `CrystalReportSource` as the report source for `CrystalReportViewer`.

The `CrystalReportSource` control includes two properties you can use to customize your report:

✦ **DataSource** — Set the report's data source by using an ASP.NET data source control, such as `SqlDataSource`.

✦ **Parameters** — Pass parameters to the reports by using values you specify or from controls on the page.

You access these properties from the Report object's properties in the Properties window. Figure 4-23 shows the Parameter Collections Editor with a parameter that uses values from a drop-down list named lstReportParams.

Figure 4-23:
Use the Parameter Collections Editor to pass parameter values to your report.

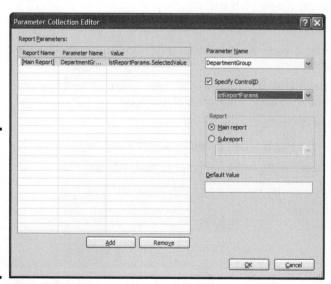

The `CrystalReportSource` control has an `EnableCaching` property that caches a report rather than create a new report each time the report is opened. Set the `EnableCaching` property to `true` when you have reports that can be easily shared across users. A current-period financial statement is a good example of a report that should be cached. A report that a user runs based on her own criteria isn't a good candidate for caching.

Deploying Your Reports

For the reports you create with Crystal Reports to run, they must have access to required files for Crystal Reports. For example, clients who want to run your application must have the Crystal Reports engine installed on their machines. If your reports aren't embedded in your project, you must include your report files.

**Book VI
Chapter 4**

**Building
Professional Reports
with Crystal Reports**

Visual Studio 2005 provides several deployment scenarios for deploying all kinds of applications. You can use the following Visual Studio 2005 deployment services to deploy Crystal Reports files:

✦ Use ClickOnce deployment with Windows applications.

✦ Create a Windows Installer for Web sites.

No matter which route you choose, you must include the Crystal Reports for .NET Framework 2.0 as a prerequisite when you deploy. To read more about deploying projects by using ClickOnce and Windows Installer, see Chapter 2 in this mini-book. Figure 4-24 shows the Prerequisites window.

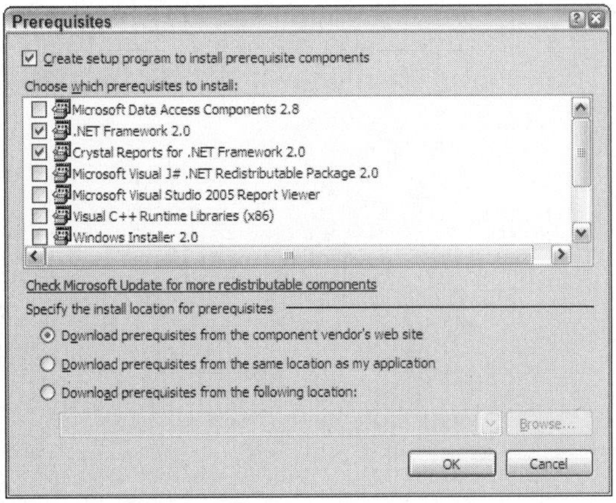

Figure 4-24: You must include Crystal Reports as a prerequisite when you deploy a report.

Chapter 5: Using SQL Server Reporting Services

In This Chapter

✔ **Creating local reports with the Report Designer**

✔ **Displaying local and server reports with the** `ReportViewer` **control**

✔ **Building parameterized server reports**

✔ **Deploying reports to SQL Server Reporting Services**

✔ **Accessing server reports in a browser**

Crystal Reports may be the official reporting solution for Visual Studio 2005, but it certainly isn't the only reporting tool in town. Visual Studio 2005 provides two tools for building reports with any data source:

✦ `ReportViewer` control

✦ Report Designer

In addition to these two tools, SQL Server Developer Edition, which comes with Visual Studio 2005 Professional, provides the Business Intelligence Development Studio. The BI Dev Studio adds business intelligence project templates to Visual Studio 2005 that allow you to create SQL Server Reporting Services reports with a wizard.

Building Reports

Visual Studio 2005 provides a new control for working with reports: the `ReportViewer` control. You use it to

✦ Display an existing report.

✦ Wire up a report that uses the SQL Server Reporting Services architecture.

✦ Fire up the Report Designer to create a local report.

The `ReportViewer` control creates reports using the Report Definition Language (RDL). RDL is an XML language created by Microsoft as a standard way of declaring report elements. Microsoft created RDL in an attempt to provide a standard file format for defining reports. Current reporting tools, such as Crystal Reports, use proprietary file formats.

Because RDL is an XML language, you can extend RDL to include your own elements and attributes.

You access the Report Designer by using the `ReportViewer` control. The Report Designer provides a visual design surface for building reports. Behind the scenes, the designer generates RDL files that describe the report. The designer adds reports to the Solution Explorer by using the file extension .rdlc.

RDL is the language for declaring report files. Reports using SQL Server Reporting Services are .rdl files, and local Visual Studio report files are .rdlc files. The c in the filename stands for client. Both file types use the RDL specification.

Using the Report Designer

The Report Designer consists of a design surface and toolbox for creating reports. You use strongly typed DataSets created with the Data Sources pane to drag and drop data fields onto the report.

To create a new report using the Report Designer, follow these steps:

1. **Create a new Windows project.**

2. **Press Ctrl+Shift+A to open the Add New Item dialog box. Add a Report file to the project.**

The file opens in the Report Designer.

The Report Designer opens the Data Sources pane.

3. **Use the Data Sources pane to add a new data source for the report to use.**

See Book IV, Chapter 2 for examples of working with the Data Sources pane.

4. **Press Ctrl+Alt+X to open the toolbox.**

The Report Items tab is visible.

5. **Drag and drop a Table item from the toolbox onto the Report Designer.**

A table appears on the designer. The table has one row apiece for header, details, and footer.

6. **Drag and drop data fields from your data source in the Data Sources pane to the Details row of the table, as shown in Figure 5-1.**

The designer fills in the Header row by using the names of the data fields.

Click the cells inside the Header row to change a field's name.

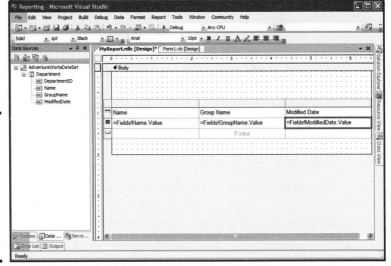

**Book VI
Chapter 6**

**Using SQL Server
Reporting Services**

Figure 5-1:
Drag and
drop data
fields from
the Data
Sources
pane to
create the
table.

7. **Click the selector for the Details row to highlight the row. Press F4 to open the Properties window.**

8. **Set the `BorderStyle` property to Solid.**

9. **Drag and drop a Textbox item from the toolbox onto the designer.**

10. **Type the report's title in the text box and use the Report Formatting toolbar to make the title bold and centered.**

Use the Properties window to set formatting properties for items on the Report Designer.

To display the RDL generated by the Report Designer, right-click the report file in Solution Explorer. Choose Open With from the shortcut menu and choose XML Editor.

Displaying a report with the ReportViewer control

The `ReportViewer` control displays reports that use the RDL file format. Your reports can be stored locally with your application or served from a SQL Server reporting server. The `ReportViewer` control is freely distributable, which makes it a great choice for providing useful reports to users.

There are different versions of the `ReportViewer` control for Web and Windows applications. Each version includes slightly different menu controls that allow users to navigate the report and export it to an Excel or PDF file. The Windows version of the `ReportViewer` control supports printing.

Here's how to display a report with the ReportViewer control in a Windows project:

1. **Open a Windows Form.**

2. **Drag and drop a ReportViewer control from the Data tab of the toolbox onto the Windows Form.**

   The ReportViewer control appears on the form.

   Press Ctrl+Alt+X to open the toolbox if it's closed.

3. **Select the Dock in Parent Container option in the ReportViewer's Tasks smart tag window.**

   The ReportViewer control expands to fill the Windows Form.

   Click the little arrow in the upper-right corner of the control to display the ReportViewer's Tasks window, if the Tasks window is closed.

4. **Choose your report from the Choose Report drop-down list.**

   The control adds your report's typed DataSet, BindingSource, and TableAdapter controls for populating the report.

   You can select the Design New Report option to create a new report using the Report Designer.

   To see how to use the ReportViewer control to display a server report, see the section "Consuming reports," later in this chapter.

5. **Press Ctrl+F5 to run the form.**

   The form displays your report, as shown in Figure 5-2.

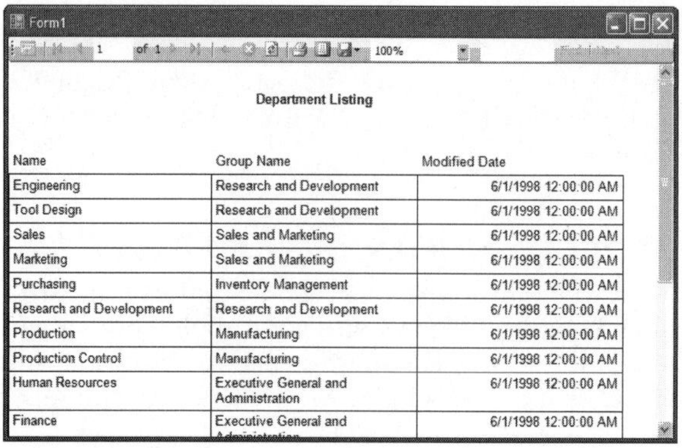

Figure 5-2:
Your report appears in the Windows Form.

Form1		
1 of 1	100%	

Department Listing

Name	Group Name	Modified Date
Engineering	Research and Development	6/1/1998 12:00:00 AM
Tool Design	Research and Development	6/1/1998 12:00:00 AM
Sales	Sales and Marketing	6/1/1998 12:00:00 AM
Marketing	Sales and Marketing	6/1/1998 12:00:00 AM
Purchasing	Inventory Management	6/1/1998 12:00:00 AM
Research and Development	Research and Development	6/1/1998 12:00:00 AM
Production	Manufacturing	6/1/1998 12:00:00 AM
Production Control	Manufacturing	6/1/1998 12:00:00 AM
Human Resources	Executive General and Administration	6/1/1998 12:00:00 AM
Finance	Executive General and Administration	6/1/1998 12:00:00 AM

The ReportViewer is available for ASP.NET Web site projects. You add a ReportViewer control by using Step 2 in the preceding set of steps. Step 4 is the same, except that the control uses an `ObjectDataSource` control to bind your report's strongly typed DataSet to the `ReportViewer` control. Figure 5-3 shows the same report in a Web site.

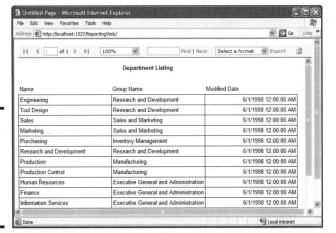

Figure 5-3: The `Report Viewer` control works in Web sites.

Check out this helpful resource for the `ReportViewer` control — the Got ReportViewer? Web site, at `www.gotreportviewer.com/`.

Use a free add-in, available for Visual Studio Web Developer Express Edition, to add the `ReportViewer` control. Find the add-in and other reporting downloads at `http://msdn.microsoft.com/sql/downloads/default.aspx`.

Accessing Server Reports

Creating a single repository for storing and distributing reports is a challenge for companies of all sizes. Users of the popular Microsoft SQL Server database have access to a server-based reporting infrastructure named SQL Server Reporting Services.

SQL Server 2005 includes the Business Intelligence Development Studio, for building SQL Server Reporting Services (SSRS) reports. The Business Intelligence Development Studio, which uses the Visual Studio 2005 shell, includes project types, wizards, and designers for SSRS reports.

You can access the features of the SSRS report designers by installing the Business Intelligence Development Studio from SQL Server 2005 Developers Edition. See Book IV, Chapter 6 for more information.

Install the client tools for SQL Server 2005 Developer Edition on top of the SQL Server 2005 Express Edition. It gives you access to powerful tools without the overhead of installing all the services of SQL Server 2005 Developer Edition.

Creating new server report projects

The SQL Server business intelligence projects include a Report Designer that's similar in functionality to the regular Visual Studio Report Designer. The Report Server Project Wizard project type has these features:

+ **Report Designer** — Allows you to view data sources and lay out and preview your report

+ **Report Wizard** — Walks you through creating a new server report

+ **DataSets tab** — Helps you view report data

+ **Shared Data Sources folder** — Saves data sources that can be deployed to the server

+ **Reports folder** — Saves reports that can be deployed to the server

The Report Server project includes on the Build menu a Deploy Solution command that deploys your shared data sources and reports to the SQL Server Reporting Server.

You create server reports with the Report Server Project Wizard; however, you must deploy the reports to the server before you can access them.

The easiest way to create a new server report is with the Report Server Project Wizard. To start the Report Wizard, follow these steps:

1. **Press Ctrl+Shift+N to open the New Project dialog box.**

2. **Click to select Business Intelligence Projects in the Project Types pane.**

A list of project templates appears.

3. **Click the Report Server Project Wizard icon.**

4. **Type a name for your report project and click OK.**

The Report Wizard opens.

To use the Report Wizard to build a report using the AdventureWorks sample database, follow these steps:

1. **Start the Report Wizard by following the preceding steps.**

Alternatively, you can start the Report Wizard by using the Add New Items dialog box to add a new report to a report server project.

2. Click the Next button on the wizard's Welcome page.

The Select the Data Source page appears.

3. Type AdventureWorksDataSource **in the New Data Source field.**

4. Select Microsoft SQL Server as the type of data source.

5. Click the Edit button.

The Connection Properties window appears.

6. Create a new connection to the AdventureWorks sample database.

The Connection Properties window returns the connection string to the Report Wizard.

See the section about connecting to databases in Book IV, Chapter 2.

7. Select the Make This a Shared Data Source option, as shown at the bottom of Figure 5-4.

The wizard saves the connection string in the project's Shared Data Sources folder.

**Book VI
Chapter 6**

**Using SQL Server
Reporting Services**

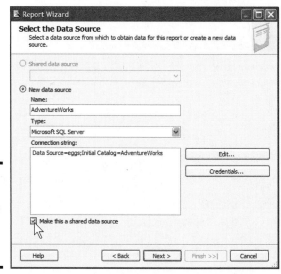

Figure 5-4:
Share the
data source
with other
reports in
the project.

8. Click the Next button.

The Design the Query page in the wizard appears.

9. Type the following SQL statement in the wizard:

```
SELECT DepartmentID, Name, GroupName, ModifiedDate
FROM   HumanResources.Department
```

Alternatively, click the Query Builder button to build a query.

10. **Click the Next button.**

The Select the Report Type page appears. Your choices are Tabular or Matrix.

11. **Select a Tabular report type and click the Next button.**

The Design the Table page in the wizard appears.

12. **Move the DepartmentID, Name, and ModifiedDate fields to the Details section.**

The Design the Table page in the wizard shows a list of fields and three options for displaying them:

- **Page** — Displays the field at the top of the page

- **Group** — Creates groups by using the selected fields

- **Details** — Lists the detailed data for the selected fields

To move fields, click a field to highlight it and click the button that corresponds to the section of the report in which you want the field displayed, as shown in Figure 5-5.

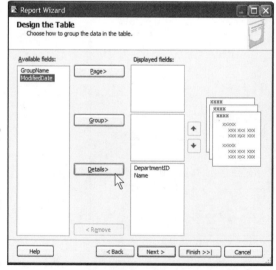

Figure 5-5:
Move fields to the area of the report in which you want the field to appear.

A matrix report allows you to select the fields you want displayed in columns and rows.

13. **Move the GroupName field to the report's Group section.**

14. **Click the Next button.**

The Choose the Table Layout page appears.

15. **Select the Stepped option and click the Next button.**

The Choose the Table Style page appears.

16. **Select a style for the report from the list of available styles, and click the Next button.**

The Completing the Wizard page appears.

17. **Type a name for the report in the Report Name field.**

18. **Select the Preview Report option and click the Finish button.**

The report appears in the Report Designer, as shown in Figure 5-6.

**Book VI
Chapter 6**

**Using SQL Server
Reporting Services**

Figure 5-6:
Select the
Preview
Report
option to
view the
report in
the Report
Designer.

The report server Report Designer gives you three views of your report:

✦ **Data** — Manage your report's data sources

✦ **Layout** — Build your report using data fields from the Datasets tab

✦ **Preview** — View your report's output

The next section walks you through using the designer's three tabs.

Creating parameters

Most reports require user input to set the report's parameters. *Parameters* allow users to enter a date range or select a customer on which to base the report. Parameters filter the data displayed in the report. The Report Designer provides extensive support for building parameterized reports.

SQL Server Reporting Services supports two kinds of parameters:

✦ **Query parameters** — Parameters specified within the query itself, in the form of *@parameter*

✦ **Report parameters** — Parameters created in the report

You can use parameters to

✦ Filter data.

✦ Sort data.

✦ Link reports.

You can cascade parameters so that the values of one parameter drive the values in another parameter — for example, in Category and Subcategory parameters.

To create a query parameter, follow these steps:

1. **Click the Data tab for the report you create in the preceding section.**

2. **Click to select the Filter cell for the GroupName field.**

3. **Type a name, such as** @GroupName, **in the cell, as shown in Figure 5-7.**

4. **Press the Tab key to move off the cell.**

The designer adds the following line to the SQL pane

```
WHERE     (GroupName = @GroupName)
```

Run the query to test your query parameter:

1. **Click the Run button (the big red exclamation point) on the Data tab's toolbar.**

The Query Parameters window appears.

2. **Type a value, such as** Manufacturing, **in the Value field, as shown in Figure 5-8.**

3. Click OK.

The query is executed and returns two records, where the value of the GroupName field is equal to `Manufacturing`.

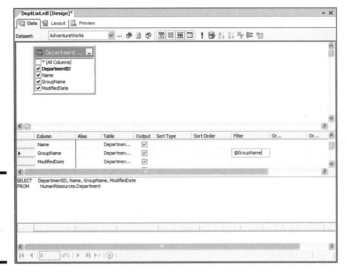

Book VI
Chapter 6

Using SQL Server
Reporting Services

Figure 5-7:
Type a
parameter
in the Filter
cell.

Figure 5-8:
Enter a
value for
the query
parameter.

A professional report should provide a list of valid values from which a user selects a value. Report parameters provide a list of valid values. Before you create the report parameter, you first create a new DataSet that provides the list of valid values.

To create a new DataSet of unique department groups, follow these steps:

1. **On the report's Data tab, click the Dataset drop-down list.**

2. **Select <New Dataset> from the list.**

   The Dataset window appears.

3. **Type a name for the DataSet, such as** DepartmentGroups, **in the Name field.**

4. **Use the AdventureWorks data source you create in the section "Creating new server report projects," earlier in this chapter.**

5. **Type the following SQL statement in the Query String field:**

   ```
   SELECT DISTINCT GroupName
   FROM HumanResources.Department
   ```

   The DISTINCT keyword retrieves a list of the unique GroupName values in the table.

6. **Click OK to create the DataSet.**

7. **Click the Run button to test your query.**

   The query returns a list of unique GroupName values, as shown in Figure 5-9.

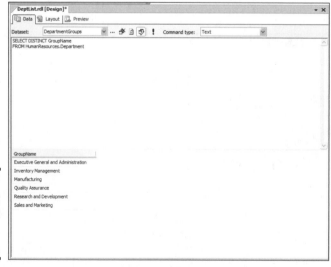

Figure 5-9:
The DataSet returns a list of unique values.

Here's how to create a report parameter that uses the DepartmentGroups DataSet as its source:

1. **Choose Report⇨Report Parameters.**

The Report Parameters window appears.

2. **Click the Add button to add a new report parameter.**

3. **Type a name for the parameter, such as** DepartmentGroup, **in the Name field.**

4. **Type a question or phrase to prompt the user for the parameter in the Prompt field, such as** Select a department group from the list.

5. **Select the From Query option in the Available Values section of the dialog box.**

6. **Select the** `DepartmentGroups` **DataSet from the Dataset drop-down list.**

7. **Select GroupName from the Value Field and Label Field drop-down lists, as shown in Figure 5-10.**

8. **Click OK.**

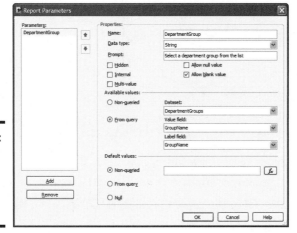

Figure 5-10:
Select the
value to
use for
the report
parameter.

The final step is to wire up the query parameter to use the report parameter so that when a user selects a report parameter, the value is passed to the report's query.

To wire up the parameters, follow these steps:

1. **On the Data tab, select the AdventureWorks DataSet from the Dataset drop-down list.**

2. **Click the Edit Selected Dataset button, which is the ellipsis button next to the Dataset drop-down list.**

The Dataset dialog box appears.

3. **Click the Parameters tab.**

4. **Type a name for the parameter, such as @GroupName, in the Name field.**

5. **Select the report parameter from the Value field's drop-down list, as shown in Figure 5-11.**

6. **Click OK.**

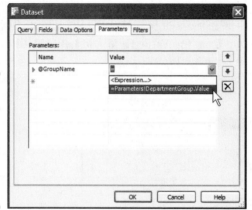

Figure 5-11: Select the report parameter from the Value field's drop-down list.

To test your report parameter, follow these steps:

1. **Click the report's Preview tab.**

   The report parameter appears at the top of the report.

2. **Select a value from the report parameter's drop-down list.**

3. **Click the View Report button.**

   Figure 5-12 shows the report and the report parameters.

Sometimes, you want to give users the option to select multiple values for a parameter. The designer supports multi-value parameters. To change the single-value parameter from the example in the preceding set of steps to a multi-value parameter, follow these steps:

1. **Click the Data tab.**

2. **Change the where clause to the following:**

   ```
   WHERE     (GroupName IN (@GroupName))
   ```

   The IN keyword allows the parameter to accept a comma-separated list of values.

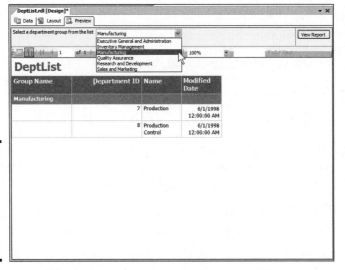

Figure 5-12:
Use the
report
parameter
to filter the
report's
output.

3. **Choose Report⇨Report Parameters.**

   The Report Parameters window appears.

4. **Select the Multi-value option and click OK.**

5. **Click the Preview tab.**

   The report parameter allows you to select multiple values, as shown in Figure 5-13.

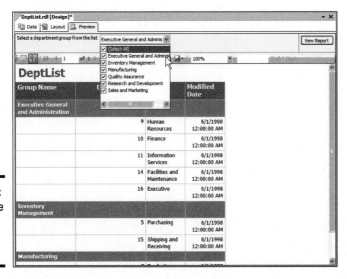

Figure 5-13:
Use multiple
values to
filter the
report.

Deploying reports

Server reports run, well, on a server. SQL Server Reporting Services (SSRS) provides an infrastructure for storing, managing, and viewing server reports. You can deploy server reports and data sources that you create with Visual Studio to the SQL Server Report Server by using the Deploy Solution command on the Build menu.

Here's how to deploy a server report:

1. **Create a new server report project by following the steps in the section "Creating new server report projects," earlier in this chapter.**

2. **Right-click your project in Solution Explorer.**

3. **Choose Properties from the shortcut menu.**

The project's Property Pages dialog box appears.

4. **Choose Production from the Configuration drop-down list in the upper-left corner of the Property Pages dialog box.**

5. **Type the URL to your report server in the TargetServerURL field, as shown in Figure 5-14.**

A report server's URL is usually in the format `http://servername/ reportserver`. In Figure 5-14, my server's name is `eggs`. (I was hungry the day I named it.)

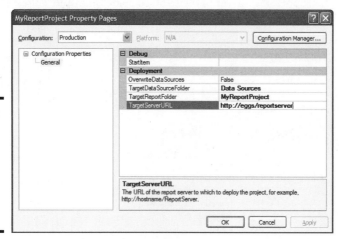

Figure 5-14: Set the report server's URL in the Target-ServerURL field.

6. **Click the Configuration Manager button.**

The Configuration Manager window appears.

7. Set the Active Solution Configuration drop-down list to Production.

8. Click the Close button.

The Configuration Manager closes.

9. Click OK.

The Property Pages dialog box closes.

10. Choose Build⇨Deploy Solution.

Visual Studio builds your reports and data sources and deploys them to your report server. Figure 5-15 shows the output from the deployment.

Figure 5-15:
The Deploy Solution command deploys the project's reports and data sources.

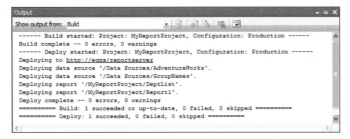

By default, you can deploy only projects whose active solution configuration is set to Production. However, you can use the Configuration Manager to configure the Debug configuration to build and deploy.

Be sure to set the `TargetServerURL` field for the Debug configuration in the Property Pages dialog box.

Consuming reports

SQL Server Reporting Services (SSRS) is a server that delivers reports. The primary means of accessing those reports is through a Web browser. Before a report can be viewed, it must be deployed to the server. To view the report deployed in the preceding section on my reporting server, I use the following URL: `http://eggs/reportserver/?/MyReportProject/DeptList`. Figure 5-16 shows the report displayed in Internet Explorer.

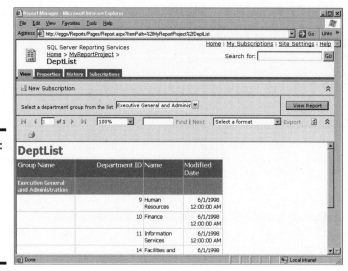

Figure 5-16:
You can
access
server
reports
through
a Web
browser.

Most users want their reports embedded within their applications. You have several options for consuming server reports in your applications:

✦ **ReportViewer control** — The ReportViewer control accepts the server and path to your server report and displays your report with navigation controls.

The ReportViewer control displays reports that use the Report Definition Language (RDL) specification. SSRS reports use RDL. See the section "Building Reports," at the beginning of this chapter, to read more about RDL and the ReportViewer control.

✦ **URL access** — Your application can dynamically build the server report's URL and display that report in a Web browser. In the case of Windows applications, you can embed a Web browser inside your Windows Form.

✦ **Web service** — SSRS provides extensive support for administering reports through a Web service interface.

Using the ReportViewer control

Using a ReportViewer control is the most straightforward approach to displaying server reports. To display a server report in a ReportViewer control, follow these steps:

1. **Drag and drop a ReportViewer control from the toolbox's Data tab onto the Windows Forms Designer or Visual Web Developer Designer.**

2. **Click the arrow in the upper-right corner of the control to display the control's tasks list.**

3. **Choose <Server Report> from the Choose Report drop-down list.**

4. **Type your Report Server URL. Report server URLs are in the format** `http://servername/reportserver`.

5. **Type the path to the report in the Report Path field, as shown in Figure 5-17.**

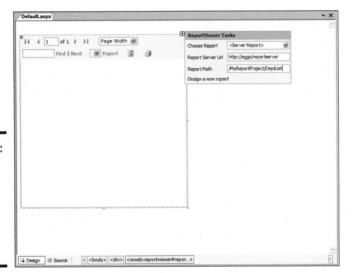

Figure 5-17: Type the report's path in the `Report Viewer` control's tasks list.

Copy and paste the report's path from the Output window when you deploy your server report project. An example of the Output window is shown earlier, in Figure 5-15.

Accessing reports with a URL

You can access server reports through a URL. You have several choices, depending on whether you want to display your report in a Web or Windows application.

If you choose to display a report in a Web application, you will

✦ Use the report's URL to access the report.

✦ Use a POST request to submit the name/value pairs of the URL to the report server.

If you choose to display a report in a Windows application, you will

✦ Fire up a Web browser from your form.

✦ Use a Web browser control on your form.

The SQL Server Books Online documentation provides several examples of using URL access in Windows and Web applications.

To use URL access, you have to understand the URL syntax for accessing a server report. A server report's URL has these parts:

✦ **A protocol** — such as http:// or https://.

✦ **The reporting server's name** — It's in the form *servername*.

✦ **The virtual root of the report server** — An example is reportserver.

✦ **An optional item path and parameter list** — It can include these items:

   • A question mark (?) that marks the beginning of the parameter list

   • The item path, in the form /MyReportProject/MyReport

   • Additional name/value parameters separated by an ampersand (&)

You can pass two kinds of optional parameters to your server report:

✦ Report parameters are defined in the report as described in the section "Creating parameters," earlier in this chapter.

   Send report parameters in the format &*reportparameter=value*.

✦ Access parameters control the appearance and output of a report. Access parameters use access prefixes to denote the kind of parameter being sent. The access prefixes are

   • **rc** — Sets values for how content is rendered

   • **rs** — Sends commands that specify the format in which the report is rendered, such as HTML or Excel

   • **dsu** — Sends a username

   • **dsp** — Sends a password

   Send access parameters by using the format &*access prefix:tag= value*, such as &rs:Command=Render.

Figure 5-18 shows an example of a server report's URL.

Figure 5-18:
Build a URL in your application to access a server report.

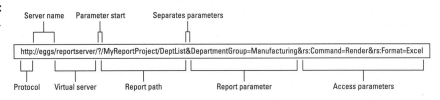

Server name Parameter start Separates parameters

`http://eggs/reportserver/?/MyReportProject/DeptList&DepartmentGroup=Manufacturing&rs:Command=Render&rs:Format=Excel`

Protocol Virtual server Report path Report parameter Access parameters

Serving up reports with Web services

SQL Server Reporting Services provides access to more than 100 services using Web service access. Using the SSRS Web service, you can do the following:

✦ Manage reports.

✦ Administer the report server.

✦ Render reports.

Reports rendered with the SSRS Web service don't include the HTML Viewer and navigational aids of URL access. However, you can build your own custom display and navigation.

Use the SSRS Web service any time you want to use a custom report viewer or provide access to report server management features.

For more information on using the SSRS Web service, search for the topic **SOAP** in the SQL Server 2005 Books Online documentation. SOAP is the name of the protocol used for Web services.

See Book V, Chapter 6 to read more about Web services.

Using other Reporting Services tools

SQL Server Reporting Services provides several additional tools for managing server reports and data sources, such as the following:

✦ **Report Manager** — Access and manage reports on the report server

✦ **Report Builder** — Build reports based on predefined data sources called Report Models

By using the Report Manager, you can access and manage

✦ Data sources

✦ Report projects and reports

✦ Report models

✦ The Report Builder

✦ Server security

You access the features of the Report Manager by clicking hyperlinks. You can configure your server by clicking the Site Settings link in the upper-right corner of the screen.

You access the Report Manager through the URL `http://servername/reports`. Figure 5-19 shows an example.

Figure 5-19:
Use the Report Manager to access and manage reports.

The Report Builder is intended to be used by business professionals. The data source for a Report Builder report is a report model. A *report model* is a simplified representation of a database that makes it easy for a power user to build reports without knowing the database schema.

You create report models using the Report Model Project in Visual Studio. You use the Report Model Project to access the Report Model Wizard and Model Designer to create report models. You deploy your report models to the report server so that users of the Report Builder can access the models.

You start the Report Builder by using either the Report Manager or the URL `http://servername/reportserver/reportbuilder/reportbuilder.application`.

Figures 5-20 and 5-21 show a matrix report, populated with data, in the Report Builder Design view. The report model makes it possible to drill down into detailed data by simply dragging and dropping data entities onto the Report Builder's design surface.

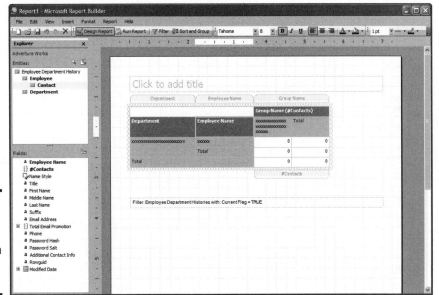

Figure 5-20:
Drag and drop data entities from the report model.

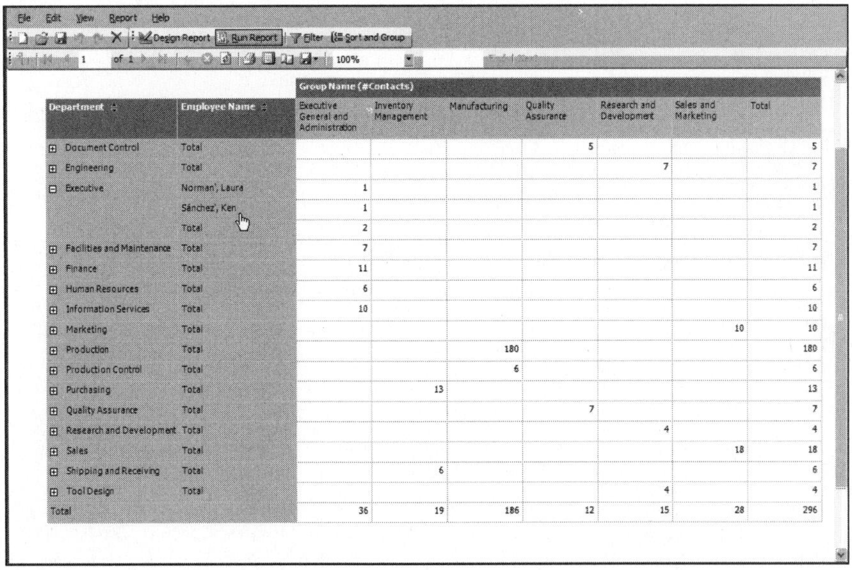

Figure 5-21:
Report Builder creates sophisti-cated reports based on a report model.

Book VII

Extending the Family

The 5ᵗʰ Wave   By Rich Tennant

"I assume everyone on your team is on board with the new system deployment."

Contents at a Glance

Chapter 1: Exploring Visual Studio Extensions

In this Chapter:

✔ **Getting the most out of Visual Studio now**

✔ **Building the next generation of Web sites with Atlas**

✔ **Looking ahead to the future of Visual Studio**

The name of this chapter should be "Getting Everything You Can Out of Visual Studio 2005 Now and in the Future." Since Visual Studio's release in Fall 2005, Microsoft has released a ton of free add-ons you can download from the Web.

Extending Visual Studio

There are many opportunities to extend Visual Studio. Some are add-ons from Microsoft; others are cool toys created by the community. In this section, I list a few of both — and share some additional resources with you, including how to get hold of trial versions of development tools.

Tools for administration and troubleshooting

One of the best things about add-ons is that all you have to do to get them is download them. Some help you administer and troubleshoot development projects; others provide new tools for programming Vista and Office 2007.

Administrative and troubleshooting downloads available from Microsoft include the following:

✦ **MSBuild Toolkit** — Use the MSBuild Toolkit to develop solutions that target the .NET 1.1 Framework using Visual Studio 2005. You can download the toolkit at

```
www.codeplex.com/Wiki/View.aspx?ProjectName=MSBee
```

✦ **Team Foundation Server Admin Tool** — As an administrator, add users to Team Foundation Server through a single user interface. Download the tool at

```
www.codeplex.com/Wiki/View.aspx?ProjectName=TFSAdmin
```

- **Managed Stack Explorer** — Investigate application hangs, using the Managed Stack Explorer. Download it at

      www.codeplex.com/Wiki/View.aspx?ProjectName=MSE

- **Web Application Projects** — Create ASP.NET 2.0 Web sites using the familiar project model of ASP.NET 1.1. Download at

      http://msdn.microsoft.com/asp.net/reference/infrastructure/
          wap/default.aspx

- **Web Deployment Projects** — Create a project to deploy your ASP.NET 2.0 Web sites. Download at

      http://msdn.microsoft.com/asp.net/reference/infrastructure/
          wdp/default.aspx

- **CSS Control Adapter Toolkit** — Take control of the elements rendered by Web server controls, using Cascading Style Sheets. The toolkit makes it possible to use CSS to override many server controls' default behavior of using `<table>` tags to render themselves to the browser. Download the toolkit at

      www.asp.net/cssadapters/

If you're not that familiar with using CSS for Web-page layout, I suggest you pick up a copy of *CSS Web Design For Dummies*, by Richard Mansfield (Wiley Publishing, Inc.). The book goes way beyond your basic CSS styling and shows you how to create multi-column Web pages without using HTML tables.

- **ASP.NET Providers source code** — Download the source code for all the built-in providers in ASP.NET 2.0, such as Membership and Site Navigation, at

      http://download.microsoft.com/download/a/b/3/ab3c284b-
          dc9a-473d-b7e3-33bacfcc8e98/ProviderToolkitSamples.msi

- **Developer Highway Code** — Access and use an e-book that features guidance and security checklists for .NET 1.1 and 2.0. It's a 147-page PDF file about writing secure code, brought to you by the Microsoft Patterns & Practices group. Download the e-book at

      www.microsoft.com/uk/msdn/security/dev_highway.mspx

- **Spec# Programming System** — Use the Spec# programming language to extend design-by-contract features to C#. Get more information at

      http://research.microsoft.com/specsharp/

The MSBuild Toolkit, Team Foundation Server Admin Tool, and Managed Stack Explorer are part of the Visual Studio Power Toys. They are released under Microsoft's Shared Source initiative. You can read more about Shared Source and find additional downloads at

      www.microsoft.com/resources/sharedsource

You may have noticed that several of the resources in the list are on the CodePlex Web site. CodePlex is a Web site that Microsoft dubs as a "new collaborative development portal." CodePlex was formally launched in June 2006 with 30 open-source projects for developers using Microsoft platforms. Be sure to check out the CodePlex Web site at `www.codeplex.com/`.

New programming tools for Vista and Office

With the release of Windows Vista and Office 2007 coming right on the heels of the Visual Studio 2005 release, Microsoft is making available a number of tools that target these new programming models. At the time of this writing, many of these downloads are betas or community technology previews. I suspect that final releases will be available from the Microsoft Web site. Here are a few resources you should check out:

✦ **Extensions for Windows Workflow Foundation** — Provides support for building applications that use Windows Workflow Foundation.

✦ **Orcas WinFx Development Tools** — Supports building applications that target WinFx with XAML support and project templates.

✦ **.NET Framework version 3.0** — Provides the libraries you need to target all the new features of Windows Vista.

✦ **Windows Software Development Kit** — Includes documentation and samples that demonstrate the new features of Windows Vista.

You can find the latest version of these resources on the Vista Web site at `http://msdn.microsoft.com/windowsvista/downloads/products/getthebeta/`.

See Chapter 3 in this mini-book for more details on Windows Vista and WinFx.

Many resources for programming Office 2007 are available at the Office Developer Center on MSDN. Some of these resources work with Visual Studio Professional 2005 while others require Visual Studio Tools for Office. Visit the Tools and Technologies page at `http://msdn.microsoft.com/office/future/tools/`.

Development resources and new server products

Microsoft has created a Web site where you can order several resources on DVD. The resources are free; you pay shipping and handling. The following resources are available for order at `www.tryvs2005.com`:

✦ **Visual Studio 2005 Team Suite 180-day trial** — Includes 180-day trial of SQL Server 2005 Enterprise Edition and Team Foundation Server.

✦ **Visual Studio 2005 Professional Edition 90-day trial**

✦ **SQL Server 2005 Enterprise Edition 180-day trial**

✦ **Microsoft Developer Security Resource Kit** — Includes articles, whitepapers, webcasts, and code samples. Also includes an e-book sample from *Writing Secure Code* by Michael Howard.

✦ **Visual Studio 2005 Accelerator Kit** — Includes guidance for migrating to .NET 2.0, code samples, articles, and a free e-book called *Refactor!*.

✦ **Microsoft Patterns & Practices (January 2006 release)** — Includes several patterns & practices guides and the complete January 2006 release of the Enterprise Library.

✦ **Windows Mobile 5.0 Developer Resource Kit** — Includes resources to get started developing applications that target Microsoft's next mobile platform.

The kits are guided tours of the resources available for a given topic, conveniently available on a DVD. Figure 1-1 shows an example of the Security Resource Kit.

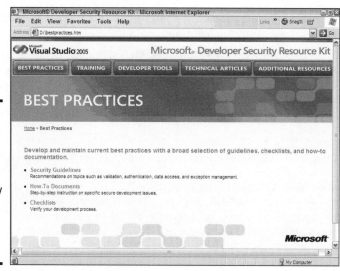

Figure 1-1: Order kits from Microsoft that conveniently bundle resources on a given topic.

In addition to its kits and other development resources, Microsoft is releasing a slew of new enterprise-server products. Many of these products have been developed closely with the architecture of the .NET Framework, and are integrated with Visual Studio 2005:

✦ **Commerce Server 2007** — A server product for creating out-of-the-box e-commerce Web sites that integrate with a company's back-end systems. Commerce Server 2007 releases in the Fall 2006 and includes a starter site. Commerce Server was built using ASP.NET 2.0, and uses Visual Studio 2005 to build and customize Commerce Server sites.

✦ **SharePoint** — There are two SharePoint products:

   • Windows SharePoint Services version 3 provides the collaboration services of SharePoint sites.

   • Microsoft Office SharePoint Server 2007 is a portal product that's part of Office 2007.

   Microsoft intends to release a set of SharePoint extensions for Visual Studio about six months after the release of Office 2007. These extensions add a SharePoint project template to Visual Studio.

   In the meantime, you can download Software Development Kits for Windows SharePoint Services version 3 at `www.microsoft.com/downloads/details.aspx?familyid=05E0DD12-8394-402B-8936-A07FE8AFAFFD&displaylang=en`. The SharePoint Server 2007 SDK can be found at `www.microsoft.com/downloads/details.aspx?familyid=6D94E307-67D9-41AC-B2D6-0074D6286FA9&displaylang=en`.

✦ **Internet Information Services 7** — The next version of IIS has integrated support for ASP.NET. IIS7 has its own dedicated Web site at `www.iis.net` where you'll find technical resources, articles, blogs, and other community resources. Write your own modules — using the .NET Framework to target the IIS application programming interface — or become more knowledgeable about how to configure and tweak IIS. The Downloads section features an IIS7 Managed Module Starter Kit for C# or C++.

Other fun items you might want to download from the community include

✦ **Spell checker for ASP.NET** — Spell-checks the text you add to your ASP.NET Web pages. This was written by one of the developers on Microsoft's Web Development Tools Team in his spare time. In other words, the tool isn't supported by Microsoft. You can download the spell checker at `http://blogs.msdn.com/mikhailarkhipov/default.aspx`.

✦ **NDepend** — Code analyzer that visually displays your source code's architecture and allows you to apply many code metrics against your source code. Download for free at `www.ndepend.com`.

✦ **MSBuild Community Tasks Project** — An open-source project that's building a library of common MSBuild tasks. You'll find just about everything you need to automate your nightly builds. Visit the project's Web site at `http://msbuildtasks.tigris.org/`.

✦ **RSS Toolkit** — Created by a member of the ASP.NET development team for consuming and publishing RSS feeds. Download the toolkit at `http://blogs.msdn.com/dmitryr/archive/2006/03/26/561200.aspx`.

Microsoft has embraced blogging. A *blog* (short for *Web log*) is a Web site where a blogger posts entries and visitors post comments on the blog entries. Here's a short list of blogs you might want to keep tabs on:

✦ **Web Development Tools Team Blog** — These are the folks that develop Visual Web Developer. Read their blog at `http://blogs.msdn.com/webdevtools/`.

✦ **S. "Soma" Somasegar's blog** — Soma is the corporate vice president for the Microsoft Developer Division. His blog always features the latest news about Visual Studio 2005. Find his blog on MSDN at `http://blogs.msdn.com/somasegar/`.

✦ **Developer Division Customer Product Lifecycle Experience Team (DDCPX) Team Blog** — These are the folks responsible for bringing aftermarket solutions — such as the Visual Studio Power Toys and software-development kits (SDKs) — to you. Find them at `http://blogs.msdn.com/ddcpxblg/`.

✦ **MSBuild Team Blog** — MSBuild is the build engine for Visual Studio. Read the team blog at `http://blogs.msdn.com/msbuild`.

You can find more Microsoft blogs at `http://blogs.msdn.com/` and `www.microsoft.com/communities/blogs/`.

MSDN has created a number of developer centers that provide links to blogs, downloads, articles, and other resources of interest to developers. Some centers you might want to visit include:

✦ **Security Developer Center** — `http://msdn.microsoft.com/security/`

✦ **Visual Studio Developer Center** — `http://msdn.microsoft.com/vstudio`

✦ **Data Access and Storage Developer Center** — `http://msdn.microsoft.com/data/`

✦ **Smart Client Developer Center** — `http://msdn.microsoft.com/smartclient/`

✦ **Office Developer Center** — `http://msdn.microsoft.com/office/`

Find even more developer centers on MSDN at `http://msdn.microsoft.com/developercenters/`.

Exploring AJAX and the Atlas Library

Atlas is the codename for a framework created by Microsoft to provide the AJAX approach to developing user interfaces for Web applications. AJAX stands for Asynchronous JavaScript and XML. Developers use a combination of client-side JavaScript and server-side programming to create a Windows-like user experience. AJAX offers an important benefit: the browser and the server can communicate without a postback; from an end-user standpoint, that means no screen flash while the page refreshes. Popular Web sites using AJAX include

✦ Google Suggest

✦ Google Maps

✦ Flickr

✦ Gmail

✦ Outlook Web Access

✦ Yahoo! Mail Beta

To get a feel for some of the things you can do with AJAX, go to the demos page at `http://openrico.org`.

To get a feel for the underlying technologies of AJAX and what it takes to AJAX-ify your Web sites using technologies besides .NET, pick up a copy of *Ajax For Dummies*, by Steve Holzner (Wiley Publishing, Inc.).

The technologies used in AJAX are nothing new. They've been around for a long time; only recently have folks applied the name AJAX to this style of programming. The technology that underlies AJAX is the object `XMLHttpRequest`. This one object makes it possible to send data back and forth between the client and server without a page refresh.

Atlas is Microsoft's version of AJAX. It consists of:

✦ **Client-side library** — Atlas provides object-oriented access to the client-side features you would usually have to write in JavaScript. With Atlas, you can apply what you know about object-oriented programming in .NET without diving into JavaScript.

✦ **Server controls** — Server-based controls similar to existing Web server controls, such as buttons and text boxes.

Atlas makes extensive use of Web services to provide the server-side features of the client-server interaction of AJAX. It's quite common for developers to wire up the elements of their user interfaces to Web services that provide data (such as specific items for a drop-down list). Of course, you aren't limited to consuming only Web services you create. You can also use an Atlas-enabled Web page to connect to third-party Web services.

Web sites that use content from other sources are called *mashups*. Mashups often utilize several technologies including Web services, RSS, and AJAX. Mashups are a driving force in the *Web 2.0* movement (the term often used to refer to the next generation of Web applications).

Installing and setting up Atlas

Atlas is essentially a library provided by Microsoft. To use Atlas, you must first download and install the library. The download includes Visual Studio project templates for Visual Basic and C#. To download Atlas, follow these steps:

1. **Browse to the Atlas Web site at `http://atlas.asp.net/`.**

The Atlas Web site features a Get Started tab that walks you through downloading, installing, and using Atlas.

2. **Click the Download button in the Web site's header, as shown in Figure 1-2. The Atlas Downloads page appears.**

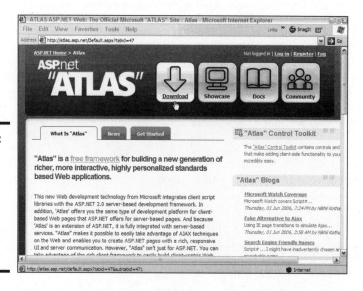

Figure 1-2: Click the Download button on the Atlas Web site to get the latest release.

3. **Click the link for the latest release of Atlas. You are taken to the Download Center on Microsoft's Web site.**

The examples in this chapter use the April Community Technology Preview (April CTP).

4. **Click the Download button to download the file, as shown in Figure 1-3.**

Your browser may prompt you to download or run the file depending on how your browser is configured. You can choose to run the file now or save it to your hard drive and execute it later.

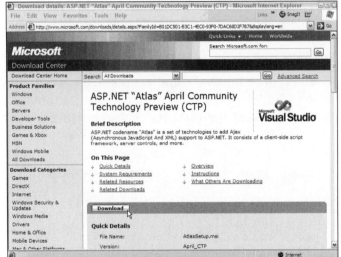

Figure 1-3:
Click the
Download
button at the
Microsoft
Download
Center to
download
the setup
file.

The instructions and screenshots in this section use the April CTP version of Atlas. Later releases of Atlas may look slightly different. Generally speaking, you should expect to successfully install Atlas by simply following the installation wizard. In the event you have problems, see the official Atlas Web site at `http://atlas.asp.net/`.

To install the file you downloaded, perform these steps:

1. **Execute the setup file from where you saved it, or directly from the browser.**

The Setup Wizard starts.

2. **Click the Next button.**

The license agreement appears.

3. **Read the license agreement; click** *I agree* **if you agree with the terms of the license.**

4. **Click the Next button.**

   The Install Project Template step appears.

5. **Accept the option to install Visual Studio project templates.**

6. **Click the Next button.**

   The Register `.asbx` File Extension step appears.

7. **Leave the option to register the .asbx file extension checked if you intend to use Atlas to communicate with external Web services.**

8. **Click the Next button.**

   The Confirm Installation step appears.

9. **Click the Next button.**

   The installation begins. After Atlas installs, the Visual Studio Content Installer appears.

10. **Accept the default entries in the content installer to install Atlas project templates in Visual Studio, as shown in Figure 1-4.**

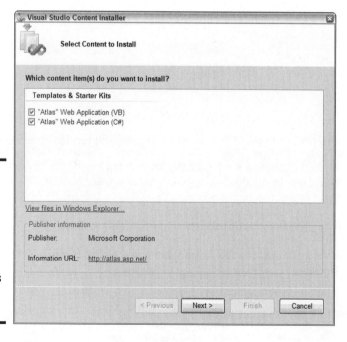

Figure 1-4:
The Visual Studio Content Installer prompts you to install Atlas project templates.

11. **Click the Next button.**

A confirmation step appears.

12. **Click the Finish button.**

13. **Click the Close button after the wizard confirms that installation is complete.**

You create a new Atlas project using the New Web Site window in Visual Studio. The Atlas project templates provided for Visual Studio wires up Atlas to an ASP.NET Web site for you by doing the following:

✦ Adding a reference to the `Microsoft.Atlas.Web.Atlas.dll` assembly.

✦ Adds a `ScriptManager` component.

✦ Adds Atlas configuration settings to the site's `web.config` file.

Before you dive in and fire up your first Atlas Web site, I suggest you download the Atlas Control Toolkit — which includes controls built using Atlas. The toolkit allows you to start using the features of Atlas without digging into the details of how the architecture works. To download and install the toolkit, follow these steps:

1. **Click the Atlas Control Toolkit link on the Atlas Downloads page of the** `http://atlas.asp.net` **site.**

The file AtlasControlToolkit.exe downloads to your computer.

Alternatively, you can download the toolkit at

```
www.codeplex.com/Wiki/View.aspx?ProjectName=
    AtlasControlToolkit
```

2. **Execute the AtlasControlToolkit.exe file.**

You are prompted for a location to unzip the toolkit's contents.

3. **Enter the name of the file directory in which you want to unzip the file.**

4. **Click the Unzip button.**

The toolkit unzips and launches a Web-based setup walkthrough that includes instructions for installing Atlas, configuring Visual Studio 2005 to use the toolkit, and samples of the controls in the toolkit.

Adding the Atlas Toolkit controls

Before you can start using the controls, you must add them to the toolbox in Visual Studio. To add the Atlas Toolkit controls to the Visual Studio 2005 toolbox:

1. **Create a new Web site using the Atlas Web Site template, as shown in Figure 1-5.**

The Atlas Web Site template is installed when you install Atlas. See Chapter 4 in Book III for more information on creating Web sites.

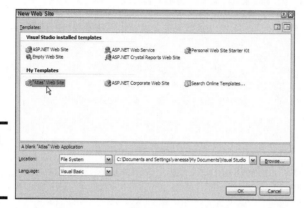

Figure 1-5:
The New
Web Site
window.

2. **Press Ctrl+Alt+X to open the Toolbox.**

3. **Right-click on the Toolbox and click Add Tab.**

   A new tab appears in the toolbox.

4. **Type** Atlas Control Toolkit **as the name for the new tab.**

5. **Right-click in the tab you just added.**

   A shortcut menu appears.

6. **Click Choose Items from the shortcut menu.**

   The Choose Toolbox Items window appears.

7. **Click the Browse button.**

   The Open window appears.

8. **Browse to the location where you unzipped the Atlas Control Toolkit in Step 4 of the preceding set of steps.**

9. **Open the** SampleWebSite **folder.**

10. **Open the** Bin **folder.**

11. **Click the file AtlasControlToolkit.dll and click the Open button.**

    A link to the dll file appears in the Choose Toolbox Items window.

12. **Click OK.**

    The controls appear in the Atlas Control Toolkit tab of the toolbox. As with all controls in the toolbox, these controls are visible only if a Web page is open in the designer, as Figure 1-6 shows.

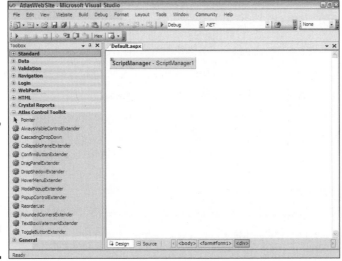

Figure 1-6:
The Atlas controls appear in the Atlas Control Toolkit tab in the toolbox.

The controls provided in the Atlas Control Toolkit aren't controls in the strict sense that a text box or a button are controls. Rather, they are control *extenders* — they add properties to existing controls.

The toolkit provides templates for creating your own extenders. Refer to the toolkit's documentation for more information.

To use one of the sample extenders provided in the toolkit, follow these steps:

1. **Select a sample you want to use from the toolkit and determine which controls it extends.**

For example, the `ToggleButton` extender works with the `CheckBox` control. (Refer to the toolkit's documentation for information on each of the control extenders.)

2. **Add Web server controls to your Web page that are extended by the Atlas toolkit to your Web page.**

For example, add the buttons, panels, check boxes, or other controls that are extended by the toolkit.

3. **Add the control extender from the Atlas Control Toolkit tab in the toolbox.**

4. **Open the Properties window for the control you're extending.**

5. **Expand the extended properties for the control, and then enter values for the properties.**

**Book VII
Chapter 1**

**Exploring Visual
Studio Extensions**

For example, the toolkit includes a `CollapsiblePanel` extender that you can use to collapse and expand a panel. Follow these steps to use the `CollapsiblePanel` extender:

1. **Drag a** `LinkButton` **control onto the Web page.**

2. **Drag a** `Label` **control inside the** `LinkButton` **control.**

3. **Drag a** `Panel` **control onto the Web page.**

4. **Drag a** `Label` **control inside the** `Panel` **control.**

You can place any server control inside a `Panel` control. Most often, the `CollapsiblePanel` extender is used with a panel to collapse and expand a list or a grid view.

5. **Set the label's** `Text` **property to** Hello world.

6. **Drag a** `CollapsiblePanelExtender` **onto the Web page.**

The extender adds a set of extended properties to the panel control added in Step 3.

7. **Click the** `Panel` **control you add in step 3 and press F4 to view the panel's properties.**

8. **Expand the** `CollapsiblePanelExtender` **properties.**

9. **Set the extended properties as shown in Figure 1-7.**

Note the `LinkButton` you create in step 1 is set as the `CollapseControlID` and the `ExpandControlID`. The label created in Step 2 is the value for the `TextLabelID` property.

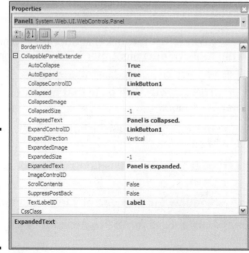

Figure 1-7: Set the properties extended by the Atlas Control Toolkit.

Press Ctrl+F5 to run the Web site. The page displays a link button that toggles between "Panel is collapsed" and "Panel is expanded" as you click the link.

Looking Ahead to the Next Visual Studio

Microsoft has plans for two future versions beyond Visual Studio 2005:

+ **Codename Orcas** — Orcas is supposed to allow developers to tap into the new features of Windows Vista and Windows Longhorn Server. Orcas is expected to release in the second half of 2007.

+ **Codename Hawaii** — Hawaii is supposed to be a complete rebuild — from the ground up — of Visual Studio.

Keep up to date with the future offerings for Visual Studio at `http://msdn.microsoft.com/vstudio/future/`. You'll find previews for future versions of Visual Studio, as well as extensions for the current version.

Orcas features

Given that Visual Studio 2005 released late and Office 2007, Windows Vista, and Longhorn Server all slipped their schedules, it seems that Visual Studio 2005 is stealing much of the thunder from Orcas. Many of the tools slated for Orcas are being made available for Visual Studio 2005.

Some of the features you can expect to find in Orcas include:

+ **WinFX** — A library for accessing the features of the Windows Vista operating system. WinFX is a framework similar to the .NET Framework.

+ **LINQ** — Extensions to the .NET Framework that support the next generation of data access in .NET applications.

+ **Visual Basic 9.0** — Read more about the features of the next version of Visual Basic at `http://msdn.microsoft.com/vbasic/future/`.

+ **C# 3.0** — Read more about the proposed changes to the C# language at `http://msdn.microsoft.com/vcsharp/future/`.

+ **Visual Tools for Office** — Updated development tools for taking advantage of Office 2007.

+ **XAML** — XAML, pronounced *zamel*, is a new declarative language for describing user interfaces. XAML makes it possible for designers to use graphic design tools that describe the user interface in an XML file. Developers can easily open the file in Visual Studio and work with the elements of the user interface.

TIP

A key player in XAML is Microsoft's new line of graphic-design tools called Expression. Read more about Expression at www.microsoft.com/ products/expression/.

The LINQ Project

LINQ is short for Language Integrated Query. In essence, LINQ creates a query language right inside the .NET Framework and the programming languages of the .NET Framework — mainly Visual Basic and C#. LINQ can be used to query any kind of data, but its primary targets are XML and SQL data.

The LINQ query architecture defines a generic set of query operators, but can be extended to handle more specific operators. Two such extensions already exist:

- ✦ **Xlinq** — These XML query operators provide XPath/XQuery features.
- ✦ **Dlinq** — These SQL query operators build on the existing SQL support in the .NET Framework.

The significance of LINQ is that you can write queries using C# or Visual Basic. You can use the standard query operators to query data in arrays or collections and use Xlinq and Dlinq to query XML and SQL data sources, respectively. Instead of specifying queries using strings as is done now, the queries are part of the language syntax.

The LINQ operators use a set of SQL-like syntax. For example, the LINQ specification defines the following operators:

- ✦ Where
- ✦ Select
- ✦ SelectMany
- ✦ Join
- ✦ GroupJoin
- ✦ OrderBy

There are many more operators, but you can see the resemblance to SQL.

Take a test drive with the CTP

A *community technology preview* (CTP) of LINQ was released in May 2006 for Visual Studio 2005. You download the CTP and read more about LINQ at the Project LINQ Web site at http://msdn.microsoft.com/data/ref/linq/.

TIP

You can find many other CTP downloads for Orcas at `http://msdn.microsoft.com/vstudio/future/ctp_downloads/default.aspx`.

The CTP includes code samples and documentation about LINQ for Visual Basic and C#. The CTP installs Visual Studio project templates you can use to create your own LINQ-enabled projects.

The code samples demonstrate all the query operators for LINQ, Dlinq, and Xlinq. The samples also show how to use Dlinq with DataSets. Figure 1-8 shows code sample that demonstrate Dlinq queries.

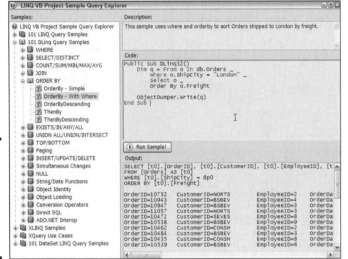

Figure 1-8: The code samples demonstrate LINQ's query operators.

**Book VII
Chapter 1**

**Exploring Visual
Studio Extensions**

The LINQ CTP includes a Dlinq Designer which is a visual designer for creating DLinq queries. Essentially, you drag and drop tables from Server Explorer to the designer — and the designer translates relational database objects (such as tables and relationships) into graphic objects. You write Dlinq queries that target the objects. Figure 1-9 shows an example of the Dlinq Designer. The shapes on the designer represent entity classes generated by the designer to represent relational tables.

A peek at Hawaii

For obvious reasons, not much information is available about the version of Visual Studio after Orcas, codenamed "Hawaii." It has been reported that Microsoft plans to completely re-architect the product. I interpret that to mean a completely new approach to software development.

My guess is that this next-generation approach to development will allow developers to immerse themselves in modeling their business problem — and in generating code from that model — rather than getting stuck in a "code zone." Three development resources that I suggest accessing for a closer look are as follows:

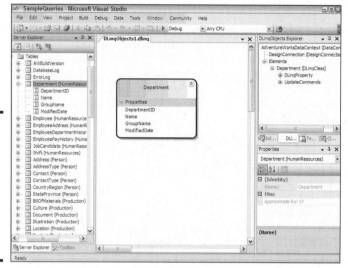

Figure 1-9:
The Dlinq Designer generates entity classes from relational tables.

✦ **Microsoft's Center for Software Excellence** (`www.microsoft.com/Windows/CSE`) — A group in Microsoft Research focused on developer productivity at Microsoft.

✦ **Intentional Software** (`www.intentionalsoftware.com`) — The company founded by Charles Simonyi to bring to market the next generation of software development. Simonyi is the man behind Microsoft Word and Excel. He also created the Hungarian notation naming convention.

✦ **Software Factories** (`www.softwarefactories.com`) — The idea of being able to mass-produce code from a model is being used now in Visual Studio Team System. Expect to see this concept trickle down to the individual developer in the future.

You can see how Visual Studio Team System is already using models to generate code in the next chapter.

Chapter 2: Being a Team Player with Visual Studio Team System

In this Chapter:

✔ **Figuring out the products in Visual Team System**

✔ **Exploring the tools of the new role-based editions**

✔ **Using Team Foundation Server**

*I*f you've ever worked on a team project, then you've probably experienced the frustrations of trying to collaborate via e-mail and folder shares. Invariably, an important document gets overwritten or an important stakeholder is left off the distribution list. Either way, the project suffers.

For most teams, the thought of implementing software to help with collaboration is about as much fun as having a root canal. Even if you decide on a vendor and manage to get the budget approved, you know the software's benefits are overshadowed by its daunting complexity.

Microsoft's approach to solving this problem is a bit different than most other vendors' approaches. Instead of creating an entire new set of tools for people to learn, they decided to create a solution that allows team members to keep using the same tools they've always used. The project managers keep using Excel and Project. The developers use Visual Studio. The architects get modeling tools that actually synchronize with code, and the testers finally get real software. The name for this make-everybody-happy approach to supporting team development is Visual Studio Team System.

Introducing the Visual Studio Team System

Visual Studio Team System isn't an edition of Visual Studio. Rather, it's a platform for building software in a team environment. The platform is composed of the following product offerings:

✦ **Four role-based editions of Visual Studio** — Each edition features a different set of tools tailored to a role in the software development life cycle. The current roles offered are:

- Architect
- Database Professional

- Developer
- Tester

✦ **Visual Studio Team Suite** — This product suite includes all four role-based editions.

✦ **Team Foundation Server Standard Edition** — This server product's features enable the members of a team to collaborate and manage projects. All versions of Visual Studio 2005 — except the Express Edition — can access a Team Foundation Server.

Each edition of Visual Studio in the Visual Studio Team System comes with a client access license (CAL) that allows access to TFS. You must purchase a CAL separately for Visual Studio Standard or Professional editions. Each user accessing TFS must have a CAL.

You aren't required to use Team Foundation Server. You can use any of the role-based editions without TFS.

✦ **Team Foundation Server Workgroup Edition** — This product provides the same features as TFS, but is limited to five connections. TFS Workgroup Edition is included with any of the role-based versions of Visual Studio or the Team Suite.

If you have five or less members on your team, then TFS Workgroup Edition is the way to go. You can upgrade to Standard Edition any time.

Each product in Visual Studio Team System comes with an MSDN Premium Subscription. Table 2-1 lists many of the tools you'll find in VSTS. (Descriptions for many of these tools appear later in the chapter.)

Table 2-1	Tools and Editions
Tool	*Edition*
Application Designer	Architect
Logical Infrastructure Designer	Architect
Deployment Designer	Architect
Class Designer	Architect, Developer
Visio and UML Modeling	Architect, Developer
Team Foundation Client	Architect, Developer
Visual Studio Professional	Architect, Developer
Dynamic Code Analyzer	Developer
Static Code Analyzer	Developer
Code Profiler	Developer

Tool	Edition
Unit Testing	Developer, Test
Code Coverage	Developer, Test
Load Testing	Test
Manual Testing	Test
Test Case Management	Test
Build Automation	Team Foundation Server
Change Management	Team Foundation Server
Work Item Tracking	Team Foundation Server
Reporting	Team Foundation Server
Project Site	Team Foundation Server
Integration Services	Team Foundation Server
Project Management	Team Foundation Server

Visual Studio Team System is more than a new suite of tools. VSTS supports the entire application lifecycle and enables processes to improve continuously.

Still, implementing VSTS is not a light-hearted undertaking. VSTS integrates with several Microsoft server and client products — as a result, VSTS requires a *big* honkin' server. The server products required by VSTS include

✦ Windows Server 2003

✦ SQL Server 2005 Enterprise Edition

✦ Windows SharePoint Services

Compared to other products of this type, VSTS is relatively simple to implement. A single server can support several hundred developers.

If you'd rather not deal with implementing yet another server, you can find a service provider who will host a Team Foundation Server for you. Developers connect to the hosted server just like it was sitting in your server room. You get all the productivity of Team Foundation Server without any of the hassles of implementing and administering a server. You can find out more about hosted Team Foundation Servers on my Web site at www.sharepointgrrl.com.

There are a number of clients you can use to access Team Foundation Server. These include:

✦ Visual Studio 2005

✦ Microsoft Office Excel 2003 or later

+ Microsoft Project 2003 or later

+ Internet Explorer

All the clients except Internet Explorer require the installation of Team Explorer (the Team Foundation Client). See the section "Accessing Team Foundation Server," later in this chapter, for more about Team Explorer.

To take Visual Studio Team System for a test spin, you can download a 180-day trial edition from Microsoft's Web site at

`http://go.microsoft.com/fwlink/?LinkId=64135`

If you prefer a DVD of the trial software, you can order one at `www.tryvs2005.com`.

If you want a Virtual PC image of a fully-functional Team Foundation Server with Visual Studio Team Suite, it's available to MSDN subscribers for a limited time.

To learn more about Visual Studio Team System, check out these resources:

+ **Team System Rocks Web site** — A Web site dedicated to VSTS that features blogs, forums, and tutorials. The site has dozens of videos on using VSTS. Visit the site at `http://teamsystemrocks.com/`.

+ **Visual Studio Team System Developer Center** — View the VSTS portal on MSDN at `http://msdn.microsoft.com/vstudio/teamsystem/`.

+ **Visual Studio Team System Virtual Labs** — Access tutorials hosted on MSDN at `http://msdn.microsoft.com/virtuallabs/teamsystem/`.

Exploring the New Role-Based Editions

The new role-based editions of Visual Studio introduce several new tools. Some of these tools are brand new, such as the Application Designer in the Architect Edition. Other tools (such as static code analysis in the Developer Edition) simply integrate existing tools that many developers have used for a while. Either way, the new editions are long on features and compatibility.

Before you decide to spring for any or all of the new editions, consider that you can achieve the same effect as many of these editions using third-party tools. Depending on your situation, you may come out ahead by sticking with Visual Studio 2005 Professional and using a set of third-party tools such as these:

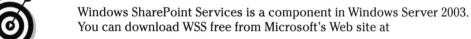

- ✦ **Unit Testing** — NUnit and NMock.
- ✦ **Modeling** — Visio for Enterprise Architects and Class Designer.
- ✦ **Build automation** — Use MSBuild and NAnt.
- ✦ **Static code analysis** — FxCop analyzes your code for compliance to standards.
- ✦ **Project portal** — Use Windows SharePoint Services or create your own portal with ASP.NET 2.0 portal pages.

  Windows SharePoint Services is a component in Windows Server 2003. You can download WSS free from Microsoft's Web site at

  ```
  www.microsoft.com/downloads/details.aspx?FamilyId=
      B922B28D-806A-427B-A4C5-AB0F1AA0F7F9&displaylang=en
  ```

- ✦ **Source code control** — Visual SourceSafe or WinCVS.
- ✦ **Team Foundation Server** — Access TFS using the Team Explorer add-in for Visual Studio 2005.

Visual Studio Team System for Software Architects

The Team System for Software Architects edition of Visual Studio includes a set of designers that allow architects to model their application designs. The models are more than just pretty pictures; they evaluate a design model's validity before it's ever deployed. For example, if you designate that a Web site must use an SSL security certificate then your model warns you if it attempts to deploy your Web site to a Web server that doesn't have an SSL certificate.

Of course, the models can't stop your technical staff from installing the application on the wrong server. The designers create models of logical server configurations. How those logical servers relate to physical servers is something that happens in the physical world.

The set of designers in the Architect edition are collectively known as the Distributed Systems Designers. The four new designers are as follows:

- ✦ **Application Designer** — Model the deployable units of code such as a Windows application and an ASP.NET Web site that constitute the system under development.
- ✦ **Deployment Designer** — Map your deployable application systems to logical server configurations in your Logical Datacenter model.
- ✦ **Logical Datacenter Designer** — Model the logical server configurations on which applications will run.
- ✦ **System Designer** — Model application systems, which are comprised of applications modeled in the Application Designer.

What's so significant about these designers is that the models are linked together and can communicate with another. For example, you can specify that your application needs to run on an IIS6 server. If you try to deploy your application to a logical server configured to run IIS5, the designer will warn you.

Further, the Application Designer can generate the projects defined in your model. As projects are developed, the models are synchronized to reflect any changes. In essence, your system becomes self-documenting. As team members go about doing their day-to-day jobs, the documentation takes care of itself.

The Distributed System Designers are a component in Microsoft's Dynamic Systems Initiative. DSI hopes to make it less costly to administer technology systems. You can read more about DSI at

www.microsoft.com/windowsserversystem/dsi/

Distributed System Diagrams are solution-level items; they don't belong to any one project in your solution. Figure 2-1 shows a DSD item-template icon in the Add Solution Items window.

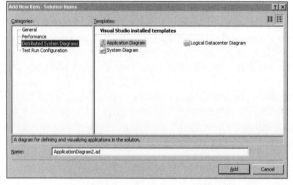

Figure 2-1:
Distributed
System
Diagrams
are solution-
level items.

In most cases, your architects create the DSD models before any coding ever starts. Architects generate Visual Studio projects from the applications they model in Application Diagrams. Figure 2-2 shows an example of an Application Diagram.

You can easily create a System Diagram by clicking a set of applications that define a system. For example, your Application Diagram may show a class library, a Web site, and a Windows application. You generate two system diagrams: one shows the Windows application and the class library; the other shows the Web site and the class library. Figure 2-3 provides an example.

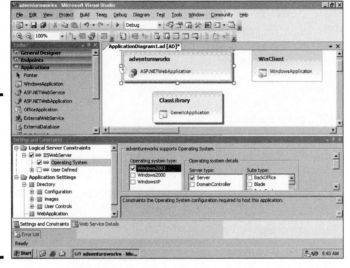

Figure 2-2:
Application
Diagrams
model the
application
in the
system
under
develop-
ment.

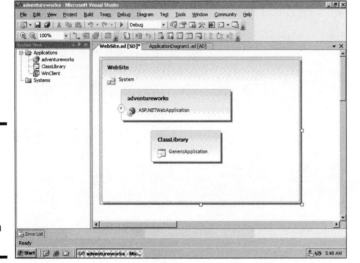

Figure 2-3:
System
Diagrams
are
generated
from
Application
Diagrams.

You can test deployment scenarios for your system using the Deployment
Designer. Using either an Application Diagram or a Systems Diagram, you
associate a Deployment Diagram with a Logical Datacenter diagram. Create
a Deployment Diagram for each Logical Datacenter scenario you wish to
evaluate.

Visual Studio Team System for Software Developers

The Developer Edition of Visual Studio Team System provides additional tools that developers can use to write better code. Many of these tools are available elsewhere as free downloads or open-source software. VSTS for Software Developers integrates the following tools into the development environment:

✦ **Static code analysis** — This tool uses rules and patterns to detect errors and bad coding form.

✦ **Dynamic code analysis** — This code profiler monitors an application's performance while it's running.

✦ **Unit testing** — This is a framework for generating and managing unit tests.

✦ **Code coverage** — This tool provides feedback on how effective your unit tests are at covering all your code.

The testing features in Visual Studio Developer Edition overlap with the Testers Edition. Developers generate unit tests from the code editor, as shown in Figure 2-4.

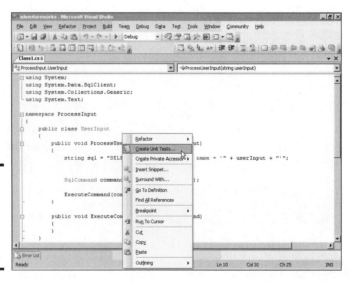

Figure 2-4: Generate unit tests from the source-code editor.

Visual Studio Team System for Software Testers

Team System for Software Testers provides resources for creating and managing many kinds of tests. You can use the Tester Edition to:

✦ Create unit tests.

✦ Record Web tests.

✦ Execute a sequential list of tests.

✦ Measure your application's performance by running any combination of unit tests and Web tests over and over again.

✦ Capture the steps for manual tests.

✦ Turn any code into a test.

You organize your tests into projects using a Test Project template in Visual Studio, as shown in Figure 2-5.

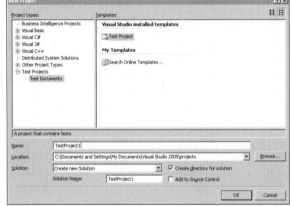

Figure 2-5:
Add a Test Project to your solution for organization tests.

**Book VII
Chapter 2**

Being a Team Player with Visual Studio Team System

A new test run configuration is added by default to the solution when a Test Project is added. Use the Test Run Configuration to configure the testing environment and code coverage, as shown in Figure 2-6.

You add a Test Project like you add any project in Visual Studio by using the New Project window.

Visual Studio Team System for Database Professionals

Team System for Database Professionals brings the database developer closer into the software-development loop. With the Database Professional Edition, you can do the following:

✦ Refactor database schema objects.

✦ Automate testing with unit tests.

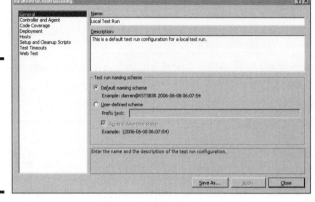

Figure 2-6:
Use a
Test Run
Configu-
ration to
configure a
group of
tests.

✦ Place database schemas under source control.

✦ Use `SchemaCompare` and `DataCompare` to compare two databases and generate scripts to synchronize the databases.

✦ Populate test databases based on production data, using the `DataGenerator`.

Getting to Know Team Foundation Server

Team Foundation Server is the bedrock of collaboration features in Visual Studio Team System. Team Foundation Server provides the following:

✦ **Source control management** — Create check-in policies that define the actions your developers must complete before integrating source code.

✦ **Work item tracking** — Create tasks, assign tasks to team members, and associate tasks with actions such as code check-in.

✦ **Build automation** — Step through a wizard to create complex automated build processes.

✦ **Reporting** — Generate reports on all activities in your Team Foundation Server.

✦ **Centralized project site** — Set up a project site where all stakeholders can access project artifacts.

✦ **Project management — Perform project management tasks in familiar tools like Excel** and Project.

CodePlex is coming

You may be wondering why you should install the Team Explorer add-in if you aren't planning on using Team Foundation Server. You can use Team Explorer to access Team Foundation Servers hosted on the Web. For example, CodePlex is a Web site created by Microsoft for community development. CodePlex is a custom Web site that uses Team Foundation Server as its backend. In fact, accessing CodePlex from Team Explorer is the same as accessing a Team Foundation Server installed in your office.

At the time of this writing, CodePlex is still in beta. According to the CodePlex Web site, registered users will be able to create projects on the site. You can browse the CodePlex Web site at www.codeplex.com. See the topic "Connecting to a CodePlex Project using Team Explorer" in CodePlex's help wiki for more information.

Many of the features in Team Foundation Server are possible using the technologies of Windows SharePoint Services. WSS version 2 is available as a free download from Microsoft's Web site. Before you take the plunge with VSTS, I suggest you install WSS. Also, pick up a copy of my book *Microsoft SharePoint Server 2003 For Dummies* (Wiley Publishing, Inc.). You'll find scenarios that show you how to use SharePoint in many different business contexts.

Accessing Team Foundation Server

You must install the Team Explorer client before you can access Team Foundation Server. Team Explorer is an add-in for Visual Studio. You can install the client using the Team Foundation Server software or download the add-in from Microsoft Downloads. It's not necessary to have any edition of Visual Studio to use Team Explorer.

To download the client from Microsoft, access this link:

```
http://download.microsoft.com/download/2/a/d/2ad44873-8ccb-
    4a1b-9c0d-23224b3ba34c/VSTFClient.img
```

To access an existing project on a Team Foundation Server using Team Explorer:

1. **Click Team Explorer on the View menu.**

The Team Explorer window appears.

2. **Click the Add Existing Team Project button.**

The Connect to a Team Foundation Server window appears.

3. Click the Servers button.

The Add/Remove Team Foundation Server window appears. Alternatively, you can select an existing server from the Connect to a Team Foundation Server drop-down list.

4. Click the Add button.

The Add Team Foundation Server appears.

5. Type the server's name in the name text box.

If your administrator has instructed you to use a different port or protocol, enter those in the Connection Details section. (Figure 2-7 shows a connection to CodePlex.)

Figure 2-7:
Type the connection information for your Team Foundation Server.

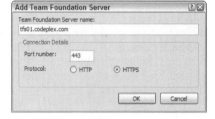

6. Click OK.

7. Type your username and password if prompted.

8. Select a project from the list of projects, as Figure 2-8 shows.

9. Click OK.

The project appears in the Team Explorer.

Figure 2-8:
Select projects to explore from the Team Foundation Server.

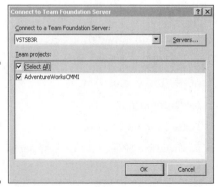

Creating a new team project

You may be wondering why Microsoft didn't create a Team System edition for project managers. It's probably because project managers don't use Visual Studio that often. And VSTS accommodates their style of work by interfacing with Excel and Project.

Some tasks, such as creating new team projects, must be completed using Visual Studio. Visual Studio provides a group of predefined environment settings specific to project managers. To reset your settings to use the Project Management Settings, use the Import and Export Settings Wizard as described in Chapter 1 of Book II. The project manager environment settings eliminate most of the menu items used by developers and other roles.

The New Team Project wizard walks you through the process of creating a new team project. To start the wizard, follow these steps:

1. **On the File menu, click New Team Project.**

The New Team Project wizard appears.

Alternatively, you can click File ➪ New ➪ Team Project. If you're not connected to a team server, the Connect to Team Foundation Server dialog box appears; you complete it to connect to a Team Foundation Server.

2. **Type a name for the project in the name field.**

The name must be unique on the team server.

3. **Click the Next button.**

The Select a Process Template step appears. The *process template* defines workflow for your project. Team Foundation Server includes two process templates from the Microsoft Solutions Framework; you can extend them or create your own.

4. **Select a process template from the drop-down list, as shown in Figure 2-9.**

The steps that appear next depend upon the process template you select. (Steps 5–9 in this list are based on the MSF for the Agile Software Development process template.)

Visit the Visual Studio Team System Developer Center on MSDN to get more information on using development processes from the Microsoft Solutions Framework at `http://msdn.microsoft.com/vstudio/teamsystem/msf/`.

5. **Click the Next button.**

The Specify the Settings for the Project Portal step appears. The values you enter in this step appear in your SharePoint-based project portal. The URL you use to access your project portal also appears in this step.

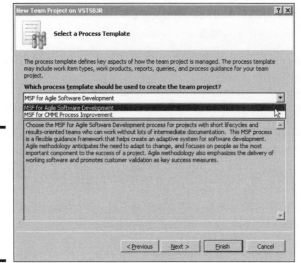

Figure 2-9:
Select a
process
template in
the New
Team
Project
wizard.

6. **Type a site title and description in the wizard and click the Next button.**

   The Specify Source Control Settings window appears.

7. **Select your settings to establish source control for the project.**

8. **Click the Next button.**

   The Confirmation Page appears.

9. **Review your settings and click the Finish button. The wizard creates your project.**

   The project is accessible from the Team Explorer and its project portal. Figure 2-10 shows a sample project portal.

Browsing with the Team Explorer

Team Explorer is the premier client for browsing resources in a Team Project. You open the Team Explorer from the View menu. The Team Explorer displays the following:

✦ **Work items** — Lists the work-item queries in your team project. Click on a query to expand a list of work orders.

✦ **Documents** — Displays the document libraries from the project portal. The project's process template determines which document libraries are created.

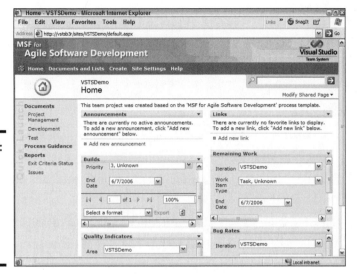

Figure 2-10:
VSTS
creates a
project
portal for
the new
team
project.

+ **Reports** — Displays a list of reports available for your projects. Reports are created using SQL Server Reporting Services.

+ **Team Builds** — Displays a list of build types for your team project.

+ **Source control** — Define check-in policies for the project.

Figure 2-11 shows a work-item query accessed using Team Explorer.

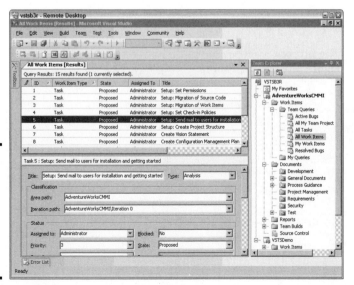

Figure 2-11:
Use Team
Explorer to
browse
team
artifacts
such as
work items.

Creating work items with Excel

You can connect to projects in a Team Foundation Server using Excel or Project. Team Explorer adds a Team toolbar you can use to get work items and to publish new or modified items to the server. To connect to a new work-item list in Excel, follow these steps:

1. **Click the New List button on the Team toolbar.**

The Connect to Team Foundation Server window appears.

2. **Connect to your server, as described in the preceding example.**

3. **Select a team project from the list of projects and click OK.**

The New List window appears.

4. **Click the Query List radio button to access a list of work items.**

Alternatively, click Input list to enter new work items and get individual work items.

5. **Click the Select a Query drop-down list.**

A list of predefined work item queries appears.

6. **Select a query from the list and click OK, as shown in Figure 2-12.**

The query's results appear in the spreadsheet.

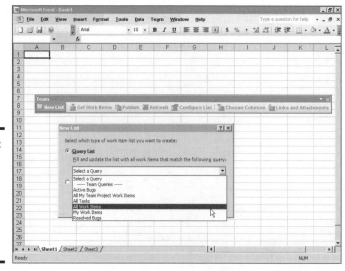

Figure 2-12: Select a pre-defined query to retrieve a set of work items from the server.

The work items are retrieved into an Excel list. You can add new work items or update existing items. Click the Publish button to save your changes to the server, and your saved changes are immediately available to other team members. Figure 2-13 shows a work item being added to a list.

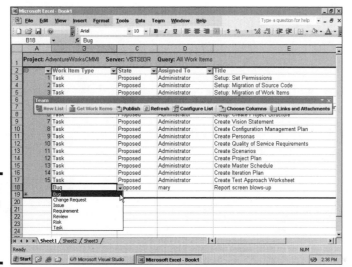

Figure 2-13: Adding new work items to an Excel list.

You can add work items in Excel, Project, Team Explorer, or during source-control check-in.

Chapter 3: Using Visual Studio with Vista and Office 2007

In this Chapter:

✔ Exploring the technologies of Vista

✔ Using the Windows Software Development Kit

✔ Taking a peek at Windows Workflow

✔ Getting a head start with Project Glidepath

✔ Starting to develop applications for Office 2007

✔ Running virtual machines

*M*icrosoft's next generation of operating systems and productivity software is here. Finally. It's been a long time coming, but Microsoft is poised to release a whole slew of software that includes

✦ **Windows Vista** — Microsoft's newest desktop operating system.

✦ **Longhorn Server** — Next-generation server platform, in beta 2 as of this writing. The product will likely be named Windows Server 2007 when it's released.

✦ **Office 2007** — Latest release of Office products.

In this chapter, I hit some of the highlights of this new software — and give you some hints for how you can get started developing applications that target Vista and Office 2007. I also show you Project Glidepath, which is Microsoft's latest attempt to help developers wrap their arms around all this new technology. Finally, I show you how you can use Virtual Server 2005 to cut down on the number of physical servers you need (and the headaches they bring) to run all this new software.

Exploring Vista

Microsoft plans to release several editions of Windows Vista. As you might expect, the lower-end editions have fewer features than higher-end editions; each higher edition is a superset of the lower-end features. The Vista Editions you should expect to see include

- ✦ Home Basic
- ✦ Home Premium
- ✦ Business
- ✦ Enterprise
- ✦ Ultimate

Microsoft will likely also release a Starter edition that doesn't carry the Vista moniker. The Starter edition is more limited than Home Basic and is intended for emerging markets.

Rumor has it that customers will be able to upgrade to a higher edition of Windows Vista simply by using a new product key. (Fascinating rumor.)

A simple of list of features can't do justice to Vista. You need to experience Vista in order to get your mind around what it can do. It's completely different.

The most visible change in Vista is the new Windows Aero interface. The new interface is intended to create an immersive user experience, similar to what you experience while playing a video game. This change means there's a learning curve with Vista's interface. Businesses typically don't *like* learning curves because they cause a short-term loss in productivity. To accommodate this, Vista has four levels of user experience you can choose from:

- ✦ Windows Classic
- ✦ Basic
- ✦ Standard
- ✦ Aero

Vista is more than a slick new user interface. It has to be. Vista is the next generation of desktop and server computing on the Microsoft platform. With Vista, Microsoft has "componentized" everything — and eliminated overlapping technologies.

If you've had an opportunity to see Vista, you must be wondering what all this means for software development. The experience is more immersive and graphically intense than anything you can create right now with Windows Forms in Visual Studio. Before I can discuss what this means for the future of Windows development, I must first explain some of the technologies that underlie Windows Vista:

- ✦ **Windows CardSpace** — Manages a portfolio of digital identities for use on the Internet. Examples of *digital identities* include credit cards, usernames, and passwords.

✦ **Windows Communication Foundation** — Next generation of Web services, intended to be used for all communications among applications. WCF replaces all presently existing communication technologies, regardless of whether the message is moving within the machine, from machine to machine, or across networks.

✦ **Windows Presentation Foundation** — The presentation subsystem responsible for user experience in Vista. With WPF, Microsoft separates user interface from the source code into a separate markup file.

✦ **Windows Workflow Foundation** — Designers and a framework for building workflow-enabled applications.

Another key technology slated for Windows Vista is Windows File Storage or WinFS. As a major technology that improves search and enables the use of structured data among applications, WinFS is a database that sits on top of a standard hard drive and provides access to resources. Unfortunately, WinFS won't ship with Vista. Microsoft had indicated WinFS would ship with Longhorn Server and would work on Vista and Windows XP, but in June 2006 the WinFS team quietly announced that's no longer the case. Instead, WinFS will be rolled into SQL Server and ADO.NET. At some point in the future, a relational file system may be made available for Windows.

All the technologies in Vista are part of version 3.0 of the .NET Framework, which works with Windows XP and Windows Server 2003. Even if you don't intend to move to Vista or Longhorn Server right now, you can start building applications that are capable of running on them.

Book VII
Chapter 3

Using Visual Studio with Vista and Office 2007

Now that you have some understanding of the technologies, you must be wondering what this means to you as a developer. Presently, you use Windows Forms to create Windows applications. But how do you create Vista applications? You have the same options that you have now:

✦ **Managed** — Create managed applications using version 3.0 of the .NET Framework (formerly known as WinFX).

✦ **Unmanaged** — Create unmanaged or native applications using Win32 or COM.

You can still create applications using Windows Forms. Vista provides you with another choice for user interface. Your applications can target the new Aero interface. Similar to how you can create a Windows UI and a Web UI using a core set of logic, you can add an Aero interface as well.

When talking about Vista, it's important to discuss both existing *and* new development. You want to make sure that your existing applications that work fine in Windows XP will continue to work with Vista. For starters, you can download the Windows Vista Jumpstart Toolkit from the Microsoft community site (`http://devreadiness.org/`). The toolkit provides access to videos, presentations, white papers, and tools designed to help you make the transition to Vista.

Getting started with Vista

You might think getting started with Vista means installing Vista. Oh no, that's too easy. I want to get you developing for Vista. There are a few tools you need to get started:

✦ **.NET Framework version 3.0** — Formerly known as WinFX, this is the managed API you use to access all the technologies of Vista.

✦ **Windows Software Development Kit (SDK)** — Includes documentation, samples, and tools for building managed and unmanaged Vista applications.

✦ **Orcas Development Tools** — Orcas is the codename for the next version of Visual Studio. In the meantime, Microsoft is providing this extension to Visual Studio 2005 so you can start working with Vista technologies now.

✦ **Visual Studio 2005 Extensions for Windows Workflow Foundation** — Project templates, IntelliSense support, and documentation for Vista's new workflow technology.

You can find information about downloading and installing these tools at `http://msdn.microsoft.com/windowsvista/downloads/products/getthebeta/`.

Many of these tools are beta or CTP releases. You should avoid installing them on production machines. I recommend using a test machine or a virtual machine. See the section "Going Virtual" later in this chapter for more information on using virtual machines.

After you install, you end up with several new project types as listed in Table 3-1. The templates are available for Visual Basic and C#.

Table 3-1	Vista Project Types and Templates
Project Type	*Project Template*
Windows (WinFX)	WinFX Windows Application
	WinFX Service Library
	WinFX Web Browser Application
	WinFX Custom Control Library
Workflow	Sequential Workflow Console Application
	Workflow Activity Library
	State Machine Workflow Library

Project Type	Project Template
	Sequential Workflow Library
	State Machine Console Application
	Empty Workflow Project

You create projects using these project types in the same way you create any Visual Studio project.

Creating Vista applications

Everything changes in Vista. Of course, your applications don't have to change. But chances are you'll want to take advantage of those changes. If you want to get started creating applications for Vista, you should start with the Windows Software Development Kit (SDK).

The Windows SDK consists of the following:

+ Extensive documentation on every aspect of the Vista operating system and its underlying technologies

+ Samples that demonstrate every aspect of Vista.

+ Tools to help you create, deploy, and manage all kinds of Vista applications.

After you install the SDK, you access its contents via your All Programs menu. The SDK can be quite overwhelming; I suggest you start out with the Getting Started section of the SDK documentation. The documentation appears in the familiar Document Explorer, which is the same tool used to display help for Visual Studio, as Figure 3-1 shows.

SDK samples

The SDK offers an amazing number of samples, including samples for Vista and version 3.0 of the .NET Framework. You can find these in the samples folder of where you installed the SDK. The SDK installs by default to C:\ Program Files\Microsoft SDKs\Windows.

The samples are organized by feature or technology. I suggest you pick a technology in which you have some interest — such as Windows Workflow Foundation — and browse through the samples. For example, I'm most interested in Windows Presentation Foundation because it represents the most visible change to Vista.

Windows Presentation Foundation

You can find the WPF samples in the file WPFSamples.zip. Once you unzip the samples, you'll find an Intro folder that contains a number of quick start tutorials. The first quick start is a simple `Hello World` application. Figure 3-2 shows an example of the output from this sample.

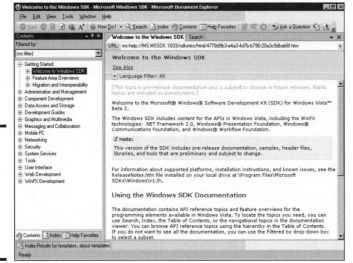

Figure 3-1: Start with the Getting Started section of the Windows SDK.

Figure 3-2: Your first Hello World from Windows Presentation Foundation.

Not very impressive — but (as I'm sure you've surmised) the samples in the SDK aren't intended to be sophisticated. Their intent is to demonstrate new features. What you're looking at in Figure 3-2 is an example of a Page. You can still use good old-fashioned Windows Forms in your development, but WPF also uses Pages to display content.

WPF applications are intended to create immersive user experiences. Think about where you're most likely to see applications with intense graphics, video, and other eye candy. It's usually on the Web. WPF applications use Pages to create rich browser-like experiences on the desktop.

Another way that WPF applications are like Web applications is that they use a markup language to describe the user interface. Web applications use HTML. In Visual Studio, you use a combination of HTML and ASP.NET markup to create the .aspx file that becomes your Web page. You write your code in a separate *code-behind file*. The same is true of Vista applications.

Extensible Application Markup Language

All Vista applications, whether they use pages or Windows Forms, use markup to describe the user interface. The markup language was created by Microsoft, and it's called Extensible Application Markup Language (XAML, which sounds like *camel* with a *z*, for short).

XAML is an XML language that you use to describe everything about the user interface. Why XAML? By describing user interfaces using an XML file, you can easily transfer user interfaces between members of a team. For example, user-interface designers can work on a UI. They can pass off the XAML file to a developer who is writing the code-behind logic. XAML is used by Visual Studio and Microsoft's new line of graphics design tools called Microsoft Expression. Designers will use an Expression product such as Microsoft Expression Web Designer to create rich user interfaces in XAML. Developers consume the XAML in Visual Studio.

Visit the Expression Web site where you can download trial versions of the new Expression products at www.microsoft.com/products/expression.

Don't worry — you don't have to learn a new language. Visual Studio will still use visual designers. However, the beta versions don't include those designers yet, so you'll have to get your feet wet with XAML. There's IntelliSense support for XAML, so it's fairly intuitive. Figure 3-3 shows an example of a typical XAML file being edited.

I suggest you take a look at the samples gallery to get more examples of using XAML. You can find the samples gallery in the Gallery folder of WPFSamples. The samples gallery shows code and previews of animation, controls, data-binding, graphics, and layout. It's a great way to get acquainted with WPF. Figure 3-4 shows an example of a control that uses XAML and C#. You can view a description, the code, and a preview.

Book VII Chapter 3

Using Visual Studio with Vista and Office 2007

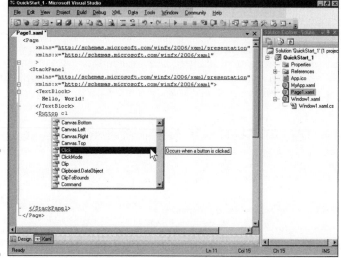

Figure 3-3:
Create user interfaces for Vista applications using XAML.

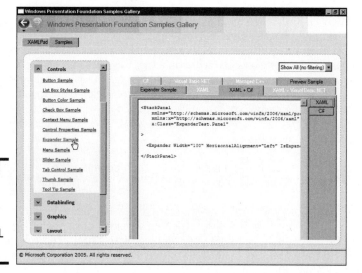

Figure 3-4:
Use the samples gallery to view XAML samples.

Another feature demonstrated in the samples gallery is XAMLPad. You type XAML markup in the lower pane in XAMLPad, and the upper pane displays the user interface. Figure 3-5 shows an example of XAMLPad.

If you're starting to feel like you're not in Kansas any more, you aren't alone. All this Vista stuff is strange new territory. Microsoft has created mountains of documentation to help you figure all this out. I suggest you set aside some quality time to read the Vista User Experience Guidelines. The guidelines walk you through the new user interface changes for Vista applications. You can find the guidelines at

```
http://msdn.microsoft.com/library/?url=/library/en-us/
    UxGuide/UXGuide/Home.asp
```

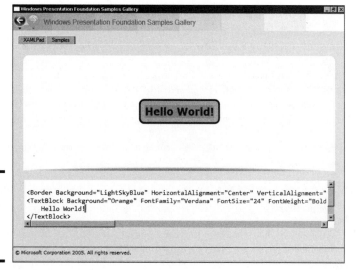

Figure 3-5:
Take XAML
for a test
drive with
XAMLPad.

Creating workflow applications

Version 3.0 of the .NET Framework has a new kind of application called a *workflow* — which is a long-running application that represents a model of a process from beginning to end. For example, think about the workflow required for getting a travel-expense reimbursement at work: It starts when you fill out an expense reimbursement form. The form is routed to your boss for approval. Then it's routed to accounts payable. If there's a problem with the form, AP may kick the form into a separate problem queue. At some point (hopefully before the credit card payment is due), you get a check. Windows Workflow Foundation allows you to create workflows that model other such processes.

There are two parts to WF applications. There's the WF model that defines the workflow itself. Workflows can't be executed directly; rather, you create an instance of the workflow model inside an application — which can be a Windows, Web, or console application — and host the workflow there. The application that hosts the workflow is the second part of a WF application. You need the workflow and an application to host it to create a workflow application.

The basic unit of a workflow is an *activity* — which you might think of as a step in the workflow. Windows Workflow Foundations supports the following three kinds of workflows:

✦ **Sequential** — Activities execute one after another.

✦ **State machine** — Activities execute when an event occurs.

✦ **Data-driven** — Activities execute when a condition is met.

Workflow models use XAML, C#, or Visual Basic. You can create a workflow by typing XAML markup in a text editor. Visual Studio provides a visual designer for creating workflows.

The mother of all workflow applications is SharePoint. You can host WF workflows in SharePoint — and visual workflow designers are available in Share-Point Designer. To see SharePoint workflows in action, you can download the Enterprise Content Management Starter Kit from Microsoft's Web site at

```
www.microsoft.com/downloads/details.aspx?FamilyID=38CA6B32-
   44BE-4489-8526-F09C57CD13A5&displaylang=en
```

Also, be on the lookout for my book *SharePoint Designer For Dummies* (Wiley Publishing, Inc.).

The Windows SDK includes a number of samples that demonstrate the technologies of WF. You can find the samples in the `WFSamples.zip` file in the SDK's samples folder. Figure 3-6 shows a sequential workflow in a designer in Visual Studio.

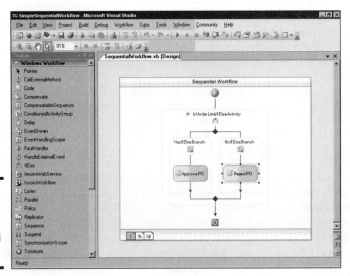

Figure 3-6:
Design workflows using Visual Studio.

In addition to demonstrating all the features of WF, the SDK includes a number of applications that show workflows in action. For example, the `OrderStateMachine` application demonstrates a state machine workflow. The sample has the following four state activities:

✦ `WaitingForOrderState`

✦ `OrderCompletedState`

✦ `OrderOpenState`

✦ `OrderProcessedState`

The workflow's events include `OnOrderUpdated`, `OnOrderProcessed`, `OnOrderShipped`, and `OnOrderCanceled`. As events are fired like a string of firecrackers, the order moves through the state activities. The sample includes a simple host application you can use to move an order through the states. The buttons in the application fire the workflow's events. Figure 3-7 shows an example.

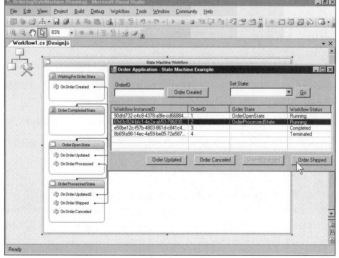

Figure 3-7:
The SDK includes sample workflow applications.

Gliding along with Project Glidepath

Does the idea of plowing through the Windows SDK make your head swim? Well, there is one way you can shortcut your way through the documentation. Microsoft is working on a new initiative called Project Glidepath to help you start developing applications for Vista. Glidepath provides much of the same content you'll find in the SDK, but it presents it to you within Visual Studio in the context of creating an application.

Project Glidepath consists of a framework that you install that extends Visual Studio. Once you install the framework, you use RSS to download content. Glidepath is intended to provide some context for building software. It uses a software factory and a set of viewpoints to help you with the process of building software.

When you install Glidepath, you get the Windows Vista Client Application Architecture package (eventually more application architectures will be available). The package includes a set of *viewpoints* — different perspectives for building an application. The package includes both technical and non-technical viewpoints; they contain workflows that walk you through creating your application.

Each Glidepath project starts out with a `_Viewpoints` project. This project has an application-architecture viewpoint that contains the starting workflow for building your application.

Even if you have no intention of developing applications for Vista, you'll want to check out Project Glidepath. It contains viewpoints and workflows for building more than just Vista applications.

Installing Glidepath

To get started with Project Glidepath, follow these steps:

1. **Download the software from Project Glidepath's Web site at www. projectglidepath.net/.**

2. **Run the GuidanceAutomationExtensions.msi installer.**

3. **Run the GlidepathGuidancePackageSetup.msi installer.**

4. **Run the GlidepathSetup.msi installer.**

Note that it isn't necessary to install version 3.0 of the .NET Framework — or any other software — to use Project Glidepath. You may need other components to take advantage of additional features in Glidepath, but you can install those later if necessary.

Project Glidepath is a framework that extends Visual Studio 2005. In order to use the framework, you must download content. To update Glidepath's content, follow these steps:

1. **Launch Visual Studio 2005.**

   You need at least the Standard Edition of Visual Studio to use Project Glidepath.

2. **Press Ctrl+Shift+N to open the New Project window.**

3. **Expand Guidance Packages and click the Glidepath Software Factory project type.**

4. **Click the Glidepath solution template.**

5. **Type a name for the solution and click OK.**

Visual Studio creates a new Glidepath solution with a project called _Viewpoints. A Workflow window appears (as shown in Figure 3-8) and walks you through the steps for using Glidepath to build a Vista application.

**Book VII
Chapter 3**

Using Visual Studio with Vista and Office 2007

Figure 3-8:
Glidepath solutions display a Workflow window.

6. **Click the Done button to close the Workflow window.**

7. **Right-click the _Viewpoints project in Solution Explorer.**

8. **Click Update from the shortcut menu.**

The Update Project Glidepath Software Factory window appears.

You should run the Update command periodically to download updates for Glidepath.

9. **Click the Update from RSS Feeds button.**

Glidepath connects to the RSS feeds listed and downloads any updates.

10. **Upon completion of the download, click Update History to view the packages downloaded, as shown in Figure 3-9.**

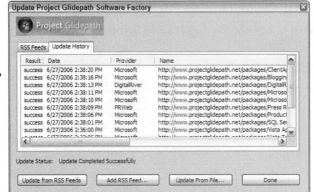

Figure 3-9:
View the
Update
History tab
to see the
downloaded
packages.

Project Glidepath uses RSS feeds to retrieve downloads. Anyone can produce content for Glidepath. Eventually there will be pay content on Glidepath; for now, make the most of what you can get for free.

Using Glidepath

When you have Glidepath installed and updated, you can start using it to build software. Not sure where to start? Let Glidepath tell you. The heart of a Glidepath solution is the _Viewpoints project, which has a workflow that walks you through using Glidepath.

To open the workflow window, follow these steps:

1. **Right-click the** _Viewpoints **project folder in Solution Explorer.**

2. **Click Workflow on the shortcut menu.**

    The Workflow window appears — yep, the same Workflow window shown in Figure 3-8 — an essential element in using Glidepath. The window has the following three tabs:

    • **Overview** — Provides a high-level overview of the package you're using.

    • **Workflow** — Provides a set of steps to guide you through the specified process.

    • **Next Step** — Provides the current step on which you're working.

To use the Workflow window, start by reading the Overview. Then take a quick look at the Workflow steps. Finally, read through the text in the Next Step tab. Here you'll find guidance and instructions on completing the step.

After you follow the guidance and instructions on the Next Step tab, click the Advance to Next Step button. This places a check mark next to the step in the Workflow tab, and displays the next step's details in the Next Step tab.

Understanding viewpoints

Viewpoints are different perspectives of the same project. For example, when you build an application, you have to think about architecture, user interface, and domain logic. You also have to think about nontechnical issues such as marketing your application. Viewpoints provide a set of technical and nontechnical workflows that remind you of all of the things you need to do when you build an application.

Each viewpoint you use in Glidepath has its own content for the Workflow window. Figure 3-10 shows the Workflow tab for Project Glidepath. The first step in the Glidepath workflow is to update Glidepath. Click the Advance to Next Step button to place a check mark next to the first step. The next step is to configure the Application Architecture Viewpoint.

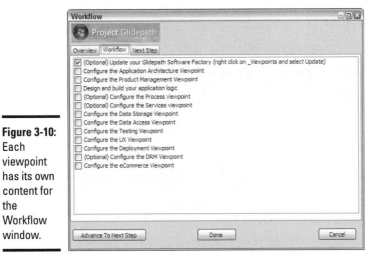

Figure 3-10: Each viewpoint has its own content for the Workflow window.

Book VII Chapter 3

Using Visual Studio with Vista and Office 2007

Glidepath has a limited number of viewpoints. Eventually, more viewpoints will be added. Table 3-2 lists some of the viewpoints you can find and the workflows they contain. The viewpoints listed here are a sampling of what you can expect to see in the future. You can get an overall mind-map of these viewpoints by viewing the `_viewpoints.mht` file in Internet Explorer.

Table 3-2		Viewpoints in Project Glidepath
Type	*Viewpoint*	*Workflow Packages*
Technical	Application Architecture	Windows Vista, Service, Client+Service, Web Site
	Data Storage	XML, SQL Server
	Data Access	ADO.NET, Data Access Block
	Deployment	MSI, ClickOnce
	eCommerce	Digital River, SSK
	Process	WF
	Services	Windows Communications Foundation, Web Service
	User Experience	Desktop WinForms, Desktop Windows Presentation Foundation
Nontechnical	Product Management	Market Analysis
	Marketing	Advertising, Website, Affiliate Programs
	Community	Blogging, Podcasting, Forums, Support
	Search	Download registries, PAD files, SEO
	Legal	EULA, eCommerce

The Application Architecture Viewpoint is the starting viewpoint in Glidepath. With this viewpoint, you decide whether you wish to work on a Vista, Service, Client+Service, or Web Site. For now, the only workflow available is for Vista. To use the Application Architecture Viewpoint, you must configure it. The configuration process adds the viewpoints contents to your Glidepath solution.

To configure the Application Architecture Viewpoint, follow these steps:

1. **Right-click the** `ApplicationArchitecture.viewpoint.txt` **file in Solution Explorer.**

2. **Click Configure on the shortcut menu.**

   The Configuration Selector appears.

3. **Click Windows Vista Desktop Client.**

4. **Click the OK button.**

   The _Viewpoints project expands to include the viewpoints listed in Table 3-2. A workflow window opens to walk you through how to use the Windows Vista Client Application Architecture Package, and the package adds an `ApplicationLogic` project to your solution (as Figure 3-11 shows). You add your domain specific logic to this project. You can right-click this project and click Worfklow to display the Windows Vista Client Application Architecture Package Workflow window.

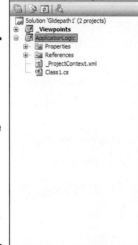

Figure 3-11: The Windows Vista Client Application Architecture Package adds the Application Logic project to your solution.

The Windows Vista Client Application Architecture Package has seven steps to complete, as shown in Figure 3-12.

Book VII Chapter 3

Using Visual Studio with Vista and Office 2007

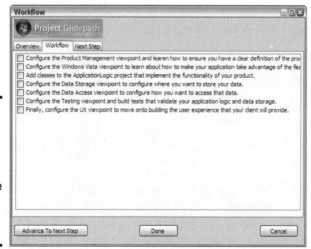

Figure 3-12: The Windows Vista Client Application Architecture Package has seven steps.

The first step is to configure the Product Management viewpoint. Six of the seven steps involve configuring viewpoints. Each viewpoint you configure has its own set of workflow packages you can select. For example, jump ahead to Step 2 in the workflow in Figure 3-12, where you configure the Windows Vista viewpoint. You configure all viewpoints the same way:

1. **Locate the viewpoint file in the** `_Viewpoints` **project.**

2. **Right-click the file and click Configure from the shortcut menu.**

It's the same way you configured the Application Architecture viewpoint, only this time you're looking for `WindowsVista.viewpoint.txt`.

When you configure the Windows Vista viewpoint, you're presented with the following packages from which to select:

- Planning for Windows Vista Logo Certification

- Top Ten things to do to get your application Vista ready

- Application Compatibility Information for existing apps

3. **Place a check mark next to the packages you wish to select, as shown in Figure 3-13.**

You don't have to select everything now. You can run the Configure command again to select additional packages.

4. **Click OK.**

Figure 3-13:
Select a
package to
add to your
solution.

The first package you select appears in Solution Explorer and the Workflow window appears. After you close the Workflow window, any additional packages you selected in Step 3 are installed.

Each added project has its own workflow. The Vista viewpoint adds the following projects to your Glidepath solution:

✦ Vista Top Ten

✦ Vista Application Compatibility

✦ Windows Vista Logo Requirements

Within each package, the workflow has its own set of tasks. Here are some typical examples:

✦ Thirty-minute Vista Compatibility Check

✦ Run the Application Verifier on your current project

✦ Follow the Windows Vista style guidelines

✦ Design for reliability and manageability

✦ Review the Windows Vista Logo Requirements

Everything you need to execute the workflow steps can be found in the projects added by the Vista viewpoint, as Figure 3-14 shows.

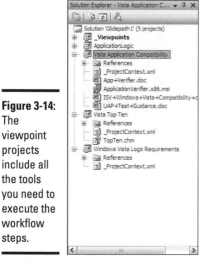

Figure 3-14: The viewpoint projects include all the tools you need to execute the workflow steps.

With all these packages and workflows, how do you keep track? You execute the Overview command on the _Viewpoints folder. Figure 3-15 shows the Workflow Overview window.

Getting Ready for Office 2007

Microsoft expects to release the latest version of Microsoft Office in early 2007. The new version of Office has the mainstays you expect (Word, Excel, and the usual crew), along with a few new client applications, such as the following:

Figure 3-15: Use the Overview window to keep a high-level view of your progress.

✦ **Communicator 2007** — Integrate communication into Office applications to enable a single identity across applications and communication modes.

✦ **Groove 2007** — Enable collaboration among team members in a workspace.

✦ **InfoPath 2007** — Create forms that integrate with other Office applications such as Outlook and Excel.

✦ **OneNote 2007** — Take notes and organize them in a digital notebook.

✦ **SharePoint Designer 2007** — Design, customize, and contribute to SharePoint sites.

Another new development for Office 2007 is the use of server products. SharePoint Portal Server and Project Server have been around for awhile, but they're both beefed up. The server offerings in Office 2007 include

✦ **Forms Server 2007** — Serve up InfoPath forms.

✦ **Groove Server 2007** — Implement and administer enterprise-level Groove services.

✦ **Project Portfolio Server 2007** — Organize, measure, monitor, and create workflows for a portfolio of projects.

✦ **Project Server 2007** — Manage a project's life cycle.

✦ **SharePoint Server 2007** — Provide a portal for collaboration, content management, and process workflow.

Office 2007 has a completely revamped user interface. A primary feature of the new interface is the Ribbon, which goes across the top of applications and is used to access menu commands. The ribbon allows more commands to be accessible with fewer mouse clicks, as Figure 3-16 shows.

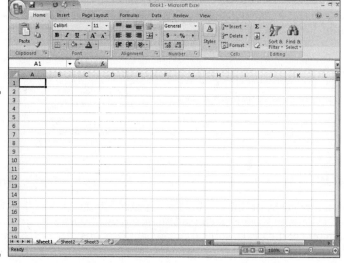

Figure 3-16: The new Office 2007 user interface replaces the standard menus with a ribbon of commands.

Another new feature of Office 2007 is the Office Open XML Formats. All your Office data is now saved as XML files instead of using proprietary file formats. Using XML enables data to be moved easily across Web services.

The increased use of servers, XML, and Web services makes it easier for developers to use Office 2007 as a development platform. They make it so easy, in fact, that you can actually create full-blown applications that use Office 2007 clients as their interfaces. The advantage of this approach is that your users are using clients they already use every day. They don't need to learn a new interface to use your application.

Microsoft will release a new version of Visual Studio Tools for Office (VSTO) to complement Office 2007. VSTO simplifies Office development by cutting down on the amount of code required to develop Office applications. If you're doing Office development, you should check out VSTO.

You should also check out the Office Developer on MSDN for tutorials and downloads for using Visual Studio to develop Office applications at

```
http://msdn.microsoft.com/office/default.aspx
```

A hard disk that makes a difference

Virtual machines use virtual hard-drive files as their hard drives. You can create a special kind of virtual hard disk called a *differencing hard disk* that lets you create parent/child relationships between virtual hard disks.

For example, you could start by creating a (virtual) *parent* hard disk, on which you install your operating system. Then you create a second, *differencing* hard disk that uses the first disk as its parent. When you fire up a virtual machine to use the differencing hard disk, the new virtual machine merges the two existing virtual disks. Any changes you make to the virtual machine are saved to the differencing hard disk. For instance, you could install beta software on the differencing hard disk. When you decide you don't want to use the beta software any more, you just discard the differencing hard disk. Your parent hard disk remains intact and can be reused.

Going Virtual

With the releases of Office 2007, Vista, Visual Studio 2005, and many other products comes the headache of finding enough hardware to run everything. If you're one of the brave souls running beta versions of this software, then you frequently find yourself reformatting your hard drive and installing software.

Instead of running all this software on individual machines, why not run it on *virtual* machines? Microsoft has released Virtual Server 2005 which gives you the capability to create multiple virtual machines on a single physical server.

Virtual Server 2005 includes support for networking, which includes these capabilities:

+ Create a virtual network that consists of virtual machines only

+ Network virtual machines to the local machine only

+ Network virtual machines to the larger network

Virtual servers work equally well in development and production environments. Officially, Virtual Server supports server operating systems such as Windows Server 2003. However, it will also run Windows XP. Microsoft doesn't support running Windows XP in a virtual machine because Windows XP is a desktop operating system.

You need to have adequate hardware to run virtual machines. Virtual Server 2005 runs as a service, but it isn't necessary to run all your virtual machines at once. For example, I have a dozen or so virtual machines configured on one of my test servers. At any given time, I'm usually only running at most two of those virtual machines.

Virtual Server 2005 is available as a free download from Microsoft's Web site at

`www.microsoft.com/windowsserversystem/virtualserver`

While you're there, be sure to check out other resources such as the Virtual Server 2005 Migration Toolkit (which you can use to migrate physical servers to virtual servers).

The administration and remote-control features of Virtual Server are Web-based. You use the administration Web site to do the following:

✦ Create, add, and configure virtual machines

✦ Create virtual hard drives

✦ Create, add, and configure virtual networks

✦ Configure and maintain the virtual server

Figure 3-17 shows an example of the Virtual Server administration page.

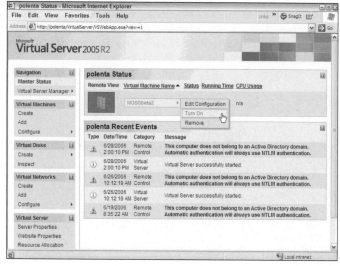

Figure 3-17: Use the Virtual Server administration page to start and stop virtual machines.

You have two options for accessing your virtual machines:

✦ **Virtual Machine Remote Control** — VMRC uses a client embedded in Internet Explorer to remote control the virtual machine's desktop, as shown in Figure 3-18. VMRC works best when you have only a few tasks to complete.

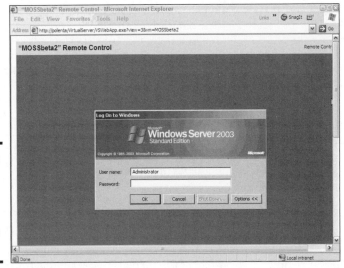

Figure 3-18: Remote control the virtual machine's desktop in a browser.

✦ **Terminal Services Remote Desktop** — Terminal Services allows you to create a new desktop session using a Windows application, as Figure 3-19 shows. Remote Desktop is a good choice when you have extensive work to do in the virtual machine. You can even maximize the Remote Desktop to cover your entire desktop.

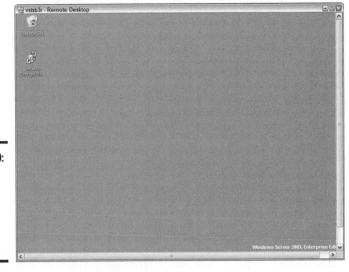

Figure 3-19: Remote Desktop creates a new desktop session.

I made extensive use of Remote Desktop while writing this book. I set up multiple virtual machines so I could run different scenarios in desktop sessions. For example, I often installed beta software and extensions on a virtual machine — for example, the software listed in the section "Getting Started with Vista" (earlier in this chapter). It worked like gangbusters.

Index

Numbers

123456 value, storing in view state, 247–248

Symbols

& (ampersand), using with access keys, 150
, (comma), using with multi-dimensional arrays, 483
. (dots), using in namespaces, 43
. XPath expression, syntax for and description of, 388
. . XPath expression, syntax for and description of, 388
... (ellipsis) button, accessing complex properties with, 151
/ XPath expression, syntax for and description of, 387
/ / XPath expression, syntax for and description of, 388
? (question mark) shortcut in C#, declaring nullable types with, 492
@ XPath expression, syntax for and description of, 388
[] (brackets), using with arrays in C#, 483
{} (curly braces)
  in C# class body, 507
  using with arrays, 483
  using with C# statements, 467
<%@ Page...%> directive in ASP.NET, explanation of, 194
<!DOCTYPE...> entry in ASP.NET, explanation of, 194
= (equals) operator, assigning variable values with, 466, 471

A

abstract classes, implementing with IntelliSense, 560
abstraction, relationship to object-oriented programming, 504
acceptance test, explanation of, 622
AcceptButton property
  description of, 154
  setting for, 155
access keys, setting for controls, 150
AccessDataSource control, description of, 316
Accessibility category in Properties window, description of, 149
Action category in Properties window, description of, 149
Active Template Library (ATL), description of, 178
ActiveSync, downloading for use with mobile Web sites, 271
Add Connection dialog box, changing database source in, 303–305
administration, tools for, 780
ADO.NET. See also data controls; providers
  binding components available in, 308
  capabilities of, 280
  components of, 392
  connection pooling feature of, 396
  data access in, 280–281
  displaying data with, 282–283
  executing offline downloads with, 281–282
  opening and closing database connection with, 600–601
  providers for, 393
  purpose of, 391
  retrieving data from data sources with, 281–282
  reusing connections in, 399
  supporting XML with, 418–419
  tools for, 284
  updating data with, 283
  using DataReaders with, 406–409
  using in applications, 419–420
ADO.NET connection string builders, using, 404. See also connection strings

C

D

F

P